WAIT FOR THE WAGGON

1794 THE ROYAL WAGGONERS

1799 THE ROYAL WAGGON CORPS

1802-1833 THE ROYAL WAGGON TRAIN

1855 THE LAND TRANSPORT CORPS

1856 THE MILITARY TRAIN

1869 THE ARMY SERVICE CORPS

1881 THE COMMISSARIAT AND TRANSPORT CORPS

1888 THE ARMY SERVICE CORPS

1918 THE ROYAL ARMY SERVICE CORPS

1965 THE ROYAL CORPS OF TRANSPORT

The Colonel-in-Chief, Her Royal Highness Princess Alice

WAIT FOR THE WAGGON

The Story of the
Royal Corps of Transport and its Predecessors
1794-1993

edited by
Brigadier John Sutton

Leo Cooper

First published in 1998 by
LEO COOPER
an imprint of
Pen & Sword Books Ltd
47 Church Street
Barnsley
South Yorkshire
S70 2AS

A CIP record for this book is available from the British Library

ISBN 0 85052 625 6

CONTENTS

vi

The British Army has enjoyed the loyal and thoroughly professional support of The Royal Corps of Transport and its predecessors for 200 years. A tradition that was founded on 7 March 1794 when the Royal Waggoners were formed.

Since then, titles, uniforms and organisations have changed no less than nine times and this latest reorganisation will lead to the disbandment of The Royal Corps of Transport as we know it. However, the achievements of The Royal Corps of Transport will not be lost because they will be carried forward, with the proud heritage of the other contributing Corps, into The Royal Logistic Corps.

Like you, I am sad to see the demise of such a distinguished Corps but I acknowledge the need for change. I have been proud to have been so closely associated with The Royal Corps of Transport and it gives me enormous pleasure to contribute to this historical record, which marks and celebrates the bicentenary of its formation.

However, while we celebrate our past achievements with justifiable pride, I am sure you will join me in wishing our successor corps, The Royal Logistic Corps the best of good fortune.

COLONEL-IN-CHIEF

FOREWORD

by

GENERAL SIR PETER de la BILLIÈRE

KCB, KBE, DSO, MC

When the Royal Corps of Transport passed into history in 1993 it did so with its reputation as the provider *par excellence* of Combat Service Support to the British Army. Its passing brought to a close a significant chapter in the story of the life and work of our Army, a story which started long ago in Flanders. It gives me great pleasure to write the foreword of this timely book and indeed it is a privilege to do so for a Corps which, in my experience, made such a magnificent contribution to the Gulf War of 1990/1991. Just two years later the Corps' significant achievements in that campaign were to become a fitting valediction not only to the Royal Corps of Transport, but to the Royal Army Service Corps and the predecessor Corps which between them had rendered loyal support to the British Army over a 200-year period.

As the eighteenth century entered its ultimate decade the Low Countries became once more the cockpit of Europe and British troops were committed there as part of a Continental coalition; however, warfare had moved on since the days of Blenheim and Minden and the expeditionary forces at our disposal needed urgent improvements. The Duke of York, Commander-in-Chief and King George III's second son, was able to give momentum to reforms designed to give the British Army essential mobility. In 1793 the Royal Horse Artillery was formed to provide manoeuvrable fire power during the battle and, also an innovation, with horses and drivers permanently established. In the following year the same sound principle of a permanent corps of drivers, horses and waggons was applied to the delivery of supplies, food and essential stores to the Army with the formation of the Royal Waggoners, the British Army's first logistic corps.

The long years of peace at home which followed Britain's crowning achievement at Waterloo brought hard times to the Army, much retrenchment and little progress. Few resources were made available for the retention of a proper supply and transport service, and the Royal Waggon Train was disbanded. The penalty for such parsimony and neglect was later paid by our troops in the Crimea. This campaign saw the urgent re-establishment of logistic support in the form of the Land Transport Corps, which went some way towards making up for the inadequacies of the much-maligned civilian-run commissariat. Nevertheless the small wars of empire were now mounted and fought with the aid of an increasingly professional nucleus of experts charged with supplying and transporting the Army. Various methods and organizations were tried along the evolutionary path as the British Empire grew. Finally a modern system and recognizable Corps, initially the Military Train and subsequently, in 1869, the first Army Service Corps, emerged. It combined proper staff functions with a balanced capability embodied in adequately manned and equipped units.

The vision and driving force behind the Army Service Corps of 1888 was provided by General Sir Redvers Buller, an infantry soldier and VC hero of the Zulu War. Buller is rightly regarded as the father of the British Army's modern logistic Services. The tool he forged so carefully was tested in the furnace of the Anglo-Boer War, the first war of the twentieth century and a chilling precursor of what was to follow. The Army Service Corps survived the ravages of friend and foe alike, while, ironically, Buller's reputation as a commander did not. The Anglo-Boer War provided a timely warning that once again Britain was in poor shape to take on a modern Continental land power and a remarkable programme of modernization was initiated in the Army. Such were the great improvements achieved by 1914 that the British Expeditionary Force sent to France that summer, with its integrated Supply and Transport Staff and Army Service Corps support, is widely accepted as possibly the finest Army Britain has ever fielded.

The war itself was ultimately resolved not by small professional armies but by vast citizen armies numbering millions. The work of the Army Service Corps, which itself grew to the size of an army, was vital on every front and in every theatre of operations. The Corps' leadership in technology enabled it to play a part in many of the most significant innovations of the war, most notably in providing drivers and maintenance mechanics for the first armoured car and tank units. Granted the title Royal in 1918, the Royal Army Service Corps carried the baton of technological advance through the inter-war years, despite limited resources, and when the second round with Germany began in 1939 the British Army was blessed with a fully mechanized transport system, while the French and Germans still retained huge numbers of horses.

The role of the Royal Army Service Corps in the Second World War and its successors in the modern era may be summed up by the words of Winston Churchill, who remarked that 'transport was the stem without which the bright flower of victory could not bloom'. Consummate masters of their trade by land, sea and air, the men and women of the Royal Corps of Transport and its predecessors have always provided a loyal service to their comrades, mainly unsung, sometimes in the forefront, but most often providing, by day and night, the myriad of ordinary but essential necessities for living and fighting. They have done their job quietly, efficiently and well; however, throughout the years, the members of these Corps have above all remained soldiers, as their record in providing volunteers for special duties shows. The men and women wearing the RASC or RCT cap badge have been no strangers to flying, parachuting, special forces, intelligence and a whole range of other duties calling for essential military skills, courage and determination. In the darker days of the last war, when an airborne force was urgently being created, a young RASC driver was the first to give his life while helping to develop military parachuting; more recently an RCT pilot won the Distinguished Flying Cross during the Falklands War and of course many RASC and RCT officers and men have also served with distinction in the Special Air Service.

The story of those men and women who kept the Army fed, who moved it and its equipment wherever it needed to go and who provided it with fuel and delivered its ammunition has been little told in the past and has not attracted the many writers who prefer to dwell on the popular appeal of combat. It is, however, a marvellous story, here simply told, of a vital and fascinating part of the Army; and because the work of the RCT and its predecessors affected every aspect of Army life, whether fighting or at peace, it also reflects the story of the Army as a whole. The Royal Corps of Transport existed for just 27 years but its passing marked 200 years of military logistics.

A new Corps, The Royal Logistic Corps, has now inherited the mantle of provider and sustainer to the Army. It has a proud tradition; one which is so lucidly described in this book which I commend to you.

Preface

The material for this book, required to cover 200 years, has been found from many sources, much being obtained from previous histories, which are listed in the Bibliography and for which help from contributors has been previously acknowledged in those volumes. For this new history we are particularly indebted to those individuals who undertook the difficult task of evaluating, extracting and incorporating the essential information from those past records to provide the earlier chapters of this book, up to and including the Second World War.

Unfortunately, even those who have personal memories of the Second World War and can still verify facts, are becoming rarer and this serves to emphasise the value of recording events 'whilst the memory serves' for future histories. However, we are fortunate in having some contributors who still have clear recollections of this last major war in which the Corps played such an important part. This has been of tremendous value in both checking and adding information for that time.

The story from the Second World War onwards covers the part played by the Corps in their activities, still world-wide, through the Cold War era. This included participation in a number of widely-differing operations and campaigns, ranging from the Berlin Air Lift to the Gulf War. We greatly appreciate the work of all those who were personally involved in these many activities and, in a time of great change, have contributed to these latter chapters, either by their personal accounts or in reading or advising on drafts. Their help enabled us to produce not only the new material necessary to cover the exceptional period since the 1982 history, but also to update and in some cases correct, versions of previously-recorded events.

The Editorial Committee, listed below, with overall responsibility for the production of the book, was initially established in March, 1992 by the Institution of the RCT, as part of the Historical and Publications Committee. This was then the part of the Regimental Headquarters Organization of the Royal Corps of Transport concerned with the Regimental Affairs of the Corps. The synopsis for the History submitted by the Editor had been agreed in October, 1991. With the formation of The Royal Logistic Corps in April, 1993, the Committee became responsible to the Committee of Management of the newly-created and separately organized Institution of the Royal Army Service Corps and Royal Corps of Transport, for the production of the book. A serving RLC, ex-RCT, Officer was then appointed as the Committee's chairman.

EDITORIAL COMMITTEE

Chairman:	Until March, 1993, Brigadier A C Massey OBE
	From March, 1993, Colonel M F I Cubitt, CBE
Editor:	Brigadier D J Sutton, OBE
Picture Editor:	Lieutenant Colonel T A Danton-Rees
Secretary:	Lieutenant Colonel R F Grevatte-Ball, from January, 1996
Members:	Lieutenant Colonel I H W Bennett
	Major C W P Coan
	Brigadier D W E Hancox, until his untimely death in April, 1996
	Lieutenant Colonel L A Huxtable
	Colonel J C Lucas, OBE
	Lieutenant Colonel M H G Young

From the start of the Book to its completion there were three Institution Permanent Staff Secretaries, Lieutenant Colonels J G Hambleton MBE, C J Doland and R F Grevatte-Ball. Lieutenant Colonel Hambleton was the last Regimental Secretary of the RCT and greatly helped in the initial preparations for the writing of the History, before becoming Regimental Secretary of the Royal Logistic Corps in April, 1993. Lieutenant Colonel Doland was the first Secretary to the RASC/RCT Institution, and as such his hard work in the post paved the way for the sound structure that followed. Lieutenant Colonel Grevatte-Ball, who took over in 1996 was not only a tireless Secretary, but by virtue of his experience while still serving made invaluable contributions to the text.

HEADQUARTERS AND REGIMENTAL CONTRIBUTORS TO THIS VOLUME

HQ Director General Transport & Movements, Logistic Executive (Army)
Transport & Movements Branch, United Kingdom Land Forces
Transport & Movements Branch HQ, British Army of the Rhine
HQ Training Group RCT
The School of Transportation RCT
4 Armoured Divison Transport Regiment RCT
7 Tank Transporter Regiment RCT
8 Regiment RCT
10 Corps Transport Regiment RCT
17 Port and Maritime Regiment RCT
27 Regiment RCT
29 Transport & Movements Regiment RCT
The Gurkha Transport Regiment

LIST OF CONTRIBUTORS TO THIS VOLUME

Lieutenant Colonel R P Arlidge
Captain G G Barraclough
Major General I S Baxter, CBE
Major General P H Benson, CBE
Lieutenant Colonel I H W Bennett
Brigadier M W Betts, CBE
Colonel F A Bush
Major General V H J Carpenter, CB, MBE
Colonel J R Cawthorne
Lieutenant Colonel P Chaganis, OBE
Major C W P Coan
Colonel C J Constable
Colonel M F I Cubitt, CBE
Lieutenant Colonel T A Danton-Rees
Lieutenant Colonel C J Doland
Colonel B A Edridge
Major General G A Ewer, CBE
Lieutenant Colonel B L Fox
Lieutenant Colonel R F Grevatte-Ball
Lieutenant Colonel D A Griffin
(Co-ordinator Transport & Movements BAOR)

Captain J Gutteridge
Colonel G J Haig, OBE
Lieutenant Colonel J G Hambleton, MBE
Brigadier D W E Hancox
Lieutenant Colonel L A Huxtable
Colonel J C Lucas, OBE
Brigadier A C Massey, OBE
Lieutenant Colonel F C Matthews
(Co-ordinator United Kingdom Land Forces)
Major Helen E McMahon
Colonel I W B McRobbie, OBE, TD, ADC, DL
F O'Connell Esq
Colonel J D Payne
Lieutenant Colonel G T Pearce, MBE
Major General F K Plaskett, CB, MBE
Colonel J S Riggall, MBE
Colonel D W Ronald
Lieutenant Colonel A C Scott
Lieutenant Colonel T C Street
Brigadier D J Sutton, OBE

Major J T Tatham
Major J E Tong
Colonel J S M Walker
Major General M S White, CBE

Brigadier W M E White, CBE
Lieutenant Colonel R F. Wills
Lieutenant Colonel M H G Young

PICTURE SOURCES

Our grateful thanks are due to the following providers of pictures for this volume.
The Dust Cover was designed and drawn by David Bennett
Photographs kindly loaned by:
MOD Library
H J Compton Esq
Illustrated London News
Lieutenant Colonel I H W Bennett
Imperial War Museum
Royal Air Force Club, Piccadilly, London
Lieutenant Colonel R F Grevatte-Ball
Major W Wynn-Werninck
Major D Balcombe
Major General M S White CBE
The Royal Hospital, Chelsea
Colonel N H G Beard MBE
The Institution of the RASC/RCT

In addition to the considerable overall help given to the Editor by all the Committee in the checking of material, obtaining additional coverage, and proofing-reading of chapters, particular members also undertook the preparation of complete chapters based on their specialized knowledge and expertise. In this respect special thanks for their major contributions are due to Lieutenant Colonel I H W Bennett, Major C W P Coan and Lieutenant Colonel M H G Young who were instrumental in producing the early chapters of the book. The challenge for the Picture Editor, Lieutenant Colonel T A Danton-Rees, to find suitable representative pictures covering 200 years was considerable. Through his persistence the resulting selection made a most valuable contribution to the Book.

The Committee Chairman from the final days of the Royal Corps of Transport, Colonel M F I Cubitt, gathered much material from serving officers now in the Royal Logistic Corps and undertook the initial onerous task of marshalling, annotating, scheduling and word-processing all the material from wherever obtained. This essential task was of the immense help in the subsequent editorial process. It was necessary at the end of 1996, when editing of the book had reached an advanced stage, to find a secretarial organization to undertake the now-changing and more instant computer activity required. We were fortunate in obtaining the services of Mrs Julia Harvey, who with the utmost help and patience saw the preparation of the book through to the publishers. With her husband, Commander R C Harvey OBE, Royal Navy (Retired), Mrs Harvey also undertook the preparation of the index to the Book.

John Sutton, Editor
March, 1998

Glossary

An explanation of some of the terms and abbreviations used in this book

'A' Vehicle	A tracked or wheeled armoured combat land vehicle primarily designed for offensive purposes.
AA	Anti-Aircraft. Term used to cover organizations, units, weapons and equipment having the primary role of defence against air attack.
AAC	Army Air Corps
AASC	Australian Army Service Corps
AASO	Army Air Supply Organizations. Units established in 1960 to provide full air despatch capabilities, commanded by an RASC Lieutenant Colonel and containing an HQ and a number of Air Despatch Companies RASC. The HQ could deploy three Air Supply Control Sections. Attached personnel from other Corps, eg. RAOC, enabled the organization to cover the full range of tasks previously carried out by RASOs and FASOs. The organizations became Air Despatch Regiments in 1965 on the formation of the RCT.
AATO	Army Air Transport Organization – HQ AATO. A Staff organization used particularly in SEAC to control the operation of supply by air and air movement and transportation
ACC	Army Catering Corps or Air Control Centre
ACE	Allied Command Europe – the command including all NATO land forces in Europe
ACF	Army Cadet Force
ACOS	Assistant Chief of Staff
AD	Air Despatch. Supply by air, by parachute or free drop
ADG	Armoured Delivery Group formed during Op GRANBY in the Gulf 1990-91 to hold reserves of crews and armoured vehicles.
ADMT	Assistant Director of Military Transport, located at Woolwich, and responsible for the control of the WD Fleet until 1940
ADP	Automatic Data Processing using computer systems
ADST	Assistant Director of Supplies and Transport. A Corps officer (Colonel or Lieutenant Colonel) on the staff of the Corps Directorate at the War Office/MOD or at Headquarters, prior to 1965
ADTR	Armoured Division Transport Regiment
AER	Army Emergency Reserve
AFCENT	Allied Forces Central Europe
AF G1098	A table listing all the equipment required by a unit to go to war
AFHQ	American Force Headquarters. The Headquarters of the American Forces in the battle for Tunisia 1942/43
AFNEI	Allied Forces Netherlands East Indies 1945
AFV	Armoured Fighting Vehicle such as a tank or armoured personnel carrier
AHA	Administrative Harbour Area
ALFSEA	HQ Allied Land Forces South East Asia. The HQ responsible for the operations of the Second World War campaign in Burma
AMC	Air Mounting Centre
AMF(L)	ACE Mobile Force (Land). A force capable of deployment mainly to its northern and southern flanks
ANZUK	Australia, New Zealand and UK
AOC	Army Ordnance Corps
AOP	Air Observation Post used for directing artillery fire
AOT	Annual Operational Test
APC	Armoured Personnel Carrier used by infantry and others
APSC	Army Personnel Selection Centre

AQMG	Assistant Quartermaster General. A 'Q' Staff Officer at War Office/MOD or lower formation in the rank of Lieutenant Colonel. On the introduction of NATO nomenclature became ACOS G4
ARH	Army Rail Head
ARP	Army Restructuring Plan, 1974/75. One of many economy plans
ARRC	ACE Rapid Reaction Corps – a multi-nation force under the command of SHAPE
ARU	Annual Report on a Unit: a formal inspection by the chain of command on a unit to check its fitness for operations and peacetime administrative procedures. Also Army Rugby Union
ARV	Armoured Recovery Vehicle used by REME to recover tanks
ASM	Artificer Sergeant Major: a REME artificer in the rank of Warrant Officer Class 1
ASMT	The Army School of Mechanical Transport located at Leconfield
ASV	Armoured Staff Vehicle: an armoured office truck
AT	Animal Transport. Transport Units using a variety of animals, eg. horses, mules, camels, bullocks etc. with pack or wagon-drawing capability
ATAF	Allied Tactical Air Force
ATF	Air Transport Force
ATGW	Anti-Tank Guided Weapon
ATLO	Air Transport Liaison Officer
ATR	Army Training Regiment formed on rationalization of training in 1993
ATS	Auxiliary Territorial Service, formed for women in 1938. It became WRAC in 1949
AVLB	Royal Engineer Armoured Bridging Vehicles
AVRE	Armoured Vehicle Royal Engineers
AWD	All Wheel Drive Vehicle or Advanced Workshop Detachment of a field workshop
AXP	Ammunition Exchange Point
'B' Vehicle	A wheeled or tracked land vehicle, self propelled or towed, which is not primarily designed for offensive purposes
BAD	Base Ammunition Depot
BAOR	British Army of the Rhine. HQ at Rheindahlen near Moenchengladbach
BAS/RARS	Battle Attrition Study and Review of Ammunition Rates and Scales in the 1980s in BAOR
BATUS	British Army Training Unit Suffield; in Canada
BCR	Battle Casualty Replacement
Bde	Brigade. A formation of fighting units (infantry, armour) with supporting arms (artillery, engineers and signals) and services (RCT, RAOC, REME) commanded by a one-star brigadier
BDR	Battle Damage Repair: emergency repairs to keep equipment in action in the field
Beach Study	A review of the selection and training of RCT, RAOC and REME officers made by General Sir Hugh Beach GBE, KCB. MC, (late RE) in the late 1970s
BEF	British Expeditionary Force
BEM	British Empire Medal
BEME	Brigade Electrical and Mechanical Engineer. Major or Captain
BER	Beyond Economic Repair. Repair is possible but not economic; equipment is then scrapped or cannibalized
Berm	Sand barrier for defence as used in Gulf. Literally, an edge, the space between a ditch and a parapet in fortifications
BETFOR	British Element Trieste Force
BFME	British Forces Middle East
BGN	British Gurkhas Nepal

Black Box	A box containing electronic equipment, eg a Line Replaceable Unit or a Centrally Repairable Module. It is not necessarily black
BLOWPIPE	A hand-held, wire-guided, ground-to-air missile fired from the shoulder
BLR	Beyond Local Repair. May be repaired elsewhere, eg in Base or by contractor
BMA	Base Maintenance Area from which maintenance support, eg ammunition, petrol, oils and lubricants, spares, rations are provided for forward troops
BMATT	British Military Advisory & Training Team. Deployed to such countries as Zimbabwe
BMH	British Military Hospital
BMM	British Military Mission, eg to the Saudi Arabian National Guard
BMP	Russian-made tracked APC used by Iraqis in Gulf 1991
BQMS	Battery Quarter Master Sergeant in Royal Artillery
BR	British
BRASCO	Brigade RASC Officer. A Captain attached to the Staff at a Brigade Headquarters to advise on and handle S&T matters
BSD	Base Supply Depot. A major depot at Theatre base holding bulk supplies
BSE	Brigade Surety Evaluation
BSM	Battery Sergeant Major in the Royal Artillery. Warrant Officer Class 2
BV 202	The Volvo BV 202 is an articulated tracked vehicle. Particularly used in Arctic training by British Forces in Norway. It proved its worth in the Falklands bogs and mud in the campaign of 1982: REME used the vehicle with a winch for recovery
'C' Vehicle	A wheeled or tracked item of earth-moving equipment, either self-propelled or towed; self mobile, self steering cranes; cable laying ploughs; certain tractors including rough terrain fork lift tractors
CADWS	Close Air Defence Weapon Systems
CALM	Crane Attachment Lorry Mounted. A form of fixed Mechanical Handling Equipment
CALTF	Combined Air Lift Task Force (Berlin)
CAM	Chemical Agent Monitor
Cannibalize	To remove serviceable parts from a repairable item of equipment in order to install them on another item of equipment
CASC	Ceylon Army Service Corps formed during the Second World War
CASCOM	(Fort Lee USA) United States Army Combined Arms Support and Command
CASEVAC	Casualty Evacuation
CASCOM	United States Army Combined Arms Support Command – Fort Lee, USA
CB	Companion, Order of the Bath; Counter Battery or Container Body
CBE	Commander, Order of the British Empire
CCG	Control Commission Germany established in West Germany at the end of the Second World War to supervise the rehabilitation
CDP	Central Distribution Points. Distribution points located at Ordnance depots as part of the BAOR Freight Service
CDS	Chief of the Defence Staff. The most senior Service officer in the Ministry of Defence. Found from the Navy, Army or Royal Air Force
CES	Complete Equipment Schedule eg accessories and tools for a vehicle
CGS	Chief of General Staff – the most senior Army officer in the Ministry of Defence (Army)
CHALLENGER	Main Battle Tank after CHIEFTAIN. Based in UK and BAOR and used in the Gulf 1990-91
CHARRV	Chieftain Armoured Repair and Recovery Vehicle (RECLAIMER). See ARRV
CHIEFTAIN	A Main Battle Tank. Replaced CENTURION, mainly in

	BAOR throughout the Seventies and Eighties. Replaced by CHALLENGER
CHINOOK	Large helicopter with twin rotors used logistically for freight and troop carrying
CIGS	Chief of the Imperial General Staff. The most senior Army officer at the War Office
CinC	Commander-in-Chief, eg Commander BAOR or UKLF
CCIS	Command and Control Communications and Information Systems
CL	Commercial, as opposed to military designed vehicles
CLAMOR	Commonwealth Liaison and Monitoring Organization in Rhodesia 1979/80
CLANSMAN	Army mobile radio system used in the field by all arms and services
CLE	The Central Landing Establishment. An organization formed in 1940 as part of the development of airborne forces
CMA	Convoy Marshalling Area
CMG	Commander of the Order of Saint Michael and Saint George
Contingency Plans	Plans made for a possible emergency or operation
CORPORATE	Operation to recapture the Falkland Islands in 1982
Corps	An operational formation of divisions and supporting arms and services commanded by a lieutenant general; or a body such as the Royal Corps of Transport
COSLOG	Chief of Staff Logistics at LE(A) Andover
COXE	Combined Operations Experimental Establishment
CPU	Corporate Planning Unit: the QMG's corporate planning staff
CRASC	Commander Royal Army Service Corps. The senior RASC officer – Lieutenant Colonel – in a formation or unit, until 1965
CRCT	Commander Royal Corps of Transport. The senior RCT officer – Lieutenant Colonel – in a formation or unit
CRG	Corps Reinforcement Group (BAOR)
CRNZASC	Commander Royal New Zealand Army Service Corps
CSM	Company Sergeant Major. A Warrant Officer Class 2
CTAD	Commander Training and Arms Directors UKLF. He later became Inspector General Doctrine and Training in 1991. A central focus for all Army training except collective training
CTC	Combined Training Centre. A centre for training with assault landing craft formed in 1943
CTMO	Chief Transport and Movements Officer at a Headquarters in the rank of Brigadier or Colonel
CT Vehicles	Combat Vehicles. Vehicles specifically designed for military use
CVHQ	Central Volunteer Headquarters at Grantham
CVR(T) or (W)	Combat Vehicle Reconnaissance (Tracked or Wheeled)
DAA	Divisional Administrative Area
DAAG	Deputy Assistant Adjutant General. An 'A' Staff Officer at War Office/MOD or lower formation in the rank of Major. On introduction of NATO nomenclature, became DACOS G1
DAA&QMG	Deputy Assistant Adjutant Quartermaster General. A Staff officer in the rank of Major normally on Brigade Headquarters staff dealing with both A and Q matters prior to the introduction of NATO nomenclature
DADST	Deputy Assistant Director of Supplies and Transport. A Corps officer – Major – on the staff of the Corps Directorate at War Office/MOD or a Headquarters prior to 1965
DAMA	Director of Army Management Audit (replaced in 1992 by Director of Manpower Audit (DMA))
DAQMG	Deputy Assistant Quartermaster General. A 'Q' Staff Officer at War Office/MOD or lower formation in the rank of Major. On the introduction of NATO nomenclature became DACOS G4

DAR	Director of Army Recruiting
DCM	Distinguished Conduct Medal
DDef LOG Mov	Director of Defence Logistic Movements
DDST	Deputy Director of Supplies and Transport. The senior Corps officer at a Headquarters (Brigadier or Colonel), prior to 1965
DESERT SABRE	The 1st (BR) Armoured Division part of DESERT SWORD
DESERT SHIELD	The early operation to defend Saudi Arabia during the Gulf War 1990-91. Op GRANBY was the British operation codename
DESERT STORM	The operation to liberate Kuwait during the Gulf War 1991
DESERT SWORD	The land operation to liberate Kuwait during the Gulf War 1991
DFC	Distinguished Flying Cross
DGEME	Director General Electrical Mechanical Engineers. Head of REME prior to Logistic Support Review implementation
DGES	Director General Equipment Support. Head of REME on implementation of Logistic Support Review, April, 1993
DGLogSP(A)	Director General Logistic Support (Army). Head of Royal Logistic Corps after implementation of Logistic Support Review April, 1993
DGLP(A)	Director General of Logistic Policy (Army) at MOD (Army)
DGTM	Director General of Transport and Movements. The designation of the Head of the Corps from 1978 to 1993
DGTN	Director General of Transportation. The designation of the Head of the Corps for an interim period in 1977
DID	Detail Issue Depot. An RASC depot responsible for the breakdown of bulk supplies and issue to units
Div	Division. A formation made up of brigades and supporting arms and services, commanded by a major general
Divisional Column	The RASC element within a Division to provide supply and transport support and commanded by a lieutenant colonel – CRASC
Divisional Slice	Resources required to maintain one division, eg a division's 'share' of Corps or Army transport
DL	Deputy Lieutenant. One of a number of deputies, within a county, of a Lord Lieutenant
DMA	Divisional Maintenance Area
DMAO	Director Military Assistance Overseas
DMov	Director of Movements. A Staff appointment in the rank of Major General at Ministry level. From 1966 a designated RCT Major General's appointment, when the Head of the Corps became DGTM. The appointment downgraded to Brigadier in 1978 on becoming part of DGTM's HQ
DMZ	Demilitarized Zone supervised by United Nations between Iraq/Kuwait
DOMS	Defence Operational Movements Staff
Downtime	Time out of action, non-effective or non-productive time
DP	Delivery or Distribution Point. The location to which ASC, RASC and RCT transport delivered its consignments in the field
DRAWDOWN	Reduction of Army Strength in 1990s under 'Options for Change'
DROPS	Demountable Rack Off-Loading and Pick-up System: a logistic load carrying system mounted on lorries
DSC	Distinguished Service Cross
DSO	Distinguished Service Order
DSP(A)	Director of Support Planning (Army). A one star officer responsible for initial support planning for all new Army equipment projects; on QMG's staff
DST	Director of Supplies and Transport. The Head of the Corps at Ministry level – Major General – or senior Corps officer at Theatre level – Major General or Brigadier – until 1965
DUKW	A Second World War 2.5 ton GMC American-manufactured truck. A

	very versatile vehicle used extensively by the RASC in both the campaigns in Europe and the Far East, and continued in service with the RCT until the early Seventies. The initials, forming a convenient nick-name stood for General Motors technical specification – D Year of manufacture 1942: U type of frame: K Front wheel drive, and W six wheels
DUS(ARMY)	The Deputy Under-Secretary of State in the Ministry of Defence Army Department; Secretary to the Army Board. The post remained until 1984
Eager Beaver	A rough military designed rough terrain fork lift truck used for handling army stores
EAASC	East African Army Service Corps
EAM	Greek National Liberation Front
ECAB	Executive Committee of the Army Board. Deals with top policy
ECP	Equipment Collecting Point for equipment casualties awaiting backloading
EFC	Expeditionary Force Canteen, part of the ASC supply organization
EKA	A type of commercial Swedish recovery gear used on the Scammell and Foden recovery vehicles
ELAS	Greek People's National Army of Liberation
Equipment Management	All activities involved in meeting the users' requirements for fit equipment at the lowest overall cost to the public
EME	Electrical and Mechanical Engineering or Engineer (a REME officer)
EMPS	Equipment Management Policy Statement issued by the General Staff for major Army equipments giving availability required and repair policy
Enosis	Campaign by Greek Cypriots for the union of Cyprus with Greece
EOD	Explosive Ordnance Disposal. RE or RAOC bomb and other explosive devices disposal experts
EOKA	National Organization of Cypriot fighters founded in 1955 by Colonel Georgios Grivas, supported by Archbishop Makarios, to bring about Enosis
EOM	Ease of Maintenance
ERE	Extra Regimental Employment. An officer or soldier employed outside own Regiment or Corps
ERB	Executive Responsibility Budget covering all costs, both cash and non-cash, of the budget holder, typically a Commanding Officer
ESO	Equipment Support Organization. Organization formed at Ministry of Defence to embrace functions of REME after Logistic Support Review
FAD	Forward Ammunition Depot
FAIR VALUE	A study into cuts in the QMG's department of civilian manpower in the mid-seventies after the Defence Review of 1974
FANY	First Aid Nursing Yeomanry. A women's independent voluntary organization formed in the First World War for driving duties, eg. staff cars and ambulances. Continued in being until the Second World War when it continued with similar duties
FARELF	Far East Land Forces
FASO	Forward Air Supply Organization. An RASC air despatch controlling HQ commanded by a Major working with RAF Mobile Staging Posts on forward airfields in the North West Europe campaign
FFMA	Forward Force Maintenance Area for logistic support in Op GRANBY in the Gulf 1991
FGA	Fighter Ground Attack
Field Ambulance	The RAMC Unit within a field force providing immediate front line medical support for casualties and their evacuation to a field hospital.

	An ASC RASC/RCT element was part of the unit to drive ambulances and other First Line transport
FILOG	The short title for the Logistic Battalion in the Falkland Islands
FIPASS	Falklands Intermediate Port and Storage System (or Flexiport). Accommodation provided for the garrison after the Falklands War
First Line Repair	Description of the first level of repair available to the Field Force, eg Light Aid Detachment, which provides immediate equipment engineering support to one or more units or a HQ
First Line Vehicles	Vehicles organic to a unit, provided for its own logistic use
FLT	Fork Lift Truck
FMA	There are two definitions: Force Maintenance Area, as used in Op GRANBY in the Gulf 1991 and Forward Maintenance Area as in normal military usage
FMC	Field Maintenance Centre
FMI	The Government's 1982 Financial Management Initiative which required greater emphasis on value for money in the public sector
FMIS	Financial Management Information System to monitor progress for the QMG's Corporate Plan
FOB	Forward Operational Base
FOX	A Light Armoured Car CVR(W) equipped with a 30mm Rarde Cannon
FSD	Field Supply Depot. A static forward depot holding bulk supplies
FTX	Field Training Exercise. A major field training exercise, normally annually in BAOR
FV 430 / 432	A family of 6-wheeled reconnaissance vehicles: included Armoured Personnel Carriers known as SARACENS and SALADIN armoured car
FVRDE	Fighting Vehicle Research and Development Establishment. The Defence Establishment responsible for the design of vehicles specifically for military use, eg. CT vehicles
FWD	A make of Tractor in the First World War
G3	NATO standard designation for operations and training branch of the Staff. Sometimes also used as an oral abbreviation of GSO3 (a captain on the General Staff
G4	NATO standard designation for Logistics and Quartering Staff
GASC	Gurkha Army Service Corps, predecessor to the Gurkha Transport Regiment (GTR)
GAZELLE	Helicopter used by the Army for attack and reconnaissance
GBE	Knight Grand Cross, Order of the British Empire
GCB	Knight Grand Cross, Order of the Bath
GCLO	German Civil Labour Organization in post Second World War Germany
or	
GCLO	Ground Control Liaison Officer – an Army Officer attached to the Royal Air Force
GDP	General Deployment Plan (BAOR)
GHQ	General Headquarters – applied to ASC Companies operating in rear areas, eg. GHQ Ammunition Parks
GOC	General Officer Commanding, eg District or Divisional Commander
GPMG	General Purpose Machine Gun; 7.62mm belt-fed
GPR	Glider Pilot Regiment – 1942-1949
GPS	Global Positioning System. A satellite-based navigation system
GPT	General Purpose Transport
GRANBY	Operation GRANBY, in the Gulf War 1990-91
GRAPPLE	Operation GRAPPLE: the provision of cover by the United Nations Protection Force (UNPROFOR) to the delivery of humanitarian aid in Bosnia/Herzogovina. The UK contribution was supplied in November 1992 by 1st Battalion

	The Cheshire Regiment with logistic support from RCT, RAOC and REME
GS	General Service eg. applied to equipment in common army use
GSE	Group Surety Evaluation
GSL	General Service Launch. A harbour and general communications vessel
GSR	General Staff Requirement. A staff statement in broad terms of the function, main features and performance required of a proposed equipment, eg for the new DROPS vehicles
GT Companies	General Transport Companies. Transport companies with varying types of vehicles allotted to formations as required
GTR	Gurkha Transport Regiment
HANWOOD	UN operation in the former Yugoslavia, setting up UN protected areas up to September, 1993. The British contribution was a Field Ambulance deployed to Croatia, with RCT and REME support
HAVEN	Operation HAVEN, a humanitarian operation to protect the Kurds in North Iraq and SE Turkey following the Gulf War in 1991
HGV	Heavy Goods Vehicle with a load capacity of over 3500kgs
HKMSC	Hong Kong Military Service Corps, which became part of the Gurkha Transport Regiment
HL	Harbour Launch
HMLC	High Mobility Load Carrier, eg. the Alvis Stalwart
HRS	Heavy Repair Shop
HT	Horse Transport. Transport employing horses as pack animals or for drawing wagons
IASC / RIASC	Indian Army Service Corps, subsequently Royal Indian Army Service Corps, the Supply and Transport organizations of the Indian Army
IGDT	Inspector General Doctrine and Training. Formerly Commander Training and Arms Directors until April, 1991
ILHB	Intermediate Higher Level Budget, eg those held by District GOCs and Arms and Services Directors
ILS	Integrated Logistic Support. The procurement system introduced in 1989-90
INLA	Irish National Liberation Army
IRA	Irish Republican Army. The main Nationalist terrorist group in Northern Ireland which has a number of splinter groups including the INLA (above) and the Provisional Irish Republican Army, or Provisionals
IRG	Immediate Replenishment Group
IS	Internal Security. Aid to the civil power in the maintenance of law and order
ISD	In Service Date. The date by which a new vehicle, weapon or other equipment is due into service with full logistic backing available in the field (such as spares, tools and technical publications)
ISO	International Standards Organization: applicable particularly to containers used in freight distribution
IT	Individual Training
or	
IT	Information Technology: all systems for communicating information including the use of computers
JEHU	Joint Experimental Helicopter Unit
JHSU	Joint Helicopter Support Unit. An Army unit with RAF elements to support the operation of Chinook helicopters.
JMCC	Joint Movements Control Centre (BAOR)
Job Evaluation	A method of analysing jobs to establish their relative worth for pay
JSPU	Joint Services Port Unit, eg. Hong Kong and Cyprus
JSTU	Joint Services Trials Unit

KBE	Knight Commander of the British Empire
KCB	Knight Commander of the Bath
LAD	Light Aid Detachment REME. A small first line workshop attached to units, including RASC and RCT
LARKSPUR	Army mobile radio system used in the field before CLANSMAN
LCA	Landing Craft Assault.
LCL	Landing Craft Logistic. Successor to the LCT
LCM	Landing Craft Mechanised
LCT	Landing Craft Tank. Operated by RASC/RCT
LCU	Landing Craft Utility. Designed to carry up to 100 men or two main battle tanks in assault role and operated by Royal Marines
LE(A)	Logistic Executive (Army) at Andover, formed April, 1977 as part of MOD (A)
LHS	Load Handling System
LMG	Light Machine Gun
LMLC	Low Mobility Load Carrier. A vehicle not designed for cross-country performance
L of C	Line(s) of Communication
LSF	Logistic Support Force
LSG	Logistic Support Group set up in the Gulf after hostilities ended in 1991
LSL	Landing Ship Logistic. Large RoRo vessel designed for military use and operated under contract by British India Line until 1970, thereafter by the Royal Fleet Auxiliary
LSR	Logistic Support Review 1990-91. The review was headed by Major General A N Carlier (late Royal Engineers). Implementation resulted in formation of RLC
LST	Landing Ship Tank
LTC	Long Term Costings of the Defence Budget which is compiled in MOD every year covering the next ten years
LTCC	Local Transport Control Centres. Part of the BAOR Freight Service
LVT	Landing Vehicle Tracked. A tracked amphibious vehicle – BUFFALO
LYNX	Army helicopter larger than GAZELLE; faster and armed
LZ	Landing Zone
MAC	Motor Ambulance Column in the First World War, consisting of motor ambulances used for rearward evacuation of casualties
MACC	Military Aid to Civilian Communities
MACM	Military Aid to Civilian Ministries
MASC	Malaysian Army Service Corps – formed in 1957
Mau Mau	Nationalist Movement in Kenya headed by Jomo Kenyatta which was involved there in the independence campaign in the early 1950s
MBE	Member of the Order of the British Empire
MBT	Main Battle Tank, eg CHIEFTAIN or CHALLENGER
MC	Military Cross
or	
MC	Movement Control
MCCP	Movement Control Check Point
MCLU	Movement Control Liaison Unit
MCTG	Mobile Civilian Transport Group. Transport units formed originally from ex German POW in 1945 to work for the Corps which continued as part of the RASC/RCT ORBAT
MEDLOC	Mediterranean Line of Communication. Provided by Train Services, controlled by Q Movements from Hook of Holland to Austria, Italy and Trieste
MELF	Middle East Land Forces
MEXEFLOTE	Rafts used to carry vehicles or stores ashore. They can be connected

	together in various configurations. Operated by RCT from 1965 and normally carried for operations on LSLs
MFVs	Motor Fishing Vessels. General purpose vessels employed within the RASC fleet
MGC	Machine Gun Corps
MGO	Master General of the Ordnance
MHE	Mechanical Handling Equipment
MICV 80	Mechanical Infantry Combat Vehicle later named WARRIOR, which replaced FV432. Issued to BAOR and first used on operations in Op GRANBY in the Gulf 1990-91
MINURSO	United Nations Mission for the Referendum in Western Sahara, for which UNMOs were provided starting in 1991
MLRS	Multiple Launch Rocket System. A US artillery system, first used on operations in the Gulf War 1991
MM	Military Medal
MMLC	Medium Mobility Load Carrier. A vehicle with better cross-country mobility than a normal commercial truck, but not so mobile as some all-wheel drive or tracked vehicles
MMP	Marchwood Military Port
MOD	Ministry of Defence – the Joint Service Ministry under the Secretary of State for Defence of which MOD (Army) is one of three single service departments: MOD (Army) took over the functions of the War Office on the formation of the Ministry of Defence in the early 1960s.
MOR	Malayan Other Ranks
MOSCO	Ministry of Supply Communications Office, which gave its name to Moscow Camp in Belfast
MRLA	Malayan Forces Liberation Army – 1948
MSO	Mixed Service Organization. Formed originally in 1945 for the same purposes as MCTG, to provide transport companies for the RASC, but from Polish and other displaced persons who could not at that time return to their own countries
MSR	Main Supply Route, eg from FMA to forward areas in Gulf 1991
MT	Mechanical Transport. Transport using vehicles driven by any form of engine
MTSD	MT Stores Depot
MV	Military Vigilance
MVC	Motor Volunteer Corps – a pre-First World War Volunteer organization providing chauffeur-driven motor vehicles for use by the army
MVO	Member of the Royal Victorian Order
NAAFI/RASC/EFI	Navy, Army and Air Force Institute and RASC/Expeditionary Force Institute supplying canteens and shops for the Forces and providing part of the ration scale not issued by the RASC. At outbreak of Second World War were badged RASC and became part of the overall supply organization as RASC-EFI. Re-badged RAOC in 1965
NATO	North Atlantic Treaty Organization. The treaty was signed 4 April, 1949 by twelve nations: Greece and Turkey acceded in 1952, Western Germany in 1955 and Spain in 1982
NBC	Nuclear Biological and Chemical. Protective clothing was sometimes referred to as a 'Noddy Suit'
NCO	Non-Commissioned Officer. Non-Commissioned Ranks range from Lance Corporal to Staff Sergeant. See also WO
NMS	New Management Strategy introduced by Ministry of Defence in 1991, creating a hierarchical budgetary management structure. (See 'PROSE')
NORTHAG	Northern Army Group in post-war Germany with its headquarters located alongside HQ BAOR

NSI	Nuclear Surety Inspection
O GROUP	Orders Group; to whom a commander at any level gives orders for an operation or task to those under command
OBE	Officer of the Order of the British Empire
OCTU	Officer Cadet Training Unit
OOA	Out of Area. The term for British troops operating outside the NATO area
Op CORPORATE	Operation to recapture the Falkland Islands in 1982
Options for Change	The review of Defence Policy and reduced requirements following the breaching of the Berlin Wall, the collapse of the Warsaw Pact and the ending of the Cold War in Europe
Op GRANBY	The British operation in the Gulf in 1990-91 as part of the American DESERT SHIELD, DESERT STORM and DESERT SWORD. GRANBY 1 was concerned with the deployment of 7 Armed Bde from BAOR and other troops up to November 1990. GRANBY 1.5 was concerned with the deployment of HQ 1 (BR) Armd Div, 4 Armd Bde and other troops, raising the number of ground troops in the Gulf from 16,000 in November 1990 to more than 33,000 at their peak.
ORBAT	Order of Battle. A list of units in a force or formation
PAIC	Persia and Iraq Command – 1942
PE	MOD Procurement Executive which obtains new weapons and equipment
'Pig'	Humber 1 ton wheeled APC which was converted for use in N Ireland
PIRA	Provisional Irish Republican Army; also known as the Provisionals or Provos. See IRA
POL	Petrol, oil and lubricants. Includes diesel fuel used by tanks and most heavy vehicles
POW / PW	Prisoner(s) of War
PSA	Property Services Agency, the successor to MPBW – Ministry of Public Building and Works, responsible for Government buildings including building and maintenance of barracks
PSI	Permanent Staff Instructor
QGO	Queen's Gurkha Officer
QMG	Quartermaster General
QMG 3	The QMG Staff branch at the War Office responsible for MT, the appointments being filled by ASC/RASC officers
QMG 6	The QMG Staff branch at the War Office responsible for Supplies and POL, the appointments being filled by ASC/RASC officers
Q (Movements)	The Staff Branch in MOD and Formation HQs responsible for Movement policy and its execution
QTO	Qualified Testing Officer. One licensed to test for driving fitness for a particular range of vehicles, eg HGV
RA	Royal Regiment of Artillery
RAASC	Royal Australian Army Service Corps
RACT	Royal Australian Corps of Transport
RAMC	Royal Army Medical Corps. The medical service of the Army, all transport in support being the responsibility of the ASC/RASC/RCT. Now provided by RLC
RAOC	Royal Army Ordnance Corps. The providers of ammunition, equipment, vehicles, spare parts, and from 1965, those functions taken over from the RASC: Supplies, Petroleum, Barrack Services, Clerical Services, Army Fire Service, RASC/EFI and Boat Stores
RAPIER	Ground-to-air anti-aircraft missile system. As used by the Army on operations in Falkland Islands 1982
RAPWI	Release of Allied Prisoners of War and Internees – Far East – October 1945

RASC/ASC	Royal Army Service Corps and Army Service Corps. The immediate predecessors to the RCT, having both a Supply and Transport function
RASO	Rear Air Supply Organization. An RASC Unit commanded by a Lieutenant Colonel established for the operations in North West Europe, to control Air Despatch operations. Commanded one or more Air Despatch Companies with attached personnel to carry out full logistic support for Air Despatch duties, eg. RAMC, RAOC, RMP, RPC, NAAFI/EFI etc
RCASC	Royal Canadian Army Service Corps
RCL	Ramped Cargo Lighter
RCT	Royal Corps of Transport. Formed in 1965, to provide transport and movement support for the Army
RCZ	Rear Combat Zone
RDI	Relief Driver Increment. A pool of extra drivers on a Units establishment
RE	The Corps of Royal Engineers
RE(MC)	Royal Engineers Movement Control. That part of the Royal Engineers with the executive responsibility for the Movement Control Service which passed to the RCT in 1965
RE(PCS)	Royal Engineer Postal and Courier Service absorbed into The RLC in April, 1993
RE(TN)	Royal Engineers (Transportation). That part of the Royal Engineers responsible for Port Operations, associated Inland Water Transport functions and Railways, which passed to the RCT in 1965
Recovery	The process of extracting a vehicle or equipment which has broken down or become disabled and moving it to a place where it can be backloaded or repaired
REME	The Corps of Royal Electrical and Mechanical Engineers
RFA	Royal Fleet Auxiliary, providing support ships such as oil tankers and LSLs, and their crews
RFC	Royal Flying Corps. Predecessor to Royal Air Force in First World War
Rigid Raider	A small semi-rigid inflatable boat used by the Royal Marines for patrolling and landings
RLC	The Royal Logistic Corps. Formed in April, 1993 and encompassing the functions of the Royal Corps of Transport, Royal Army Ordnance Corps, Royal Pioneer Corps, Army Catering Corps and the postal responsibilities of the Royal Engineers
RM	Royal Marines
RMP	Royal Military Police
RNZAF	Royal New Zealand Air Force
RNZASC	Royal New Zealand Army Service Corps
RNZCT	Royal New Zealand Corps of Transport
RO-RO	Roll on-Roll off. Ferries which allow vehicles to drive on and off at bow or stern
Roulement	A temporary tour of duty, usually for a few months only, employed in Northern Ireland and elsewhere for formed units or sub-units coming from Britain or BAOR from the Seventies onward
RPC	Royal Pioneer Corps
RPL	Ramped Powered Lighter
RQMS	Regimental Quarter Master Sergeant; a Warrant Officer Class 2
RSA	Royal School of Artillery, at Larkhill, Wiltshire
R SIGNALS	The Royal Corps of Signals
RSM	Regimental Sergeant Major, in the rank of Warrant Officer Class 1
RTCH	Rough Terrain Container Handler
RTE	Rail Transfer Equipment. Equipment to enable loads to be transferred from road to rail flats in association with DROPS

RTR	Royal Tank Regiment
SACEUR	Supreme Allied Commander Europe: a NATO appointment
SAGW	Surface to Air Guided Weapon, eg RAPIER
SAS	Special Air Service
SATCOM	Satellite Communications
SBA	The Sovereign Base Areas in Cyprus under British control
SCORPION	CVR(T): a light tracked armoured vehicle equipped with a 76mm gun and issued to armoured regiments for reconnaissance. Used in Falkland Islands 1982 and the Gulf 1991
SCOUT	An Army helicopter
SDF	Sudan Defence Force
SEAC	South East Asia Command. The command covering the war against the Japanese in the Second World War
SEA KING	A helicopter used by the Royal Navy to carry men or to operate against submarines
Second Line	Vehicles other than unit vehicles used for forward logistic support of divisional units and operated by the ASC/RASC/RCT
Services	The Corps such as RAMC, RCT, RAOC, REME as distinct from the 'Arms' such as RAC, RA, RE, R SIGNALS and Inf
SHAEF	Supreme Headquarters Allied Expeditionary Force
SHAPE	Supreme Headquarters Allied Powers Europe
SHFHQ	Support Helicopter Force Headquarters based at RAF Benson
Somerville Study	The Logistic Reorganization Committee headed by Major General R M Somerville (late RA) VQMG, set up in 1974 and which reported in 1975. It led to the formation of the Logistic Executive (Army) at Andover in April, 1977
SOP	Standard Operating Procedure
SPEARHEAD	A UKLF codeword for an infantry battalion group at 72 hours' notice to deploy in any operational role worldwide, with a leading company group at 24 hours' notice
SPEARPOINT	A series of exercises in BAOR for 1(BR) Corps. It was the 1(BR) Corps insignia
SRD	Supply Reserve Depot. A major supply depot holding bulk supplies
S&T	Supplies and Transport. The generic term for the tasks carried out by the Corps from 1869 to 1965
ST 2	The RASC branch responsible for petroleum from 1945 to 1965 at War Office, MOD (Army) and major headquarters, replacement QMG 6
Staff	A commander's advisers and planners who issue orders and instructions on his behalf, eg Military Secretary, Operations (G3), Intelligence (G2), Personnel (G1) and Logistics (G4) staffs: prior to NATO nomenclature Military Secretary – G Staff, A Staff (Personnel), and Q Staff
STALWART	6 wheeled load carrier with all wheel drive and an amphibious capability; highly mobile with an armoured cab. Extensively used by the RASC/RCT as second line vehicles
Star	NATO terminology refers to 'one star', a brigadier in UK or 'brigadier general' in some other armies, eg Canada; 'two star', a major general; 'three star', a lieutenant general; 'four star', a general; 'five star', a field marshal in the British Army. In some NATO armies the number of stars on the badges of rank reflect the rank of the officer. In the British Army the stars were mounted on red plates on Army staff cars and Jeeps to show the rank of the occupant. This practice was restricted when the security threat led to senior officers travelling in plain clothes and civilian cars without Army registration plates
STUFT	Ships Taken Up From Trade, exemplified by British merchant ships requisitioned for the Falkland Island Operation CORPORATE in 1982

Sustainability	The ability of a force to maintain the necessary level of fighting power for the duration required to achieve its objectives. This requires sufficient personnel, equipment and stocks on hand plus the ability to resupply and reinforce as necessary
SW	Special Weapons
TA	Territorial Army; established in 1908 and reformed in 1947
TA&VR	Territorial Army and Volunteer Reserve; formed in 1967 and became TAVR soon after
'Tail'	Army slang for that part of the Army which is not in the 'Teeth' Arms, eg the medical, logistic and engineering support services – RAMC, RCT, RAOC, and REME
TAVR	Territorial Army Volunteer Reserve; became TA again in 1976
TCV	Troop carrying vehicle
TD	Territorial Efficiency Decoration
'Teeth' Arms	The fighting arms of the British Army, eg Royal Armoured Corps, Royal Artillery, Royal Engineers, Infantry
TLDT	Training and Logistics Development Team. That part of Headquarters TO in C (Army) dealing with the development of new vehicles, training techniques and the publication of the associated training manuals
TN	Transportation. That part of the Corps of Royal Engineers concerned with Port operations and Inland water transport, transferred to the RCT in 1965
TLB	Top Level Budget, eg that held by a CinC
TO in C (A)	Transport Officer in Chief (Army). Title of Head of Corps 1965-1976
TOW	Tube launched Optically tracked and Wire guided US anti-tank system fitted to Army helicopters, eg LYNX
Trickle Posting	The system of posting individuals to and from a unit in a particular station, rather than replacing the whole unit at once in the manner of infantry battalions and armoured regiments etc
TTF	Truck Tanker Fuel, ie fuel tankers
UAE	United Arab Emirates (formerly the Trucial States)
UE	Unit Entitlement; the authorized scale of equipment holding
UKFCSS	UK Future Command Structure Study, known as the Stainforth Committee, headed by Major General C H Stainforth CB, OBE (late RASC), leading to the creation of UKLF in 1972
UKLF	United Kingdom Land Forces. Replaced Army Strategic Command on 1 April, 1972 with HQ at Wilton near Salisbury. It commanded the UK-based field forces for operations overseas, and Army districts in the UK
UKMF	United Kingdom Mobile Force formed by 3rd Division with 38 Group RAF 1969-1977 to reinforce NATO forces in Europe. It was the Division's primary role
UN	United Nations
UNFICYP	United Nations Forces in Cyprus
UNHCR	United Nations High Commission for Relief – Bosnia 1992
UNICOM	Unit Computing. A new peacetime administrative computer system for all regular and reserve units worldwide. Introduced in the mid-1990s for personnel, pay, finance, stores, training, mechanical transport etc
UNIKOM	United Nations Iraq/Kuwait Observation Mission for which UNMOs were provided, starting in April, 1991
UNMO	United Nations Military Observer. Individual officers provided for UN missions worldwide for verification of forces and implementation of agreements

UNPROFOR	United Nations Protection Force – Croatia 1992
UNTAC	United Nations Transitional Authority in Cambodia for which which again UNMOs were provided
UOR	Urgent Operational Requirement. There were many such requirements for Op GRANBY 1990-91
USAAG	United States Army Atomic Group
V	Volunteer, as in title of TA units, eg. RCT(V)
VOR	Vehicle Off the Road, awaiting repair or backloading
VRD	Vehicle Reserve Depot
WA	West African
WAC	Women's Auxiliary Corps
War Office	The Government department under the Minister for War prior to the formation of the Ministry of Defence (Army)
WARRIOR	Armoured tracked troop carrier for infantry battalions, equipped with a turret mounting a 30mm Rarden cannon and a Hughes Chain Gun. First used on operations in the Gulf War in 1991. Replaced FV 432
Warsaw Pact	The Eastern Bloc Communist Defence Alliance
WD	War Department. A designation of anything pertaining to the War office prior to the formation of the MOD (Army)
WD FLEET	The War Department Fleet. A civilian-manned fleet of vessels to meet the Army's requirement for water transport, formed in the 19th century and locally controlled by the ASC/RASC. Operated worldwide
WESSEX	An early troop-carrying helicopter
WMR	War Maintenance Reserve: stocks kept in peace for use in war
WO	Warrant Officer Classes 1 or 2. An officer intermediate in rank between the highest non-commissioned rank, ie. Staff Sergeant and a commissioned officer, the rank being granted by virtue of a Warrant
WRAC	Women's Royal Army Corps, formed 1 February, 1949 from the Auxiliary Territorial Service and disbanded 6 April, 1992 when their integration within Regiments and Corps took place and they were re-badged accordingly
WSG	Weapons Support Group. The organization responsible for the carriage of special weapons
XP	Exchange Point
Z Craft	A shallow draft powered lighter locally designed by RE(TN) and manufactured in India/Egypt during the Second World War for use in the Middle East area. Subsequently used worldwide for harbour work
ZNA	Zimbabwe National Army, formed from former Rhodesian and guerilla armies
ZULU	ZULU Time is Greenwich Mean Time as distinct from local time. ALPHA time is one hour ahead of GMT

Introduction

This is the story of a Corps and its Predecessors (collectively or singly being referred to as 'the Corps' in this Volume), that over a period of two hundred years from 1794 provided support for the British Army on land, sea and, later, in the air. Despite modifications to role and the twenty-two year period of the Government moratorium on the Army's supply and transport organization in the mid-1800s, the Corps carried forward its traditional regimental connections and pride, to each successive re-named organization. The story starts at a time when Great Britain was a major colonial power with its Empire spread worldwide. Many parts of that Empire provided armies in support of the British Army for local peace-keeping in their own countries and overseas in two world wars. Their overall contribution to the defence of the Empire was immense. Over the years the Corps played a major part in the highly successful development and training of sister Supply & Transport Corps of these Colonial Armies throughout the Empire. This reached its peak during the Second World War, and the understanding and trust built up during the development of these Corps was to be invaluable when the Corps served together. A large number of individuals from the Empire also joined the British Army in the Corps, and many served with distinction.

For a large part of this period, the Corps carried out both the supply and transport tasks for the Army. These tasks, which started from the onset with responsibility for transport, were not fully integrated until the mid-nineteenth century, and at times before then varied in structure and detail. In 1965, with the formation of the Royal Corps of Transport (RCT), the roles were again split and additional transport and movements tasks were taken on, whilst the supply functions were shed. The importance of the Corps' differing responsibilities to conform to the overall organization, technical advances and activities of the Army during this whole period are clearly illustrated in the chapters that follow. How well it fulfilled its duties across a wide and ever-changing spectrum of war and peacetime duties readers will be able to judge for themselves.

A number of official and unofficial histories chronicling detailed activities of the Corps, for various periods, have been written since its formation, the last comprehensive one covering the period from 1945 to 1982. These are listed in the Bibliography. The Corps' life evolved from a troubled birth and many times of uncertainty were to follow in its long and varied history, serving the British Army worldwide in peace and war. Throughout, the dedication and sustained efforts of its individual officers and soldiers recorded in this volume were to ensure that the Corps carried forward collectively its skills, and a proud record of overall achievement, to its new existence.

At the end of 1991, when it became clear that under the Government's Options for Change Defence Review the Corps would not have a separate identity after 1993, it was agreed that a final official recorded history should be written to that date. Initially it was proposed that this version should only encompass the last eleven years of the life of the Corps starting where the last history finished in 1982. However, the suggestion was accepted that, with the ending of its own identity, a more fitting alternative would be to produce in one volume the story of the Corps' life over 200 years. This would give sufficient detail of its long and varied heritage to ensure that no important milestone would be forgotten.

To give wider coverage within available space, the layout of this volume has been changed from that used in the 1982 History. The Elements of the Corps, eg. Transport, Supplies, Maritime, Territorial Army etc, covered in that history, are now covered in appropriate slots in the general chronological order of overall activities. To help the flow of the story, however, some chronological overlapping between chapters and periods has been made in describing ongoing situations, eg. development of vehicles or equipment, major organizational changes, overseas commitments etc.

The story now told is the product of many contributors and the Corps gratefully acknowledges all their efforts. Some have drawn on past histories of their particular interest, sifting through much material to produce the essential outline of the Corps' evolution. Others, dealing with the latter half of this century, have been able to draw on extensive personal experiences, as well as more familiar contemporary reports. Individual styles of contributors have largely remained unaltered, since they convey the spirit and purpose of the time that they cover.

Inevitably, in order to trace two hundred years of activity in this one volume, the material, coming from many sources, has had to be condensed. This process has necessarily been selective, to ensure that the outlines of the principal campaigns, the role of the Corps in them and important issues and events are properly included. It has necessitated, though, limiting to examples descriptions of many of the worldwide range of activities of the Corps and of those organizations, units and individuals who participated in them. In turn, the number of officers and soldiers mentioned by name, as well as the activities, anecdotal stories and pictures of individual units are not as numerous as some might wish. Nevertheless it is hoped that this story will provide both a credible and interesting overall record of the life and achievements of a great Corps and all those who made its invaluable contribution to the Army possible. The Bibliography at the end of the book records the main sources of material, and readers requiring more detail of activities in particular periods or concerning specialized tasks can refer to the appropriate related volume.

The life of the Royal Corps of Transport and its Predecessors started with the Royal Waggoners in 1794. Its first century of existence, when it saw service under a variety of titles in campaigns in many parts of the world, was bedevilled by parsimonious governments and local commanders lacking knowledge of what is now termed logistics. Both were ignorant of the need for efficiently organized supply and transport for the Army in the field, and there were many operational failures as a result. Some commanders, too, who had the means of operating a sound system lacked perception and, with ill judgement, interfered disastrously in the operations of those capable of producing sound results. Not all was gloom in the development, however, and, as this story will show, the most successful commanders were those who understood the importance of sound logistics, which in turn gave the incentive to those who developed them. By the end of the South African Wars the Army Service Corps, which the Corps had now become, had the skilled and enthusiastic officers and soldiers capable of taking the Corps into the new mechanized age. In describing its role the modern term logistics is used throughout the book to encompass all those varied tasks carried out by the Corps, throughout its history, in the provision of its particular support for the Army. Other Corps and organizations were also involved in the overall provision of logistic support, and these are described when their roles overlap.

During the period covered by this book, not only the potential threat to the security of this country, but also public opinion and considerable changes in social attitudes have influenced the size, shape and activities of the British Army, and correspondingly, the Corps. There have been many changes instigated by those serving within the Army across a wide spectrum, resulting in both success and failure and other examinations of even greater significance by the Government in power at the time. The latter have in most cases had the aim of achieving financial savings. After the end of the First World War, for example, the Army (and the Royal Navy and Royal Air Force too) were subjected to constant financial scrutiny of size and structure by Government Committees, to achieve greater cost-effectiveness, particularly in every aspect of manpower, employment and logistic support. This undoubtedly slowed down the development of mechanization. During the period leading up to the Second World War it was only the enthusiasm and dedication of officers and soldiers in the RASC and other affected Regiments and Corps that ensured that, on mobilization, mechanization by various means was so well advanced. This continuing process is covered in Chapters 5 and 6.

Following the Second World War, the Government examination over the years, in addition to covering the wider structure, organization, strengths and tasks of the whole Army, involved many changes of great significance to all the Logistic Corps. The ending of the Cold War in 1989 finally gave the Government the impetus to effect the major overall Tri-Service changes under the Options for Change Defence Review. This review was to lead to the end of the RCT's separate identity in 1993 and the formation of The Royal Logistic Corps (RLC). The decision and effects of those Government Committees since the Second World War, which had a direct bearing on the functions and organization of the Corps at the time, including the major change on the formation of the RCT in 1965, are examined in detail in the chapters relating to the period in which they occurred.

An example of social attitudes affecting the composition of the Army is that which started with the introduction of voluntary women drivers to replace men in the First World War. Initially this was a wartime necessity because of the manpower shortage, but no place was found for women in the Services when the war ended. All this was to alter in the Second World War, when the social attitude to the employment of women in what had hitherto been considered unsuitable careers gradually changed. In 1914 women drivers were found from a number of volunteer organizations, including the First Aid Nursing Yeomanry (FANY) and the Women's Legion, later to form the basis of the Women's Auxiliary Corps (WAC). They were associated with the ASC in driving ambulances and cars, in both UK and France and Belgium, where they served with distinction and released men to go to other combatant areas overseas. When the war ended no women were allowed to serve in the Regular or Territorial Army until 1938 when war again threatened. The Auxiliary Territorial Service (ATS) was then formed with a strength of 20,000. By this time the attitude to the employment of women in the Services had changed considerably. Not only were the ATS mobilized in 1939, as the men were, to become part of the Regular Army, but women were now conscripted into the ATS in a wide range of 124 trades spread throughout the Army. They were not at this stage, though, allowed to serve in combatant units. ATS drivers served in the Corps in all types of Mechanical Transport (MT) units other than those in forward areas, but remained ATS badged. Some RASC MT units were mixed and had both RASC and ATS drivers, whilst others became completely composed of ATS, all of whom drove both cars and load-carrying vehicles.

At the end of the war, although many of the ATS trades were no longer required, it was decided that women would still be needed for many tasks, and on 1 February,

1949, the Women's Royal Army Corps (WRAC) was formed. An increasing number began to serve in the RASC, but still retaining their own cap badge. Subsequent changes in the role of the WRAC attached to the RASC, and from 1965 the RCT, when the number of trades for women in the Corps increased, are dealt with in appropriate chapters of the book. Gradually the role of servicewomen was developed and combat zone responsibilities were introduced, these being fully tested in the Corps during the Gulf War. The complete integration within the Corps of a range of trades took place on 5 April, 1992, when the WRAC was disbanded and those serving with the Corps were re-badged RCT. Thus the initial association which had started over seventy-five years earlier, between the Corps and the Volunteer organizations, having followed a most successful development pattern of co-operation, reached fruition in both the Regular and Reserve Army.

During the Corps' lifetime, as suggested in the previous paragraphs, it was certainly no stranger to change in its responsibilities and the means of carrying them out. It is perhaps understandable that, in meeting some of its wide-ranging tasks, the Corps was often stretched to the limit. At times the resourcefulness, determination and skills of its officers and soldiers were all that stood between success and failure in achieving the successful support required of it. Hard lessons were learned and, as with all Arms and Services, the changing scenes of modern conflict, political aims and structures, and military capabilities had to be matched with technical advances, new concepts and organizations.

It is hoped that this book, tracing as it does a worldwide coverage of its peacetime and battlefield tasks in all their forms, will illustrate the very considerable contribution that the RCT and its Predecessors made to the logistic support of the Army over two centuries.

CHAPTER ONE

The Wars of the French Revolution and the Empire

Introduction. Campaigns in the Low Countries; The Royal Waggoners; North Holland; The Royal Waggon Train. The Peninsular War; The Royal Waggon Train; Waterloo. The Crimean War; The Land Transport Corps. The Indian Mutiny. The Military Train; China. New Zealand. Abyssinia.

INTRODUCTION

The Wars of the French Revolution and Empire, and the British involvement once again in war on the mainland of Europe, created a period of mixed military fortunes and of reputations made and lost. Within the British Army the period also saw progression towards a structured supply and transport system, albeit with many inadequacies. The organization to provide this system was to be developed over the years, despite numerous false starts and setbacks, into one that was ultimately to prove its essential worth in the logistic support of the British Army. The birth of the Corps and its place in British military history over 200 years stem from the period of fitful evolution outlined in this chapter.

The French Revolution and the establishment of the First Republic in 1789 had produced a French Army which bound together the fervour of a citizens' army with the strength and arrogance of the *ancien régime*. It was conditioned in many battles as France continually sought to establish itself as the dominant power in Europe. With Napoleon Bonaparte at its head, and with the enthusiasm and entire resources of the French nation to support the army in a new-found ferocity, France plunged Europe into a war which lasted nearly a quarter of a century.

CAMPAIGNS IN THE LOW COUNTRIES

In 1793 France invaded the Low Countries and declared war on Britain, who then faced up to an enemy which threatened her prestige, her influence and indeed her homeland.

Revolutionary France was bankrupt and when her armies sallied forth to plunder Europe it was with the firm intention of living off the land where they campaigned, without payment. This policy confronted them with guerrilla enemies they might otherwise not have faced.

The British Army was conditioned differently. The Duke of Marlborough in the early 1700s had established a system for the payment of agents in a theatre of war and the appointment of men of local importance to provide both supplies and transport. Failure to supply these essentials, which often occurred, was due at best to inexperience, generally to bad contractors and insufficient funding, but more importantly to a lack of professional military interest in the problems.

The Commissaries in the British Army played a major part in the local provision

1

and management of transport and supplies in the field, but they were under the control of and financed by the Treasury, which often had little comprehension of the military requirements or the conditions existing in a particular theatre of operations. Regiments had their own baggage train which consisted of a motley collection of carts and coaches. Some were hired or otherwise acquired locally by the regiments themselves and these generally carried the officers' baggage and messing arrangements. There was no fixed army establishment for regimental transport, their number and type often depending on the wealth of officers of the regiment. However, some of the waggons or mules with their drivers or handlers for use by the regiments were often hired by the Commissariat to carry supplies. The control of transport and its load was a regimental responsibility and a regimental officer was appointed as a Regimental Waggon Master.

In 1793 an expeditionary force under the Duke of York was sent to the Low Countries to assist the Austrians and the Prussians against the French. The British Army at this stage, though, was in no fit state to undertake a campaign. In the previous decade establishments had been cut, political interference was a way of life, and elegantly attired inefficient officers were indifferent to the skills of their profession and the needs of the soldiers under their command. With characteristic lack of planning, the first contingent of this force which arrived in Holland was without any Commissariat support, a situation which was partially rectified two weeks later when Commissary Brook Watson arrived to take charge of the supplies and transport of the army. He, at least, had some experience, having seen active service during the American War of Independence.

Against this background the first uniformed Transport Corps, designated the Royal Waggoners, was raised by a warrant dated 7 March, 1794, which in part was intended to allay the all too familiar complaints of past failures of the supply and transport support of the British Army. A Corps of Waggoners was established to serve with the forces under the command of the Duke of York but to operate under the control of the Commissariat. James Poole was appointed Captain Commandant of the Corps and he was to recruit five companies of foot, each comprising one Captain, one Lieutenant, one Ensign, four Sergeants, four Farriers, four Collarmakers, four Wheelwrights and one hundred Privates. The recruits were not found by conscription, as in the French Army, but from those sources from which the British Army was usually recruited: 'the jails of England continued to yield the Army their drunks, felons, debtors and psychopaths'. No attempt was made to recruit men experienced with horses, except that the Chelsea Hospital was asked by the Treasury to call upon any of its cavalry pensioners to volunteer, if they so wished, and they were offered a substantial bounty. As could be expected with this motley collection, the reputation of the new Corps was not likely to be enhanced when it joined the campaign in the Low Countries in July, 1794, four months after the warrant raising the Corps was signed. It is perhaps not surprising that their duties and activities were not recorded.

One other corps had been formed at the same time, the Corps of Artillery Drivers, which was intended to relieve the Commissariat of the burdensome task of finding horses and drivers for gun teams on the Continent.

In early 1795 the campaign in the Low Countries came to an ignominious end when the Duke of York decided to agree very easy capitulation terms with the French and withdraw his force to England. This was mainly because, unknown to the French, his supply and transport arrangements had broken down. However, the French having other aims in Europe, were more than pleased to see his force leave. The British Army boarded transports at Bremen, leaving the hazards of mainland Europe for the safety of Britain. If the work of the new Corps was unsatisfactory, it was neither better nor worse than the rest of the army during the campaign, but nevertheless the Royal Waggoners were abolished and a chance to establish a proper system at that time was lost.

No comment concerning the Royal Waggoners would be complete without that made by Sir James Craig, the Chief of Staff: 'a greater set of scoundrels never disgraced an army. I believe it to be true that half of them, if not taken from the hulks, have visited them...they have committed every species of villainy and treat their horses badly'. It is fair to say that the rest of the Army was not much better, but, being dressed in blue, the Royal Waggoners attained an evil reputation and were known as the Newgate Blues, Newgate being a particularly unsavoury prison in London.

By 1797 only Britain and Portugal stood against the French who were occupying the Low Countries, the Rhineland and Northern Italy. When a small French force did land in South Wales it was rounded up by a local Volunteer Force, the Pembroke Yeomanry, aided by the apparent imminent intervention of reinforcements, actually Welsh women in red shawls. This engagement is commemorated by the only battle honour awarded for action against a foreign enemy on the British mainland. Bestowed on the Pembroke Yeomanry by Queen Victoria in 1853, the inscription 'Fishguard' was later worn on the collar badges of 'A'(Pembroke Yeomanry) Troop, 224 (West Wales) Squadron, Royal Corps of Transport, the successors of that original yeomanry. This incident, and the fear of a general French invasion of Britain, provoked a patriotic response, and a variety of local amateur units, such as the yeomanry, were raised to meet the threat.

NORTH HOLLAND

The Royal Waggon Train

In an effort to break the French hold on the strategically important Scheldt estuary, the British mounted an expedition to North Holland in August, 1799, under Sir Ralph Abercromby. For this expedition another attempt was made to provide a Corps of Waggoners to support the Force. An establishment of five companies was sanctioned and Digby Hamilton appointed a Lieutenant Colonel and Waggon Master General, a slight variation from the title of the previous transport commander. The first depot in England was at Bromley, later at Croydon, and the Corps served at Windsor, Canterbury, Eltham, Ramsgate and East Ham.

There appeared to be some difficulty in deciding on a title for the new Corps, and this lack of decision continued for some years. In September, 1799, appears the first mention of the title 'Royal Waggon Corps', and 'troop' described the sub-unit instead of 'company'. On official letters the title was variously given as 'Corps of Waggoners', 'Royal Waggon Corps' or 'Corps of Royal Waggoners'. In the Army List corrected to 1 September, 1799, the title appears as 'Royal Waggon Corps' to 'serve with rank in the Army on the continent of Europe only'. By August, 1802, whilst at Canterbury Barracks, the name 'Royal Waggon Train' appears to have been settled on and from June, 1803, the Corps ranked as a mounted corps after the 29th Dragoons, then the junior cavalry regiment, and in which position it remained until 1833.

Within a month of being created, part of the Corps arrived in Holland. However, because of the parsimony of the Treasury the vehicle establishment of one hundred bread waggons, one hundred forage carts, twenty hospital waggons and ten forge carts were not in fact constructed even by the time the campaign ended and only a few were made available from local sources in Holland. The lack of supplies and transport, together with bad weather, affected the British Army to such an extent that consolidation of their initial success became increasingly difficult. Little wonder that the Corps was reported as inadequate for the needs of the Army. It was fortunate that the French proposed an Armistice and the Army was able to be evacuated from Holland. However, good came out of this campaign as it was generally recognized that an organized transport service was essential and that disciplined persons accustomed to horses must be recruited.

Four more troops were raised in September, 1799, including a troop for recruiting duties. When later three more troops were added, the Commandant of the Corps, Digby Hamilton, was promoted to Colonel and eventually Major General. An established transport service for the British Army appeared to be becoming a permanency, but appearance was one thing, ultimate fulfilment quite another.

The French presence in Egypt at the end of the eighteenth century and their ultimate defeat in 1801 and Napoleon Bonaparte's victories against Russia in Switzerland, and Austria in Germany and Italy, did not involve the Royal Waggon Train. Similarly the Allied successes in India (where Arthur Wellesley was promoted Major General in 1802) are but a backcloth to the main event of this part of the logistic story which will centre on the Iberian Peninsula.

A pause in hostilities brought about by the Peace Treaty of Amiens in 1802 gave a short breathing space for the contending powers. By May, 1803, Britain and France were at war again and, with Napoleon massing an army for the invasion of Britain, the British Army's prime task was the defence of the home base.

THE PENINSULAR WAR

The Royal Waggon Train

Following Nelson's defeat of the combined French and Spanish fleet at Trafalgar, the threat of invasion receded and Napoleon marched away from the Channel to campaign against his continental enemies. In 1807, determined to close all European ports to Britain, he invaded the Iberian Peninsula where the people of Spain and Portugal eventually rose in revolt in May, 1808, and appealed to Britain for aid.

In 1808 Sir Arthur Wellesley, commanding a British expeditionary force, sailed from Ireland to seize the naval base at Lisbon and took with him two troops of Irish Commissariat Waggon Corps. By October these two troops had been incorporated with the Royal Waggon Train, bringing the strength up to twelve troops.

The total strength of the Royal Waggon Train in 1805 was two thousand all ranks and it was significant that there were 'one hundred and twenty Privates armed' among them. With the threat of invasion passed, the Corps was reduced to four troops, but in 1807 it was increased again, this time to ten troops. Echelon duties in support of the Commissariat continued but now, where the transport columns had to be protected, the Royal Waggon Train was increasingly involved in providing close support to the combat arms. It ultimately became a normal practice to split troop organization into small detachments in direct support of infantry or cavalry.

4

The landing in Portugal was effected to the north of Lisbon over the beaches at Mondego Bay; a long-drawn-out process due to the conditions, but it did give Wellesley the time to arrange his logistic support in a manner which was to become familiar throughout his campaigning.

The task which had been given to Wellesley was to ensure 'the final and absolute evacuation of the Peninsula by troops of France'. Whitehall, though, continued to lack an understanding of the logistics involved in a military campaign fought by one army, but ranging over a large country with difficult terrain. Fortunately

Letter authorizing change in colour of the Royal Wagon Train Dress from blue to red.

HORSE GUARDS,

25th September, 1811.

Sir,

 I have received His Royal Highness the Commander-in-Chief's directions to acquaint you that His Royal Highness The Prince Regent has been pleased in the name and on behalf of His Majesty to approve of the colour of the clothing of The Royal Waggon Train being changed from Blue to Red; the Clothing with the exception of this change of colour to continue in every respect the same as at present.

I have the honour to be,

Sir,

Your most obedient Servant,

(*Signed*) R. DARLING.

Deputy Adjutant General.

(Colonel Ralph Darling, 51st Regiment of Foot.)

Wellesley was a master of solving his logistic problems, having learned his lesson whilst fighting in many battles in India. If he was ill-served by inexperienced commissaries, he was quite capable of quantifying the requirement and issuing orders to ensure a timely delivery of necessities to his forces. Wellington was ever ready, however, to commend competence and Commissary General Robert Kennedy, who accompanied Wellesley at Mondego Bay and the subsequent march to Lisbon, gained favour for his zealous contributions to the logistic plan.

Within a month of landing in Portugal, Wellesley gave the French a foretaste of the capabilities of the British Army by the defeat of the French at Rolica and Vimeiro. The first Peninsular awards of bars to the Military General Service Medal 1793-1814 to members of the Royal Waggon Train resulted from these victories.

The command of the British Army in the Peninsula during the winter campaign 1808-09 now passed to Sir John Moore, Wellesley having temporarily fallen from favour; he was blamed for his involvement in the Treaty of Cintra which allowed the defeated French to evacuate Portugal and sail home in British ships.

In October, 1808, a British force under General Sir David Baird landed at Corunna, on the north-west coast of Spain, and it was followed a month later by reinforcements which contained three troops of the Royal Waggon Train. This force was to join Moore who by this time was preparing to march from Portugal into Spain to confront the French. A careful plan of supplies and transport was essential for success, but Moore began his advance with little support from the Spanish government and local population. With few reliable supply resources and with bad weather and indifferent transport arrangements, the regular distributions of supplies became increasingly difficult.

It was Moore's intention to strike at the French lines of communications with his Army, which had concentrated on 20 December. This threat was countered by Napoleon who directed his army, with a superiority of over six to one, to attack Moore's force. Against such odds Moore was forced to retire towards Corunna, where transports were at anchorage and evacuation of his force by sea was possible. But his retreat there, which began just before Christmas, was no easy matter in appalling weather conditions and with a growing lack of logistic support. Waggons provided from local resources broke down and the hired drivers deserted with their teams. Other waggons were too cumbersome for the narrow roads, which varied from seas of mud to ice-covered, from which many slid over the precipices. In these conditions extra horses had to be harnessed to each waggon so that the number which could be horsed was reduced, affecting the overall carrying capacity for supplies. The sprung waggons were used as ambulances due to the increased number of casualties. They had a load of two men lying or eight sitting, but each waggon required four horses and they often blocked the road.

Soon there was little food, no fuel, no shelter and nothing to drink but snow. Morale and discipline of the troops began to suffer, but, given the opportunity to engage the French, the spirit was still there. Small depots that had been set up by Baird *en route* to Corunna were sacked by Moore's hungry soldiers, and the stocks vanished, watched by hapless commissaries. Villages were plundered for wine and what little food there was, and almost every sign of a disciplined fighting force disappeared. It was only when Moore, who had been marching with the Rearguard, arrived forward with the main force on 2 January that order was restored.

The terrible winter retreat of some 300 miles will best be remembered for the culminating battle at Corunna on 16 January, 1809, where Moore was mortally wounded, but not before he had been able to revitalize and reorganize his Army to face the French and defeat them. When one of the sprung waggons arrived to take him from the battlefield the six Highlanders who were carrying him in a blanket respectfully asked that they might continue, as they would march in step and carry him more comfortably – a soldierly tribute to a popular commander. The victory at Corunna allowed the British Force to be evacuated, and by the end of the 17th, following Sir John Moore's carefully laid plans, all were on board ship and set sail for England.

It is easy to understand that much of the blame for lack of logistic support and the ensuing suffering and chaos was directed at the Royal Waggon Train, starting with the Waggon Master General who was referred to as that 'fat General Hamilton and his useless Waggon Corps'.

Apart from an overall lack of experience and transport skills in the Royal Waggon Train, it had insufficient waggons and animals, and many of the waggons were unsuitable for the tasks and terrain. The fact that the waggons and animals that they had were used in small detachments, instead of being concentrated and carefully controlled, also contributed to the failings of the organization.

The Commissariat were no better, lacking experience and being confronted with a task beyond their comprehension. Looting of what supplies there were was commonplace, but sheer inadequacy of supplies and poor distribution compounded the situation on the ground. The deeper reason for the supply and transport failures was, however, the vital lack of understanding at the highest level of how the logistic needs of an Army should be met when operating at an abnormal distance from the supply ports. Hitherto the Royal Navy had for many years ensured that the British Army enjoyed an uninterrupted build-up of supplies which remained accessible to the battlefields close to the ports. Moore's route from north of Lisbon to Corunna was, however, extended over a long distance in very difficult conditions of terrain and weather. In these circumstances the absence of a professional appreciation of logistic and administrative support had a disastrous effect.

Sir Arthur Wellesley was now appointed to command another Army which disembarked at Lisbon in April, 1809, and thus began a period of five years campaigning against the French which was to become a personal and national epic. Wellesley considered that successful campaigning in the barren lands of the Peninsula depended upon an established system of supplies and transport and the prudent use of his seaward communications.

Having arrived in Portugal, he pushed north across the Douro, forcing the French to retreat and then faced by a greater force, he retreated first to a defensive line at Talavera, from where, having lost a quarter of his strength, he withdrew to Portugal. In these actions Wellesley had found the Transport Corps 'of the greatest use on the march and while stationary'. Some of the transport was poorly designed for the terrain and the sprung waggons in particular were used mainly on the good roads. These sprung waggons had been indispensable in the retreat at Corunna for the carriage of the wounded and more and more were they used for this purpose, two or three being attached to each division. The forward transport, supplying the Army with food, was carried on the backs of mules on the insistence of Wellesley because mules did not block the roads and were more flexible in their use than waggons. They operated under the direction of the Commissariat.

Among such loads would be fodder for the horses and mules, and a most important item for the British soldiery, the rum ration, set at a third of a pint per

Commissary Waggon Train operating under the Commissary General. Seen here with horse and bullock-drawn carts.

soldier per day. The requirements of mules for this organization produces some interesting statistics; for example: an Army of 50,000 would require one mule per seven soldiers: a cavalry brigade of 1300, with more horses than soldiers, would require one mule per two soldiers.

By now years of hard campaigning by the British Army had produced an efficient and confident fighting force. Little by little also the logistic support for the Army improved and the presence of Wellesley with his order and system made a substantial impact on its effectiveness.

After Talavera Wellesley withdrew the exhausted Army behind the impregnable defensive lines constructed at Torres Vedras, and the tasks of victualling the Army eased as it could now be supplied through the port of Lisbon and by local merchants. The French confronting Wellesley at the end of long lines of communication were prey to guerrillas, and with the country around devoid of food, were reduced to starvation.

In 1811 local transport proved inadequate to support the Army's needs and to help the mule transport attached to the Divisions it was decided to build 600 bullock carts to carry 800 lbs each. These were built during the winter at Lisbon, Oporto and Almeida and formed a Commissariat Waggon Train under the Commissary General. By this time the Commissariat had been given relative military ranks whilst remaining Treasury Officials, which added to the confusions of those who endeavoured to sort out the duties of the Royal Waggon Train with those of the Commissariat. Commissary General Kennedy returned to England and Wellington asked for Commissary General John Bissett as a replacement.

In 1812 a well-organized British Army with sound logistic backing took the offensive. A series of successes by Wellington against the numerically superior French encouraged Austria and Prussia, alongside Russia, back into the war against Napoleon. The Peninsular campaign ended with the advance north to the Pyrenees and beyond into France. With his armies defeated in each battle and in spite of his tactical flair, Napoleon finally abdicated with the fall of Paris on 31 March, 1814, and his exile to Elba followed.

The Royal Waggon Train had been represented at most of the battles fought in the Peninsular War and many of its members were recipients of bars to the Military General Service Medal 1793-1814 which was ultimately issued in 1848. These included thirty-six members who were awarded the bar – Corunna.

Wellington paid the Commissariat a high compliment 'Notwithstanding the increased distance of our operations from our magazines and that the country is completely exhausted, we have hitherto wanted nothing, thanks to the diligence and attention of Commissary General John Bissett and the officers of the department under his charge.'

The Royal Waggon Train gained the battle honour – PENINSULA.

When Wellington's campaigns ended in 1814 his well seasoned Army was scattered and the Royal Waggon Train was reduced to five Troops. At home, the headquarters and depot had settled at Croydon where, amongst its activities, it established an unofficial band much enjoyed by the local populace and HRH The Duke of York, a close friend of the Commander, Colonel Digby Hamilton. A transport service was provided for the varying demands of the British Army at home and the following detail gives an idea of the nature of the work performed: fifty-five horses on the Royal Military Canal, Hythe, for works and roads; forty-eight on the Isle of Wight, for removal of sick and wounded, baggage, works and roads; eighteen at Portsmouth for sick; four spring waggons in Kent to convey sick from shore to hospitals in the south; sixty at Croydon for the transport of treasure and various duties and at Wormwood Scrubs, to make a field for exercise and roads to it; sixty at the Royal Military College for general duties.

WATERLOO

In 1815, Napoleon returned from exile and resumed power and hostilities against his old enemies, and the British Army was once again to be involved. But it was without the essential element of a supply and transport organization as the system which Wellington had so carefully built up between 1809 and 1814 had, in a short space of time, been dissipated. It was now necessary to repeat all the troublesome processes to re-establish it.

The Royal Waggon Train

To raise the number of Royal Waggon Train troops once more to twelve, four Hanoverian troops were recruited in June. The establishment of eight troops of Royal Waggon Train at this time was sixty-seven Officers, 1,005 Other Ranks, and 1,440 horses; one hundred spring waggons, five store, five forage and twenty-seven forge waggons. The record of the manner in which this establishment was used indicates that it was again employed in attachments to cavalry and to infantry regiments with the spring waggons carrying the sick and wounded.

Napoleon's plan was to deal first with the Prussians, whom he attacked and defeated at Ligny on 16 June, 1815. Wellington in the meantime held the French at Quatre Bras and withdrew to prepared positions at Waterloo.

The battle of Waterloo has been much written about and it is sufficient for this account to say that the cream of the Napoleonic war machine was defeated on that battlefield. The British Army, together with its allies, won a great victory and the hastily organized logistic support stood the test over a short period of time. Wellington's Army had reached the stage when he could say that with it he could go anywhere and do anything; an essential element of its perfection was the organization, slowly and painfully evolved, for supply and transport, it having been clearly established that the two must ever go hand in hand.

Napoleon abdicated a second time on 22 June, 1815, and died in exile on 5 May, 1821.

A detailed account of the day-to-day operation of the Royal Waggon Train during the Waterloo campaign exists only in the undertones of the regimental histories of others. One such history relates how a driver of the Royal Waggon Train, Private Brewster, drove a waggon of much-needed ammunition through the French lines at Hougoumont Farm to supply the beleaguered 3rd Guards.

The final duty of the Royal Waggon Train at Waterloo was the clearance of the battlefield, a task which involved burying the dead and burning the dead horses in great funeral pyres. Whatever their duties, it prompted Wellington to write, in the face of threatened Army reductions by the Treasury, 'No person can be more impressed than I am of the absolute necessity of a corps of the description of the Royal Waggon Train'.

As a mark of esteem, all officers present at Waterloo had the letter 'W' placed against their names in the Army List; all men were styled 'Waterloo men' and were granted special pensions.

The Royal Waggon Train gained its second battle honour – WATERLOO.

The Battle of Waterloo marked the end of a long series of wars with France and major British involvement on the continent of Europe.

At home the Army diminished to the boundaries of regimental influence and tribal attitudes became more important than military cohesion. National economy and the political suspicion of a victorious army after Waterloo reduced the ability of the British to raise a field army.

The Royal Waggon Train was employed on mundane transport tasks, having been reduced in December, 1815, to six troops and a year later to five. One such duty was accompanying the conveyance of military stores and personnel by fly boats on the canals of England. Pickfords, a name synonymous with British Transport since the early 18th Century, were contracted by the government to provide this relatively cheap transportation. The fly boats travelling at three and a half miles per hour required a crew of two steerers and two drivers. A trip would usually be divided into four or five stages, allowing relays of horses to do about forty miles per day.

In 1818 a General Order stated that only one private, two horses and one forge waggon were to be attached to each cavalry regiment and all others of the Royal Waggon Train to be maintained at their depot in Croydon. Only two troops remained at the end of 1818, with a detachment in Gibraltar in 1820, and thus it remained until disbandment in 1833.

THE CRIMEAN WAR

In 1854 Britain, with her ally France, drifted into war with Russia, who was threatening the Turks in the Middle East. The outbreak of the Crimean War on 24 March laid bare the neglect of the British Army during the previous forty years. The British expeditionary force, arrayed in their colourful uniforms, setting sail for Malta, whence they were gradually transferred to Gallipoli or Scutari, was hardly a field force. It lacked the cohesion that a staff organization and supporting service could have given. No land transport organizations existed and trained Commissariat officers were not available. Commissary General William Filder, an aged veteran of the Peninsular campaign, was given the task of collecting local transport, forage and fuel in a country which had even fewer such resources than he had found in impoverished Spain.

The force was transferred to the Black Sea port of Varna in Bulgaria to support the Turks who were resisting a Russian advance to Constantinople. When this threat withered in the face of the resolute Turks in May, the British troops remained to suffer many deaths from dysentery, cholera and typhus.

At the end of August, orders were received to attack Sebastopol, Russia's most important arsenal and naval station on the Black Sea. The battles in the Crimea which were to follow were marked with pride by Victorian England in naming streets, squares and barracks in their memory, but also with anger levelled at politicians, the General Staff and a system which brought needless suffering to her soldiers.

Delay in the arrival of supplies, no organization for receiving and distributing those items which did arrive but remained on board the ships or on the dockside rotting in the adverse weather conditions, inadequate clothing, no cooking arrangements and a casualty rate from disease which halved the numbers of the fighting troops at the battle front were all part of the Crimean scene. The appalling weather of the winter of 1854-55 added to the misery. The supply route from Balaclava, which had been captured in September, to the Sebastopol plateau known as the Uplands, where the British Army lay in siege of Sebastopol, covered a distance of eight miles. In many cases provisions were carried along this route by soldiers knee-deep in mud as there was little or no alternative transport.

Under the stress of the public indignation at this confusion, a new administration began to set things right. The Commissariat was transferred from the Treasury to War Office control, a Hospital Conveyance Corps was raised, a corps of labourers was sent from England to build a railway from Balaclava to the camp on the Uplands and a Land Transport Corps was to be formed 'to establish a more perfect system of land transport in the Army in the field'.

The Land Transport Corps

On 24 January, 1855, nearly a year after the start of the war, a warrant for a transport corps was signed. It was not raised until April when the Land Transport Corps was recruited with its headquarters in Horfield Barracks in Bristol. By 1856 it was in good shape, having been culled and then brought to a state of efficiency under the command of Colonel William McMurdo; but a real weakness still remained in keeping the Commissariat responsible for the load and the transport service responsible for its carriage.

The ultimate strength and disposition of the new Corps admirably fitted the organization of the Army it was supporting. Colonel McMurdo introduced a double echelon system in which one wing worked forward one day and the other the next, between the base and the trenches. Agencies were opened throughout the Middle East to purchase mules, and when sufficient officers arrived McMurdo took control of the Commissariat transport and absorbed the Hospital Conveyance Corps. All requisitions for transport were sent to a Land Transport officer. The animals and transport at this time consisted of horses, ponies, mules, camels, bullocks and buffaloes with Arabian waggons and carts, and mules in the pack role. When the pack mules arrived at the front from the base during an engagement they were unloaded to be ready for carrying ammunition further forward, supplying water and medicinal comforts and carrying seats *(cacolets)* for the wounded.

As the size of the Army in the Crimea increased, a fresh organization of the Land Transport Corps was approved on 1 March, 1856. It was all military and based on the need for each Army Division to be supported by its own affiliated transport. As there were six Infantry Divisions and one Cavalry Division seven regiments of the Land Transport Corps were each divided into two battalions thus:

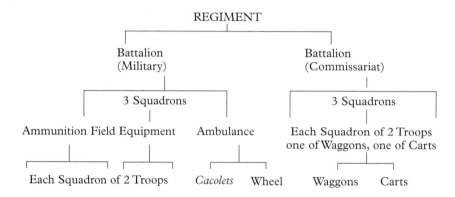

To clear the congested port of Balaclava a railway was constructed by civilian contractors with labour from Britain. It was ultimately supervised by the Land Transport Corps and the animals were drawn from an 8th Battalion. It was far from being just a simple track. The first two miles were operated by five twelve/eighteen ton locomotives driven by Royal Engineers. Then the side-tip waggons of the Land Transport Corps, fitted with railway wheels, were hauled up, eight at a time, by a stationary engine operated by engineers at Kadikoi. From there a team of horses hauled two waggons at a time up the steep gradient, then along a fairly level stretch, after which each waggon coasted down a hill which gave sufficient momentum to climb up the next and last one. Then each waggon was hauled by another team of horses to the end of the line on the Uplands in reach of the front line.

The final transport-carrying capacity of the Land Transport Corps in the Crimea amounted to three days' rations for 58,000 men and 30,000 horses, 200 rounds of ammunition per man for 36,000 men and 2,500 casualties in ambulances.

The final assault on Sebastopol in September, 1855, led to an armistice being signed in February, 1856. The winter in between these dates was in stark contrast to the first winter. The British force was well fed, well clothed and well sheltered. No one would have taken the smart, clean troops seen on the Uplands in January, 1856, for the same care-worn, overworked and sickly soldiers of the trenches of January, 1855. That this changed situation was directly related to properly organized, well-

The Land Transport Corps supervising railway operations in the Crimea 1855-57

balanced logistic support was not in doubt. However, when the Land Transport Corps was renamed the Military Train in August, 1856, as a permanent basis for transport support, all the old ills returned. The Military Train was reduced to 1,200

A general view of the Land Transport Corps bringing supplies ashore in the Crimea 1855-57.

13

men, in spite of the Commander in Chief Crimea, Sir William Codrington, protesting strongly that such a small train would only suffice for a Division. By setting supply upon a civil basis (the Commissariat) and transport upon a military basis (Military Train) a separation was created that became an ever-widening breach.

The evolution of the Military Train from the Land Transport Corps continued as a War Office committee met to report on the 'supply of stores to an Army in the field'. At the same time the Army Transport committee met to examine the question of transport services. These separate deliberations with their subsequent findings were overshadowed by the mutiny of Sepoy troops in Bengal and attention became diverted to the British Empire and the Indian Mutiny.

THE INDIAN MUTINY

The Indian Mutiny involved the entire native Army in Bengal. For the usual parsimonious reasons the European troops were spread too thinly and were without a transport service. Concentration could not be achieved and the Commissaries were unaware of what stocks of food were available. Delhi fell, the Cawnpore garrison was massacred and Lucknow was besieged.

In early 1857 the 2nd Battalion Military Train, commanded by Major J P Robertson, were under orders for China. When news of the Indian Mutiny reached their ship they were diverted to India, where, at Calcutta, they were equipped as light cavalry. The battalion fulfilled their new task admirably drawing praise from one commander, General Sir James Outram, and the Viceroy of India for a career 'short but brilliant and eminently serviceable to the country'. This service, which included the relief of Lucknow and operations around Azimghur, was marked by the awards of the Victoria Cross to Farrier Michael Murphy and Private Samuel Morley for gallantry in saving the life of the Adjutant of the 3rd Sikh Cavalry.

The Military Train gained its battle honour – LUCKNOW on 3 September, 1863.

The Mutiny led to the administration of India passing from the East India Company to the British Government.

THE MILITARY TRAIN

When fifteen battalions of the Land Transport Corps were reduced, and the Military Train was formed, Colonel William McMurdo was appointed Director General. He formed the Military Train from the pick of his old Corps, retaining the best officers and other ranks, supplemented from various cavalry regiments. There were three battalions, each of six troops and having twenty-seven officers, 480 other ranks and 546 horses. But by January, 1857, the strength had been increased to six battalions, each of four troops, with the Depot at Horfield Barracks in Bristol. In 1859 a 7th Battalion was raised to replace the 1st Battalion which had been sent to China.

In 1860 Colonel McMurdo was appointed to reorganize the Volunteer Forces for Home Defence and Colonel John Clark-Kennedy became Colonel Commandant of the Military Train. He had barely taken up his new appointment when he accompanied the 1st and 3rd Battalions Military Train to Canada. Neither battalion

14

The Military Train with horse-drawn waggon on home duties 1857.

saw active service, the 1st Battalion returning to Aldershot in July, 1862, and the 3rd Battalion to Woolwich in September, 1864. During this time the 3rd and 6th Battalions were employed on general transport duties at home stations.

The initial organization of the Military Train continued until 1865 when it was changed to a twenty-four troop establishment. The numbering of these troops from one to twenty-four have been carried through to the succeeding units of the Army Service Corps, the Royal Army Service Corps and Royal Corps of Transport who celebrated their centenaries in 1965, as a part of their on-going histories. In early 1857 the Military Train was stationed in Aldershot, which had just been established as a military camp and their Corps successors were in residence, in 'the home of the British Army', until the formation of the Royal Logistic Corps in 1993.

The troop organization allowed for one Captain, one Lieutenant, one Sergeant-Major, three Sergeants, four Corporals, one Trumpeter, one Harness-maker, one Farrier, one Sergeant Wheeler, one Smith, and fifty-six Privates – total seventy-one. The transport consisted of five general service (GS) waggons, one corrugated iron waggon with four horses, one forge cart, one pack saddle, a total of forty-one horses.

The glowing reputation of the 2nd Battalion affected the morale of the whole of the Military Train and a cavalry spirit tended to enter into the attitudes of the other battalions. In reality two or three cavalry charges proved a poor exchange for lack of skill in their own legitimate business and, whilst the Commissariat continued to carry out their task with considerable efficiency, the Military Train, in which officers purchased their commissions similarly to officers of the cavalry and infantry, drew scathing comments about its efficiency.

China

The 1st Battalion Military Train served in China in 1860 where a combined force of British and French were campaigning to ensure that the Chinese government honoured a peace treaty signed in 1858. When the battalion arrived in Hong Kong it was split into three divisions. The first division was sent to Japan to buy horses and cattle and the remaining divisions made arrangements for transport, but language difficulties hampered their efforts severely.

Large numbers of Chinese coolies were used to offset the work of the few animals that were available and horses, asses, mules, bullocks and every conceivable beast that could be found were used to move supplies.

The allied force of fourteen thousand British and seven thousand French, including the two divisions of the Military Train, embarked and sailed for the mainland. With little effort the defensive Taku Forts were taken and the troops marched into Tientsin, where, during a short delay, all the hired drivers and their animals disappeared. The force then advanced on Pekin where the Chinese government surrendered and operations came to an end.

The 1st Battalion Military Train gained the battle honour – TAKU FORTS and PEKIN on 4 November, 1861.

This small campaign underlined all the usual problems of the separation of responsibility for transport and supplies. There was constant friction between the Commissariat responsible for supplies and the Navy and Military Train responsible respectively for transport afloat and ashore. Both declined to take orders from the Commissariat, although the Military Train were reported as knowing nothing of transport work and having little regard for it in any case, preferring to retain their light cavalry image gained in India. Additionally, the Maltese carts and the waggons sent to them from England, originally destined for the Crimea, were of faulty construction and the wood rotted and the harness perished through overlong storage.

Arguments of control continued but the final words appeared to be those of Colonel Clark-Kennedy: 'Any system based on the provision of food by the Commissariat and its independent conveyance by the Military Train would result in failure'.

New Zealand

In the Maori Wars of 1861-71 the first Commissariat Transport Corps was formed by the General in command and by 1863 there were thirteen companies dividing their responsibilities between land and water. The 200-mile line of communication varied from roads to rivers of varying depths and size and there were ten changes from land to water carriage.

When the 4th Battalion Military Train arrived in 1864, General Sir Duncan Cameron, who was in command, ordered that they were to be employed in and about Auckland and thus their field operations were restricted to only one cavalry charge at Nukumaru where Captain Thomas Witchell was commended for his leadership and the vigorous and effective charge over difficult ground.

Abyssinia 1867

The Abyssinian expedition of 1867-1868 did not directly involve the Military Train. The expedition was mounted from India under the commander-in-chief of the Bombay Army, Lieutenant General Sir Robert Napier, to secure the release of imprisoned Europeans from the tyrannical King Theodore of Ethiopia. A transport officer who had served in the Land Transport Corps in the Crimea, Major John Warden, was appointed, as was a senior supply officer from the Commissariat. Mules for the expedition came from Mediterranean countries and their collection and organization was supervised by Colonel Clark-Kennedy with detachments of the Military Train. The expedition's success in overcoming the hazards of climate and terrain was due to effective improvisation and the spirit and discipline displayed by the troops. Initial logistic problems were overcome and there was no dissent between Commissariat and Transport as the Indian Army favoured companies in which these duties were combined under a unified command. This only served to emphasize the shortcomings in the British Army logistic system which was to have to wait until the evolution of the Army Service Corps later in the century before a clear system was established.

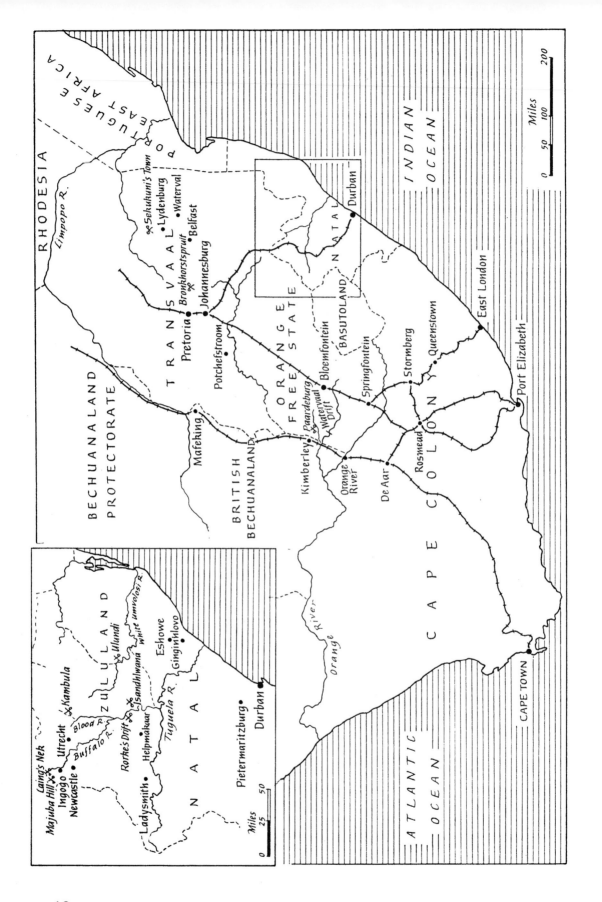

RHODESIA

PORTUGUESE EAST AFRICA

Limpopo R.

BECHUANALAND PROTECTORATE

TRANSVAAL

Sekukuni's Town
Lydenburg
Waterval
Belfast
Bronkhorstspruit
Johannesburg
Pretoria
Potchefstroom

Mafeking

BRITISH BECHUANALAND

ORANGE FREE STATE

Paardeberg
Waterval Drift
Kimberley
Bloemfontein
Springfontein

BASUTOLAND

NATAL

Durban

INDIAN OCEAN

200
Miles
100
50
0

East London

Queenstown
Stormberg
Rosmead

Orange River
De Aar

CAPE COLONY

Port Elizabeth

Orange River

ATLANTIC OCEAN

CAPE TOWN

ZULULAND

White umvolosi R.
Ulundi
Eshowe
Gingihlovo
Isandhlwana
Kambula
Laing's Nek
Majuba Hill
Ingogo
Utrecht
Newcastle
Blood R.
Buffalo R.
Rorke's Drift
Helpmakaar
Tugela R.
Ladysmith
NATAL
Pietermaritzburg
Durban

Miles
50
25
0

18

CHAPTER TWO

The Evolution of the Army Service Corps and Campaigns in Africa and the 19th Century

Introduction. South Africa 1805-1877, British Army Supply and Transport 1867-1878; Background; The Ninth Frontier War, The Zulu War 1879. The Sekukuni Campaign, The First Anglo-Boer War 1880-1881; The Commissariat and Transport Staff, Egypt and the Sudan 1882-1885; Egypt 1882; Sudan 1884; Nile Campaign (Relief of Khartoum) 1884. Bechuanaland Expedition 1884-85. Formation of the Army Service Corps 1888. The Boer War 1889-1902. Epitaph.

INTRODUCTION

The last quarter of the 19th Century saw turbulent years on the continent of Africa, particularly in southern Africa where war followed war in almost continuous succession. This era coincided with a period of great change and reform in the British Army and was a crucial time in the development of the supply and transport services. It was during this time in South Africa that the Army Service Corps evolved from the Military Train and was tested in war. South Africa was the setting for much of the war experience which culminated in the major Anglo-Boer War of 1899-1902. Space does not permit more than an outline reference to the campaigns, enough only to illustrate the part played by the supply and transport services in them.

SOUTH AFRICA 1805-1877 – BACKGROUND

British involvement in South Africa began when they took control of the Dutch colony at the Cape of Good Hope during the Napoleonic wars as a strategic base on the sea route to India, and permanently annexed the territory in 1814. The Dutch had started a settlement in the Cape in 1652 and it had been augmented by French Huguenot and German immigrants over the years. These had fused together into a fiercely independent Protestant people, the Boers. Skilled riders and marksmen, adept at bushcraft, they were averse to the imposition of central government and were soon at loggerheads with the British authorities over taxation and native affairs. As in all contemporary colonial societies, some slavery existed. When slavery was abolished throughout the British Empire in 1834, inadequate offers of compensation to the Boers was the last straw for many of them and between 1835 and 1837 large numbers left Cape Colony and moved to the interior. This mass exodus, known as the Great Trek, resulted in the setting up of new independent Boer Republics. By 1875 South Africa was composed of two British Colonies, two Boer Republics and a clutch of ill-defined native kingdoms, including the Zulus.

Having achieved a confederation of the English and French-speaking Provinces in Canada, the Colonial Secretary, Lord Carnarvon, appointed Sir Bartle Frere as Proconsul in South Africa tasked to bring about a similar unification. Carnarvon took the first step by annexing the Boer Transvaal in April, 1877, under the pretext of its bankruptcy and state of conflict with several native kingdoms, including the Zulus. He alleged that the Zulus seriously threatened peace and stability in the region. Bartle Frere, who had been a distinguished and decisive Governor of Bombay during the Indian Mutiny, quickly formed the opinion that the Zulu King Cetewayo was behind the widespread native unrest and that the Zulu army of 40,000 formidable warriors could bring about an uprising of Indian Mutiny proportions. Added to this, it was clear that the Boers and Colonists both disliked the idea of federation and the Transvaal Boers were determined to regain their independence. Against this turbulent background the British Army was again about to be severely tested.

BRITISH ARMY SUPPLY AND TRANSPORT 1867-1878

Background

During the twelve years from 1855 to 1867 which followed the administrative débâcle of the Crimean War, no less than seventeen Royal Commissions and nineteen War Office Committees examined the supply and transport needs of the Army. The outcome was the creation in 1869 of the Control Department, under the orders of the Secretary of State for War, with the express purpose of exercising effective control over military expenditure. This department consolidated into one organization the fragmented logistic services of the day. However, it did not completely shed its Treasury-orientated civilian character, despite the formation of a small Army Service Corps which was manned by soldiers commanded by officers drawn from the Control Department. The Army Service Corps companies were raised during 1870, in the first instance from volunteers drawn from the Military Train, the Commissariat Staff Corps and the Military Store Staff Corps. By 1871 there were twelve Transport Companies, each of 107 non-commissioned officers and men, seven Supply Companies and three Ordnance Store Companies, each of 105 non-commissioned officers and men. This experiment continued until 1875 when the Control Department was abolished and divided into two separate organizations, the Commissariat and Transport Department and the Ordnance Store Department. Although the Commissariat and Transport Department now assumed a more military character and the status of the ASC was enhanced, the numbers of ASC companies had only increased to seventeen by 1878, insufficient to support the Army in war. Officers of the Commissariat and Transport Department served in most garrisons around the world except in India. The Headquarters Office was located at Woolwich Arsenal where two ASC Transport Companies provided the departmental Depot. The operational ASC Companies were deployed mainly at Woolwich, Aldershot and in Ireland. The original Supply Companies were amalgamated to form 18 Company which became the Depot for all Supply personnel and was at Aldershot.

The scale and complexity of the problems which confronted the Commissariat were never more graphically illustrated than in the vast hinterland of southern Africa during the campaigns between 1877 and 1881 when the lines of communication reached nearly 1,000 miles in extent. There were no navigable rivers and the construction of a railway system had only just started. The few roads were little more than pot-holed tracks which quickly broke up in wet weather to become impassable. Bridges over the fast-flowing rivers were few and flooded crossings could delay traffic for days. The main method of freight transport was the ox-waggon, capable of

A general impression of bullock-drawn waggons moving in convoy and up to six abreast.
(Illustrated London News)

carrying three or four tons when drawn by sixteen oxen yoked in pairs. Each waggon required an expert native driver and an ox leader called a *voorlooper*, whose main task was to keep the animals moving. Every three or four hours he also had to turn them out to graze to prevent them from rapidly deteriorating in condition. In this way fifteen miles a day was considered good progress. With each ox-cart and team needing some sixty yards, convoys became unmanageably long, not to mention vulnerable, and it became military practice to move the waggons up to six abreast. Given a choice, the military preferred faster and more mobile mule waggons, but these required fodder which had to be carried, whereas oxen fed off the land.

A group of waggons, whether owned by the military or hired, were managed and controlled by a Conductor, usually a Boer or Colonist. This title was not to be confused with the British Army rank which was introduced in 1879 for a new class of Warrant Officer in the Commissariat and Transport Department. Designated Conductors of Supplies, they took precedence over all other non-commissioned officers in the Army and had full powers of command over non-commissioned officers and men of any arm placed under their orders. Similar Warrant Officers, denominated Conductors of Stores, were appointed to the Ordnance Stores Department. All wore uniform similar to a junior officer but, curiously, no badge of rank.

The Ninth Frontier War

In the autumn of 1877 a tribal brawl on the Eastern Cape frontier flared up to become the Ninth Frontier War. The Cape Government, which opposed confederation, took this opportunity to assert its independence by insisting that the insurrection should be put down by Colonial troops alone. The Imperial troops, under Lieutenant General Sir Arthur Cunynghame, looked on in frustration while a poorly equipped colonial force lacking supplies and ammunition suffered a series of humiliating defeats. A proposal from Cunynghame that the entire Commissariat be placed under the British Army was flatly rejected by the Cape's Prime Minister who would rather 'supply costs double than the administration be placed in the hands of an Imperial officer'. The result was an absurd competition between the Imperial and Colonial Commissariats which achieved little other than pushing up costs.

When finally the Cape Government was forced to ask Cunynghame to intervene, he refused to move until all supply and transport was put under his Commissary General, Edward Strickland. Cunynghame later applauded Strickland, a veteran of the Crimean and Maori Wars, for working wonders in collecting in supplies and transport despite innumerable difficulties. Strickland, whose handful of Commissariat officers and ASC soldiers were scattered throughout the Cape, Natal and the Transvaal, supplemented his small staff by employing experienced civilians. One such civilian was a retired ASC staff sergeant then living in South Africa, James Dalton. Dalton was the only civilian mentioned in despatches by Cunynghame who wrote, 'The columns never waited for rations or wanted for ammunition'. Dalton was later awarded the Victoria Cross for his gallantry at Rorke's Drift.

A painting by Lady Butler depicting the action during the defence of Rorke's Drift.

The acrimony between Cunynghame and the Cape Prime Minister deteriorated and both were removed from their posts. Cunynghame was replaced by Lieutenant General Thesiger, soon to become Lord Chelmsford. On arrival, together with large reinforcements, he found Strickland was already being accused by the new Cape Prime Minister of extravagance and mismanagement.

Although Chelmsford brought the war to an end in a matter of months, a major political dispute arose between the British and the Cape Governments as to who was to pay for the war, in particular the commissariat costs. London issued a sharp directive to Chelmsford not to incur any further transport expenditure. A minor campaign in itself, the Ninth Frontier War exposed the flaws in the recently reorganized supply and transport service which left an understaffed Commissariat and Transport Department wholly dependent on primitive local resources and susceptible to political interference and pressures. Close observers of these logistic problems were Colonel Evelyn Wood VC, the field Commander in the Ninth Frontier War, and Major Redvers Buller.

THE ZULU WAR 1879

The Zulu War of 1879 is one of the best remembered of the Victorian colonial campaigns, but the effects of the supply and transport problems on the conduct of the war, and their profound consequences for the future development of these services, is little recognized.

Moving to Natal after the Ninth Frontier War Chelmsford, under the political direction of Bartle Frere, was confronted with three military situations spread over an area larger than France. He was required to plan for a war against the Zulus, keep a watchful eye on the Transvaal Boers who were showing signs of rebellion, and subdue Chief Sekukuni and his people who were threatening the peace of northern Transvaal.

Chelmsford found the Governor of Natal, who was far from convinced of the necessity of war with the Zulus, not prepared, for economic reasons, to sanction martial law enabling the Army to requisition transport. This important issue was to create a brittle relationship between the Natal government and the Army which was to endure throughout the war.

Strickland, still struggling with the finances of the Ninth Frontier War, viewed with foreboding the forthcoming operations. He reminded Chelmsford that 'These must be carried out over a vast extent of country, at isolated posts separated from each other by vast distances and in wild impracticable country almost destitute of commissariat resources'. He pleaded for a few trained officers and NCOs, dreading his task without them. The total commissariat strength at the time, spread throughout the Cape, Natal and Transvaal, numbered nineteen officers and twenty-nine men, several of whom were still sick or injured as a result of the Ninth Frontier war.

The extent of the transport problems was accentuated as an exceptional drought brought ox waggon transport in Natal to a virtual standstill, preventing the movement of stores inland from Durban to stock the bases for the invasion of Zululand. Simultaneously the operations against Sekukuni were aborted because of a lack of water and the exhaustion of the transport animals.

Chelmsford, labouring under the impossible restrictions placed on transport expenditure imposed by the Home Government, immersed himself in the minutiae of transport planning. Initially he considered invading Zululand with five columns but the shortage of transport and the need to leave sufficient troops in the Transvaal to contain Sekukuni and watch the recalcitrant Boers made him reduce the number to three. Number 1 Column, under Colonel Pearson, would cross the Tugela River near its mouth and drive up the coast; another, Number 4, under Colonel Evelyn Wood would march from Utrecht, while a Central Number 3 Column, under Colonel Glyn, accompanied by Lord Chelmsford would enter Zululand at Rorke's Drift. This plan necessitated moving all stores required inland from Durban 260 miles to Utrecht and 155 miles to Helpmakaar, the base for the Rorke's Drift crossing.

Attempting to resolve the transport problems, Chelmsford discarded the advice of his Commissary General and set up a Board under an infantryman, Colonel Evelyn Wood, to assess the options. After only three days' deliberation this Board recommended that vehicles be purchased for regimental and hospital transport, the remaining requirements being met by hiring from civilian contractors. The Board further recommended that regimental officers take over transport duties as there were insufficient commissaries for the task.

Chelmsford accepted these recommendations and at this critical time took the drastic step of imposing an untried transport system on his Commissary General. Strickland objected, stating that after forty years' experience he did not believe the system would work. He was to be proved correct. By this reorganization Chelmsford effectively split the responsibility for transport away from supplies. The War Office approved the changes with reservations, insisting that, while the combatant arms must be used to expand the Commissariat in war, it was contrary to the principles of the service to divide the responsibilities for supplies and transport.

Having made his protest, Strickland loyally attempted to implement the plan and prepare for the campaign. Once again the Commissariat and Transport Department, lacking strength and status, had proved vulnerable to inexpert military and political pressure.

On 10 January, 1879, as they waited for a response from the Zulu Chief, Ceteswayo, to their ultimatum the British were poised in three columns to invade Zululand, supported by a veritable transport armada comprising some 10,000 oxen and 400 mules to draw 977 waggons and fifty-six carts. The story of the disaster which befell the Central Column at Isandhlwana and the dramatic defence of Rorke's Drift are too well known to need retelling. However, it is seldom acknowledged that the waggons at Isandhlwana had not been formed into a defensive laager because they were being prepared to return to Rorke's Drift to collect rations essential before any further advance could be made. Nor is full credit given to the Commissariat personnel for the vital part they played in the defence of Rorke's Drift, Acting Assistant Commissary J L Dalton being awarded the VC, Assistant Commissary Walter Dunne, unsuccessfully recommended by Chelmsford himself for the VC, and Corporal F Attwood, the only ASC soldier present, awarded the DCM for gallantry.

In the aftermath of the disaster at Isandhlwana, where 1,500 animals and 300 waggons and carts were lost, the British were forced on to the defensive, with Pearson's Column, besieged in Eshowe, having lost 1,000 oxen to the Zulus, Glyn at Rorke's Drift, and Wood with his Column still intact at Kambula.

Chelmsford directed his main effort to replacing his crippling transport losses, but even in this crisis was quite unable to persuade the Governor of Natal to impose martial law.

At the end of March Chelmsford took personal command of a force to relieve

Waggons on the slopes of Isandhlwana after the battle. (Ian Bennett)

Eshowe, in the process inflicting a significant defeat on the Zulus at Ginginhlovo. His advance had been painfully slow, eliciting the prophetic remark, 'Ox waggon transport is enough to destroy the reputation of any number of commanders'.

Simultaneously with the relief of Eshowe, Wood inflicted a decisive defeat on the Zulus at Kambula. So ended the second phase of the war as huge reinforcements began to arrive from England.

The chaotic state of the Commissariat Services can be imagined as Strickland and his staff wrestled with the dual problem of making good the transport and provisions lost to the Zulus and providing logistic support for the new enlarged army deploying in Natal. The system imposed by Chelmsford was foreign to the experience of his Commissaries, while the infantry and cavalry officers now primarily responsible for running the transport were completely untrained. Strickland complained to Chelmsford of their incompetence, while Chelmsford in turn complained to the War Office that once or twice the Commissariat had been on the verge of breakdown because their officers had not been trained in peacetime to prepare them for war.

Among the reinforcements from England were 3, 4 and 5 Companies ASC, complete with horses and GS waggons. In the event the waggons designed for use in Europe proved top-heavy and unsuitable for the rough veldt.

With transport costs soaring, the problem was compounded when Major General H H Clifford VC, a personal choice of the Duke of Cambridge, was appointed to command the Lines of Communication. He was specifically tasked to monitor and curtail the alarming increase in expenditure. Chelmsford also hoped that Clifford would resolve the martial law issue with the Natal government, but events were to prove him disloyal to Chelmsford and unconstructive in his criticism of Strickland and the Commissariat. When Clifford was forced to advise the Governor of Natal that if transport was not forthcoming the Army might be forced into an ignominious retreat he, with Chelmsford, put the whole responsibility on Strickland, leaving him to find a solution. Strickland deftly contrived an acceptable political compromise

Destruction of Transport near Suakin. (Illustrated London News)

which allowed the military to commandeer waggons for individual journeys.

Under these inauspicious conditions, the British began the advance on the Zulu capital, Ulundi, at the end of May, 1879. Movement was ponderous in the extreme due to over-caution, appalling weather and difficult terrain. The main Column only covered thirty miles in six days before they halted to build a defended supply depot and off-loaded fourteen days' supplies. The Column then remained stationary while an enormous escorted convoy comprising 600 waggons returned to base to replenish. The ox waggon convoy stretched for fifteen miles and took eleven days to complete the round journey.

On 16 June, 1879, as he approached Ulundi, Chelmsford received a telegram from London advising him that he was to be superseded by General Sir Garnet Wolseley. The Government specified the reasons as 'Delay in the progress of the war and the manifest lack of harmony between the civil and military authorities'. Ignoring his dismissal, Chelmsford continued the laborious advance at the rate of five or six miles a day until he finally met and defeated the Zulu army at Ulundi on 4 July, 1879.

Wolseley assumed command soon after the battle of Ulundi and immediately began criticizing his predecessor, fuelling the vexed topic of transport with vitriolic comments on the ability of Strickland, who had recently been knighted for his services. However, in a final speech prior to leaving South Africa, Chelmsford sought to close the controversy, saying he had placed great strain on the Commissariat and

Transport Department, but that his demands had been met in full and had enabled him to carry his plans to a successful issue.

Evelyn Wood earned a considerable reputation for logistic skill during the Kaffir and Zulu wars. In particular, aided by his assistant Redvers Buller, he had ensured that his men received fresh bread and meat every day while the rest of the Army fed on ships' biscuits. They evolved a system of sending ASC bakers with their ovens in waggons under escort ahead of the Column to the next camp site. There they produced fresh bread to await the arrival of incoming men. After the war Brigadier Evelyn Wood, later to become a Field Marshal, was offered but declined the appointment of Commissary General at the War Office.

The Sekukuni Campaign

The Zulu War over, General Wolseley personally commanded a short, sharp campaign to defeat Chief Sekukuni in the Transvaal. The campaign was fraught with supply and transport problems, causing Wolseley to make a garbled entry in his journal, 'It is a fatality, apparent in our Army, that to rely on a Commissariat Officer is to be destroyed, and so it must always be until the commissariat men are gentlemen or at least as much gentlemen as the average British officer' (sic).

Ironically, among those leading the final assault on Sekukuni's stronghold was Commissary H S E Reeves, destined to become the first functioning head of the ASC on its formation in 1888.

THE FIRST ANGLO-BOER WAR 1880-1881

The first Anglo-Boer war was a revolt by the Transvaalers against the refusal by the British Government under Gladstone to grant them independence, reversing the annexation of 1877.

The war was mainly remarkable for the defeats which the Boer commandos inflicted on the British and the death in battle of the Governor General, Sir George Colley, at Majuba Hill. The peace, which gave local independence to the Transvaal but with remaining doubts over the British suzerainty, left the Army with a feeling of frustration and bitterness which was to manifest itself in the great Boer War of 1899.

The war added little to the Army's logistic experience but there were a number of memorable incidents involving the Commissariat and ASC personnel. At the battle of Laing's Nek an ad hoc cavalry squadron commanded by Major Brownlow, King's Dragoon Guards, composed of thirty men of the KDG and thirty men of 7 Company ASC commanded by Quartermaster F Battersby, unsuccessfully charged the Boer position. The same men were again engaged in the battle of Ingogo. 7 Company suffered several killed and wounded in these actions.

When, shortly after the outbreak of war, the Boers ambushed the 94th Regiment (Connaught Rangers) at Bronkhorstspruit, the entire column was killed, wounded or captured. Conductor R Egerton, although wounded, was released by the Boers to walk forty-two miles to Pretoria to bring medical assistance for the wounded. Unbeknown to the Boers, Egerton wrapped the Colours of the 94th round his body, carrying them to safety and covering the distance in eleven hours. He was rewarded with a commission in the 94th.

In the siege of Lydenburg a civilian Conductor, Charles Jurgenson of Danish origin, was awarded the DCM, and Conductor W Parsons was commissioned as a Quartermaster, both for gallantry.

At Potchefstroom Assistant Commissary General Walter Dunne, of Rorke's Drift fame, again distinguished himself in the defence of a fort the size of a tennis court which held out under continuous rifle and cannon fire for ninety-five days.

The Commissariat and Transport Staff

The failings of the Commissariat and Transport Department exposed by the Zulu war had brought a remarkably swift reaction from the War Office. In 1880, barely a year later, the Department was replaced by the Commissariat and Transport Staff, and in 1881 the ASC was abolished, being succeeded by the Commissariat and Transport Corps. Direct Departmental commissions to the new corps were discontinued except for Quartermasters commissioned from the ranks.

Army Service Corps horse-drawn water cart.

Army Service Corps horse-drawn ambulance.

The main purpose in creating the Commissariat and Transport Staff was to build up a reserve of experienced regimental officers trained in supply and transport duties. These officers could then augment in war the permanent cadre of Commissariat officers who had originally been transferred from the old Department. The idea was to attract regimental officers of five years' standing from the cavalry, artillery and infantry with an offer of extra pay. Initially these officers would serve for five years, extendable to ten years, with the Commissariat Staff. At the end of ten years they could revert to their parent regiment or elect to join the Commissariat Staff as Departmental officers. However, the viability of the scheme was never tested, as before the ten years 1880 to 1890 had expired the ASC came into being under the reforms initiated by General Sir Redvers Buller, then Quartermaster General. One of the factors leading to the creation of the ASC was the refusal of some seventy seconded officers to give up their combatant commissions and become Departmental officers.

Redesignating the ASC in 1881 appears to have had the sole purpose of finally separating Commissariat and Transport companies from units of the Ordnance Store

Army Service Corps convoy on the road.

Army Service Corps at a convoy staging camp. (all Ian Bennett)

Corps. Junior officers for the Commissariat companies were found by conferring commissions on warrant officers who became Quartermasters but performed normal subalterns' duties, as Conductors of Supplies frequently did. The companies were commanded by officers from the superior Commissariat and Transport Staff.

Following the experience of employing an improvised unit during the Zulu War, the Army Medical Department in 1880 introduced bearer companies manned by the Army Hospital Corps to collect casualties in battle and evacuate them to Mobile Field Hospitals. Commissariat and Transport Corps companies provided officers, NCOs and men to control and drive the horse-drawn ambulances and pack mules for these Medical Units. So began the Corps' association with the transport for Field Ambulances RAMC which has continued to the present day.

EGYPT AND THE SUDAN 1882-1885

Financial and strategic interest in the Suez Canal involved Britain in the affairs of Egypt and the Sudan throughout the last two decades of the nineteenth century, giving rise to several military campaigns.

Egypt 1882

In 1882 a power struggle in Egypt led Britain to despatch a force of 24,000 men, under Sir Garnet Wolseley, to reinstate the legitimate ruler, Khedive Tewfik. The force included eight companies of the Commissariat and Transport Corps each allocated to the support of a Division or Corps Troops, under overall command of Assistant

The Army Service Corps.

Commissary General H S E Reeves with Deputy Assistant Commissary General C H Bridge as his adjutant. After capturing Alexandria, Wolseley switched his base to Ismailia on the Suez Canal. He planned a rapid advance on Cairo, supplied along a fresh-water canal and a poorly equipped railway. The arrangements for landing supplies were defective and when regimental transport, together with transportation along the waterway and railway, all broke down, the feeding of the troops caused great anxiety. The decisive victory at Tel el Kebir retrieved the situation, but to achieve a quick decisive result Wolseley had gambled on landing more troops than the Commissariat could be expected to feed. Success vindicated his judgement but it was a close call. The War Office history of the campaign succinctly stated 'It is only necessary to add that in England we have not hitherto maintained, during peacetime, any transport adequate to supply even a small army'. Among the awards for this Campaign, Assistant Commissary General Reeves was promoted to the relative rank of Lieutenant Colonel, and Conductor A Brook received immediate promotion to Quartermaster for distinguished service at Tel el Kebir.

Sudan 1884

A Sudanese uprising against Egypt, inspired by their religious leader, the Mahdi, caused the appointment of General Gordon as Governor of the Sudan in 1884. The Sudanese inflicted a series of defeats on the Egyptian Army which isolated Gordon in his capital, Khartoum. To aid Gordon, the British landed troops, including Commissariat and Transport Corps soldiers, at Suakin, on the Red Sea coast of the Sudan in 1884. The force was withdrawn after only a month having defeated local Sudanese at El Teb and Tamai.

Nile Campaign (Relief of Khartoum) 1884

Wolseley's campaign of 1884, extending 1400 miles down the Nile in an attempt to relieve Gordon besieged in Khartoum, is well documented elsewhere. However, apart from mentioning his use of a fleet of specially built boats manned by Canadian voyageurs, little attention has been given to reporting the overall logistic arrangements. This reflects Wolseley's lack of understanding of the need for coordinated control of supply and transport by the Commissariat and Transport staff.

Before leaving England, Wolseley declared his intention of taking the control of transport out of the hands of the Chief Commissariat Officer. Lieutenant Colonel Furse, Black Watch, was appointed Director of Transport. Wolseley also decided that, as an experiment, the Chief Commissariat Officer should be attached, not to the staff of the Commander in Chief where Major General Redvers Buller was Chief of Staff, but to the General Commanding the Lines of Communication, the ubiquitous Sir Evelyn Wood.

Away from the Nile the force was dependent on pack camels, some 8,000 of which had been purchased, 2,000 less than the Commissariat said was required. Only two Commissariat and Transport Corps companies, 9 and 11, were deployed at cadre strength to supervise native camel drivers. The Commissariat privates were to prove impatient and unintelligent in their treatment of the natives, and more trained Commissariat and Transport officers were essential. However, Furse tried to make

The Khartoum Relief Expedition. (Illustrated London News)

good the deficiency with inexperienced regimental officers, whose mismanagement caused the loss of a great number of the transport camels. More successful were the Conductors of Supplies serving with 9 and 11 Companies. They did sterling work and were singled out for high praise. Staff Sergeant P O'Malley was awarded the

Unloading Supply Boats on the Nile. (Illustrated London News)

DCM for bravery at Abu Klea and immediately promoted to Quartermaster.

The role of the Director of Transport proved confusing and ineffective, and, had Wolseley's plan to separate supplies from transport been fully implemented, chaos would have ensued. However, Evelyn Wood and Buller unostentatiously reversed the policy and restored some degree of system.

Undoubtedly the expedition failed in its objective because it had started too late, but it is for conjecture whether the outcome might have been different if the business of supply and transport had been left in the hands of Commissariat staff. In the event, the final last-hope dash across the desert to reach Gordon was delayed for eight precious days because there were insufficient camels to convey the essential supplies in one journey.

Suakin 1885

In February, 1885, the British again landed a force at Suakin with the dual purpose of building a railway across the desert to link up with Wolseley on the Nile and to destroy the local Mahdist leader, Osman Digna. The expedition, about 1400 strong, was supported by 3, 5, 12 and 17 Companies of the Commissariat and Transport Corps. These Companies, at little more than cadre strength, operated a total of over 1000 mules and 8000 camels, all led by native drivers. This time the business of supply and transport was wisely entrusted to the Senior Supply and Transport Officer whose major problem was the distribution of drinking water. Sea water was distilled in condenser ships off shore, then carried to units of the force by hundreds of camels.

The expedition had only penetrated a few miles inland by April when the Government halted operations and ordered a withdrawal. The force had by then won two hard-fought engagements at Hasheen and Tofrek. At Hasheen, Conductor Samuel Reid earned the DCM, but at Tofrek, where the Mahdists penetrated the British square, twelve men of the Commissariat and Transport Corps were killed, together with 700 transport camels.

Bechuanaland Expedition 1884-85

While Wolseley's expedition to relieve Gordon was taking place, the British sent a force to Bechuanaland to prevent Boer infiltration. In this militarily insignificant campaign Assistant Commissary General W Richardson and Deputy Assistant Commissary General F T Clayton, with 10 Company Commissariat and Transport Corps under command, provided supplies and transport for the force 1200 miles from their base in Cape Town. Both men were to find their experiences invaluable a few years later when war broke out with the Boers in 1899.

FORMATION OF THE ARMY SERVICE CORPS 1888

Between 1878 and 1885 only three additional transport Companies were raised. In 1887, in order to meet the provisions of a War Office Mobilization Plan for two Army Corps plus Lines of Communication and Base Troops, the ASC was expanded by the expedient of splitting sixteen of the eighteen existing Transport Companies into two cadres each, which gave a total of thirty-two capable of expansion in time of war. It

The Army Service Corps Reading Room, Buller Barracks.

was in 1887 that the Quartermaster General, Sir Redvers Buller, who had a wide knowledge of commissariat affairs in Africa and Egypt, drew attention to the need to reform the supply and transport service. He pointed out that mobilization plans required 224 officers for the Commissariat and Transport Staff, but only half that number existed. While the higher ranks were full, there was a serious deficiency of subalterns. He wrote, 'I do not myself believe that we shall ever get a ready flow of officers into a service which offers no permanent prospects of promotion or employment.'

Clearly the attempt to attract combatant officers to what was regarded by the Army as a non-combatant Department had failed. Under Buller's initiative it was decided to make a sweeping change, replacing the Commissariat and Transport Staff and the Commissariat and Transport Corps with a wholly combatant branch of the Army to be called by the old name, Army Service Corps. An officer would join the Corps when young and make supply and transport his career. Pay, promotion and pensions were fixed on the lines of the Royal Engineers. The principle of taking officers from line regiments was to continue as it was considered that such experience would give an understanding of the needs of the fighting men, and also a capability to defend their convoys. There was to be a great change in the status of Army Service Corps officers, who were now to enjoy the same rights and privileges as all combatant officers, unlike the Commissaries who had been regarded as inferior. For the first time all officers were to be accorded normal combatant ranks.

At the very top the Quartermaster General assumed responsibility for supply and transport at the War Office, and the appointment of Commissary General was abolished, along with his large staff. Army Service Corps officers were now eligible to become members of the Quartermaster General's staff, including the Assistant Quartermaster General, designated head of the Army Service Corps. The first to hold the appointment was Colonel H S E Reeves. There was a plan for thirty appointments on the General Staff to be allotted solely to the Army Service Corps for staff work on all Headquarters which dealt with Army Service Corps matters. The officers filling these appointments were to be appointed Deputy Adjutant Generals, Assistant Adjutant Generals, or Deputy Assistant Adjutant Generals as appropriate. In common with all other regiments and corps, the highest regimental rank was to be lieutenant colonel; an Army Service Corps officer promoted to the rank of colonel would become eligible for further advancement in the Army as a whole. To reinforce this new image, the Royal Warrant of 11 December, 1888, which authorized the new Army Service Corps, laid down that the Permanent List of the Corps would only consist of combatant officers who had transferred from regiments and corps. There was to be a Supernumerary List made up of those officers who had previously only held commissions in the Commissariat and Transport Staff. These, being Departmental officers, would not have the same rights and privileges as those on the Permanent List. In effect there was no prospect of promotion beyond the rank of colonel for Departmental officers. The Conductors of Supplies were also affected by the new combatant status of the Army Service Corps. In 1889 their title was changed to Conductor and they appeared in the Army List above the Warrant Officers of all Regiments and Corps of the Army. The title was again changed in 1892 to First Class Sergeant Major, but they retained their precedence.

During the ten years which followed the formation of the new Army Service Corps, members of the Corps were engaged in several campaigns but never in large numbers: 1893 Matabele Rebellion, 1895 Ashanti, 1896 Mashonaland, 1896 to 1898 the Sudan. While these campaigns provided wide-ranging experience, the Army Service Corps organization as such was not put to the test, although Captain H G Morgan was awarded the DSO for service in the Sudan in 1896. For example, in his campaign to reconquer the Sudan in 1898, Kitchener employed a supply and transport system of his own design. He personally commanded both the fighting troops and the L of C, and though supplies were administered by Army Service Corps officers, not an ounce was issued without the direct sanction of Kitchener. The Director of Transport was Lieutenant Colonel Kitchener, brother of the Commander, and he was assisted by four British infantry officers. The Army Service Corps appears to have been excluded from any real transport responsibilities. Kitchener divided the detailed conduct of supply and transport work, but exercised personal control over both functions. This was possible on a campaign of limited scale and suited Kitchener's autocratic style of command. Despite the restrictions on their employment, a large proportion of the Army Service Corps officers and men involved received awards; a CB, two Distinguished Service Orders and nine Distinguished Conduct Medals, as well as numerous Mentions in Despatches.

In this decade the scope of ASC activities was widened when, in 1891, the WD Fleet was transferred to the Corps and, in 1893, when the Corps of Military Staff

Clerks was absorbed into the Supply Branch of the ASC. A comprehensive detailed handbook entitled [cf2]Army Service Corps Duties in Peace and War[cf1] was published in 1897. It was written by Colonel Edward Ward, late Army Service Corps, who was to play an important part in the first year of the Boer War.

By 1898 mobilization plans requiring the Army to form into Brigades, Divisions and Army Corps had finally taken shape. The strength of the ASC was increased by forty officers and a thousand men to meet the war requirement for transport units. Mobilization instructions laid down the organization for supply and transport. Regimental Transport manned by their own soldiers would carry the unit's immediate needs of warlike equipment, ammunition, rations and forage. ASC companies designated Supply Columns, carrying one or two days' rations and forage, were allocated one per Brigade and one each to Divisional and Corps troops. These companies replenished from the ASC Supply Park, composed of ASC companies with supply personnel carrying at least three days' rations and forage for all the formations being supported. Forage for animals was as vital a commodity in war then as petroleum fuels were to become in the Second World War. The Supply Park was in effect the mobile reserve which drew stocks from a railhead. In the absence of a railway it was intended that the ASC improvised auxiliary road transport. At this time the ASC had no formal role in the ammunition replenishment system, a task usually performed by Royal Artillery Ammunition Columns. The reorganization envisaged by Buller was now complete and in place.

Since 1888 the ASC had rapidly developed a regimental identity and esprit de corps. Much of the credit for this impetus was due to Lieutenant Colonel Ernest Grattan, commanding the ASC Service Companies at Aldershot from 1888 to 1892. A highly respected Corps officer, he was responsible for the Corps motto [cf2]Nil Sine Labore[cf1] and it was his idea to start publishing a Corps Journal in 1891. A great innovator, he created the Corps cricket ground, later irreverently known by many as 'God's Acre', and was instrumental in having the Corps Theatre built. For

On trek in the Transvaal. (Ian Bennett)

generations this was the venue for social and regimental events until the levelling of the old barracks in the 1960s.

The old wooden R, S, X, Y and W lines, which had been the Aldershot home of the ASC's predecessors since 1859, were at last replaced by the substantial red brick Buller Barracks in 1895. Lieutenant Colonel Bridge and the officers at Aldershot invited representatives of the Corps from all stations in the United Kingdom to a formal house-warming dinner in the new Buller Officers' Mess on 30 January, 1895. The newly built ASC School of Instruction housed a Corps Museum. From this time Aldershot became increasingly regarded as the headquarters station of the ASC. In 1893 the officers formed a Dinner Club to meet annually on Derby Day. In the same year the ASC Branch of the Army Temperance Society was inaugurated, some two hundred pledges being made by the ASC in Aldershot.

A mounted gymkhana was held at Aldershot in June, 1894, which, it was hoped, would develop into an annual Corps Week. Freemasons serving with the ASC formed the [cf2]Nil Sine Labore[cf1] Lodge in 1895. St George's Church Aldershot, the only church for which Queen Victoria laid the foundation stone, was consecrated in 1893 and became affectionately known as the 'Corps Cathedral'. Many memorial tablets in the church stand witness to the worldwide service of the Corps down the years. The first ASC memorial tablets were placed in the church in 1898 in memory of those who died in the Nile campaigns of 1884, 1885 and 1886, Suakin 1885 and 1886, Ashanti 1895, and the Nile 1898.

THE BOER WAR 1899-1902

The great test for the newly organized Army Service Corps came with the South African War of 1899-1902 – the second Boer War.

The image of the ASC at that time is caught by Sir Redvers Buller in a letter written by him at sea to Colonel W W G Robinson, on his way to assume command in South Africa. W W G Robinson was a Colonel ranking as Major General, who had been the senior ASC officer on the formation of the Corps on 11 December, 1888. Buller is referring to Lord Wolseley, then the ageing Commander-in-Chief at the War Office:

'Dear Robinson

I must write a line and thank you for your letter of the 11th and tell you how gratified I am by your remembering me. The Army Service Corps will be all right, for them I think this war has come at a crucial moment. There has to some extent, at the WO, arisen a king who knew not Daniel and the Corps have of late had neither him nor even fair treatment – the natural result followed, and a spirit of dissatisfaction, not to say of disaffection, was being engendered.

I hope this war, which will involve the employment of almost the whole Corps, will sweep that away and give the fillip the Corps wanted.

The fact is Lord Wolseley has never been able to get out of his head that Supply and Transport are civil duties, and will always go like clockwork, provided the GOC is prepared occasionally to hang a commissary.

We are escaping from that view but only slowly. I look forward to the end of this campaign proving what the ASC are and what they can do.'[cf1]

Ever since the Transvaal Boers had defeated the British in the war of 1880-81, the political contest between the British and the Boers over the mastery of South Africa had continued. Diamonds and gold had attracted a swarm of foreigners into the Transvaal. Known as Uitlanders, most of these newcomers were British. The Boers refused to grant Uitlanders any say in government, despite taxing them, thus creating another rift between the Transvaal and British Governments, which negotiations failed to close. The new mineral wealth had enabled the Transvaal to establish a military force. Modern magazine rifles, sixty to seventy of the latest field guns and stocks of ammunition were bought from Germany and France. A corps of regular gunners was formed, the officers trained in Germany. The British response to all this was the despatch of meagre reinforcements to the Cape. Among them were five ASC officers led by Colonel C H Bridge. Bridge, who had recent local experience, having been the DAAG responsible for supplies and transport as well as ordnance depots during the Matabele War of 1896, was tasked with planning the provision of draught animals, vehicles and harness as a contingency measure against the outbreak of military operations. Two ASC Transport Companies were also sent out. With further deterioration in the political situation, the British Government decided to mobilize the 1st Army Corps under the command of General Sir Redvers Buller for service in South Africa.

On 16 September, 1899, General Sir George White sailed from England to command the troops already in Natal. He was accompanied by Colonel Edward Ward, late ASC, who was to be his chief supply officer. Ward, described by White after the siege of Ladysmith as 'the best Commissariat officer since Moses', was to be knighted in 1900 and became Permanent Under-Secretary of State for War.

Embarking on the same day was Colonel Wodehouse Richardson, who had been appointed to overall command of the ASC in South Africa. Colonel Bridge, already in the country, was to be Director of Transport under him. Richardson was to be responsible for supplies and transport by land, other than regimental transport, but including embarkations and disembarkations, coast-wise transport by sea and railway transport. He had considerable experience of war in South Africa, having been on the staff of Commissary General Strickland during the Frontier and Zulu wars. He served in the first Boer war, and was subsequently Senior Commissary on the Bechuanaland Expedition of 1884. Before sailing from Southampton, Richardson wrote to General Buller recommending that the ASC companies be despatched as soon as possible to arrive before the fighting formations. This would ensure that preparations for supply and transport could be completed before the Army Corps disembarked. Buller accepted this advice and, consequently, ASC staff and companies were in position and ready to support the army as it arrived.

On his arrival in October, 1899, Richardson found a major difference in the transport situation from his previous campaigns; railways now traversed the country, eliminating the old complete dependence on slow, cumbersome ox and mule waggons for long hauls. There were three main lines which were to become the arteries of communication:

The Western Railway – linking Cape Town through Kimberley and Mafeking to Rhodesia.

The Midland Line – linking Port Elizabeth through Bloemfontein to Johannesburg and Pretoria.

The Eastern Line – linking East London to Queenstown and joining the Midland Line at Springfontein.

These three lines were also linked by a cross-country line from Stormberg, Rosmead to De Aar. All these stations were destined to become important logistical centres. Additionally, in Natal a main line now connected Durban with Johannesburg on the Midland Line to Pretoria. Thus from all the four main sea ports in South Africa the railways converged on the Transvaal capital, Pretoria.

Richardson and the ASC were responsible for railway transport, until the arrival of Major Girouard RE, who later was to distinguish himself in that capacity. Richardson drew up detailed plans with the Management of the Cape Government Railways for the forward deployment of troops with their equipment as they disembarked, and introduced such innovations as the use of refrigerated trains to distribute meat. Richardson's foresight in deploying the ASC and his use of the railways made possible the stocking of peacetime garrisons such as Ladysmith, Mafeking and Kimberley, which were to prove so critical in the war. Supplies were also stockpiled at strategic points on the railways, while contracts were made for food and forage including one for four million pounds of meat.

A key task of the ASC at this time was to provide and issue the animals and vehicles needed for regimental transport. Some vehicles were also provided by the Ordnance Department and issued through the ASC. The arrival of the ASC ahead of the main Army enabled them to acquire sufficient transport to equip every unit on disembarkation. As this transport was best driven by local drivers, some 600 ASC drivers were initially surplus and able to be loaned to the Royal Artillery who had requested assistance. Other ASC drivers were employed in the Remount Depots.

The majority of the ASC companies sailed in one contingent from England on the *Braemar Castle* on 6 October, 1899, under the command of Lieutenant Colonel F T

Typical Terrain in South Africa over which Mule Transport operated. The mounted officer in the foreground is General Sir Redvers Buller. (Ian Bennett)

Clayton, later Lieutenant General Sir Frederick Clayton. It was intended that the companies should be deployed as planned under the Buller organization of 1888, one company to each infantry and cavalry brigade, one to each Divisional HQ, Corps HQ and Army HQ. Three companies, 4, 29 and 42, were to provide the Supply Parks and the Mobile Bulk Supply depots; four more companies were allocated to the L of C.

40 Company, the Bakery company, was immediately split into sections which were attached to the Supply Depots being set up all over the country as required. Supply personnel were sent out to South Africa in varying sized detachments without any coherent organization. On arrival they were all included in the establishment of 38 Company, which was the Supply Company formed in 1892 by splitting 18 Company. 38 Company with its headquarters in Cape Town and supply depots spread throughout South Africa, eventually comprised nearly 2,000 all ranks.

The war officially started on 11 October, 1899. By the next day 23,000 Transvaal and 15,000 Orange Free State armed Boers, mostly mounted, were in the field. Considerably outnumbered, the British were fortunate in that the Boers lacked the cohesion and enterprise to exploit their advantage in numbers and mobility. After some sharp engagements, General White ignominiously withdrew his troops into Ladysmith to be closely invested there by the encircling Boers who also laid siege to the mining towns of Kimberley and Mafeking. The Boers next marched south to threaten the unprotected supply depots which had been set up by Richardson at the railheads of Orange River Station, De Aar Junction and Queenstown.

In early November, 1899, significant reinforcements began to arrive from England. An attempt to relieve Kimberley was launched and three brigades deployed in Natal, where Sir Redvers Buller took personal command. Before leaving he issued orders dividing the control of supplies and transport, believing that for the moment the combined task was too much for one man. He made Richardson Director of Supplies and Bridge Director of Transport. Buller wrote, 'It is recognized that the duties of these two officers have no sharp dividing line. The above decision is merely made for the adjustment of details. In a time such as the present the duties of these officers must be mutually performed, and many minor points decided by the senior.'

Richardson's response was predictable disagreement, 'I think this arrangement is a mistaken one as Colonel Bridge and I must now work together as a kind of Siamese twins, and if one happens to disagree with the other the troops will suffer. However, the great thing is to try and run the show with as little friction as possible.'

During the second week of December, 1899, dubbed 'Black Week' by the Press, the British suffered a series of humiliating defeats. The Government, having lost faith in Buller, appointed Lord Roberts, 'Bobs', to supersede him as Commander in Chief in South Africa, with Kitchener as Chief of Staff. Both were popular idols with the British public as a result of past victories, Roberts in Afghanistan, and Kitchener in the Sudan. Neither, though, had in-depth knowledge of the organization and administration of the British Army, in particular the course of events in the administrative field which had led to the reconstruction of the Army Service Corps in 1888. When Colonel Bridge spoke to Kitchener about Supply Parks, Kitchener simply stared at him and ejaculated, 'I don't know what you mean'.

Roberts and Kitchener, together with large reinforcements, reached Cape Town on 12 January, 1900. Roberts' new strategic plan was to cut loose from the Western railway and strike across country at Bloemfontein, capital of the Orange Free State. Both Roberts and Kitchener appear to have arrived in South Africa with a preconceived notion that the existing transport system was inflexible and wasteful and not capable of supporting their planned offensive. They were particularly opposed to dedicated regimental transport on the grounds that, if a unit was not actually moving, its waggons were idle and a waste of resources. They did not appreciate that, under British Army regulations, such transport was at the disposal of the senior ASC officer in the area. Throughout the war Kitchener was to display an extraordinary ignorance of transport and animal management.

The British Army replenishment system laid down in the current Mobilization Instructions provided for:

1. Regimental Transport manned by unit personnel under a unit officer. This was divided into:

> ● First Line, which included water carts, and carried ammunition, tools, medical stores, machine guns.
> ● Second Line, which carried one or more days' rations and forage, together with blankets, tents and similar regimental baggage. This Regimental transport was drawn by mules.

2. Supply Columns – ASC Companies allocated on a scale of one per Brigade, and one each to Divisional, Corps and Army troops, carrying on mule waggons one day's rations and forage plus an emergency ration.

3. A Supply Park – ox waggons under ASC Supply and Transport officers carrying at least three day's rations and forage for all the fighting formations; in effect a mobile reserve.

4. Auxiliary Transport – mainly ox waggons organized for L of C work commanded by ASC officers, used for tasks such as restocking the Supply Park from a rail head.

5. Technical Transport – Royal Artillery Ammunition Columns, Royal Engineer equipment waggons, medical unit transport.

REORGANIZATION OF ASC SUPPLIES AND TRANSPORT

Biased by their personal experiences in India and Egypt, at the stroke of a pen Roberts and Kitchener swept away the progress achieved in the British Army over a quarter of a century. They directed that all transport other than technical transport, must be concentrated into a general pool of transport companies under ASC officers. Waggons would then be allocated to units as and when they were required to move, returning to their parent ASC company having completed their task. Unit officers and men released by the abolition of regimental transport returned to duty and were lost to the transport system. To absorb and control this additional influx of waggons, the fourteen ASC companies which had been the Supply Columns were each split into two, their old title numbers, eg 19, 20, 36, were replaced by letters A to Z plus AA and BB. It was immediately obvious that there were insufficient ASC officers to man this number of companies, and therefore available officers from any regiment or corps were drawn in and attached for transport duties. Very few had any experience of transport or animal management, but for some inexplicable reason they were paid more than their ASC counterparts. The new companies were organized into mule-drawn companies each of forty-nine waggons, to support either an infantry brigade of four battalions or a cavalry brigade of three regiments. Some were equipped as ox companies of 100 waggons to fulfil the function of the old Supply Parks. Each company had a complement of fifteen to twenty ASC non-commissioned officers and drivers to supervise the native drivers. This reorganization was accomplished in a very short space of time under the able direction of Lieutenant Colonel Clayton, but it placed an enormous strain on the ASC. Only Colonel Richardson among the senior ASC officers supported the change, and he seems to have had an old prejudice against regimental transport. The problems created by the reorganization were compounded when the experienced Colonel Bridge was relieved of the control of transport and replaced by Major General Sir William Nicholson, then Military Secretary to Lord Roberts. Nicholson was an able Royal Engineer officer but had no special knowledge of transport or supply. Fortunately for the outcome of the war and the future of the Army, Major General French, commanding the Cavalry Division and Buller's army in Natal, insisted on retaining the old system.

On 11 February, 1900, Roberts, with 30,000 men, moved east across country away from the railway. His objective was the capture of Bloemfontein a hundred miles

A Fowler Traction Engine and Train fording a Drift in the Transvaal. The Traction Engine in the foreground is a Burrell 224.

away. Simultaneously the Cavalry Division was despatched on an 80-mile forced march to relieve Kimberley. The new ASC Companies were divided up into penny packets attached to units. They were mainly commanded by inexperienced regimental officers who were lucky to find an ASC sergeant and one or two experienced ASC drivers to support them. With the ASC Supply Columns abolished, this motley collection of ad hoc units was expected to draw rations and forage directly from the main ASC Supply Park. This Supply Park, carried in over 200 ox waggons, was the responsibility of Major S S Long, destined to be a key figure later in the campaign. Despite repeated requests by Long for a proper escort for the vulnerable Park none was forthcoming. Only four days into the offensive the Boers ambushed the Supply Park while it was passing Waterval Drift and, despite belated attempts to rescue it, were able to make off with 200 waggons, 150,000 rations and forage for 30,000 animals. Roberts was then forced to put the troops on half rations as they surrounded the Boers at Paardeburg. Even this was only possible by the return of French's Cavalry Division, whose ASC Companies still had the flexibility and resources to respond to the crisis situation.

The subsequent surrender to Roberts of a large Boer Army at Paardeburg on 27 February, so early in the campaign, was a major triumph, but the loss of the Supply Park at Waterval effectively prevented him from exploiting his success for a week. He eventually entered Bloemfontein unopposed on 13 March, 1900. After a little over one month's activity in the field the Army was exhausted. The losses in animals had been very severe and there was now a general shortage of supplies and serviceable transport. This paralysis lasted for two months. The Roberts and Kitchener transport system had broken down, mainly because there was no intermediate support between the units and the single main Supply Park. To find waggons to draw rations, regimental transport would have to offload blankets and equipment. Kitchener's assumption that pooled transport, once having delivered to units, would return to the parent ASC Companies foundered because the front line units, learning from bitter experience, retained the transport for their own immediate use. ASC transport remained dispersed round the battalions and regiments which were themselves constantly being redeployed. Within a fortnight of the campaign starting, no ASC Company was complete and few could locate more than a quarter of their men and vehicles.

In stark contrast, in the army in Natal commanded by Buller, where the old system had been retained, all supply and transport arrangements were working smoothly. When, after several bloody battles, Buller's troops relieved Ladysmith on 1 March, 1900, he was logistically prepared to resume his advance within three weeks. Because Roberts' own force was still incapable of offensive action, he directed Buller to delay any movement until 7 May, 1900. The delay of some ten weeks before Roberts resumed the advance on Pretoria was due in no small measure to the chaotic state of the supply and transport situation, which had resulted largely from Kitchener's interference.

The Army was now struck by an epidemic of the killer enteric fever and severe criticism of the Army Medical Corps resulted in a Royal Commission being set up to investigate the circumstances. Commenting on the supply of medical comforts the Commission found that the ASC had given a satisfactory service. Colonel Richardson was, however, of the opinion that 'the consumption of medical supplies is very large, I fancy that the patients do not get all that is expended'. Colonel Walter Dunne, veteran of Rorke's Drift, as AQMG at the War Office responsible for all Army supplies and forage, considered the complaints surprisingly few. Most seemed to be concerned with the quality of the port and claret, also the rawness of the whisky!

After the relief of Ladysmith Colonel Ward became Director of Supplies for the field Army while Richardson returned to Cape Town as Director of Supplies for the Lines of Communication. His pressing task was to hasten the replenishment of stocks at Bloemfontein where acute shortages still existed. The Boers now frequently disrupted the railways and it took until May to accumulate the thirty days' reserve needed to sustain an advance. During this static period an attempt was made to reorganize the failed replenishment system. Something reminiscent of the old ASC system was introduced. ASC waggons were permanently allocated to units and these drew on ASC mule waggon companies in support of each division, called Supply Columns. These were in turn replenished by ASC Supply Parks which shuttled ox waggon convoys from the railhead.

This system continued in use until the Boers were beaten in the last set-piece battle of the war at Belfast on 27 August, 1900. Kitchener, on meeting with Buller at Pretoria, remarked that only the columns of Buller and Methuen had proper transport arrangements. Buller pointedly replied, 'These were the only two who stuck to the original ASC system'.

After Belfast the whole nature of the war changed, becoming a campaign against mobile guerrilla forces which dragged on for another 18 months. Roberts and Buller returned to England, Kitchener taking over as Commander in Chief in South Africa. Under his command the Divisions and Brigades vanished, to be replaced by ad hoc columns of various sizes which relentlessly pursued the Boer guerrillas across the whole country. ASC detachments went with the columns, but there was no overall transport organization or supporting depots. The Ordnance provided the columns with vehicles, harness, wheels and other essential stores, while the animals came from the remount department. There was no way of validating requisitions and one staff officer described the waste as 'like water being poured through a sieve'. The mobility needed to catch the elusive Boers was dissipated by mismanagement.

This unhappy situation was retrieved by the initiative of Major Long ASC, who had been in charge of the great Supply Park captured by the Boers at Waterval Drift. Now DAAG responsible for transport at Bloemfontein, he initiated a system to monitor the location of animals and vehicles. He then set up ASC depots to issue vehicles and draught animals and carry out repairs. In this way he was able to identify the needs of the units in the field and only draw the actual requirements in equipment and animals from Ordnance and the Remount Depots. Instead of abandoning damaged vehicles and sick or worn out animals, Columns now had to return them to the ASC Depots for repair or recuperation. The new system worked well and was extended to cover the whole area of operations. In this way the ability to redeploy resources was speedily restored so that all Columns were able to get the vital support needed. Long, the innovator, was to become Director of Supplies and Transport in 1914.

The guerrilla war phase was weary and costly, but in retrospect it proved to be of inestimable benefit to the Army in terms of training and experience for the great struggle of the First World War yet to come. The South African War represented the greatest overseas military effort that had ever been mounted by the British. The numbers in rations at the end of the war were 327,000 men, 265,000 horses and mules and 19,000 oxen. The ASC sent to South Africa 233 officers from a total strength of 264 and was supplemented by 250 officers seconded from other regiments and corps. A total of 4,672 warrant officers, non-commissioned officers and men went to the war for supply and transport duties from a Corps strength of 5,067. Of these 600 drivers were loaned to the Royal Artillery and earned great praise. By mid-1900 the ASC was operating sixty-six mule and ox companies, and the number of supply depots reached 100 in 1902.

The impact of modern technology was experienced with the wide availability of an established railway system, while steam traction engines and motor cars made their first appearance in a British Army at war.

In spite of the disruption caused by the reorganization imposed by Roberts and Kitchener in the midst of the war, the hopes and expectations of Buller for the ASC had been realized. Giving evidence before the Royal Commission on the War in South Africa Field Marshal Lord Roberts stated, 'The Army Service Corps did well throughout and deserves great credit'. The awards received by members of the Corps reflect this praise. Colonels Richardson and Ward were knighted (KCB), other decorations were seven CBs, eight CMGs, nineteen DSOs and eleven DCMs. Many were Mentioned in Despatches.

Epitaph

On 11 April, 1903, the stained glass windows in Saint George's Garrison Church at Aldershot were unveiled and dedicated to the memory of 392 officers, warrant officers, non-commissioned officers and men of the Army Service Corps who died during the South African War 1899 to 1902.

CHAPTER 3

1902-1914

The Early Development of the Army Service Corps and Mechanical Transport

General Organization and Staffing. Initial Trials of MT. ASC responsible for MT. Major Trials and Repair responsibilities. MT becomes accepted part of Army Movement. Registration and Subsidy Schemes. Introduction of Motor Cycles. The Petrol-Engined Lorry accepted. The Volunteer Force. Eve of War situation

General Organization and Staffing

In 1902, in recognition of the Corps' services in South Africa, His Majesty King Edward VII appointed his brother, His Royal Highness Field Marshal The Duke of Connaught and Strathearn, to be Colonel of the Army Service Corps. In 1932 the

A Horse Transport Company ASC parading in the horse lines, Buller Barracks, Aldershot.

appointment was changed to Colonel in Chief, which he held until his death in 1942.

The year after the end of the Boer War saw a blossoming of regimental activities as the confidence gained from successful operations in South Africa took hold. In St George's Church, Stanhope Lines, Aldershot, the ASC South African Memorial East Window was unveiled and dedicated in April; and on a wet and rainy day in June the first general Corps gathering took place, the forerunner of subsequent Corps Weeks. Cricket matches were played against the Royal Artillery and Royal Engineers and on the last day of the sports a luncheon was served in the Corps Theatre next to the Recreation Ground for all officers in station and their ladies. In 1905 the first ASC Quarterly was published, which was devoted to professional papers on general military matters. Subsequent issues not only continued to inform ASC officers of military matters of importance to them but also provided an opportunity for the more serious and ambitious officers to publish their views on ASC matters for the education of their fellow officers. In June, 1907, a new web girdle (the future stable belt) was introduced, which led to a full-page cartoon in the ASC Journal showing a smart ASC soldier walking out in his blue uniform, exhibiting his new blue and white belt. A street paper boy, something of an urchin, shouts, 'Hie! Tommy, you've got your braces round yer waist.'

Every war has its post mortem and the period following the end of the Boer War was no exception. The Esher Report of 1904 made major recommendations for reform of the army organization, including the formation of a General Staff, and the reorganization of the responsibilities of two key posts which impacted on the ASC, the Adjutant General and the Quartermaster General. Transport and Supply were to be under separate Directorates in the War Office and the Director of Transport and

Remounts was to have the Director General of Army Veterinary Services under him. A new Director of Movements and Quartering took over responsibility for railways in war and the custody and equipping of barracks. However, after the mistakes of the previous century and developments in the Boer War, this split, while following the example of Continental armies, was less than practical.

The 1888 stipulation that the ASC should fill thirty staff appointments was effectively cancelled by the Esher Committee. Colonel F T Clayton, Assistant Quartermaster General for the ASC at the War Office, however, obtained approval for the creation of Assistant Directors as well as Deputy Assistant Directors of Supplies and Transport at the various Command headquarters. The Assistant Director Supplies and Transport appointment at least ensured that the best ASC officers would be promoted to Colonel, the most senior rank available to them at the time. Widespread recognition of the worth of the Corps' officers, however, and further pressure by Colonel Clayton ensured that the Army Council accepted in 1904 that ASC officers 'would be eligible equally with officers of other arms, thus giving opportunities of promotion to general officer's rank'. This important decision soon bore fruit: Colonel E C Heath was promoted in 1905 to Brigadier General in Aldershot: Colonel H N Bunbury was promoted in 1906 as Major General Administration in Ireland: in 1908 Brigadier General Heath moved to the War Office as Major General, Director of Transport and Remounts and in 1908 Colonel G A Hadfield was appointed Major General Administration in South Africa, to be succeeded in 1909 by Colonel Clayton himself. It can thus be seen that within four years of the Army Council decision in 1904 the ASC had produced four Major Generals, which much strengthened the position of the Corps in the Army and enabled it to develop along practical lines, not those dictated by staff officers from other Arms with limited knowledge and vision of the detailed logistic requirements.

In 1902 the Corps consisted of a number of horse transport companies, largely abroad: 7, 9, 12, 19, 21, 24, 28, 30, 31, 33 and 37 Companies were still in South Africa; 15 and 22 Companies were in Somaliland: 68 Company was in Gibraltar, 69 Company in Malta and 70 Company in Egypt. In 1902 six more companies were formed and a further eleven in 1903, bringing the total to seventy-seven. Most of these companies were at lower strength. In addition, the Corps had small detachments in a variety of stations throughout the world, in Bermuda, Cyprus, Jamaica, Mauritius, North and South China, Sierra Leone and Singapore. In 1902 A and C Supply Companies were in Aldershot, B Supply Company in South Africa, D Supply Company in Dublin and E Supply Company in Woolwich. In 1906 an additional F Supply Company was formed in Tidworth.

Initial Trials of Mechanical Transport (MT)

At this stage mechanical transport came on to the scene, with the army taking advantage of civilian technology and keeping abreast of developments in Continental armies. The Royal Engineers had used steam traction engines in the Boer War, but essential water and coal were not readily available and the dust and low speeds led to limited success. Diehards in the army did not consider mechanical transport had any place in 'real soldiering', although some in South Africa took notice when a traction engine recovered a bogged-in waggon which eighty oxen had failed to move!

During the war the War Office established a Mechanical Transport Committee which included Royal Artillery, Royal Engineers and Army Service Corps representatives (Colonel Heath and Lieutenant Colonel Clayton were the ASC

German Milner Daimler 5-Ton Lorry No 16, 1905, The driver is E J Grubb.

members). The committee set up War Office trials in 1901 in the search for lighter vehicles with a radius of more than thirty miles, suitable for British and European roads. Prizes of £500, £250, and £100 were awarded and the War Office had the option of buying any of the vehicles for its own use.

These trials in Aldershot were followed in subsequent years by other trials, but it might be of interest to look at the early mobility requirements in these first trials. Specifications included a need to be able, with a crew of one, to work on rough roads, go where country carts could go (including through a seven feet six inch gate), carry five tons (three tons on board the prime mover and two tons in a trailer), be capable of a maximum speed, fully laden, of eight miles per hour and an average speed of five miles per hour, able to climb a gradient of one in eight without assistance and run for forty-eight hours without overhaul or cleaning. There were eleven entrants, all except the Milner-Daimler being steam-driven, of which only five started. With a maximum speed of ten miles per hour on the level the Straker was very fast, but a Thornycroft won the first prize and a Foden the second. The two latter vehicles (they were then called 'lurries') were sent to South Africa in February, 1902, and were trialled for four months. The Thornycroft was the more reliable of the two, and Lord Kitchener's report to the Royal Commission on the war in South Africa stated that, 'Thornycrofts are the best'.

At the same time a few motor cars were purchased by the War Office for the Royal Engineers in Chatham and for the ASC in Aldershot for experimental work. A letter of 21 January, 1902, from the War Office informed the General Officer Commanding 1 Army Corps Aldershot that, 'It is proposed to purchase a motor car for your use in order to facilitate the inspection of works in progress in the district under your command and also in order that this class of vehicle may be tried as to its suitability for aiding, by its capabilities of rapid locomotion, the command of troops in the field.'

With senior officers becoming more interested in a convenient and speedy form of transportation which required no effort from them as passengers, trials in 1902 and 1903 were carried out with internal combustion engines, with the emphasis on cars. An interesting Volunteer unit, the Motor Volunteer Corps, was formed in 1903, consisting of a number of gentlemen who provided their cars and chauffeurs to support the General Staff, including General Sir John French, on annual manoeuvres. They took part in a number of manoeuvres over the next few years, providing sterling support for officers who were essentially horse-orientated. Motor cyclists were also included, being authorized by the War Office in 1904. The MVC took part in the 1905 Great Royal Review at Holyrood Park in Edinburgh. With the development, however, of full-time ASC MT Companies, the MVC was disbanded in 1906, having served its purpose, not before showing the staff, however, that headquarters' staffs needed their own allocated transport and should no longer be reliant on four-legged chargers. Their full dress uniform was olive green with gold ornaments, but otherwise khaki service dress was worn.

ASC Responsibilities for MT

1903 was a key year in the history of military transport in the Army. The War Office decided that mechanical road transport should be the responsibility of the ASC. Steam engines, as well as experimental cars and lorries held by the Royal Engineers, were transferred from Chatham to Aldershot. The first Officer Commanding was Major C E I McNalty ASC and he was supported by Corporal Langley and eleven other men who transferred from the Royal Engineers – in a predominantly horse transport world they were known as 'the mucky dozen'. They brought with them a Bush car and twelve heavy steam-traction engines. At the same time the traction engines of the Royal Engineers in Malta and Gibraltar were also transferred to 77 Company ASC. The ASC Journal of the day provides an insight into the ponderous nature of these lumbering beasts: 'The cleaner is the man who sits in the last truck when the engine is on the road – he applies the brakes to the truck, notifies the driver of overtaking traffic and generally makes himself useful. The cleaner lights the fire while the driver and steersman are having their breakfast. When finished they relieve the cleaner who, in turn, has his meal.'

In 1903 war in Somaliland persuaded the War Office to buy several Stirling lorries (made in Edinburgh). Although their internal combustion engines used petrol, which was declared too dangerous for use on English roads, it was considered that the risk was acceptable for use abroad. In the event the vehicles did not go to Somaliland and they were converted to paraffin fuel, clearly not successfully, as the nine-day journey by one of them from Chatham to Aldershot, full of accidents and breakdowns, showed. The lorry concerned was nicknamed 'spit and cough machinery'. In 1903, therefore, the ASC had several forms of mechanical transport to complement the horse transport units around the world; cars, lorries and traction engines. All of them, however, were held on an experimental basis and were not part of the main field force. In these early days there was already a division of opinion between the relative virtues of steam traction or internal combustion, which would take several years to resolve. Indeed the years until 1905 were occupied in consolidating ground won in the overall fight for recognition of mechanical transport at the same time as deciding the relative advantages of tractor and lorry.

The Army's guiding body in the early development of mechanical transport was the

8 Horsepower Panhard Lavassor staff car. Seated on left is Lieutenant General J D P French with members of staff and ASC driver, Aldershot, 1904.

Mechanical Transport Committee, initiated in 1900 with four sub-committees: Experimental, Royal Artillery, Royal Engineers and ASC. In 1903 an Inspectorate of Mechanical Transport was established within the ASC, which not only dealt with all technical aspects of military transport but also acted as technical adviser to the War Office. Major W E Donahue ASC was Chief Inspector of this organization, with two inspectors. They acted as a focal point within the ASC for the increasing number of officers who saw a bright future in this new form of mobility.

Major Trials and Repair Responsibilities

The War Office trials of 1903 were won by a thirteen-ton Hornsby-Ackroyd tractor, which, being too heavy for army use, was later converted with caterpillar tracks. A smaller version, the 'baby caterpillar', which was subsequently (1910) purchased from Hornsby in Grantham, took ten days to reach Aldershot. In 1903 the speed limit had been raised from fourteen to twenty miles per hour, with ten miles per hour allowed in towns, so it was not the national speed limit which made it take so long. Its slow progression apparently resembled the action of a small ship in rough seas and

A Steam Tractor Lorry of 52 Coy RASC.

the vehicle was at once christened 'Rock and Roll'.

An early decision had been made concerning the repair of vehicles. The Army Ordnance Department was made responsible for base overhauls, but otherwise the ASC was responsible for all running repairs. In 1905 the first static workshop was built at Thornhill Road, Aldershot, which served mainly 77 Company and its sister 78 Company formed in 1904, the year when MT was first used on manoeuvres. In 1905 mobile workshop trailers were designed, which contained a lathe, drilling machine, tool-grinding machine, a fitter's bench and vices, the tools being driven by a dynamo from the towing traction engine. It was not long before these mobile workshops were built on to lorries, which saw service until the end of the 1914-18 war.

MT becomes accepted part of Army Movement

As a result of the latest manoeuvres it was evident that mechanical transport had now become a regular feature of movement for the army. The ASC Training Establishment in Aldershot took steps to train all its officers in mechanical transport duties, with the most promising being selected for further training as workshop officers. The first mechanical transport instructor was Captain T M Hutchinson ASC, who was later to be a member of the War Office Mechanical Transport Committee. To show what advances were being made a scheme was instituted in 1906 for the inclusion of a

London Omnibuses used in trials to move troops from Hounslow to Shoeburyness.

small amount of MT to be incorporated into mobilization plans, on the basis that MT could travel twice the distance of horse-drawn transport in a day. Light steam tractors were allocated to the third echelon of supply in the field (ie the Parks). Practical demonstrations of the efficacy of MT were still needed, however, and these were given in 1906, the year in which the London General Omnibus Company invested £1 million on converting their horse-drawn buses to MT. These were predominantly Dennis, Leyland, Maudsley and Thornycroft vehicles. Except when using ships or railways, the mass movement of troops had always been on foot. Buses provided a new opportunity for speedier movement.

The London General Omnibus Company and Eastern Command Headquarters co-operated in trials involving twenty-four omnibuses in 1908, moving troops from Hounslow to Shoeburyness. The following year, on a freezing St Patrick's Day. 17 March, a composite battalion of Guards was moved from London to Hastings by 316 privately owned cars, all organized by the Automobile Association. Crowds greeted them *en route* and the resultant publicity reinforced the potential of mechanical transport for a permanent role in the Army.

Registration and Subsidy Schemes

No doubt influenced by the success of these demonstrations, Colonel G R C Paul, late ASC, the Assistant Director of Transport, obtained approval for 900 vehicles in war mobilization plans over and above those already held in units. Needless to say the army did not possess this number of vehicles, so the problem was solved by introducing a Registration Scheme. In 1908 the sum of £2 a year was paid to owners of steam lorries of approved pattern if they agreed to be registered for call-up 'in the event of unpleasant developments'. In 1911 its successor, the Subsidy Scheme, included petrol driven lorries, with the amount paid rising to a sum varying from £38 to £52. In 1912 1,000 vehicles were registered, the price now being £110 a year. Times were changing!

Many manufacturers and owners were keen to register under the Subsidy Scheme since the sums paid were a real aid to their businesses. There was a catch, of course. On the owner's side he hoped war would not be declared, and on the army's side there was an insistence on certain standardization measures, essential in a newly developing industry in which all makers went their own way. The following were demanded by the army: four forward gears and one reverse: the gear lever knob should be round, but the brake lever should be square. A shaft-driven transmission was also considered essential, but industry could not provide this at the time, so in the event, a good number of chain-driven Albions, Commers, Guys, Halleys and Hallfords were impressed for war use.

Introduction of Motor Cycles

Two-wheeled locomotion has yet to be mentioned. In 1911 Olympia staged a Motor Cycle Show, which was visited by army representatives, who then invited various manufacturers to send their machines to Brooklands for trials. The average speed of the motor cycles sent was extremely high for those days, forty miles per hour. Ten machines were bought for field trials with ASC units, among them Douglas, Phelon

T Model, Motor Cycle, with chain cam belt drive, on trial, Grantly Barracks, Devonport.

Moore, Premier, Rudge-Whitworth, Triumph and Zenith.

It was intended that a motor cycle should take the place of a horse for convoy work, but opinions on suitability and usage varied. The ASC Journal of 1909 gave a view: 'At present section sergeants are mounted on bicycles. No mounts (ie horses) are provided for Staff Sergeants who might, with advantage, ride the motor cycles allotted to the company. For working with traction engines nothing can be equal to a steady horse, as the average speed of a loaded engine is about 4-5 miles per hour. For fast lorries a motor-car is best, while motor cycles are useless for accompanying convoys. If they take it into their heads to run well, one gets miles ahead: if they run badly one is soon left behind trying to make the necessary adjustments. They are not an officer's mount.'

The Petrol-Engined Lorry Accepted

It was the custom before the 1914-18 war to attach officers to foreign armies to observe developments and for liaison. An Austrian petrol-engined Saurer lorry was imported into Aberdeen from the Continent, even though petrol was still banned for private users. This vehicle was trialled extensively between Elgin and London and as a result the army bought a batch of petrol-driven Thornycrofts. At the same time ninety steam tractors were hired for the 1910 manoeuvres for trials at divisional level, although their use merely illustrated that they did not have the necessary eighty-mile radius envisaged for MT vehicles in war.

This limitation in radius had an unprecedented influence on the method of supply. For reasons of economy there were no manoeuvres in 1911 and the time was used to redesign the supply system. Petrol-engined lorries were to distribute supplies from a forward railhead to refilling points, from which point ASC Train or regimental transport would take over. This was a radical introduction, with a possible war in Europe in mind. This new idea was successfully trialled in 1912 and immediately written into operations manuals. This resulted in the ASC being in a position in 1914 to provide the army's needs with up-to-date equipment and a new method of supply which solved the problems of time and distance experienced in South Africa. It was a system that provided a flexibility never before available. At the same time Divisional Ammunition Parks ASC were created, with steam tractors earmarked, to carry 3rd line artillery stocks, under the Inspector General of Communications. A Royal Artillery officer was allotted to each Ammunition Park to ensure that the lorries sent up to the various refilling points contained the right types of ammunition and fuses. In other respects the supply of artillery and small arms ammunition remained the responsibility of the Royal Artillery.

In 1911 the War Office decided that there was no future for tracked vehicles in the army and, although caterpillar vehicles continued in use, they were not trialled or developed further. In fact, it was discovered that the Admiralty had conceived a Landships Committee with the intention of designing forty-foot-long caterpillar landships capable of carrying fifty men as well as guns and ammunition. This concept was well in advance of its time but the results were very cumbersome. The trial models were transferred to the army, who handled them with masterful inactivity and they were never seen again.

The UK base in the meantime was not sitting idly by. Between 1904 and 1914 an increasing number of horse transport ASC companies were mechanized, converting at Aldershot before returning to their various stations around the United Kingdom, 'spreading the gospel' of a new form of locomotion. Many horse transport companies

Mechanical Transport of 77 Company ASC. The motor car second from left is a Clement Talbot, others are Wolseleys. The steam tractors are Fowlers.

were on lower establishment and a typical establishment was of two officers, one company sergeant-major, two sergeants, two corporals, one trumpeter, two lance corporals, fifteen drivers, and a wheeler, saddler and farrier staff sergeant or corporal, as well as a shoeing and carriage smith.

Regimental Matters

The ASC Old Comrades Club was initiated in July, 1910. Among the earliest to join were Major T W Reynolds, who had served in the Military Train, and Assistant Commissary General E Litchfield, who had served in the Crimean War. The first annual dinner was held in the Holborn Restaurant in London on 20 October, 1910, with some 260 members, the chair being taken by Major General H N Bunbury, CB.

Also in the same year was formed the Corps Club, in order to control the various other clubs and activities which had developed in recent years: the ASC point-to-point, cricket, dinner, the band, the Ascot Lunch, the Journal, Quarterly and Seniority List. The stated aim was that 'The Corps, past and present, be a united family and work together for the general benefit of the Corps'. The Corps Band made its first appearance at the Royal Navy and Military Tournament at Olympia in July, 1910, and is recorded as having acquitted itself with credit. During this period teams from Aldershot and Woolwich, the two main ASC centres, competed regularly at Olympia in waggon dismounting and mounting competitions.

The Volunteer Force

The Volunteer Force, whose first formed ASC unit was the Hampshire Brigade Company ASC in 1885, had gradually seen the appearance of more ASC companies, with many individuals volunteering for service in South Africa. The Royal Commission after the Boer War had recommended a separate Volunteer Transport Corps, but the time was not opportune. Much work was done in the War Office, however, and the army was reorganized in 1908 to provide six Regular divisions, each with its own Transport and Supply Column ASC.

The Territorial Force (as it was renamed in 1908) was to consist of fourteen divisions and fourteen mounted brigades, one for each of the military Districts (two for London), each with its own Transport and Supply Column. Each Divisional Column had a strength of nineteen officers and 450 men (plus a Regular Adjutant and four Permanent Staff Instructors), while the mounted Brigade Column was of company strength. In addition to ASC units for both Regular and Territorial Divisions, there were additional ASC units for Army Troops and for specialist purposes (eg wireless, cable, field HQs and medical units).

The early recruitment of volunteers was slow, with critics hurling taunts and nicknames at every opportunity, but 'Haldane's Horse' or 'The Saturday Night Soldiers' carried on, encouraged by King Edward VII's personal intervention through Lords Lieutenant of the counties. Because their establishments were small and they were able to recruit from civilian sources, where occupations generally matched military functions, the volunteer ASC units had quite the best recruiting results in the entire Territorial Force. In May, 1912, a great boost was given to the MT section of the Corps when Their Majesties King George V and Queen Mary inspected the MT of the ASC on parade in Aldershot. By 1913, with war looming, every ASC unit had experienced more than once the duties of transport and supply in support of its formation on manoeuvres or at camp. The summer camps of 1914 saw all units on collective training with their formations so that they too, like their Regular counterparts, were as ready as they could be for war.

Eve of War Situation

On the eve of the First World War the ASC was scattered throughout the world, in every Army garrison except India. Prior to May, 1916, the ASC did not serve in India, and similar duties there were undertaken by the Supply and Transport Corps of the Indian Army, although that Corps varied in constitution and scope. For the Indian S & T Corps a limited number of captains and subalterns were seconded from the British service for periods of five years and this proved a great advantage when, later, the time came for the two services to co-operate in the field. At that time the ASC numbered 500 Regular officers and 6,000 men, largely in seventy-three companies as follows: five Depot companies (three horse transport and one each for MT and supply), thirty-three HT companies and twenty MT companies, two station HT companies at lower establishments, four service companies for supply, four remount companies and five HT companies in the Middle East or in South Africa. In peacetime the soldier's daily ration at home consisted simply of one pound of bread and one pound of meat, while the officers received no rations at all. Abroad groceries were issued to everybody. This situation was about to change and the issue of a more comprehensive ration for all ranks had been planned by the outbreak of war.

CHAPTER 4

The First World War – 1914-18

The Role of the Army Service Corps

Mobilization. The Expeditionary Force. France and Belgium. Italy. Egypt and Palestine. Mesopotamia (Iraq). The Balkans (Salonika). The Dardanelles (Gallipoli). East Africa. Russia. The Home Front.

Mobilization

The duties of the Corps were defined in the King's Regulations and Orders for the Army 1912 (reprinted with Amendments published in Army Orders up to August, 1914): 'The officers of the ASC are entrusted with furnishing transport, provisions, fuel, light, and supplies, for the use of all branches of the army, and with the allotment of barracks and quarters and their equipment, as laid down in the Regulations for Supply Transport and Barrack Services.' In August, 1914, when mobilization came, these duties provided a wide range of problems for the ASC.

The supply and transport plans were well thought out and in place, but the manpower difficulties were enormous and soon worsened as the Army grew ever larger.

Thanks to Brigadier General S S Long, who had progressed from the Officers' Training Establishment in Aldershot to the Supply Reserve Depot in Woolwich and then to the position of Director of Supplies and Quartering, the Army at least had sufficient supplies for its immediate commitments. With war imminent, contracts had been placed and plans complete even to the extent of using refrigerated ships as cold stores for frozen meat from overseas. In the transport field, previously under Major General F W B Landon, Director of Transport and Movement, establishments had been revised, vehicle provision and issue planned, spares and equipments earmarked, repair workshops allocated and mobilization plans drawn up. It had never been possible, however, to practise mass mobilization arrangements, but plans had been made, under the Assistant Director of Transport, Lieutenant Colonel F W Stringer, and a location in London earmarked, for its control.

At 1600 hrs on 4 August, 1914, the order for the mobilization of the Expeditionary and Territorial Forces was issued by the government. Barracks and quarters were emptied, tented camps blossomed, buildings were hired and men were billeted on the local population. 3 August had been a Bank Holiday and Territorial units were on the move to camps for their annual training; nevertheless mobilization went smoothly and 120,000 horses were collected. The Expeditionary Force's embarkation for France was delayed until 9 August, with the advance parties going on 7 August, including Major H O Knox ASC, in command of the Supply Detachment, for the first overseas base. He is credited with being the first Expeditionary Force member to land on the continent, closely followed by Captain G E Terry ASC.

On 4 August the orders to requisition the 900 vehicles initially needed by the Army were signed, and officers were sent to America, Canada and Egypt to buy additional mules. The Officer in Charge of ASC Records in Woolwich was also instructed, according to prepared plans, to bring units up to strength and to provide MT personnel for field force formations. All garrisons were recalled in August from Egypt, Gibraltar, Malta and South Africa.

In Yorkshire over a thousand men of the Yorkshire Waggoners Special Volunteer Reserve, more recently known as the Wolds Waggoners, were enrolled under the guidance of Sir Mark Sykes of Sledmere.

In the event the pre-war vehicle planning figure was inadequate and this is when the Vehicle Subsidy Scheme bore fruit. Some 1,200 vehicles in all were called in, also private cars and motor cycles. This was still not enough and the Army took over much of the vehicle factory output throughout the land.

In September, 1914, Major General Landon was appointed Inspector of QMG Services and Brigadier General Long the Director of Supplies and Transport. Quartering remained an ASC responsibility under Major General C E Heath.

The Expeditionary Force

Priority in everything was given to sending the Expeditionary Force to France, with initial movements involving the concentration of four divisions and the cavalry division in the neighbourhood of Le Cateau. By 20 August this deployment to locations pre-planned with the French in 1911 was completed. The sixth division followed on 8-9 September. In addition Army and Line of Communications troops were sent. The initial ASC units of the Regular Army and mobilized Territorial Army totalled some 15,000 men in thirty-four HT and nineteen MT Companies, three remount depots and sixty supply units of various sizes, with a total of 1,200 MT vehicles of all types, of which only eighty were Army owned.

Movement for the embarkation of infantry units at Southampton was largely achieved by train, with whole units completing a train load. Movement for ASC units was necessarily more complicated:

- Avonmouth was used for MT and petrol
- Newhaven for stores and supplies
- Liverpool for frozen meat and MT, and
- Southampton for HT units

Ports of disembarkation in France were Le Havre, Rouen and Boulogne, where Base Depots were opened in August, 1914.

FRANCE AND BELGIUM

From their initial contact with the German Army the Expeditionary Force was hard-pressed, but during the retreat from Mons the Corps was able to keep the Army supplied, despite the difficulties. Many ASC units had a variety of strange adventures. They were frequently in close contact with the enemy, having to defend their own positions and glean news of the tactical situation from any source available, information which was usually conflicting. It was not uncommon for contact to be

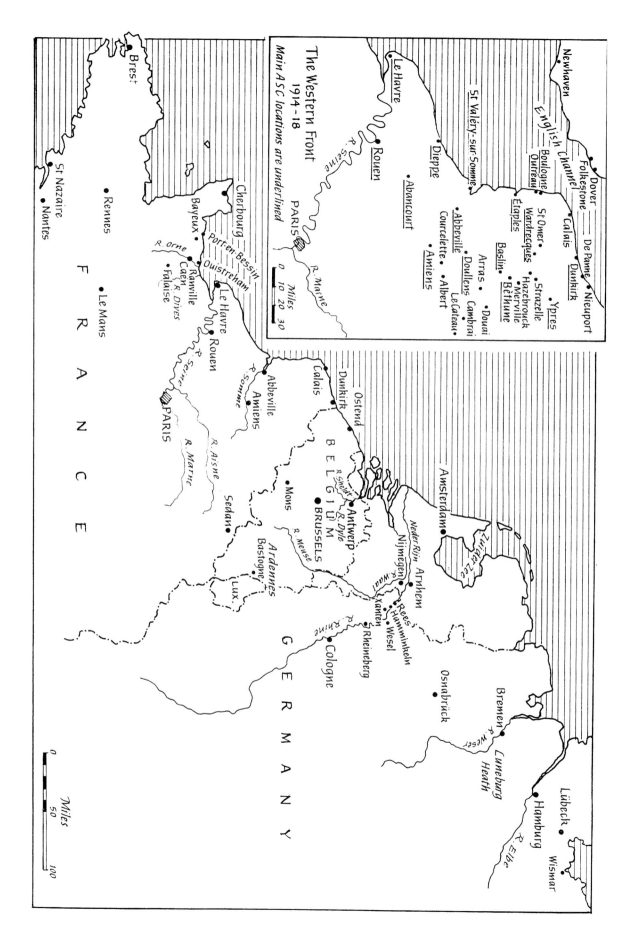

A painting depicting a column of thirty ASC vehicles attacked by a force of German cavalry after refusing to surrender during the retreat from Mons, Belgium, late August, 1914. Only two vehicles were lost.

lost with units being supported, so ASC supply points issued food and ammunition to any grateful units which had lost contact with their own ASC support. Convoys were attacked by Uhlan cavalry, with little loss, however.

Early lessons were learnt in the achievement of mobility. The great majority of field ambulances were horse-drawn, motorized ambulances then being not widely available. The speed of the withdrawal from Mons affected the horses badly; they got little rest and inadequate food and shelter, which severely reduced their efficiency. Many workshop trailers were towed by steam tractors, which proved unable to keep up with the retreating troops, so had to be left behind, immobilized by breaking radiators and cylinder blocks with sledgehammers or picks. These were subsequently recovered, repaired and taken back into use on the retreat of the German Army in September, the Germans having been unable to operate them.

Major General F T Clayton took over the post of Director of Supplies in France from Brigadier General C W King MVO, who was invalided back to UK. The Director of Transport was initially Brigadier General F C A Gilpin, but he was replaced in November, 1914, by Brigadier General W G B Boyce, who remained in post until the end of the war. Major General Clayton was promoted to Lieutenant General in the appointment of Inspector General of Communications in Abbeville, the first of what was eventually three such appointments for Corps officers.

By the middle of September, 1914, the BEF was 240,000 strong, with an additional 25,000 men from the Indian Army, and some 100,000 animals. All needed support from the ASC.

A new form of military transport appeared on the scene at the start of the war – the London omnibus. Sixty AEC 'B' Type omnibuses with their civilian drivers were requisitioned by the Admiralty to transport a force of Royal Marines to Antwerp to counter the German attack in Belgium. On the unsuccessful conclusion of this adventure, forty-eight escaped to join the rest of the BEF, driven with great cheerfulness and courage by drivers who had not long before been plying the streets of the capital. The Germans must have been amazed to see these omnibuses, still painted in their original livery, advertising commercial products and London shows.

Three hundred more omnibuses were taken over, formed into omnibus companies in London and driven by ASC drivers for the first battle of Ypres in October-November, 1914. Each could carry twenty-five armed and equipped men, and were painted battleship grey, probably due to the availability of that particular paint. Their windows were boarded up and they were equipped with picks and shovels to give them a military air, though it did, in the event, prove difficult to dig buses out of Flanders ditches.

At the start of the war the strength of the ASC had been 498 officers and 5,933 other ranks. The original six divisions were clearly not enough to support operational developments and the Secretary of State for War, Lord Kitchener, initiated plans for the famous 'New Armies'. Territorial Divisions were embodied and underwent six months' training before taking to the field. By the spring of 1915, however, the

Troops embussing in boarded up London omnibuses.

casualty rate forced the War Office to deploy Territorial Divisions in the Western Front. The first to go was the North Midland Division.

The reception, testing and training of the thousands who flocked through Army Recruiting Offices for the MT ASC needed a new organization, since the pre-war training companies in Aldershot and Woolwich could not cope. In September, 1914, a large workhouse in Grove Park, south-east London, was taken over and became 1 MT Reserve Depot ASC, in due course the nucleus of the later Lee Reception and Training Area.

The main method of supply on the continent had great flexibility, which was, in the event, often needed with formations switched from one part of the front to another. Essentially stores from the UK base were moved by train and ship to an entry port and then moved by rail, through a regulating station, to which other stores were delivered and then to a railhead. Motor transport took the supplies, including small arms ammunition, from there to Refilling Points where second-line horse transport (ie the Divisional Transport and Supply Column) collected to deliver forward to battalion or unit lines. Gun ammunition, which was delivered direct to the guns, was initially carried by the Divisional Ammunition Column (an Artillery organization), but this was soon handed over as an ASC MT responsibility, though the Royal Artillery were still responsible for stock control. Units along the Line of Communication collected their stores from depots in their area.

It is understandable to think of the Corps' work in terms of transport, since it is more visibly active. Supplies, however, constituted a large part of the ASC's responsibilities and credit must be given to a large organization which worked with

ASC mobile workshop vehicle set up in the field.

Mobile repair unit repairing a broken front axle in the field.

high efficiency and little notice throughout the war. Initially the feeding strength of the Army in France was 12,000 men and 40,000 animals; by the end of the war the figures were 3,000,000 and 500,000 respectively. Advanced Supply Depots were established at Abbeville, Abancourt and Outreau, with a separate depot for Indian troops at Orleans. Field Supply Depots were opened at Barlin, Béthune, Doullens and Wardrecques. Bakeries were established at Boulogne, Calais, Dieppe, Etaples, Le Havre, Marseilles and Rouen. Until May, 1915, when the Perkins oven was introduced, bread was cooked in the old 'Aldershot' ovens, taking a batch of 108 loaves in each oven. Members of the Queen Mary's Auxiliary Army Corps were employed as bakers to supplement ASC men.

Whereas the pre-war work of the ASC involved only the provision of supplies and transport, the war saw a great widening of responsibilities. A cooperative, efficient organization became something of a 'maid of all work', notably in the fields of heavy vehicle repair, gun towing, ambulance operation, support for Engineer units, water, petrol and troop carrying, agricultural units, and Expeditionary Force Canteens. In the Middle East the Corps also operated armoured cars and armed motor boats, whilst in North Russia reindeer units were a further diversification. On the formation of the Tank Corps the ASC provided skilled drivers on transfer to the new Corps, as well as those later sent to other Arms to replace casualties.

The repair of vehicles had been the responsibility of the Corps since the introduction of internal combustion-engined vehicles in the Army. The theoretical division of responsibility was that the ASC, as the sole operator of MT, would carry out unit repairs, and the Army Ordnance Corps (AOC) would carry out the heavy work at a base depot. Circumstances of a war situation, coupled with the shortage of transport and spares, militated against this and January, 1915, saw the return from the AOC to the ASC of base repair. The AOC Base Depot in Rouen continued its skills in the repair of artillery equipment. Quite apart from the extensive base repair

Base repair, 2nd ASC Repair Shop, Chautiers, 20 August, 1917.

organization centred on Heavy Repair Shops, the ASC recovered its own vehicles by means of Mobile Repair Units, each MT company also having its own mobile workshop vehicle.

In October, 1914, the War Office directed that the Territorial units of the ASC should be incorporated into the Regular Order of Battle, and that the term 'Transport and Supply Column' should be replaced by 'Train'. At the same time a Divisional Supply Column MT, consisting of a transport company, was added to each Train in an Infantry Division.

1915 saw a large increase in RA Siege Batteries for the static warfare that had developed, and this had a considerable impact on the Transport Corps of the Army. The ASC Depot Company in Aldershot, 52 MT Company, had incorporated a caterpillar section in 1914 and it moved at the beginning of 1915 to Avonmouth to become the ASC Tractor Depot, providing caterpillar tractors and drivers for heavy gun towing. Until the end of the war ASC Siege Park Company tractors, initially FWD, Foster Daimler and Fowler, and later Holt caterpillars from America, towed all the guns and carried the ammunition of the heavy artillery. This artillery consisted of 60 pdr guns, 6 inch guns and howitzers, 8 inch howitzers, 9.2 inch guns and howitzers, 12 inch guns and howitzers and 13 pdr and 3 inch anti-aircraft guns.

In 1915, at the request of the Adjutant General, the Director of Supplies and Transport undertook the driver and MT technical training of the newly formed 'Heavy Branch of the Machine Gun Corps', using 711 Company ASC as the MT

Workshops and calling for volunteer ASC drivers. The Heavy Branch of the MGC (Machine Gun Corps) was the cover unit for the initial trials and deployment of Britain's new secret weapon to break the stalemate of trench warfare, 'the tank'. Tank crews came as volunteers from all army cap badges and every crew member was taught to fire the guns and drive the tank, but an early report comments that in battle the professional ASC driver would always be the driver. Thus it came about that, on 15 September, 1916, all the fifty or so tanks that fought the first-ever tank engagement against the Germans, now called the Battle of Flers-Courcelette, on the Somme, were all driven by cap-badged ASC soldiers. Most of these ASC men then transferred into the Tank Corps, as the Heavy Branch of the MGC subsequently became known, and many fought again as tank crews at the better known Battle of Cambrai.

From Peninsular War days through to the Crimea and beyond, the ASC and its predecessors have been responsible for the transport of wounded men for the Medical Services. In addition they now provided ambulance support for Field Ambulances, Royal Army Medical Corps (RAMC), both AT and MT, to carry wounded from Regimental Aid Posts to Advanced Dressing Stations and from there to General Hospitals. If a 'Blighty' was involved (ie a wound which necessitated return to UK) train and ferry to the UK base was the method of transport of patients and transport to and from trains was an ASC task. Railways lacked the inherent

ASC Driven Caterpillar Tractor towing an 8in Howitzer, September, 1916.

flexibility of road transport and, either to replace or complement trains, a number of Motor Ambulance Columns (MACs) were formed. Each one consisted of an ASC transport company, forty-eight being provided in all.

The need for the provision of canteens for the Army was acknowledged by the Army Council in February, 1915, and Expeditionary Force Canteens, pioneered by Lieutenant Colonel E C Wright in France, increasingly supplied small comforts such as the troops were accustomed to buying in their own canteens in peacetime.

Later Lance Corporal E Seaman won a posthumous Victoria Cross on 29 September, 1918, shortly after transferring from the EFC ASC to the Royal Inniskilling Fusiliers, as part of the transfer of ASC manpower mentioned earlier and described in the following paragraphs.

By the middle of 1916 the manpower situation was causing anxiety at the War Office. The results of the recently introduced

Issues being made from an Expeditionary Force Canteen Store, biscuits predominating.

Horse-drawn ambulance east of Moricourt Montauban road, September, 1916.

Conscription Bill were yet to make themselves felt and heavy casualties were anticipated in the operations planned on the Somme. In May the Director of Supplies at the War Office initiated an exchange of 5500 category 'A' men of the ASC for men of lower category and a wholesale examination of establishments at home and abroad was instituted. Some 80,000 men, mostly HT drivers, with large numbers coming from the Divisional Trains, were transferred to the Infantry, Cavalry, Tank Corps and RFC. Later, in 1917, some battalions of the 60th Rifles were badly mauled by the German Marines near Nieuport. These units had recently received large drafts of ASC men and the Adjutant of one of the battalions wrote to the OC of the ASC Depot asking whether it could be arranged that more men from the same source could be provided for the reconstitution of his unit, as those who had been previously incorporated had conducted themselves so splendidly in the face of the enemy. Less well-known is that over 100 officers were attached or transferred to the Royal Flying Corps.

The manpower shortage was, to a certain extent, improved by the employment of women, there having been none in the Army in 1914. From April, 1916, women were increasingly used in munitions factories and, in the Army, the ASC led the way.

In 1916 Lady Londonderry, President of the Women's Legion, was authorized to form a section of female motor drivers, with Miss Christobel Hills in charge. At first these drivers were attached to MT Companies in London, but after a year they were placed under the direct control of the War Office and were more widely employed. A number of Women's Legion drivers later replaced men in the Rhineland in 1919 to assist in demobilization.

FANYs with their motor ambulances at Etaples, 27 June, 1917.

Mention must also be made of the First Aid Nursing Yeomanry (FANY), who provided the first replacements for British soldiers during the war, particularly for driving MT, when they took up their duties at Calais in January, 1916. From their early pre-war training days to practical help with fuel and maintenance in France the FANYs had close links with the ASC, which continued into the Second World War.

Lorries collecting ammunition at railhead.

There were also, in addition to personnel changes, organizational changes instituted in 1916, which continued into 1917. These changes essentially involved the pooling of transport to provide greater efficiency and flexibility, especially in the face of a possible major breakdown in railway support. In particular the control of certain units was changed: Divisional Supply Columns, which had been Lines of Communication troops under the Inspector General of Communications, were placed under command of a Corps. Similarly, Divisional Ammunition Parks and Lines of Communication units were broken up and GHQ Ammunition Parks were formed in their place. Each Corps had its own GHQ Ammunition Park and each Division its own Ammunition Sub-Park.

Perhaps the most interesting and certainly the most successful of reorganizations concerned troop carrying. The five omnibus companies were centralized under GHQ; the unit was known as the Auxiliary Omnibus Park (MT). They formed at St Valéry-sur-Somme at the end of 1916 and were complemented by two other companies, one of charabancs, the other of troop-carrying lorries.

With 650 vehicles and 1,800 all ranks the Park could carry the dismounted troops of a division. After the unit had moved to the

Drawing rations at ASC roadside Supply Depot.

71

Amiens area in March, 1917, and had established its routines, bus columns were available within an hour of the order being received. The actual embussing and debussing of a division seldom took more than half an hour; the record for a brigade was four and a half minutes. This centralized form of transport really came into its own during the German offensive of March, 1918.

On 6 May, 1918, Field Marshal Sir Douglas Haig, Commander-in-Chief of the British Armies in France sent the following letter to the Commanding Officer of the Auxiliary Omnibus Park:

> 'Please convey to all ranks of the Auxiliary Omnibus Park my great appreciation of the services rendered by them since 21st March. The details of the work they have accomplished, in circumstances of peculiar hardship and difficulty, have been brought to my notice and constitute a record of which every officer and man may well be proud. They may rest assured that in meeting the heavy demands recently made upon them, through long hours of continual duty both on the road and in the workshops, they have greatly assisted the operations of our troops and have contributed in no small degree to the frustration of the enemy's plans. I thank them for the work they have done, and count with confidence upon the same loyal service and devotion in the future.'

An example of those buses, No B43, called 'Ole Bill', is currently on display in the Imperial War Museum, reconditioned and gleaming in its original livery. HM King George V inspected a number of ex-Great War ASC bus drivers at Buckingham Palace in 1920 and actually climbed on to the running board of B43, the first monarch ever to take such a proletarian step!

It was during this last major German assault in 1918 that two members of the Corps were awarded the Victoria Cross. Lieutenant Alfred Herring, who was attached to 6 (Service) Battalion, the Northamptonshire Regiment, held up the German attack on 23 March at Montagne Bridge at Jussy, thus enabling the rest of the

Motor ambulance recovering casualties in the ruins of Bazentin.

Wounded being placed in an ambulance for evacuation.

A wounded collecting point.

Ambulances waiting at the Forward Field Dressing Station.

battalion to withdraw. The day after his capture he was introduced to the Kaiser at St Quentin. He was imprisoned at Graudenz (now in Poland) where his medal ribbon was later presented.

Private George Masters was an ambulance driver attached to 141 Field Ambulance at Béthune. In April, 1918, he made repeated journeys over difficult roads, constantly under shell and machine-gun fire, even bombed by an aeroplane, in order to evacuate a number of severely wounded men. His ambulance was the only vehicle to get through, and on his final trip he was even gassed. His bravery was so inspiring to the front-line soldiers that he was awarded the Victoria Cross on 9 April, arguably the only Corps VC winner who received such an award for performing purely Corps duties.

One of the other and perhaps lesser known developments during the war concerned labour. An Army Order of 4 August, 1914, authorized ASC Labour Companies, the first of which arrived at Le Havre on 26 August. More followed in due course along with labour units for the Royal Engineers, AOC railways and the Directorate of Works, mainly men from Africa and China.

By November, 1918, the total of men on labour duties had risen to 249,000. In December, 1916, a Directorate of Labour was formed at GHQ, the first Director being Brigadier General Evan Gibb, late ASC, with appropriate staff at Army, Line of Communication, Corps and Base HQ levels. This newly formed Labour Corps provided sterling service for the BEF, but was disbanded immediately after the war.

Salvage was an important function within the Supply Branch of the ASC. Divisional Salvage Companies were formed in 1915 and salvage dumps were established for rearward transmission to the base. The ASC was specifically responsible for salvage within the fields of supply and transport, mainly derelict or damaged vehicles and empty containers.

The last few months of the war, although rarely highlighted in general histories, were in fact times of great difficulty for the ASC. It had poured new blood into the teeth arms to replace the losses of 1916; it had been partially reorganized in 1917 and had survived the German onslaught of March – April, 1918. In supporting a decisive breakthrough a great strain was put on the ASC, both in men and material, horse transport as well as mechanical transport. Personnel were exhausted and the vehicles were becoming very battered. Fortunately the Armistice of 11 November, 1918, stopped the war before any diminution of support occurred.

The Western Front is, for many reasons, that which attracts the most attention. However, the contribution made in other theatres to the successful outcome of the war should not be understated and was essential for overall victory. Although the operations in each Theatre took place under very different conditions, each was a test of the fortitude and resourcefulness of our armies, and some were stretched to the very limit before victory was achieved. The following paragraphs outline the widely differing operations in these theatres. For the Corps each presented their own special problems in maintaining our Forces, the solving of which was vital for success.

Italy

Italy was one of the Western Allies in the fight against Germany and Austria and contingency plans were drawn up in 1917 for the involvement of British and French troops. The major defeat of the Italian Army at Caporetto led to 200,000 British and French troops moving speedily to reinforce Italy and keep her in the war. The British formations involved were 7, 23 and 48 Divisions, their units moving from France by rail and on the coastal road via Modane. ASC mechanical transport units drove the 1,100 miles for this move.

Within two months Brigadier General W S Swabey, who had been sent to Italy as the Director of Supplies, was appointed the Director of Supplies and Transport. The Base Supply Depot at Arquata, north of Genoa, was commanded by Lieutenant Colonel C Rowe ASC. Part of the contingency planning which was implemented immediately was the loan of 500 1-ton Fiat lorries and drivers.

In March, 1918, the British troops were moved to the Asiago plateau in the north, to counter a likely Austrian spring offensive, where they were to be involved in mountain warfare. The ASC inevitably needed to adapt its organization for its first ever involvement in Alpine terrain. Two sectors were established, each quite different: the left sector entailed the use of a rack and pinion railway between Rochette and Asiago, and the right sector enabled only road transport to be used. The railhead town of Chiuppana for the left sector had its exciting moments as it was in full view of the Austrians in the mountains and was occasionally shelled; the staging point of Rochette near Chiuppana was even under enemy searchlight observation and was therefore frequently shelled. Limbered waggons and mule transport carried supplies forward from the railhead. For the right sector the railhead was at Villaverla, from which Divisional Trains initially moved supplies the six miles to Fara, where first-line units took over for onward movement to Granezza. Mountainous roads and the twenty miles involved were too much, however, and a mule company operated a double echelon system to solve the problem.

Fiat vehicles operated by ASC in the Italian Alps, 1915.

In the event the Austrians opened their attack in June but were forced to accept an Armistice on 4 November, 1918, not before the right sector formation (48 Division) needed to capture Austrian forage to ease its supply problems. In addition, the Division had to use fifty light Fiat lorries with Italian drivers during its advance to Trent and Levico in lieu of the Divisional Train heavy draught horses, which could not be used on the steep mountain roads. There was also an exchange of vehicles between the ASC and their Italian counterparts: six Pavesi tractors for nine British four-wheel drive lorries to enable guns to be moved on difficult roads, a good bargain under the circumstances.

The maximum strength of the ASC in Italy was 275 officers, 4,180 MT other ranks, 2,120 HT other ranks, 900 Supply personnel and 1,534 vehicles.

Egypt and Palestine

There were in fact two campaigns in the Near East: a minor campaign in 1914-16 to defend the Suez Canal by defeating the Senussi in the Western Desert and a major campaign in 1916-18, advancing from Egypt through the Sinai, Palestine and Syria, ending with the defeat of the Turkish Army near Aleppo. In the former campaign Alexandria was used as the base. British forces 8000 strong progressed westwards along the coast by rail, road or camel, eventually to Sollum, 350 miles away. In this minor foray there was little significant ASC activity except for the provision of over 2000 gallons of petrol in Sollum for a raid westwards for 120 miles by armoured cars to rescue the survivors of two British ships, *Tara* and *Moorina*, who were held prisoner. Light ASC MT lorries were also used as troop carriers to assist in the capture of the Siwa Oasis, 180 miles south-west of Mersa Matruh.

The main campaign in 1916-18 involved 250,000 men, the senior ASC officer being Brigadier General G F Davies (later to be the Director of Supplies and Transport in the War Office), brilliantly supported by Colonel W Elliott, a Reserve officer with pre-war service in Egypt and the Middle East and war experience in Gallipoli. The initial aim was to safeguard the Suez Canal from the Turks, whose main force was at El Arish on the eastern edge of the Sinai Desert, 100 miles from Qantara on the Suez Canal.

With the Sinai an effective barrier to movement, transportation took on a special significance. To solve the problem the Royal Engineers built a standard gauge railway

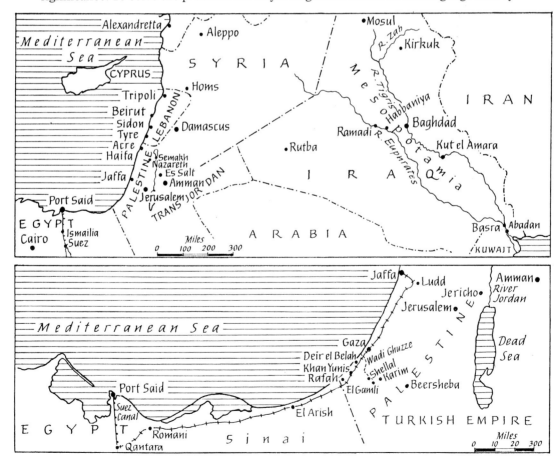

The Camel Transport Corps in Egypt.

from Qantara to Wadi Ghuzze near Gaza. Qantara soon developed into the main base. At the same time a new form of transportation was introduced, the pipeline, essential for the supply of water. Until the pipeline was ready, however, water was moved in bulk on the new railway and then distributed to the forward troops by ASC camels. A Camel Transport Corps, organized in companies of 2,000 animals each, totalling 35,000 animals, was formed under Colonel C W Whittingham, an ASC Reserve officer, and was employed as first line transport and as special columns – the ASC provided supervisory staff (111 officers and 208 NCOs) for the Egyptian drivers. Later, reservoirs and wells were established forward, but the capture of the wells at Beersheba eased the water supply situation.

After fighting against the Turks in the Romani area, which opened the way to El Arish, Rafah on the Palestine border was occupied in January, 1917. A track along the coast was laid, with wire netting laid on the sand and pegged down. Mounted troops were forbidden to use this track as horses' hooves would have cut the wire.

General Sir Edmund Allenby replaced General Sir Archibald Murray as Force Commander in June, 1917. He moved GHQ from Cairo to Rafah and reorganized and revitalized the Army for its next offensive against the Turks. Ultimately there were fourteen trains and four auxiliary mule transport companies on the Line of Communication with a total strength of nearly 17,000 men, of whom just over half were Egyptian. Two donkey companies were also formed for employment in the difficult going of the Judaean Hills. Reserve and advanced depots were also created in a wide area occupied by British troops. The depot at Karm was set up in full view of the Turkish positions and was subjected to attack by gun fire.

General Allenby's Force, reinforced by two additional divisions, mounted a surprise attack on the Turks and took Beersheba, which forced a Turkish withdrawal from the Gaza area to a precarious line between Jerusalem and Jaffa. At this stage, excluding Line of Communication units, General Allenby's army had thirteen MT companies available to him, made up of one Ford van company and twelve caterpillar tractor companies, eleven of which towed the heavy guns of the Royal Artillery. On the eve of the attack three more lorry companies were brought up from Qantara.

The subsequent pursuit lengthened the distances over which the ASC worked, but Jerusalem fell in December and Jericho in February, 1918. Camels working in three echelons along the coastal sand dunes overcame the problems caused by a lengthy period of rains, saving the operational situation, but in some places camels sank up to their girths in mud and had to be abandoned. By the end of December, 1917, fresh supply depots had been formed along the entire front, from Jerusalem to Jaffa, and other depots were opened.

After something of a delay in operations in early 1918, the offensive continued in September. Within thirty-six hours the Turkish 7th and 8th Armies were broken and forced to retire, which forced their 4th Army east of the Jordan to conform. Thereafter the fighting developed into a general pursuit and harassment of a fleeing enemy. In this welter of constantly developing operational scenarios the ASC, with its forty companies, was at full stretch in close support of the Teeth Arms. Maintenance of the force was assisted by coastal landings at Haifa, Tyre, Sidon, Beirut and Tripoli, with the Camel Transport Corps cooperating until the MT could take up the work on the repaired coastal road north of Beirut and on the Haifa-Nazareth-Galilee road to Damascus. East of the River Jordan the Cavalry Division in pursuit of 4th Turkish Army was supported by MT from Jericho and by mule transport.

This campaign was a memorable achievement in which logistic support necessarily matched the determined brilliance of the forward troops, with the brunt of the transport work being borne by the MT companies.

The first British lorries (Peerless) to enter Damascus, 1918.

In support of a force (in September, 1918) of 466,750 men and 159,900 animals, the ASC operated a total of 1,601 lorries, 1,467 cars and vans, 530 ambulances, 1,487 motor cycles and 288 tractors, with 1,094 officers and 17,817 other ranks, complemented by 2,725 Indians and 32,744 Egyptians. The best traditions of the Corps had been upheld, their efforts described by the Commander-in-Chief as 'a triumph of organization and perseverance'. This striking tribute was equalled after the war by the Turkish General Refet Pasha's offer to General Allenby to fight the Palestine campaign over again with an equal Commissariat.

MESOPOTAMIA (IRAQ)

Moving further to the east, Mesopotamia offers another little-known campaign, in which the most intense demands were placed on the vehicles and men of the Corps.

In 1914 the Indian government landed a force at Basra to protect the Royal Navy's oil supplies from the Turks. The scope of the operations was expanded, with the aim of capturing Baghdad, but, after some initial success, the British and Indian forces under General Townshend were forced back to Kut el Amara and surrendered in April, 1916, after a gallant defence. The first known air supply drop took place during this siege. At this stage only the Indian Army Supply and Transport Corps was involved in support of the Western forces, but with understrength animal transport.

In early 1916, with British prestige at stake, the War Office was directed to recover the situation and assumed responsibility for the maintenance of the forces in Mesopotamia. Problems abounded, however: roads were non-existent, the only railway ran north of Baghdad; no maritime methods had been employed in an area of rivers and waterways; in the rainy season the country was almost impassable and in summer dust and the lack of water supply made movement highly uncomfortable; and furthermore the Indian logistic system was totally inadequate.

The appointment of General Maude in August, 1916, set in train a range of improvements. On the Supply and Transport side Brigadier General P J C Scott was appointed Director of Supplies and Transport, at the head of 659 officers and 12,200 other ranks of the ASC who eventually served in the campaign.

Lieutenant Colonel F W Leyland was appointed as Assistant Director of MT and the War Office was requested to send a number of MT companies. By the end of December two Ford van companies, two Holt caterpillar tractor companies (for howitzer towing) and another Motor Ambulance Column had arrived; ultimately there were forty-two ASC MT companies. Additionally infantry battalions were provided for the first-time with their own first line MT lorries.

General Maude was now able to go on the offensive and 1917 and 1918 were a story of uninterrupted success based on good administrative support and operational mobility, both provided by the ASC. Kut was recaptured in February and Baghdad taken in March; the Lines of Communication were thereby extended to some 500 miles from the base in Basra and the Army reached a total strength of 300,000 men and 66,000 animals.

In September, 1917, the 3,000-strong Turkish garrison at Ramadi was attacked and for this operation the ASC, commanded by Major E Snepp, concentrated 350 Ford vans and ten Fiats as a column for troop-carrying duties, the first time the ASC had performed this task outside Europe. In a subsequent aborted attack on Hit, 100 cars carrying infantry and Lewis guns moved at night, without lights, over unknown and difficult country, a remarkable operation. The success of these rapid concentrations was immediately reinforced and four columns were organized, each under the command of a lieutenant colonel; the composition and strength of these columns varied according to the operational requirements, but the largest number of vans was 1,200 for one specific operation.

The extensive demands for vehicles in this theatre could not, however, be met from the UK base. Model T Fords from America provided the answer and some 3,300 were eventually used; their lightness and ease of maintenance made them ideal for the desert and rough going in Mesopotamia. Many Fords were driven by Indian and Burmese drivers, armed mostly with ineffective, outdated weapons. Another American vehicle, the Packard 3 tonner, provided the heavy lift in two transport companies. Ultimately there were forty-two MT companies, of which twenty-two were Ford van companies, the total number of vehicles amounting to 6,930.

An interesting additional task carried out by the ASC was the provision of men, vehicles, spares and repairs for six light armoured motor batteries, six anti-aircraft sections and a railway armoured motor battery; not to be forgotten either was the use of a large river barge, converted by an ASC officer, into a double-decker floating mobile MT workshop, as no suitable building was available ashore. Even the Expeditionary Force Canteen took over a barge, the *SS Masoodi*, on the Tigris.

Ford convoy on the Jebel Hamrin, Mesopotamia.

When the Armistice was signed on 31 October, 1918, the ASC had reached a strength of 12,660, of which 3,000 were Indian or Burmese and 800 Arabs. Just under 400 ASC died or were killed. You will find their graves, but you will look in vain for mention of the ASC in the index of the Official History of the campaign!

THE BALKANS (SALONIKA)

The Balkans provided something of a messy campaign. The British High Command, in its own way, distinguished itself by the decision to send formations without organic transport, both at first and second line. From this chaotic start things could at least only get better, and inevitably much improvisation and hard work on the part of the ASC saved the day.

The deployment of British and French troops – 150,000 were promised – was designed solely to save the Serbian Army and persuade Greece to honour her treaty obligations to side with the Western Allies against the Austro-Bulgarian Army. Both aims failed.

The advance party, which landed at Salonika in September, 1915, included Lieutenant Colonel O Striedinger, Assistant Director of Supplies and Transport. 10th Division followed in a disorganized manner, not helped by the torpedoing of the *Marquette* carrying the Ammunition Column, which left ASC units short in transport and supply numbers. Energetic action, however, and the cooperation of the French, recovered the situation and a Base Supply Depot was established just outside Salonika. Initial movement was based on animal transport, but then MT vehicles started arriving and a Base MT Depot was established in the town of Kalamaria, Salonika.

In spite of unhelpful Greek authorities, who requisitioned all available horses and mules to delay the allies, the British moved to the Doiran area in November to assist the French with their two Divisions. By December the mountainous forward areas were badly affected by heavy snow and rain and the few roads and tracks became morasses, thus making resupply difficult. Instead of six mules to a waggon, ten or twelve were often necessary, which had a knock-on delaying effect. In December blizzard conditions and the deteriorating operational situation forced a withdrawal by both the French and the British to a new defensive line north of Salonika, and 29 Divisional Supply Column (244 Company ASC) had to make a difficult conversion to a pack transport role, the only way to operate in the mountains

This campaign, perhaps more than in any other theatre of war, had elements of farce which would have been suitable for any comic opera. There was, for example, the incident of the Nehamas barn in Salonika: several hundred tons of hay had been bought locally by the British and it was under Army guard; meanwhile the ever-unhelpful Greeks forbade its removal and added a sentry of their own to reinforce their orders. The wily local vendor, an entrepreneur to his back teeth, then sold the hay to the unknowing French, who posted their own sentry. The three guards happily watched each other for several days.

The UK base in Salonika was not immune from well-meaning advice. A cable arrived from home proposing the use of olive trees for fire wood, in spite of their importance to the local community, each mature tree being then valued at £80. The Greeks also prohibited the sale of petrol and placed a guard on the Standard Oil Company premises, but fortunately the ASC depot was next door and the Greeks

Field Bakery operating in Salonika, using Aldershot ovens.

never noticed that fuel stocks were passed over the wall.

By December, 1915, the British force was 90,000 strong, with 25,000 animals. Colonel P C J Scott arrived in November as the Director of Supplies and Transport and Brigadier General A Long took over from him in January, 1916, with Major General F W G Koe as the Inspector-General of Communications. The Army was expanding rapidly, with four more Divisions (22, 26, 27 and 28), each with its own Train, so that by February the force being supported was 120,000 men and 50,000 animals strong, later to increase even more. Additional ASC supply units and motor transport arrived, some seventy lorries, which allowed resupply to be carried out by a combination of rail, mechanical and animal transport. Each division had 4,000 mules and a mix of waggons, in addition to the large number of Army and Line of Communications units.

In May, 1916, the Allies began preparing for a move north from the Salonika area, towards Struma, moving over the mountains north of Lakes Beshik and Langaza. This greatly influenced the transport and supply situation and Divisional Trains needed to be doubled in size (to eight companies in each Train) for mountain warfare. The war situation with the BEF in Europe meant that the extra men could only be obtained 'locally' and some 4,700 muleteers were recruited from Cyprus, who complemented the 2,100 muleteers already recruited in Greece (the Macedonian Mule Corps).

Extra manpower and mules for the British Army and six MT companies arrived in October, 1916, their sole purpose being to provide support for the Serbian Army. Under extremely difficult circumstances, in vile weather and with sickness rife, Lieutenant Colonel L C Bearne's command performed magnificently. 688 Company, which had operated over primitive roads in South Croatia constantly exposed to enemy gun fire and aircraft attack, had the honour of being awarded the French Croix de Guerre, along with eleven other units of the British Army. 688 Company, however, was the only unit to receive the cross 'with Bronze Star'.

As in every other theatre of war the ASC found itself involved in duties outside its normal role. In December, 1916, 33 ASC Motor Boat Section was established, with one boat on Lake Beshik and one on Lake Langaza. Thirty feet long and armed with machine guns, these patrol boats kept all native boats off the lake at night and prevented any landings on the northern shores. In June, 1916, when the Royal Navy took over, they moved to Lake Tahinos, where they led a much more exciting life with exchanges of fire with the Bulgarian Army.

18 August, 1917, provided a different sort of activity when a fire broke out in Salonika which destroyed a square mile of the town. Two ASC fire engines, from the Base MT Depot at Kalamaria and the docks, provided assistance – one engine for ten days, the other for seventeen. One driver remained at his post without sleep for almost sixty hours. Innumerable ASC lorries and vans transported refugees out of danger.

Towards the end of 1918 the concentrated effort of the Anglo-Greek and Franco-Serbian armies in the areas east and west of Doiran led to the defeat of the Bulgarian army and an armistice was signed on 29 September. At the end of the campaign the ASC was supporting a ration strength of 385,000 men and 120,000 animals, with 19,959 ASC officers and men and 6,800 Cypriot and Greek muleteers. The Corps suffered just under 700 dead.

Winter in Serbia, 1916. The vehicles are Albion 3 tonners.

THE DARDANELLES (GALLIPOLI)

If the Balkans campaign was messy, the Dardanelles campaign was a disaster, an embarrassing operation that has been the source of controversy and acrimony ever since.

After the unsuccessful naval attack to force a passage through the Bosphorus in March, 1915, the Army sent 29 Division to gain the Gallipoli Peninsula, along with the Royal Naval Division, the Australian and New Zealand Army Corps (ANZAC), and an Indian brigade, a total of 60,000 men and 13,000 animals. The French were also to contribute 17,000.

The force assembled at Alexandria under the command of General Sir Ian Hamilton. The designated Advanced Base was split between the Aegean islands of Lemnos and Imbros, sixty and fifteen miles respectively from the landing area. A Supply Depot and a Horse Transport Depot were established at Mudros and an Advanced Supply Depot and Horse Transport Depot on Imbros; a cold store ship was also chartered and used as a floating cold store at Mudros and 10,000 tons of hay were obtained from India. Brigadier General F W G Koe, located at Mudros, was the Director of Supplies and Transport and he dealt personally with Cape Helles, while his staff at Imbros dealt with Suvla Bay. Brigadier R Ford was DST in Egypt.

Unfortunately the Intelligence Branch of the War Office was unable to advise on roads and Lord Kitchener directed that no transport of any sort was to be taken. He was persuaded to change his mind by Major General S S Long, Director of Supplies and Transport. Instead of standard 3-ton lorries, 29 Divisional Train was re-equipped with 30-cwt vehicles, and this in spite of Lord Kitchener being informed by General Hamilton that 'pack transport is necessary'. In the event these vehicles were used in the Alexandria base.

The landings took place over the period 25 April-1 May at a considerable cost in lives. The British, French and Indian Brigade landed at Cape Helles and the

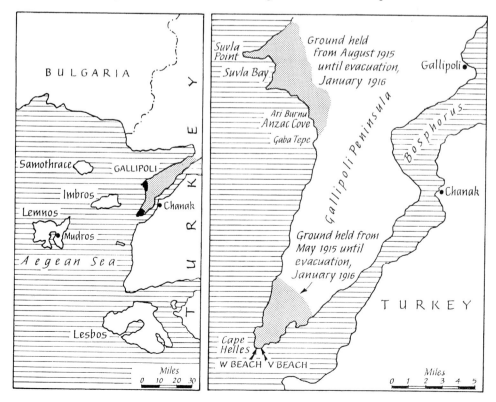

Australians and New Zealanders at Anzac Cove between Ari Burnu and Gaba Tepe in the north. In the south the allies fought their way two miles inland, in the north 1,500 yards. All areas were under constant observed shelling and rifle fire from the Turks.

Under these circumstances normal transport and supply arrangements could not operate. After initial difficulties in getting the animals ashore, animal transport was used as far as possible, although several Holt caterpillar tractors were later used at Cape Helles, and twenty 30-cwt lorries and a few Ford cars and ambulances were used at Suvla Bay.

Field Supply Depots were established at Helles, Anzac Cove and later at Suvla, with a Field Bakery at Helles. Because of the limited size of the bridgehead, these were located on the beaches and duties were carried out under enemy observation and shell fire. Extremes of climate were a problem: the weather varied from torrid heat to icy cold weather, with a blizzard raging for days on one occasion which caused a number of deaths from exposure. Initial landing problems were eased by a temporary reorganization of the system of food and ammunition supply; all surplus animals had been left in Egypt and officers' kits and men's blankets were left behind; troops were provided with 200 rounds of ammunition and three days' food; each sea transport put ashore a reserve of 300 rounds and seven days' food. Although in the event a good supply of wells was discovered ashore, water was supplied by means of a chartered water tank steamer, and a variety of skins, tanks, oil tins and other receptacles were used for the purpose of storing water on the beaches or sending it forward. Carriage forward was by pack transport or fatigue parties of men who were already exhausted from their duties in the trenches.

At the end of May the transport situation eased when a remarkable organization known as the Zion Mule Corps disembarked, the first transport unit to come ashore. This unit of 750 pack mules, formed in Egypt from Russian Jews who had fled from Palestine, was commanded by Lieutenant Colonel J H Patterson, an ASC Reserve officer; he was supported by eight Jewish officers selected from among the 500 refugees. One of the men, Private Groushkonsky, distinguished himself when his ammunition convoy was shelled and he was awarded the Distinguished Conduct Medal. An Indian mule cart Train of some 700 carts and 1,500 animals, was also employed in the wheeled or pack role supporting formations at Cape Helles and Anzac Bay.

In May 42nd East Lancashire Division and a French Division arrived as reinforcements, followed by 52nd (Lowland) Division in June. Further reinforcements arrived in July and August, bringing the strength of the force up to twelve divisions, all of which enabled a three-pronged attack to be made on the Turkish positions in August. Sadly, for a variety of reasons, these attacks were unsuccessful, although some ground was gained.

A number of troop and hospital ships were used in the campaign, the latter to handle the flood of casualties, 250,000 alone from the British, Anzac and Indian contingents. Enteric fever and dysentery were major contributors to the high casualty rate. One incident involving the ASC should be recorded: HM Transport *Royal Edward* was torpedoed by a German submarine on 13 August in the Gulf of Kos. Among the 1,400 troops on board were 300 men of the ASC, the majority of whom were elderly and not fit for service in the infantry. Most perished but reports of survivors place the calmness and magnificent discipline of those who died on a level equal to the heroic story of the loss of the *Birkenhead* in 1852.

86

On 16 October, General Sir Charles Monro succeeded General Sir Ian Hamilton, and he immediately recommended evacuation of the Force, a view confirmed by Lord Kitchener when he visited Mudros. Suvla and Anzac Cove were evacuated in December, and only such guns, animals and stores which were needed until the last were abandoned. Helles was evacuated in early January, 1916, but in this case a considerable amount of supplies, material and animals had to be left behind. Both evacuations were carried out in great secrecy at night and were described by a German writer as a 'hitherto quite unattainable masterpiece'. 118,000 men, 5000 animals and 300 guns were withdrawn and redistributed to Egypt, France and Salonika. Thus ended the intended spear thrust into the heart of the Turkish empire, a tragic, ill-judged and badly planned and executed campaign, the only opposed amphibious operation of the war, one, however, in which thirty Victoria Crosses were awarded.

East Africa

The Colony of German East Africa lay between the British Colony of Kenya in the north and Northern Rhodesia and Nyasaland over 600 miles to the south. Reaching to the Indian Ocean to the east of Nyasaland, lay Portuguese Mozambique. allied to Britain. In 1914 the Germans invaded Kenya. Widely dispersed and confused fighting continued until 1916 in which mainly Indian and South African troops were used against the invaders, but as time went on British troops were increasingly employed and the Germans were eventually driven back into their own Colony. They consisted of a force some 5000 strong, of which only the Command and Supervisory element were German. The enemy native troops, Askaris and porters, lived off the country they knew well, moving on foot carrying portable boats for river crossing, but otherwise unhindered by pack or mechanical transport. Using the difficult climate and terrain to their advantage, the German forces ranged far and wide over a vast territory, evading capture or destruction until an armistice was signed in late November, 1918, at Abercorn in Northern Rhodesia.

The British field force in 1916, when the ASC was first employed, consisted of 1st and 2nd East African Divisions. After service in France, Brigadier General P O Hazleton took on the post of Director of Supplies and Transport in January, working hard to regularize the situation. Transport support until then had been provided by a volunteer East African MT Corps raised in Nairobi, and the South African ASC. From now on animals provided the main means of transport, but the wastage of horses, mules, oxen and donkeys was extremely high, largely due to the ravages of the tsetse fly, some 28,000 animals dying in one operation alone. The ASC with mechanical transport were then sent to the theatre. 30-cwt lorries with solid tyres for the Divisional Supply and Ammunition Columns arrived in June, but they proved unsuitable in that in dry weather they quickly ground the surface into dust, and in the rains they sank axle deep. The main movement was along the line of the railway wherever possible, which eased the ASC task, ameliorated in turn by the arrival of ox transport formations from South Africa, some of whose animals were butchered as difficulties in feeding the Army at the end of a long line of communication developed.

During August, 1916, MT reinforcements began to arrive from England and South Africa, 300 Ford vans forming the majority of the vehicles. The 3-ton vehicles were relegated to the bases and Line of Communication. Spare parts remained a critical problem throughout the campaign and placed great demands on the imagination and adaptability of the fitters. European drivers, however, quickly contracted malaria and

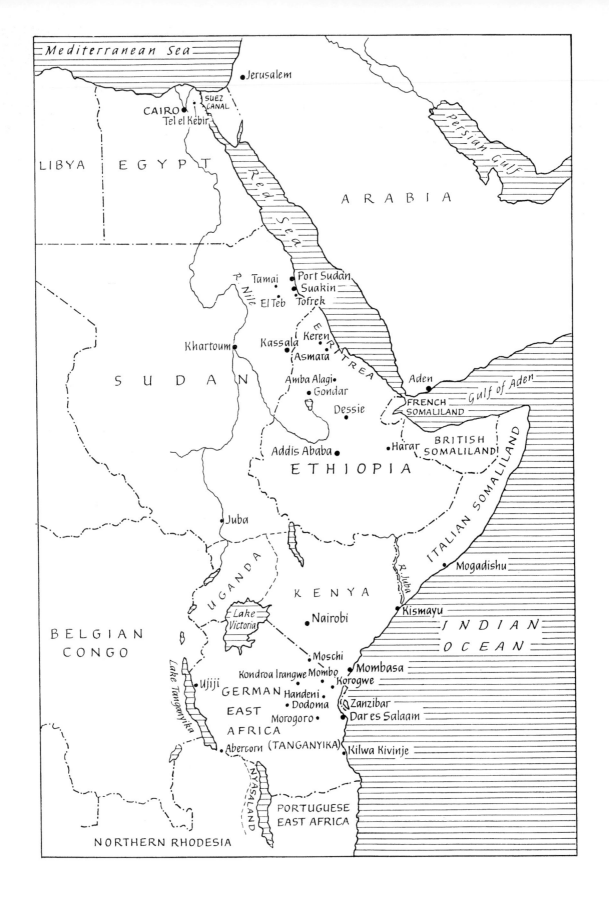

Mediterranean Sea

Jerusalem

SUEZ CANAL

CAIRO
Tel el Kebir

LIBYA | EGYPT

Red Sea

Persian Gulf

ARABIA

Nile

Tamai
El Teb
Port Sudan
Suakin
Tofrek

Khartoum

Kassala
Keren
Asmara
ERITREA

SUDAN

Amba Alagi
Gondar

Dessie

Aden

Gulf of Aden

FRENCH
SOMALILAND

Addis Ababa

Harar

BRITISH
SOMALILAND

ETHIOPIA

ITALIAN SOMALILAND

Juba

R. Juba

Mogadishu

UGANDA

KENYA

Nairobi

Kismayu

INDIAN

OCEAN

BELGIAN
CONGO

Lake
Victoria

Moschi

Lake Tanganyika

Kondroa Irangwe Mombo
Ujiji
GERMAN
EAST
AFRICA
Handeni
Dodoma
Morogoro

Korogwe
Mombasa

Zanzibar
Dar es Salaam

Abercorn (TANGANYIKA)

Kilwa Kivinje

NYASALAND

PORTUGUESE
EAST AFRICA

NORTHERN RHODESIA

88

During the campaign, the Ford vehicle was nicknamed the Jigger, after the Jigger flea, for, like the insect, it could get anywhere.

operations had to be postponed owing to sickness and casualties among the drivers of Supply and Ammunition Columns. Some 1,000 Swahili, Ugandan, Indian and Nigerian drivers were engaged to make up the deficiencies, a driving school being set up for them in East Africa, while Chinese were recruited as artificers.

In April, 1916, a Base MT Depot of 201 all ranks arrived in Mombasa and set up initially in Nairobi, moving in September to Dar-es-Salaam. Advanced MT Depots were opened at Mbuyuni, Mombo and Handeni as the advance progressed that summer. During 1916 and 1917 some 3,000 vehicles were bought in South Africa and two motor ambulance convoys, a light armoured motor battery and two MT companies used, as special long-distance supply columns were added.

The war in this theatre is notable for the largely unknown employment of a unit of four heavy armoured cars of 322 Company ASC, named 1 (Willoughby's) Armoured Motor Battery, raised and trained in February, 1915, in England by Sir John Willoughby. The armoured cars, actually converted Leyland lorries, were wholly manned by the ASC, a remarkable enterprise at a time when armoured vehicles were in their infancy. They arrived in East Africa in 1917 but were disbanded in July that year.

At the time of the armistice the strength of the Army was 111,731. At its strongest the ASC numbered just over 4,000 all ranks, of whom 270 died in East Africa.

RUSSIA

The revolution in Russia caused her to withdraw from the war in 1917 and make a separate peace with Germany. In June, 1918, the British committed a brigade strength force in North Russia, part of which was landed at Murmansk to prevent the Germans using the Kola Inlet as a submarine base, the other part in Archangel to assist the anti-Bolshevik forces, thereby ensuring that the Germans could not withdraw entirely from the Russian front. The British were involved in a few minor skirmishes but in the event achieved nothing and withdrew in September, 1919.

The ASC was commanded by Lieutenant Colonel T C R Moore as Assistant Director Supplies and Transport in Murmansk, and Major H N G Watson was located in Archangel. It is of interest that Major W J English, who had won his VC in the Boer War on 3 July, 1901, with the Scottish Horse and was commissioned in the ASC in October, 1906, served with the force in North Russia.

With units located up to 400 miles from base, poor communications and extremes of climate, resupply was not easy. Transport was mixed. Initially the horse transport

ASC horse-drawn sleighs, Murmansk.

units were used with limbered GS waggons but these proved unsuitable and the ASC turned its hand to manufacturing a local type of cart, which was successful; a shortage of saddlery and harness also involved local manufacture under ASC control. As no Veterinary Service personnel were in the force the ASC also became responsible for this as well as for remount duties. In summer pony carts and pack transport were used to supplement the ASC ration boats and barges on the rivers, but in winter sleighs were drawn by ponies, Canadian huskies and reindeer. Mechanical transport was tried but was not successful due to the bad weather and absence of proper roads. Ford cars, ambulances and vans were used in Archangel, as well as 3-ton and 30-cwt lorries, a section being attached to 1152 Company in 1919.

In 1919 a 'Reindeer Transport Corps' was formed under Captain E M Squarey, ASC, with Laplanders as drivers, each sleigh carrying 600-800 lbs, three reindeer pulling with one at the back to act as a brake. Some 2,000 reindeer, 500 sleighs and 1,000 Laplanders were employed in this example of local innovation. Sleighs were demanded from England, but, pending their arrival, a small sleigh factory was established locally, which was so successful that within a short time it provided sufficient sleighs.

An officer with the Murmansk Force wrote home:-

> 'I have got two reindeer which constitute our ASC transport, and are very kind creatures. They are quite easy to drive; you lead them to the road, turn their heads in the right direction, smack them on the rump and take a flying leap into the sledge. When you come to cross-roads you jerk the one rein, and if they do not grasp your

Reindeer and sleigh operated by the ASC.

wishes they stop and you have to get out, turn them into the right track, and start again. They pull by a single trace with passes between their legs; there are no shafts, and of course the sledge swings very erratically behind.'

To illustrate how this campaign created some other unusual involvements for its ASC members, the following is the Military Cross citation for Second Lieutenant W C Wannell:

> *'When carrying out a reconnaissance on Lake Onega on 8th July, in close touch with enemy vessels, the motor boat caught fire and a petrol tank exploded. Though badly shaken himself, he assisted three wounded mechanics on to the upper deck, and then returned to the engine room and drove the one engine which was still working, until the boat was within a mile from the shore, when a second explosion wrecked her. His pluck and devotion to duty in driving the engine, at great risk to himself, got the boat near the shore and saved lives.'*

Before leaving Russia, mention must be made of a strong Military Mission which assisted the anti-Bolshevik forces in South Russia in 1918-19, based mainly at Odessa. A number of ASC officers, clerks and car drivers were attached to this Mission, whose work was mainly advisory or connected with the distribution of supplies and war material made over by the Allies to General Denikin, the South Russian leader. These people, albeit under different circumstances, had as difficult and adventurous a time as their compatriots in the north.

THE HOME FRONT

Literature on the Great War tends naturally to concentrate on the theatres of war overseas, and it is not generally appreciated to what extent the UK base was the heart of a great and dynamic war machine. Out of a total strength of 3.8 million men just under half were in the UK; 73,000 were ASC, 5% of the whole. Of these, 48,000 men were under training or were otherwise non-effective, 12,000 were in units awaiting embarkation and 13,000 were unfit for service overseas. The numbers of unfit men may seem high but it will be remembered that there were regular trawls to find men suitable for other Corps, and some 82,000 men, irrespective of trade or value to the ASC, were exchanged for others of lower medical category.

The affairs of the Corps were controlled by two Directorates under the Quartermaster General in the War Office, through the Headquarters of the major UK Commands: Northern, Southern, Eastern, Western, Scottish, Irish and Aldershot, each of which had appropriate ASC staffs. Subordinate to them was a network of Districts and Garrisons in which were located almost eighty transport units and some forty remount units. The large Corps depots (for Mechanical Transport, Horse Transport and Supply and other Corps functions) came under the technical control of the QMG's Directorates but under local Commands for administration.

The MT Training organizations in the Grove Park and Osterley Park areas sent its trained men to the Bulford Mobilization and Embarkation Area, which opened in September, 1914, under the command of Major F L Lindsay Lloyd. Its functions were the mobilization of MT units, the repair of vehicles and the despatch of units and individuals overseas. This was achieved by its four organic companies and two embarkation depots, the former using camps, billets and tents for the large numbers of men who passed through. The Workshop and Stores Department, commanded by a lieutenant colonel, dealt with up to 100 vehicles at a time which came in from civilian factories or firms, or from units overseas. At any one time 700 vehicles were held in covered accommodation for issue to units being formed. Bulford and Salisbury photographers did a roaring trade by photographing all these new companies. The elongated pictures, still to be seen today, are typical of the period.

Subordinate to Bulford were the embarkation depots of Avonmouth and Portsmouth, the latter being opened in January, 1917, when the former could not handle the necessary throughput. To give an idea of the size of their task, 30,000 men and 22,000 vehicles passed through Avonmouth during 1917 and 13,200 men and 7,840 vehicles through Portsmouth during the first five months of 1917 alone. Bulford also controlled the ASC Tractor Depot in Avonmouth, which saw nineteen officers, 532 men, 1,500 caterpillar tractors and 200 lorries pass through its hands on their way to support heavy gun batteries of the Royal Artillery.

At the end of the war all vehicles were returned to an MT Vehicle Depot established in the western outskirts of London at Kempton Park Race Course, where the race track and central area soon became completely covered with vehicles; however, Prime Minister Lloyd George, who understood the gambling needs of the public in the immediate post-war days, had the Vehicle Depot moved to Slough in early 1919.

Mechanical transport needs constant repair and the timely provision of spares, stores and equipments. Before 1914 this had been handled by twelve men in the Aldershot-based Inspection Branch Mechanical Transport (IBMT) for the relatively small fleet of ASC vehicles. When war was declared the work load increased considerably and October, 1914, saw the staff increased to seventy-five, and ultimately to 2,431 military and civilian staff in December, 1918. In addition to serving the British Army, they provided vehicle spares for the Admiralty, Royal Air Force, Dominion, American, Belgian, Greek, Italian, Portuguese and Serbian Armies, as well as a host of government organizations in UK (eg Foreign Office, YMCA and the British Red Cross).

The IBMT moved in February, 1915, to Short Gardens in London, where it was augmented by a number of sub-depots in various parts of the city, Camden Town, Carlow Street, Gray's Inn Road and Cressy Road and in Liverpool. The variety of vehicles and operating conditions around the world presented enormous problems in forward planning and storage, as can be inferred from the fact that the MT stores issued during the war were valued at approximately £60 million. In 1916, when Lieutenant Colonel M S Brander took command, the unit's name was changed to the Home Repair Depot ASC.

Horse transport training in the Corps was provided by three HT depots, in Aldershot, Bradford and Woolwich, whose training included saddlers, wheelers and farriers. These depots dealt with some 7,000 reservists on mobilization before they turned their attention to recruit training. Bradford and Woolwich each dealt with 25,000 recruits during the war, while the depot in Aldershot formed no less than thirty-one Divisional Trains, thirty Reserve Parks and five Trains for Army Troops by the end of 1915. Shortly after mobilization a Reserve HT Depot (661, 662 and 666 Companies) formed at Deptford, which later moved to Park Royal, Willesden; a second Reserve HT depot (665, 667 and 668 Companies) then formed at Blackheath.

At the instigation of Brigadier General Long complete equipments were issued through one of the HT depots. The Army Ordnance Department, which issued waggons, saddlery, harness and other transport equipment, and the Remount Department, which provided animals, normally issued items separately to units. This greatly benefited infantry battalions and TA units, which generally had neither saddlers nor men accustomed to putting together and fitting saddlery or harness.

The Supply side of the Corps was based on supply companies in Aldershot, the Supply Reserve Depot in Deptford, and a host of base, main or field supply depots in the various theatres of war. Troops in the home base were fed by local contractors. The essential trades were butcher, baker, clerk and issuer.

Since pre-war days A Supply Company had provided the depot functions of reception and training, while C Supply Company held the trained men and provided drafts for units. In fact C Supply Company was totally used up in providing men for the BEF in August, 1914, so, after A Company 'held the fort' until December, K Supply Company was formed to fill the gap. By the end of 1914 the two companies had handled almost 300 men, and during the first half of 1915 10,000. An additional task thrown on the supply companies was the recruitment and training of men as skilled labourers, stevedores, packers and loaders of the Labour Companies ASC, 21,000 having joined up for this purpose by the end of 1915.

As the strength of the Army grew, K Company took over from A Company, which moved in February, 1916, to Catterick, only to move again in December to Southport. The company's new duties were to receive men invalided from overseas and, after medical boards, either retrain or discharge them.

Conclusion

The end of the Great War saw the strength of the ASC worldwide rise to 13,112 officers and 315,334 men. It operated, in total, 56,659 lorries and tractors, 23,133 motor cars and vans, 7045 motor ambulances and 34,865 motor cycles, variously in 715 horse transport units, 648 mechanical transport units and 346 supply units. Casualties were 280 officers and 8,187 men killed, with almost the same number wounded. Twenty-two officers and ninety-eight men were taken prisoner-of-war. There were no deserters. In addition to the two Victoria Crosses and 688 Company's Croix de Guerre, there was a host of national and international awards and decorations, including 296 DSOs, 519 OBEs, 512 MCs, 1,762 MMs and 9 Albert Medals.

When Major General Sir Alban Crofton Atkins KCB, CMG, vacated the appointment of Director of Supplies and Transport at the War Office on 20 January, 1919, he caused to be published the following Special Corps Order:

'On vacating his appointment at the Headquarters of the Army, Major General Crofton Atkins wishes to place on record his high appreciation of the work accomplished by all ranks of the Royal Army Service Corps, including the civilian subordinate establishments and the women who have undertaken military obligations. The important results achieved are not due to the efforts of any particular individuals, but to the collective determination of the whole Corps to secure at all costs the welfare of their comrades in fighting formations. In this spirit only has it been possible to maintain the troops in all theatres of war in food and transport, and to contribute so materially to the victorious success of the military operations.'

CHAPTER 5

1918–1939

Between The Wars

Introduction. Postwar Commitments; Training; Ireland; Mesopotamia and the Balkans; India and the North-West Frontier; The British Army of the Rhine; Shanghai. Supplies. Mechanical Transport. Requiem for the Horse. Petroleum. The Road to War. Rearmament; General Planning; The Middle East; The Territorial Army.

INTRODUCTION

Less than three weeks after the Armistice was signed His Majesty King George V conferred the title of Royal upon the Corps in appreciation of its valuable services during the war, and the Royal Army Service Corps was ready to face up to the many challenges that lay ahead. With the First World War now over the British Army was once again facing a period of retrenchment. However, the introduction of mechanization during the war had set in train a progression which could not be halted. Its effects had to be assimilated and the momentum of change maintained.

The Corps entered this uncertain post war period on a high note. Not only had it firmly established its position in the Supply and Transport role, having gathered in the responsibility for delivering ammunition previously resting with the Royal Artillery, but it had been in the forefront of the development of mechanical transport. This was now well advanced in replacing the horse as the means of providing the Army with mobility. The development of wheeled vehicles with multi-axle drive and pneumatic tyres, vehicles which could move off roads, was to greatly improve this mobility on the battlefield and bring about a change in the Army's support requirements. The increasing reliance on mechanical transport not only made the provision and effective handling of motor fuel a vital concern, but also made access to the natural sources of oil of greater strategic importance. The provision and distribution of petroleum fuel was now added to the Corps' role. This, with the responsibility for the carriage and distribution of all ammunition, including artillery, greatly strengthened the Corps' position. Its capabilities and vital overall contribution in the logistic support role of a modern mobile Army were now fully recognized.

Despite the acceptance of new concepts, the years that followed were to be very difficult for those trying to ensure an effective Army for the future and seeking to profit from the many lessons learned and the many changes brought about by the war. The final victory had left all nations, winners or losers, exhausted. There was a determination that there should be no repetition and the politicians hoped that, by the establishment of the League of Nations, an institution had been created that would ensure a lasting peace. The people were sick and tired of war and nobody wanted to give much thought to the Armed Services, except those whose duty it was to effect as large economies as possible in public expenditure. Disarmament was the order of the day and so the 'Geddes Axe' fell, resulting in the reduction of the Army to little more than cadre strength. To quote Sir John Fortescue, 'It is the misfortune of our Army that, as soon as it has been brought to high efficiency by a great war, it is instantly pulled to pieces by the nation.'

Fortunately there were those of a similar mind and with an equal understanding of the nature of things. They also foresaw that a prolonged period of peace was unlikely, and that the nation's guard should not be lowered completely. However, despite aggressive attitudes stirring again in Europe, the desire in Britain for peace at all costs provided unpromising conditions for a smooth continuation of the Army's mechanization programme. It was left to a dedicated few to ensure that so much was achieved in the continuing modernization of the Army and when the threat was at last plainly recognized much had been done which would help the Army prepare to meet it.

The postwar strategic concept, as expressed by the War Cabinet in 1919, was that the British Empire would not be engaged in any great war during the next ten years and therefore no Expeditionary Force would be required. This was the premise on which Service departments were to base estimates and the assumption was periodically reviewed. It was not until 1934 that it was reluctantly accepted that a real threat to peace existed and the assumption was abandoned.

The pillars of our defence strategy were the security of the UK base, the protection of the sea routes on which our existence as an importing country depended, the maintenance of the free international use of the Suez Canal and the security of Middle East oil. A small regular Army and Navy with the help of the newly-formed Royal Air Force would be sufficient, it was assumed, to meet these commitments. In the event of a sudden emergency there were ample reserves of trained personnel with recent active Service experience.

POSTWAR COMMITMENTS

Between 1914 and 1918 the ASC strength, which in 1914 had been around 500 officers and 6,000 other ranks, expanded to some 13,112 officers and 315,334 other ranks. During the years immediately following 1918 the RASC, in company with the rest of the Army, had to suffer a reduction to almost its 1914 size.

But this could not happen all at once. The war had left stricken areas which needed the help of the Allied Armies and there were enemy and Mandated Territories in which occupation forces were required for the maintenance of order until the peace treaties were ratified. It is probable that the Corps was more stretched and more widely dispersed throughout the world during the years immediately following the Armistice than at any other time in its existence. Wherever British troops were deployed at home or abroad, RASC units were required to carry out supply, transport and barrack duties. Overseas, peacetime garrisons extended from British Honduras and Jamaica in the west, to Gibraltar, Malta and Cyprus in the Mediterranean, and to Ceylon, Singapore, Hong Kong and North China in the east. In addition substantial forces were still maintained in Germany, Northern Russia and the Black Sea area and commitments continued in the Balkans, Egypt, Palestine, Mesopotamia and in East and South Africa. In India the Corps had inherited, since 1916, a heavy commitment which was to continue until 1928.

Training

Great importance was always placed on the RASC Training Centre and on the care in selection of the officers to command and staff it. At exercises and on collective training, and in studies at the RASC Training College, the organization of supply and transport services in the field was the subject of continuous study and experiment. However, until 1929 theoretical studies at the Training College represented the extent of training for war carried out by the Corps. RASC units could do little more than complete their individual training because of their heavy commitments. Fortunately there remained in the Corps a great wealth of surviving experience from the war.

Ireland

The official end of the war with Germany, formally declared by an Order in Council on 10 January, 1920, the date when the Treaty of Versailles was ratified, did not immediately signify the end of hostilities everywhere. In Ireland there was no peace. In 1914 the Home Rule Act had been put into suspension on the assumption that the war with Germany would not last long. By 1916 the Sinn Fein party had lost patience and broke into open rebellion at the Easter Rising. Barbed wire, armed convoys, interrupted communications and a strict curfew were the lot of the soldier in Ireland. A fragile peace treaty was signed in 1921. Under this Irish Peace Treaty, Great Britain was granted the right to occupy certain offshore defences in order to control, in time of war, the eastern approaches to the Atlantic. These consisted of Spike Island, the outlying forts at the mouth of Cork Harbour, Bear Island in Bantry Bay, the base in Lough Swilly in County Donegal and finally Forts Lenan and Duntree. These treaty rights continued until 1938 and Corps detachments served in these unusual stations. The Donegal forts were resupplied on a regular basis from Belfast by the ASC Companies in Ulster, the convoys travelling at 12 miles an hour and taking eight hours each way – a stiff task in the winter with open cab lorries.

Troop-carrying lorry waiting to go into Belfast.

A typical 15cwt open-cab lorry.

Mesopotamia and the Balkans

Heavy demands were placed on the Corps in Mesopotamia (renamed Iraq in 1921) until 1926. Whilst unrest continued in the Balkans it was necessary to keep an Allied force in Constantinople. War broke out between Greece and Turkey which ended in the complete defeat of the Greeks. When the Turks then threatened to occupy the Gallipoli Peninsula a British force was hurriedly assembled, including a small RASC detachment. The Turks were not anxious for further trouble and by the end of 1923 most British troops had left Turkey.

India and The North-West Frontier

At the end of the war more Corps units arrived from East Africa and Mesopotamia to add to the growing number of MT units operating in India. Operations on the North-West Frontier during 1919 and 1920 were important to the RASC and the Indian Army Supply and Transport Corps, for this was the first time that mechanical transport was used on a large scale for the maintenance of troops in forward areas. Most of the Corps units in India were employed on the frontier, with their base at Chaklala, three miles from Rawalpindi. Very few of the British officers and men of the Corps who served in India missed this experience and the contribution made by the Corps to the Indian Army was considerable.

In July, 1923, the Supply and Transport Corps became the Indian Army Service Corps and speculation was rife that an amalgamation with the RASC was imminent. This did not happen, but the reorganized Indian Army Service Corps was entirely dependent on the permanent transfer of a substantial number of RASC officers and other ranks. Almost 1,000 all ranks finally transferred voluntarily and this represented nearly 20% of RASC strength. This amounted to a considerable loss of

View of the Khyber Pass.

experience and ability to a Corps which had already suffered heavily in the reduction of its establishment. The RASC left India in 1928 and from that time the IASC took over full responsibility there.

The British Army of the Rhine

When the British Army of Occupation first arrived in Germany at the end of 1918 it was a large force scattered over a wide area. 2 Corps Troops MT Company RASC played a leading role in supporting the move into the Rhineland. The number of units was gradually reduced and concentrated into an area with its centre at Cologne. Bulk supplies were sent from France and England to Antwerp and Rotterdam, and thence by rail and barge to Cologne. Not many local resources were available. In January, 1920, a small British force, which included a Corps supply section and MT detachment, arrived in Danzig from Cologne to supervise the plebiscite which resulted in Danzig becoming a Free City. This was completed by November, 1920, and the British troops were back in Cologne in December.

There was a small RASC detachment in Berlin as part of one of the missions and the Corps was also involved in other plebiscites in Upper Silesia and the Saar.

A great deal had to be done in restoring conditions to normal and transport was at a premium. At the end of 1925 the Rhine Army moved from the Cologne area to Wiesbaden and by 1926 all Corps units were accommodated there.

In 1929 the British Army of the Rhine withdrew from Germany. It had been a popular and happy station and our soldiers had been good ambassadors.

Shanghai

Shanghai, straddling the Whangpoo River, a tributary of the mighty Yangtze-Kiang, is the commercial gateway to China. Ample berthing facilities exist for the biggest ships and it is one of the largest ports in the world.

Ever since the Republic of China was established in 1912 the country had been in turmoil. Strong opposing factions developed in North and South; in 1925 civil war had broken out. Anti-European riots had occurred from time to time and when they broke out again in 1927 the foreign powers decided that the time had come for strong measures. The Shanghai Defence force was formed and despatched from Britain in the beginning of that year. Its role was the protection of the lives, property and interests of British subjects. The RASC contingent included MT and supply units and a bakery detachment.

The international force included British, French, American, Dutch, Italian and Japanese naval units, British, French and Italian army units and the 4th United States Marines. The British Army force (Shanghai Defence Force) numbered 15,000 at its highest figure and was strongly backed up by the Shanghai Volunteer Corps and the Shanghai Municipal Police.

The strong force which had been sent to Shanghai had its effect and its reduction started in the autumn of 1927. By November, 1928, the strength of the Corps in Shanghai itself was only 228. There would continue to be a garrison in the city of Shanghai; China would be a three-year station of which only one year would be spent in Shanghai.

A little more than two years after the emergency had begun, the situation in Shanghai was, for the time being, settled. But although the emergency was over and for the next four years life in Shanghai was comparatively uneventful, the garrison was retained.

SUPPLIES

As to the detailed business of the Corps, there were major changes. On 1 January, 1921, the Navy and Army Canteen Board became the Navy, Army and Air Force Institute (NAAFI). It was then decided that considerable savings could be made by using this organization for the peacetime distribution of rations. The soldier's ration was divided into three parts; certain staple items such as bread and meat were issued from RASC supply depots, the main bulk of the ration was drawn from the NAAFI, and the third element was a messing cash allowance to buy extras to add variety to the diet. This made it unnecessary to retain more than a few supply depots, less than a dozen being left worldwide. This system had two serious defects. First, virtually no supply units existed in peacetime to provide a nucleus on which to expand in emergency. Secondly, only limited reserve stocks could be held and such a quantity of reserves was totally inadequate for any major emergency. Training in the operation of the supply service was limited to theoretical study and the minimal opportunities provided by large-scale exercises.

MECHANICAL TRANSPORT

Perhaps the most revolutionary change to affect the Corps during these two decades was the total eclipse of horse transport by mechanical transport. During the 1914-18 war MT more than fulfilled the expectations of those who worked for its introduction. The totals in all theatres on 11 November, 1918, were 46,659 lorries and tractors, 23,133 cars and vans, 7,045 ambulances and 34,865 motor cycles. Before the war the ASC MT Inspection branch had been responsible for technical research and development under the direction of the Mechanical Transport Committee. This responsibility continued to be borne by the RASC MT School of Instruction after 1918. The School was responsible for developing the ideas of the War Office MT Advisory Board, set up at the end of 1920 as a successor to the pre-war MT Committee. This board was responsible for the development of all wheeled

Bogey Drive Motor Cycle. Built by RASC Workshops, 1923, and shown here on trials.

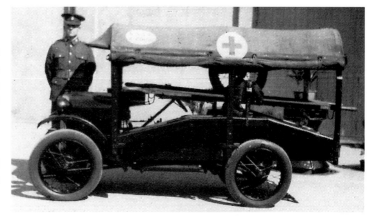

Austin 7 HP ambulance used in hill districts in Hong Kong in 1932 and having adjustable stretchers for hills, working on a pivot.

A Pavesi (Italian) Agricultural 4-wheel-drive tractor, fitted with winch (FWW) on trial.

vehicles used by the Army. The Chairman of the board was the DST.

The co-operation between the War Department, represented by the RASC experimental workshops, and commercial motor manufacturers and users, was a good augury for the future and ensured that large numbers of the same types of vehicle which the Army used in peace could be rapidly taken into service in the event of future mobilization.

Because the RASC was the chief user of mechanical vehicles for general transport purposes, the responsibility for certain duties connected with research, design and experiment, as well as the provision and maintenance of a large number of vehicles of non-RASC units, had remained with the Corps. In 1928 these responsibilities were transferred from the Quartermaster-General to the Master-General of the Ordnance. As a result the MGO became responsible 'for the research, experiment, design, manufacture, inspection, provision, storage, issue and repair (other than first line repair) relating to mechanically propelled vehicles of all kinds except for the provision, inspection, storage, issue and repair of all MT vehicles on the establishment of RASC units, including vehicles in Medical units, which continued to be the responsibility of the QMG, who also remained responsible for the impressment of vehicles on mobilization.

REQUIEM FOR THE HORSE

The end of the war brought a swift reduction in the number of horse transport units. By the end of 1920 and the beginning of 1921, when the size of the peacetime Army had been settled and the regular RASC units reorganized and renumbered, there were only thirty-one HT companies left, nine fewer than in 1914. During 1922 and the beginning of 1923 twenty-three HT companies had been either amalgamated or disbanded; some were converted to mechanical transport. By 1924 there were only eight HT units left in the Corps.

The reduction in horse transport was a sign of the times. Military thinking focused on the concept of mobile forces, and collective training exercises were designed to test mobility and the administration of fast-moving mechanical units. Although it appeared certain that MT would eventually replace the horse, it was accepted that mechanical cross-country performance still needed improvement and that in some areas animal transport would remain essential.

The 1928 manoeuvres were designed to test a new divisional organization in which

RASC Horse Transport Training in Aldershot.

there was no provision for the Reserve Horse Transport Company in the Divisional Train. A year later, in September, 1929, a new RASC divisional organization was introduced in place of the Divisional Train. The Horse Transport Company was omitted, completing the mechanization of the divisional RASC.

This was the beginning of the end. Early in 1929 it was announced that two more HT companies would be disbanded. In May Woolwich, which for seventy-five years had been one of the chief RASC stations and for over 30 years the home of HT training, bade farewell to 'Y' Depot Company, which together with the Corps coach, moved to Aldershot which now became the centre for all RASC training.

The disbandment of HT service companies followed and 'Y' (HT) Depot Company, shortly to be renamed HT Training Company, Animal (Transport) Training Company and finally Transport (Animal) Company, was left as the only HT unit in the British Army. Henceforth its role was to be the training of RASC officers and men in the technique of animal transport in case this form of transport might be required in a future theatre of war.

PETROLEUM

Despite the rapid adoption of mechanization, during the first ten years of peace following the 1914-18 war, little effort was made to study the problems of petrol supply in the field. Collective training was not resumed until 1924. Large-scale manoeuvres seldom lasted more than four days. Most units had no difficulty in carrying sufficient fuel in their petrol tanks and unit reserves made replenishment unnecessary before the end of the exercise. Even as late as 1937, when manoeuvres were designed to last ten days in order to give a realistic trial of the problems of maintenance of an infantry division, little attention was paid to the supply of petrol.

An important decision had to be made on how the distribution of petrol within an operational theatre should be organized. In 1928 the first serious attempt was made to study the whole problem of petrol supply in the field. A special exercise was designed by the RASC Training College to examine all aspects.

These studies examined the relative merits of bulk supply and distribution in containers. Although the trend of commercial practice was to go over to bulk supply, and the use of cans was rapidly decreasing, the existing tankers in commercial use were unlikely to be suitable for field operations. In the forward area it was considered that bulk supply would be less flexible and more vulnerable than supply in cans.

THE ROAD TO WAR

The 'War to End Wars', the Armistice of 1918 and the League of Nations had not cured the world's ills. In the USA, the Wall Street crash on 29 October, 1929 had repercussions throughout the civilized world. The effects on the British economy were not immediate but sufficient to bring about the collapse of the second Labour Party administration and the establishment of a National Government on 26 August, 1931. In less than a month the gold standard was abandoned and this crisis led to a severe economic recession. Drastic economies were made which inevitably did not exclude the Services. Expenditure on the mechanization programme was postponed, large scale training exercises were cancelled, TA training was reduced, establishments were pruned and cuts were made in rates of pay.

Disarmament, though, was proving illusory. The failure of the Disarmament Conference in Geneva in 1932 was a disappointment and destroyed many people's faith in the League of Nations. The growth of the National Socialist Party in Germany cast a shadow over central Europe. Disturbances in Palestine, which grew in seriousness until two regular divisions were needed there, underlined the growing influence of that area on Imperial strategy and the importance of Egypt as a military base.

Development in mechanical transport and in armoured fighting vehicles since 1918 gave clear signs that a future major conflict would be quite a new experience. Highly mobile forces supported from the air would alter the whole character of conflict and would prevent a repetition of static trench warfare. The emphasis in training exercises was therefore on mobility, traffic control, air defence and the development of an administrative organization able to support rapid advances over long distances. In this concept the Corps had a major role to play.

REARMAMENT

In 1934 the Chiefs of Staff assessed that Germany might be ready for war by 1938 or 1939 and recommended a five-year rearmament plan. Accordingly the Government abandoned the 'no major war for ten years' assumption. Reorganization in RASC training opened the way for a vigorous and enlightened approach. Although there was no significant expansion of the Corps before the mid-1930s, a number of important changes in organization took place which had far-reaching effects. Foremost was the creation of divisional RASC companies as an integral part of the formation which they served, and the formation of separate petrol companies foreshadowed the development of a complete system of petrol supply. Later, the double echelon supply system was introduced as an integral part of the maintenance system for supplying fast-moving mobile forces.

The emergency measures introduced in 1935 also produced a sudden demand for vehicles to equip the units being sent to Egypt and Palestine, which could not be met from existing stocks. The staff of QMG3 showed considerable resourcefulness in obtaining, at extremely short notice from the General Motors Corporation, 300 Bedford lorries suitably modified for Army use. The same firm proved equally co-operative when it was decided, after the Munich crisis in 1938, to stockpile a reserve of 500 load-carrying vehicles in the Middle East.

The DST carried out his responsibility, under the QMG, for the impressment of vehicles by setting up an enlarged Inspectorate of Supplementary Transport. Detailed records of civilian vehicles suitable for military use were compiled. In the event of mobilization the owners would be instructed to drive their vehicles to selected collecting centres. In the event the scheme proved invaluable in the impressment of the planned 14,000 vehicles required on mobilization and went on to provide many more later to cope with the massive expansion of the Territorial Army.

With these urgent preparations for a possible war in Europe, supplies were of vital importance. The building up of reserves, together with the necessary accommodation, became a matter of urgency. Foodstuffs were obviously plentiful and easily available in the civilian market and authority was given for the expenditure of £250,000 on thirty days' reserve for 170,000 men. In addition, document contracts (which only became effective on the declaration of war) were concluded by the Services with many of the principal food manufacturers.

Authority was given for the number of supply depots, where reserves could be held, to be increased to forty. At this time there was only one Supply Reserve Depot at Deptford. Agreement was obtained in 1936 for a second SRD at Barry. This was immediately followed by the creation of the Chief Provision Officer (Food Supplies) with the responsibility for controlling the stocks in the SRDs and all arrangements for contracts and overseas shipments.

The provision of sufficient personnel trained in supplies remained a problem right up to the outbreak of war. By 1937 an agreed petroleum policy envisaged that the main reserves for the Army would be held in the UK and that detailed distribution in an overseas theatre of war would be in the 4-gallon container – the flimsy non-returnable tin can – crated in pairs in wooden boxes. At the same time, wherever possible, reserve holdings and distribution in bulk would be resorted to. This policy involved the construction of plants for the manufacture of containers and the establishment of reserves in bulk and in cans, both at home and overseas. In Egypt a reserve of a million gallons in cans was built up at Abbassia on the outskirts of Cairo.

The decision to rely initially on container distribution instead of developing a bulk system has been criticized, but records show that there was no petrol supply failure which had any appreciable effect on operations in the early years of the 1939-45 war.

In the four years between 1935 and 1939 great strides were made in preparations for war. Bulk reserves were located in safe areas both at home and in the Middle East near Suez. Manufacturing plants for 4-gallon tins were set up at Llandarcy and Avonmouth. All these arrangements were put in hand in close co-operation with the civil oil industry, particularly Shell and the Anglo-Iranian Oil Companies, and involved a comparatively small outlay.

The Middle East

No unified Middle East Command existed before the outbreak of war; British troops in Egypt, with Cyprus and the Sudan, formed one command, and British troops in Palestine and Trans-Jordan formed another. Each of these commands had its own RASC organization on the usual peacetime lines. There was a general lack of RASC personnel and the very low peace establishments had to be supplemented by the employment of local civilians.

There were a dozen MT companies in Egypt and Palestine, most of them having the standard establishment of twenty-four vehicles. 39 Company, which was stationed at Abbassia (Cairo), with Repair Shop, Vehicle Reception and MT Stores components, served both Egypt and Palestine. On the supply side there were four small depots in Egypt and two in Palestine and each contained a reserve of two months' supplies. A few static field bakeries were in operation, manned largely by native civilians, and cold storage facilities existed at Port Said.

A reserve of two months' fuel was held to meet initial requirements in the event of war. Civilian bulk storage for petrol existed at the Suez refinery, at Alexandria, and at Haifa, and plants for the manufacture of 4-gallon tins were in operation at these places, and also at Port Sudan, whilst considerable additional tinning facilities existed at Abadan. The only method of distribution envisaged was by means of the 4-gallon tin.

The lack of reserve bulk storage for petrol had caused anxiety for some time before the war, but in January, 1939, a joint War Office and Air Ministry mission investigated the matter and it was decided to construct buried storage to hold six months' reserve should the Suez Refinery be put out of action. The storage was to be located in the Geneifa area, between Suez and Fayid.

All these preparatory measures required a great deal of forethought and initiative, and the fact that RASC units were fully equipped and ready for active service on mobilization in 1939, that there were no disasters on the supply front and an effective petroleum system was in place, was largely due to the resourcefulness of the dedicated RASC staff officers who filled the appointments in the QMG (QMG3 and QMG6) branches of the War Office.

The Territorial Army

Events in Europe gave clear signs to all who wished to see them. In 1933 Hitler became Chancellor of the German Reich and denounced the Treaty of Versailles on 16 March, 1935. Mussolini launched his Abyssinian campaign the same year. A proper structure for the air defence of the country was now set up as part of the Territorial Army and two dedicated anti-aircraft divisions were formed. The RASC of three territorial divisions were re-roled to support the new anti-aircraft divisions and at the same time set about recruiting up to their war establishment of 1350 all ranks. When the Spanish Civil War broke out in 1936 both Dictators saw the opportunity to put their military training and equipment to the test and gave renewed impetus to the expansion of the Territorial Army. Hitler invaded Austria in March, 1938, and Czechoslovakia a year later. By the spring of 1939 five Territorial Army anti-aircraft divisions had been formed and two were in the process of forming. Altogether the RASC had recruited upwards of 20,000 Territorials, officers and men, to provide support for the new formations. As the international situation worsened the Government decided to activate a large part of the nation's air defences, including the whole of Greater London, by putting the Territorial Army on a voluntary 'partial' deployment between June and August. The RASC responded magnificently to the appeal and many columns were therefore already busily deployed when the normal camping season started. The turnout was remarkable, with few columns fielding less than 800 Volunteers. At this moment the Government announced that the Territorial Army was to be doubled and the process of splitting units, recruiting and training began again, but by now the core of trained and experienced officers and NCOs was spread very thinly.

As the political situation deteriorated and the prospect of war became more certain, urgent steps were taken to expand the Corps by the creation of many new units, by increased recruitment of officers and men. Eventually the nation introduced compulsory military service and a new militia under the Compulsory Training Act of 19 May, 1939, and the Territorial Army was further doubled. At the same time urgent preparations were made to increase reserves of supplies and petroleum both at home and abroad.

As the fine summer of 1939 wore on, the German threat against Poland materialized and the ultimatum which was to plunge Europe once more into war was at last delivered to Adolf Hitler.

CHAPTER 6

The Second World War 1939-1945

Introduction. The RASC in the British Expeditionary Force – France and Belgium, September, 1939, to June, 1940. Norway, April to May, 1940. The Home Base Gears Up. The Middle East – The First Campaigns. The Western Desert – The 8th Army Campaigns and Final Victory in North Africa. The Build-up of GHQ Middle East and Tasks and Expansion of RASC, 1941 to 1943. North West Africa and the Mediterranean. The Outbreak of War in South East Asia and Loss of Hong Kong and Singapore. Burma – The First Campaigns. The Home Base. Airborne Forces and RASC Air Despatch. The Liberation of Southern Europe – RASC Tasks. Preparations for the Invasion of North West Europe – Operation OVERLORD; RASC Tasks; The Normandy Landings, Arnhem and Advance to the Rhine. From the Rhine to the Baltic. The Final Offensive in Italy. Return to Greece. Victory in Burma. Miscellaneous Overseas Stations and Minor Theatres. Achievements at the end of the War.

INTRODUCTION

With war now inevitable, mobilization was ordered on 1 September and two days later the country went to war. The immediate priority was to get the British Expeditionary Force (BEF) to France as quickly as possible and the first units crossed the Channel on 10 September. Originally to be only two divisions it had been decided in April, 1939, to increase the planned BEF to four divisions in two corps. Following mobilization, the main problems facing the RASC were to assimilate the great numbers of reservists, conscripts and volunteers now flocking to reporting centres, receive into service thousands of civilian vehicles under the 'impressed vehicle' scheme and at the same time fashion all this into a Supply and Transport structure to support the Army in the field many times larger than the peacetime strength. This had to be done rapidly and while the BEF formations were moving to France.

Although a great deal had been done in the period immediately before mobilization towards achieving the sort of organization with the right equipment that the RASC needed, there were still in both respects considerable shortcomings at the outbreak of war. The overall situation in the Corps' main roles at this stage is outlined in the next few paragraphs.

Supplies

At the start of hostilities QMG 6 was the Branch at the War Office which was responsible for both food (rations) and petroleum, oils and lubricants (POL) supply to the Army through the RASC maintenance chain. In the few years immediately before 1939, when rearmament started, it was confronted with the major tasks of adapting and improving the Army ration, and in producing a system to meet the vastly increased requirement for petroleum products. Both were essential to maintain a modern mechanized Army in mobile warfare.

107

Units drawing supplies from a Field Supply Depot. (Illustrated London News)

Whilst a Supply organization existed for food, albeit inadequate in some respects, it could be built on. However, there was not even a nucleus of an RASC POL organization, nor any settled policy on equipments or the methods that should be adopted for supply and distribution of POL in a theatre of war, both functions in peacetime being carried out by civilian contractors. Although before the war started the need for a separate organization was recognized within the Corps, neither the money nor the manpower was then available to create one. It was only as a result of the early experiences of the BEF, related later, that such an organization was established at the War Office and down through the RASC system with formed POL units. Because of its increasing importance, the POL system is described in the narrative separately from Supplies from now on.

The work by QMG 6 on a new field service ration produced a scale that was more in keeping with modern nutritional practices and included a complete range of tinned or preserved food to replace the old 'hard fare' which used to be issued when fresh rations could not be distributed. Despite opposition, as many in Government Departments considered that stockpiling of food was unnecessary and money for it short, QMG 6 pressed its case for a reserve of the field service ration for the initial maintenance of a field force.

As 1939 approached, it was ultimately agreed that this reserve should consist of those items which took time to produce, and that the balance of staple commodities should be met rapidly by the Ministry of Food, then in an embryo state. With war imminent, the new arrangement was that the Ministry of Food to be should provide all the staple items of food for the Services, whilst the War Office remained responsible for items that had to be specially manufactured to meet Service specifications. This was a major change of system and an Inter-Service committee was established to work with the Defence Plans Department in co-ordinating the supply of military food with civilian requirements. For this co-ordination, an RASC Colonel represented the Services Supply Branch with the Ministry of Food throughout the conflict to come.

By early 1939 the triple plans of purchasing reserves, completing detailed arrangements for the supply of Ministry of Food commodities, and the inclusion of dormant contracts with the Food Industry to take effect if war occurred, were well in hand. With the formation and build-up of additional Supply units, and the establishment of new Base Supply Depots in UK to hold reserves, the Corps was now better poised to carry out its Supply role in support of a field force.

POL

The immediate concern of QMG 6 was for the arrangements for supplying the BEF because they depended almost solely on the production of new tin-making and filling plants for the 4 gallon flimsy tins (Flimsies) now agreed as the method of carriage and supply of MT fuel in the field. When planning to meet the estimated initial requirements for the BEF, QMG 6 had only relied on obtaining a 50 per cent output from the factories to start with. They had provided a small cover against any possible failure by placing 5,000 tons of MT fuel in France just before war was declared. But it only took a few weeks' working to show that even the predicted output from the UK factories was not being attained because of unexpected mechanical problems. Shipping placed at Avonmouth and Swansea to load supplies was soon lying idle and GHQ BEF began to express some apprehension about their MT fuel stock situation.

Fortunately the consumption of MT fuel in France did not reach the expected level and the movement of the forces was not impaired for lack of it, but the passing shortage and preliminary adverse reports on the utility of the 4-gallon tin both served to precipitate the development of a new POL supply organization.

From a War Office point of view the MT fuel supply arrangements made for other potential operational areas were satisfactory. The civil bulk plants and tin-filling factories in Egypt and Palestine were running concerns and work on providing military protected bulk storage and filling apparatus in Egypt was already proceeding. Singapore had adequate bulk supplies and tin-making plant and the supply situation in Hong Kong was also satisfactory. Work was in hand at Gibraltar to provide protected storage accommodation for service liquid fuels and, although similar plans for Malta had been delayed, increased packed reserves and a small filling plant had been established there.

There was now no delay in settling the organization and establishments of the new POL units required, and the first unit, a Bulk Petrol Storage Company, was in France by December, 1939, and followed shortly after by a second. Two base petrol filling centres were formed and were in France by early 1940. They were static units and were equipped with heavy plant which necessitated a good deal of preliminary engineering work before it could be installed. Mobile petrol filling centres were introduced later in the war. Petrol depots, formed from a section of base supply depots, were organized for holding packed reserves of spirit and other fuels and lubricants, but were still within the Supply organization.

Stockpiles of fllimsy petrol tins after manufacture in Egypt.

All these units required a high proportion of officers and men skilled in executive and technical petroleum duties who could only be drawn from the oil industry. An appeal for the manpower needed was met at once, and it did not take long before those who had been commercial rivals a few weeks before were presenting a complete unity of enthusiasm and endeavour.

Mechanical Transport

The mobilization plans worked smoothly and well. The first and heaviest burdens within the Corps fell on the provision branch of ST 3 at the War Office and on the Chief Inspector of Supplementary Transport (CIST). The latter implemented the impressment plan and the former was particularly concerned with the production of technical vehicles.

The war had not been in progress many days before there were claims for additional transport. Such tasks as the equipping of the Territorial Army and the

110

expansion of maintenance work in the United Kingdom brought a heavy and sudden demand on our resources. Furthermore, demands were soon received from the newly established Expeditionary Force in France for transport units over and above their original order of battle.

New types of transport companies began to emerge. Works Companies were one such type needed to operate with the Royal Engineers on airfield and road construction. Under their later designation, Tipper Companies, they were found to be indispensable in most theatres of war.

Water Transport

The Army's peacetime requirement for water transport at the beginning of the war was met by a fully civilian-manned organization, The War Department Fleet, which was locally controlled and administered by the RASC through local transport offices, under the direction of the Assistant Director of Military Transport, located at the Royal Arsenal, Woolwich. It operated worldwide in all military stations where local water transport facilities were required. Its tasks included target towing and range safety launches, moving WD cargoes between the main UK ports, including RN and RA artillery pieces from the Royal Arsenal to shipbuilding yards and emplacements, a wide variety of personnel movement tasks and the maintenance of outlying sea forts. The Fleet operated a range of vessels that included coasters, MFVs and Fairmile Launches, with a worldwide pre-war strength of 66 vessels and launches.

It had been realized that in the event of war a large expansion of the Fleet and its range of tasks would be necessary, and this would involve decentralization of command and control to Formations and Commands and the formation of operational units outside the normal role of the current civilianized Fleet. The existing element would still continue with its same role, and in the event the crews were to be subjected to their full share of wartime hazards, and to suffer casualties. At the beginning of 1940, to provide the operational capability, RASC Motor Boat Companies were formed, and at the same time the ADMT's organization at Woolwich was disbanded and absorbed into the Supply and Transport Directorate of the War Office as part of ST1 Branch. The civilian element of the new fleet with its increased tasks was to remain throughout the war, with only a few posts becoming militarized, whilst the new military element now beginning to take shape was to expand rapidly and to play a major part in many operations to come. It was to rise in strength to over 1600 vessels.

The Motor Boat Companies were equipped mainly with requisitioned launches and early in 1940 two motorboat training units were raised and located at Salcombe in Devon and St Austell in Cornwall. These were officered chiefly by Emergency Commissioned Officers RASC with a knowledge of small boats and navigation, and with soldier crews found from volunteers from all arms and services with similar seafaring knowledge. 1 Motor Boat Company was raised at Salcombe in Devon and 2 Motor Boat Company at Falmouth, later moving to West Mersea near Colchester.

As the impact of war increased, the meagre resources of the RASC Fleet became heavily strained, and additional craft, mostly of the launch and cabin cruiser type, were quickly requisitioned. Rapid expansion demanded a greater decentralization of control, and in January, 1940, the first Water Transport Companies, RASC were formed at Woolwich, Barry Docks, Leith, Portsmouth and in the Far East at Singapore, under the command of specially selected RASC officers.

About this time also the decision was made to form RASC waterborne units whose job was to provide essential RASC water transport services in future field force formations and their role, broadly speaking, was to be analogous to that of general transport companies.

THE RASC IN THE BRITISH EXPEDITIONARY FORCE
FRANCE AND BELGIUM
SEPTEMBER 1939 – JUNE 1940

Preparation

In its support of the BEF the RASC was to take the field for the first time as a completely mechanized Corps. Each division was to be provided with a Commander RASC, Headquarters, and three transport companies: one company for ammunition,

RASC of the BEF embarked for France. (Imperial War Museum)

one for POL, spare blankets and anti-gas stores, and the third, which had two echelons of vehicles, for rations. A similar organization was allowed for Corps Troops, and each corps was allotted two companies, designated by the old fashioned term 'Park', for holding reserves of ammunition and POL. The Park was commanded by a CRASC with a Royal Artillery officer on its establishment. Separate companies were provided for carrying the general needs of GHQ troops and non-divisional artillery, and five units were allotted for the carriage of casualties. Four companies were reserved for troop-carrying, and one for bridging material, and there were seven companies for general duties on the lines of communication. The standard equipment was the 3-ton lorry, but two of the lines of communication companies were equipped with 6 and 10-ton vehicles. When war broke out all the available six-wheeled vehicles held in peacetime were to be converted into ambulances and workshop vehicles.

The twelve companies required for the four divisions were in existence at the outbreak of war but only in cadre form; the remainder of the fifty companies in the order of battle had to be formed on mobilization from static transport units which too were only cadres. In 1939, for instance, the three RASC companies stationed in Northern Ireland held only fifteen of the GS 6x6 3-ton trucks each, and a similar situation prevailed throughout the Corps.

There were no counterparts in peacetime for all the Supply units required in war, so these had to be formed on mobilization and manned with officers and men drawn from other types of RASC units. Also, as described earlier, no special organization for storing and distributing petroleum was provided, as, in addition to rations, POL were to be handled throughout within the existing Supply organization.

The Landing in France – September, 1939 onwards

Cherbourg and Brest were chosen as ports of entry for a northern base at Rennes while St Nazaire and Nantes were selected for a southern base. Their choice meant that the everyday needs of the BEF would have to be carried forward by rail over a distance of up to 400 miles; but the apparent advantages of security from air attack outweighed every other consideration.

The first body of troops landed in France on 10 September, and although in many cases other planned locations proved unsuitable or inadequate, it was possible to establish the Headquarters L of C at Le Mans. From the outset the staff were handicapped by the wide dispersion of the base areas and with communications difficulties. Distances to be covered were great and transport was scarce. The French telephone system, too, was unreliable and its use had to be restricted for security reasons, whilst for despatch riders, who provided the reliable and secure alternative, countryside and language were unfamiliar. Unexpected conditions also arose at the ports, where there was considerable difficulty in finding enough labour, and the port facilities provided by the French proved inadequate. The railway resources for clearance also fell below the expected standard. The immediate result was that delays began to occur in the turn-round of ships and there was congestion at the docks. The plans made at home for the shipment of balanced trainloads of rations to be received at the ports in France also went awry, as, in the event, balanced consignments were split between different ships.

The arrangements for shipping RASC transport were inefficient and there were many delays before units could become operational. In one instance the 220 vehicles of a company were split up by being loaded in ten different ships. The first general transport (GT) company was not scheduled to land until several days after the force started arriving in some strength, and divisional ammunition and POL companies were landed before supply companies.

The general lack of storage and other accommodation was to be made good by new construction, but the decision to start work on a new defence line along the frontier, on the sector held by the BEF, meant that additional labour and vast quantities of materials would also have to be provided there. Extra transport would thus be wanted for all these new commitments and for the support of TA divisions due to arrive after completion of their training in UK.

Because of all these increasing tasks the original decision to maintain the force through the southern ports of Brittany and Normandy had to be revised, as the Admiralty was emphatic that more ports should be opened to the north, to reduce the turn-round of ships plying between UK and the base ports. In consequence it was decided to open a new base in the area of Le Havre and Rouen and to take into use all the available ports as far north as Calais.

Transport

If the word 'phoney' could be used to describe the period between the landing of the BEF and the beginning of active operations the next year, it certainly did not apply to the task of the RASC transport in the force. All divisional and corps units when not under training were fully employed and the severe winter conditions and ice-bound roads made their task more difficult.

The Corps had played a major part in developing highly mobile military vehicles between the wars such as the 6x6 models, but there were very few of them. Most task vehicles had been obtained by requisitioning under the impressment scheme and were a very mixed bag of makes and types. The RASC organization for vehicle maintenance was well tested in bringing this motley fleet up to standard, but it was quite a common sight in France to see a well known trader's name or logo clearly visible through the hastily applied khaki paint on a passing lorry. By March, 1940, there were 104 RASC transport units in France with this mixed range of vehicles.

The unit which handled vehicle spare parts, the MT Stores Depot (MTSD), was established about fifteen miles from the Heavy Repair Shop, but, as stores took as much as ten days to reach the BEF, an advanced section was set up near Rouen. The MTSD kept pace with the 1,300 demands received each week, which sometimes involved handling and packing some 4,000 different spare parts.

POL

One of the implications of the high degree of mechanization in the BEF was the greater prominence that the supply and distribution of MT fuel now demanded. It soon became obvious that a separate organization from supplies was required for handling POL, and that better use should be made of existing bulk petroleum storage facilities in France, for which a new petroleum company was now provided. During the first few weeks, however, the main MT fuel stocks for the force were stored in the tin flimsies by the Number 5 Sections of the two Base Supply Depots and they continued in this role as petroleum depots for packed stocks.

114

An exercise code-named PUNCH to practise ship-to-shore bulk refuelling.

Before the Storm

As the months passed by the BEF grew stronger. A fifth division had been formed in France and, between January and April, 1940, the 42nd, 44th, 48th, 50th (Motorized) and 51st Divisions had arrived from home. A third corps (III Corps) was formed in April, so that, just before the battle broke out, the BEF had three corps with nine divisions on the main front and a tenth, 51st, disposed with the French armies in the Maginot sector.

The original deficiency in general transport and troop-carrying companies had partly been made good by the arrival of more companies from England, and the supply organization had again been strengthened by a third supply personnel company, a fourth bakery, and cold storage units. However there was little that could be done to rectify the extreme shortage of experienced RASC officers, warrant officers and senior NCOs. Despite several hundred RIASC officers returning to the Corps, on average there was hardly one pre-war regular officer per company by the time the campaign started. It should also be remembered that no one, not even First World War veterans, had experienced the problems of providing logistic support for such a large mechanized and mobile force.

The Campaign

On the morning of 10 May, 1940, the German armies began their invasion of France, Luxembourg and the Netherlands and the French and British forces in the north were ordered to leave their prepared positions and move forward to a new line from Holland to Sedan with their main front along the line of the River Dyle. That afternoon the four RASC troop-carrying companies, which had the distinction of being the first RASC companies to be engaged, started lifting the leading brigades of 1st, 2nd and 3rd Divisions forward to their new positions. The next day all formations followed with full echelons of POL, ammunition and supplies.

All went well with the divisional and corps RASC as they moved forward to replenish their formations. There were, however, minor hindrances caused by some enemy air activity, by movement in a strange country heavily intersected with small bridges and level crossings, and by refugees appearing in considerable numbers on the three main routes of advance.

Although engaging the BEF heavily, the main German thrust was through the Ardennes and across the River Meuse with the intention of breaking through at Sedan and then dashing towards the Channel along the valleys of the Rivers Somme and Aisne to cut off the northern group of Allied Armies. By 15 May the Panzers had smashed a gap thirty miles wide through the French 9th Army, Paris lay unguarded and the road to the coast clear. The 1st Army group, including the BEF and the Belgian Army, began to withdraw towards the Channel ports. By now there were heavy attacks by low-flying aircraft on the rear areas, against both military and civil traffic and on refugees who by this time were tending to paralyse all movement. Many RASC columns suffered casualties, and vehicles were destroyed. Unit anti-aircraft teams were in action throughout the day. Many awards for gallantry were earned in these actions in the ensuing days, for example by Lance Corporal J H Fairchild, who fought off fourteen enemy aircraft, by Driver W H Hall, of 50th Division, who carried on firing although seriously wounded, and by Drivers B Wallsworth and J G Lee, of 42 Division, who were given immediate awards of the Military Medal.

As the withdrawal went on, some confusion arose from the various cross movements of formations, continued changes in the location of units, and alterations in the points used in the chain of replenishment. This caused temporary loss of touch between RASC units and formations, but, in the absence of detailed information about future movements, POL and supply points were established on the main withdrawal routes. The chief preoccupation of Divisional Commanders RASC was how to maintain communications with the ST staff at Corps headquarters, with their own divisional Q staff and with their own units.

RASC motorcyclists played an important part during the campaign in maintaining communication, marking routes and in guiding packets and convoys, as did also car drivers. Many motorcyclists were recognized with awards for their devotion to duty in acts such as those of Driver E Shepherd, HQ RASC 42nd Division, Driver V Askew, 44th Division, and Driver J W Priest, 45 Company, who were each awarded the Military Medal.

The frequency with which brigades and artillery units were detached from their parent formation showed up a weakness in the divisional RASC organization in that each transport company was only organized to carry a specific commodity, that is ammunition or POL or supplies. Therefore the detachment of a brigade involved drawing on three different companies to provide the requisite complement of RASC vehicles with their specific commodity loads.

By 21 May the German leading elements had reached the sea near Abbeville and the lines of communication and supply between the BEF and its bases to the west were cut. The general situation was such that a further withdrawal on the main front of the BEF was inevitable in order to shorten the line and free troops for what was from then onwards to be a fight on two fronts.

With the communications cut, the efforts that had been made to amass six days' rations for nearly 400,000 men and millions of gallons of petroleum and other fuel oils along the lines of communication were completely nullified and the stocks lost. The situation for the further maintenance of the force was now critical. Only the three Channel ports of Boulogne, Calais and Dunkirk remained available to the Force for further supply from the UK, but their usage was doubtful since under the conditions now prevailing they could not handle the 2000 tons of stores a day that the Force required. Although only of minimal significance against the overall requirement, during this period there was an early example of supply by air when eighty tons of supplies and small arms ammunition were flown from Croydon airport to Merville.

At this stage it was in fact already clear that, despite all the efforts of the Corps officers and soldiers who had now reached the port of Dunkirk, to where some supplies had been diverted, that getting them unloaded and the stores distributed was not a sustainable operation. The hazardous and chaotic state of the port due to continual air attack, with fires and major destruction everywhere, and lack of transport and labour, meant that by 27 May it had to be abandoned for use by further supply ships. All ships already at the port had been unloaded and there were many gallant acts by those involved in this work in their endeavours to continue maintaining the Force under the rapidly deteriorating situation.

The Transport Situation

On 27 May Belgium surrendered, leaving the left flank of the BEF exposed, although the Belgians did open the dykes to provide a water obstacle. As the withdrawal to the coast in the general direction of Dunkirk went on, the rear area of the BEF became smaller and uncertainty regarding the proximity of the enemy to the region where RASC transport was operating increased. There were, consequently, many brushes with the enemy and some pitched battles. One of the two railhead companies had a series of encounters and, although they fought off enemy tanks with the aid of their few weapons, they eventually suffered severe casualties. Major C B Langdon was awarded the Distinguished Service Order for his part in one of these encounters. In another instance Driver A N Sanson, a motorcyclist of 4 Company, was awarded the Military Medal for repeated reconnaissance and message-carrying through the enemy lines.

There were also many other cases of individual gallantry and determination, like that of Corporal Merrivale of 7 Motor Ambulance Convoy, Driver Lilley, 150 Field Ambulance, and Driver Burrows, 4th Division.

The Last Phase

There was great congestion in the area around the Dunkirk perimeter as units were directed to the beaches. Roads became almost jammed with a flow of French military and civil vehicles converging from all directions, and instructions that units should abandon their vehicles in selected places outside the bridgehead do not seem to have reached them. There was also some initial uncertainty as to whether vehicles should be put out of action and how this was to be done, but this was later put right and clear instructions given for destroying them.

With the rail Lines of Communication cut, the conventional maintenance system broke down and improvisation became the order of the day. 522 Company, the ammunition company of the 50th Division, resorted to salvaging ammunition from abandoned and wrecked vehicles with some success and at one stage loaded ammunition from a burning train. Captain K Mansfield of 522 Company was awarded the Military Cross for the train episode and other acts of gallantry during the withdrawal.

Although it eventually became clear that an evacuation was to take place and that vehicles and equipment were to be destroyed, details did not filter down to platoon level until a very late stage. In 50th Division RASC destruction of vehicles was done in parking areas by removing the sump plug and releasing oil, smashing the radiator and leaving the engine running. The final approach to the beaches was on foot in darkness and the evacuation was completely improvised, especially along the coast between Dunkirk and De Panne where the shallow waters meant that shore-to-ship ferrying had to take place in ships' lifeboats with soldiers manning the oars. Morale and discipline remained good, but one of the biggest problems came from lack of sleep. By the time of the evacuation mental and physical exhaustion tested junior leadership to the full.

The evacuation from Dunkirk, Operation DYNAMO, was the first big operation in which the RASC Fleet took part. Eight of the fastest launches in the water transport companies – the 45 ft range launches *Grouse*, *Kestrel*, *Pigeon*, *Swallow* and *Vulture*, the RASC high-speed launch *Wolfe*, and the 57-ft target-towing launches

A WD Fleet launch of a type used in the evacuation of Dunkirk.

Haig and *Marlborough* – were diverted to the task and did valiant work, as the following letter (extract from Special Fleet Order No. 1 dated 8 June, 1940) from General Sir Walter Venning, then Quartermaster General to the Forces, to each of the masters records:

> '*I wish to thank you, your engineer and crew for the very fine part which you played in the recent evacuation of the BEF.*
>
> '*In particular I wish to convey my admiration for the way in which the personnel of the WD vessels participating volunteered to perform a dangerous task quite outside their normal duties.*
>
> '*To have been successful in saving the lives of over 1,300 British and Allied soldiers is a feat of which all of you concerned may well feel proud. The damage done to so many of the craft engaged is a testimony to the dangers which you and those serving under you faced with cheerfulness and gallantry.*
>
> '*I am proud to think that, as Quartermaster General to the Forces, the War Department Fleet comes within my sphere.*'

NORWAY

On 5 April, 1940 the Germans moved to establish a strategic position in Norway and seized Oslo, Bergen, Trondheim and Narvik, establishing themselves firmly to pre-empt any Allied action. As a consequence, and while the momentous events in France were building up to a climax, the ill-fated expedition to Norway was hastily planned and launched.

Headquarters 49th (West Riding) Division was modified to form HQ 'Avonforce', which was charged with the recapture of Narvik. Under command were 24 Guards Infantry Brigade and administrative units, the RASC element of which comprised a special petroleum depot, a special transport section, a field bakery section, a field butchery section and 4 Supply Personnel Company with three sections. The transport was extremely limited, consisting only of a car for the GOC, six light ambulances, four Bedford Scammell tractors with 5-ton semi-trailers, and four Austin two-seater cars for the use of the Guards Brigade. The intention was that all general transport needed should be hired locally, a forlorn hope based on over-optimistic information.

The RASC staff of 'Avonforce' was not formed from 49 Divisional RASC, but posted in to fill a special establishment consisting of ADST (Lieutenant Colonel H M Hinde), two DADSTs and two staff captains.

'Avonforce' embarked at the end of the first week in April and arrived on 12 April in the Vaagsfjord. After turning south the convoy anchored off Harstad, a small fishing port on the island of Hinno. The decision was made to disembark the force there and set up a base before marching on Narvik some fifty miles to the south.

The ADST landed with the first reconnaissance party, and the remainder of the ST headquarters an hour later. Contact was made early with the British Vice-Console, Mr Per Sanvig. a Norwegian, and a representative of the Anglo-American Oil Company. The help rendered by this gentleman was of immense value, especially to the ST staff. The immediate task was to locate suitable supply and petrol depots and organize transport, as unloading of stores was to begin the next day. Unloading of troops began immediately.

The Maintenance Situation

The transport picture was depressing. There was only one contractor, who was also owner of the main garage and workshops. It was arranged that he should provide as many load-carriers as possible as well as taxis and private cars for use as staff cars. The first night only four 30-cwt trucks could be raised. These were used to help clear kit from the quay, while a few private car owners helped by transporting staff officers about the town.

The only points at which stores could be landed were the town quay, which could berth two ships, the coal quay (one ship up to 5,000 tons) and the oil wharf, served by a very narrow road (one ship).

In view of the extreme scarcity of transport, hired vehicles were allocated according to three degrees of priority, the first operational as ordered by the G Staff, the second for dock clearance and the third to meet individual demands. On an average daily hirings were fourteen cars and fourteen lorries, the peak being twenty-one lorries.

The RASC transport landed about three days after disembarkation began and did sterling work, especially four tractors and trailers, which were put on to dock clearance and worked twenty-four hours a day with drivers in shifts.

By this time the supply depot was firmly established, prodigious efforts having been made by the RASC supply men who, working with little sleep in foul weather, managed in one period of four days to unload 350 tons of supplies without outside help.

The field bakery had to clear three feet of frozen snow before it could erect its Aldershot ovens, but it came into action within three days and rapidly attained an output of 5,000 lbs of bread a day, backed up by a further 3,000 lbs daily from local resources. Fuel for the Aldershot ovens was a constant worry, wood being scarce and of poor quality.

The petroleum depot had to abandon its first location after the blizzard as the site was unworkable while the land was under snow. It was moved to the Anglo-American Oil Company's jetty, on which a packed POL depot was opened when the first shipment of cased petrol (14,000 gallons) arrived on 26 April. This site was unsuitable in that it did not allow for any dispersion and, in consequence, late in May the packed stocks were destroyed during one of the air raids. Luckily local bulk stocks were untouched and proved to be adequate for all purposes.

The Withdrawal from Narvik

Air raids occurred daily, and for some time the only anti-aircraft protection were the guns on the RN ships lying in the fjord and from units' own Bren guns.

Meanwhile in the south of Norway the British forces landed at Namsos and Andalsnes, but were driven back by the Germans and had to re-embark and return to the UK. This left the North-Western Expeditionary Force (NWEF) alone in their assault against Narvik.

Early in May further reinforcements arrived, including a Polish brigade which was landed on the mainland north of Narvik and passed straight on to join up with the Norwegian 5 Division which was advancing south on Narvik through the mountains. A heavy mobile anti-aircraft regiment and a mobile light anti-aircraft regiment arrived each with their attached RASC sections. The former section was fully employed with its parent unit, but the latter was able to contribute daily to the

120

transport pool and greatly eased the situation.

Towards the end of May Narvik was captured, but it became evident that, with the turn of events in France, no further troops could be sent to Norway and that the maintenance of the forces already there would be an unwarrantable drain on our naval resources. Evacuation of the Force there became inevitable.

The Andalsnes Operations

The allied force at Andalsnes suffered similarly. Luftwaffe air raids were continuous. There was an acute shortage of transport and forward supply was hazardous owing to the cratering and collapse of the one road and single railway track.

The tasks set to the ever-diminishing transport strained it to the utmost, but it succeeded in rescuing wounded from various isolated sanatoria and private houses before they were overrun, and also distributed rations to retreating troops and dumped 1,000 rations in each of the three base defence sectors.

On the night of 29 April about 300 wounded and some surplus base sub-area personnel were evacuated in destroyers. This work was continued on the following two nights in face of determined enemy efforts to prevent it. Daily the Luftwaffe fired the surrounding woods to give them light enough to bomb the destroyers, which could not manoeuvre in such narrow waters, but the enemy had no success. On 30 April the remaining wounded and as many others as possible were got away, including half of 2 L of C MT Company, the two supply sections and some RASC clerks.

On 1 May the few remaining vehicles moved up to ferry the last of the forward troops across a seventeen-mile gap between two craters on the railway, but they were not needed. Instead they brought in wounded, Royal Marine outposts, demolition parties and stragglers, and then stood by to bring in the troops, including the remaining half of 2 L of C Company, RASC, holding the port perimeter some three miles up the valley. In the end all were successfully evacuated.

The general opinion of all who took part in this operation was that, from the RASC point of view, it was hopelessly impracticable from the start; at the same time many valuable lessons emerged and were recorded.

France under Marshal Pétain sued for peace on 17 June, 1940, and the immediate priority at home was to put together a defence against invasion and to reconstitute the field Army.

THE HOME BASE GEARS UP

While the war on land was unfolding in France and Norway and what measures that could be taken to strengthen overseas garrisons were put in hand, the home base set about gearing up for a protracted war.

MECHANICAL TRANSPORT

Vehicle Maintenance Units

As the number and type of RASC road transport units was increased in the early years of the war, there had to be a corresponding development in the three main types of RASC MT maintenance units on which the transport companies were so dependent for the replacement of vehicles and spares, the provision of stores, and for the execution of repairs beyond the resources of unit workshops. The three units concerned were the Vehicle Reserve Depot, the MT Stores Depot and the Heavy Repair Shop, all sited before the war at Feltham, Middlesex. In late 1939 and throughout 1940 more of these units had been established in the UK, but this expansion had only just been completed when there was to be a profound change in the allocation of responsibility for the maintenance of MT. This caused the RASC to hand over complete responsibility for heavy repairs to a new corps, the Royal Electrical and Mechanical Engineers, of which more detail is given later.

Vehicle Reserve Depots

The growth of the RASC led to increasing demands on the vehicle reserve depots, the MT store depots and the heavy repair shops. The first two types of unit were increased to three of each (at Feltham, Slough and Ashchurch). The Heavy Repair Shop (HRS) was not so easy to triplicate, or even duplicate, owing to its requirements in machinery and skilled workers, but a site at Ashford, near Feltham, which had been acquired for an extension of the VRD, Feltham, was converted into a new HRS, while an entirely new shop was set up, on a smaller scale, in requisitioned premises at High Wycombe. These three shops, with a further one which had been opened in Northern Ireland, coped with the load at home, with the help of the Ministry of Supply 'Army Auxiliary Workshops', which were civil workshops run under Ministry of Supply control for the repair of B and RASC vehicles at home.

Auxiliary Territorial Service (ATS) Drivers with the RASC

Between the two world wars no women were allowed to serve in the Armed Forces, but in 1938 Royal Assent was given to the recruitment of 20,000 women to form the ATS, and these were mobilized in 1939 for non-combatant roles in the UK, releasing men for overseas service. Many took their place in the Corps as drivers, and the numbers employed in this trade increased enormously as the war progressed. Many of the ATS officers employed with the Corps on MT duties were found from the First Aid Nursing Yeomanry (The 'FANYs'), the unofficial women's organization which had existed with limitless enthusiasm since the South African War, the Corps having helped by undertaking their technical training and general sponsorship.

Although mixed RASC MT Companies were formed having both RASC and ATS officers and drivers, others were completely composed of ATS, and they drove every type of vehicle from staff cars to load carriers.

ATS drivers played their part in supplying MT units with replacement vehicles.

Establishments of Transport Units

From 1941 the establishment of our transport units was reorganized on a platoon and section basis. The section was composed of seven vehicles, with a section commander mounted normally on a motorcycle. The platoon consisted of a headquarters which included a platoon officer, a platoon sergeant and a fitter and four sections. The total strength of the platoon was thirty vehicles. This platoon was not only the exact counterpart of the infantry platoon but also, if equipped with 3-ton lorries, it could carry in one lift the marching element of an infantry battalion. This made troop-carrying a simple matter to plan and execute. If a second driver was required on each vehicle, the platoon remained unaltered but was given a Relief Driver Increment (RDI), a number of which were established in companies as necessary according to their role and specific tasks.

The company consisted of a headquarters, one or more workshop platoons, and as many transport platoons and composite platoons as were necessary for it to fulfil its role. Where, as in a division, armoured division, army corps, lines of communication or base area, a number of RASC companies were required to perform the RASC duties for a formation or area, these companies were grouped into a 'column' under a CRASC, the column being the equivalent of a battalion in the infantry. The term 'column' was a timely revival of the early nomenclature for grouped ASC companies.

ANIMAL TRANSPORT

Not long after Dunkirk orders were given to form a RASC pack transport company in the United Kingdom. Reorientation of strategy after the fall of France included the possibility of at least one division being required for operations in mountainous country generally assumed to be Norway. Later, in 1941, a second company was formed; both were composed of British officers and men. In France animal transport companies of the RIASC, as well as a company manned by Cypriot muleteers, were in operation. The arrival of the RIASC companies so early in the war made history, as they were the first units of the Indian Army to take the field.

WATER TRANSPORT

The evacuation of the BEF and the threat of German invasion brought in their train many problems for the RASC Fleet, although applications from volunteers for duty with the motorboat companies continued to flow in and selection and training afloat went on rapidly.

Intensified defence measures on the east, south-east and south coasts created additional transport and ferry commitments on estuaries, rivers and any stretches of water suitable for enemy seaplane landings, enemy mine-dropping and to challenge any suspicious craft entering the special defence zones. The patrol craft – a most motley array of cabin cruisers and launches of all types and condition – were operated by sundry units, both of the Regular Army and of the Home Guard. In several cases they had been 'requisitioned' locally by their operators.

By the end of 1941 the strength of the RASC Fleet had increased to 200 vessels, and two years later had reached 1,110 worldwide.

SUPPLIES

The System of Supply

The preparations which were made by QMG 6 before the war were necessarily limited in their scope. The reserves of food which had been acquired were only sufficient for filling the supply pipeline to the BEF and for part of the additional reserves required by the principal commands overseas. The organization in the commands at home for supplying the Army and RAF after mobilization was only a nucleus, and additional accommodation for holding War Office reserves was still under construction when war broke out.

The maintenance of the Army at home and abroad once war was declared was therefore largely dependent on how quickly pre-war plans for supply could be implemented. These plans outlined earlier were now operating.

The home commands had put into effect the detailed plans for expanding their organization by setting up new depots and complementary NAAFI stores. As soon as war was declared, the partly finished depot for holding War Office reserves (2 SRD at Barry, in Wales) was taken into use and construction work hastened, as, although the existing depot at Deptford was adequate for immediate needs, its location was thought to be so vulnerable that it was to be cleared and shut down as soon as possible. Plans for a third SRD, located at Taunton, were also hastened and work on construction began at once.

By early 1940 the total requirement for food reserves had risen to 100,000 tons, exclusive of the everyday needs of the Army at home, which were being supplied by the Ministry of Food and NAAFI. It soon became clear that the Army's requirements would have to be forecast for over a year or more ahead, so as to give the food industry the necessary opportunities for advance planning and developing their productive capacity. Forecasting the amount of food required was an art and not a science, and was one of the most important duties which had to be performed by the supply service both at the War Office and at the headquarters of all the theatres of war. Even if there had been only one ration scale for the whole of the Army, it would have been a difficult matter, but account had to be taken of many basic scales, as it was no uncommon thing for a single command overseas to have to design and administer up to as many as fifty different scales to cater for the needs of the many nations which formed part of the British Army and our Allies.

At the War Office ST 6, the new designation for QMG 6, had many other duties apart from procurement and the wide field of work connected with rations and rationing. One of the first questions which had to be explored was the reorganization of the supply system in the theatres of war. The internal organization of BSDs was altered in such a way that they could be used singly or in groups. They were provided with their own transport specially designed for depot work and labour-saving equipment which could be used under field conditions. The supply personnel company was abolished and eventually replaced by a system of standard-sized supply platoons and Detail Issue Depots (DIDs), each self-contained and of such a size that they were easily adaptable for the various supply duties which they would have to perform.

The arrangements for producing bread in the field were considerably improved by the introduction of mobile bakeries which were completely self-contained for transport, power and plant. They could move quickly from place to place and come into action within a few hours of arrival at their site. The organization for providing frozen meat in the field underwent little change and perhaps lagged behind progress made in other directions. Mobile, or rather movable, cold stores were designed which could be erected in the field, but their size was limited.

There were many changes made before the war ended, but generally speaking it can be said that the ration was maintained at a level of about 3,800 calories gross for the rest of the war. This included the food value of these items obtainable with the small cash allowance of $2\frac{1}{2}$ old pence per person which supplemented the articles issued in kind.

Tribute must be paid to parts played by the Ministry of Food and the NAAFI. The Ministry had the difficult role of combining the duty of poacher and gamekeeper for the national good. At the same time they took good care that the serviceman received his due share of the national larder and that he received perhaps just that little bit extra of the few luxuries which were popularly known as 'being in short supply'.

The NAAFI was faced with a double task of acting as the agents of the Government for supplying a considerable portion of the ration for all three Services at home and at the same time endeavouring to satisfy the demands of the serviceman in their canteens throughout the world. NAAFI also undertook the whole of the responsibility, on behalf of the Ministry and the Services, for the administration of the rationing procedures for canteens, for the control of sweets rationing, and for instituting unofficial rationing for such much-sought-after articles as cigarettes. They had a great deal to contend with throughout the war and deserve the fullest praise.

POL

Meeting the UK Needs

The threat of enemy invasion of Britain made ST2, a new branch designation for the POL staff of the old QMG 6, turn to home defence. Up to that time the Army at home relied very largely for its petrol supplies on the civil system of distribution. The first need was to provide reserves of canned petrol for each command for use in the event of the normal systems of distribution being dislocated. The tin-filling factories were ordered into full production, and arrangements made to open petrol depots at each of the eight strategic points which had been selected for siting similar strategic reserves of food in main supply depots.

In the event of invasion detailed instructions were issued and equipment provided for the destruction of bulk stocks in the coastal belt and inland areas which the enemy might make his objective.

As soon as the preliminary measures for defence were in train ST2 began to extend the arrangements for bulk storage, can-filling and packed reserves in such a way that they would not only serve to support large-scale defensive operations in these islands, but would serve to support the launching of future operations against the enemy overseas when the Army was again in a position to take the offensive.

THE MIDDLE EAST

The war in the Middle East broke out in June, 1940, when Mussolini belatedly declared war on Britain. A small British army, reinforced by Australians and Indians, was based in Egypt to guard the Suez Canal. Italian armies were guarding the Italian Colonies in Somalia, in Libya, including Cyrenaica and Tripolitania, and were occupying Abyssinia. Above all both sides needed a military victory rather than a tactical or territorial advantage. The Italians wanted to demonstrate their prowess as a credible partner in the Berlin-Rome axis and the British desperately needed to restore confidence and morale after the disastrous campaigns in France and Norway.

General Wavell, the British commander in chief in the Middle East, had set up his GHQ in Cairo and had at his disposal about 45,000 men with the bulk, 30,000, in Egypt. Of the rest he had 7000 in the Sudan, 2000 in British Somaliland and 6000 in Kenya. With these he had to deal with 200,000 Italians under General Graziani in Libya and another colonial army of over 200,000, including 90,000 Italians, holding down Somalia and Abyssinia.

Expansion of RASC Services

The entry of Italy into the war and the threat to our sea communications in the Mediterranean made the holding of large stocks of essential commodities a matter of vital necessity. The creation of a large base involved not only the despatch of enormous quantities of RASC supplies and stores from the United Kingdom but also the provision of Corps personnel to man the additional RASC depots and units.

The arrival of men and stores was delayed when the Mediterranean was closed to merchant shipping and convoys had to follow the long sea route round the Cape of Good Hope, a voyage of ten weeks or more. It was necessary to offset the deficiencies in British manpower by the formation of units with British cadres but composed of other nationalities, for example Cypriots, Maltese, Sinhalese and Palestinian Jews. This was a successful venture, particularly in the case of transport units.

A RASC Middle East training school was established in February, 1940, for the training of officers and other ranks, and courses were run with a comprehensive syllabus on supply, petrol and transport subjects. A RASC base reinforcement depot was formed at Geneifa, in Egypt, in September, 1940, to receive, acclimatize and hold RASC reinforcements from the UK.

THE FIRST CAMPAIGNS

SUDAN AND ABYSSINIA

Against the Italians in Abyssinia General Wavell operated from three bases: Cairo, from where he controlled his reserves, Khartoum in the Sudan and Nairobi in Kenya. In June, 1940, all Wavell could do in the south was mount a mobile harassing campaign and on the Sudan front delay the Italians as much as possible.

At the outbreak of war with Germany in 1939 it was decided to amalgamate HQ British Troops Sudan and HQ Sudan Defence Force. Local difficulties in administrative methods made the fusion of the service a difficult and lengthy progress, but a unified ST directorate was eventually achieved. Even then the supply and transport services of the SDF proper, requiring specialized knowledge and experience, was left largely in the hands of El Kaimakam E R Goode Bey, the senior RASC officer at that time still seconded to the SDF.

Following Italy's entry into the war in June, 1940, reinforcements began to arrive to build up the British forces in the Sudan. However, there were no second or third line administrative units to deal with any large influx of troops. Spare storage space was non-existent, although depots to hold 150 days' reserve for about 30,000 troops were planned. However, supplies, ammunition and other stores soon began to pour into the country.

The magnitude of the task confronting the small ST staff at HQ Troops Sudan and the pressure on the limited RASC and RIASC units committed to the battle at that time can be well appreciated, since there were soon five separate fronts stretching from Equatorial Province in the southern Sudan to the Red Sea littoral, about 1200 miles to the north. Also the total ration strength was now about 28,000 all ranks and the MT resources available consisted only of two sections of an SDF reserve MT company, second-line transport of 5th Indian Division, and one MT company of the Sudan Defence Force; altogether totalling about 500 military vehicles, together with a limited number of hired civil lorries.

On 4 July the Italians attacked and drove the British out of Kassala and the frontier posts, but then failed to advance further. By the end of 1940 the situation was much better, with more troops arriving all the time and a revolt being successfully fomented in Abyssinia.

In December it was decided to reinforce the Sudan further, so that defence could be turned to attack and the Italian forces in Eritrea destroyed. The reinforcements allotted were 4th Indian Division, together with a considerable number of non-divisional units, including a squadron of infantry tanks and anti-aircraft units. The fighting formations arrived first, followed by a very inadequate administrative backing. It soon became obvious that, with the large distances to be covered in the advance into Eritrea, the provision of extra transport was vital. After repeated requests, four South African Cape Corps MT companies were allotted. They arrived by overland route from South Africa in the middle of January, 1941, and helped to relieve the fraught MT situation.

In January Lieutenant General W Platt with his Indian troops counter-attacked from the Sudan towards the Red Sea and at first made rapid progress. However, it had become clear by the beginning of February that the enemy intended to stand on the heights of Keren dominating the plain in which our forces were now deployed. The position was a formidable one with no way round. Its capture would need the full strength of both divisions. This required a comprehensive administrative plan.

Between 1 and 28 March some 16,000 tons of supplies, ammunition, petrol etc, were moved forward by road, that is 550 tons a day. The transport available consisted of 480 Cape Corps vehicles, of which at least one-third were always off the road for lack of springs and tyres, the second-line vehicles of 4th and 5th Indian Divisions and part of the SDF MT Company. There were no replacement vehicles.

The battle for Keren lasted twelve days from 15 to 27 March and, with the continued advance, Asmara was occupied on 1 April. The campaign ended with the capture of Amba Alagi on 15 May, 1941, when General Platt was able to link with General Cunningham's Force which had come up from Kenya.

EGYPT AND CYRENAICA

During these early days of the war when General Wavell's forces held the Egyptian frontier there had been established a number of dispersed reserve dumps of ammunition, food, water and petrol. From these, troops could have been maintained for a short period in the event of the extended lines of communication being cut by

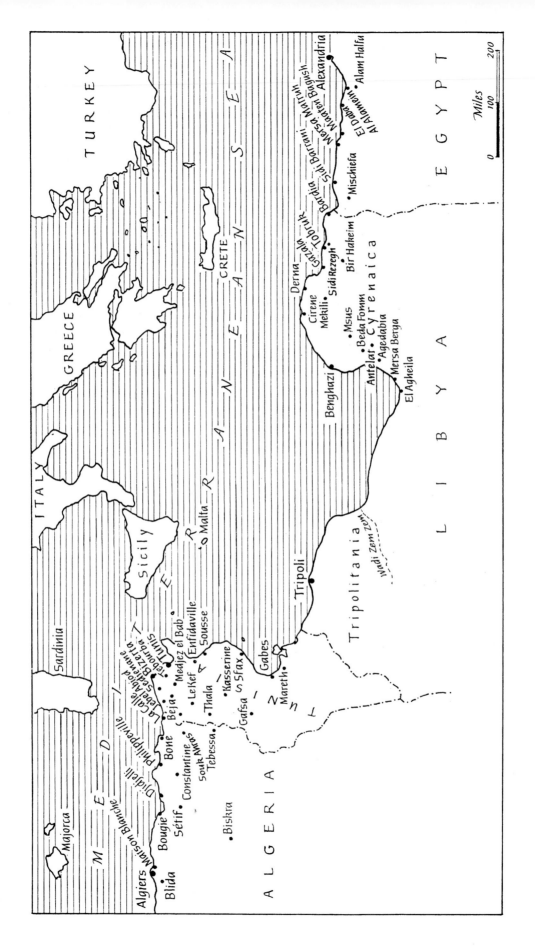

sea raids, parachute attacks or other methods. The dumps, for lack of a better name, were called field supply depots (FSDs) although they held much more than supplies. For a planned advance, available transport would be used to establish FSDs well forward. When the advance took place, second-line transport would switch to these FSDs and third-line begin to build up further depots.

On 4 August, 1940, the Italians had opened the Middle East campaign by driving the garrison out of Somalia, but in the west Marshal Graziani, the commander of the Italian forces in Cyrenaica, delayed his attack there until 13 September. By then the British, by risking a massive sea convoy, had doubled Wavell's forces and the Italian assault, aimed at Alexandria, ground to a halt at Sidi Barrani. General Wavell went over to the attack which went better than expected and 7th Armoured Division (by which title the Armoured Division (Egypt) was now known), made a rapid advance. On 9 December 4 Armoured Brigade cut the coast road west of Sidi Barrani, and then went on to do the same west of Bardia. This strained administrative resources almost to breaking point; 5 Company drove continuously night and day collecting captured petrol from Sidi Barrani and delivering it to the Brigade – a turnround of some 175 miles on the desert road

Several RASC companies were working with 4th Indian Division, 61 as a water-tank company and 231 for troop-carrying 16 Indian Brigade. The latter company was one of those locally raised, composed of Cypriots and Maltese, with British officers and NCOs. During the operations leading up to the capture of Sidi Barrani it was very hard hit, coming under heavy shell and machine-gun fire and being dive-bombed and machine-gunned from the air. Its casualties were fifteen other ranks killed and fourteen wounded, while fourteen vehicles were destroyed and fifty-four were damaged. The unit did well under fire and gave the infantry all the fire support it could. Two men were given the immediate award of the Military Medal in this action, Lance Corporal J Zoumberis, a Cypriot, for saving three men under fire and

The road to Sidi Barrani.

Lance Corporal W Sonnino, a Maltese, for courage and coolness under artillery fire and bombing. After the attack on Sidi Barrani 4th Indian Division was withdrawn and its place was taken by 6th Australian Division.

General Wavell was now able to send 4th Indian Division to help mount an offensive in Abyssinia and in January continued the advance into Tripolitania. Tobruk fell on 13 January, 1941, the Italians were again routed at Beda Fomm on 6 February and Wavell pushed forward to prepare a position at El Agheila.

The possibility now existed of pressing on to Tripoli, but this was abandoned. The rapid advances after December, 1940, of the Western Desert Force (later known as XIII Corps) from east of Sidi Barrani to the frontiers of Tripolitania, where it arrived in about two months, put an enormous strain on the logistic system. The Lines of Communication, with no suitable port readily available, now extended 1000 miles and were stretched to the limit. The main reason, however, was the decision to send a large force to Greece to help oppose an Axis invasion.

GREECE

In February, 1941, the British Government agreed to send a force from North Africa to support the Greeks, despite the protests of the hard-pressed Navy and Army commanders. The Government hoped to achieve a land victory in Greece to boost morale. The despatch of the main Commonwealth force began early on 7 March, 1941, and by early April amounted to Force HQ Australian Corps, HQ 2nd New Zealand Division, 6th Australian Division, 1st Armoured Brigade (from 2nd Armoured Division) plus supporting Arms and Services, amounting in all to about 58,000 men. Before the end of April 43,000 of this force had been driven out, many to be lost at sea or in Crete and the remainder dead or POW. On 21 April the Greek Army capitulated and the date of British evacuation, already fixed for 28 April, was advanced to 24/25 April.

For some months after the campaign odd parties of officers and men who had escaped capture made their way back by various 'underground' channels; several who remained hidden eventually joined British special service missions and operated very successfully. Lance Corporal S Rochberg, 285 Company, who helped with sabotage, and later escaped, was awarded the Distinguished Conduct Medal; the Military Medal went to Private E S Buhayar, who helped two officers to attack a strongly held German airfield and to destroy three aircraft. Other awards to RASC personnel included the DSO to Lieutenant Colonel H H E Geddes and the MC to 2nd Lieutenant P W Valentine.

CRETE

In November, 1940, a brigade had been sent to Crete. This garrison was greatly increased in April, 1941, by troops evacuated from Greece. In Crete the ad hoc defending force was seriously unbalanced in terms of logistic support and transport was at a premium throughout the subsequent operations. The detachment of 231 Company possessed thirty-six 3-ton lorries, and was later increased by forty-four personnel who had been in Greece. All other RASC detachments were similarly reinforced, so that a base supply depot and sufficient minor supply and petrol units to meet all requirements were made available. There was no lack of food and petrol and reserves were held in all sectors.

The main German attack on our positions in Crete began on 20 May with the air-landing of paratroops and glider-borne forces. Once more we had to evacuate and only half of the total Allied strength was able to escape. Not only did this attempted intervention severely hinder the campaign in North Africa but it had a disastrous effect on the RASC. Of the 138 officers, 4424 other ranks and 2700 vehicles, only 75 officers and 2076 other ranks eventually returned to Egypt, without their vehicles. The large Australian ASC and New Zealand ASC contingents suffered equally.

The Effect on the Campaign in Cyrenaica

Whatever the political advantages of intervening in Greece and Crete, militarily it was disastrous for the situation in North Africa. Wavell's hold on Cyrenaica was precarious, with his reduced force having to guard 1000 miles of lifeline with worn-out equipment. Despite the continuous build-up of reinforcements, most of these were far to the rear in reserve in Egypt. A second armoured division had arrived, only for the largest part to be redirected on to Greece. In the meantime the Germans, determined to bolster up their Italian allies, had been shipping in through Tripoli an armoured force for a counter-offensive. Under Lieutenant General Erwin Rommel this started at the end of March, 1941, with a surprise attack at El Agheila which was immediately successful.

On 31 March Rommel advanced from El Agheila, and the partially equipped elements of 2nd Armoured Division and 9th Australian Division, which had relieved the better equipped and very desert-worthy 7th Armoured and 6th Australian Divisions, were soon in full retreat, the former by the desert route to Mekili and the latter over the Jebel. Eventually the headquarters and remnants of units of 2nd Armoured Division surrendered at Mekili but the 9th Australian Division were able to withdraw to Tobruk and joined the garrison there to begin its historic defence, under the command of Major General Morshead of the Australian Army. By 11 April Rommel had encircled Tobruk's 30-mile-long perimeter, but the Australians repulsed all attempts by the Afrika Korps to capture the advanced base and harbour which Rommel needed for any further advance. By 4 May Rommel had pulled back his forces from attacking Tobruk after suffering heavy casualties, and, although without a land link, the garrison held out until relieved in December, 1941.

Throughout the siege of Tobruk the RASC, with some Australian Army Service Corps (AASC) assistance, ran supplies, transport, petrol and ammunition there, while many of the AASC of 9th Australian Division did gallant service as infantrymen. RASC units included 9 BSD, 48 DID, 115 Petrol Depot, a section of 1 Bulk Petroleum Storage Company, a field bakery section, 25 Motor Ambulance Company, 61 Company and 345 Company. Starting in mid-August 70th British Division and Indian, Polish and South African troops relieved 9th Australian Division using fast craft to ferry between Alexandria and the damaged harbour at Tobruk under cover of darkness. The RASC element of 70th Division was composed of 61, 145 and 419 Companies.

In June Wavell had tried to break the deadlock in the Western Desert and relieve Tobruk, but was repulsed, the British suffering the effects of the 88-mm gun for the first time. Fortunately, in failing to capture Tobruk Rommel had outrun his administrative resources and both sides were for the moment incapable of any great activity. This condition of stalemate continued throughout the summer of 1941.

In mid-August, 1941, it was agreed that Auchinleck, C-in-C in India, would change places with Wavell, but before giving up his command in the Middle East Wavell launched two new campaigns in Iraq and Syria.

IRAQ

When the lawful government of Iraq was overthrown in a *coup d'état* in March, 1941, by Rashid Ali and his faction the only British forces in the country were the RAF units at Shaiba, a few miles from Basra, and at Habbaniya. These were maintained from India via the Persian Gulf. German agents had been relentlessly spreading propaganda against the Allies, and the rebels soon showed their real intention. On 16 April they despatched an infantry brigade with artillery and tanks to the plateau overlooking the RAF cantonment at Habbaniya, and on 2 May bombarded the airfield.

On the same day an airlift was started, using Valentia aircraft of 31 Squadron RAF, to move the 1st Battalion King's Own Royal Regiment, the only British troops immediately available, from Karachi via Basra to Habbaniya. Thanks to the prompt action of the British Ambassador, an Indian Infantry brigade bound for Malaya had already been diverted to Basra and a second brigade also from India was on its way.

Action had also been taken to draw on 1 Cavalry Division then in Palestine and to assemble a force which was to secure the communications across the desert to Habbaniya, relieve the beleaguered RAF station and then strike at the rebels and restore the situation around Baghdad. Units, which were horsed, had to be quickly mechanized for the purpose, but by the evening of 13 May 'Kingcol', a column made up of headquarters 4 Cavalry Brigade, the Household Cavalry Regiment, a company of infantry and some artillery, engineers and signals, with 51 and 552 Companies RASC, were assembled at the H4 station on the oil pipeline. The remainder of the force, which included the divisional headquarters and their CRASC headquarters and 543 Company, was to follow, to open up the long new line of communication which was to stretch from the Haifa base to Habbaniya. On the morning of 14 May 'Kingcol', with 1800 men and 500 vehicles, of which 300 were of the RASC, reached Rutba which had been cleared of its rebel garrison the day before by the Arab Legion. This was followed by further feeble attacks by the rebel forces, but the situation in Iraq was quickly restored.

After the rebellion had been dealt with, two brigades of 50th (Northumbrian) Division moved into the Kirkuk/Mosul area and the RASC, 522 and 524 Companies, had a very difficult support task in extreme winter conditions. They were without winter clothing and equipment, in bivouacs, and had no anti-freeze for vehicle cooling systems. When the Zab River flooded resupply was by improvised rafting.

SYRIA 1941

The revolt was assisted by the Vichy French in Syria who had been allowing German aircraft the use of Syrian airfields. Syria could not be allowed to remain as a potential threat to the British position and in May, 1941, it was decided to bring the country under British control.

The General Staff plan provided for the invasion of Syria with a force consisting of 21 and 25 Australian Brigade Groups, 5 Indian Infantry Brigade Group, with certain Free French forces in Palestine and that part of the 1st Cavalry Division 'Habforce' which had completed its task at Habbaniya and Baghdad. The Australian brigades had their own second line, and 4 and 5 British Reserve MT Companies (50 and 97 Companies RASC) provided their troop-carrying vehicles, 4 Reserve MT Company (50) was re-equipped with diesel-engined buses and Ford V8 scout cars, which latter vehicles, with a Lewis gun mounting, were used as defence vehicles. 'Habforce' had 552 Company (late Cavalry Divisional Supply Column), 3 Reserve MT Company (51) and 543 Company RASC. Active operations began on 8 June and, after a spirited resistance, the Vichy forces asked for an armistice on 11 July.

The maintenance system was similar to that adopted in the Western Desert and Greece. Field supply depots were stocked with all commodities as far forward as was safe operationally. The narrow gauge railway from Haifa via Semakh to Damascus and farther north had a limited capacity. Its use beyond Damascus could not be relied on, as it was subject to interruption from demolition by hostile retreating forces. Up to three days' rations and petrol were held in first-line transport. Ammunition dumps seldom exceeded two first-line refills. Water was limited to one gallon per head per day and was, on the eastern flank, obtained from local wells.

EAST AFRICA

In Kenya the autumn of 1940 had been spent building up and training the force as troops arrived from East and West Africa, Rhodesia and South Africa. Although no RASC unit served on the mainland of East Africa during the war, there was not a single unit of the East African Army Service Corps (EAASC) from 1941 onwards that did not contain a high proportion of RASC officers and other ranks.

A great strain was placed on the supply system. By the end of January, 1941, the feeding strength reached 122,000, comprising a heterogeneous collection of races which required six main and numerous subsidiary ration scales.

The War Office had undertaken to reinforce the EAASC with drafts of RASC officers and other ranks. Shipment was promised of 5,000 4-ton lorries, including some of workshop, stores and breakdown vehicles, over a period of six months. About 3,000 lorries and many smaller vehicles were bought through local agents. These would make possible the formation of fifteen new reserve MT companies and three more infantry brigade group companies. However, after the arrival of the first 1,500 lorries, Middle East claimed the remainder, and this loss caused a shortage throughout the campaign and the dearth of MT spares continued.

Until November, 1940, petrol was controlled by the staff, through ADS (Petrol), of the King's African Rifles, which was unsatisfactory from the ST point of view and arrangements were therefore made for this service to become the responsibility of the DDST in Kenya. In addition to the oil companies' bulk storage, a reserve stock of nearly 8,000,000 gallons of packed petrol was built up just before the advance. In the event of the source of supply from the Middle East, Persia and Iraq being cut off, 9,000,000 gallons were held in Durban, representing about three months' supply, of which one-third was packed ready for immediate despatch.

By December Lieutenant General Sir Alan Cunningham, with his Force, was able to start aggressive raiding and on 24 January, 1941, he crossed the border and forced the line of the Juba on 16 February into Somaliland. So far as the supply and transport services were concerned, their enthusiasm and loyalty were unbounded, which evoked the finest praise that can be given to any Logistic Corps, when General Cunningham, on saying farewell to the East African Command, spoke these tense and significant words, 'You boast you are a service – and, by God, you are!'

As General Cunningham's Force moved forward he was able to shorten his difficult lines of communication by using the ports of Kismayu and Mogadishu before swinging north west along the good Italian roads. The pursuit to Jigjiga was achieved in an astonishing seventeen days for the 744 miles. Moving into the mountains, Cunningham's Sappers overcame demolition barriers to enable the advancing forces to reach Addis Ababa by 6 April and on 16 April, at Amba Alagi, he connected with General Platt's Division moving south from Keren. Here the British finished the active campaign by capturing the Duke of Aosta and the last remaining significant body of Italian troops. General Cunningham and many of his troops now moved up to join the Western Desert Campaign

Immense administrative problems, involving the services, especially supplies and transport, still remained in the evacuation of the forces now freed for service in Egypt and in the organization of the maintenance of the forces left to occupy the former enemy territory.

THE WESTERN DESERT

After five comparatively quiet months of preparation the British desert army in Egypt, now called the 8th Army, under General Cunningham fresh from his success in Abyssinia, opened a new campaign for the reconquest of Cyrenaica. This period had been of great value to the RASC in building up its strength and in training for desert work the third-line companies which were now coming forward in satisfactory numbers.

Moreover, two most important events occurred which were to influence the operation of the Corps in all theatres for the rest of the war. These were, firstly, the formation of the Field Maintenance Centre and, secondly, the provision of RASC column headquarters for command of third-line transport.

The Field Maintenance Centre (FMC) grew out of the FSDs, whose formation has been already outlined. What had become evident during the advance to the Tripolitanian frontier became even clearer during the summer of 1941; the FSD had become a focus of all maintenance and evacuation traffic behind division and had, therefore, come to stay as part of the administrative machine. No longer could the RASC captain commanding the DID control this centre and perform his own duties as well. An FSD was not merely an RASC organization, but a small formation dealing with every aspect of administration, including such diverse elements as NAAFI and prisoners of war. To meet the situation a small headquarters named a 'Field Maintenance Centre' was evolved. Although not an RASC responsibility, the first trial FMC was formed by HQ 30 Company RASC, all of whose platoons happened to be temporarily detached.

The column headquarters were something quite new both to the DDsST of the Corps who were to control them and to the Lieutenant Colonels in command. For forthcoming operations, four column headquarters were allotted to 30 Corps and one to 13 Corps. It should be mentioned that in October Desert Force Headquarters had been replaced by HQ 8th Army and Force HQ had reverted once more to 13

Corps. The first DDST Eighth Army was Brigadier W d'A Collings. Brigadier F S Clover took over in November, 1941, and Brigadier H A Kelsall rather more than a year after that.

As the FMCs were three days' turn-round from railhead and the third-line transport was barely sufficient to meet requirements, no vehicles could be held at FMCs under load and commodities had either to be accepted or returned – and it took a strong-minded man to send a load back all that way. Scales and load tables had been carefully worked out, but inevitably there were over-estimates as well as under-estimates. Rations and water were simple. Petrol was in such demand that the infamous 4-gallon flimsies scarcely had time to leak. However, because of the large percentage of new or practically new vehicles in units, the normal six per cent lubricants against petrol proved much too generous and some types of ammunition were not being discharged at intensive rates.

On 18 November, 1941, General Cunningham launched 30 Corps at Sidi Rezegh, but things did not go according to plan and after 10 days with little to show for intense fighting, the Commander in Chief Middle East, General Sir Claude Auchinleck, replaced Cunningham with Lieutenant General Ritchie as commander of the 8th Army. The dogged fighting continued, Tobruk was relieved, Benghazi captured and our forces advanced well towards El Agheila. On 2 December Rommel, having overstretched his logistic capabilities, lost his nerve and ordered a retreat, falling back to El Agheila, which he reached on 10 January, 1942.

Loading precious food supplies on to trucks during the retreat from Libya.

Ritchie decided to maintain his forward dispositions while he built up troops and supplies for an offensive. Piling up dumps, he guarded them with all troops available. However, Rommel was not deterred for long, mounting troops in every available vehicle, he reverted to blitzkrieg methods and on 21 January, 1942, struck back from El Agheila only 11 days after arriving there. Ritchie was taken by surprise, and, with the Army off balance and overstretched, it was quickly driven back to Gazala. The second Libyan offensive had ended like the first in failure, with Rommel capturing valuable stocks of petrol and stores, and cutting off some of our forces in the Benghazi area. Despite the confusion and destruction, Richie, however, managed to stabilize the 8th Army into a solid front in the area south of Gazala. Here the Army stayed until Rommel started his great effort to drive the British out of Egypt a few months later. The rapid advance from Tobruk to the frontier, and subsequent rapid withdrawal when once again Rommel counter-attacked, gave rise to much troop-carrying, and RASC vehicles were involved in many scattered fights.

The weather and the condition of Benghazi placed out of question any material assistance from that port, so that maintenance was on a six days' turn-round across the desert from Tobruk to FMC at Msus, sixty miles south-east of Benghazi, all available transport being concentrated on this task. The twenty or more GT companies employed on these runs worked with almost complete regularity, with a turn-round of up to 400 miles and they never failed to deliver the daily quota of essential supplies of all sorts, proving once again that RASC transport could operate in the desert, running for continuous periods with reliable results, provided that the mileages were not above sixty a day. This allowed time for meals, rest and maintenance, and could not be exceeded, except for brief periods, without a risk of breakdown.

During December, 1941, 1st Armoured Division had joined 8th Army. Its RASC companies were 10 (22 Armoured Brigade), 925 (2 Armoured Brigade), 903 (Support Group) and 910 (Divisional Troops). The two third-line companies, 911 and 918, became GT units. Early in January the division was facing the Germans in

A tank being recovered by a tank transporter crew.

their El Agheila position, much as the ill-fated 2nd Armoured Division had been nearly a year before. To make up for the absence of an FMC at Agedabia, a link had to be found from 13 Corps' slender transport resources, working forward sixty miles from Msus; then 10 Company took over and delivered to the second line twenty-five miles farther on and it was still forty miles to delivery point.

In February, 1942, with the new threat from Rommel, now a Field Marshal, the part of 50th Division in Iraq was hastily moved to the Gazala Line and this involved a very long and testing journey by road and desert for the Divisional RASC, equipped as they were with old wooden-bodied vehicles taken over from 5th Indian Division prior to it going to Iraq.

Tank transporters were now at work in the forward area, though as yet only in small numbers. There was one company (144) and an independent section. The company moved both 7th and 1st Armoured Divisions forward and then delivered reinforcement tanks from Tobruk to Msus and later to Antelat, 230 miles across the desert. On arrival at delivery point, the transporters would be used for operational moves to be sent back to fetch up tanks from Mischiefa or even Mersa Matruh. On the return trips the company always asked for loads of 'dead' tanks for evacuation, but at that time the organization for the recovery of tank casualties was not fully developed and the unit had enough to do without going round the desert looking for them.

During the withdrawal Captain W M Nichol of 144 Company, with twenty-one Tank Transporters, was ordered to recover as many tanks as possible. In spite of interference from enemy armoured fighting vehicles and artillery, he succeeded in recovering twelve tanks and crews. For this action he was awarded the DSO.

The Retreat to the Alamein Line

All thoughts were now directed towards preparations of a new offensive and a new swing of the pendulum in the right direction, from which it was hoped that there would be no return. However, Rommel was ready first and on 27 May, 1942, launched his attack on Bir Hakeim and other key points along the 42-mile front between Bir Hakeim and Gazala. Rommel failed to take Bir Hakeim but switched his concentration on other points of the British line and breached it in two places. Returning to Bir Hakeim, he forced its evacuation and, having secured his flank, swung once more on the main line, throwing the centre into disarray. Against the odds, magnificent fighting by the South Africans and 50th Division foiled Rommel's trap, allowing the British to fall back in order. Lieutenant Colonel S T Divers, CRASC 50th Division, was awarded the Distinguished Service Order for his part in keeping the RASC support effective during the retreat from the Gazala Line. Rommel now had Tobruk, although once more cut off, as a threat to his lines of communication, and he had to waste time and effort in reducing it. When it fell on 19 June, 1942, some 2000 RASC all ranks were among those captured. Ritchie continued his retreat back to Egypt, reaching Mersa Matruh on 25 June. After a sharp rearguard action there by the New Zealanders, the withdrawal continued to the prepared lines at El Alamein, 110 miles further back, where General Auchinleck had decided to make his stand. In August General Auchinleck was transferred back to India as Commander-in-Chief and replaced by General Harold Alexander, while Lieutenant General Bernard Montgomery succeeded General Ritchie in command of the 8th Army.

Composite Rations at a Supply Point.

An Ammunition Point.

With the 8th Army, 1943. Supplies of packed petrol moving forward.

The Battle of Alam Halfa

Now followed a particularly busy period for the RASC. Many companies in all echelons were in a battered condition after a long retreat and many months of previous campaigning in the desert. This called for re-equipping and reorganization. 8th Army was built up of a great variety of formations from all parts of the Empire and indeed outside it – all on different ration scales – Australians, New Zealanders, South Africans, Indian Army, Greeks and Free French.

This process of reorganization and training was carried out with a general feeling of suppressed tension and expectation, but with growing confidence. That Rommel would attack, everybody knew, but the Army Commander, now General Montgomery, had prophesied the lines on which this attack would occur and how it would be met. His prophecy proved to be accurate. On 30 August Rommel attacked at Alam Halfa. Against the carefully planned defensive positions and the subsequent vigorous counter-attack he was repulsed. He had shot his bolt and the second phase of El Alamein began with the British building up for their offensive. The Corps had responsibility for a great number of vehicles and stores well forward and camouflage took a high priority,. There were many artillery reinforcements and ammunition of all types had to be dumped in gun positions for the opening bombardment of the enemy's Alamein Line of defences. This bombardment was to be on a massive scale and most of the dumping had to be done at night. A further interesting undertaking was the siting of reserves for the armour, which were to be drawn on after the breakthrough had been accomplished. It was necessary that these reserves should be well forward so that the second line of the armoured division should not have long and difficult return journeys to the area behind the Alamein Line.

The Battle of El Alamein

The battle of El Alamein opened at 2130 hours on 23 October, 1942, and after ten days of strenuous fighting the German divisions were put to flight and most of the Italians surrendered. Flexibility of operation was crucial. For example the infantry element of 151 Brigade of 50th Division during the Alamein battle moved from under command its own divisional headquarters in turn to 2nd New Zealand Division, 9th Australian Division and 30 Corps reserve. The RASC second-line support, a detachment of 524 Company, had to make the changes, support the battle and keep the second-line stocks topped up, and all of this without radio communications. It speaks highly for the training of the RASC MT units of all echelons that 30 Corps was able to advance with such rapidity in pursuit of the Germans and without any administrative hitch to the area of Mersa Brega, a distance of nearly 800 kilometres from El Alamein and 400 from Tobruk. This was all the more significant since for some units, and indeed formations, it was their first experience of a 'desert gallop', and even 7th Armoured Division found themselves breaking new ground. It was during this advance that Lieutenant Colonel H J Gilman, CRASC 7th Armoured Division, gained an immediate award of the Distinguished Service Order. Tobruk was, of course, opened without delay, and a start was made at feverish speed to build up stocks. A prerequisite to any future advance on Tripoli was the formation of an advanced base considerably further west than Tobruk. Benghazi was the obvious location. With great effort the port and docks were gradually got into working order and, simultaneously with Tobruk, the stocks in

Casualty evacuation by motor ambulance.

Benghazi began to mount steadily, coming in by both sea and land. Luck was not with us, however, and by the middle of this build-up an unprecedented storm destroyed the harbour mole, while ships broke their anchorage and bounced about like corks.

El Agheila

By 12 November General Montgomery had thrown the Axis forces out of Egypt with massive losses. He continued his pursuit, but was held up for fifteen days by a rearguard action at El Agheila. When sufficient stocks had been built up, the attack on the Agheila position was launched with the New Zealand Division doing their first wide left hook. It was eminently successful and once more the Afrika Korps was in retreat with the 8th Army in full pursuit. The achievements of all Corps transport units from the divisional second line back along the lines of communication towards the advance base were beyond praise. At each pause they were called upon to redouble their efforts to build up stocks in the minimum of time for the next advance. This could not have been achieved without the determination of the individual driver not to be 'out of the hunt'. It was largely this urge in the individual which was responsible for the high standard of vehicle maintenance. Each driver 'nursed' his vehicle, and the development of individual improvisations was quite remarkable.

Wadi Zem Zem

The next pause came in the area of Buerat on the Wadi Zem Zem, now a distance of 300 kilometres from Benghazi and 950 from the far distant point of El Alamein. A big goal was in sight – Tripoli – and everybody knew it, not the least the RASC driver. But the terrain was changing. The coast line was more developed, and it was obvious from the map that units would be unable, as in the past, to leave the coast road at will for the wide open spaces of the desert. To the south of Tripoli lay foothills passable only by road and track. These new features called for careful study and planning by all RASC transport units, and particularly by the divisional second line.

The well-developed maintenance drill established between Army and Corps staffs made certain that if the expected distance of the forward move did not warrant a new army base corps FMC stocks were maintained at a minimum level. This meant that when the advance did take place stocks were already partly consumed, leaving no great transport problem. When a new army base was envisaged the FMC was built up as far as time permitted. In the event the army roadhead for the final attack on Tripoli was located at Nofilia, 350 miles to the east.

Tripoli and the build-up for the next phase

The capture of Tripoli ended another phase of the campaign. The main tasks for the moment were the reorganizing and re-equipping of the army, the opening up of Tripoli as a port and the establishment of yet another army base. This re-equipping presented many a problem. The distance from the great Middle East base of the Delta was considerable. Maintenance by road was out of the question. Supply by sea was limited by the number of craft available and by the port facilities of the already bombed Tripoli. The wear and tear of the RASC vehicles in all echelons in the advance from El Alamein was very great, so a repair organization was set up at various civil factories in Tripoli to which all RASC workshops contributed personnel and equipment. Most of these same vehicles eventually completed the African campaign and some went on to Sicily!

The Mareth Line

The attempt to pierce the line between the sea and the road on the northern flank failed in spite of the tremendous efforts of the gallant 50th Division. As at El Alamein, this attack on a strongly defended position provided the ambulance drivers with the opportunity to distinguish themselves. Drivers G Houghton, S Crompton and S Francis all won the Military Medal. It once more fell to the lot of 2nd New Zealand Division to carrying out another and possibly their most difficult 'left hook' in a wide sweep through the difficult mountainous terrain south of the main position. The Division, supported by additional armour under the command of General B C Freyberg, moved south followed by 'Crump's Private Army', the New Zealand Division ASC under its CRNZASC Lieutenant Colonel S H Crump, which was reinforced by additional RASC companies. They carried four days' maintenance for the force. The intensity of the Mareth battle caused some ammunition supply problems which at one stage necessitated, for example, the Brigade RASC Officer (BRASCO) of 151 Brigade guiding RASC vehicles, containing 3-inch mortar ammunition, from the AP direct to the infantry battalion areas. After much hard fighting the New Zealanders reached the rear of the Mareth Line, the Germans pulled out and the Force once again resumed maintenance from the normal lines of communication along the north coast.

The Final Stages

With the fall of the Mareth Line the back of the campaign was broken as far as the 8th Army was concerned. The advance continued via Sfax and Sousse up to the mountains in the Enfidaville area. Again the lines of communications grew longer and longer, and were now based on Tripoli. Once more the MT companies were strained to the limit, but the old and well-used vehicles, most of which had started from Alamein, stood up to it and kept going.

Thus ended a long, trying and finally victorious campaign throughout which the RASC driver had played a not only decisive but determined and at times gallant part. The next act for which most of the veteran desert units were to plan was the invasion of Sicily. To one and all at the time it appeared a tremendous undertaking, and so it undoubtedly was. But the 8th Army had many advantages: all the MT units were trained and battle-worthy; divisions knew what they would want; staffs knew each other and everyone was full of confidence.

The Air Arm

From the battle of El Alamein onwards one of the greatest contrasts to the previous periods of the campaign was the situation in the air. Superiority had gradually been wrested from the enemy, with obvious advantages to the RASC transport units. They were subject to occasional bombing and low-level sneak raids, but that solitary ribbon road along the north coast was no longer a death trap.

During these latter stages of the campaign a high degree of co-operation was developed between the fighter wings and squadrons and the RASC. The Desert Air Force provided fighter squadrons operating far behind the enemy lines. To obtain the

142

range it was necessary that these fighter squadrons should be based as far forward as possible. The solution lay in the maintenance of these squadrons being made a Corps responsibility. A Corps Troops RASC liaison officer was attached to the RAF and a firm friendship was formed between members of the two services.

THE BUILD-UP OF GHQ MIDDLE EAST AND EXPANSION AND TASKS 1941-1943

GHQ Middle East, which had been formed at the outbreak of the war, was to see a tremendous expansion of its responsibilities and countries of operation in these years. They grew from the early operations in North-East Africa – Sudan, Eritrea, Somaliland, Abyssinia and in the Egyptian Western Desert and Cyrenaica, to responsibilities in 1941 for the provisioning of Malta, quickly followed by the operations in Iraq and Syria the same year. Additionally, in January, 1942, the 10th Army in Persia and Iraq passed from the control of GHQ India to GHQ Middle East. For the Corps, expansion of the ST Directorate and the resources which it controlled was essential to meet the ever-widening and diverse tasks required of it.

At first the Directorate consisted of two branches only, supplies and transport, but in 1940 a POL branch was added, as the increasing importance of petrol supply in operations soon became all too apparent. A local resources branch was also formed, which, by exploiting various sources of supply within the countries of the Middle East, helped to save shipping and to provide fresh supplies for the forces. It was also found essential to have a planning branch to manage the organization, formation and disbandment of all types of RASC units, including questions of war establishments and the RASC manpower ceiling.

Supplies

There were more than thirty different ration scales in force to meet particular needs. The British field service scale applied, with modifications, to among others, Americans, Belgians, French, Ceylonese, Greeks, Jews, Maltese, Mauritians, Poles, Czechs, Yugoslavs, South African Union Defence Force (European, Cape-coloured and Indian), Seychellois and Trans-Jordan Frontier Force. Then there were the scales for Indian troops (Hindu and Muslim), the Sudan Defence Force, troops from French and Belgian Africa, Ethiopians and so on. There were also special scales for the women's services, operational air crews, prisoners of war and internees, and for a variety of animals. In the early days as in the first battle of Libya numbers of POW far exceeded estimates and in certain cases there was also the civilian population in occupied areas. The RASC also assumed responsibility for the provision of common user commodities for the Royal Navy in the Mediterranean, including many items from local resources.

The exploitation of local resources, which began in quite a small way in 1940, gradually assumed large proportions and it is estimated that in the year ending March, 1943, over a million tons of shipping were saved by this means. Perhaps the most important of these schemes was the growing, in Egypt and Syria, of potatoes, without which the British soldier does not consider himself properly fed.

There was insufficient cold storage at the beginning of the war to meet war-time needs and a large cold storage project was carried through between 1940 and 1943.

This met the requirements of the theatre but the fluidity of the operations and the lack of rail communications made the supply of all fresh food a tremendous problem for our troops fighting in the Western Desert. The aim was always to provide fresh food, particularly meat and bread, to as many troops as possible, as far forward as possible.

During the seige of Tobruk in 1941 it was difficult to supply fresh food, which is more important than ever in siege conditions. Bread was produced throughout by the existing bakery, and dehydrated vegetables were sent up. The normal ration was modified to meet the special conditions and such items as chocolate and lime juice were introduced.

Malta convoys were sent at irregular intervals and at moonless periods, when fast shipping became available. Each time elaborate cover plans were made in an attempt to disguise the destination of these vessels from enemy agents at the port. Every ship was loaded 'balanced' , so that ships which arrived safely carried a complete ration. Until command of the Mediterranean was regained, however, no convoy ever reached Malta without serious losses.

POL

Throughout the war, for several reasons, the provision and distribution of petroleum products raised greater problems in the Middle East than did any other forms of RASC supply. First, as mentioned earlier, there was no separate RASC POL organization and no petroleum units existed at the start of the war. Secondly, there had been little pre-war planning, and provision had not been made for a large-scale organization for the storage, transportation and distribution of petroleum products, particularly overseas. Thirdly, the flimsy 4-gallon (non-returnable) can, designed as the sole means of distribution in the field, proved not stout enough for use in war and the effect is discussed later.

However, starting from zero, a large and efficient organization was built up, which never failed to despatch from the base the quantities required to meet the needs of the field forces. The oil firms in the Middle East placed their technical skill, their advice and material resources unreservedly at the disposal of the Army. Without their help there might well have been a failure to meet operational needs in 1940/41.

As in the case of supplies, lack of men at the outset was the main problem. No petroleum units arrived from Britain until August, 1940, and later many units were excluded from convoys, giving place to fighting troops. But gradually an organization was built up and by August, 1941, there were in operation more than a dozen petroleum companies and some bulk petroleum transport companies.

The main source of supply of petrol was by tanker from Abadan. There was an initial lack of tankage for the reception of bulk stocks until the completion of the Jebel Dave scheme, but the tanks for holding MT fuel were installed and filled during 1940 and those for aviation fuel were ready by mid-1941. When orthodox equipment started coming through from Britain, bulk distribution became the normal system of supply in all base areas, where well over nine-tenths of petroleum was issued by this means.

This did not, of course, solve the more important problems of distribution in the field, where the flimsy remained the normal means. Its one merit was easy local production. While adequate for normal commercial purposes in peace-time, the flimsy was not strong enough to stand up to constant handling and rough usage under war conditions. At times losses reached thirty per cent or even more. As consumption increased, many additional can-making plants became available from Abadan and elsewhere, but even so all plants had to be worked day and night in continuous shifts in order to meet demands. At the peak, the factories were producing at the rate of more than four million cans a month.

In 1941, when the German forces arrived in the Western Desert, they brought with them a petrol container superior to any other type, the existence of which was known in the United Kingdom before the war. This was the German 20-litre steel welded can, which became known universally as the 'jerrican' which was produced eventually for all Allied Armies. Luckily, large numbers of jerricans fell into British hands from time to time and were invaluable in supplementing our supplies of flimsies.

Transport

In the early days local Cypriots and Maltese had been trained as drivers and two MT companies were formed, with British officers and NCOs. One of these companies was employed in the desert in the first battle of Libya. Many companies were formed composed of Palestinian Jews, and these did good work in an operational role. Later Palestinian Arabs were trained as drivers and were formed into companies with British cadres for work at the base. The Sudan Defence Force provided many GT companies with Sudanese drivers, and two of these units took part in the final advance in the desert. Ceylon was found to be a good source of supply of personnel and a RASC officer was sent there from the Middle East to take charge of a training school. In consequence, several Sinhalese companies took their part in operations. A company was formed in Mauritius and later worked in the desert. East African and later West African transport companies also arrived. Dominion forces provided third line transport and there were Australian and New Zealand companies and also many RIASC companies. After the arrival of the South African Division, third line units were made available manned by the Cape Coloured Corps.

Horse transport companies were formed with civilian native drivers and were usefully and economically employed for short hauls in base installations, on dock clearances, road and airfield construction and on the building of the Haifa-Beirut railway. Eight of these companies were formed and released a considerable amount of mechanical transport.

When the retreat in the summer of 1942 had been stopped on the Alamein line, many RASC units with the 8th Army had sustained heavy losses of vehicles and nearly all the remaining vehicles required overhaul or replacement after hard service in the desert. The problem was to provide the greatest amount of transport for the offensive in October and the target agreed upon with the 8th Army for third line transport was the equivalent of thirty-six 3-ton GT companies, nine water tank companies, six tank transporter companies and one bulk petrol transport company. The refitting of existing companies and the provision of new ones was a heavy task and required much ingenuity, but by 23 October, when the battle began, the target had been reached and seven other GT companies were also available in GHQ reserve. Later, as the advance progressed, yet another three and a half companies were made available from the Delta by depleting base transport, and a Sudan Defence Force GT company was moved to the 8th Army from the Sudan via the oasis of Kufra. A further 10-ton company was produced from the personnel of a tank transporter company for which no transporters were available. This improvisation was only made possible by the arrival of more 10-tonners from overseas. Even so, it was necessary for 8th Army to retain second-line transport from divisions withdrawn from the battle, raising the number of third-line companies to fifty-eight. This was just sufficient to maintain the 8th Army to Tripoli, which was entered on 23 January, 1943.

Middle East depended largely on the United States for its supply of vehicles and, as a rule, units from Britain arrived with men and headquarters vehicles only and were equipped with load carriers on arrival. In 1940 4,000 Chevrolets (with an agreed proportion of spare parts) were shipped from the United States to the Middle East to equip RASC and Dominion ASC transport units. Requirements of RASC vehicles for 1941 were estimated at 14,000, but deliveries did not reach this figure and the deficiency was made worse by heavy losses in Greece. Up to May, 1941, vehicles were received assembled and this was heavy on shipping space, but on arrival of assembly plants vehicles came in cased and 'completely knocked down'. Initially the assembly was an RASC responsibility but the newly formed REME took over in October, 1942.

At an early stage the problem of water carriage became acute. During peace training this had been met, in first line, by 150-gallon water tank vehicles augmented by a supply of $12\frac{1}{2}$-gallon camel tanks (the beautiful copper tanks which were carried one on each side of a baggage camel) and by the use of local 'birs' or tanks. But the water tank vehicles were few in number and stood up poorly to desert conditions. The supply of $12\frac{1}{2}$-gallon tanks was also unequal to the demand, and it was feared that, if the 'birs' were used too extensively, the local Arabs would be deprived of water for themselves and their camels.

For the purpose of bulk distribution in third line, 350-gallon water cistern lorries could be used but they were not suitable for second line because of the delay in decanting which would arise at the replenishing point. The 2-gallon petrol can therefore had to be used in second line with the resultant heavy requirement of steel plate.

As time went on the Royal Engineers, by magnificent work, brought water by pipe from Alexandria far into the desert beyond Matruh, but in 1940, except for a source being developed at Maaten Bagush, which was of use to rearward troops, the main source of supply was from an old Roman system at Mersa Matruh supplemented by distillation.

NORTH-WEST AFRICA AND THE MEDITERRANEAN

Operation TORCH

The agreement made in the summer of 1942, between the British and the United States Governments to invade French North Africa was one of the most far-reaching decisions of the war. If the assault was successful and the immediate objective, the seizure of the enemy's airfields in Tunisia, could be fully exploited, there was a good hope that the enemy could be driven out of Morocco, Algeria and Tunisia. The Mediterranean sea routes could then be opened up for Allied shipping and firm bases established for the invasion of Sicily and Italy.

It was a serious decision because French reactions to an incursion into their territories were unpredictable, and so much depended on whether the move of our forces could be conducted over many thousands of miles by sea without the enemy learning of our intentions.

The outlined plan for the operation, which was finally confirmed in September, was that three separate task forces, the western, central and eastern, would land at Casablanca, Oran and Algiers respectively, the eastern force being predominantly British. The British Force and the 34th United States Division were to be mounted in Britain, and the western and central forces in America. The specific role of the British force, after landing and capturing Algiers, was to strike at once for Tunis which lay over 500 kilometres to the east.

The British Force was to land at Algiers only. There were other ports nearer Tunis, notably Bougie, Philippeville, Bone and Bizerta, but they were closer to the enemy's airfields in Sicily, and the Royal Navy had not enough escort ships to guarantee the passage of convoys with safety. The best that could be done was to provide for a floating reserve, to land at Bougie, if all went well at Algiers. The British task force was named the First Army and placed under the command of Lieutenant General Kenneth Anderson. It was to consist of two corps, 5 and 9 Corps, with the 1st, 46th and 78th Infantry Divisions, the 4th (Mixed) Division and the 6th Armoured Division and 25 Tank Brigade. The American element in the force consisted of two combat teams.

Brigadier H M Hinde, who was appointed DDST First Army, had many new problems to consider in planning the RASC organization required for this expeditionary force. The supply organization had been remodelled since the days of the BEF and the RASC petroleum organization was also a post-1939 development. Water transport units would be wanted for work along the North African coastline, and provision had to be made for a pack transport organization which could be expanded at short notice by using local animals and locally enrolled muleteers.

The ultimate RASC order of battle which was decided upon included seventy transport units of various kinds in addition to the usual complement of companies which formed part of formations. There were about thirty supply units and about the same number of petroleum units, which included sufficient units for four separate bases. It was hoped that all three ports east of Algiers – Bone, Bougie and Philippeville – could be used for that purpose as soon as the striking force had cleared Algiers and air superiority in Algeria and Tunisia had been achieved.

The Plan

The role of the eastern force was to land on the beaches on either side of Algiers, whereupon 11 Brigade (78th Division) was to seize the airfield at Blida, south of Algiers, and cut the main road leading to the south. 39 Combat Team and some US Rangers were to make for Maison Blanche airfield, a few miles to the east of Algiers, and then march on the city; while 168 Combat Team was to attack Algiers from the west. Parties of Commandos and Rangers had the task of seizing Algiers harbour to prevent sabotage.

As immediate land-based fighter cover was vital to the plan: five squadrons of the RAF were to fly from Gibraltar to Maison Blanche a few hours after the assault began, and one squadron of Spitfires was then to fly on to Djidjelli.

Once Algiers was in our hands, a striking force of 78th Division, less a brigade, the 17/21st Lancers Armoured Regimental Group (BLADEFORCE), and two battalions of paratroops were to be employed in the dash for Tunis.

The administrative plan for the initial period was largely based on the hope that the striking force could be maintained through the three ports which lay to the east of Algiers, thereby obviating the need for transport for the long carry from Algiers over the main inland road and rail systems, which led over the hills and mountains through Setif and Constantine to Tunis.

At 0100 hours on 8 November, 1942, Operation TORCH forces landed on the beaches around Algiers in the face of negligible opposition. The RASC contribution to the assault force was detachments of second-line transport for 11 and 36 Brigades, a DID, a small POL depot, a transport platoon for each of the two beach maintenance groups, and six other transport platoons, which included tippers, ambulances and one platoon for Bailey bridging. A DID, petroleum depot and one platoon of transport were also included in the floating reserve for the development of the port of Bougie.

The second convoy, which was due to arrive on the fourth day (D plus 3), was to carry a transport detachment for the striking force, BLADEFORCE, a troop-carrying company, a tank transporter company, four other platoons of various kinds, and five platoons of general transport. The rest of the second-line transport for 78th and 6th Armoured Divisions and their third-line companies were not due until the third convoy, which was scheduled to arrive from D plus 14 to D plus 18.

All troops in the force were to be provided with a 48-hour mess tin ration and thereafter with the new 14-man composite ration until base supply depots could be established and the normal field service ration taken into use. Petroleum was to be provided in packed form, although it was hoped that the existing bulk storage facilities could be developed within a short time to allow can-filling to be done on the spot and distribution in bulk where possible.

The Corps Tasks after landing

Three days after the landings a 'cease fire' was broadcast throughout all French territory in North Africa.

The first task for the RASC was to get supplies of aviation fuel to the airfields at Maison Blanche and Djidjelli, as it was vital to refuel the fighters, which were arriving from Gibraltar. One platoon of tippers, specially loaded with 100 octane fuel, was put ashore in landing craft over the beaches, and made straight for Maison Blanche with an escort which cleared up some minor opposition. Later in the day one of the two petroleum depots which had been landed with the beach maintenance parties was able to begin passing more supplies to the airfield.

Twelve hours after landing the DIDs were in operation, issuing composite rations and water, and reconnaissance parties were at work on the sites which had been selected for the base depots due to arrive on the second and third convoys. Complete information was obtained about the petroleum facilities in the country thanks to the help of the local Shell Company headquarters, and tentative arrangements were made to take over 60,000 tons of bulk storage and to plan for their cleaning and rehabilitation before bulk supplies arrived.

As soon as the two DIDs at Algiers could be relieved one was sent forward to Bone. Its convoy was heavily attacked on the way, but it was in action again issuing supplies on D plus 7. The other reached Philippeville on D plus 12 but it also had an adventuresome journey owing to accidents on the mountain roads. The DID and petrol depot landed at Bougie were also in action by the same date.

For the first six weeks of the campaign the Army was fed entirely on composite rations and transport was extremely restricted. The arrival from home of the normal field service ration commodities coincided with the first issue of fresh bread, although only one of the mobile bakeries which had been landed at that time was accompanied by its equipment, a deficiency made good by taking over French bakeries. The hope that fresh meat could be obtained locally was not fulfilled, as, contrary to intelligence reports, the supposed vast sheep population of North Africa proved to be illusory. During these early weeks the only transport available for the force was the second-line companies which at their assault scale amounted to little more than a platoon each, although they were gradually brought up to strength as further convoys arrived. At one time two brigade companies, designed to maintain 9000 men, were working to support 20,000.

Essential water transport support for the TORCH operation force was provided by 247 Motor Boat Company RASC. Ten vessels were shipped in the convoys from the United Kingdom, and, as soon as a base had been established at Algiers, steps were taken to acquire further craft locally. Some were requisitioned, and some were 'prize' vessels. These varied from 40-50 ft launches to 400-ton schooners and coastal craft. The wide variety of engines – diesel, petrol and even steam – gave the workshop officer many a sleepless night, and it says much for the spirit and training of the men, both deck and engine room staff, that they could take on the operation of these craft. In addition to the usual duties which its small launches performed in all the harbours from Algiers to Tunis, the coastal cargo-carrying vessels of the company did valuable work.

Additional craft were urgently required by 247 Company at Algiers and two drifters, the 100 ft *Ocean Breeze* and the 92 ft *Boy Phillip*, were refitted in Britain for despatch. The two vessels were delivered safely to the motorboat company and two more trawlers, the *Lucien Gougy* and *Elizabeth Therese*, were delivered soon afterwards. The 500-ton RASC vessel *Malplaquet*, with its civilian crew, was also diverted from the United Kingdom for duty in the Mediterranean.

By 24 November the Allied forces striking eastwards were within sixteen miles of Tunis and then a series of adverse circumstances brought our attacks to a standstill. The Axis forces were being heavily reinforced from Sicily and Sardinia, more than fifty troop-carrying aircraft arriving daily. Our small force of fighters had the almost impossible task of covering the forward area and communications which stretched back towards Algiers for over 400 miles. The Germans' main bases in Sicily were only half an hour's flying time distant. The spearheads of our advance were over 100 miles ahead of the nearest railhead and second line transport. In addition heavy and continuous rain began to fall, turning the roads into mud-covered slippery tracks with boggy verges.

Medjez el Bab was held by 1 Guards Brigade, the third brigade of 78th Division which, on its arrival in North Africa, was immediately carried forward by a GT company to occupy that keypoint. In the meantime a Franco-American force had seized the important pass, Faid, on the Kasserine-Sfax road. It was at Tebourba that Lance Corporal G Bowyer, of 563 Company, won the Military Medal when in charge of a section of water-tank lorries. He organized the defence of his section and supplied units under heavy fire. Sergeant B Philips, who was one of the RASC clerks at 36 Brigade Headquarters, was awarded a Military Medal for helping to remove a blazing ammunition lorry and extricating a wounded man from an adjoining burning building.

Due to winter weather conditions, movements off the roads became practically impossible and airfields were becoming unusable. The enemy had been able to mass about 40,000 men to oppose us and so a postponement of operations towards Tunis became inevitable.

The Initial Petroleum Organization

During the initial drive to Tunis by the striking force the amount of POL required was relatively small and supply was at first maintained in the form of packed stocks forwarded by road and rail and by sea from Algiers and the other base ports. On the other hand the fuel which was in four-gallon flimsies was already showing the effect of much handling and it was not uncommon to see lorries leaving for the front with petrol streaming from them. The principal task of the petroleum organization was to build up and develop supply in bulk so that the amount of road and rail transport required for packed stocks could be reduced.

As sections of the bulk storage companies began to arrive, existing civil storage for about 8,000,000 gallons was taken over at Algiers and 6,000,000 at Bone. There was a great deal to be done before the tanks could be filled, but with the aid of the civil oil companies, who collaborated in the work in every possible way, and of the French authorities, tanks and pipes were cleaned and put into order and the installations made ready for use. At the same time active steps were taken to develop the system for distribution in bulk.

The first bulk supplies to be handled into the main installations came by rail from Oran in the American sector and in railcars which had been filled by a short sea line fitted up from a torpedoed and beached ship. The first ocean tanker to discharge its cargo arrived on the twenty-second day after the first landing and small coastal tankers were obtained for carrying supplies to Bone.

Building up the Supply Organization

By the end of January, 1943, the strength in the theatre was nearly 250,000, which included 45,000 Americans. Only about 87,000 were in the army area forward of the railheads, the remainder, about 160,000, being engaged at the bases or on the lines of communication.

Although the general stock position often lagged behind the official levels, reserves and working stocks were generally adequate by the end of February. The chief problem which exercised the ADSTs and base provision officers (now called CsRASC supplies) was how to provide sufficient units and accommodation to handle the stocks which were pouring into the theatre. Supply had outrun the pace at which supply units were being sent from England, so that any type of unit which could be spared, such as field butcheries and the composite platoons for anti-aircraft artillery regiments, had to be diverted to operate DIDs.

The Second Phase – On the Defensive

The Axis force knew that it was only a matter of time before the Allies would develop their full power and therefore they needed to mount an offensive as soon as weather conditions would allow. The storm broke on 14 February, when the enemy struck in force against the widely dispersed United States 1st Armoured Division, inflicting heavy losses in men, tanks and equipment on the Americans as they withdrew. By nightfall of 17 February the enemy had captured Kasserine and Gafsa and was infiltrating through the Kasserine pass. Then, breaking through the pass, two armoured columns were directed on Tebessa and Thala, and for some days the situation was critical. It was at Thala that 4 Company, RASC, was ordered to stand by to fight as infantry in support of the Royal Leicestershire Regiment. Allied reinforcements were already on their way, but the situation became so serious that regiments and even companies had to be committed to the battle as they arrived. These reinforcements were, however, able to turn the tide, and a week later the enemy had withdrawn to almost his original starting line while the attacks made on the British in the north gained little success, although the fate of Beja at one time was in the balance.

Almost all types of units took a share in carrying out special tasks. One GT company detailed to convey an American combat team from Biskra to the battle position at Thala covered 497 miles of difficult terrain in forty-one hours. Tank transporters performed some quite spectacular deeds, such as the ferrying forward of the Churchill tanks of 25 Tank Brigade, when drivers had little or no rest for several weeks. Their work is instanced by the award of the British Empire Medal to Driver R Roberts who drove his 70-ton load for fourteen days with never more than a few hours' rest. On some of the mountain passes the speed of these vehicles was reduced to about four miles an hour, and the general road conditions were so bad and the expenditure in tyres so high that replacement stocks became depleted.

The individual gallantry of many members of the ambulance units, operating over a huge area, was recognized by various awards. Company Sergeant Major Rowe of 16 Parachute Field Ambulance received a Military Medal for a series of actions which included maintaining a supply of water to an advance dressing station, the rescue of a badly damaged ambulance and repairing another vehicle under heavy fire. Driver R Willshire was awarded a Military Medal for driving under fire over a road which was known to be heavily mined, and Driver A Stern of 88 Company was given a similar award for gallantry in bringing wounded to safety.

Meanwhile 46th Division had arrived from home. The divisional RASC consisted of 519, 520, 521 and 570 Companies. Of these the first three had originally belonged to 49th Division. The first company to go forward was 520 Company, which remained in the Sedjenane area until April. Two of its soldiers soon earned immediate awards of the Military Medal: Lance Corporal R Butler for continuing to issue ammunition until the site of his dump became untenable after being machine-gunned and bombed, and Driver P Murphy, who delivered supplies to an isolated unit, although his route was under direct fire from snipers and his lorry was hit three times.

The other unit of 46th Divisional RASC came forward in February to the Beja area. It was there that Driver A A Lawton, a motorcyclist attached to 128 Brigade HQ, earned a Military Medal for reconnoitring the enemy's movements and that Driver W J Hughes of 183 Field Ambulance was awarded the Military Medal for collecting casualties under heavy fire.

Developing the Petroleum Organization

The gradual transfer of American troops from the central and western to the eastern forces considerably increased the rate of petrol consumption in the First Army area until, in February, about 1,000 tons a day were being used. A petroleum section was set up at AFHQ to co-ordinate supply, with the rather wide charter of 'controlling and co-ordinating all problems of petroleum products brought to and stored in and distributed to naval, military, air force and civil agencies'. Although each army was to preserve its responsibility for the intake and storage of its supplies, the planning and development of all main pipelines became an integrated responsibility of the new petroleum section. Ocean-going tankers began to arrive at Algiers and RASC personnel responsible for discharging them soon became experts at the task.

For the final offensive half the total fuel required was to be held at the bases and half divided over an advanced base and the forward area, a grand total of 180,000 tons. The first step was to stock an advanced depot at El Guerrah about eighteen miles south of Constantine. The depot was staffed by a base petrol filling centre early in March, and stocks were built up at a rate of about 800 tons a week, brought forward in the main from Philippeville by road.

The build-up in the army area was completed by 20 April, much of it in the form of barrelled stocks which were distributed over the axis La Calle Souk el Arba Le Kef and at Souk Ahras. The organization on the lines of communication had made great progress and work was done at great speed. Ocean tanker storage was installed at Philippeville by an American unit, in the form of thirteen bolted tanks of 1,000 tons capacity each, in a matter of six weeks, while the 'stringing' together of two 4-inch pipelines and the setting down of pumping stations went on simultaneously.

The same American unit then left for Bone, where it erected four 500-ton tanks for the British base and at the same time completed a line sixty-nine miles long to the British pipehead at Souk el Arba. This work was finished in a month, after which the line was handed over in working order to the British engineer unit detailed to maintain it.

Transit of petroleum by road and rail was also developed with the aid of 8,000-gallon railcars imported from America and additional rolling stock obtained from Morocco.

While the enemy was making his last efforts, it was decided that the two converging Allied armies, the 8th Army and the 1st Army, with Americans and French, should operate under the unified command of Headquarters 18 Army Group, with General Alexander at its head. The army group had two clear-cut tasks: to reorganize the 1st Army into British, American and French formations to simplify administration and to build up reserves for the future combined efforts of the unified command.

On 20/21 March the 8th Army began its famous onslaught on the Mareth Line which forced the enemy under the Italian Marshal Messe to fall back to the Wadi Akarit. The month closed with 46th Division and French troops of the Corps d'Afrique pushing back the enemy in the north to beyond Jebel Abiod.

The Axis forces were given no time to rest and were forced to withdraw into their predetermined stronghold behind the hills running north from Enfidaville to Bizerta and so reduced their frontage to about 100 miles. A redistribution of our forces became necessary. The American 2 Corps was switched to the north, and the 1st Army was joined by 1 Armoured Division from 8th Army. Railheads were moved forward, and forward reserves were replenished in preparation for the first onslaught against the enemy's new positions, which took place on the night of 19/20 April, when the 8th Army attacked and captured Enfidaville.

The final great offensive began on 5 May with 5 Corps gaining the hills which dominated the Tunis plain and 9 Corps advancing in bright starlight on the morning of 6 May. By the afternoon their infantry had gained their objective, and 6th and 7th Armoured Divisions (the latter from the 8th Army), swept forward and entered Tunis on 7 May. On the same day the American 2 Corps and Free French Corps d'Afrique gained Bizerta.

By 9 May the Axis force in the northern pocket had been completely mopped up, while the divisions of the 1st Army then turned to assist in the encirclement of the

Pack Mules moving into the hills of North-West Africa, March, 1943.

southern force, which they achieved between 11-13 May. The Axis force had been cast out of Africa, and the Mediterranean was open to our ships. The way was clear for the final phase in the invasion of Europe from the south.

The RASC could look back on the seven-month campaign with considerable satisfaction. The British North Africa force had been well fed. The 6000-odd RASC 'task' vehicles had covered 35,000,000 miles between them. The vehicles of one bulk petrol company averaged over 15,000 miles and one vehicle held a record of 30,000 miles. The record of the companies' workshop sections was one to be proud of, as during the whole campaign only 418 task vehicles had to be evacuated. The petroleum organization had shown what good planning and the use of modern equipment could achieve. Pack transport had established its reputation which was to be excelled later in Italy. RASC casualties were 103 officers and men killed and 146 wounded.

Malta GC

During the critical months of the war the island of Malta had held out against axis air attack from both Libya and Sicily. Playing an active part in supporting the garrison was the RASC water transport section which had long been established there, the vessels in pre-war days carrying out the normal administrative and target-towing details. Civilian officers of the W D Fleet were sent out from home on special agreements; a few officers and all ratings were engaged locally. The craft were controlled and administered by the local RASC Officer-in-Charge Transport, Valetta being the main station.

The difficulties and dangers under which the vessels operated during the years of seige need little emphasis. By 1943, of the six craft there, one had been lost, one sunk (but subsequently salved and recommissioned), and the remaining four had suffered damage of one sort or another, all from enemy air attacks. In one engagement the Master of Vessel HMV *Lord Plumer*, Mr E V Elson, was awarded the OBE for his gallantry

THE OUTBREAK OF WAR IN SOUTH EAST ASIA AND LOSS OF HONG KONG AND SINGAPORE

When war broke out in Europe Japan was already in possession of parts of China as well as Korea, Manchuria and Formosa. Japan's expansionist policy in the Far East and continued aggression in China caused a trade embargo to be imposed by the United States and by mid 1941 this was beginning to bite. In July Japanese troops were sent deep into French Indo China and the important naval base in Camranh Bay secured. On 7 December, 1941 without warning, Japanese planes attacked the American base at Pearl Harbor and on the next day Japan declared war, launching attacks on British Malaya, both from the sea and overland through Thailand, and on the British colony of Hong Kong from positions on mainland China. Following up the establishment of secure bases in northern Malaya and southern Thailand advance parties of Japanese troops crossed the Kra Isthmus on 15 December, 1941, and advanced towards southern Burma.

Hong Kong

There were only 207 RASC personnel in the Hong Kong Garrison who provided the small MT Company (No 12), a supply depot and a bakery, and the usual barrack and transport office. There were a few WD vessels, most of their crews being locally enrolled Chinese, and there was also one Indian Army unit, the Hong Kong Mule Corps, equipped with small (AT) carts and pack equipment.

Reserves of supplies were only enough for two months and did not include provision for the Indian troops or local forces, or forage for the animals, while petrol was held by contractors. The transport scheme for mobilization called for drivers for 600 vehicles. There were insufficient RASC and local European drivers, and Chinese had to be hired by the day.

In mid-1940 the RASC took over all food stocks from NAAFI, a full war-time ration was introduced, reserves were brought for the local forces, and stocks of petrol were amassed. Supply stores, petrol dumps, goat stables, a flour mill, a bakery, and other installations, were built or improvised in the country on the east, west and south sides of the island, away from the vulnerable north. By the middle of 1941, four and a half months' reserve of supplies was in hand, nearly all the new storehouses had been erected, the stocks were dispersed, 3000 goats were in their stables, and the mill was working.

The Japanese Attack

The Japanese attack on the mainland began on 8 December, 1941, and soon overran the forward defended localities. The evacuation of the mainland was ordered on 11 December. During this period, RASC water transport had been operating at full scale to evacuate the military hospital from Kowloon and move NAAFI stores from their mainland godowns to the island.

Supply was maintained, though in the face of many difficulties. The CRASC (Lieutenant Colonel K T Andrewes Levinge), had to cope with broken communications, constant changes in order and in the location of units, desertion of Chinese drivers with their lorries, and the employment of his few technical and supply men on operational duties.

The final withdrawal from the mainland on the night of 12 December was at once followed by a peremptory Japanese demand for the surrender of the Colony. This was categorically refused. The island was now open to direct fire from all directions. By 19 December troops had been in action for eleven days without respite, but the small garrison, although hopelessly outnumbered, continued the struggle for six more days. For his bravery throughout the defence Major A J Dewar RASC was awarded the DSO.

Malaya

Before the war the RASC had a distinctly limited liability – a liability restricted to maintaining a small garrison in Singapore, an Indian battalion stationed at Taiping (in Perak) and a small body of troops which garrisoned the island of Penang. In 1939 the overall strength increased to about 10,000.

Transport available to the Officer Commanding RASC was 52 MT Company and a small water transport detachment, the only British members of the company being one officer and twelve other ranks. The twenty-five lorries and ten ambulances in the unit were manned by Malay civilians. The water detachment also had Malay crews, but was supervised by a British Master Mariner. There was a plan for providing civil road transport in the event of war, but not for the RASC. A total of 500 civil vehicles were to be impressed to bring units' first-line transport up to their higher scale, but the movement of their stores and equipment to their places of deployment was to be effected by hired civilian vehicles. The RASC was forced to rely entirely for the additional MT companies required on locally raised companies backed by small cadres of British officers and NCOs. Political considerations debarred the use of the vast Chinese population of the Peninsula, so the field of recruiting was confined to Malays and local Indians. The bar on Chinese was not lifted until just before the outbreak of hostilities.

The Officer Commanding RASC was more favoured in his supply arrangements, as a new supply depot, modern bakery and small cold storage had just been completed at Alexandra in Singapore, the bakery being a model of its kind. The supplies commitment was mainly a British one, as a large part of the food eaten by the few Indian troops and the Malay Regiment was indigenous to the country and was procured from contractors who were also nominally responsible for holding reserves and for providing all fresh vegetables and fruit.

There were no special military reserves of petrol because units normally refuelled their vehicles from kerb-side pumps installed in their barracks, which were kept refilled under contract by the civil oil companies.

By 1941 reinforcements comprised British, Australian, Indian and Gurkha troops. The RASC had the primary responsibility for the supply and transport services in the command. By September, 1941, the DDST had become responsible for supplying, in round figures, 55,000 Indian, 21,000 British, 15,000 Dominion troops, 3,400 Malayan enlistments and 1,400 Chinese, each of which had their different ration scales.

The growing strength of the command and increased transport commitments entailed new plans being made to build up reserves of food and petrol and the setting up of a supply organization to cover the whole of the Malayan Peninsula and the expansion of the arrangements for providing transport.

On 1 December a state of emergency was declared and the volunteer forces were mobilized. Six days later Japanese convoys of warships and transports were reported to be steaming westward, and on 8 December the enemy began to land elements of the 25th Japanese Division at Singora and Patani in southern Thailand and at Kota Bharu. At the same time the remainder of the division plus supporting troops moved overland through Thailand from Indo-China.

Inadequate Defences

So far as the RASC were concerned, preparations for the supply and transport services were almost complete when hostilities broke out. On the west coast stocks of food and petrol for 11th Indian Division were held as far north as Alor Star, backed by twenty days at Sungei Patani, while a month's supply had been built up at Bukit Mertajam, to be drawn on if Plan MATADOR (advance into Thailand) was put into effect. 9th Division was also well provided for, since twenty days' stock had been laid down at Kuala Krai for replenishing Kota Bharu, and twenty days at Jerantut for replenishing the small garrison at Kuantan on the east. To enable the garrison at Penang to hold out if by-passed by an enemy advance, six months' supplies had been laid down there. Various other stocks were held at other centres such as Ipoh and Seremban on the main Western Railway, the main forward reserves being stored in the advanced base supply and petrol depots at Kuala Lumpur.

In view of the enemy's rapid advance, all stocks from Kuala Krai were successfully back-loaded to Singapore by rail, and the evacuation of the Indian brigade afforded the first opportunity for the RASC (Malay) transport to prove its worth. If there were any doubts about these untried men, they were soon dispelled as the platoon of 43 Company, which was the last to leave, earned the commendation of the divisional commander for its work.

The island of Penang was soon left uncovered from the mainland, and, as heavy air attacks had completely disorganized the civil services, it was decided to evacuate the garrison by sea to Singapore. Efforts were made to destroy the stocks of food and petrol, and the MT Platoon, after its arrival at Singapore, was sent forward to join 43 Company at Kuala Lumpur.

During the withdrawal the stocks at Taiping had to be abandoned, although partially destroyed, but the supply depot at Ipoh was successfully evacuated, two days' rations being left to be collected by 11th Division on its retreat to the south. The two MT companies at Ipoh were withdrawn to Kuala Lumpur. They were a useful reinforcement as there was a great deal to be done in the way of forming dumps behind the Perak and the Slim Rivers (many of which had to be retrieved soon after), carrying RE demolition parties and collecting and backloading of stores of all kinds as part of the scorched earth policy, on which directions had been received from the home Government in mid-December. This policy involved the denial of anything in the wake of the withdrawing army that might be useful to an enemy.

The Battle of Singapore

The withdrawal of the British Forces from the mainland to the island of Singapore was completed by the morning of 31 January, 1942, when a gap was then blown in the only road link – the causeway – with Johore. The future battle ground was not, as popularly supposed, a fortress; it was only a large area of land and water with permanent defences designed to meet seaborne attacks and with reasonably good anti-aircraft defences. The total area in which our forces were concentrated only measured about thirty-seven miles by fifteen, but even so there were insufficient troops to man the perimeter in any strength, and there were no tanks to support them. There was a huge Asiatic population, and even if the facilities had been available, there was an almost insuperable civil defence problem to be overcome.

The general resources behind the RASC when the offensive against the island began were more than adequate. But the fighting strength of all formations had been sadly depleted. Orders were given early in February to 18 Divisional RASC, the only RASC organization with a full strength of British ranks, to form two companies for an infantry role. The order was carried out quickly by drawing on about three-fifths of the available strength of 54 and 55 Companies and men from two field ambulances and within twenty-four hours the two RASC 'infantry' companies were on their way to take their place in the future battle zone. These two units did well and took their full share of the fighting that followed, and, although they suffered many casualties, they came out of the fight with high morale – a morale which they maintained during three and a half long years as prisoners of war, in spite of being separated from their officers.

On 8 February the enemy crossed the Straits of Johore. The continued pressure of the enemy towards Bukit Timah directly menaced the main reserves of both food and petrol which were held in that area. On 10 February a large quantity of petrol was destroyed, on 11 February the main petrol depot fell into enemy hands, and the same evening the base supply depot was captured.

The depth of the enemy's advance into the island had led to the loss of all our main reserves of food and petrol, and of the many subsidiary stocks at various points which were already in enemy hands. As late as 10 February the DDST, who had been in constant touch with the Civil Food Controller, confirmed that supply ships were still being unloaded by improvised labour, as most of the regular civilian labour had deserted their tasks. There was still a large quantity of meat in the Government cold storage at Orchard Road and there were sufficient other commodities to have provided a modified form of ration if the general conditions had allowed. There was some petrol remaining at a dump at Balestier Road formed from stock which had been backloaded from more forward dumps and from supplies obtained by draining the tanks of unwanted vehicles which had been directed there for the purpose, also in many civilian pumps.

On 15 February the Commander-in-Chief had no option but to order a cease fire. Capitulation followed and all officers and men passed into captivity.

BURMA – THE FIRST CAMPAIGNS

Leading elements of the Japanese 15th Army had crossed the Kra Isthmus on 15 December, 1941, and started advancing north through Thailand towards south Burma. On 20 January, 1942, at Moulmein they launched their main attack on the Anglo-Burmese forces comprising 17th Indian Division and a Burma division as part of their drive on Rangoon. Geographically Burma is a huge valley containing two rivers, the Irrawaddy and the Sittang. Crossing the valley from east to west some 600 miles north of Rangoon was the Burma Road linking China and India. This was vital to Allied strategy as the Americans believed that the Chinese would make a massive impact in the fight against Japan if their forces could be adequately supplied. In the autumn of 1941 the Army in Burma was gravely deficient in ancillary troops and services, the Burma Army Service Corps being still in its infancy. Our forces were driven back, in spite of the arrival of reinforcements. Apart from individual officers, the only RASC unit engaged in the retreat from Burma was 65 Company RASC, supporting 7th Armoured Brigade, which landed at Rangoon on 21 February, 1942.

An RASC officer in charge of the BSD at Mandalay had managed to move a large part of the stocks across the Irrawaddy and so ensured the supply of rations during the final withdrawal. This began with a race for the Chindwin crossing at Kalewa, 7th Armoured Brigade covering the retreat. The last place in the order of march was given to 65 Company, which therefore had to act as a rearguard, with some untrained Gurkhas attached; but when night came, contact with the enemy was lost. Rangoon was evacuated on 7 March, 1942. On 29 April the Japanese captured Lashio on the Burma Road, Mandalay on 30 April and by 12 May when the monsoon broke, the British and Indian troops were back over the Indian border and the enemy were within striking distance of India itself.

Air Despatch Introduced

In Burma law and order collapsed as the British and Indian troops withdrew, fighting between rival factions broke out and a general state of banditry prevailed. Large numbers of the local population decided to follow the British into India down the Hukawng Valley. Soon over 20,000 Burmese refugees were struggling through the Naga Hills along three tortuous roads towards Ledo in appalling conditions and without food. It was clear that large numbers would soon die of starvation and exposure unless more help could be provided quickly. On 9 May, 1942, a single RAF transport squadron, No 31, started dropping supplies to the refugees and retreating troops in the North. For this early attempt at air supply the RIASC provided the supplies and ground support on the airfield and quickly identifying the essential requirement of the hour, put together a small organization to improvise containers and supervise packing and loading. This, the first Air Despatch unit, was raised by Lieutenant Colonel A W Cawthorn and was based in Tinsukhia, drawing supplies from RIASC FSDs in Assam. On occasions RIASC soldiers flew on sorties to 'kick out' the bundles, but generally this tiring task was undertaken by the RAF aircrew wireless operator and gunner and anyone else from the crew that could be spared, frequently only the pilot remaining in the cockpit when over the dropping zone. By 31 July when the refugee operation ended 3,000 tons of supplies had been dropped but the Air Supply task for the Army and RAF was only just beginning.

For the time being the main opposition to the Japanese armies in the field was

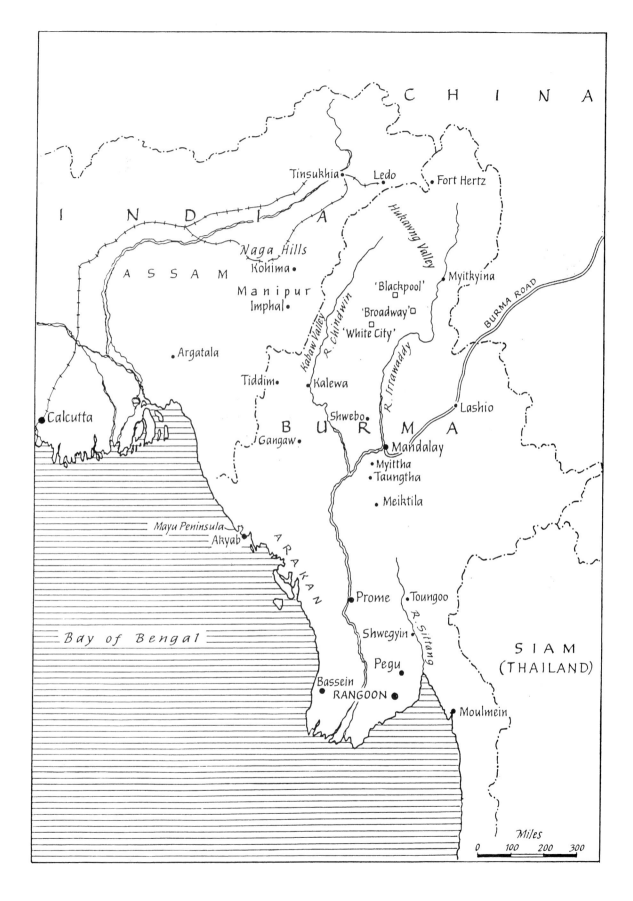

being provided by the Nationalist Chinese under Generalissimo Chiang Kai-shek, aided by the American General Joseph Stilwell ('Vinegar Joe'). With the Japanese astride the Burma Road the only way to support the Chinese with supplies and equipment was across the Eastern Himalayas in North Burma and this needed a new road into China and an air bridge to be established over the mountains, but any further advances north or east by the Japanese would cut the corridor and isolate the Chinese.

The British were now faced with the problems of maintaining the troops in their remote positions with hardly any land communications. In many cases there was no alternative to supply by air, but this too was made more difficult not only by the shortage of aircraft but by the poor location of available airfields which had not been sited with the defence of the North Burma border in mind. Throughout the summer and autumn of 1942 the isolated garrison of Fort Hertz, responsible for the Burma Road, was supplied almost totally by parachute, although two landings were made, primarily to evacuate casualties and refugees.

Kachin and Chin irregulars, patrols of 'V' Force and some Chinese units were also maintained entirely by Air Supply. V Force was an intelligence-gathering operation of European officers and RAF signallers, assisted by local tribesmen. Each officer, originally found from those with local knowledge, but eventually from others who had volunteered, had responsibility for 100-200 tribesmen covering several hundred square miles. Between May and December, 1942 over 1,000 tons were dropped to some of the most difficult DZs. One, little larger than a tennis court, was on the top of a cone-shaped hill and demanded pinpoint accuracy and perfect timing for each drop or the bundles would be lost irretrievably down the steep hill.

The Army and RAF now found themselves fully committed to Air Supply operations for which they were unprepared and ill-equipped. Despite the fact that air landing and supply dropping had been used frequently since Kut, nearly every lesson had to be learned all over again and improvisation, trial and error were once more the order of the day. Out of necessity came much practical experience. This was quickly put to good use and valuable work in developing and standardizing containers, equipment and parachutes was done by the Air Landing School, which had originally been set up at Willingdon Airport, New Delhi, in late 1941 to train parachutists. This work, and the parallel evolution of ground and air operating procedures, was carried out with the assistance of a RIASC Supply Company which looked after the purely Army aspects. The school soon moved to Chaklala where an offshoot, the Air Transport Development Centre, was set up, and in late 1942 the Army element was expanded to establish the Air Despatch Training Depot RIASC. By December, 1942, a formal organization for Air Supply Companies had been approved and the first unit formed up at Chaklala that month, pre-dating the first Composite Company RASC by six months and the first Air Despatch Company in the European Theatre by more than a year. Air Despatch companies were required to pack stores for air drop, transport them from depots to airfields, load and lash them in the aircraft and then provide despatch crews. Salvaged parachutes and equipment, expensive and always in short supply, had to be sorted and returned to RAF maintenance units. In addition the Air Despatch companies were to hold reserve stocks of all commodities likely to be needed, some ready-packed for dropping, and the necessary quantities of supply dropping equipment. On forward airfields they were also responsible for unloading incoming supplies and organizing their onward transportation to formation maintenance areas. In practice the enormous demands

1. The Royal Waggoners raised by Royal Warrant, 7 March 1794 *(Institution of the RCT(IRCT))*.

2. An Officer of the Royal Waggon Train, 1803 *(IRCT)*.

3. A Field Officer, a Subaltern and a Veterinary Officer of the Royal Waggon Train, 1822 - 1827. The Household Cavalry and the Royal Waggon Train were the first to allow their veterinary officers to adopt regimental dress *(IRCT)*.

IRCT

IRCT

4. The Royal Waggon Train moving a barge loaded with a Company of the 95th of Foot (the Rifle Brigade) on the Royal Military Canal, Hythe, 1809 *(H.J. Compton)*.

5. Private Brewster driving an ammunition waggon through the gates of Hougoumont Farm to supply the 3rd Guards during the Battle of Waterloo *(IRCT)*.

6. An artist's impression of the action at Azimghur during the Indian Mutiny when Farrier Michael Murphy and Private Samuel Morley of the 2nd Battalion Military Train each won the VC *(IRCT)*.

7. Left, Captain, Commissariat Staff Corps, 1859-69 *(IRCT)*.

8. Right, Assistant Commissary, Control Department, 1869-75 *(IRCT)*.

9. Painting of the *Braemar Castle*, sunk while trooping in the Aegean in 1916 *(IRCT)*.

10. A painting by Michael Turner, Guild of Aviation Artists, depicting York freighters at RAF Gatow, Berlin, in 1948 during the Berlin Air Lift *(Royal Air Force Club, London)*.

11. HM The Queen receiving the Keys of the City of Portsmouth from Lieutenant Colonel TC Street, the Commanding Officer of 20 Maritime Regiment, RCT, at the start of her official visit to that city in 1977 *(IRCT)*.

12. HM The Queen inspecting the Queen's Baggage Train which is provided by 20 Squadron RCT *(IRCT)*.

13. Crane Attachment Lorry Mounted (CALM) fitted to an 8-tonne Bedford TM; also a JCB 410 Rough Terrain Fork Lift Tractor (RT FLT) unloading ammunition *(IRCT)*.

14. RCT Port Operations – Marchwood Military Port *(R. Grevatte-Ball)*.

15. RCT Railway Operations in Germany *(IRCT)*.

16. The Berlin Military Train with the RCT Movement Control Train Staff. *(IRCT)*.

17. HRH Prince Philip, Duke of Edinburgh, inspecting the Royal Staff Cars at Buckingham Palace, accompanied by Major General VHJ Carpenter, CB MBE, the Representative Colonel Commandant RCT *(IRCT)*.

18. School children in BAOR boarding RCT school buses with MCTG drivers *(IRCT)*.

which came to be made on the Air Supply organization meant that the numbers of trained Air Despatch personnel were always insufficient and considerable numbers of untrained troops had to be used. Of necessity Air Despatchers found themselves mainly involved in supervising others. Indian Pioneer units were brought in to do much of the packing and additional personnel were drafted from British reinforcement camps. The comparatively simple despatch methods used on routine drops were entrusted to local volunteer 'kickers' of all arms under the critical eyes of the RAF aircrews.

Success and Failure

The second half of 1942 was a period of general consolidation in India and Burma. The British long-term aim was to recapture Burma while the Americans wished to reopen the Burma Road. To these joint ends much effort was put into improving the roads and railways and building much-needed airfields. Although the position in Burma after the initial retreat had been stabilized along the Indian border, General Wavell, as Commander-in-Chief India and overall Commander, realized that his forces – the Eastern Army as it was then known, under its GOC-in-C, Lieutenant General N M Irwin – were not yet in a position to launch a major offensive against the Japanese. However, some effort was needed at least to restore confidence and morale, and a limited operation down the Mayu Peninsula of the Arakan, with the aim of retaking the airfield at Akyab for future operations, was planned to start in December, 1942. At the same time Wavell had agreed to a raid into Burma, of brigade strength – the first Chindit operation – led by Brigadier Orde Wingate, with the aim of disrupting Japanese communications. The Chindit operations are discussed in later paragraphs.

This first Arakan campaign ended in failure, and by 11 May, 1943, the force was back where it started, a sad ending to a much-heralded offensive, and a setback for the morale of the whole Force on the Burma front. The actions of Wingate's force did much to offset the failure of the Arakan offensive, and was, although not a strategic success, a great boost to morale of both our troops on the ground and to all at home.

Command Reorganizations

At this stage in 1943 major changes were about to take place in the command structure of our forces in the Far East and the Commanders, which were to have a profound effect on the future success of our operations against the Japanese in Burma. Field Marshal Earl Wavell became Viceroy of India, and was succeeded by General Auchinleck as Commander-in-Chief India, but no longer to be Commander-in-Chief for the operations in Burma. South East Asia Command was formed (SEAC), with Admiral Lord Louis Mountbatten as Supreme Commander, General Sir George Giffard as Commander-in-Chief Allied Land Forces, and General Sir William Slim as GOC-in-Chief 14th Army, as the Eastern Army now became. The fight back was about to begin.

In the campaign against the Japanese on the eastern frontiers of India, and in Burma, the RASC were the subsidiary partners in the supply and transport services, as the theatre was the responsibility of GHQ India, which had its own Directorate of ST services performed by the Royal Indian Army Service Corps.

There was no great number of RASC in India and SEAC during the war. The largest groups were the RASC components of HQ 4 Corps, ie the ST staff, the staff

RASC DUKWs, amphibious 2½ ton trucks, carrying supplies on the River Chindwin in Burma.

clerks and some drivers. This formation had originally been sent to Persia, but it eventually arrived in India, and in May, 1942, it took over in Assam the organization for the reception of the retreating Burma Army and the defence of that frontier. Gradually the RASC officers in it were replaced by those of the Indian Army and were absorbed into the general pool of RASC/RIASC officers; but HQ 4 Corps, still retaining its RASC other ranks, was to see the campaign through to the end. A motor ambulance convoy (928) worked for over three years in East Bengal on casualty-clearing duties far behind the line, but it was specially valuable for work in connection with the evacuation of patients by air. A higher standard of driving was required for the specialized work with aircraft than could generally be found at this stage among the Indian drivers, most of the experienced ones being in the Middle East. At the end of 1942 two artillery companies, 92 (Northern Ireland) and 169, and 102 GT Company were used to form four mixed tank transporter companies, 553, 554, 589 and 590 Companies, RASC-mixed, because the headquarters and workshops were British, half the drivers British and half Indian.

A small but important RASC contingent was the cadre of some twenty all ranks sent out from the Amphibian Training Centre in England to organize the Indian

RASC DUKWs ferrying West African and Sikh troops across the River Chindwin in Burma.

Amphibian School at Cocanada on the east coast of India. The school was commanded by Lieutenant Colonel Bill Lucas RASC. There, several Indian transport companies learnt to handle the amphibious 2½ton trucks, known as DUKWs, and tracked amphibians. One of these units successfully effected the ship-to-shore transfer of supplies as XV Indian Corps worked its way down the coast of Arakan.

The Chindits

The only light on an otherwise dark horizon came from the northern end of the Burma front with the first Chindit operation. In February, 1942, Wavell had rescued Brigadier Orde Wingate from sick leave in England. Wavell had always believed that the myth of the Japanese soldier being invincible could be exploded by hard, aggressive action and, remembering Wingate's exploits in Abyssinia, he tasked him with organizing a force to undertake guerrilla operations behind the Japanese lines. Wingate was given 77 Indian Brigade which he used as the basis for two Long-Range Penetration Groups. These were to operate as a number of self-contained columns relying on mules for first-line transport and aircraft for resupply. On the night of 14 February, 1943, the two columns, with 3,200 men and 1,000 mules, crossed the Chindwin River; accompanying them were RAF liaison officers with radio equipment whose job it was to co-ordinate the air supply. This was to be mounted from Argartala as the main base, using a detachment of DC3s and Hudsons from 31 and 194 Squadrons RAF, with No 4 Air Despatch Company RIASC providing the army element.

The demanding nature of the undertaking was quickly brought home to the aircrews who had to locate with pin-point accuracy the tiny DZs in featureless jungle, often at night. When close to the location DZs would be marked by flares and smoke but then the drop had to be made with precision on to the smallest areas, too small to permit stick dropping. As many packs as possible were stacked in the open door of the aircraft and on the signal from the navigator were literally kicked out by every available crewman. Even so numerous circuits and dropping runs would be needed to complete the despatch, keeping the aircraft overhead half an hour or more, both risking the arrival of Japanese fighters and advertising the presence of the column. Altogether 300 tons of supplies were dropped in 178 sorties to the seven LRPG columns before they crossed back into India in mid-April, 1943. The force had marched nearly 1,000 miles and, although its campaign of disruption had succeeded in drawing off two enemy divisions for a while, it had suffered 30% casualties and lost most of its equipment. From a results point of view this first 'Chindit' operation proved to be of only limited strategic value, nevertheless it had shown what could be done, and the air supply operation which supported it, with over 80% of supplies dropped being recovered, was an outstanding success. The conclusion of the campaign in Burma will be described later but significant events were taking place meanwhile on the Home Front.

THE HOME BASE

The RASC hands over its Workshops

As a result of an investigation into the availability and services' usage of technical manpower by an Army Council Committee it was directed that RE workshops were to confine themselves to repair and maintenance of electrical and mechanical equipment, the RASC were to give up the provision, storage and issue of their own vehicles and spare parts, and the heavy repair of their vehicles, and the RAOC, while acquiring full responsibility for vehicle and spare part provision, storage and issue, were to give up the whole of their engineering side and to cease to be responsible for the repair of their own or other arms' equipment, from guns to bicycles. To bear this immense combined inspection and repair load for all arms, a new corps was to be formed, combining the technical elements of the RE, RASC and RAOC. This was to be called the Corps of Royal Electrical and Mechanical Engineers. For the present, the RAC, RA, RE and R SIGNALS would retain their technical personnel engaged on maintenance within their units, and the RASC would retain the men in their workshop platoons. As a second phase, when opportunity offered, the whole of the remaining technicians and their functions would pass to the new corps.

The Army Council adopted the report *in toto* and ordered its immediate implementation, in essence as from May, 1942, and in fact from 1 October, 1942, when the new repair corps would officially come into being, its initial make-up being about 1% ex RE, 4% ex RASC and 85% ex RAOC.

Plans for Return to the Offensive

Operationally, the first half of 1942 was still disastrous overseas, with the retreat of the 8th Army to the Alamein line, the loss of Hong Kong, Singapore and Malaya, and the overrunning of Burma, but at home preparations were in hand for launching two offensive enterprises, both entailing amphibious assaults. These were the minor operation for the snatching of Madagascar from Vichy French control, and the much larger and more ambitious plan for the invasion of North Africa, Operation TORCH.

The Corps was closely concerned with the new task of waterproofing vehicles for both these operations. The question of amphibious operations had been studied at the Combined Operations training centres in Scotland and, later, at a Combined Operations Experimental Establishment (COXE) which was set up at Westward Ho! in Devon. These were 'all arms' establishments, with strong RASC representation.

The period 1941-1943 saw the increasing use of the ATS to drive vehicles in transport units and VRD convoys at home and the emergence of the mixed station transport companies, manned by RASC and ATS drivers.

During this period, too, the strength of the Corps in tank transporter companies increased steadily to match our growing strength in armour. Most of these units were equipped with United States 'Diamond T' tractors and Rogers or Crane multi-wheeled trailers. The purchase of these tractors and of a quota of the trailers built in America was fortunately put through before the big switch of American production to meet the needs of the American Army was fully felt. The companies did excellent service, first in the Middle East and in North Africa, in which chapters their activities are fully described.

Barrack Services

Barrack Services was an organization found only in the British Army. In other armies the provision of quarters, furnishings, lighting, fuel, window cleaning and chimney cleaning were controlled and carried out by a variety of agencies. The co-ordinated service provided by the Corps was of particular value, for in providing proper arrangements for men to be housed, to have beds and bedding, and to be provided with heating, lighting and cooking facilities much was done to sustain the morale so vital to the fighting forces. Possibly the biggest single job of the Barrack Services was the provision of coal and coke for the forces in the United Kingdom and in operational theatres overseas. At home, as the war went on, the availability of solid fuel grew less and the demand increased. Supply diminished through falling output and lack of transport, due to bombing, non-repair of wagons, lack of staffs, and rail priority for troop movements and operational equipment. Demand was increased by the swelling production of armaments and, on the military side, by the needs of the growing British army at home and the large influx of American troops. By May, 1944, three and a half million troops, including well over a million Americans, were being supplied with fuel in the United Kingdom, requiring a yearly total of 2,500,000 tons. It was inevitable in the circumstances that at times reserves fell to low levels and rigid economy measures had to be applied.

PETROLEUM

Resources

The resources of petroleum which could be drawn upon were world-wide. Before the war Britain drew about 43 per cent of its supplies from the Caribbean area (Venezuela, Columbia and Trinidad), about 24 per cent from Persia and about 18 per cent from the United States. Fortunately, all these remained available to the Allies throughout the war. The maintenance of war supplies was thus primarily a matter of protecting the sea lanes and maintaining sufficient tanker tonnage in the face of continued and often heavy losses by enemy action.

The strategic importance of POL as a national resource meant that the War Office, through ST 2, continued to mastermind petroleum provision and supply from the Home Base, even though most active operations were outside Western Europe. By the end of the first phase of the operations in the Western Desert, in September, 1940, it was evident that the petrol supply arrangements would have to be greatly expanded. The pre-war scheme of providing exclusively military tankage of 15,000 tons in the foothills of Suez and on the border of the Great Bitter Lake was just completed. The scheme was a sound one, as the two separate tank farms were connected by pipeline and the intake of petrol, from ocean tankers, could be effected either at Suez or at Fanara. But the tankage was only sufficient for holding about fifty days' supply for a small force of three divisions. The scheme also provided for two plants for filling returnable containers but the principal means of distribution was the 4-gallon flimsy and the capacity of the tin-making and filling plants, at Suez and Alexandria, was only about 15,000 tins a day.

When the future situation was appraised in September, 1940, it was estimated that an additional 155,000 tons of tankage would be required, to provide for a sixty-day reserve for twenty-one divisions, and that extra filling plant would be needed for 76,000 tins a day. The general scheme for the 155,000 tons of tankage and filling plant was called the 'Reserve Storage Egypt' scheme. It was authorized by the Treasury in October and work began on the new filling plants and expanding the existing bulk storage installations at the end of the year. Supplies for the forces in the Western Desert and the Nile Delta was only one of the Middle East petroleum problems as the Command had also to cater for operations in East Africa, Iraq, Palestine and Syria, and for the maintenance of garrisons in Cyprus and on the Red Sea littoral. Each territory presented a different supply problem.

Petroleum Distribution and the Jerrican

Ample supplies of refined petroleum were available in the Middle East area. The whole territory was supplied from the output of crude oil in Iraq, central and southern Persia and to some extent from the Egyptian oilfields. The refineries at Haifa, Suez and Abadan provided petrol and derv. Aviation fuel was produced at the Abadan refinery. Early in 1942 the output from Abadan was 200,000 tons of 100 octane and 100,000 tons of 90 octane. It was doubled by the end of 1942 and a target of 800,000 tons had been set for a later date. The principal problem was storage and distribution in each of the widely separated areas where our forces operated. There was usually some bulk storage at the bigger towns in each territory but the distribution of civil supplies was mainly in 4-gallon tins which were in common use in these eastern regions.

At the end of 1941 there was a serious shortage of tin plate in the Middle East owing to the increasing demand and the non-arrival of shipments expected from America. An emergency demand for 10,000 tons of plate, followed by a second demand for a similar quantity, had to be made by the War Office on the Ministry of Supply whose stocks were low. There were, at that time, some twenty tin-making plants operating in the Middle East. Some were civil plants, some had been obtained from the USA, a few were ex-enemy ones and others had been purchased second-hand from India. More plants were on order from India, Australia and the USA. The combined output of all the plants in operation was in the region of 3,000,000 tins a month. A year later it rose to 4,300,000.

The Middle East Command had, some months before, recommended to the War Office that the German Jerrican should be adopted as a standard container, but a considerable interval of time elapsed before the pattern was accepted and put into full-scale production, a matter which has been much criticized. The production of jerricans started in 1942 and 1,000,000 had been despatched to Africa by the end of the campaign in 1943. In spite of the growing population of returnable jerricans built up between 1942 and 1943, and the capture of about 1,500,000 enemy cans, it was still necessary to use 4-gallon tins, to the extent of over 4,000,000 a month, to keep the forces maintained.

During the time when ST2 were engaged on the development of returnable containers, Operation TORCH had been put into action by the invasion of North Africa in November, 1942. The early maintenance of the force presented a considerable problem as 8,000,000 gallons of petrol had to be accumulated in the home depots for the purpose, and, for example, the shipments for the assault convoys took 126 train-loads of petrol for loading over 106 different ships. Initial supplies had to be in packed form, as, although the expedition was the first to have a complete petroleum organization with it, no reliance could be placed on utilizing bulk supply until local facilities had been reconnoitred, rehabilitated and supplemented.

Operation TORCH was the first joint Anglo-American large-scale expedition and, as petrol was a common user commodity, ST2's responsibility for supply eventually passed to an Allied organization set up by AFHQ when they were established in their new operational zone.

AIRBORNE FORCES

From almost every chapter of this book it emerges that the Corps was constantly faced with the need to solve new and unforeseen problems by adapting old and well tried principles. In few cases was adaptability stretched to such limits as in meeting the needs of the completely new airborne arm.

It was not until the middle of 1940 that the first few seeds of the airborne army were sown. In June of that year a handful of officers and men assembled at Ringway in Cheshire to offer themselves as experimental material for parachute development.

German parachutists in the Netherlands in 1940 had shocked the British out of a complacent attitude. The airborne arm was seen suddenly to be not only practicable, but powerful indeed, for a nation isolated on an island, it now seemed to the more perceptive to be a really essential factor in any plan for resuming the attack on the enemy's territory.

By early 1941 parachute battalions were being formed. They were soon to develop into brigades, which came together to form the nucleus of 1 Airborne Division in April, 1942. The importance of forming an airborne force was not realized until the effectiveness of such troops was demonstrated by the Germans in 1940. Shortly after Dunkirk it was decided, although in rather vague terms, to establish a 'parachute training centre'. The movement was given a much-needed boost by Winston Churchill who, by then Prime Minister, expressed his desire in a minute to the War Office that 'We ought to have a corps of at least 5,000 parachute troops' and asked the War Office to come up with a plan.

As a result the Central Landing School was set up at Ringway Airport near Manchester in late June, 1940, and, despite an almost total lack of parachutes, equipment and aircraft, training started almost immediately. With the decision to create a considerable airborne force and the formation of a training centre which could also act as a focus for planning and tactical development, the ultimate provision of an adequate logistic support system together with the necessary specialized equipment was more or less assured. It would be, though, over two years and outside the 'main' theatre of the war before Air Supply in its own right would be seen as a valuable method of supporting forces generally, and a great expansion of the capability put in hand. However, when this did occur, the work done in developing supply-dropping techniques, parachutes and equipment for the airborne forces was to be of great benefit. Indeed, an early product of the renamed Central Landing Establishment was a supply-dropping container designed in conjunction with the 'GQ' Parachute Company to fit on standard bomb racks, but, at six feet in length large enough to accommodate rifles, machine guns and mortars. Destined to be made in millions, the container and subsequent variants became known simply by the initials of the establishment, CLE. The first British drop of troops and containers from the same aircraft was made in December, 1940.

Despite the enthusiasm of the Airborne community in the British forces, the path was not smooth. Efforts were soon split to include provision for glider-borne troops, leading ultimately to the formation of the Army Air Corps and the Glider Pilot Regiment in December, 1941, and throughout there was a chronic shortage of aircraft. None of the aircraft which were available were particularly suitable for dropping military parachutists and the priority given to producing bombers eventually meant that Britain would not produce a new cargo or troop-carrying aircraft before the end of the war.

In February, 1941, the first, small, British airborne operation was mounted when six Whitley aircraft of No 91 Squadron dropped thirty-eight men from the 11th Special Air Service Battalion with their arms and explosives into Italy to blow up the strategically important Tragino aqueduct. Despite two aircraft failing to drop their supply containers, Operation COLOSSUS was a success, with the aqueduct being breached, although the effect of this was less than had been expected and the whole party was captured. Among the important lessons learned was the critical nature of packing and loading containers, as the failure to release them properly on the two aircraft was attributed to the centre of gravity of the containers being misplaced.

The Airborne Divisional RASC and Air Despatch

Before the war airborne forces had never been seriously thought of as a part of the British Army. Any suggestion that the technique of maintenance of several airborne divisions should be worked out or studied would have been considered eccentric. Yet when the need came to launch a whole corps of troops by glider and parachute deep into enemy territory, a complete, efficient, highly-trained RASC organization was ready to deliver its daily load from base depots in England to fighting men on the ground.

In April, 1942, work started to create 1st Airborne Division and soon after this the RASC of the division began to take shape. After many trials, a fairly firm organization emerged which endured for most of the war. Under the control of HQ CRASC (of whom the first was Lieutenant Colonel T H Jefferies) were two Heavy Companies (Airborne Divisional Composite Companies) and one Light Company. The former were equipped with 3-ton vehicles and the latter with jeeps and trailers. Airborne formations were not always withdrawn immediately after action, but could find themselves fighting on for long periods in a ground role, needing all their second-line transport, which therefore could not be left behind with the maintenance task in the Airborne Base; and the dumps themselves were growing so fast as to be beyond the capacity of the divisional column to hold. A completely separate organization being seen to be necessary, the Air Despatch Group began to develop.

Air Despatch

In 1942 supply by air was still a developing function for the Corps and was made a practical proposition by the improvement in the reliability and capacity of aircraft, and made a necessity with the increasing difficulty experienced in many theatres of maintaining lengthy lines of communication. These lines were so extended that not only did their organization absorb an inordinate proportion of the 'ration strength' in the theatre, but also it became impracticable to protect them from being cut by the enemy. This was particularly true in Burma where the first large-scale resort to air supply started, following experiences in early 1942, but in that theatre was largely the responsibility of the RIASC.

In January, 1944, 81 (West African) Division were dependent on head-load African carriers for ground transport. Auxiliary Groups, raised by RASC officers and NCOs, were deployed in inaccessible jungle-clad mountain country as flank guards to the main Arakan offensive. The Division became the first normal formation to be entirely maintained by air. The daily resupply lift of 51,000lbs, including ammunition, required twenty-two aircraft, with twelve in reserve, and was loaded and despatched by the RIASC Rear Air Supply Organization. These operations continued for six months.

Formation and Tasks of the Air Despatch Group

Technically the tasks of the Air Despatch Group now to be formed were divided into two types of maintenance by air: the air maintenance and re-supply which meant the maintenance, normally by dropping, of ground or airborne troops as a routine task, after they had established themselves in an operational area, and, secondly, supply by air. The latter means the loading of aircraft with stores and supplies straight from dumps without special packing and landing the complete aircraft and load at the destination. In the United Kingdom the executive portion was at first under a CRASC Air Despatch. Later, as the task grew, an Air Despatch Group was formed. This consisted of a Headquarters Air Despatch Group RASC, three HQs RASC, air despatch companies and airborne divisional companies (attached from 1 and 6 Airborne Divisions). There were also general transport companies for collecting from supply and ordnance depots the stores for despatch, small RASC and RAOC depots for holding commodities at ready availability, and an air maintenance company, RAOC, for holding and packing specialized and delicate RAOC stores. There was also a detachment RAOC for operating the 'cushion' ammunition depot, and a Pioneer company for labour. The aircraft for the carriage of the stores were controlled and operated by the Royal Air Force. In South-East Asia Command, where there were no civilian or well established military communications, a Royal Signals regiment was also part of the organization.

Air Despatch in North-West Europe

The problems to be faced in North-West Europe, however, differed from those in the Far East in several respects. With the exception of airborne operations, supply and maintenance by air were planned as emergency measures rather than as a normal system. For this reason the Air Despatch Group was only used spasmodically and was never stretched to its full capacity except for short periods. The enemy opposition from air and ground was very much heavier in North-West Europe and this had considerable influence on the technique for dropping, which was designed to eject the whole load in one run over the dropping zone.

The airfields used for supply operations were served by excellent roads, had good rail facilities and were connected by a first-class system of telephone and teleprinter communications. This made the central control of RASC transport and air despatch personnel reasonably simple, and enabled transport, stores and men to be switched rapidly from airfield to airfield in order to meet the frequent changes of aircraft and airfield availability brought about at short notice by casualties and bad weather.

The heavy companies of 1 Airborne Division were the predecessors of the Air Despatch Group, to whom they handed over a complete technique for packing, holding, loading and despatching stores not only for airborne formations, but for any others requiring emergency supply. The Airborne Column did not entirely relinquish its base work. There was always a heavy company of one of the divisions working with the Despatch Group, concerned more particularly towards the end of the war with the delivery of stores by night to Special Air Service units operating on secret missions in France, the Netherlands and Belgium, to individual agents, and to the underground organizations of those countries. Besides this, the heavy companies of the divisional columns retained the duty of mounting airborne operations – that is, of moving their divisions to sealed camps adjacent to the base airfields, and thence to their aircraft for emplaning, before themselves travelling by sea to join up later in a normal second-line role. From these companies also came the steady flow of parachute volunteers who replaced the casualties in the light companies of their own columns.

A Second Airborne Division is Formed

1 Airborne Divisional Column RASC left UK by sea in May, 1943, for its first taste of active service in North Africa. The North African campaign was over by the time

the column was established there, and about two months were spent in the completion of training, under somewhat difficult conditions. While 1 Division was away, the formation of a second division, which would be necessary to form the spearhead of an invasion of Europe, was begun. Early in 1943 the units from which the division was to form began to assemble in the Salisbury Plain area. Among these was 398 Company RASC, which had been detached from the Royal Marine Division, then undergoing reorganization. For some months this was the only unit to represent the RASC column. In September it was decided to complete the column and 716 and 63 Companies arrived for conversion. A CRASC headquarters was formed at the same time.

THE LIBERATION OF SOUTHERN EUROPE

With the elimination of Axis forces in Africa new impetus was given to planning for the inevitable invasion of mainland Europe, but the build-up of forces in Britain and preparations for an assault on the coast of France would require another year to guarantee success. To keep the pressure on the Axis and tie up their forces it was decided to activate plans for the invasion of Sicily. Some 160,000 Allied troops were committed to the invasion and for the first time the Allies involved a significant airborne force. The prelude was to secure the islands of Pantellaria, Lampedusa and Linosa which were bombarded and captured in two days in June, 1943. 1 Airborne Division, with two parachute brigades and one air-landed brigade, landed in Sicily on the night of 9/10 July, and by 17 August the whole of Sicily was in Allied hands.

In the invasion of Sicily and the subsequent campaign in Italy the RASC had to develop each of its activities to the fullest extent, as, in addition to an extensive supply and transport organization, both animal and water transport were used on a large scale. The campaigns also provided the RASC with their first opportunity of demonstrating the values of their new form of transport – the amphibious vehicle.

On the beaches the RASC carried out the stores landing task with its new vehicle, the $2\frac{1}{2}$-ton amphibious DUKW. It is no exaggeration to say that this wheeled amphibious vehicle revolutionized the business of beach maintenance. By being able to unload direct from LSTs into DUKWs, which could deliver their loads to beach maintenance dumps without any intermediate handling, we were able to speed up enormously the rate of discharge of stores over beaches. We became less dependent on the weather and calm seas, and were not so restricted in our use of beaches. It is easy to divert DUKWs from an unfavourable beach to a better one without the necessity of moving landing ships and craft and without causing congestion at the beach exists. With less handling there was also a great saving in labour.

Beach maintenance was undertaken by beach groups in the case of formations mounted from the United Kingdom or from North Africa, and by beach 'bricks' in the case of formations mounted from the Middle East. These beach 'bricks' consisted of an infantry battalion with the necessary service units and depots attached. In the case of the RASC these consisted of two platoons of a general transport company, a small petrol depot and a detail issue depot. They had been rapidly formed and trained in the Middle East and carried out their beach maintenance functions admirably.

There was no real problem in connection with supplies. All troops landed in Sicily with a 48-hour mess-tin ration. 'Compo' rations were issued until D plus 18 (28

July), after which normal bulk rations were issued. Fresh bread was supplied from D plus 13. To begin with, this was baked in Malta and despatched daily by LCT. Later two field bakeries were set up in Sicily, and contracts were made with civil bakeries in Syracuse and Catania.

Although plans had been made for the supply of petrol in bulk to airfields in Sicily, it proved impossible to develop bulk supply until the campaign was over. Good bulk storage existed at Syracuse and Catania but this was extensively sabotaged by the Germans and took several weeks to put in order.

It had been foreseen that there would be a need for pack transport in the mountainous areas in central Sicily and six pack transport companies had been included in the order of battle. However, these were very low on the priority list and there was little chance of their arriving until the end of, hopefully, a short campaign. Plans were also made to make use of local Sicilian mules and saddlery. Two troops of an RASC pack transport unit did actually take part in the final stages of the advance on Messina and 50th Division requisitioned local mules and donkeys for use along the coast road where enemy demolitions prevented the use of road transport. The pack saddles and equipment were drawn but use was limited.

The Landings in Italy; Operation BAYTOWN

Before the Sicily campaign was completed it had already been decided to invade Italy to hasten its collapse, to gain access to the Foggia airfields and to complete Allied control of the Mediterranean. On 3 September two divisions, 5th British and 1st Canadian, landed at Reggio in the Straits of Messina. During the landings and the subsequent advance they were maintained by four amphibious companies RASC, plying backwards and forwards across the straits from dumps in the neighbourhood of Messina to the beaches just north of Reggio. The DUKWs of 385 Company were off-loading on the beaches within one and a half hours of H hour. Because of the early withdrawal of the enemy, there had been little expenditure of ammunition, and the beach maintenance areas were rapidly stocked up. The DUKWs presented a considerable traffic problem in the narrow walled roads just north of Reggio and, until traffic circuits had been made and roads widened, the congestion was a vulnerable target to the enemy air force. A subsidiary operation was now carried out in Apulia. 1st Airborne Division was landed by sea at Taranto on 9 September and on the same day elements for 5th US Army began landing in Salerno Bay.

Operation AVALANCHE

The landings at Salerno were timed to coincide with the announcement of an armistice with Italy. Although distracted by the armistice, the Germans mounted a determined resistance. Anticipating such an assault, the enemy had strengthened his defences and at the time a German division was engaged on an exercise in Salerno Bay. Instead of being demoralized by the defection of the Italians, the Germans redoubled their efforts and fought fiercely to annihilate the assaulting forces, to give themselves time to reorganize in Italy and to meet the possible threat to their communications from their turncoat ally.

For a week 5th Army's position at Salerno was precarious. During this period the RASC played their full part in keeping the forces in the beachhead supplied. By the evening of D Day 519 Company and a detachment of 521 Company, part of 46 Divisional Transport Column, were ashore and maintained the division for the first

172

week. 58 Detail Issue Depot was also ashore on D Day in 56 Divisional area and the DUKWs of 239 Company worked continuously from ship to shore.

During the campaign in Italy pack transport came into its own. In 1942 pack transport (a cadre) figured for the first time in the initial order of battle for an expeditionary force – for North Africa; but it was not until the opening of the campaign in Italy that it was required on a really extensive scale. Towards the end of the campaign no fewer than 30,000 animals were being employed by the Allied armies. All the pack units employed by our own Army were led by British officers and NCOs.

No account of pack transport would be complete without mention of the close liaison between the Corps and the officers and men of the Royal Army Veterinary

RASC DUKWs going aboard an LST in Salerno harbour.

Corps who tend and care for animal casualties. A special tribute is paid also to those officers and men from other Corps of the armed forces who, when the need for expansion arrived, willingly joined the ranks of the Corps and played such a large part in the success of pack transport.

The advance northwards produced no food supplies problems. In the case of petroleum the rapid east coast advance had outrun its stocks and, until a ship could be unloaded at Taranto, convoys consisting of whatever transport could be made available (including DUKWs) were run across from the west coast from Salerno and Sapri. Bulk storage tanks at Naples, Taranto and Bari, many of them damaged, were

RASC DUKWs approaching the stern ramp of an LST.

soon repaired and two bulk petroleum storage companies were set to work in order to introduce bulk supply as soon as possible.

With the British advancing on the right and the Americans on the left the Germans made excellent use of the defensive mountainous country. After three days hard fighting the Trigno/Volturno line was forced on 15 October. With the weather deteriorating the many rivers flowing across the line of advance became increasingly severe obstacles. By the middle of December the Allies had only managed to advance 40 miles in two and a half months and the Germans were holding a winter line, known as the Gustav Line, in which the mountain and river at Cassino provided an almost impregnable stronghold. To bypass this line, outflank the Germans and open the way to Rome another amphibious landing at Anzio was planned. The seaborne attack was to be made in conjunction with a new assault on the main German positions and sufficient landing craft would be retained in the theatre to meet the needs of the assaulting formations. This action is covered later in this chapter.

A Mule Pack Team loaded with supplies going through the damaged streets of Adrano.

The mountainous terrain in the region made road and rail transport particularly susceptible to the disruption of war. However, the shape of the Italian peninsula, and the coastlines of Yugoslavia, Albania, Greece, Corsica, Sardinia, Malta and North Africa, with their many small ports, made the Central Mediterranean an ideal theatre for the employment of RASC water transport. For years the Italians had made extensive use of coasting schooners and consequently there were many suitable vessels available on the spot. 247 Company RASC soon had far more commitments than it could properly handle and from it three more water transport companies, 797, 798 and 801, of special establishment were formed in October, 1943, and April and June, 1944. The motorboat company was then restored to strength with enthusiastic volunteers from all arms.

As the Allied armies advanced, a reorganization became necessary and in the autumn of 1944 247 Company assumed responsibility for the waters around Southern Italy, Sicily and Malta, 797 for the Northern Adriatic from Ancona, 798 for the Northern Tyrrhenian Sea from Naples, and 801 for the Southern Adriatic, Yugoslavia, Albania and Greece.

Some of the schooners were manned entirely by military crews, especially in the early days when shipments to Yugoslavia first began, for the Yugoslavs firmly refused to allow an Italian-manned vessel to call at their ports. Vessels were loaded in Bari and sailed to Manfredonia, where they anchored until darkness fell. Then they would surreptitiously make the passage to the island of Vis with their cargo of ammunition or stores for the British forces and the Partisans. Another route used was that to the Yugoslavia port of Split and trips were made even down to Kalamata in Greece.

The RASC Fleet with the Middle East Forces

Farther to the east, yet another RASC Fleet unit had come into being. In November, 1943, 782 Company (Motorboat) was formed at Alexandria to take over all small craft operated by the military forces in the Middle East. Military crews were trained from local volunteers with the help of the RAF air/sea rescue instructional centres. Four 68 ft and one 57 ft high-speed target towing launches were quickly manned and operated at Alexandria, Port Said and Haifa. Within a short time of its formation, the unit itself was training soldiers in handling the local sailing vessels known as *caiques*.

As crews became available, they manned *caiques* allotted by the Sea Transport Officer, GHQ Middle East, for duty in the Eastern Mediterranean, sailing between Alexandria, Port Said, Haifa, Cyprus, Beirut and northwards. They ferried high-octane aviation fuel to forward bases on Kastellorizo ahead of the RAF, ferried urgently required supplies from Famagusta to the recently occupied Dodecanese, carried Italian prisoners of war and enemy agents, and a hundred-and-one other cargoes.

By 1944 the small craft commitments covered the whole coastal area from Tripolitania to Palestine and stretched as far south as Aden, much too large a parish for the one company. Consequently 782 Company was disbanded and two new units were formed – 698 Company RASC (Water Transport) based at Port Said, covering the Mediterranean coast and eventually reaching as far north as Piraeus and 698 Company RASC (Water Transport), based at Port Suez, covering the Suez Canal and the Red Sea ports.

Serving these companies was 3 Boat Stores Depot RASC, formed towards the end of 1943 and originally located at Tahag, near Tel-el-Kebir. Its staff consisted of one British officer and some Sinhalese who soon adapted themselves to this specialized job and also became quite skilled in making fenders, splicing cordage and the like. In 1944 the depot was moved to Alexandria, where it remained until the end of hostilities, when it moved to Port Said.

PREPARATIONS FOR THE INVASION OF NORTH-WEST EUROPE – OPERATION OVERLORD

RASC TASKS

The latter part of 1943 and the early months of 1944 were periods of intense preparation of formations and units for participation in the coming invasion of Normandy. The volume and variety of the work done by the ST branches in the War Office in preparation for the mounting of Operation OVERLORD was enormous.

Supplies

Of major importance as far as Supplies were concerned was the introduction of the new 24-hour pack ration, devised and produced at short notice and which proved light, compact and highly nutritious. A reserve of 75,000,000 bulk rations and 60,000,000 special pack rations had to be built up in spite of a world scarcity of foodstuffs and shipping. Many other intense activities were taking place as part of the preparations and these will be covered in the paragraphs that follow.

MT

The vehicles of all the assault formations and of the follow-up formations had to be put into first class mechanical condition and then to be waterproofed. The operating crews had to be taught the technique of waterproofing and of driving through deep water. As a 'target' they and their vehicles had to be prepared for at least six minutes' immersion in salt water five feet deep, with a 'wave height' of eighteen inches and they had, moreover, after landing, to know how to de-waterproof their vehicles immediately and to carry on with their transport tasks without a break. All this kept our training centres and our formation transport companies fully stretched, while, superimposed on their normal full-time programme, the home transport companies were given the heavy task of moving and delivering the numerous articles of equipment to the concentration and embarkation areas which were being prepared in southern England. Some 200 MT Companies were formed to cope with these tasks and what lay ahead, despite the inevitable manpower difficulties and lack of certain types of equipment.

Water Transport

In Scotland new motorboat companies (467, 571, 624, 625 and 626) were raised to assist with the invasion. The first – 467 Company – was located in April, 1943, at Rothesay. This was the first RASC unit to receive the standard Admiralty 36 ft open harbour launches which were then becoming available for issue to the RASC Fleet. They were sturdy, seagoing craft which gave yeoman service in every theatre. They would carry a platoon in full battle kit on an up-river or coastal fighting patrol or three tons of cargo. In due course the four other units moved to the areas of Inverary, Irvine and Rothesay. To further their training and to overcome the lack of naval manpower, they took over from the Royal Navy the manning and operation of assault landing craft used at the Combined Training Centres (CTCs) in Scotland. For this task they were placed under the command of CRASC CTCs. It was work which really suited them, and soon they were handling LCTs, LCMs, LCAs and the like with confidence and skill.

Early in 1944 these units, with the exception of 467 Company, were required to re-equip and reform for Operation OVERLORD. The assault landing craft were handed back to the Royal Navy and the companies were gradually concentrated in the West Mersea area on the East Coast near Colchester, to which the Central Training Unit, 246 Motor Boat Company, had already been moved.

The remaining unit, 467 Company, remained in Scotland and acted as a continuation training unit under War Office control.

Petroleum

Long-term planning for the invasion of mainland Europe may be said to have begun during 1941 and 1942 when the War Office decided to increase the bulk reserves in England, to create six petrol reserve depots for packed stocks, to build satellite tin-making plants and to install two large filling plants for returnable containers.

To save further construction of military-owned tankage it was arranged that the additional military bulk reserves would be held in civil installations and would be administered by the Petroleum Board on the Army's behalf. By this means the military holdings in early 1941, of 227,000 tons of bulk tankage, was raised to nearly 1,000,000 tons by the end of the war. The six War Office-controlled petrol depots were designed to hold 50,000 liquid tons of packed petroleum products. The plans to provide more filling facilities were changed as the strategic situation turned from defence to offence and the use of tins changed to that of cans.

By the time that active planning of OVERLORD began a great deal of experience had been gained in the Middle East, North Africa and Italy and in the Far East. The original concept of the functions of the various types of British petroleum units proved to be quite sound, although various changes were made in their organization as further experience was gained. The speed with which new tankage could be erected and pipelines laid over both short and long distances had been amply demonstrated, as had the rate at which bulk distribution could be introduced on lines of communication.

The plans for supply for OVERLORD differed in many respects from those made for previous operations inasmuch as initial supplies were to be in returnable cans (jerricans). For this during 1943 more than 17,000,000 jerricans and 3,000,000 returnable containers of other kinds were produced in the United Kingdom. Bulk supply for refilling cans was to be developed immediately after the first landings and not deferred, as had been formerly done, until civil installations were captured and rehabilitated. Portable and prefabricated tankage was to be landed quickly and supplied from floating tank barges and bulk petrol lorries used to carry forward supplies to mobile filling centres. The supply of bulk fuel from England was to be maintained by a fleet of small shallow-draft petrol carriers and by a submarine pipeline which rejoiced in the code name of PLUTO (Pipe Line Under The Ocean). The whole scheme was gigantic and involved the co-operation of the Navy, the Royal Engineers and the Oil Industry, and the production of huge quantities of material. Perhaps the most spectacular achievement of the petroleum planners was the provision and training of the units required to operate the terminal installations of PLUTO. Men were specially picked and were trained for their task on a submarine pipeline running from Swansea to Ilfracombe.

The provision of marine craft portable tankage and pipelines was not a direct ST2 responsibility, although they were concerned with their ultimate use. Some idea of the overall effort involved will be of interest. The equipments on order in July, 1943, included 1,400 miles of pipeline, 900 rail tank wagons, 130,000 tons of 'quickly erected' tankage, 200 prefabricated 1,000-ton tanks, 200 barges and a programme for thirty dual-purpose carrier vessels for the carriage of petrol in bulk or in cans.

There were 121 contractors employed in producing the equipment which had to be provided by ST2 alone. The items on order ranged from 155,000,000 clips, for identifying the contents of jerricans to fifty-five mobile filling plants.

Raising and training the eighty-five RASC petroleum units which appeared in the order of battle was a critical task. It was greatly assisted by the existence of a Petroleum Technical Training Centre where courses were arranged for both technical and general duty men. A special headquarters (a HQ CRASC) was set up at 4 Mobilization Centre. This HQ arranged for realistic training and rehearsals of units' future tasks in France and Germany.

The Formation of the Airborne Corps

With the experience of 1 Airborne Division now available and with the competitive spirit induced by the presence hard by of 101 United States Airborne Division, the 6th Airborne Divisional Column, spurred also by the knowledge that D Day could not be far ahead, rapidly gained in efficiency and within a matter of weeks was fit for war.

The arrival of 82 United States Airborne Division in the United kingdom led to the formation of an American Airborne Corps headquarters under General Matthew Ridgway. About the same time the return of 1 Airborne Division to the United Kingdom was the signal for the formation of Headquarters 1 British Airborne Corps. This had long existed, but in a much reduced form under the title of HQ Airborne Forces. As a Corps HQ it now received a DDST in the person of Colonel T H Jefferies, who was promoted from 1 Airborne Division in which he was succeeded as CRASC by Lieutenant Colonel M St J Packe, who had been the first airborne company commander, RASC.

Air Supply

In QMG House at the War Office was a room in which, by early 1944, all information regarding supply and maintenance by air could be found. It contained, among other statistics, the availability and locations of road transport and stocks of various kinds, and from it all RASC air despatch activity was co-ordinated. The RAF Air Freight Control Centre was in the Swindon area, and around it the airfields used for air supply and maintenance were grouped. The headquarters of the RASC Air Despatch Organization, commanded by Colonel S W Walsh, was located with this centre and received orders direct from ST 3 at the War Office. Colonel Walsh's command consisted of three air despatch companies, comprising twelve air-dropping platoons, each of fifteen air-dropping crews of four men. These 180 crews had an approximate capacity of 360 tons a sortie. Two sorties could be flown daily in an emergency, but not for any length of time. A pool of six general transport companies under CRASC War Office Transport Column divided its services between the Air Despatch Organization and DDST Airborne Forces. All RASC units in this organization were trained with the RAF for emergency supply (in case of severed sea communications), for schedule supply (a daily service in which about twenty-five tons of urgent ordnance stores, blood plasma, mail and newspapers were carried) and for temporary maintenance of ground formations. Air supply was to be effected by air landings and air maintenance by parachute dropping of pre-packed panniers.

THE NORMANDY LANDINGS

Introduction

The OVERLORD plan provided for simultaneous landings on the Normandy coast by eight equivalent brigades, of which three were British, two were Canadian and three were American combat teams. Commandos and Rangers also took part. The Americans assaulted on the right because they were to be partially maintained and supported direct from the United States through Cherbourg. Airborne forces were used on both flanks; 6 British Airborne Division was given the task of seizing the crossings over the Caen Canal and operated on the British left. General Montgomery commanded all the land forces for the assault, for which task he had an American increment attached to his headquarters.

The Seaborne Assault

After delays because of bad weather the assault took place on 6 June, 1944. On the extreme left of the British assault by sea was 3rd Division (1 Corps) supported by an armoured brigade. The RASC of these formations had the additional task of maintaining 6th Airborne Division for the first ten days of the operations. The bridges leading to the Ranville dumps were bottlenecks and naturally received attention from enemy aircraft as well as intermittent shell, mortar and small arms fire. Major J R Cuthbertson, commanding 27th Armoured Brigade Company (90 Company), was responsible for the task of maintaining the division and was awarded the Military Cross for his part in its successful accomplishment. The first RASC units ashore in this sector were two assault platoons of 172 Company, with one platoon of 90 Company attached.

In the right sector of the British area 30 Corps assaulted on a one-division front. 50th Division was supported by 8 Armoured Brigade, and was followed up immediately by 7th Armoured Division. CRASC and elements of HQ RASC 50th Division landed on D Day and 522 Company was the first of the 50th Division RASC Companies to land with detachments of 346 and 552 Companies. The latter company served 8 Armoured Brigade. One of the first tasks of 522 Company was the maintenance of 47 Commando at Port-en-Bessin, which was destined to be the PLUTO port and which was still well inside enemy territory. Delivery of vital requirements to this Commando was continually effected in the face of small arms fire and shelling from enemy tanks. Captain B W M Linden and Staff Sergeants T Burt and W J Tams received immediate awards of the Military Cross and the Military Medal respectively for their part in these operations. Two hours after the first landing 39 GT Company came ashore. Their first task was to deliver anti-tank guns required for the defence of the beach maintenance area. Delivery was effected under mortar and small arms fire and three awards of the Military Medal were made to members of the Company. A platoon of 127 Company, which had been with 30 Corps since 1941, and detachments of 30 Corps HQ Car Company were also ashore on D Day.

The absence of a port in the invasion area was partially overcome by the construction of two artificial ports (code name: MULBERRY) in the United Kingdom which were towed across the channel in sections. These in themselves were brilliant engineering constructions and a considerable shipping skill was required to position them. They were a major factor in the subsequent successful maintenance of the Force. Until these were in position DUKWs of the eleven RASC DUKW companies played a vital role in unloading the maintenance stores from vessels anchored offshore, carried them over the beaches, and evacuated casualties from the beaches to LSTs. Thereafter the DUKWs continued to support and supplement MULBERRY in a wide range of tasks. This was particularly vital when a storm on 19 June severely damaged the British MULBERRY and swept away the American MULBERRY, which was further west.

During the twenty-four hours ending 1800 hours 11 June, DUKWs carried 10,850 tons of stores over the beaches. On 12 June one DUKW brought Mr Winston Churchill and General Eisenhower ashore and, on 14 June, another, known thereafter as the 'Royal DUKW', had the honour of carrying King George VI. Two

Mulberry Harbour. Huge concrete caissons, each weighing 7000 tons, were towed across the Channel and positioned at Arromanches.

DUKW drivers were awarded the Military Medal on the recommendation of the United States Army authorities.

Until sufficient GT companies had been landed, DUKWs had to carry their loads through to the dumps, but as soon as possible transhipment areas were established in the vicinity of the beaches where the DUKWs dropped their loads and returned through a control point to the sea.

There were two beach groups with each of the assaulting divisions and each group included, as beach maintenance area units, a detail issue depot and a petrol depot. Maintenance areas for 50th and 3rd Canadian Divisions were established without much incident and within three days of landing. DDST 30 Corps landed at about H plus 6 on D Day and found a Detail Issue Depot (DID) and a petrol depot with stock on the ground and actually making issues – a truly remarkable achievement.

During the battles which followed the establishment of the bridgehead a great deal of artillery ammunition was expended. In 50th Division it was quite normal for up to 400 rounds of twenty-five pounder ammunition to be dumped per night at the gun positions. This task was carried out by 508 Company (the Division Troops Company), together with the Gunner Regiments echelon vehicles which came under RASC control for the duration of the dumping programme.

The Airborne Assault

The parachute brigades dropped in the early hours of D Day, before the seaborne assault approached the beaches, to seize the vital bridges over the Orne and the Caen-Ouistreham Canal and secure the left flank of the intended beachhead. Reinforced later in the day by the air landing brigade in gliders, they were to extend the territory held and destroy bridges over the River Dives to prevent the approach of enemy reinforcements.

The plan of CRASC 6th Airborne Division was to send two parachute platoons and three jeep-trailer platoons by air on D Day, the remainder of the light company travelling by sea. One heavy company would be engaged solely in air despatch duties, while the other, loaded with second-line holdings, was to go by sea with the assault force.

The honour of being the first RASC unit to land in France on D Day, belongs to the Light Composite Company of 6 Airborne Division (716 Company). Two platoons of this Company were among the earliest who parachuted in some hours before the beach landings. The company's task was to organize the supply of the division and to collect the containers which had been jettisoned by the aircraft from which the men had jumped. By 0600 a dump had been formed in a quarry north of Ranville, from which units were drawing direct. The company commander was wounded soon after landing, leaving Lieutenant F J Bland in command for that day. The jettison drop had fallen over a wide area occupied by the enemy, but in spite of this difficulty, which entailed working under fire most of the time, with very slender resources, Lieutenant Bland kept the fighting troops supplied with ammunition until

Air Despatch in North-West Europe. Supply containers being dropped to glider-borne troops during Operation Overlord. (Imperial War Museum)

the link-up with the beach assault force, the only shortage being of 75 mm Howitzer ammunition, of which 15,000 rounds were expended the first day, 13,000 the next, and 2,500 on 8 June, when the first pre-loaded vehicles managed to get through by land. Lieutenant Bland was awarded the Military Cross and Sergeant Wilson received the Military Medal for collecting mines and delivering them to the Royal Engineers in a captured lorry while under constant mortar fire.

By the morning of D plus 1 the Divisional Maintenance Area (DMA) was in full working order and the men, although very tired, were doing their job with great enthusiasm. For some time afterwards all were overworked, for from D plus 1 onwards 1 and 44 Special Service Brigades (Commandos) came under command. They had no RASC units of their own and in consequence one attenuated company was supplying the needs of five brigades.

The airborne phase gradually lessened, the Division becoming an infantry formation for the ensuing operations. A Belgian and a Netherlands brigade came under command, presenting certain ration problems, but bringing some second-line transport with them which was a great help, particularly when, without warning, the RASC was called on to provide troop-carrying transport for the first break-out from the beachhead.

The Column's casualties during the early phases had been two officers and twenty other ranks killed, three officers and forty-one other ranks wounded, and fourteen missing. The heavy company which had remained in England to carry out the air despatch suffered no losses: they performed the same duties later, however, on behalf of 1 Airborne Division at Arnhem, where their casualties numbered forty-four.

The men of the 224 Parachute Field Ambulance were widely dispersed after the drop. Lieutenant G C G Phile, RASC, unit transport officer, rallied them and led them through enemy-occupied territory. That same night the main dressing station at Le Mesnil was crowded with wounded and there was no transport available. Lieutenant Phile, with four men, forced sixty-three Germans to surrender and captured their five vehicles and a motorcycle. This transport made possible the rapid collection of wounded all over the brigade area and saved many lives. Lieutenant Phile also received the immediate award of the Military Cross.

Water Transport Companies and MULBERRY

The first motorboat company craft to be involved in OVERLORD were three harbour launches of 626 Company which carried Sappers for erecting the MULBERRY Harbour. They left in the convoy of D minus 1. The main body of the harbour launch company arrived off the beaches on 9 and 11 June (D plus 3 and D plus 5). The advanced HQ CRASC, thirty fast motorboats and six motor fishing vessels of 624 Company crossed on D Day. Thereafter small parties of craft from both units left each day.

Until the MULBERRY harbour had been constructed, it was not possible for craft to get nearer than one mile off shore, and so all crews had to live on their launches and MFVs. This was most arduous, especially for the harbour launch crews in their open boats. Eventually, however, they were accommodated in the unsubmerged portion of one of the sunken block ships around MULBERRY. With the exception of certain smaller vessels which were able to enter the harbour, shipping lay some three miles off shore. The fast launch company was used in the control of this and to maintain contact between the DUKW companies and the ships to be unloaded.

Although it may be invidious to give individual examples of the exploits of these

184

A painting depicting the action of MFV 610 skippered by Sergeant Yeabsley BEM, RASC in which 160 gunners marooned on an isolated caisson were rescued.

RASC crews, mention must be made of the following. It was the crew of MFV 610, skippered by Sergeant R J Yeabsley, RASC, with Corporal K Popperwell, RASC, as second coxswain, who earned renown on 19 June, 1944, when they battled for five hours in an appalling gale to rescue 160 gunners marooned on an isolated caisson. The newly-fashioned emplacement, swept by enormous waves, was in constant danger of breaking up. Sergeant Yeabsley was subsequently awarded the British Empire Medal for Gallantry.

Harbour Launch 278, with Sergeant A E Smith, RASC, as coxswain, distinguished herself on 10 and 11 June, 1944, in gallant work before being wrecked in a third valiant rescue attempt ten days later. On the first occasion a motor launch blew up a mine while engaged on the demolition of a wreck. The coxswain of HL 278 immediately went to the rescue and, in spite of the warnings of further explosions, succeeded in saving three lives. The next day another motor launch blew up one and half miles off shore. The same coxswain, although the crew were in the midst of doing gearbox repairs, quickly improvised a gear lever by using a Stillson wrench and hurried to the scene of the explosion. They saved six of the crew. On 21 June HL 278 was ordered to the assistance of the destroyer *Fury*, which had struck a mine, caught fire and had been blown on the rocks. HL 278 made many attempts to take a line from the destroyer to one of the tugs which could not get alongside because of the enormous seas. It was during these heroic efforts that the harbour launch was flung on the rocks and completely wrecked. Fortunately, her gallant crew were saved.

Significant early supplies into Normandy were achieved by RASC ingenuity. Two weeks after D Day bread with special keeping properties was flown in for consumption in hospitals and RASC bakeries were established and in production by early July. British beer made its first appearance in the beach-head in July. The first bulk petrol transport company (252 Company of 37 Transport Column) landed on 23 June, and on 30 June the first cargo of bulk petrol was discharged from a coastal tanker to prefabricated storage in Port-en-Bessin.

It was during the final phase of the Falaise fighting on 20 August that the Air Despatch Group in England made its first appearance over Normandy, when they dropped sixty tons of ammunition to a Polish armoured brigade. By late August the RASC presence in the rear maintenance area was eight BSDs, eight DIDs, thirteen field bakeries, two field butcheries, fourteen petrol depots and six mobile filling centres.

The huge build-up of Allied Forces put demands on Barrack Services for necessities often taken for granted, such as coal. During the early stages of operation OVERLORD it was necessary to manhandle coal over the beaches. About 18,000 tons was bagged in 80 lb sacks, a sack being the equivalent of a one-man load, and for this purpose 250,000 rot-proofed sacks were obtained under Ministry of Supply arrangements. A buffer stock of 5,000 tons in bulk had been laid down at Swansea, and was subsequently shipped.

Advance to the Rhine

The immediate tasks for 21 Army Group after crossing the Seine were:

- The destruction of the enemy in North-East France;
- The clearance of the Pas de Calais and the elimination of 'V bomb' sites;
- The capture of airfields in Belgium, and
- The capture of Antwerp.

The axis of 2nd Army advance was north-east, that is towards central Belgium. The First Canadian Army was given the task of advancing up the Channel coast with its series of heavily fortified ports. 30 Corps was the spearhead of the Second Army's advance. Amiens was entered on 31 August, Brussels on 3 September, and Antwerp the following day.

Operation MARKET GARDEN

On 11 September orders were given for the advance to Arnhem. The outline plan was for the 2nd British Army to advance approximately seventy miles to seize the Grave-Nijmegen-Arnhem area and then to penetrate still further northwards to the Zuider Zee in order to cut off the enemy forces in the Low Countries from those in Germany. This was to be an airborne and ground operation and the whole operation was given the code name of MARKET GARDEN. The Airborne forces consisted of the 1st Airborne Corps commanded by Lieutenant General Sir Frederick Browning and the ground force of 30 Corps commanded by Lieutenant General Sir Brian Horrocks.

The task given to the 1st Allied Airborne Army, which now comprised two British and three United States divisions, was to seize the bridges over the Maas, the canal at Grave, the Waal, and the Neder Rijn, all of which were big obstacles and hold them until 30 Corps could cross them all and debouch into the Eastern Netherlands and the North German plain. The seizure of the Neder Rijn bridge at Arnhem, which was the northernmost and some sixty miles in advance of the forward troops of 30 Corps, was allotted to 1st Airborne Division, the other bridges being the responsibility of the 82nd and 101st United States Airborne Divisions.

The plan of CRASC 6th Airborne Division was for one parachute platoon to fly in with each of the three brigades of the first airlift, collect the large quantities of ammunition which were to go in simultaneously in gliders and, after delivering it to their brigades, return to the pre-selected supply dropping point which would by that time be captured. This they were to lay out and prepare, at the same time seizing any German and Netherlands transport which they could lay hands on. In the second lift on the following day, CRASC's headquarters and the remainder of the light company would arrive, their jeeps fully loaded, and begin ferrying supplies from the abandoned gliders and from containers of the jettison-drop to the divisional maintenance area, which would be completely under RASC control. On the third day would come the first supply drop, followed by further daily missions to maintain the force until 30 Corps reached them.

The plan miscarried. Not being able to bring his whole force in a single air-lift, Major General Roy Urquhart, the divisional commander, found himself compelled to engage an unexpectedly large enemy force piecemeal. In spite of this, the bridge was held for longer than was planned, but 30 Corps was unable to reach it and it had to be given up.

The RASC contingents landed as planned, but one of the parachute platoons was cut off with its brigade at the Arnhem bridge, could not return to the Supply Dropping Point (SDP), and all its men became casualties. The SDP itself was never captured. Signals sent to divert the supply drop on D plus 2 failed to get through and in consequence the armada of Stirling and Dakota aircraft flew through murderous fire right over the now restricted divisional perimeter and dropped their cargoes to the enemy.

There were many acts of great heroism on the part of the RASC air despatch crews and their RAF colleagues. Of scores of accounts, one only, written by an infantry officer, need be quoted as an example: 'It was with excited hopefulness and an almost painful admiration that those on the ground watched these aircraft day by day flying in to drop their loads. Through a continuous curtain of fire they flew on unwaveringly and very slowly – and so low that it seemed wonderful that more of them were not destroyed – to drop their loads which floated down mostly behind the enemy lines. Many were hit and set on fire, but continued to despatch their panniers until they fell from view; one unknown aircraft was already on fire when it arrived over the target, but dropped the remainder on the second run until it went down in a sheet of flame. There were many acts of great gallantry in the air and there were fairly heavy casualties among the RASC despatchers. But it is consoling to know that the small proportion of the many hundreds of tons dropped which did reach our lines enabled hungry men to have some sort of a meal on the fifth day and also provided sufficient ammunition of all kinds to keep weapons firing and to keep the RASC dump 'in issue' right up to the withdrawal.'

On the ground, the situation steadily became worse, and the defended area progressively smaller. Mortaring and shelling, always continuous, increased to tremendous intensity after each supply drop. The ammunition dump repeatedly caught fire and was put out several times with great difficulty. CRASC had a personal interest in this, as his headquarters, a slit trench, was between the 3-inch mortar stack and the small arms fire. The jeeps were knocked out one by one. By the end there were no supplies of any sort, nor a single vehicle left.

On the sixth day the remnants of the last parachute platoon, now without a job, were organized into a force some seventy strong and sent to hold a sector of the perimeter, which they defended successfully to the end. Then, with the other survivors, they retired across the swift-flowing Rhine in the pouring rain, some in boats and some by swimming. Ten RASC officers and 243 other ranks had flown in to Arnhem. Five officers and eighty-three other ranks came out. Of those who did not, two officers and thirty-six other ranks were killed and many more were wounded.

From September to early March bitter fighting took place clearing the Scheldt Estuary, at Arnhem and through the Reichwald Forest. The Americans fought from the south and on 3 March the pincer movements had linked up and 21 Army Group was lined up on the western bank of the Rhine as far south as Dusseldorf.

During this phase every artifice had to be employed to make the limited resources keep pace with the advance; the range of all echelons was extended to the limit. In emergencies first-line transport drew from Forward Maintenance Areas (FMA), and second-line from army roadheads. In 50th Division RASC in the Nijmegen area one

A petrol filling point in the forward area where jerricans are filled from motor tankers.

A roadside bulk petrol filling point.

Brigade Company (522 Company) ran all the ammunition, POL and supply points for the whole division as well as local tasks such as troop-carrying for relief of battalions in the line. The rest of the divisional RASC was tasked with bringing loads forward from FMA and Army roadheads.

8 Corps and two independent brigades were grounded and their transport thrown into the general pool ferrying between RMA and roadheads. Fortunately the capture of many bridges intact allowed the bridge companies to be released for general transport purposes, and anti-aircraft and tank transporter units were also made available for similar work. Later, eighteen transport units from AA Command and driver training sources were improvised and sent to France to operate in the ever lengthening L of C.

The system of lifting forward and establishing dumps of stores which were then rapidly consumed was adopted as standard practice during the advance to the Meuse. It maintained a long and rapid advance and kept transport in centrally controlled pools. Transport control using radio at terminals and staging points became standard practice in 30 Corps. Daily tasks were passed to Transport Columns by DDST staff during the night and the progress of convoys, all with serial numbers related to tasks and loads, was constantly monitored as they moved forward during the day enabling redirection to take place and dumping to be controlled by DDST staff. It proved to be a simple but effective system.

By 10 September, 1944, the railway lines from Bayeux to the Seine had been repaired and rail was introduced in the L of C as far as the Seine. Second Army set up an organization on the Seine for the clearance of railheads on the south of the river and for movement of stocks by road transport to railheads on the north of the river. A ST rear link formed part of this organization, and was later supplemented by representatives from Q and Q(Movements) staff. It continued to control the transfer of stores across the Seine until such time as 6 Army Railhead (ARH) was established, when HQ 21 Army Group set up a special control at Amiens.

FROM THE RHINE TO THE BALTIC

While the Battle of the Rhineland was being fought, the Rhine crossing was being planned. The failure of Operation MARKET GARDEN to secure a bridgehead across the Rhine through which the main forces could enter Germany meant that a

full-scale assault of the river would have to be mounted and this operation was deferred until the spring of 1945. In the intervening months most of the territory west of the high ground which flanks the river was cleared up, an extensive series of muddy operations took place in the flooded Northern Netherlands, and the Germans staged their last great counter-attack through the Ardennes, into Luxembourg and Belgium, cutting off 101 United States Airborne Division in Bastogne. 6th Airborne Division, in a ground role, was sent to help restore the position, and when this was done, was withdrawn again to England to prepare for the assault of the Rhine in the vicinity Xanten-Wesel, a joint Anglo-American, land, air and partly amphibious operation known by the code word VARSITY PLUNDER. Roads and railways had been repaired and developed and Second Army depots had been stocked with some 130,000 tons of stores.

The attack began on the night of 23 March and by the next morning all the assaulting divisions (two British and two American) and the British Commando Brigade had accomplished their initial crossings between Rheineburg and Rees. The key to the crossings was the important communication centre of Wesel, which was captured by the Commando Brigade after an intense air attack by Bomber Command. On the morning of 24 March 18th United States Airborne Corps, with 6th British Airborne Division and one American airborne division, dropped on the east bank of the Rhine, within supporting distance of our guns on the west bank. These drops were successful and the British and American bridgeheads were quickly joined.

Buffaloes of 4th Royal Tank Regiment moving towards the Rhine mounted on RASC Diamond T transporters.

Hitherto, airborne forces had been employed as the spearhead of assault, to make the fullest use of the factor of surprise inherent in their rapid approach. On this occasion however, surprise was impossible – our intention to cross was only too obvious to the Germans watching from the other bank. So it was decided, by a really heavy artillery bombardment, to drive them as far back as possible. This would allow a night assault in boats and amphibian vehicles by ground forces. However, on the German side excellent cover was available in dense woods a mile or two from the river, and the bridgehead would be precarious if the German counter-attack forces were allowed to build up. So 6th Airborne Division was to be dropped some four miles on the German side in the general area of Hamminkeln after the assault phase had been completed to cover the consolidation of the bridgehead and the initial advances from it. American plans in the adjoining sector to the south were similar.

This was a short-range operation and the CRASC's plans for maintaining 6th Airborne Division for this operation were simple. The light company, less two transport platoons (ie three parachute platoons and one transport platoon), equipped with twelve tracked carriers and trailers instead of jeeps, were to fly in with the division, the transport being in Hamilcar gliders, which also stowed as many pannier loads of stores as could be got within the weight limit. The company's first duty on landing was to select a divisional maintenance area and begin stocking it, the initial stores comprising the panniers from the Hamilcars, two boxes of composite rations from nearly all other gliders used in the operation and whatever could be recovered from the jettison drop.

Dumps Established

The DMA was quickly reconnoitred and stores dumps began to be established, transport consisting only of three carriers, one trailer and a captured lorry. At 1300 hours the first supply drop took place and it was a bad one. Not only was it widely dispersed but much of it was dropped from too low a height, giving the parachutes insufficient time to open, so that a great many containers burst open. This was not wholly a disadvantage, since it was decided to open all containers in situ, to save transport, instead of carrying them complete to the DMA. Clearance continued through the night, in spite of parties of enemy infiltrating through the woods and crossing the dropping zone.

RASC Air Freight Handling team, Evere, Brussels, September 1944.

19. An RCT-manned Bedford TM 8-tonne Medium Mobility Load Carrier (MMLC) *(IRCT)*.

20. An RCT-manned Bedford TM 14-tonne MMLC *(IRCT)*.

21. An RCT JCB loading ammunition on standard NATO pallets on to a Demountable Rack Offload and Pickup System (DROPS) *(IRCT)*.

22. A view of the enlarged military port at Marchwood showing three Landing Ships Logistic (LSL) and a civilian cargo vessel alongside *(R. Grevatte-Ball)*.

23. RAF Chinook with underslung 20-tonne container load in the Falklands Campaign *(IRCT)*.

24. Ammunition being unloaded from a merchant ship to an RCT-manned Mexeflote raft in the Falklands Campaign *(IRCT)*.

25. Offloading Mechanical Handling Equipment (MHE) at Al Jubayl prior to receiving main stocks *(IRCT)*.

26. A convoy of 35-tonne Leyland Crusaders each carrying two FV430 Armoured Personnel Carriers led by a Leyland DROPS vehicle *(Martin White)*.

27. Convoy marshalling area, A1 Jubayl *(Martin White)*.

28. B Troop of 38 Squadron RCT loaded and ready to move forward *(Martin White)*.

29. DROPS vehicle loading with ammunition *(Martin White)*.

30. RHQ and Workshop of 27 Regiment RCT moving into location *(Martin White)*.

31. A Scammell Commander of 7 Tank Transporter Regiment moving tanks forward *(Martin White)*.

32. Commander 4 Brigade, Brigadier Christopher Hammerbeck, and officers and NCOs of 38 Ambulance Squadron GTR meet Corporal Parsad Gurung, later Mentioned in Despatches *(Martin White)*.

33. Officers and NCOs of 28 Ambulance Squadron GTR. In the background are Land Rover 1-tonne ambulances *(Martin White)*.

34. Artillery units on the move, carried by 7 Tank Transporter Regiment RCT *(Martin White)*.

35. 17 Squadron RCT running the Administrative Harbour Area on the Main Supply Route (MSR) Dodge *(Martin White)*.

36. Supplies moving on the MSR *(Martin White)*.

37. All-important fuel tankers coping with desert conditions *(Martin White)*.

38. A unit of 10 Regiment RCT refuelling en route *(Martin White)*.

39. A DROPS vehicle taking on and filling a water tank *(Martin White)*.

40. A DROPS vehicle delivering water to a flexible (pillow) tank *(Martin White)*.

41. The RCT Medal Collection – general view *(IRCT)*.

42. The RCT Medal Collection showing the Victoria Cross case *(IRCT)*.

43. Ex-RASC/RCT In-Pensioners, The Royal Hospital, Chelsea *(The Royal Hospital)*.

44. Major General JD MacDonald CB CBE, the last Director of the RCT in 1992, with Regimental Sergeant Major
RW Cass and In-Pensioner Sergeant L Varley MVO MBE, formerly RSM at the RCT Training Centre *(IRCT)*.

45. The interior of the Garrison Church of St Michael and St George, Aldershot *(IRCT)*.

46. The Royal Waggon Train in the Peninsular War – a painting by Johnny Jonas *(IRCT)*.

47. The Silver Centrepiece *(IRCT)*.

48. The RCT Corps Band on Public Duties at Buckingham Palace, March, 1973, before the new headdress, the Shako, was taken into service *(IRCT)*.

In the meantime progress from the far side of the river had been satisfactory. The first crossings had been made about ten hours before the airborne landings, and CRASC's adjutant, arriving about 0945 with HQ RASC of 15th (Scottish) Division, set out on his reconnaissance to establish a dump to be called PEGASUS. That day eighteen DUKWs crossed and by the evening of the next eighty-four DUKW loads had been delivered at the PEGASUS dump. At this point amphibious transport was stopped, through fear that a breakdown might cause a DUKW to be swept by the swift current against the newly-built pontoon bridge a little below the crossing point. Thereafter all supplies crossed the bridge in the vehicles of the heavy companies, which were given bridge priority. Soon after this, normal supply to 6th Airborne Division from the PEGASUS dump began and the division became to all intents an infantry formation for the rest of the operation. With the crossing of the Rhine, the last airborne operation was complete and no more actually took place (though others were planned), during the remainder of the war.

On completion of its task in crossing the Rhine 6th Airborne Division was used in the role of an infantry formation. With the addition of five transport platoons its RASC Column was able to support the division during the advance to the Baltic Sea where it arrived at Wismar at 1430 hours on 2 May, 1945. The Royal Navy played a considerable part in this operation with craft which had been carried by road across Belgium, the southern Netherlands and the Rhineland.

Within four days the bridgehead over the Rhine had been established and on 28 March the advance to the Elbe began. Second Army advanced with its left flank directed on Hamburg. The main drive to the Elbe continued towards Luneburg, which was reached on 18 April, when the British forces began to line up on the southern bank of the river to mask the city of Hamburg. The Elbe was crossed on 29 April and spearheads made straight for Lübeck in order to seal off Schleswig-Holstein peninsula. Across the Elbe there was hardly any opposition and on 2 May a German party came out from Hamburg to negotiate its surrender. The countryside was crowded with masses of German soldiers and refugees fleeing, in opposite directions, from 21 Army Group and from the Russians with whom contact was established on 2 May.

The negotiations which began in Hamburg led, on 3 May, to the despatch by Admiral Doenitz of envoys to Field-Marshal Montgomery's tactical headquarters on Luneburg Heath. On the evening of 4 May General-Admiral Friedeburg, Commander-in-Chief of the Germany Navy, signed the instrument of unconditional surrender of all German naval, land and air forces opposite 21 Army Group. The cease-fire was ordered on 21 Army Group front as from 0800 hours on 5 May.

Road Transport

Once the advanced base had been established in Belgium, the main task of the GHQ transport pool became dock clearance at Antwerp and the Channel ports. But there were many other and varying jobs to be done, from bridge-building and airfield construction all over the BLA area, which involved general transport as well as the ubiquitous tipper lorries, to civil affairs tasks. As always, the calls for transport exceeded the availability and the strain was increased in February by Operation GOLDFLAKE. A road line of communication was organized between Italy and BLA, for which the Corps provided a headquarters RASC. Along this line of communication 1 Canadian Corps and 5 British Division were transferred from Italy to 21 Army Group. They brought their own formation transport, but not their quota of GT companies. In order to relieve this pressure, a large number of Belgian and Dutch companies were formed and trained by the Corps. Captured German and civil horse transport was also brought into use and played quite a large part in short dock clearance hauls in Antwerp.

A further strain on the transport organization was the pruning which took place at the end of 1944 to provide more fit officers and other ranks for the infantry. One divisional RASC had to find eleven captains and subalterns for transfer, while a group of four GT companies produced 140 other ranks.

In early March, 1945, there were the equivalent of eighty 3-ton companies working on the lines of communication, whilst 1st Canadian Army had nine and 2nd Army had eight from the GHQ pool. In the GHQ pool itself there remained only about twenty equivalent 3-ton companies, all of which were committed on permanent tasks, such as timber haulage and construction work. In the period before the Rhine assault as much as possible was moved by rail right up to within three miles of the front line. But the tonnages to be lifted by road were still formidable.

It took Second Army four weeks to get from the Rhine to the Elbe and, although this advance was not so rapid as the one across France and Belgium, the strain on transport was as great. Large commitments, apart from those connected with the advance of our own troops, arose. The backloading of German prisoners of war as well as our own, whom we continually uncovered, the clearance of refugees and inmates of concentration camps, including the notorious Belsen, and relief to the starving population of the Netherlands, were all added to the battle tasks of troop-carrying, dumping, bridging and normal maintenance.

Supplies

Naturally supply units were hard-worked like everyone else in this phase, and the unexpected calls on their resources and initiative for prisoners, refugees and starving populations were many. Perhaps the only aspect of special interest was the drill which was evolved for GHQ to take over successive roadhead stocks with their units from Second Army, thus relieving Army of unwanted responsibilities far behind their operational area. By the time of the surrender in May GHQ-controlled supply units and installations stretched from Hamburg to Antwerp and the total feeding strength of the theatre eventually reached two million.

Petroleum

By the end of the campaign 7,500 tons of petrol a day were being issued in the British area alone. But the supply of fuel never caused any anxiety. By 15 March the 'PLUTO' pipehead was the source of bulk petrol for both armies and this was coming into the theatre at the rate of 15,000 tons a day. The total quantity of petrol and oil imported for 21 Army Group during the campaign in bulk shipments alone mounted to nearly 1,200,000,000 gallons and at the end the RASC was operating 300,000 tons of bulk storage. In addition, 2,500,000 jerricans and over 4,500,000 4-gallon tins were sent over.

Aftermath

Major General W d'A Collings, DST 21 Army Group, issued the following message

A pipeline taking bulk fuel to forward refilling point.

to all ranks of the Royal Army Service Corps and Royal Canadian Army Service Corps on 'Victory in Europe Day', 8 May, 1945:

> *'The achievement of victory in Europe provides an opportunity to review the work of our Corps in this campaign, upon which we entered determined to enhance the high traditions earned in many others.*
>
> *Throughout the campaign, from the beaches of Normandy over many rivers to the banks of the Elbe, the Corps has been working almost continuously at the highest pressure. It has endured almost every form of enemy attack, from small arms fire to V 2s, and every condition of weather. It has been called on with almost monotonous regularity to make 'that extra all-out effort' whenever vital operations were in preparation or in progress, and it has never failed.*
>
> *This has been the greatest military operation ever conducted by the British Army and, in some of its phases, the fastest moving. These are the conditions which throw the greatest strain on the RASC and it is safe to say that not only did it never fail, but it never appeared in any danger of being unequal to the strain. This magnificent result is the reward of good training, good leadership, good discipline and comradeship, and above all a determination to live up to our traditions. This applies equally to the Royal Army Service Corps and the Royal Canadian Army Service Corps. As Director of Supply and Transport in 21 Army Group, the ultimate responsibility for all that you have done falls upon me, and I wish to place on record that I have never once during the campaign been called upon to answer criticisms on the work of the Corps. I send you my congratulations, grateful thanks, and best wishes for the future.'*

The rounding-up, amid dispersal, of the remnants of the German armies in

Schleswig-Holstein, the cleansing of concentration camps, repatriation of prisoners of war and staging, direction and transport of displaced persons became the pressing military commitments immediately the surrender had been signed, and the Corps was probably more deeply committed in most of these tasks than any other arm or service.

THE FINAL OFFENSIVE IN ITALY

The Capture of Rome

General Alexander's final offensive against the Gustav Line opened on 11 May, 1944. After several days of strenuous fighting, a breakthrough by the French Expeditionary Corps in the Fifth Army sector was the prelude to victory. Finally, on the evening of 4 June, the leading troops of the Fifth Army entered Rome, hot on the heels of the last Germans hurriedly withdrawing to the north without waiting to demolish the bridges over the Tiber.

Up to the capture of Rome the armies were based for their maintenance on the port of Naples for formations operating on the west side of the Apennines, and on the ports of Tarranto, Brindisi and Bari for those operating on the east coast. From the ports the greatest possible use was made of the railways following the coastal plains on the east and west coasts and of the arterial roads, Highways 6 and 7, which converge on Rome.

Supplies in the Anzio Bridgehead handled by 37 BSD containing enough food for three days.

Corps maintenance areas were established as far forward as possible, and during the period of static warfare on the Gustav Line were only a few miles behind the forward positions, with an army roadhead (or maintenance area) not far in rear. The stocks in these maintenance areas proved invaluable once the pursuit began, while the reserves laboriously built up in the Anzio beachhead, which were located some eighty miles nearer Rome, helped to sustain the rapid advance beyond Rome, without the inevitable delay usually involved in moving stocks forward. Petroleum pipelines were constructed for the first time as far forward as corps maintenance areas and mobile petrol filling centres were set up under corps control. Right up to the fall of Cassino great reliance was placed on supply by jeeps, mules and porters.

The Pursuit North of Rome – Capture of Florence

The capture of Rome gave no respite to the Allied armies. It was imperative to continue the pursuit of the beaten enemy as far as our advancing columns could go without having to pause for administrative reasons. The enemy's powers of recuperation were sufficiently well known for there to be no room for complacency.

The immediate task of the Allies was expressed as: 'to destroy all German forces south of the Pisa-Rimini line'. This was greatly hampered by the withdrawal of substantial forces from Italy to support the projected landings on the French Riviera. The whole of the American 6 Corps was withdrawn between 14 and 27 June and the French Expeditionary Corps followed soon afterwards.

Nevertheless, the advance went relentlessly on. By the middle of July the River

A section of RASC Bridging Vehicles in Italy, winter 1943/44.

Arno was reached, Pisa, Ancona and Leghorn were captured and the most important administrative centre of Arezzo was in our hands.

Arezzo was rapidly developed as a railhead and a system of rail pack trains was introduced. Although this system no doubt effected considerable economies in the road transport lift, it caused great difficulties in front of railhead. This was mainly because of the irregularity in the arrival of trains, the time wasted by road transport waiting for them and the frequent discrepancies in the contents of the various packs they contained. It made the establishment of railhead depots absolutely essential, with the additional handling that this involved. With the capture of Florence in the first week of August resistance south of the River Arno came to an end and the Allied armies found themselves coming up against what was to prove the last great German defensive position in Italy – the Gothic Line. This extended from north of Pesaro on the east coast, through the Futa Pass on the crest of the Apennines, to south of Spezia on the west coast.

Winter in the Apennines

The last account of the adventures of pack units in Italy should not only describe the most arduous and protracted period of the whole campaign, but should also recount the work of a group composed of Italian companies strengthened by a single company of one of the well-tried units of the RASC.

Whatever opinions may be held about the part played by the Italian Army in some phases of the Second World War, there is no doubt that the men of the pack units led by their British cadres displayed the greatest gallantry, night after night, under the

Pack Mules crossing the River Ronco, Italy.

most appalling conditions. The operations north of Florence before the final breakout to the River Po were most protracted and trying, starting as they did in the autumn of 1944 and lasting for twenty-two weeks.

This was to be the last drawn-out stand by the enemy, who craftily encouraged the advancing American formations and the 1 and 78 Infantry and 6 Armoured divisions to pursue him along the difficult Route 65 and then contrived to force them, still in pursuit, to two axes – one the road leading to the Futa Pass and the other the track which led to Castel del Rio. Rain and traffic were both heavy. The divisions, with their mules, had floundered on over the top and down to the valley until just after Castel del Rio, where they came up against solid enemy resistance on the last range of hills before the Po Valley. This was exactly what the enemy wanted. He had about two miles of supply lines, whereas we had thirty-five over desolate, wild, mountainous country crossed by only one track. Motor transport managed to supply to divisions as far as just north of Castel del Rio, but from there on everything had to be carried by mule. This last range of hills, where the infantry were to stay for some twenty-two weeks, was one of the bleakest spots in the Apennines and – except for a rare farmhouse – offered no shelter at all.

The conditions for pack transport were miserable. It was a grotesque sight to see the columns lurching, splashing and floundering up steep muddy tracks, the mules sweating and grunting, and the men with the mud over their rubber knee boots hanging on to the odd strap to keep up and going.

The End of the Campaign

In the later stages of the campaign men of the RASC continued to earn their share of awards for gallantry. Space alone precludes a recital of their many achievements. The battle casualties sustained by the RASC during the campaign in Italy amounted to five officers and 156 other ranks killed, thirty-four officers and 679 other ranks

Landing Vehicle Tracked (LVT) - Buffalo

wounded and two officers and forty-eight other ranks missing.

As the campaign progressed, the army began to assume an almost international appearance, as, in addition to American, French, British and Indian formations, there were divisions from the Canadian, New Zealand and Brazilian Armies, a Polish Corps, and also single brigades of Palestine Jews and from the Royal Greek Army. When the Italian Army was reformed, a number of *gruppi* joined the Allies.

The RASC, whose strength rose to almost the same as the total strength of the pre-war Regular Army at home, had an even greater diversity of nations in its ranks, with companies manned by Sinhalese, Cypriots, Mauritians, Basutos and Arabs from both Arabia and North Africa. The Corps also had a large number of units manned by Italian co-operators, former prisoners of war who volunteered to serve. In the last stages several RA anti-aircraft units were converted into GT companies.

The spring offensive opened with an attack by the 8th Army in the Adriatic sector, making use of Tracked Landing Vehicles (LVT) to overcome the flooded areas around Lake Comacchio, on 9 April, 1945. This was followed by the attack of the Fifth Army on 12 April. From the start everything went well. Bologna was captured on 21 April, followed swiftly by Genoa on 26 April, Padua and Venice on 29 April, and Milan on 30 April. The Germans in Italy were finally defeated, and on 2 May, 1945, the German Army Group in Italy surrendered unconditionally and the war in this theatre was at an end.

General Montgomery landing in Italy on 3 September, 1943, from an RASC DUKW.

THE RETURN TO GREECE

After the British troops had been forced to withdraw from Greece in 1941 a continuous and relentless war was carried on by Greek guerrillas against the German occupying forces. During the years that followed, the Allies continued to plan for an eventual return to the country and close touch was kept with the Greek Government, which was exiled in Egypt, so that when the opportunity arose we would be ready to assist in re-establishing law and order and to provide the relief that would be so sorely needed by the stricken Greek people.

Early in 1944 there was good hope that the combined efforts of the guerrillas and the gradual encirclement of the Axis Powers would cause the Germans to withdraw. Plans for a return to Greece were then perfected. A separate organization for supply and relief had been set up in Egypt under the name of Headquarters Military Liaison Greece, which was to assist in the rehabilitation of the civil economy. The force placed at the disposal of the GOC, Lieutenant General Sir Ronald Scobie, was small, and consisted of 3 Armoured Brigade, 4th Indian Division, 2 Independent Parachute Brigade and ancillary services.

The situation moved quickly and on 14 October, 1944, British troops re-entered Athens amid scenes of the wildest enthusiasm and rejoicing by the civil population. Internal politics soon changed the situation as the strong left-wing element of the guerrillas, who were numerically superior to other factions, saw the opportunity of seizing political power. Open attempts by the left-wing political party known as EAM, who controlled the Communist-dominated guerrillas referred to as ELAS, to undermine the newly returned Government, led to growing tension in November, and the first shots of what developed into a civil war were fired on 3 December. On the same day 139 Infantry Brigade (46th Division) began to arrive in Athens by air to reinforce General Scobie's command.

The Beginning of Civil War

RASC units had been allotted to the force on the basis that civil transport for general purposes would be obtained locally and that the supply and petrol organization need only be sufficient for static conditions. It was considered that the RASC brigade companies with each of the brigades and a small supply depot, bakery, butchery and static petrol units would be quite adequate. The account of their actions does not rest so much on their prescribed activities as on their conduct when called upon to defend their lives and their positions.

To overcome the lack of transport, the DDST arranged for the withdrawal of about 250 vehicles originally landed for the Greek Government. At the same time agreement was given to the employment of the transport of 66 Light Anti-Aircraft Regiment RA as a temporary transport company.

RASC Units in Defence

The first and most serious attack against our forces took place early on 13 December against the collection of units in the infantry barracks, which included 331 Company, RASC. There were many acts of individual gallantry on the part of the garrison, such as that of Driver W Prickett who performed one hazardous task after the other until badly burned, but even then refused to give up until the enemy had been cleared. Captain V H Band, in spite of enemy fire organized the clearance of petrol stocks to a safer point and later went in search of wounded under enemy fire, until, wounded himself, he was rescued under heavy fire by Drivers J W E Carter and H Hobson. Captain Band and the three drivers were given immediate awards of the Military Cross and the Military Medal respectively.

While 4th Division was arriving and the enemy were being gradually cleared from the Piraeus area, the work of building up stocks went on steadily at Faliron. Strenuous efforts had been made to provide some bread in place of biscuit. 2 Parachute Brigade were able to extricate men of the field bakery who were set to work in civil bakeries. The feeding strength had been increased considerably because the large number of Greek police and gendarmerie and units of the newly formed Greek National Guard had no means of subsistence and had to be taken on the British ration strength. By the end of December the original figure of 16,000 to be fed had risen to more than 70,000.

During the first three weeks of hostilities the bulk petrol storage section and 2 Mobile Petrol Filling Centre, which were located at the Shell, Socony and Secombel plants, had remained at their posts. For his part in the defence of the petrol installations Major A S Mackay RASC received an immediate award of the Military Cross.

The Civil War Dies Down

By early in January, 1945, the city was gradually being cleared of the remaining insurgents and ships could be unloaded again at the Piraeus, but the tragic war did not come to an end until 12 February. Many of the inhabitants were near starvation and thousands had been dispersed from their homes and the civil economy was hopelessly disorganized. Bread was the first need. A committee under the presidency of the DDST was set up and mill owners, the Greek Ministry of Supply, the Red Cross and other authorities were gathered together to make a plan for immediate relief. With the help of the Navy a grain ship was unloaded, supplies of oil and petrol were provided by the Army and, as soon as the mills were in action again, bread was put on the market at a reasonable controlled price. All available transport was also set to work to help in carrying relief stores and supplies.

VICTORY IN BURMA

The Struggle to Victory

During the monsoon period at the end of 1943, during which time 14th Army were preparing to go on the offensive both on the Assam and Arakan fronts, the Japanese had doubled their forces and were also planning to go on the offensive. On 3 February, 1944, in the Arakan, they struck at two of the Indian divisions facing them, cutting their communications. Lieutenant General Slim immediately placed the two divisions on air supply, whilst the Army Commander, General Giffard, sent in two more divisions. The Japanese force was itself enveloped and, after bitter fighting, it was broken up and fled, leaving 5,000 dead. The British had won their first victory over the Japanese.

The Chindits

Meanwhile Wingate had launched another expedition with his Chindits, this time at divisional strength, based on 70th British Division. It was successful in keeping the Japanese communications cut for a long time, but failed in one of its objectives which was to force the withdrawal of the Japanese division facing General Stilwell's force in the north. The Chindits were again entirely maintained by air. It was decided that, although an RIASC air despatch organization was in existence, the British Chindits must be served in this respect by their own RASC. 61 Company was reorganized as an air despatch company and continued with this task until the Chindits withdrew. Its duties included the establishment of air bases in the advanced strongholds of the Chindits such as 'Broadway' and 'White City', deep in Japanese-occupied territory. After this special task, the company continued to be employed as part of the great Army-Air Transport Organization, on which Fourteenth Army depended to an ever-increasing extent for its maintenance as it drove south through Burma.

Another air despatch unit, 799 Company, took part in the later stages of the maintenance of Fourteenth Army. Having supplied the French resistance forces, our troops in Normandy and at Arnhem, and the Americans in the Ardennes, it was sent out East and began operations with the United States Army Air Force in May, 1945.

As the tide of war began to turn against the Japanese at sea, in the South Pacific and in Burma, plans were evolved for the recapture of Rangoon, Malaya, Singapore, Hong Kong and the other Far Eastern territories. In these plans provision was made for a large number of RASC Fleet units of all types, including such new companies as floating workshop companies, coaster companies and ambulance launch companies.

In September, 1944, the HQ CRASC, 56 Water Transport Unit, was formed at Stranraer, quickly followed by 856 and 884 Companies RASC (Motorboat). Cadres of trained and battle experienced men were provided from forty-two Water Transport Units, and the units were built up to strength from the output of 467 Company, at that time engaged on continuation training at Stranraer. The demand from Headquarters Allied Land Forces, South-East Asia (ALFSEA), for these companies was urgent.

2nd Division in Action

On 15 March, 1944, the Japanese launched their main offensive in Assam with a strength of four divisions against the three Indian divisions in the area Kohima-Imphal-Tiddim. Slim had foreseen what would happen and the besieged garrisons at Kohima and Imphal were put on air supply, whilst two Indian divisions were flown in from the Arakan front and 2nd British Division was brought down from the Manipur Road railhead, one of its brigades also being flown into Kohima. The ensuing battle was one of the longest and most bitter of the war, both during the Japanese offensive and after, when 14th Army took the initiative. It lasted for three months at the end of which the Japanese broke and fled across the Chindwin in rout.

Everywhere the administrative troops took their share of the fighting. At Kohima this was particularly severe, and the siege, which lasted sixteen days, has justly become famous. It was here that 2nd Division with its RASC Column entered the battle. The fighting troops of the division were flown in and with them went the CRASC and his staff and elements of the composite platoons. Casualties in the infantry made necessary the attachment of 300 men of the divisional RASC to battalions to fill the gaps in their ranks. They earned the commendations of the infantry commanders for their splendid efforts. However, with these men attached to the Infantry there was a shortage of drivers in the Transport units and the situation became increasingly difficult, and the two remaining Companies were hard-pressed and had to be helped by the RIASC.

At last the Japanese began to withdraw and the division pursued them hotly.

Troop-carrying and maintenance made the greatest demands on all transport. Guns and all materials had to be ferried forward, and this involved a double mileage. Dumps were carried forward a few miles but were no sooner unloaded than the battle moved forward, and the loads had to be lifted again. Every available man in the transport companies was continually loading and unloading vehicles, and drivers were often driving for twenty-four hours at a stretch over the tortuous mountain road to complete one delivery.

Beyond the Chindwin

The East African Division crossed the Chindwin in December, 1944, and established a bridgehead opposite Kalewa. The plan for 2nd Division was to go through the bridgehead and make for Shwebo but the road on the far side of the river was broken down for several miles and only passable for light vehicles. One of the DUKW platoons was called in and, towing pontoons, moved all the troops, tanks, guns and transport of the Division some eight miles downstream to Shwegyin, where the road could be picked up again. The same platoon towed into position the sections of the 1,000-foot Bailey bridge built to span the river at Kalewa; it also stocked the bridgehead with thousands of tons of stores.

DUKWs from RASC companies were by now becoming heavily involved in supporting operations throughout the theatre, in particular the crossings of the Chindwin and Irrawaddy rivers. During the crossing of the latter by 2nd Division drivers of 387 Company each ferried over an average of seven loads of troops in their DUKWs to strengthen the bridgehead and every trip meant coming under machine-gun fire as they rounded the sandbank; casualties were inevitably incurred. Corporal E Eglon, Lance Corporal S B Lines and A A Meese and Drivers J Hall and J O'Brien received the immediate award of the Military Medal. By nightfall the leading brigade was over and the situation was saved. During the next seventy-two hours rafts towed by the DUKWs moved the rest of the division, 6,000 men and 200 vehicles, including tanks, guns and supplies.

With the bridgehead secure, the DUKWs turned to the task of carrying over the division's reserves of ammunition, supplies and petrol. They did this for another month as a vital link in the maintenance of 33 Indian Corps, which by then was reducing Mandalay. Another RASC unit employed on the water link was 884 Motor Boat Company, which arrived in March. The RASC's part in the crossing of the Irrawaddy had been of major importance.

RASC Motor Boat Companies in Burma

Arriving in India in February, 1945, as the Arakan campaign was drawing to its close, 856 Company was sent urgently to Akyab to assist the inland water transport situation, eight D-type tugs were taken over. The company did work there that they had surely not been taught at Rothesay or West Mersea – how to assist in mooring a 10,000-ton freighter in a six-knot tide, or to tow one, possibly two, heavy barges laden with men and supplies through treacherous waterways without charts.

In April, 1945, the company was withdrawn to Calcutta and re-equipped with its own 36 ft harbour launches, which by then were arriving from Britain in large numbers. Soon they embarked with the assault forces for Rangoon. There they took over what had once been a prosperous iron foundry on the muddy banks of the Rangoon River. It had its own jetty at the foot of the Sulei Pagoda road and operated various harbour services. Boarding and mooring craft were provided, but perhaps the most interesting and frequently exciting detail was the weekly despatch boat which ran from Rangoon to Bassein to supply the garrison there.

Tank Transporters

There were three tank transporter companies in 14th Army. One of them, 553, was engaged in an unspectacular but necessary role on the L of C. The conveyance of replacement tanks over the very long line, 3-400 miles, with the limited number of rather worn out transporters available, was a great problem, calling for Herculean efforts from the company, which were on the whole successful. The unit had also to cope with other heavy loads, such as six 21-ton locomotives and large craft for use by IWT. The movement of these awkward loads over the difficult roads of the already congested L of C presented many problems.

When the Japanese invaded Assam in March, 1944, 589 Company joined 254 Indian Tank Brigade in a 'box' or defended area on the Imphal Plain and went on ferrying tanks and stores and bridging material. When the enemy retreated it moved tanks to Nanhanwe, a round trip of 300 miles. It reached the Chindwin at Kalewa on 12 January, 1945, and, while some transporters crossed by the bridge, others were towed on pontoons by DUKWs to Shwegyin, thence the unit went forward by way of Shwebo to Myittha and eventually by way of Taungtha to Prome; this was virtually the end of the company's active role and of a task of which they could be justifiably proud.

The other transporter unit, 590 Company, served 255 Indian Tank Brigade and probably had the hardest task of them all. In order to effect a surprise crossing of the Irrawaddy at Pakokku, and from there make a dash for Meiktila, 4 Corps, which included this tank brigade, was switched from the left flank of 14th Army to the right and sent down by way of the Kabaw and Gangaw Valleys. The route was difficult; it was 400 miles long, of which 110 through the Kabaw Valley were over a fair-weather road, already the main L of C of 33 Indian Corps and deep in dust. The difficulties encountered by 590 Company in moving the tank brigade over the last 200 miles, without using too much track mileage, were immense. The whole move took eight weeks to complete because of the arduous nature of the route and the lack of transport. Throughout this period the company worked extremely hard in terrible conditions and earned much praise for their sustained efforts.

The End in Burma

During the later part of the war in Burma a growing flow of RASC units and individuals arrived in India and SEAC, mainly because of the build-up in preparation for the intensive war against Japan which was planned to follow on the defeat of the Germans in Europe. For the final drive to reach Rangoon before the monsoon broke General Slim decided that 33 Corps should move on a feint down the Irrawaddy Valley, while 4 Corps should make the real attack on foot and in road transport, crossing the Irrawaddy and advancing down the line of the Toungoo-Pegu railway. The British and Indian troops, having overcome fanatical Japanese resistance, entered Rangoon on 3 May. Ultimate victory was achieved by the subsequent shattering defeat of the Japanese east of the Sittang River, and by 4 August Burma was secured.

MISCELLANEOUS OVERSEAS STATIONS AND MINOR THEATRES

In remote corners of the world small RASC detachments did their duty unheralded and unsung. Many of these detachments found themselves in pleasant places climatically and otherwise. Others laboured amid snow and ice and in conditions of acute discomfort. Some knew that enemy action in their neighbourhood, though possible, was unlikely, while few knew not what excitements the next day might bring forth.

An important detachment was that stationed in Iceland. When that wintry island was occupied as a precautionary measure in 1940 by 49th Division, the divisional RASC did not accompany it. Corps duties were performed in difficult terrain and climate by a base supply depot, a field bakery, four detail issue depots, four petrol depots, a field butchery, 275 (Reserve) MT Company, a detachment of 70 (WT) Company and a section of 246 (motorboat) Company. These units had a total strength of about sixty officers and 1,400 other ranks. In 1942 the force was relieved by American troops, but a small RASC detachment remained for some time to look after naval and RAF units, the officer commanding RASC also doing the duties of Officer Commanding, British Troops, Iceland.

Ceylon

Because of the strategic importance of Ceylon, a large force was built up in the island when Japan entered the war. This considerably reinforced the small British Army garrison there, then based in Colombo and in the area of the Royal Naval base of Trincomalee, where nearby there was also the Royal Air Force station at China Bay. The reinforcements, located in areas over the whole island, consisted of an Indian division late in 1941, and subsequently an East African division, followed by a British brigade from the Western Desert in 1942. Many of these forces later went into Burma after training in Ceylon, including British infantry battalions who joined Wingate's Chindits. A full administrative base was established in the Colombo area, where Ceylon Army Command was located. The S & T role on the island was shared between the RASC, the RIASC and the Ceylon Army Service Corps (CASC), for which Corps an RASC-run training organization was established.

The Corps, supported by the CASC, covered all aspects of the Corps' tasks in the base area, whilst the RIASC provided the transport requirements and all the supply units for the remainder of the island. In this they were supported by the S & T elements of the formations located throughout the Command. The DDST (Brigadier – RASC) at the RASC-manned S & T Directorate at HQ Ceylon Army Command had technical control of all S & T matters within the Command.

The importance and scope of the Command increased when, in mid-1944, Lord Louis Mountbatten, now Supreme Commander of South-East Asia Command, moved his headquarters from Delhi to Kandy, in the centre of Ceylon.

West Africa

Perhaps the most important station well away from any land operations was West Africa, comprising the colonies of the Gambia, Sierra Leone, The Gold Coast and Nigeria. These had great strategic value as the main refuelling points for our vital sea convoys en route to the Middle and Far East. Suddenly, with the fall of France in

1940, the colonies were surrounded by potentially hostile Vichy French colonies, which possessed considerably larger military forces.

Immediate steps were taken to expand the small Royal West African Frontier Force which had no indigenous supply and transport units. In late 1940 cadres of RASC officers and NCOs arrived to create and build up a West African Army Service Corps from raw and mostly illiterate African recruits. The potential French threat prevailed until the Allied North African landings in 1942. During these two years the RASC cadres, in the face of enormous difficulties, brought into being excellent transport companies, supply units and a workshop organization. Unique organizations raised by the RASC to meet the needs of jungle warfare were the Auxiliary Groups. A Group was intended to support an infantry brigade, comprising 1000 African carriers each to head-load 50 pounds. Initially all the officers and NCOs were found from the RASC.

With the removal of the French threat, two divisions, 81 (WA) and 82 (WA) were made available for service in Burma. In January, 1944, General Slim decided to deploy 81 (WA) Division in the previously inaccessible jungle-clad mountains on the flank of the Arakan to prevent the type of Japanese incursion which had frustrated previous offensives. The deployment was only possible due to the combination of air supply and the mobility afforded by the Auxiliary Groups. Major E W Childs, RASC, 5 Auxiliary Group, was awarded the MC for bravery during an attack in which the Commanding Officer and Second in Command were both killed.

The success of the West African Army Service Corps was a tribute to the RASC and to the courage, cheerfulness and hard work of the Africans they welded into a Corps.

Other Smaller Stations

The Corps also operated detachments in the Faeroe Islands, Archangel and Murmansk, the Falkland Islands, St Helena and Ascension Island, Bermuda, Jamaica and Trinidad, the Azores, Mauritius, the Seychelles and Cocos or Keeling Islands. To support the RAF in Aden a petrol depot was established by the RASC, whilst all other ST duties were provided by the RIASC.

Madagascar

Madagascar was a French possession and, after the capitulation of France, was governed from Vichy. Its long coastline and many creeks and estuaries suitable for lying-up early attracted the Japanese, whose submarines began to take heavy toll of the Allied shipping routed round the Cape. In order to stop this interference with vital traffic, Operation IRONCLAD, mounted from Britain, saw Force 121 carry out an assault landing on 5 May, 1942 and continue to the capture of Diego Suarez. Diego Suarez lies at the head of a fine large harbour at the northern tip of the island. The Force comprised 29 Independent Infantry Brigade Group and 13 and 17 Infantry Brigades. CRASC was Lieutenant Colonel R A E Dunlop.

RASC support to Force 121 comprised 55 DID with a few additional bakers and butchers and a transport detachment of twenty 15 and 30-cwt vehicles and six ambulances. 13 and 17 Brigades had their RASC companies, though initially no vehicles could be landed for them. During the operation and subsequently until all vehicles were landed, the available transport was at full stretch but was able to meet requirements because of the short distances.

Fighting continued southwards until the French forces surrendered and an armistice was signed at Ambalavao on 6 November 1942.

Persia and Iraq

Up to September, 1942, Persia and Iraq had formed part of the responsibilities of GHQ Middle East in Cairo. Persia and Iraq Command (PAIC) came into existence in September, 1942. The importance to the Allies was twofold. It contained important oilfields, including the huge refineries at Abadan near Basra, and it was one of the few routes through which supplies could reach Russia.

During the summer of 1942 the German advances had almost reached the Caucasus Mountains which separate Russia from Persia. The role of the Command was to prepare to prevent the German forces sweeping into Persia and Iraq and to quell a pro-Axis rebellion. It was also there to guard the right flank of forces in the Middle East. Headquarters 10th Army was established in Baghdad and planned to maintain a force of eleven divisions and soon RASC and RIASC were deployed throughout the theatre.

The port of entry into the command was Basra, a well-equipped port which had been developed as a military base for the Mesopotamian campaign twenty-five years before. Basra is the base for two lines of communication, one running through Iraq with a metre-gauge railway system and the other through Persia with a standard gauge.

A cold storage installation, petrol-tin-making plants and assembly plants for vehicles were among the many developments at the Base during this period. Work was also begun on an advanced base area in the neighbourhood of Baghdad, which included among its units a combined RASC/RIASC Training and Reinforcement Depot at Mussayib, to which newly arrived units were sent to complete their equipping and acclimatization and where new locally raised units took shape.

In PAIC, a command in which not a single shot was fired at the enemy, many officers and men of the RASC and RIASC took part in an operation whose direct connection with the war was obvious. This was the 'aid to Russia' operation, which continued during the whole of the active life of PAIC.

In November, 1942, the Russians fighting in the Caucasus had urgent need of ammunition and 203 and 204 General Purpose Transport (GPT) Companies, RIASC, were allotted specially for this task. As an increased lift of ammunition and other warlike stores was required, HQ 16 L of C Transport Column RASC was formed in December. Two further companies were provided almost immediately and early in 1943 the strength of the column was built up to eight companies.

The defeat of the Germans at Stalingrad in February, 1943, removed any serious threat to the theatre, but Corps units remained heavily involved in operating the supply route to Russia, a total of five million tons, plus supplying huge numbers of cattle on the hoof to Syria and Palestine.

Another task of great importance was the mobilization and training of Polish troops released from prison in Russia. A British military mission, on which the RASC was strongly represented, supervised the training of the Polish Corps which, under General Anders, served with such distinction in Italy and elsewhere.

SOME ADDITIONAL ACHIEVEMENTS

Reorganization of RASC Transport Units

The importance of these technical units in the RASC organization may be realized from a glance at the numbers of vehicles in the service. In the First World War the Corps operated about 90,000 load carriers and 35,000 light vehicles and motorcycles. At the end of the Second World War the number of B and RASC vehicles in depots and units was nearly 1,500,000, and of those with units roughly 40 per cent were in the hands of the RASC.

This immense fleet owed much of its existence to the Canadian and the United States motor industries. As the war progressed an ever-growing proportion of our vehicles were of North American origin, and the RASC were dependent for our life-blood, our vehicles, largely on the operation of the lend-lease scheme.

The Composite Ration

The introduction of the composite ration was probably the greatest acquisition provided for the Army by the supply branch. The idea of packing a complete day's ration for so many men into one box can hardly be regarded as an invention, but it was certainly an innovation in the British Army and one which was adopted by almost all our Allies.

The original ration, although a comparatively plain affair, was used for the first time in 1940 during the operations in Norway and it was voted an immediate success. The plan was then so developed that special ration packs were produced to meet many types of operational conditions and by the end of the war no fewer than 40,000,000 packs were manufactured in different varieties.

Petroleum

The development of the organization in the larger commands abroad was directly influenced by the gradual evolution of the petroleum organization and supply and distribution policy which originated at the War Office. The supply of MT fuel, liquid fuels and lubricants was a War Office responsibility throughout the war, as was providing the means of producing containers and the supply of plant and material required overseas.

The ST Directorate at home and abroad could not, however, have achieved their purpose without the co-operation of the British Oil Industry. Many members of the industry served with the Corps; those who did not also made an indispensable contribution in many parts of the world.

Barrack Services – Coal

The War Office was responsible for all further supplies of solid fuel both for the British and the American forces from D Day until May, 1945, after which part of the coal required came from the United States. From D Day to the end of July, 1945, a total of over two million tons of solid fuel and pitch was supplied from the United Kingdom against SHAEF demands.

In reviewing Barrack Services during the war it is apparent that ample proof was given of the value of the system of co-ordinating the domestic services for static accommodation within one department.

Clerical Services

Wherever the British Army served it had its supply lines covering the globe like a gigantic spider's web. General headquarters, divisional area and district headquarters had been established in each theatre of operations, while allocations for the issue of field ammunition, food, petrol and water were dotted along the supply lines. All these had one thing in common – clerical administration and support provided by clerks of the RASC.

In addition in all formations down to brigade HQ level, the clerical staff was RASC. Both in the static or field force units the clerks often became caught up in other, including infantry, roles and received awards for gallantry and distinguished service.

CHAPTER 7

The Burdens of Peace – The RASC in the Postwar Years

Introduction. Responsibilities of the RASC; Organization. The RASC in Post War Europe; BAOR; MCTG and MSO Transport Units; Effects of the Cold War on RASC Organization; The Lines of Communication; Norway; Austria; Trieste; Italy; The Berlin Airlift. Changes to the Home base; Balancing the Support Requirement; National Service and the Reserve Army. The RASC/RCT Vehicle Fleet. REME Phase II. Air Despatch – British North Greenland Expedition. The RASC Fleet. Changes in Western Europe; Belgium; Austria and Trieste. Return to the Far East, the Elusive Peace; Singapore; Malaya; Borneo; Sarawak. Malayan Emergency and Independence. Hong Kong. The Korean War. The Corps Support to Army Aviation. The Middle East – A Dangerous Highway; Palestine; Egypt; The RASC Fleet; Malta GC; Libya; Cyprus. Kenya. Singapore; Formation of the Gurkha ASC; Organizational Changes in FARELF. Aden. The Indonesian Confrontation. Towards an All-Regular Army and a New Corps; Junior Leaders; Anti-Aircraft Command; Changes in Rank of Senior Corps Appointments Training Commitments. The McLeod Reorganization.

INTRODUCTION

When the War ended Great Britain found herself with eight million British and Empire servicemen and servicewomen under arms occupying territory greater than at any previous time in the Empire's history. In addition to all the pre-war Empire land, Britain was in occupation of large parts of Germany, Austria, Italy and Greece. In Africa Britain had assumed responsibility for all the Italian colonies and countries previously occupied by the Italians, while British troops had a major presence in nearly all the countries of the Middle East, including Iran. In the Far East Empire troops took repossession of former British, French and Dutch colonies from the Japanese. The three pillars of British military strategy were: the defence of the United Kingdom, the protection of the nation's sea lanes and the defence of the lines of communication to India and Australasia through the Middle East. Our Armed Forces were dispersed worldwide to meet the commitments that this strategy involved.

Wartime formations and commands, designed for manoeuvre and the defeat of the German, Italian and Japanese enemy, gave way to static commands reflecting the occupational nature of their task. In Germany 21 Army Group became the British Army of the Rhine (BAOR), with the two other major commands of Middle East Land Forces (MELF) and Far East Land Forces (FARELF) centred on Cairo and Singapore respectively. The RASC was present wherever there were British troops. Although the war was over the peace seemed by no means certain. Jubilation at coming through the sternest of trials was tempered by apprehension for the future.

Shortly after the war ended Field Marshal Montgomery of Alamein, when addressing a parade of RASC and RCASC at 4 Training Brigade RASC in Lippstadt in Germany on 26 November, 1945, summed up his views of the Corps' wartime achievements:

'I consider that the work done by the RASC in this war has been quite magnificent. I know well that without your exertions behind, and often in front, we should never have been able to advance as we did. No Corps in the Army has a higher sense of duty than you have. You have delivered supplies in all weathers and over all roads. You have driven your vehicles in rain and snow and ice, and you have never once let us down. Without your supplies our battles could never have been won. It is a fine record and I am glad to be here, publicly, to pay the RASC the tribute that it deserves."

Field Marshal The Viscount Montgomery of Alamein KG, GCB, DSO, Investiture of Captain J G Alpe RASC with the MC.

Whilst appreciating the recognition of a job well done, the Corps was now facing up to new tasks and challenges in an uncertain world. Although equipment and methods inevitably changed, men of many races wearing the Corps badge continued to enhance the reputation gained in the Second World War.

Responsibilities of the Royal Army Service Corps

The RASC's responsibilities remained unchanged at the end of the war and were:

- The provision, storage, inspection, distribution and accounting for food supplies worldwide.
- The provision, storage, inspection, distribution and accounting for petroleum, oil and lubricants worldwide.
- Distribution of ammunition to units in the field.
- Operation of all road transport, other than unit transport, but including all transport of medical units.
- Operation of animal transport.
- Operation of amphibious transport.
- Operation of water transport, except inland water transport.
- Provision of air despatch crews and the operation of rear and forward airfield supply organizations.
- Operation of Barrack services.
- Provision of clerical services for the Staff.

Organization

At the War Office the Quartermaster General was responsible for the overall organization and policy affecting the deployment, tasking and operation of the Corps, whilst the head of the Corps, the Director of Supplies and Transport, a Major General, was responsible to the QMG for the efficient functioning of the Corps in all its resultant duties, world wide.

The DST exercised technical and regimental control of the Corps through DSTs at the three major Commands overseas, BAOR, MELF, and FARELF, and through Deputy Directors of Supplies and Transport at all other Commands at home and overseas. The appointments of DST at BAOR and MELF were in the rank of Major General, and that in FARELF a Brigadier. DDSTs were either Brigadiers or Colonels. The S & T staff organization at the War Office was mirrored in each command, but with a lower rank structure. This latter organization was often referred to as the static chain of command in contrast to the RASC in field formations. Here the staff and command organization was similar, but with titles which reflected the formations supported or units commanded. Examples are DDST 1 British Corps in BAOR and all Commanders RASC (CsRASC) of divisional columns. The Army Catering Corps, although organized and badged as a separate Corps, with its own Director, was nevertheless sponsored by the DST at the War Office and at all RASC levels of command and was therefore not an independent Corps at that time.

THE RASC IN POSTWAR EUROPE

British Army of the Rhine (BAOR)

The end of the war in Europe on 8 May, 1945, found that continent in a chaotic state. Almost six years of violent conflict had left it in a shattered and desperate condition. Whole nations and millions of people were on the brink of starvation, with the basic economic infrastructure vital to support a nation's existence largely destroyed.

Under the terms of the 1945 Potsdam Conference, the four major Allied powers agreed the post-war responsibilities and division of Germany into occupation zones to be controlled by the victors. In the case of Britain, her occupation zone covered the huge area roughly bounded in the west by Germany's normal international boundaries with Holland and Belgium, and to the North Sea as far east as Hamburg. It then followed the lines of the River Leine to the south, the boundary with the Russian zone of occupation to Hessen, then west again to Cologne adjoining the French zone. The British called their forces of occupation in this area BAOR. Berlin, the German capital, although well inside the Russian zone, was also jointly occupied by the four Allies, each having its own sector. The Potsdam Agreement allowed the Western Allies road and rail corridors through the Russian zone. The first attempts to open a rail route from the British sector to the British zone of West Germany were thwarted when members of the Berlin Railway Control Team failed to acquire from the Russians in Magdeburg a copy of the document showing which lines had been repaired and which were open. However, a service was eventually started on 14 July, 1945, initially for freight only, but in August a passenger service was added. So began the Berlin Military Train service which was to run daily, except during the period of the Russian blockade of the city in 1948, for 41 years.

In addition to controlling and reconstructing the national structure of Germany, there was, immediately after the capitulation, the pressing problem of managing the disarmed German armies. There was the added necessity of housing, feeding, clothing and transporting, by Army transport, to their own countries, hundreds of thousands of displaced persons. The RASC driver transporting these people found himself delivering anxious men, women and children to the point where a new life began.

Having set the homeless on the right road, the RASC were then called upon to assist in ensuring that the Germans should not suffer the final catastrophe of starvation with its accompanying diseases. To this end Operation BARLEYCORN was devised. This entailed the demobilization and return home of non-Nazi officers and men of the German armed forces who were required to gather in the harvest and assist in the preparation of the fields for the crops on which the existence of their own people depended. The numbers to be moved were too great for the Corps to handle unaided and so transport platoons officered and manned by other arms were formed. RASC NCOs were allotted to the platoons and each platoon was attached to a RASC parent company. These platoons collected the German prisoners of war from the prison camps and transported them to dispersal points near their own homes.

While these tasks and many others were proceeding, the release from wartime service of large numbers of Corps officers and soldiers progressed with a rapidity which produced many problems for the DST and his staff. A Reorganization and Disbandment Centre RASC was set up at Herford and this proved invaluable in controlling the interchanges of personnel, equipment and vehicles. During the winter of 1945-46 the Corps was reorganized in BAOR and Divisional Occupational Transport Companies were established, each division being allotted two companies, one company consisting of four platoons of 3-tonners, the other company comprising one platoon of 10-tonners, one of troop-carrying vehicles (TCVs), one of 1,750-gallon petrol tankers and one of 800-gallon petrol tankers. Additional transport support was provided by tank transporter companies and general transport (GT) companies. To maintain and repair vehicles, independent station maintenance sections were established.

In support of the large force in BAOR, increased by the influx of thousands of civilian members of the Control Commission Germany (CCG), RASC static supply, petrol and solid fuel depots were established together with a large barrack and quartering organization. With the demobilization of so many experienced soldiers, the demand for clerks, butchers, vehicle mechanics and other specialists became increasingly urgent. To meet these needs, 4 Training Brigade RASC was established at Lippstadt in July, 1945. Even this did not fulfil the urgent need to produce additional drivers, without which transport could not be adequately provided to meet all the requirements arising from the overall responsibilities of the Corps in BAOR, for both its military and civilian support tasks.

MCTG and MSO Transport Units

To meet this shortfall, transport units were formed from civilian sources within West Germany. Over many years to come these units were to provide invaluable assistance to the Corps and maintained a very high standard of which they were justifiably proud. The personnel recruited were of mixed origin and not only provided drivers for transport units but also for supply duties and a considerable general labour force.

The first category of recruit was found from German ex-soldiers, mainly returned prisoners of war; the second was drawn from the large number of nationals originating from countries now occupied by the Russians. The latter had become genuine political refugees in West Germany and many had a military background. Typical of these were Polish officers and soldiers, and Yugoslavian Chetniks, who, having fought with the Allies, could not return to their own, now Soviet-occupied, countries. There were also Latvians, Lithuanians and Estonians who did not wish to return to their Communist-dominated countries. Not only were these recruits, in both categories, able to fill essential driving and other roles, but they also helped to reduce the considerable problem of civilian unemployment in West Germany and established a means of rehabilitation into a normal social life.

Initially, in 1945, Dienstgruppen Transport Units (DG) were formed from German Army units, many virtually intact, marching from the East into captivity in the Schleswig-Holstein area of the British Zone. They were given the opportunity to join DG units, the majority volunteering immediately, and about 100,000 ex-prisoners of war were employed in the transport units and in other capacities.

Records of exactly how many DG transport units there were are incomplete, but the number was probably around forty-five. Until December, 1945, the men wore their German Army uniform, virtually worked within a military command structure and were largely self-administrating. Their initial form of dress was later replaced by field-grey and semi-civilian dress, and in the summer of 1946 by special dark brown battledress uniforms. Also in 1946 the military titles within the DG were abolished and replaced by civilian nomenclatures: managers, superintendents, foremen, etc, who carried out the day to day running of units highly efficiently under the close control of their RASC sponsors. From their formation there were British Supervisory Elements (BSE), headed by an RASC major, a Mechanist Sergeant Major for the workshop (later an Artificer Sergeant Major REME) and one or two senior NCOs. The units were later to be renamed, firstly from 1 April, 1947, German Civil Labour Organization (GCLO), and in 1957 Mobile Civilian Transport Groups (MCTG). The separate BSE was then dropped and integrated into the establishment with the RASC major becoming OC. These units were to become a permanent part of the RASC transport unit establishments of the static garrisons formed in BAOR and described later, but were initially also employed in support of the field force.

DG transport units were used on practically any task. These included Operation SHUTTLE, the transfer of prisoners between the American and British zones, and Operation EXODUS in September, 1945, which involved the removal of 19,000 disarmed Wehrmacht soldiers from the British sector of Berlin to the British zone in western Germany. Most units at this time had a wide variety of American, Canadian, British and ex-German Army vehicles.

The second category of civilian-recruited transport and other types of units which started to be formed in 1947 were non-Germans and were made up from nationals from countries in Eastern Europe, as described above. They were then known as the Civilian Mixed Labour Organization and the Civilian Mixed Watchman Service, all later to be renamed the Mixed Service Organization (MSO). The majority were Poles or Yugoslavs, but there were many from the Baltic States of Latvia, Estonia and Lithuania. Apart from nationality, a significant difference between the MCTG and the MSO was that the MSO carried personal weapons for unit defence, received military training and had a clearly defined operational role in direct support of military field formations.

40th Anniversary of the MCTG Parade: Major General Derek Braggins CB inspects the '40 Year Men'.

Major General Peter Blunt CB MBE GM inspects the MSO on Parade.

It has only been possible in this volume to mention overall the proud history of all the MCTG and the MSO transport units, many of which served the Corps so well, firstly as RASC units and then as RCT, until the formation of the RLC in 1993. Their more detailed history until 1982 is well recorded in the last volume of the Corps History, *The Story of the RASC and RCT 1945-1982*, and only some of the many excellent units can be specifically mentioned as appropriate examples in this volume.

Whilst the painstaking peaceful restoration of West Germany was taking place, supported by the occupying powers, United States, France and Great Britain, the situation in the Eastern Europe Communist countries developed into a political and military threat against the West's way of life. This situation became known as the 'Cold War' and meant that a military stance had to be maintained in Western Europe against potential Russian aggression. This encouraged the formation of the North Atlantic Treaty Organization (NATO) in April, 1949. This Treaty required the Occupying Powers in the West, and other Western European Countries who become members, to keep up a high standard of military vigilance and training to counter the Russian military threat.

Effect of the Cold War on RASC Organization

Over the years the pressure from Russia was maintained and exacerbated by such incidents as the Berlin blockade in 1948, which resulted in the Berlin Air Lift described later in this chapter, and the cutting of the links between East and West Germany by the building of the Berlin Wall in 1961.

Against this background, the work in BAOR of the RASC, and later the RCT, in all their varying roles, was balanced between the overall support on a peacetime basis of a large military theatre organization, with its families and other civilian elements, and the maintenance within the whole of a large continuously training field force army at a high state of readiness.

Despite the many organizational changes affecting BAOR which were made during the early postwar period, the Corps' responsibilities to support the Army changed in degree only. Directly supporting Corps and Divisional formations in the field were the RASC transport columns integral to that Corps or Division, with the vital role of the maintenance and resupply of the combat arms. Other specialist units were established to support formations, including bridge-carrying and tank transporter units, of which 612 and 617 Tank Tansporter Units MSO were examples.

Both the field force and the static elements of BAOR were co-located in garrisons which were established throughout North Germany and the British Zone in Berlin immediately after the war ended, mainly in garrison towns where German barracks existed. Each garrison contained organizations which provided a full range of logistic requirements for all units, families and attached civilians located in the area. Many included major installations providing base requirements for the whole theatre. The RASC were represented in all these Garrisons by static CsRASC establishments which, with their units, provided the complete range of Corps services – eg CRASC Celle, CRASC Paderborn, CRASC Hamburg etc. From 1947 the static Garrison transport tasks started to be taken over by DG (later MCTG) and MSO units, which were tailor-made for the particular duties involved. Ultimately, as the years passed these units took over the complete role of administrative transport for garrisons, across the whole transport range from ambulances to school buses, and were recognized as a highly effective part of the Corps.

Senior Superintendents of all the twelve MCTGs and the one MSO transport unit on a visit to Sandhurst.

The Lines of Communication

The RASC role in maintaining BAOR included the lines of communication, which, when the war ended, ran through the Channel ports and Belgium. This supply route through Belgium continued to provide essential support to the British forces stationed in Germany. An advanced base with a British garrison was established east of Antwerp. Depots were built for Engineer, Medical, RASC and RAOC stores. For the Corps the two major depots were 1 Petroleum Reserve Depot and 2 Main Supply Depot, later becoming 5 Supply Reserve Depot. An HQ RASC was established at Grobbendonk with 601 Transport Unit to meet the needs of the base with a wide range of transport.

Norway

Planning had originally started in 1943 for the liberation of Norway, in the event the complete military defeat of the Wehrmacht in Germany resulted in the unconditional surrender of 400,000 troops in the garrisons of German-occupied Norway. A British force was sent there with the initial task of demilitarizing the German units. As far as the Corps was concerned, this meant the control of some 113 German Supply Depots scattered throughout the length of Norway. Additionally, the range of Corps duties included supply by air and sea, troop-carrying, requisitioning transport, water transport and the training of the reformed Norwegian Army in Supply & Transport tasks. Some forty RASC units and sub-units were deployed. All British troops were withdrawn by the end of December, 1945.

Austria

In addition to 21st Army Group and then BAOR in the north of Germany, the RASC was deployed with other British troops in Austria. The RASC's task started with the arrival on 11 May, 1945, of HQ 5 Corps, spearhead of the 8th Army which had fought its way across North Africa and up the length of Italy. Italy had joined the Allies in October, 1943, and British troops were not present in the role of occupying forces. The advance of 5 Corps into Austria was rapid, some 250 miles in eight days, and inevitably this stretched the lines of communication. Immediately on arriving in Austria, the RASC had to start by building up stocks at Klagenfurt, a five-day turnround from the logistic bases in Italy. The Corps was issuing daily some 113,000 rations and 63,000 gallons of petrol. Other problems were the same as those facing the Corps in Germany, the feeding and transporting of vast numbers of surrendered German troops and displaced persons. A ceaseless stream poured in from the mountains and totalled some 400,000 from over thirty different nations.

Army Area Headquarters was in Vienna and under command of the CRASC were a supply depot, a POL depot, a car company and 14 Company RASC for station transport support. HQ British Troops Austria was initially at Klagenfurt, the senior Corps appointment being the DDST (Colonel). A Transport Column provided the transport support in this area, with another column in Graz.

The RASC in Austria included the Headquarters of a Pack Transport Group which had provided invaluable support to 5 Corps during their advance through the mountains of Italy. Under command of this Group four horse transport platoons were formed, manned by White Russian personnel.

A German Transport Column was put together from surrendered enemy troops under the supervision of a small cadre of RASC officers and NCOs. A total of twenty-four transport platoons, organized into four companies and supported by their own workshops, were formed, all manned by German personnel. These transport companies were invaluable in distributing food and supporting engineer and municipal work throughout the British occupied areas. This use of POWs applied particularly in the British zone, but in Vienna there was much greater use of Austrian civilian drivers to save British military manpower. One feature of this was that the RASC platoon command structure was severely pruned and the subaltern platoon commander might find himself commanding ninety vehicles and civilian drivers, the equivalent of three platoons.

There was an admirable tie-up between Movements and Transport. The main route for reinforcements, leave and release was via the Mediterranean Line of Communication (MEDLOC) route 'C', which was initially served by RASC Troop-Carrying Vehicles driving from the English Channel ports overland to Austria until such time as the European railway system was sufficiently repaired. Road gave way to rail and MEDLOC 'C' trains ran through to Villach. RASC transport units still provided the connecting links with the trains including, for example, a service from Villach to Vienna.

Trieste

Trieste was initially occupied by 2nd New Zealand Division on 2 May, 1945, followed by 24 Guards Brigade. HQ British Element Trieste Force (BETFOR) was formed from HQ 13 Corps. Together with United States forces, the role of the combined force was to support the Allied Military Government in the restoration of normal life and preserve the peace until the future of the territory could be determined, Italy and Yugoslavia being rival claimants. The British force was at brigade group strength, although artillery support was provided by the Royal Navy off-shore. Commanded by a CRASC, the Corps element was 65 Company RASC(GT) of four platoons, a Supply Depot which included a large Petrol Depot and an Army Fire Brigade. Each RASC unit included locally employed civilians employed as drivers, clerks and storemen.

CRASC BETFOR was responsible direct to the DST War Office for all departmental matters. Normal S&T services were provided and local contracts were operated. Contracts for fresh fruit and vegetables were arranged with Italian suppliers and BETFOR also became the agency for the supply of fresh produce to our Forces. Meat was shipped from the UK, the Supply Depot using refrigerated storage space in the Municipal Cold Store. Local contracts were made for the supply of petrol.

Italy

British troops continued to be stationed in different parts of Italy for over two years after the end of the war. The Peace Treaty with Italy was ratified in Paris on 15 September, 1947. At that time there were ten RASC units still in Italy all under command CRASC 29 General Transport Column. The evacuation date was fixed for 8 December, 1947, and by then all RASC units had left Italy.

THE BERLIN AIRLIFT

As a result of an agreement made in London during the war, Britain, United States and Russia undertook a tripartite occupation of Berlin, later modified to include the French. Thus the western half of Berlin was occupied by the allies with a right of access to Berlin from their respective zones. Food, coal and raw materials to assist the rebuilding of West Berlin and its industry were moved by road, rail and water through

Four members of 62 Coy RASC at the Brandenburg Gate, Berlin.

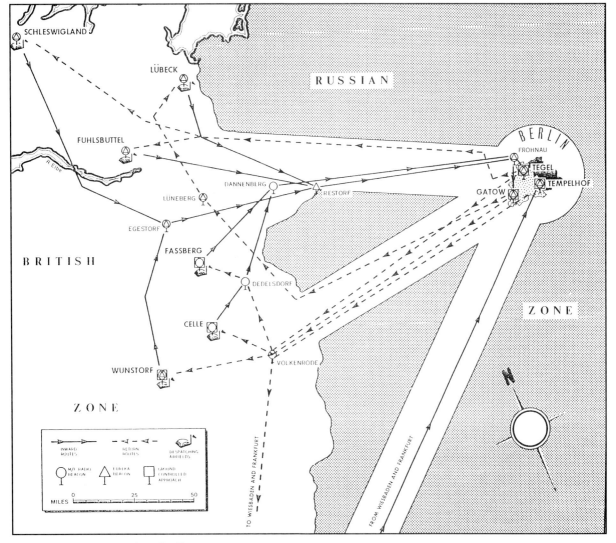

Air Routes into Berlin.

the Russian zone into West Berlin and the sectors of Allied occupation.

On 1 April, 1948, the Russians began to impose rigid checks on the movement of this traffic and in May the land surface routes were virtually closed.

There were also, by the previously established agreement, three air corridors into Berlin from the west, each twenty miles wide converging in the shape of an arrowhead, with its point in the western sectors. At the end of June an operation was mounted to supply Berlin by air using these air corridors. For fifteen months the Berlin Airlift became the focus of the Cold War.

The success of the airlift, codenamed Operation PLAINFARE for the British, and Operation VITTLES for the Americans, can finally be judged by the comparison of imports into Berlin when 13,500 tons daily had been supplied overland before the operation and, ultimately, the day's record of 12,872 tons moved by air toward the end of the airlift.

From unsophisticated beginnings, the RAF (together with the support of

Commonwealth airmen and civilian air organizations) and the United States Army Air Force combined to produce a round-the-clock flight programme.

On the ground, initially using the expertise of 749 Company RASC, the Corps gradually built up its support-producing units at each Rear Airfield Supply Organization (RASO) in the zone and Forward Airfield Supply Organization (FASO) in Berlin with units which were titled Air Freight Companies RASC. These units were established with three platoons to work in shifts to maintain the round-the-clock support of the air forces in the provision and loading of supplies at the RASO and the unloading and distribution at FASO. Transport and labour support to these units was provided by established German units and a variety of ad hoc arrangements in Berlin where the blockade had cut off all hopes of a road transport reinforcement to meet the aircraft offloading and subsequent distribution requirement from the airfield to the city.

RASOs and the FASO, with their Air Freight units under the control of the Army Air Transport Organization (AATO), an RASC department of the Combined Air Lift Task Force (CALTF), operated from the airfields opened one by one as the air traffic into Berlin increased – Wunstorf, Fassberg, Lübeck, Fuhlsbuttel, Schleswig Holstein and Celle. For a short time Sunderland flying boats were flown into Berlin, landing on Lake Havel, from Finkenwerdt on the Elbe near Hamburg. Sunderlands were able to carry salt, whereas other aircraft were not protected from the corrosive nature of the load. Bakers in Berlin continued to bake their bread!

The airfields of Berlin, Gatow for the British and Templehof for the Americans, became choked as the build-up of supplies from the airfields in the zones increased. A new airfield was built at Tegel in the French sector, much of the equipment being flown in from Lübeck, to help achieve the required airlift tonnage.

The airlift continued day and night, seven days a week, including Christmas Day, 1948. It was not an operation of war, although it caused the death of several gallant airmen, but it was an operation carried out with the intensity of war. A more damaging East/West crisis was averted.

As a major contributor, the RASC took pride in the successful conclusion of the operation. One by one the units in support of the airlift closed down, the last being at Wunstorf, in November, 1949, where it had all started in the greatest sustained air supply operation known in the history of flying.

CHANGES TO THE THE HOME BASE

Balancing the Support Requirement

At the War Office in 1946 the problems of balancing the ability of the Army to meet new military threats against the inevitable force reductions as troops were demobilized were immense. The Corps was heavily involved in the logistic aspects of the overall adjustments in role and dispositions of the Army that were now necessary. The DST and his staff at the S & T Directorate grappled with the many problems confronting the Corps across the whole range of its responsibilities, with tasks still spread worldwide. In the UK Home Base the RASC was involved not only in the maintenance of the large home defence forces spread throughout the country, but also the support of the vast overall training organization remaining from the war and the many formations in transit to overseas theatres. There was an overall Corps manpower shortage which particularly affected transport units in every theatre. The supply organization continued to deal with the worldwide distribution of foodstuffs from its Supply Reserve Depots; food rationing was still in force in UK and there were many shortages, including fuel.

In 1946 much of the Home Base wartime supply and transport organization was still in place throughout the country. It had to be scaled down and regrouped as demobilization and restructuring of the Army gradually took place. This led to a reduction and reorganization of the Corps UK training organization and the redistribution of Corps units and manpower to meet shortages as they occurred. The reconstitution of the Territorial Army with a substantial Corps strength was also being planned; this is covered later in this chapter.

The Command Supply Depots were located near every large military concentration and they were reduced in line with troop reductions. POL was an integral part of this supply organization, the major Petroleum Depot at West Moors in Dorset being the exception. Barrack Services in each garrison were heavily involved in the re-equipping of barracks designated for peacetime use and the rebuilding programme for both barracks and married quarters. Scales of accommodation and furniture were gradually improved as the country emerged from the austerity years.

Transport support for all commands, districts and garrisons was provided by transport companies deployed throughout the military centres. In Northern Ireland CRASC had his headquarters at Lisburn and commanded station transport units, supply and barracks services depots and a petrol depot. During the war the province had been an important garrison for holding and training many British, and later American, formations prior to their deployment overseas. After the war Northern Ireland was re-established as a home command with the Corps commitment reflecting the size of the garrison. By 1950 the pre-war resident transport unit, 26 Company RASC, had been reactivated in Victoria Barracks, Belfast, having ended the war in Berlin as a Tipper Company.

The large RASC training organization, developed during the war for a conscript army, was coping both with its own problems of demobilization and playing its part in training an effective but smaller army. The Boys Company of 1 Training Battalion reformed after the war at Aldershot and was subsequently to produce many of the potential Warrant Officers and NCOs of the Corps.

On 1 July, 1946, the RASC took over complete responsibility for the Army Fire Service. Firemen tradesmen had their training initially as drivers at 3 Training Battalion at Ellis Barracks, Farnborough, followed by qualifying as firemen at the Army Fire School at Colchester, this school also becoming an RASC responsibility.

With the closing of the wartime Officer Cadet Training Units (OCTUs), the Cadet Company RASC was established as part of 1 Training Battalion at Buller Barracks in 1947. After completing an All Arms Course at Mons Officer Cadet School Aldershot, all RASC Emergency and later National Service Officers received their Special to Corps training in the Cadet Company, until it closed with the ending of National Service. The Company produced the bulk of the immediate postwar officers for the Corps, many becoming Regular Officers; two became Directors of the Corps.

National Service and the Reserve Army

In 1947 Britain still had a spread of worldwide commitments which could not be given up easily. This delayed full demobilization and any thought of a speedy return

TA Soldiers in NBC equipment under training.

to all Regular Forces. Nevertheless, the steady run-down in numbers caused severe problems and the provisions for wartime national service were extended. This situation could not continue and it became clear that the unpopular measure of peacetime national service would have to be adopted. A Bill received Royal Assent in July, 1947, for peacetime national service to start in January, 1949. By the time it began, the manpower situation had become critical. The National Service Act now set the period of service at $5\frac{1}{2}$ years, two years with the colours and $3\frac{1}{2}$ with the Reserves. This Reserve commitment was essential in order to rebuild the Territorial Army, which, although embodied during the war, no longer existed in its pre-war state as a separate entity.

The Territorial Army was reformed in 1947 after a year of planning by the War Office, in which the TA & VR Council again became represented. Recruiting started on 1 April and the RASC had an establishment that was greatly enhanced from pre-war, covering the whole range of responsibilities of the Corps, with additional types of units that had been developed during the war. There were forty-three column headquarters and some one hundred and twenty MT companies with an across-the-board range of vehicles, which included DUKWS. Three supply companies, and port, supply and petroleum platoons for a beach brigade, completed the new order of battle.

Recruiting into the revived TA started slowly, but this was no surprise since it was

224

realized that few of those who had just finished their war service would wish to return to a military organization so soon. It would take a while before people began to miss the life and comradeship that the TA could provide. By August, 1948, however, RASC columns were still only at about company strength, despite prodigious efforts of those who had joined quickly, most with a great deal of wartime experience. But as word got round and the annual camps were successful, recruiting began to improve. Nevertheless, the TA overall was still greatly undermanned and the War Office needed a viable Reserve Army in the face of the military threat posed by the Soviet Union.

In 1950 the first intake of National Servicemen into the TA appeared and, despite initial apprehension on both sides, the majority settled down well to complete their not inconsiderable training liability. Many volunteered for TA service and continued to serve on beyond their National Service liability for a full TA engagement. There were to be substantial changes in the strength and structure of the Reserve Army in the years that followed, as well as title changes; these are covered later in the chapter.

The introduction of National Service in peacetime produced continuity problems in the Regular Army. This was felt particularly in the driver training battalions where there was a constant turnover of instructors. This situation was gradually improved with the introduction of civilian driver training instructors, starting with 15 Driver Training Battalion at Blandford in 1949. The throughput of the various training battalions was high, with constant reinforcements required for service overseas. The RASC National Service officer and soldier quickly found themselves involved in all overseas campaigns and their training stood them in good stead.

The RASC / RCT Vehicle Fleet

Replacement of the vehicle fleet of the RASC started in the fifties and was a gradual and continuing process. To meet changes in operational concepts and corresponding logistic requirements during this whole period needed vehicles of improved technical design within new logistic parameters. The provision of such vehicles was, however, always affected by financial constraints , and it was essential to find more economical methods of providing vehicles. Too often design faults in some new vehicles still proved an obstacle to achieving optimum efficiency, but these problems were slowly overcome. It is convenient to summarize the developing situation for standard cargo vehicles at this stage because of the overlapping of the designs and types of the vehicles in use from the end of the Second World War until the early seventies, when probably the most dramatic changes occurred. Examples of the use of specific types of these vehicles are given where appropriate in the chapters that follow. The more high technology specialist vehicles introduced in the eighties are considered in Chapter 9.

At the end of the Second World War the RASC's MT fleet was worn out. Because of the multiplicity of types and makes in use, it was both a logistic and maintenance nightmare. Brave plans were drawn up by the MOD to revitalize the UK's military heavy vehicle industry and a whole series of Combat (CT) military vehicles were designed in the UK, mainly at the Fighting Vehicles Research & Development Establishment (FVRDE), based at Chertsey. Vehicles ranged from the Austin Champ (to replace the ubiquitous Jeep), up to ultra-heavy tank transporters to carry the 65-ton Conqueror tank. CT vehicles would have the maximum of commonality in parts and would remedy several of the main design faults found in the wartime vehicles.

The Austin Champ.

These emphasized the need for multi-fuel operation, plenty of power, the ability to wade, and to have electrical screening for the radios now considered essential to battlefield command and control.

Alas, most of this came to naught as overlong development times, spiralling costs and poor design all made a mockery of this admirable concept. There were, for example, an enormous degree of redundant and technical complexity in the vehicles which proved both difficult to maintain and costly in spares! In the event, after considerable nugatory expense, the War Office was forced to turn to civilian designs to plug an urgent shortfall in logistic vehicles in the mid-1950s. The only two CT military-designed vehicles that actually saw service within the RASC in any large numbers were the Austin Champ and the Leyland Martian 10-ton Cargo-FV 1121. However, even the Martian vehicle only saw limited service (in 1 Divisional Column RASC). The main successor to the old wartime Albion and AEC Matador 10-ton vehicles (10,000 Matadors were produced throughout the Second World War) was the AEC Militant MK 1 (FV 11008) and MK 3 (FV 11047), produced in two chassis lengths and for RASC use, in both cargo and, tipper versions. The AEC Militant was a thoroughly conventional commercial design, as was the 3-ton Bedford RL to replace the Bedford QL wartime design.

The Thornycroft Mighty Antar tank transporter (FV 12001/2/3/4/6) replaced the ageing US wartime-designed Diamond T 980/981 M20. The Antar had been

The AEC Militant 10-ton truck.

designed for the Wimpey organization to haul oil pipeline in Iraq. When the FVRDE-designed CT Leyland FV 1000/1200 vehicles were recognized as being far too expensive and unreliable ever to enter service, the timely Antar purchase proved to be an excellent choice to replace the ageing Diamond Ts. The reliance on civilian designs for the RASC/RCT vehicle fleet was emphasized by the now-famous Land Rover, which at its inception was a speculative civil design.

The Diamond T Tank Transporter.

Gun ammunition for the Royal Artillery was the main Combat Supply load for the Corps. When the Bedford RL and AEC Militant series of vehicles was introduced, ammunition was mainly still supplied in boxes, each of which had to be individually manhandled. Ammunition depots soon began to band boxes together on pallets for easier storage and for through-movement from depots to users. To achieve all the economies which this system of packing offered, it was necessary to introduce Mechanical Handling Equipment (MHE) into the field. In the combat area this equipment had to be able to handle pallets of ammunition weighing over 1 ton right up to the gun lines. To work this system the Corps opted for a mix of conventional fork-lift trucks and lorry mounted cranes known as CALM – Crane Attachment Lorry Mounted.

The initial Fork-Lift Trucks, based on a simple civilian pattern, could handle large numbers of pallets fairly rapidly but were slow to move between locations. CALM would always be in the right place, being built on to the lorry, but was far slower in transferring pallets than the fork-lift. By the seventies many 4-ton (all 3-ton GS vehicles had by now been 'uprated' to 4 tons) and 10-ton cargo vehicles were being fitted with CALM, finally to a scale of one vehicle in every four and were complemented by the introduction of an excellent basic, but reliable, military designed fork-lift truck – the Eager Beaver. This used Bedford 4-ton axles and many common in-service items, but with no cab, an Eager Beaver driver was totally in the open. This allowed him an excellent understanding of what he was doing at night in a forward deployed Distribution Point (DP), but made for unpleasant road redeployment driving, especially in inclement weather.

REME Phase II

The decision to complete the implementation of the formation of REME by transferring first-line repairs of vehicles and equipment still in the hands of the RAC, RA, R Sigs and Infantry and first and second-line in the case of the RASC was finally made by the Army Council in November, 1950. The considerable reorganization involved was to take place over eighteen months, and as far as the Corps was concerned was completed in 1952, when the unit workshops became a REME responsibility. Ninety-five officers and 369 artificers of the Corps transferred to REME. Although there had been initial misgivings within the Corps over the loss of its own repair responsibilities, as with other sensible and logical reorganizations, REME Phase II was quickly assimilated into the system. Over the years the Corps had cause to be grateful to REME for the skill and professionalism displayed in its support of the Corps in its many vital roles.

Air Despatch

In 1952 a major air despatch effort was being made in the operations in Malaya; these are described in a later chapter. In the UK, 47 (AD) company, which was the operational and training company based in the Salisbury Plain area, was given the opportunity to practice its skills under very different conditions to those in Malaya. The UK Air Despatch organization was tasked with a trial of air-supply techniques in conditions of extreme cold by supporting the British North Greenland Expedition. The RAF provided two Hastings aircraft from RAF Lyneham and the RASC team was two Air Despatch crews under the command of a major. The small air transport force arrived at Thule in September and started dropping operations on 15

47(AD)Coy RASC operating over Salisbury Plain.

September. The ice cap plateau was over 9000 feet high and the combination of altitude and the northerly latitude meant that the air despatchers during long sorties and frequent dropping runs had to contend with shortage of oxygen and extreme cold. Although parachutes were used, very low level free dropping was also fully utilized; the unobstructed flat expanses of snow made such a technique possible with

Land Rover and trailer prepared for Parachute Landing.

minimum damage. In the middle of one such low-level drop, the aircraft struck the snow and crashed. Miraculously, although the air despatchers were not strapped in and the stores in the cargo bay were being prepared for despatch, injuries among the total of twelve on board were slight, Major D S Barker-Simson breaking an ankle while other crew members had broken ribs. The following seven days, before a United States Air Force aircraft could effect a rescue, became a struggle for survival. Until reinforcements could arrive from England, the remaining aircraft and air despatchers had to cope with the added burden of supplying the downed crew as well as the expedition parties. Despite this, the air supply operation concluded successfully on 12 October. 156 tons of supplies had been dropped in the course of twenty-one sorties under most difficult circumstances.

The RASC Fleet

The reduction of both the Military and Civilian Fleets at the end of the war with the finish of clearing-up operations and the ending of numerous tasks led to a reduction in military personnel from 2650 to 660. However, at the same time the Civilian Fleet took over running seven Landing Ships (Tank) (LSTs) and around one hundred Landing Craft (Tank) LCTs MK III, IV and IVa, with the result that their numbers increased from 1407 to 2350.

The military units were based on the south coast, mainly on the Isle of Wight and at Plymouth, while the Civilian Fleet passed under control of the Supplies and Transport Directorate ST3 administered by the Fleet Administration Unit; both branches were at last designated the RASC Fleet.

Shortly after VJ Day two 90-ft MFV fire tenders commanded by Captains Barr and Wood RASC were sent to Singapore, and this became the first long ocean voyage to be made by vessels commanded and crewed purely by serving Army personnel.

The main overseas action now moved to the Eastern Mediterranean based at Port Said and Port Fouad in Egypt where 697 Company RASC and 698 Company (LST Administration) operated a total of 140 vessels together with an extensive workshop and floating dock. These included six 120 ft Fairmile 'B' MLs with naval armament removed, as well as coasters, LSTs and other vessels. The Fairmiles took over from the Royal Navy the task of supplying the newly liberated islands of the Dodecanese, as well as Greece, Crete, Cyprus and Tobruk, with fresh food and stores.

This task subsequently developed into the maintenance for several years of all communications to support the indigenous islanders and was assisted by a substantial RASC detachment in Greece which supported the Military Mission. The vessels were involved in a number of operational and intelligence tasks, including coastal patrols.

The major tasks after the end of the war were the redistribution of stores worldwide. Due to the scarcity and expense of merchant shipping the Civilian Fleet had taken over seven LSTs named after distinguished Corps officers: *Evan Gibb, Charles Macleod, Maxwell Brander, Snowden Smith, Humfrey Gale, Reginald Kerr* and the *Frederick Glover*.

The LSTs were the largest landing ships used during the war and the largest ever operated by the RASC Fleet, with an overall length of 345 ft and a beam of 54 ft. They had bow doors with a ramp and could beach on slipways. Once they were taken over by the Civilian Fleet they required added accommodation to Board of Trade Regulations. Five of the vessels were sent to the Middle East and two to the Far East. During the evacuation of Palestine RASC vessels *Humfrey Gale* and *Evan Gibb* made thirty voyages each between Haifa and Port Said, lifting over 26,000 tons of vehicles and stores. Similar work was done worldwide until 1952 when the ships were handed over to the North Atlantic Steam Navigation Company, tasked by the War Office direct. Subsequently one, re-named the *Empire Gull* and tasked by Q (Mov) 1, moved ammunition between Marchwood Military Port and Zeebrugge until 1978.

Military units were steadily reduced as the military Motor Boat Companies were disbanded in 1948 and those remaining were employed in mainly local details with 71 Company RASC at HM Gunwharf, Portsmouth, 46 Company RASC at Menai Bridge, the 985 Training Company RASC (Water Transport) at Golden Hill Fort, near Freshwater, Isle of Wight, and the workshops at Fort Victoria near Yarmouth, Isle of Wight. Cairnryan, near Stranraer, became the main centre of Civilian Fleet activity from 1945 until 1958 where between 400 and 500 civilian crew members were employed on ammunition dumping and associated duties.

A large fleet of around 24 LCTs MK III, IV and MK IVa were operated, supported by five ex-Naval 'Isle class' trawlers, three steam coasters – the *Marquis of Hartington, Sir Evelyn Wood, Sir Walter Campbell*, and the motor vessel *Malplaquet*. The ramp-bowed LCTs, redesignated Ammunition Dumping Craft (ADCs), were excellent for the job of dumping old ammunition, as it was a simple matter to roll or shove the loads down the lowered ramp into the Beaufort Dyke, midway between County Down and Wigtonshire in Scotland. Some dangerous chemicals, however, were dumped beyond the Continental Shelf by the steam coasters.

These operations continued until 1958 when all vessels were sold, the oldest of which was the steam-powered *Marquis of Hartington*, taken out of service after 71 years.

At the same time the dumping programme continued in Port Said where four ADCs of 697 Company were based and a further three LCTs MK IV were permanently stationed in the Far East as part of 37 Company RASC (Water Transport) at Pulau Brani at Singapore.

CHANGES IN WESTERN EUROPE

By the early fifties the Army in the UK was coming to terms with the effects of demobilization and the introduction of peacetime National Service; much restructuring had taken place. This situation was reflected in BAOR which was now better organized to meet the Russian threat. Elsewhere in Western Europe, British Forces were being formally established for the long-term support of BAOR, or withdrawn from countries as national sovereignty was restored.

Belgium

On 12 November, 1952, the status of British units based in Belgium in support of the Lines of Communication was formalized with the establishment south-east of Antwerp of Advanced Base British Forces under a bilateral Anglo-Belgium agreement named GONDOLA. A base headquarters commanded by a Colonel was established, together with storage depots for Engineer Stores, Survey (Maps), Medical Stores, RASC Petrol and Supplies and RAOC General Stores, Vehicles and Ammunition. In addition, there was a full range of administrative services to support the large base organization. For the Corps this involved the provision of transport, the detailed issue of rations and petrol, Barrack Services and cover by the Army Fire Service. HQ RASC was located in Grobbendonk, together with 1 Petroleum Reserve Depot. 5 Supply Reserve Depot was built at Berlaar where massive reserve stocks were held. Transport support was provided by 601 Transport Unit RASC; its HQ was in Herenthals, with platoons in Geel, Tielen and Grobbendonk.

The importance of the newly created base, and in particular the functions of the RASC, was demonstrated during the 1956 Suez Emergency when enormous quantities of vehicles, stores and equipment were moved to the Channel ports. Under normal peacetime conditions some 95% of the maintenance requirements for BAOR came through the Channel ports and were controlled by British Forces Antwerp. The wartime role was much wider in scope and included reinforcement in one direction and evacuation in the other, as well as providing a vital link in the maintenance of BAOR. The same situation continued up to and through 1965 when the McLeod reorganization took place.

Austria and Trieste

In 1953 the British garrison at Graz was evacuated. Villach, where there was an OC RASC and 60 Company, was run-down. British Troops Austria remained only in Vienna and Klagenfurt, where HQ RASC was located. In 1955 Russia agreed to evacuate their forces in exchange for Austria's strict neutrality, and as a result all British forces finally withdrew on 17 September, 1955. Further south, in Trieste, where there was a CRASC and a full range of Supply & Transport services, the continued presence in 1953 of British forces began to arouse Italian suspicions of British intentions and some politically inspired rioting occurred in October of that year. As a result of political pressure, the decision was made to evacuate, only twenty-one days being allowed for this to be carried out. A few days before the final evacuation the United Nations decided to delay the withdrawal for twelve months. A year of uneasiness and tension followed. After the signing of a treaty in London by which Trieste was returned to Italy, units of the Italian Army began to take over on 25 October, 1954. On the following day the rear parties of HQ BETFOR and HQ 24 Guards Brigade including their RASC elements, embarked on the aircraft carrier HMS *Centaur* and a destroyer, thus ending ten years of occupation in which the Corps played a full part.

RETURN TO THE FAR EAST – THE ELUSIVE PEACE

The atomic bombs on Hiroshima and Nagasaki in August, 1945, had brought a rapid end to the war against Japan and the abandonment of Allied plans for a series of potentially costly major amphibious operations to re-take the Malayan Peninsula and Singapore.

Although hostilities with the Japanese ended in August, there was much to be done before the long-awaited demobilization of war-weary troops could be put into full effect. The British had to re-establish effective government in Empire and Commonwealth lands occupied by the Japanese during the war. The Japanese forces had to be withdrawn from French and Dutch possessions, whilst France and Holland, only recently liberated, struggled to exercise effective control over their colonies. This was not easy and neither was a return to the previous colonial situation. The pre-war position of superiority enjoyed by the European colonial powers had suffered a fatal blow at the hands of an Asian state – Japan. Many nationalist and communist movements had also gained in strength, organization and confidence as a result of their struggle against the occupying Japanese.

Singapore

Landing in Singapore in August, 1945, the British forces were faced with the task of first disarming the Japanese and then bringing order and stability to the British colony after nearly four years of enemy occupation.

One of the first units in Singapore was 56 Water Transport Unit, soon located on the small island of Pulau Brani. This made an excellent base for the RASC fleet in South-East Asia and continued to be used as such until the British withdrawal in the 1970s. The RASC transport organization on Singapore Island was formed from 61, 75, 799 and 986 Companies.

Late in 1946 it was decided to establish a RASC School at Nee Soon in Singapore mainly for the training of locally enlisted personnel. Initial emphasis was placed on driver training and MT maintenance, followed soon by recruit training, driver training for other arms, clerical, fire and regimental training. By August, 1947, the training establishment was expanded to include a holding platoon to receive British, Malayan, Indian, Chinese and Eurasian trainees. Over the years the RASC School ran courses for a wide spectrum of RASC trades for soldiers from Australia, New Zealand, Fiji, East Africa, Burma, Nepal, Thailand and Britain, but the majority of students were from Malaya and Singapore.

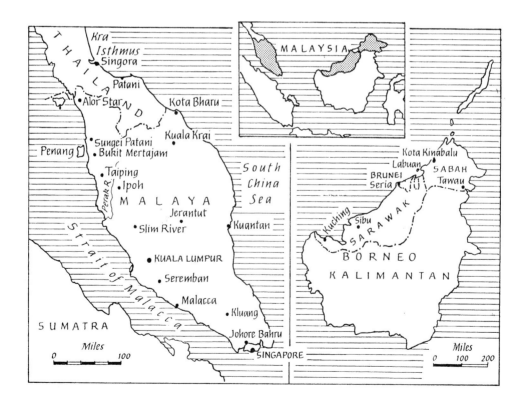

Malaya

The RASC element in Malaya was spread throughout all Army Districts created after the Japanese surrender in August, 1945. Fifty percent of S & T responsibilities were performed by the Royal Indian Army Service Corps (RIASC). The peacetime build-up of the RASC started after the return to India of the RIASC in 1947. By the end of that year the Corps was coping with all the logistic problems that arose with providing garrisons in a large country with only a small proportion of the units that existed before. The shortage of British soldiers was filled both by civilians and by locally enlisted personnel. RASC officers and NCOs were required to command and administer the Malayan Other Ranks (MOR) from all races in Singapore and Malaya. The RASC School at Nee Soon on Singapore Island met the requirement to train MORs and the first intake passed through the RASC School in July, 1947.

Netherlands East Indies

Despite the peaceful nature of the return to Singapore and Malaya, it was not long before serious trouble broke out in the Netherlands East Indies. To assist the Dutch, it was agreed that British and Indian troops would be made available to release allied prisoners of war and internees and to disarm and repatriate the Japanese forces. The Allied Forces Netherlands East Indies (AFNEI) was provided by 15 Indian Corps with Colonel C B Langdon as the DDST. The first elements arrived in Batavia (later renamed Djakarta) on 29 September, 1945. These included an air supply control cell from 70 Air Despatch Company in Burma. Major I Renwick had been sent down to Singapore shortly after its liberation to attend a conference on the situation in Java concerning the liberation of internees and prisoners of war. The inclusion of an air despatch capability in the force to be sent there was considered prudent and so 70 Air Despatch Company was moved from Burma more or less directly, followed by 799 Air Despatch Company. At first the situation was tense but under control, and the Japanese troops were compliant and able to give assistance. The RAPWI (Release of Allied Prisoners of War and Internees) organization set about its task and the air despatch company quickly started managing the air freight requirements. On 3 October the first Dutch troops arrived, which prompted nationalist groups to resort to arms to prevent a return to colonial rule.

On 13 October, the Indonesian People's Army declared war on the Dutch and, implicitly, the British. The situation deteriorated and on 28 October British troops were attacked in Surabya and a brigadier murdered. Severe fighting continued for three weeks until the local situation was brought under control, but a general state of guerrilla war now prevailed, with attacks on outposts and convoys. Supply by air became essential and the presence of experienced RASC air despatchers most fortunate. All the well-tried Burma air supply techniques were employed and in addition much novelty and improvisation. Extraction of internees, widely dispersed in remote areas, with many in no physical condition to travel overland, was a major and urgent problem. In a bold experiment loaded gliders were 'snatched' by Dakotas fitted with trailing hooks and flying low to pick up the newly available nylon towing ropes rigged up on poles. Many owed their lives to such resourcefulness and gradually all the internees and prisoners of war were recovered. Hostilities with Indonesian Nationalists continued through 1946 but in the autumn British and Indian troops were withdrawn, the last leaving on 30 November. By that time the Dutch forces had risen to 130,000. British and Commonwealth casualties were 556 killed and 1393 wounded, the great majority suffered by Indian Army units. 799 Company was withdrawn to Singapore where its air despatch role was reduced and a general transport role added. 70 Air Despatch Company, the air supply control cell, was disbanded.

Brunei, Borneo and Sarawak

The reoccupation of the Island of Borneo was more peaceful than operations in the Dutch East Indies. 32 Indian Infantry Brigade took over responsibility for Brunei, Borneo and Sarawak from 9 Australian Division on 28 December, 1945. Attached supply units included 4 Supply Company, 363 Bulk Petrol Platoon, a Control Centre for a Field Maintenance Area and 38 Indian Composite Platoon RIASC. These units took over a Base Supply Depot on Labuan Island and Supply Depots at Kuching, Sarawak and Jesselton. They were responsible for the maintenance of the Brigade, the RAF, the remaining Australian personnel and a large number of Japanese POW awaiting repatriation. Large sections of the population were starving and the Brigade RASC organization became involved in food distribution to these civilians.

The bulk petrol installation was located on the dockside on Labuan Island. In addition to responsibility for POL distribution to all military units in Borneo, the RASC Bulk Petrol Platoon provided aviation fuel for all aircraft using Labuan airfield, which soon became the major staging post between Singapore and Australia.

By June, 1946, the duties of the force having been completed, all operations were closed down and the Corps units embarked for the UK.

MALAYAN EMERGENCY

The Emergency in Malaya started in June, 1948, with acts of sabotage, intimidation and murder by the Communist movement which called itself 'The People's Anti-British Army', later changed to 'The Malayan Races Liberation Army'. The immediate operational problems facing the RASC were, firstly, the maintenance and troop-carrying requirements of the infantry units engaged in jungle operations, and, secondly, the provision of a suitable ration pack for the Gurkhas and Malays to carry with them on these operations.

Gradually, as the tempo of operations increased, with more troops moving into the jungle away from their land communications, the requirement for supply by air became apparent. In June, 1948, a platoon of 799 Company RASC (AD/GT) was located in Kuala Lumpur and this was used to cope with what at first was a light commitment. By December the platoon was given over fully to air despatch. In the following year the demand for air supply continued to grow and over 900 tons were dropped. During the same period a small air despatch detachment from 799 Company was also set up at Kai Tak in Hong Kong and another assisted with the evacuation of civilians during the civil war in Burma. The tonnage dropped in Malaya doubled once more in 1950, and the Kai Tak detachment was expanded at the same time. In September, 1950, 799 Company, with its HQ in Singapore, was renumbered and confirmed in its air despatch role as 55 Air Despatch Company RASC.

By 1950 there were six RASC companies providing transport for infantry movement. Two of these companies (3 and 27) were manned by British drivers and four (24, 29, 52 and 69) were Malayanized. At this stage all the officers and warrant officers were still British, as well as some of the senior NCOs. The high standard of

An RASC Air Despatch Crew at work on board a Dakota over the Malayan Jungle.

training of the MOR driver at the RASC School at Nee Soon, and subsequent NCO training, was to prove its worth. Malayans of officer, warrant officer and senior NCO quality developed rapidly and formed a sound nucleus for the later formation of the Malayan Army Service Corps in 1957.

There was still a shortage of infantry and other Arms and Services were called upon to act in an infantry role. 3 Company RASC provided a jungle squad which was trained by 1st Battalion, the Suffolk Regiment. The squad was soon in action and was employed in a number of jungle operations. Sadly, in one such action an officer and four soldiers were killed when their vehicle was ambushed. After a comparative lull in the intensity of operations during 1950, the communist terrorists, now calling themselves the Malayan Races Liberation Army, or MRLA, heartened by Communist successes in China, Korea and Indo-China, launched a new offensive in June, 1951, with renewed ferocity. This year proved to be the bloodiest year of the Emergency with Security Forces casualties reaching 505 killed and 668 wounded. By 1953 the situation had been stabilized, the security situation was under better control and the Security Forces were able to concentrate on offensive operations for the first time. In March, 1954, HQ 55 AD Company RASC moved to Kuala Lumpur. In 1955 air supply operations reached a climax with an annual record of 4485 tons dropped. In March alone the tonnage dropped exceeded the total for the first year of operations.

Malayan Independence and End of the Emergency

On 31 August, 1957, the Malay States were granted independence within the Commonwealth. The Federation Army was formed prior to this date on 15 July, 1957, including the Malayan (later Malaysian) Army Service Corps (MASC). It was not until 1965 that the Malaysian Army Service Corps was firmly established, having evolved from the Federation Supplies and Transport Service of the Armed Forces Maintenance Corps which had absorbed the MASC soon after its formation in 1957. A number of RASC companies, which had been previously converted to MOR-manned units, passed to the MASC, retaining their British officers. 29 Company RASC became 2 Transport Company MASC and 52 Company RASC became 3 Transport Company MASC. RASC officers played a major part in the successful establishment of the S & T element of the Federation Army. On the transport side, an Air Supply Platoon MASC was formed and trained by 55 Air Despatch Company RASC using RAF aircraft.

Many RASC officers were seconded to a rapidly expanding MASC and played an important part in establishing a training organization to meet the needs of a growing Federation Army. A school was established near Taiping to provide all-arms driver training. The next stage in the development of the MASC School was an Officers' Training Wing followed by an Officers' School, a Driver Training School, a NCOs' Wing, an Air Despatch Wing and a Catering School, all this being part of a progressive policy of grooming local soldiers to take early responsibility in the Federation Army. This led to rapid progress by the new MASC, redesignated Malaysian Service Corps (MSC), in all its activities which could not possibly have been achieved in such a short time without the expertise and dedication of RASC officers and NCOs.

The emergency continued beyond independence and the Corps maintained its operational support of the British forces involved. The end of the emergency was formally declared on 1 August, 1960. Throughout, the contribution made by the RASC air supply organization and 55 (AD) Company RASC in particular was of enormous importance. Even when the intensity of ground operations slackened, there was no let-up in the demand for maintenance by air. Corps despatchers flew in every type of transport aircraft, including RNZAF Bristol Freighters and the smaller short-range aircraft of the RAF such as the Pioneer and Auster. No formal Rear Airfield Supply Organization or RASO was set up, these duties being performed by 55 (AD) Company HQ. The climate, weather conditions and terrain in Malaya meant that air transport operations were always hazardous and the toll on RAF air crew and RASC air despatchers was high. Indeed 55 (AD) Company RASC had the highest casualty rate of any corps or regiment, four times that of the infantry. A memorial plaque to commemorate their sacrifice is installed in the Church of St Michael and St George in Aldershot.

Hong Kong

The RASC was among the first to return to Hong Kong following the Japanese surrender in August, 1945. With the relieving force was 781 Company, a Civil Affairs GT Company, which arrived in early October and also a detachment of the

RASC/EFI to repossess the former NAAFI installations and set up a service for the returning garrison. Also in October, 1945, a platoon of 387 GT Company RASC arrived from Burma, to be followed by the rest of the company in January and February, 1946.

The RASC transport task of moving and dumping Japanese ammunition was extremely hazardous work. On 21 March, 1946, Driver Joseph Hughes was killed when his lorry blew up while he was trying to extinguish a fire which had started in his load of ammunition. His attempts had delayed the explosion and warning was given to others in the locality who were able to take cover. He was subsequently awarded a posthumous George Cross.

Because of the water gap between Hong Kong Island and the mainland (Kowloon) the vessels of 79 Company RASC (Water Transport) were in constant demand for the ferrying of passengers, vehicles and stores.

Hong Kong returned to normal conditions within a comparatively short space of time, but considerable reinforcement was required in 1948 and 1949 because of the civil war in China. There was no British intervention, but substantial reinforcement was considered to be the best way of deterring Red China from an attempt to add Hong Kong to its conquests.

When, in 1949, *HMS Amethyst* was attacked by artillery and machine-gun fire

Mules of 414 Pack Troop RASC refuelling a MK10 Whirlwind.

238

from Chinese Communist forces on its way up the Yangtse River to rescue British diplomats and their families from Nanking, it was halted in mid-stream, suffering casualties. An RAF doctor and a two-man air despatch team from 799 (AD/GT) Company in Hong Kong with relief medical and other supplies were sent in an RAF Sunderland flying boat to land on the river by the *Amethyst*. The Sunderland came under heavy fire from the Chinese and was damaged, but the doctor managed to deliver the medical supplies to the ship. The plane's crew succeeded in getting the Sunderland back to Hong Kong and returned in a second plane with further supplies. These they were unfortunately unable to deliver because of the intensity of the Chinese fire. The two air despatchers, Drivers Chadband and O'Dono, were unique in the Army in subsequently being awarded the Naval General Service Medal with the bar 'Yangtse' for their part in the operation.

The force was built up to divisional strength including all supporting arms. The Corps' duties were many and varied throughout the Island, Kowloon and the New Territories. In addition to the Garrison Transport units, the RASC element of the formation was composed of 8 (Infantry Brigade) Company, 56 (Hong Kong) Company, 79 Company (Water Transport), 81 Pack Company (HT), a Base Supply Depot, a Supply Depot, 3 Supply and Petroleum Depot, and a large Barrack Services organization.

THE KOREAN WAR

Korea had been annexed by the Japanese in 1910 and ruled by them until the end of the Second World War. After the capitulation of the Japanese in 1945 the States of North and South Korea were eventually established. South Korea, allied to the West, became the Republic of Korea. North Korea remained Communist-dominated and under the influence of China when the Russians left in 1948. The border division between the states was the 38th parallel of latitude, which had been agreed at the Potsdam Conference in 1945. This demarcation line had initially been selected as a convenient line, to the north of which Russia would supervise the withdrawal of the Japanese, and south of which the United States would do the same. It quickly became a political and ideological division.

On 25 June, 1950, North Korea invaded South Korea across the demarcation line and started what came to be known as the Korean War. The United Nations condemned the North Koreans as aggressors and all member nations were called upon to give every assistance to South Korea.

General Outline of the Campaign

● **25 June, 1950-15 September, 1950**. The initial thrust of the North Koreans from 25 June resulted in their capture of the South Korean capital Seoul three days later. The United States swiftly intervened from bases in Japan and were soon helping the hard-pressed South Koreans. During September the British 27 Brigade was despatched from Hong Kong and was quickly in action with 24 United States Division. The build-up of a United Nations Force had begun.

● **16 September, 1950-24 November, 1950**. During this period the UN Force counter-attacked to drive the North Koreans out of the two-thirds of South Korea which they now occupied and by November had driven them back to the Manchurian border. In early November 29 Infantry Brigade Group arrived by sea from UK.

● **November, 1950-24 January, 1951**. China now vigorously intervened with ground forces and the UN Force was forced to withdraw south in all the severity of a Korean winter. By 4 January Seoul had been evacuated for the second time, but the Chinese advance was stemmed a few miles south along the line of the Han River.

● **25 January, 1951-31 March, 1951**. The UN Forces carried out successful counter-attacks along the whole front, but with only limited objectives. Seoul was retaken and by the end of March the UN was established on a line a little south of the 38th Parallel.

● **1 April, 1951-31 May, 1951**. The Chinese now began a Spring Offensive with some success against the South Korean formations. During April the famous battle of the Imjin River took place, in which the 1st Battalion The Gloucestershire Regiment distinguished itself. During this battle RASC units were heavily involved in close support. The main UN defences held and the Chinese advance was halted after they had sustained heavy casualties.

The RASC Participation

The part played by the RASC in this campaign in the support of the British and Commonwealth forces subsequently deployed was a remarkable one, not so much for the numbers involved but as a tribute to the fortitude and resourcefulness of all those taking part, and in particular to the individual MT drivers of the Corps.

78 Company was the first RASC MT company to arrive in Korea at the beginning of October, 1950. It mobilized for Korea as a motor ambulance company, designated to provide medical evacuation cover for 29 Infantry Brigade, also mobilizing in UK. The company personnel consisted of 80% Class A Reservists, 10% Regulars, and 10% Volunteers for Korea. On arrival at Pusan, the main UN port of entry in south-east Korea, it was to deploy in a much wider GT role from the British Maintenance Area at Zong-Song beside Pusan's enormous natural harbour, and its vehicle composition was changed. Initially some of its transport operated between the beaches, the depots and the railhead. The railway providing the link to the TCVs and ambulances continued to support 29 Brigade, now arriving. The Company HQ, Workshop Platoon, and two of the ambulance platoons, which had changed their ambulances for Bedford QL 3-tonners, went north to the front in support of 27 Infantry Brigade. The Brigade was by then in the throes of the long withdrawal and heavily involved in the fighting on the eastern front as part of 24 United States Division. 78 Company was now given operational command of a platoon of the Royal Canadian Army Service Corps, and a platoon of the Royal New Zealand Army Service Corps for its troop-carrying operations in the withdrawal. Both platoons were quickly and successfully integrated into the Company for this operation, which was carried out in increasingly severe winter conditions. For the Company the withdrawal south was finally halted in the region of Kunchon, and from late January to March the Company supported the counter-attack by the UN forces, and the slow advance northwards.

By November, 1950, 29 Brigade Group had also arrived in Pusan by sea and with

An RASC Land Rover faces the difficult Korean roads.

it was 57 Company RASC as the brigade group transport company. The Brigade with 57 Company moved at once by rail some 200 miles north to Suwon, a journey which took over two days. 57 Company had hardly settled down when news came that the Chinese had broken through to the east. Supporting their brigade, they, together with 78 Company in 27 Brigade, were now to be involved in the overall withdrawal of the whole of the UN forces from North Korea. This long withdrawal for both companies produced a dreary pattern of activity under extremely onerous conditions. Basically it was a continuous round: dump stores and load troops – take troops back to the next layback position – return to pick up the dumped stores – withdraw to behind the layback positions – wait for about 48 hours and repeat the same procedure. At one period the drivers suffered considerable hardship when the temperatures were sub-arctic and there was a shortage of appropriate winter clothing. Great resolution was shown in carrying out all that was required of them under such conditions.

By the end of January, 1951, the withdrawal had at last ceased and the United Nations line had been established. The next phase was a counter-attack with the limited objective of clearing South Korea but halting short of the 38th Parallel. This was achieved by the end of March, 1951, and Seoul retaken. With the advent of Spring, the Chinese carried out a series of heavy counter-attacks in the general area of 29 Brigade. During the third week of April the Imjin River battle took place, the brigade's biggest action of the war with 57 Company much involved in support. In July, 1951, with the front held, 1 Commonwealth Division was formed and 1 Commonwealth Divisional Column RASC came into being. 57 Company ended its successful duty as an affiliated brigade company in August and became part of the divisional column.

The formation of the 1st Commonwealth Division on 25 July, 1951, was of considerable interest. The Division was part of 1 US Corps of the Eighth US Army throughout the remainder of the war, although neighbouring divisions changed periodically. It was located two and a half hours' drive north of Seoul, and four from the west coast, and remained there for two years with the exception of a short period out of the line in 1952. The Divisional Column RASC had responsibility for maintaining three brigades: 25 Canadian, 28 Commonwealth and 29 British Infantry

RASC Vehicles carrying Australian Troops across the Imjin River.

Brigade. The Column was formed initially from 57 and 78 Companies, with the addition of 54 Company (later 23 Company) Royal Canadian Army Service Corps. This composition remained until 15 October, 1951, when 78 Company was relieved by the newly formed 10 Company Royal New Zealand Army Service Corps.

78 Company took up Lines of Communication duties in the Advanced Base in Pusan and at the base in Japan, leaving behind in the Divisional Column, with great regret, its Canadian and New Zealand Platoons. Under the technical control of the CRASC were also the various motor ambulance detachments of the British, Canadian and Indian Field Ambulances and the Divisional HQ Transport Platoon RNZASC.

Within both the Divisional and Brigade headquarters, staff officers were a mix of nationalities from all the Commonwealth countries represented in the Division and Corps officers filled a number of these appointments. At one time the Corps provided the DAQMG in the Divisional HQ, two brigade DAA & QMGs, the Staff Captain AQ and two of the three BRASCOs. In the Column HQ the CRASC was always RASC and the 2IC normally RCASC.

A commodity maintenance system was employed in Korea, each of the three Companies in the Column being responsible for the carriage and issue of supplies, POL or ammunition. Companies changed responsibility occasionally, although ammunition remained with the Canadian company throughout, because of its geographical situation and the fact that the Canadians had US-type weapons. The British and New Zealand Companies each ran an Ammunition Point.

With a mixed national ration strength in the Commonwealth Division averaging 21,000, there were complications involved with supplies, mainly because of finance, national and religious food preferences and the fact that control of provisioning above divisional level was exercised by the Americans. The US packed ration was, however, very attractive, and the fresh ration scale was excellent and abundant; the British soldier, though, often expressed a preference for simpler types of food.

All POL was an American supply and was provided in 53-US-gallon drums. There were some headaches caused by nomenclature, but the major logistic problem was the quantity of petrol used during the winter months, which was staggeringly high. This large demand was caused by the use of petrol in heating stoves. Essential as it was, heating produced a fire hazard in unit locations, and losses due to fires, of equipment difficult to replace, were considerable.

At the time of the formation of the Commonwealth Division the war entered a period of stalemate. The UN Forces actively patrolled from defensive lines against which the Chinese suffered very heavy casualties, although the UN Forces did not go unscathed. Late in November, 1951, a demarcation line between the opposing forces was agreed, with the aim of signing an armistice within thirty days. It was in fact twenty months before major fighting ceased. During that time minor and not so minor clashes were frequent and the Column's support task did not diminish. The armistice was finally agreed and signed on 27 July, 1953.

In August, 1954, the Commonwealth Division was reduced to about brigade group strength, although still retaining its divisional title. The impact on the Corps was that only 10 Company RNZASC remained with the Column. 23 Company RCASC returned home by December, 1954, and HQ RASC disbanded, the CRASC being replaced by a DADST. 57 Company remained in Korea over that Christmas but then largely dispersed, the Company remaining in cadre form at the base in Kure, Japan, where there was an RASC element, including a locally-recruited transport platoon, stationed throughout the war. The reduced Division was finally disbanded on 10 March, 1956, 10 Company RNZASC being the last of the Corps to leave what had been a highly successful organization.

The Korean War once again proved the ability of the British soldier to cope with operations against a fanatical enemy under exceptional and testing conditions of climate. The RASC driver showed undaunted spirit in ensuring that the wheels kept turning and the forward troops never lacked support. The lessons learned by the Corps from co-operation and relationships with the US and Commonwealth Forces in a UN role were to stand them in good stead in the future.

THE CORPS SUPPORT TO ARMY AVIATION

The Corps had always shown a keen interest in military aviation, this frequently being a direct reflection on the farsightedness of its senior officers of the day. The heyday of flying within the Corps was between the early 1950s and 1970, during a period called 'The Integration Scheme', when the RASC/RCT had three Army Aviation 'flights' concurrently on its establishment. One of these was to see active service throughout the Borneo confrontation. At the start of this period the RASC was also instrumental in organizing and manning the only army unit ever to fly medium-lift support helicopters, the Joint Experimental Helicopter Unit (JEHU). This also saw operational service at Suez, when it dropped the 'experimental' from its title.

Over fifty officers from the ASC trained and flew as pilots in the Royal Flying Corps (RFC) during the First World War, winning at least one Distinguished Flying

Cross, awarded to Brigadier (final rank) H A Courtenay DFC, RASC and RIASC for 'rendering inoperative' the 7th Turkish Army HQ from the air, in Mesopotamia, by dropping 20lb bombs by hand whilst they were 'debouching from a defile'! Several RASC officers were awarded RAF 'wings' in the Second World War, probably transferring into the Corps after their time as RAF pilots and at least one DFC was awarded (Lieutenant Colonel (final rank) C D C Dunford Wood DFC RASC for flying gallantry in Burma) and many RASC NCOs immediately volunteered for pilot training with the Glider Pilot Regiment (GPR) on its formation in 1942. Indeed Lance Corporal L Morris RASC was reputed to be the first successful GPR volunteer. Pilots of the GPR were expected to fight on the battlefield. Soon after the Second World War the GPR was disbanded (1949) and several RASC NCO pilots converted to flying light, fixed-wing powered aircraft, then transferring into the newly-formed Light Liaison Flights equipped with Auster aircraft, which the MOD had just formed to supplement the Royal Artillery Air Observation Post (AOP) Flights. Throughout the Second World War these Royal Artillery-piloted AOP flights had shown how essential army-controlled light aircraft were on a modern battlefield, not only for the direction of artillery, but but also for reconnaissance, aerial photography, rapid casualty evacuation and general liaison duties. Many RASC officers also trained as pilots for these Light Liaison Flights, which were attached to RA (AOP) units and under command of army formation HQs.

The American Army's use of helicopters in the Korean War had clearly demonstrated the importance of this type of aircraft on the land battlefield. In the light of this successful use, the Ministry of Defence in 1955 formed the Joint Experimental Helicopter Unit. Under the impetus of the then DST, Major General W H D Ritchie, the RASC, as the Combat Zone combat supplies and transport experts, took control of this experimental unit. They supplied many of the Tri-Service helicopter pilots, often experienced Auster pilots who converted over to helicopters on courses in the United States, plus all of the non-technical ground element. Flying Sikorsky Whirlwind Mark 2 and Bristol Sycamore Mark 14 helicopters, the trial was a great success. It deployed on the Suez operation, but very soon afterwards was transferred, as a political expediency, to the RAF. Many excellent army helicopter pilots chose to leave the Service early at this time.

In 1957 the Army Air Corps (AAC) was formed to take control of all army flying, including the Light Liaison and RA (AOP) flights, in anticipation of the expected substantial increase in the use of aircraft within the British Army. By the early 1960s it was appreciated that the only practical way for this expansion was integrating aircraft directly into cap-badge units, thus manpower and running costs would have to be found from within existing unit structures and cap-badge budget allocations. A secondary consideration was that pilots would normally come from the Arm concerned and thus already have an intimate knowledge of the specialist battlefield roles of armoured reconnaissance, infantry, engineer and signal support, etc. Thus was born the unit flight, air troop and air platoon under the general term of Army Aviation. At theatre level the RASC fought hard to win control of the old Light Liaison Flights, which resulted in three of the four Theatre Flights being cap-badged RASC/RCT. These were FARELF, BAOR and the UK, with the AAC running only the MELF Flight. The non-technical ground crew were all RASC/RCT cap-badged, as were most of the pilots, though several NCO pilots were posted in from other Arms or Services to make up shortfalls.

Also in the early 1960s the AAC had purchased the de Havilland of Canada

DHC2 'Beaver', a single radial-engined light aircraft, to replace the underpowered and ageing Auster. The Beaver proved to be an extremely rugged, reliable and powerful aircraft, able to carry six people over 500 miles. Designed for the Canadian bush, it could be operated for long periods with only the minimum of maintenance, revelled in landing on unprepared surfaces including snow, and never seemed to run out of power! There was an airstrip in Aden where all army helicopters were grounded for half of the day, due to the high ambient temperatures vaporizing the fuel. However, the Beaver never suffered from the problem. The metal was almost unbearably hot, even inside the cockpit, but the engine would start first time and the aircraft stagger into the air at its full all-up weight. The Corps was the major UK Army Aviation user of the Beaver.

The first RASC flight to form was 30 Flight RASC, as the FARELF theatre flight, under Major J S Riggall RASC. Using Beaver aircraft already deployed to that theatre with AAC flights, it was immediately heavily tasked in support of the Borneo confrontation. It flew its first operational sortie in Borneo at 0800 hours on the day it formed, signalling the DST *'30 flight RASC commenced forming today (8 April, 1964) and is operational with immediate effect'!* It expanded to a strength of nine aircraft in support of the operations in Borneo, where distances were considerable and where, because of the Beaver's versatility and high serviceability rates, all its aircraft were in constant demand, both for long-distance communication flying and also for the battlefield tasks of close reconnaissance and artillery fire control. When the Borneo campaign closed in 1966 the flight, now retitled 130 Flight RCT, returned to West Malaysia where, as well as flying a regular communication schedule throughout that country, it also provided the pilots with challenging flying detachments in both Nepal and Laos. The Nepal detachment was in support of the British Gurkha recruiting and pension payment roles, flying in the foothills of the Himalayas. Laos was a Foreign Office-funded deployment to assist the UK and the Australian Embassies there to monitor the 'Neutrality of Laos' agreement, somewhat ironical as the Americans were flying intensive combat operations throughout the region! 130 Flight RCT was the last RCT Flight to disband, flying its Beaver aircraft back to the UK over a three-week period in late 1970. The Nepal detachment was consequently closed, but the Laos detachment remained until 1975, usually manned by an RCT officer pilot. Major P Shield MBE RCT was the last pilot there, and he gained his MBE for his work in Laos over two years.

130 Flight's flying return to the UK was just one example of a series of long-distance ferry flights undertaken by Corps pilots. In 1964 Captain J H Ingram, together with another ex-RASC pilot, flew Beavers from Cyprus to Aden for onward deployment to 130 Flight by sea, and in 1968 Lieutenant R F Grevatte-Ball, with one other pilot, flew a Beaver from the UK to Ethiopia and back over a four-month period to provide support to Colonel Blashford-Snell's 'Great Abbai' Expedition, a river descent of the Blue Nile almost entirely re-supplied by the single Beaver, frequently by parachute drops. Whilst in Ethiopia the aircraft was based out in the open for two months in monsoon weather conditions, during which time its only unserviceability was one blown fuse!

The BAOR theatre flight was 31 Flight RASC, on redesignation becoming 131 Flight RCT. Flying throughout Western Europe, from Turkey in the south to Norway in the north, with three Beavers and three Sud-Aviation Alouette 2c helicopters, these helicopters were mainly used throughout BAOR for VIP trips. First commanded by Major P G C Child, a former RASC officer who had transferred to the AAC, this

A Beaver Light Aircraft and a Scout Helicopter of 130 Flight RCT. (R. Grevatte-Ball)

Beaver flying was of an entirely different nature to that in 130 Flight. In Europe precision airways procedural flying replaced 'nap of the earth' bush flying and only experienced pilots, with an aptitude for mental arithmetic, were suitable. In the UK the final Corps Flight, 132 Flight RCT, was only formed in 1967, under the initial command on Major C F L Waistie RCT, with its role exactly similar to the three Beavers of 131 Flight, but being tasked by the MOD. Exercise 'Hardfall' in Norway was regularly supported every winter by a weekly liaison flight from the UK.

By the late 1960s the period of integration with Army Aviation was coming to a close and the AAC was steadily taking back all UK Army flying units, under the guise of centralization for economy and efficiency as successive replacement aircraft became ever more sophisticated and expensive to operate. 131 Flight RCT in BAOR was retitled 131 Aviation Flight AAC in 1970 and 132 Flight RCT was similarly renamed, though remaining with an RCT officer pilot in command until just before it disbanded in 1974. 130 Flight RCT was the only theatre flight always to be in Corps hands. Fixed wing flying with Army Aviation ceased with the closure of these three flights in the early 1970s, on grounds of economy (with the exception of one specialized Northern Ireland photographic role) and nearly fifteen years of highly professional military aviation, mostly using pilots found from within the Corps, came to an end. However, the Corps continued to provide helicopter pilots for AAC units until its final days. Between 1950 and 1982 117 officers and 27 Senior NCOs were awarded the military symbols 'pl' for becoming a qualified army fixed-wing pilot, or 'ph' for a similar helicopter qualification; many earned both. Further details of flying within the Corps can be found in greater detail in the Corps history *The Story of the RASC and RCT 1954-1982*.

The final two Corps flying gallantry medals were both DFCs. Captain D J Ralls RCT (later Brigadier AAC) was awarded one in 1968 whilst flying a Scout helicopter of an AAC flight in Aden, when he successfully fired upon, and co-ordinated RAF Hunter FGA attacks against, Arab terrorists who had just ambushed a Dhala road convoy in Aden's 'Area West' in the mountains near Habilayn. Captain J G Greenhalgh RCT won his at the Battle of Goose Green during the Falkland Islands campaign, when, as an AAC detachment commander flying Scout helicopters with 3 Commando Brigade, he repeatedly flew under enemy fire to resupply ammunition and evacuate casualties.

THE MIDDLE EAST – A DANGEROUS HIGHWAY

In the aftermath of the war, the Chiefs of Staff recognized that the Middle East remained of greatest concern to Britain's defence strategy. Here the Commonwealth lines of communication and vital oil reserves around the Persian Gulf could be threatened by a combination of nationalist ambitions and Soviet subversion. Many countries were involved in this complex and unsettling situation. In several Middle Eastern countries there was a British Army presence.

Palestine

As soon as the Second World War was over, the Palestinian Jewish community immediately reopened the question of the British Government's White Paper of May, 1939. This had limited Jewish immigration into Palestine to a given maximum over a period of five years, after which no further immigration would be permitted without Arab consent. In 1944 the time limit of five years was extended because of delays resulting from the war, but no increase in the total number of immigrants was allowed. By the end of 1945 the total number (75,000) had about been reached. The Jews wanted Palestine as a home for displaced Jews from all over Europe and regarded adherence to a 1939 quota as inhuman. The Arabs disagreed. Thus the country simmered with a growing political tension and a major internal security situation had arisen.

At the end of the War 1st British Infantry Division was in Palestine and was joined by 6th Airborne Division. 3rd British Infantry Division alternated with the 1st Division between Palestine and the Suez Canal Zone. On 14 November, 1945, there were large scale riots in Tel Aviv, which was placed under martial law for six days. British internal security work became set in a pattern of 'cordon and search' for the maintenance of law and order and the rounding-up of terrorists, suspects and illegal immigrants. This was the political climate in which the Corps had to operate throughout Palestine in the first post-war year. It continued to do so right up to June, 1948, suffering its full share of problems, hardships and casualties. At the height of this difficult and most disagreeable operation there were thirteen MT companies in Palestine in addition to the divisional companies, and a full range of supply and POL units and depots.

The British Mandate in Palestine ended on 14 May, 1948, and the political and military withdrawal started. At the same time the State of Israel was proclaimed by David Ben-Gurion, the Jewish Agency leader, who became Prime Minister in a provisonal government. The final withdrawal from the Haifa enclave took place on 30 June, 1948. Thus ended the British military presence in Palestine which dated back to 1917. Left behind was a situation which, in its continuing civil, military and political turbulence, affected all those with interests in the Middle East.

Egypt – 1945 to 1956

At the end of 1945 Egypt requested a revision of the 1936 Treaty, which amounted to a request for a British withdrawal. A considerable time elapsed before the British Labour government of the day announced on 7 May, 1946, a plan for the evacuation of Egypt. Rioting had already broken out. By the end of March, 1947, the British forces had moved into the Canal Zone as a first step towards complete withdrawal. This did not satisfy Egyptian terrorists; the tension grew and the situation worsened. There was an upsurge of nationalism in Egypt and almost the whole of the nine years following Britain's withdrawal into the Canal Zone were full of dangerous internal security incidents which demanded constant vigilance. In October and November, 1951, the situation had become so serious that British forces were reinforced by some 6,000 servicemen, together with 330 vehicles and large tonnages of stores. This brought the troops in the Canal Zone to sixteen infantry battalions, seven RA regiments and two and a half armoured regiments. The Egyptian government then withdrew the bulk of Egyptian local civil labour. This crisis was resolved by the arrival of several thousand Pioneer troops from Mauritius and a civilian labour force of 3,000 from Malta and Cyprus.

Because of the strained relationship with the Egyptians, it became impossible to rely on local sources for the provision of fresh ration items for the British Forces in Egypt. These had to be imported and distributed throughout the zone by RASC MT companies and refrigerated railway waggons.

Political negotiations went on behind the scenes between the two governments for the British withdrawal. When negotiations broke down there was increased violence. Over forty British soldiers lost their lives. RASC transport companies were severely overstretched because of the need for extra manning of vehicles. Standing orders for every unit required each vehicle to have two drivers in the front and one in the rear as a look-out (a practice later adopted in Northern Ireland in the seventies). In

October, 1954, agreement was reached that British forces would be gradually withdrawn over a period of twenty months. The last British troops left Egypt on 13 June, 1956.

Egypt – The Suez Crisis

Sadly, it was not long before they returned. The Egyptian government, just six months after the final evacuation of Egypt, seized control of the Suez Canal in breach of international law and nationalized the Anglo-French Canal Company.

Britain and France immediately sought the re-internationalization of the Suez Canal through diplomatic channels. They also made joint plans to retake the Canal by force as a last resort, should peaceful negotiations fail. This included in Britain the calling up of Army reservists. 3 Infantry Division, including the Divisional Column RASC, received orders to mobilize. Corps units were also heavily involved in Malta and Cyprus on dock-clearance tasks as the build-up took place.

In September, 1956, as a result of the growing Suez crisis, the decision was taken by the Chief-of-Staffs Committee that the Army would organize and run logistic shipping in support of Army operations. General Sir Gerald Templer, Chief of the Imperial General Staff (CIGS) decreed that the Royal Engineers and the RASC would take over the project and the RASC, under the DST Major General W H D Ritchie, readily accepted the task. 76 Company RASC (LCT) was formed under command of Major D Cuff on 5 October, 1956 at Yeovil in Somerset and officers and crews were gathered together from all sources in the Corps including, especially, qualified National Servicemen.

The British and French Governments decided to retake the Canal by force and Airborne landings took place at Port Said on 5 November, 1956. The landings involved 63 Parachute Company RASC which took over Egyptian vehicles to help maintain the Force. These air landings were followed by beach landings by Royal Marine Commandos. On 10 November 3 Division, less the Guards Brigade, landed to relieve the Parachute Brigade and the Commandos who then returned to Cyprus. As the result of United States pressure, a ceasefire was ordered three days later and United Nations troops relieved British forces who withdrew finally on 22 December, 1956. 3 Divisional Column left many of its vehicles behind for UN use.

The RASC Fleet

On 19 January, 1957, as a result of the reorganization started during the Suez Crisis, the MK VIII LCT 4061, the headquarters vessel of 76 Company (LCT) was sent to Portsmouth. During the next few weeks she was joined by LCTs 4041, 4128, 4097, 4062, 4002 and finally LCT 4074, so that by the end of February, 1957, the Company was established at Portsmouth and was fully operational, manned entirely by military. These LCTs MK VIII were very different from the vessels previously operated by RASC soldiers and were 231 ft long with 38 ft beam and a speed of around 8-9 knots. From the very beginning, despite the lack of specialized experience, the RASC ran the vessels well up to Naval standards with a substantially smaller crew – two officers, a WO coxswain and twenty-six soldiers.

Operation HARDROCK, the setting up of a Guided Weapons Range in the Hebrides and on the island of St Kilda, now started up. Since there were no proper ports in the Outer Hebrides or St Kilda, the Royal Navy had been unable to provide support, so the RASC were asked if 76 Squadron could help. After a recce by LCTs

4002, commanded by Captain Michael Weston, and 4041, by Captain Tony Charles, it was advised that operations were possible. On 15 April, 1957, LCT 4002 sailed from Lochboisdale, South Uist, with the reconnaissance party from 5004 Airfield Construction Squadron RAF and landed them on St Kilda. Operation HARDROCK had begun and since then the RASC and later RCT military-manned LCTs MK VIII, and later the LCLs, operated between the south of England, Cairnryan or Rhu on the Clyde, and the Outer Hebrides and St Kilda. The operation required the LCTs to put men, stores and equipment ashore on to the beach at St Kilda, some 45 miles out in the Atlantic Ocean, west of the Outer Hebrides, from April through to September each year. After completion of the range in 1958/59 the LCTs delivered the equipment and vehicles of the Guided Weapons Wing of the School of Artillery to Benbecula annually, including the Corporal rocket missile for test firing.

In 1959 76 Company RASC (LCT) was divided into two flotillas – one in Scottish waters and one based at Portsmouth, which maintained at least one vessel at Instow, North Devon, to work with the Amphibian Training Wing RASC, 18 Amphibian Squadron RASC and Fording Trials Branch REME nearby at Fremington. January, 1960, saw three LCTs MK VIII despatched to Singapore to become the third division of 76 Squadron based with 37 Company RASC (WT) on Pulau Brani.

These vessels, in many ways, replaced the steam-driven coasters of the Civilian Fleet as maids-of-all-work, not only transporting tanks and other vehicles and stores around the UK and Far East, but also taking part in major exercises such as when HMAV *Aachen* (ex LCT 4062) (Captain I Peradon), and HMAV *Arezzo* (ex LVT 4128) (Captain T Street) loaded with a Regiment of the Royal Horse Artillery at Sylt, Denmark and sailed through the Kiel Canal to undertake exercises with German LSMs, all under the command of Korvetten Kapitän Kretshmer, the famous U-Boat commander. LCTs also sailed to the Shetlands, Norway, the Channel Islands, France, Germany and Denmark with specialized heavy loads such as transformers, radar equipment, hovercraft and snow equipment.

A War Office review of 1959 showed that there were still 111 vessels in commission with 58 in reserve, but the Civilian Fleet continued to reduce. All the old steam coasters and ADCs were scrapped and the last civilian-manned vessels left Cairnryan, Weymouth and Woolwich. The operations in the Hebrides were thus purely military with the exception of the Civilian Fleet's T-Class trawler *Mull* which continued to support operations to St Kilda, particularly in the winter.

However, range clearance for weapons ranges and proof and experimental establishments work continued to provide tasks for the Civilian Fleet, as well as the operation of the training vessels *Yarmouth Navigator*, a 90ft MFV and the smaller MFV *Yarmouth Seaman*. Operations soon started at the Royal Armoured Corps range at Lulworth, followed by the Castle Martin and Manorbier ranges in South Wales, the Royal Artillery guided missile range in the Hebrides and the Infantry Cinque Ports training area. At the same time the Civilian Fleet supported the P & E establishments at Eskmeals in Cumbria, Pendine Sands and Shoeburyness.

In addition, the RASC operated vessels in the Caribbean and Bermuda which started with the formation of 889 Company RASC (WT) at Port Royal in Jamaica and continued with operations in British Honduras (now Belize), the Bahamas and Turks Island. These vessels were mainly crewed with Jamaicans from Port Royal, although the Belize-based vessels were locally crewed.

Since it would take some time to commission the LCTs MK VIII which had been laid up in South Wales, the Army called for volunteers from the Civilian Fleet to man logistic shipping to help meet the Suez commitments. Nearly seventy Civilian Fleet members volunteered, including Frank Bourne, the last Fleet Superintendent, and three LCTs, the MK VIII L4086, (later the *Arromanches*) under command of J Bayliss, and two MK VIs, L408 with J G Scott as Master and L403 with Captain Watt as Master, sailed in a small convoy escorted by a T-Class trawler. The vessels were loaded in Malta and, after a pause off Famagusta, Cyprus, steamed to Port Said where two remained until 1957.

Malta GC

The Corps' role on the island immediately postwar was the routine support of a small number of Army units and of the relatively large RN and RAF forces of the peacetime garrison. The RASC organization was similar to that prior to the 1939-45 War, that is HQ RASC, 67 Supply Depot and its associated Bakery, 32 GT Company and 80 Water Transport Company.

During the Suez crisis the Corps became heavily involved in the preparation for

The RCT Fast Launch Call Boy *at its berth in Valetta Harbour.*

intervention by British forces. 32 Company's duties included troop lifts to ships and aircraft, stores collection to and from docks, the loading of LCTs and the evacuation of casualties from the aircraft carriers *HMS Theseus* and *HMS Ocean* to the hospitals BMH Imtarfa and RNH Bighi.

Libya

The scene of the 8th Army campaigns in North Africa remained part of the British presence in the Mediterranean area for a number of years after the Second World War. In Tripoli, under HQ Libya and Tripolitania Area, HQ RASC Tripoli initially commanded 7 and 40 Transport Companys, 123 Supply Depot, an Army Fire Brigade and a Barrack Services organization. Five hundred miles east of Tripoli, in Cyrenaica, garrisons at Benghazi, Barce and El Adem were supported by 1, 13 and 806 Transport Companys, 26 and 477 Supply Platoons and 112 Command Petroleum Depot. In Tobruk 193 Company (manned by Mauritian drivers) and 805 Company (manned by German drivers) gave transport support to the garrison. 115 Command Petrol Depot, 489 Supply Platoon and Barrack Services, together with a few RASC Harbour launches and Motor Fishing Vessels (MFVs), completed the RASC establishment.

The garrisons were reduced finally to Tripoli and Benghazi; their presence firstly being to aid a treaty of friendship signed by Britain and King Idris of the United Kingdom of Libya and to support overseas training for UK and BAOR-based units where the terrain gave limitless opportunities for manoeuvre. The formation of the RCT in 1965 meant that HQ RASC Tripoli was disbanded, leaving 38 Squadron RCT and a small Movements detachment as the only Corps presence which departed when the rest of the garrison closed down in April, 1966.

When King Idris was deposed by a group of Libyan Army officers in September, 1969, it preceded the final departure of British troops in Benghazi. The total evacuation from Libya was effected between January and March, 1970, and a Movement Control detachment, 52 Port Squadron RCT, a Freight Handling Troop with lighterage facilities, traffic operators and tank transporter drivers were all sent out from UK to assist the withdrawal. 6500 tons of cargo, over 1000 vehicles, 3,500 servicemen and their families were safely evacuated to UK or Cyprus, finally ending links with a region significantly marked in British military history.

CYPRUS

After the Second World War the Corps was represented in the Cyprus Garrison on a small scale. The largest unit was 471 (Cyprus Volunteer Force) Company RASC (GT). A substantial number of Cypriots had served in the Corps as MT drivers and muleteers during the War. Together with 695 Company RASC (Station Transport), these two units were busily engaged up to 1948 in supporting the garrison and moving illegal Jewish immigrants from docks to camps on the island.

Following reorganization in 1949, these two units were disbanded and replaced by 17 Company RASC. By 1950 CRASC Cyprus District commanded 17 Company, 74 Supply Depot, 539 Field Bakery, 252 Command Petroleum Depot and the Barrack Stores.

In 1954, in response to the impending move of GHQ Middle East Land Forces from Egypt, the Corps' presence began to grow. A detachment of 58 Car Company RASC arrived from the Canal Zone. New accommodation was built at Dhekelia for a MT company, a supply company, a supply depot, static bakery and the petrol depot. During the latter half of 1955 the British forces' strength in Cyprus grew over twenty-fold due to the build up of reinforcements for the Cyprus Emergency which had started on 1 April, and the arrival of GHQ Middle East Land Forces, located in Episkopi, and large RAF contingents. The Cyprus Emergency stemmed from the terrorist actions of the Greek Cypriot movement, EOKA, against the British in its efforts to ensure Greek rule in Cyprus, ENOSIS, and domination over the Turkish Cypriots.

The original build-up, further increased for the Suez Emergency in 1956, required a complete reorganization of S & T services. New HQs and units were formed and others arrived complete from Egypt and the UK. CRASC Cyprus District became DDST Cyprus District, 1 Transport Column RASC was formed at Famagusta, CRASC Cyprus (West) at Limassol, 40 Company RASC (MT) at Dhekelia, 42 Company RASC (MT) at Limassol and 65 Company RASC (GT) at Famagusta. At Episkopi three new units appeared, 45 Independent Transport Platoon RASC, Field Supply Platoon RASC and Field Bakery Platoon RASC. Other units which served in Cyprus during this hectic year included 138 Air Supply Platoon RASC and 63 Company RASC (Parachute Brigade) and a much-increased Barrack organization. The Corps were active in support of the operations against the terrorists and sustained a number of casualties during 1955 and 1956.

During the summer of 1957 3 Infantry Division moved from UK to Cyprus, bringing with it 1 Company RASC, this reinforcement being necessary to meet growing violence by EOKA terrorists. The internal security situation required that all vehicles be double-manned with a look-out in the rear and with all ranks being armed when out of their unit location.

Throughout 1958 diplomatic discussions took place in attempts to arrive at a solution to the Cyprus problem of unrest. An agreement was finally signed on 19 February, 1959, by the United Kingdom, Greece, Turkey and the Greek and Turkish Cypriots. Cyprus became an Independent Republic, with Archbishop Makarios as its first president, on 16 August, 1960.

The Army commenced its withdrawal into the Sovereign Base Areas (Akrotiri and Dhekelia) where the United Kingdom retained full sovereignty and jurisdiction, and the use of roads and other facilities.

After the end of the emergency there was the usual rundown and withdrawal. The DDST appointment was downgraded to CRASC and HQ RASC Cyprus (West) was redesignated HQ RASC Cyprus and established in Dhekelia, as this was destined to be the principal logistic base. 17 Company and 136 Supply Company were disbanded in May, 1960. The designation and role of 58 Company was changed from the GHQ Car Company to a GT Company and was largely civilianized with Cypriot drivers. The company moved from Episkopi to Dhekelia in October, 1962, into accommodation which had been occupied by 40 Company RASC, now disbanded except for two RASC platoons taken over by 58 Company.

A few days before Christmas, 1963, there was a shooting incident between Greek and Turkish Cypriots in Nicosia and fighting between the two communities spread all over Cyprus. The Greek and Turkish communities shortly afterwards accepted the offer of the British to establish protected lines between the main community areas, particularly the 'Green Line' through Nicosia separating Turkish areas in the north from Greek areas in the south. A British truce force was established, later replaced by a United Nations force – UNFICYP. The UK provided units for the UN force, as well as the logistic backing for the whole force, which was supplied from the Sovereign Base Areas. During this period 7 Company RASC arrived on an emergency tour from the UK, mainly to support Royal Engineers in the construction of an airstrip at Dhekalia. The emergency continued to simmer through and beyond the McLeod logistic reorganization. There was a major confrontation between Greeks and Turks in July, 1974, described later in this book.

KENYA

The immediate post-war commitments in East Africa were carried out by East African Army Service Corps units under the command of RASC officers and NCOs. East Africa Command's future involved the construction of a large base at Mackinnon Road, north of Mombasa, as the base for the British Strategic Reserve. 51 Company RASC and 4 Armoured Brigade Transport Company RASC were the first two Corps units to arrive for the Mackinnon Road project. 4 Company RASC and 242 Company RASC soon followed, but the project was later abandoned. An EAASC Depot and Training Centre had been formed, and tasked to raise nine Special Establishment Transport Companies with British and African officers and NCOs. By 1950 this had been achieved.

During this period the local Mau Mau terrorist organization had declared itself as an anti-white and anti-Christian force; its aim was to drive out of East Africa all Europeans and other foreigners by means of murder and revolt. The movement grew throughout 1951 and atrocities by the Mau Mau resulted in the declaration of a State of Emergency in October, 1952.

The Mau Mau activities were so widespread that the force of 39 Infantry Brigade of three British battalions and 70 (East African) Brigade of six battalions of the King's African Rifles was inadequate. In September, 1954, 49 Infantry Brigade arrived as reinforcement. RASC convoys had to have armed escorts. The very nature of the dense country justified the deployment of an Air Despatch Detachment RASC, an independent unit of thirty RASC soldiers. Animal Transport was also provided by 67 Animal Transport Company EAASC to support all infantry battalions operating in the high-altitude forests and mountains, particularly isolated detachments.

In August, 1953, 77 Company RASC arrived to provide additional support, not only normal maintenance but also troop carrying; its Composite Platoon packed supplies for free air drops. By the end of 1955 over seven thousand British troops were engaged in the operations against the Mau Mau, together with some seven hundred RAF air and ground crew. By 1956 the terrorists were finally defeated and dispersed.

In 1958 RASC Air Despatch provided support for the Mount Kenya Expedition and took part in a world record altitude supply drop from a Pembroke aircraft, dropping supplies from just over 17,000 feet. At that time 60 Transport Company RASC arrived in Kenya. In addition to its normal maintenance role in support of 24 Infantry Brigade, it was also employed in 1961 on famine relief. During 1961/62 the Company deployed to Kuwait with 24 Infantry Brigade, which was sent to resolve the confrontation on the border with Iraq. Later a platoon of the Company went to

Swaziland in support of The 1st Battalion The Gordon Highlanders.

In late 1961 and early 1962 16 Air Despatch Company RASC was engaged in supplying civilians in those areas of Kenya and Tanganyika isolated by flood waters. These were some of the last Corps operations in Kenya which became an independent state in 1963, the withdrawal of all British troops taking place in 1964 and 1965.

SINGAPORE

Formation of the Gurkha Army Service Corps

By the late 1950s reorganizations were taking place in Singapore. In 1958 the initial cadres of the newly raised Gurkha Army Service Corps (Gurkha ASC) were trained in MT and supply duties at the RASC School in Singapore.

The Gurkha ASC (subsequently The Queen's Own Gurkha Transport Regiment) was formed on 1 July, 1958, in Singapore and the Federation of Malaya. It was (and remains) an integral part of the Brigade of Gurkhas.

The formation of the Regiment under command of Headquarters Royal Army Service Corps, 17 Gurkha Division/Overseas Commonwealth Land Forces was beset by many unusual problems. Not least, the Gurkha soldiers had little or no experience of vehicles, or driving, or RASC operating procedures. Few spoke English. The British Command Training Team, although widely experienced in mechanical

Gurkha ASC under driver training at Kluang.

Gurkha ASC Recruits Attestation Parade.

transport and Corps procedures, knew nothing of Gurkha Brigade customs and did not speak Gurkhali. The Brigade of Gurkhas units gave the new Regiment every possible assistance to get off to a good start. The RASC British officers, posted in to fill company appointments, were sent on the Gurkhali language course held at the Gurkha Brigade Depot at Sungei Patani in Northern Malaya.

Queen's Gurkha Officers (QGOs) and senior ranks transferred into the raising Cadres for 28 MT Company Gurkha ASC and 30 Infantry Brigade Group Company Gurkha ASC arrived at the RASC School Nee Soon in Singapore in August, 1958, where they immediately began training. This was completed by December, 1958, and they, in turn, became instructors for the junior non-commissioned officers who by then had also reported to the school.

The first recruits were received from the Brigade of Gurkhas Depot in November, 1959. This batch consisted of fifty-four men recruited directly from Nepal for the Regiment and a further forty from Boys' Company training at the Depot. The soldiers recruited were selected in the same way as infantry battalions from either east or west Nepal. These potential drivers therefore included caste names such as Gurungs and Thapas from west Nepal and Rais and Limbus from the east. This tradition has continued ever since.

In May, 1960, the raising Cadres of 31 and 34 Companies Gurkha ASC were formed and moved from Nee Soon. 31 Company went to join its newly formed Composite Platoon in Buller Lines, Kluang. 34 Company moved to Batu Pahat which it initially shared with 28 Company.

In July, 1960, 28 and 30 Companies completed their initial training and 28 Company sailed to Hong Kong on the troopship *Nevasa*, arriving on 10 September to replace 8 Company RASC. 30 Company remained in Malaysia as the MT Company of 63 Gurkha Infantry Brigade and was soon deployed in direct support of operations against the communist terrorists during the Malayan Emergency.

The Major General Brigade of Gurkhas, Major General W C Walker, CBE, DSO, visits 34 Coy GASC, commanded by Major A R Price, in Seremban, 26 September 1962.

Headquarters Gurkha ASC was formed on 1 July, 1960, with the redesignation of Headquarters RASC 17 Gurkha Division/Overseas Commonwealth Land Forces. The affiliation of the Gurkha Army Service Corps to the Royal Army Service Corps was graciously approved by Her Majesty the Queen in December, 1959.

On arrival in Hong Kong 28 Company settled into Whitfield Barracks, alongside Nathan Road. In its MT role the Company had three platoons each equipped with the standard complement of twenty 3-ton task vehicles plus two 3-ton in reserve. The Company also had a heavy section of 10-ton vehicles and a section of two tank transporters with trailers. The transporters proved an awe-inspiring sight along the narrow roads of the New Territories as they carried out their annual major task of rotating the Colony's stockpile of Centurion tanks between Sek Kong and Kowloon. In March, 1961, the Regiment was advised that 30 Company would move to UK the next year to support 51 Gurkha Infantry Brigade (Air Portable). 30 Company moved between April and May, 1962, and settled into Jellalabad Barracks, Tidworth, with minimum turbulence. It flourished as a part of the United Kingdom Strategic Reserve and the Gurkha soldiers enjoyed the benefits of better accommodation, rations, scales of equipment, as well as better rates of pay. Sadly the Indonesian Confrontation and the return of 51 Brigade to Singapore led to the Company packing its equipment, returning vehicles and travelling back to Nee Soon Camp during February and March of 1964.

Organizational Changes in FARELF

HQ 3 Army Air Supply Organization was formed in Singapore in 1960 with under command 5, 6 and 7 Air Supply Control Sections, 55 Company RASC and 21 Air Maintenance Platoon RAOC. This organization was immediately and heavily involved in December, 1962, in the Borneo operations, which are described later in this chapter. A year later detachments of the Air Supply Organization were operating throughout Malaysia, Sarawak, Labuan and Brunei with one composite detachment at Changi.

By 1965 HQ RASC Singapore District was commanding both British and locally-enlisted MT Companies, including 6, 24 and 25 MT Companies, 37 Water Transport Company RASC, 47 LCT Squadron RASC, 4 SRD, supply and POL depots, Barrack and Fire Services. This, together with the Air Supply Organization, was an exceptionally large Corps representation. At this time also, a unique situation existed on the Staff at HQ FARELF where all three Q Staff Colonels were found from RASC/RCT: Colonel H B Booth-Mason Q Maint, Colonel C Boynton Q Qtg, and Colonel V H J Carpenter Q Mov.

Reorganizations also extended to Hong Kong. In the sixties, 81 Pack Company (HT) became 29 Company (Pack Transport) and 79 Company (Water Transport) was absorbed into 56 Company RASC.

ADEN

Although by the early 1960s the RAF had built up a considerable strategic airlift capability, the Chiefs of Staff had decided that it would still be necessary to maintain three bases east of Suez, Aden, Kenya and Singapore. A primary reason was the need to have acclimatized troops readily available. A number of RASC units and seconded officers supported both British and locally raised formations in the Aden peninsula from the late 1950s. In 1959 the first Unified Command was established and CRASC British Forces Arabian Peninsula appointed with responsibilities not only in Aden but elsewhere in the Arabian Peninsula, including Kuwait, Bahrein and Oman. The RASC played a vital role during the Kuwait/Iraq crisis in 1961. 2 Company RASC, a general transport unit, had the main task of supporting the Infantry battalions of the Aden Brigade and support of the forces engaged in the Radfan and Dhala areas some 60 miles north of Aden. The unit also had detachments in Muscat and Oman. 16 Company (Air Despatch) RASC, based in Kenya, detached A Air Supply Platoon to Aden in 1961. 16 Company RASC itself moved from Kenya to Aden in December, 1964. 90 Company RASC was raised for the third time on 1 December, 1957, in Aden with a largely locally enlisted establishment with Corps officers and NCOs. The unit supplied staff cars and administrative transport for Aden Garrison. 60 Company RASC was affiliated to 24 Airportable Brigade and moved its 'C' Platoon to Aden in April, 1964, at the start of the Radfan campaign. The main body of the company moved to Aden in December, 1964, when 24 Brigade redeployed there following the withdrawal from Kenya.

Civil unrest and terrorist activity in the urban areas of Crater and Ma'alla involved all RASC companies in providing an increasing number of soldiers to assist the infantry battalions in their internal security (IS) duties. At the same time, the up-country activity increased with convoys to Museimir and Abyan (Area West).

An Alvis Stalwart Rough Terrain Vehicle in typical Aden surroundings.

Similarly, all RASC transport units were involved in April to June, 1964, in supporting operations in the Radfan. A British force faced the task of expelling Yemeni-backed left-wing guerrillas from the area. The bitter fighting was supported by Corps units providing logistic support by road and by helicopter in the most rugged terrain and severe climatic conditions. Stalwart HMLC were widely employed by the Corps and one of their more unusual duties 'up country' was the daily early morning mine clearance of the main runway at Habilayn, which was constructed of oiled gravel in which the guerrillas frequently buried mines overnight! A Stalwart, with the driver safely belted into his seat and wearing ear plugs, was the most efficient and rapid way of checking on runway safety each morning. Due to the shape of the vehicle's hull, a detonating mine merely blew off a wheel station, much to the subsequent annoyance of REME, and the Stalwart returned on its five remaining wheels. This operation continued until the final British withdrawal from Aden in late 1967.

Before they left Aden in 1967, 60 Company had become 60 Squadron RCT under the McLeod reorganization described at the end of this chapter. They were, in the June of that year, to suffer a grievous incident and the first battle casualties of the new Corps. At that time the situation in Aden had become very tense, initially as a result of the Israeli victory over the Arabs in the Six Day War early in the month. The rumour spread that the British had helped the Israelis and anti-British feelings escalated. This was added to as a result of internal Arab rivalries in the newly-formed South Arabian Armed Police. On 20 June the situation boiled over. A party of two officers, Captain P Godwin being the senior, and nineteen NCOs and soldiers of 60 Squadron, returning from practice on the rifle range in front of Champion Lines, a barracks occupied by the South Arabian Armed Police, were fired upon when they were approximately 150 metres from the barracks.

The vehicle was forced to halt and the occupants, who had already sustained casualties, found what little cover there was in the immediate area. Armed only with rifles and with limited ammunition, the party, for three hours, came under sustained close-range automatic fire from the barracks, whose occupants, the Armed Police, had mutinied. After three hours an Army armoured car came on the scene and was also attacked. It took off three of the party's wounded and, leaving behind its LMG to increase the party's fire power, went for help. Although called on to surrender, the party refused to do so and an hour later all were taken out on the arrival of two 1 Ton APCs (Pigs) and a Saladin. Of the twenty-one members of the party, seven were killed, one died of wounds and six were wounded. Staff Sergeant Butler was postumously Mentioned in Despatches for Gallant Conduct, and Second Lieutenant N H G Beard was also Mentioned in Despatches for Gallant Conduct. In the Crater area of Aden there were further attacks on British troops and nine members of The Royal Northumberland Fusiliers and five from The Argyll and Sutherland Highlanders were also killed on that day. All were buried at the Silent Valley Military Cemetery in Little Aden on 25 June.

Twenty-four years later by now Colonel Beard and his wife returned to Aden with a Royal British Legion Pilgrimage to visit the Squadron graves in Silent Valley, which were all well kept, and laid a wreath at the memorial.

THE INDONESIAN CONFRONTATION

By 1962 Indonesian ambitions to expand its sphere of influence and its territories were beginning to have repercussions both in Sarawak and Northern Borneo. In December, 1962, open revolt broke out.

What started as a local disturbance became a major insurrection. Rapid reinforcement became necessary in order to quell, or at least to contain, the revolt. Simultaneously with the initial build-up of infantry through Labuan, eventually to six battalions, the maintenance backing for the force was established. In an area with few road communications and large water gaps separating areas of operation, RASC air despatch and water transport units played a vital role in the operational build-up. Road transport was still essential in those areas where land movement was possible and in the maintenance area being established on Labuan. The Gurkha ASC provided the bulk of the road transport, reinforced by 3 Company RASC from Terendak Camp in Malaya. In February, 1963, a complete Supply Platoon RASC arrived to assist in the enormous task of resupply. Accommodation was found in the docks and large refrigerators arrived with RE staff to maintain them; at this stage the Composite Platoon of 99 Brigade RASC reverted to its normal role within the brigade.

By December, 1962, the first phase of operations was completed. In the main centres of population the rebellion had been crushed and all airfields were secured.

The rebels then took to the jungle and the second phase began. This involved the redeployment of British and Commonwealth forces into the jungle to cut off the hard core of rebels from their sources of supply across the Indonesian border and to destroy them. This task continued until January, 1964.

The role of Air Despatch in Malaya and its utility elsewhere had been seen as an important supporting element for the Army's Strategic Reserve and resulted in timely changes taking place in the organization of Air Despatch. These were to be of the greatest value during the confrontation. In 1960 Air Despatch in UK and Western Europe had been formed into 1 Army Air Supply Organization (1 AASO), with its headquarters at Watchfield and commanding 47 (AD) Company RASC, an Air Despatch Training Wing and shortly after 22 (AD) Company RASC. This was followed by the formation of 3 AASO in UK which was to command 55 and 69 Air Despatch Companies in the Far East. The latter company moved to Singapore, from UK in 1965 and was subsequently deployed to Borneo for the confrontation. 16 (AD) Company RASC operating in Aden and Kenya was also under command of 3 AASO.

Once forces were deployed in the jungle, 3 AASO was quickly involved. The Air Despatch organization consisted of elements of HQ 3 AASO, HQ 55 Company (AD) RASC with two Air Supply Platoons and 21 Air Maintenance Platoon RAOC. From then on air supply became the normal maintenance system. Further reinforcement followed from the UK, provided by 1 AASO. An indication of the volume of air supply during these operations is shown in the records of 'A' Platoon 47 Company (AD) which between late December, 1962, and 11 April, 1963, despatched 529,208 pounds of stores in 110 sorties.

By the end of January, 1964, the campaign entered its third phase when confrontation between Indonesia and Malaysia started. The operations now extended over Brunei, Sarawak and Sabah, to cover the whole frontier with Indonesian Borneo to the south. Command of the British force had been raised to two-star level. The build-up of the Maintenance Area on Labuan continued and the supply systems by surface and air were functioning well and coping with the extended operations.

From the beginning of the campaign a third element of the Corps, Water Transport, was also involved. Three LCTs Mark VIII of 46 Squadron RASC from Singapore with British officers and NCOs and Malay ORs were the only service-

An RASC Landing Craft Tank MK VIII

A Hovercraft of the JSHU in Service in Borneo.

manned landing craft capable of making the passage in safety from Singapore to Borneo in the NE monsoon, in which period the initial operation took place. The daily maintenance run between Labuan and Brunei was carried out by LCT until April, 1963. Only on one occasion was a vessel unable to enter Brunei River, despite the monsoon weather conditions. From April, 1963, the maintenance of Brunei became a joint operation with a Ramped Cargo Lighter (RCL) of 37 Company RASC (WT), together with Ramp-Powered Lighters (RPL) and requisitioned Z craft of 10 Port Squadron RE. A number of launches from 37 Company played an important role in communication duties and in operational tasks carrying troops.

The Borneo campaign was to see the introduction of a new element in the field of transportation in operations. The Joint Services Hovercraft Unit (Far East) was formed in July, 1964. Of the four officers in this unit, two were RASC. There were also two RASC soldier crew members. The craft were used in the logistic support system of the operations and proved a marked success.

During the whole period of the campaign the RE Transportation and RASC Water Transport organizations worked closely together with the utmost cooperation. This augured well for the successful amalgamation of the WT responsibilities of both Corps when the RCT was formed on 15 July, 1965, a year before the end of operations in Borneo.

Defence reviews of the late Sixties heralded the withdrawal from FARELF by 1970, so the LCTs were subsequently sold locally. LCTs were also sent to the Persian Gulf and Aden for the evacuation there. At the end of the requirement HMAV *Agheila* (LCT 4000), commanded by Captain C Rawlinson, remained in Aden and made a voyage to Durban for the Rhodesian Security Forces. It became the first Army LCT to cross the equator, finally returning to Portsmouth – the only foreign-based LCT to do so. She was finally transferred to the Civilian Fleet, by then 18 Maritime Squadron RCT, in 1978, after the building of the two new Landing Craft

Logistic (LCLs), thus becoming the last large ocean-going LCT to be operated by the Civilian Fleet.

In 1965 the first LSL, *Sir Lancelot*, joined the Army-controlled ships, and the RCT, including the newly cap-badged Movements Staffs, began the long and successful association with this and subsequent LSLs.

Corps Duties in Other Overseas Stations

Between 1945 and 1965, as well as playing its part in the operations described in this chapter, the Corps carried out its normal peacetime duties in a miscellany of stations throughout the World. These were Burma, Caribbean Islands, Ceylon, Christmas Island, Cocos (Keeling) Islands, Eritrea, Ethiopia, Gibraltar, Greece, India, Indo-China, Japan, Libya, Mauritius, Netherlands East Indies, Rhodesia/Zimbabwe, Sudan, Vanuatu (New Hebrides) and West Africa. In some cases whole units and sub-units of the Corps were involved, but mostly there were individual officers and NCOs working with locally enlisted personnel. Immediately after the War there were clearing-up tasks to be done, followed by work of major importance in the training of locally-enlisted personnel, forming such troops into operational units and then commanding them. There were also occasions when British forces, including Corps support, were called in to restore order in an emergency. In all these different regions of the world and faced with a great variety of tasks, the Corps left behind a reputation for efficiency and dedication.

TOWARDS AN ALL-REGULAR ARMY AND A NEW CORPS

Junior Leaders

It was clear during the late 1950s that National Service could not be sustained indefinitely and the task of fully manning the army with regulars needed to be addressed with greater urgency. It was not surprising that Boys' units were seen as an important asset in achieving this task.

Boys Company RASC in Aldershot, 1951.

Boys Company RASC in Aldershot 1951.

Junior Leaders in Training.

The Boys' Company RASC had moved to Bordon in 1955 and here the term 'Boy' was dropped in favour of 'Junior Leader' which was considered a more accurate description. Until 1960 the unit was called Junior Leader Company RASC, but, with an increase in numbers, the unit became a battalion and moved to Norton Manor Camp at Taunton. The task was to train young school leavers to take their place in a RASC field force unit with developed qualities of leadership and character in order that they might earn early promotion. Many achieved commissioned rank.

Anti-Aircraft Command

One of the first major casualties of the changing defence policy after the Second World War was the disbandment of Anti-Aircraft Command in 1955. At this time the Command was divided into five AA Groups. The RASC representation in AA Command was high, though by 1955 predominantly Territorial Army. Each Group had one regular RASC MT company and two TA AA Group Transport Columns, except the Group in Scotland which had only one Column. At the Headquarters of the Command there was a DDST (Colonel) and a small S & T staff. The Regular Army units of AA Command were absorbed into the overall UK requirement, but some 5,000 TA RASC were lost as a result of the disbandment of the Command. This was a disheartening time for the TA.

Changes in Ranks of Senior Corps Appointments

By 1960 all Major General posts in the Corps other than the Head of Corps at the War Office, the DST, had been downgraded to Brigadier, to conform with the overall reduction within the Army.

Training Commitments

An interesting training commitment, which reflected the changing military situation in Western Europe and NATO in 1961, was undertaken by 19 Tank Transporter

An Antar Tank Transporter of 19 Tank Transporter Company RASC carrying a Leopard Tank of the German Army.

Company RASC, then located at Ranby. It was tasked to move tanks of the German Army being deployed for the first time for training in UK, at the Castle Martin training area in Wales. The movement was widely reported by the media as a significant step in the acceptance of Germany into NATO.

National Service finally ended in 1962 and one immediate consequence was a considerably reduced training requirement for the all-Regular Army, although recruiting was initially disappointing and it took several years to achieve a satisfactory manning level. The Corps, however, was able to disband 15 Driver Training Battalion at Blandford, and driver training was concentrated on 6 Driver Training Battalion at Yeovil.

THE McLEOD REORGANIZATION

During the period 1961 to 1963 there were discussions within the War Office on the need to reorganize the logistic services. The proposition put forward in general terms was that there should be:

- One Corps for supplying the Army
- One Corps for moving the Army
- One Corps for repairing the vehicles and equipment of the Army.

General Sir Roderick McLeod GBE, KCB, DL, then GOC in C Eastern Command, was appointed as Head of the Committee to examine the proposals. In the case of the RASC, the Army Council proposed that:

- The RASC should become the Transport Corps of the Army (title later to be agreed as Royal Corps of Transport). It would hand over to the Royal Army Ordnance Corps (which would become the Supply Corps, retaining its present title) responsibility for Supplies, Petroleum, Barrack Services, Clerical Services, Army Fire Service, RASC/EFI and Boat Stores.

Other proposals affecting the RASC included:

- Subsequently the Army Catering Corps gained its full independence.

- The Royal Engineers was to hand over to the new Transport Corps its transportation functions including Ports, Inland Water and Railways and also the executive responsibility for the Movement Control Service.

- The repair function remained the responsibility of the Royal Electrical and Mechanical Engineers who retained their title.

As a result of the accepted recommendations of the McLeod Committee a Royal Warrant dated 26 March, 1965, changed the title of the Royal Army Service Corps to Royal Corps of Transport to be effective from 15 July, 1965. The detailed effects of this major change are considered in Chapter 8.

CHAPTER 8

A New Corps with Worldwide Responsibilites –
The Immediate Post McLeod Effects

Introduction. Transport Units – General. Movement Control; Port Operations; Inland Water Transport and Railways. The Reserve Army and Cadet Forces. Organizational Changes from 1965-1980. Examples of Home Based Transport Units. Freedom of the Borough of Aldershot. Freedom of the Borough of Rushmoor. The New Corps in Germany and in Belgium; General; 1(BR) Corps Support; 8 Regiment; The Static Organization; The Lines of Communication; Introduction of the ISO Container System, The Gurkha Transport Regiment.

INTRODUCTION

The formation of the Royal Corps of Transport on 15 July, 1965, resulting from the McLeod Report, involved considerable changes to the structure of what had hitherto been the Royal Army Service Corps, and these broadly affected personnel, responsibilities and nomenclatures. The broad concept was the creation of a single Corps responsible for moving the Army.

Within the new Corps all the original land, sea and air transport tasks and units remained from the RASC, but the responsibilities for Movement Control and the operation of Ports, Inland Water Transport and Railways, passing from the Corps of Royal Engineers, had to be integrated in the new Transport Corps organization. After the transfer of some 400 Regular Army RASC officers to the RAOC, about 1000

The Re-badging Parade at Buller Barracks, Aldershot. Vehicle March Past. General Sir James Cassels, GCB, KBE, DSO, Chief of the General Staff, taking the salute.

remained to form the cadre of the RCT, to be joined by some 200 Transportation and Movement Control officers from the RE. A corresponding number of Reserve Army officers were similarly transferred between the three Corps involved. Both officers and soldiers were affected by the inevitable upheaval of re-badging, particularly those being transferred. They were undoubtedly apprehensive at parting from a Corps that they had served so well, and from the family of which they had grown to be a part. It was not easy for everyone to see immediately the opportunities that their new Corps offered or positive reasons for the upheaval, but most of those affected quickly adapted to the changes and successfully continued their careers with undiminished enthusiasm.

The Head of the Corps became The Transport Officer in Chief (Army) with its first incumbent being Major General Sir John Potter. This title was to change twice more during the life of the Corps. In 1977 it became Director General of Transportation during the tenure of Major General P H Benson, who held the appointment until it became Director General of Transport and Movements in 1978. The last DGTM was Major General J D MacDonald who held the appointment from 1990 to 1993.

TRANSPORT UNITS – GENERAL

On re-badging, former RASC Transport Columns were designated Regiments, with Companies becoming Squadrons and Platoons Troops. Appropriate role related titles were added, eg 1 Divisional Transport Regiment. Some were renumbered, eg: 1 (BR) Corps Troops Column RASC became 10 Regiment RCT, whilst others changed their role and grouping within the regiment. A number of Transport and Movements Regiments were introduced into the static chain. This combined functions in one regiment, offering advantages in command, control and administration, and exploited the potential for rationalization made possible by the functional span of the new RCT. The duties of the Composite Platoons in the old Divisional Transport Companies were taken over by the divisional RAOC, which provided Combat Supplies support to the redesignated RCT Squadrons.

There were many changes in unit titles in the ensuing years as new overall Army concepts of operations were established, and reductions in the Army's strength were made which had to be matched in the RCT. It is not possible in this volume to cover all the many aspects of the changes that this involved; indeed, many of the reorganizations after the initial transfers of officers and soldiers with the other two Corps involved, RE and RAOC, and the re-badging and renaming of units, were progressive over the next few years. Examples of some of the immediate changes that occurred on the formation of the RCT are, however, outlined in the paragraphs that follow, whilst many of the later changes are covered in subsequent chapters.

MOVEMENT CONTROL, PORT OPERATIONS, INLAND WATER TRANSPORT AND RAILWAYS

Although Transportation and the Movement Control Section of the Corps of Royal Engineers were transferred as part of the new Corps in July, 1965, there was no change at that stage in the staff function of 'Q' (Movements), which was the separate

268

Vehicles being checked by movement control staff before embarkation.

An RCT Movement Control Officer with his RAF counterpart emplaning equipment and troops.

staff branch responsible for Army Movements at the War Office, later the Ministry of Defence. The Director of Movements (Army), a major general, and the members of his staff followed the normal pattern and were found from staff officers of all Arms, and some specialist Movement Control officers (originally RE and now re-badged RCT). This pattern was followed with all Q (Movements) Staff in Commands and some lower Headquarters at home and abroad. Below MOD level, some responsibility for Q (Movements) gradually passed to the RCT, particularly in BAOR, and the number of RCT officers in Q (Movements) staff appointments increased. It was not, though, until 1978, when the Head of the Corps became Director General of Transport and Movements, that full responsibility for the movements function staff passed to the RCT in MOD and in all other headquarters.

From July, 1965, Movement Control operators were established in RCT headquarters and units as appropriate to the unit task, and continued to discharge their Movement Control duties with equal effectiveness. These Movement Control cells were designed to operate as necessary at ports, beaches, railway stations and marshalling yards, road and inland water transport regulating points, base depots installations and civil airports. Initially many of these integrated posts had to be filled by experienced Movement Control officers and soldiers transferred from the RE. As movements training progressed and experience gradually developed within the Corps generally, a more flexible employment of personnel in the full range of RCT duties became possible.

After the merger between the Royal Engineers (TN) and RASC Water Transport, which included both the Civilian Fleet and the military-manned LCTs, as mentioned earlier, the units were grouped into 17 Port Regiment RCT. These included the sister squadrons 51 and 52 Port Squadrons RCT, each of which had two troops of port operators with their equipment, and one lighterage troop equipped with RPLs. There were also work boats (with a Dracone towing capability), 36ft harbour launches (HLs) and a Mexeflote platoon equipped with Mexeflotes. These were large pontoons, built up on a brick system, which could measure 120ft long by 56ft wide and were powered by two giant Harbourmaster outboard engines. These Mexeflotes were allocated two to a Landing Ship Logistic, large RFA-manned sea-going Landing Craft, and secured to their sides, or disassembled and secured on board. They could thus be carried all over the world to carry out specialized lighterage tasks in remote areas. The Mexeflote craft were operated by seamen and marine engineers from the RCT Maritime units.

The LCTs, together with the Civilian Fleet were formed into 20 Maritime Regiment RCT, based at St George's Barracks, Gosport, and subsequently joined by 200 Hovercraft Squadron RCT. The soldiers then became interchangeable, and the Mexeflotes, RPLs and Dracone towing workboats undoubtedly benefited from the experience gained in the LCTs. One of the exceptional duties of the Commanding Officer of 20 Maritime Regiment was Keeper of the Keys of the Fortress of Portsmouth.

During the six-week long seamen's strike in 1966 Marchwood Military Port, commanded by Lieutenant Colonel John Lofts and operated by 17 Port Regiment, began the movement of priority military stores and ammunition across the Channel to Zeebrugge and Ostend which developed into a major long-term task. In 1968, with the second seamen's strike, container traffic through Marchwood Military Port began on an *ad hoc* basis. The LCTs MK VIII proved to be ideal for container shipping, being able to carry up to 32 x 20ft ISO containers, and also tanks and heavy

An RCT manned Ramp Powered Lighter and a loaded Mexeflote towed by an RCT Workboat.

equipment for Northern Europe. This became the pattern for the next twenty years until the end of the LCTs, but continued with their replacement, the LCLs. From 1967 to 1970 the LCTs were also employed delivering the new Chieftain tanks to BAOR and recovering the obsolete Centurions from Antwerp. At Marchwood three large Dolphins were erected to allow the LCTs to beach on the slipway and load and discharge.

Military Railways

When the responsibility for the operation of military railways passed from the Royal Engineers to the Royal Corps of Transport the railway function was already diminishing in scale. After 1965 it was to be further drastically reduced in line with both the Army's needs and the changes in transport technology available to meet them, such as the expansion of containerization. A few rail facilities remained in UK at Army stores and ammunition depots and at the Longmoor Military Railway. This had been used for training the railway trades and as a feeder for local depots, but was to become an early casualty of railway reductions. In BAOR some depots continued to be rail-served with operating and maintenance staff provided by 79 Railway Squadron RCT, located at Moenchengladbach. As railway operations declined in the UK, it was decided to close the historic training organization based on the Longmoor

Longmoor Military Railway.

Military Railway and 79 Squadron took over the responsibility for training military railwaymen.

Responsibility for the Berlin Military Train also passed to the Royal Corps of Transport. Initially, 486 Movements Troop RCT and then, from 1971, 62 Transport and Movements Squadron RCT (Berlin), were responsible to the GOC (BR) Sector Berlin for the day-to-day running of the Berlin Military Train. The train left Charlottenburg station, Berlin, at 0849 hours daily carrying British and Allied servicemen and their families out of Berlin, either on duty or on leave visits.

As the train entered the north access corridor it had to stop at Potsdam and, despite the locomotive being East German, it had to be detached from the train and searched. On arrival at Marienburg, just short of the east/west border, the train would stop again and the RCT Movement Control Warrant Officer, with an interpreter, would alight and present all the travel documents, including identity cards and passports for checking by the Soviet authorities. The train then moved on to Helmstedt and finally Braunschweig at 1230 hours. The return journey started at Braunschweig at 1600 hours and arrived back in Berlin by 1944 hours.

THE RESERVE ARMY AND CADET FORCES

The formation of the Royal Corps of Transport on 15 July, 1965, affected the two separate and distinct parts of the Reserve Army, the Territorial Army and the Army Emergency Reserve very differently. The RASC TA had been relatively little touched by the drastic reorganization and disbandments of 1960 and brought to their new Corps twenty-two columns, many with a long and proud history. The only immediate change was redesignation as regiments and squadrons and the new cap badge. This *status quo* was to continue for two more years.

The AER, on the other hand, was immediately affected. Still reeling from the 1960 reorganization, during which the RASC establishment had been reduced from 1000 officers and 25,000 men to 100 officers and 1000 men and the Royal Engineer Transportation and Movement Control units similarly heavily reduced, the two cap badges were again involved in considerable change. The RASC Supply and Petroleum Groups transferred to the RAOC leaving at Bedford, under command of the newly-reconstituted HQ AER RCT, 101 Regiment RCT (AER) of two MT squadrons and an amphibious squadron, and 104 Regiment RCT (AER) of two MT squadrons and a maritime squadron. The Royal Engineers AER, remaining for the time being at Longmoor under command of a detachment of HQ AER RCT, brought to their new Corps a sizeable force consisting of:

- 2 Railway Group RCT (AER) of three railway regiments, one railway squadron and a transportation pool

- 5 Port Group of two port regiments, two independent port squadrons and HQ 3 Port Task Force (AER Element)

- Four Movement Control Regiments

- One independent Movement Control squadron

- Two Movement Control increments

The combined strength was some 4000 all ranks.

Colonel of Volunteers

In July, 1965, the TA Colonel who advises the Director General on all TA matters affecting the Volunteer and who represents the TA on all Corps committees was Colonel L T Knights. The post was redesignated Colonel of Volunteers on 1 April, 1967. During the next twenty-eight years eleven officers held this important appointment. Both sections of the RCT TA were fully represented. Four of the officers came from Independent regiments, six from Specialist regiments and one, the late Colonel J A Butler, served an equal time with each. In addition, another thirteen officers reached the rank of Colonel, nine as District Colonels TA or Deputy Brigade Commanders and four as Commanders of the BRSC Liaison and Movements Staff.

The 1967 Defence Review

The RCT TA, as it was to be for the next twenty-five years, really dated from 1 April, 1967. That year again saw a huge reduction in the Reserve Forces and a complete change of role and purpose. The TA merged with the Army Emergency Reserve and was retitled the 'Territorial and Army Volunteer Reserve' (T & AVR). There were four main T&AVR categories, I and II forming the 'Volunteers' liable for call out for service worldwide, and III and IV 'Territorials', only liable for call out in defence of the United Kingdom. Group 'A' units were Independent, Group 'B' Sponsored. As far as the RCT was concerned, there were two Category I units, 562 Parachute Squadron RCT(V) located at Southall, Middlesex, and 490 Movement Control Troop at Bedford. The eight newly formed Independent transport regiments were Category IIA and the Sponsored units Category IIB.

The new order of battle of the RCT TA was:

Independent units

150 (Northumbrian) Regiment RCT(V)
151 (Greater London) Regiment RCT(V)
152 (Ulster) Regiment RCT(V)
153 (Highland) Regiment RCT(V)
154 (Lowland) Regiment RCT(V)
155 (Wessex) Regiment RCT(V)
156 (Lancashire and Cheshire) Regiment RCT(V)
157 (Wales and West Midland) Regiment RCT(V)

Sponsored units

160 Regiment of four MT squadrons and two artillery troops
162 Movement Control Regiment with three MC squadrons
163 Movement Control Regiment with four MC squadrons
490 MC Troop
491 and 495 Movement Control Increments
280 MC Squadron
275 Railway Squadron
HQ Port Task Force
270 and 271 Port Squadrons
264 Amphibious Squadron
265 Maritime Squadron (Fast Launch)

Apart from the formation of 161 Ambulance Regiment in 1971, minor redesignations and further considerable reductions in the Sponsored Port and Maritime unit, this grouping was to remain largely unchanged in 1983.

The reorganization caused many long-established units to disappear, and virtually all those remaining were affected by amalgamations, re-roling and retitling. Many of the independent regiments formed from four or more transport regiments and, in addition, elements of other Arms, notably Yeomanry, Royal Tank Regiment, Royal Artillery and Infantry. Sponsored units were equally affected, the Railway Group in particular, of more than three regiments, surviving as only one small squadron. A large number of loyal and long-serving officers and soldiers were declared redundant. In the Sponsored units 96 officers and 958 soldiers had to leave and the Independent units were similarly affected. The whole exercise, ruthlessly driven by financial and political pressures in the Ministry of Defence, was badly handled. The TA associations were not properly consulted, and when they were their views were generally ignored. Inadequate publicity resulted in the TAVR suffering for many years to come from the general public's widespread belief that the TA had virtually been disbanded. In particular, recruiting and the crucially important employer support were badly affected.

More insidiously, the Volunteer who had survived the changes developed a marked scepticism of the Ministry of Defence which inevitably reflected on the Regular Army as a whole. The TA, with their continuity and strong local connections, have long memories and this mistrust re-emerged most noticeably some 23 years later during 'Options for Change', described in Chapter 10.

A New Role

The much-enhanced role of the TA as an essential part of the order of battle of the Regular Army, rather than as general reinforcements, was widely welcomed. The phrase 'One Army' started to be heard as the TA, for the first time for many years, had a clear aim and purpose. The training standards to be achieved were much higher than in the past because the need for the TA to deploy immediately to their operational role precluded any period of training after mobilization. Given the limitations of time and resources in peace, it was an immensely challenging task.

The Regular Army, for their part, were involved with the TA to a far greater extent. The TA were now an essential part of the plan and this was particularly so of the logistic services. In 1st British Corps at second line the Divisional Regiments were reinforced by formed troops who were part of the regiment. At third line two-thirds of the general transport support was TA. Behind the Corps' rear boundary the bulk of the support was TA. The handful of Regular Movement Control personnel were totally dependent on TA MC units in UK and on the Continent to activate and man the L of C. On mobilization the TA took over Marchwood Military Port, as 17 Port Regiment deployed overseas. This pattern was equally widely reflected throughout the Army. In order to achieve the standard required in peace a three-year cycle of training was developed. Year One consisted of individual skills training, Year Two a regimental exercise and Year Three a full-scale formation exercise, usually in BAOR, in the mobilization role. The transport regiments were able to conform broadly to the cycle. Not so the Movement Control units who were in constant demand and found themselves repeating the third year annually. As regular army reductions and shortages of manpower took effect, the transport units came into increasing demand and towards the end of the 1970s the phrase 'over-exercised and under-trained' was coined by Brigadier J D Lofts, Commander Transport and Movement UKLF, who identified weaknesses in individual training. He had a plan to solve the problem.

The Move of CVHQ RCT TA

In 1968 the scope of training at Bedford was widened to include facilities for all Category IIA Independent units. Accommodation, pool vehicles and stores and equipment was provided for complete sub-units. In addition Independent units started sending their recruits to Grange Camp for initial training. It was the start of the totally integrated system in use today, making maximum use of instructors and facilities.

One of the few disadvantages of Bedford was the poor state of the temporary accommodation in Grange Camp. Maintenance funds were limited, and non-existent for Kempston Barracks across the road, where instructional accommodation in use was literally falling down – some parts actually being declared unsafe. Additionally, the site of Grange Camp was wanted by the local Council to develop for housing, and this was much in accordance with Government policy to alienate MOD land in towns for use by the local authorities. Fortunately the former Royal Air Force station at Grantham in Lincolnshire was being closed as part of the RAF reductions. It was offered to the Army Department and, after the briefest of reconnaissance, snapped up by the Commandant of CVHQ, Colonel J S M Walker. It was centrally situated with excellent road and rail communications and provided far superior facilities to Bedford, including a grass airfield that made an ideal back-door training area. CVHQ and the Sponsored units moved to Grantham in October, 1976, and on 21 May, 1977, the refurbished camp was formally named Prince William of Gloucester Barracks by the Colonel-in-Chief, HRH Princess Alice, Duchess of Gloucester. It was the first of several visits she paid over the next fifteen years.

In 1979 CVHQ was redesignated RCT TA Depot and Training Centre. It was more than a mere change of name. The provision of training facilities and the opening of recruit and trade courses to all units of the RCT TA, started at Bedford, was now developing quickly. Independent regiments during Year One of their three-year training cycle started to camp at Grantham. This relieved them of the burden of unit administration and allowed them to concentrate on training, making maximum use of the limited time. Brigadier Lofts' long-term plan was reaching fruition. The Charter of the Commander at Grantham was widened to include specific responsibility for trade and individual training for all RCT TA units. Less than three years later a major reorganization at HQ UKLF dismantled the Transport and Movement Branch. The CTMO, Brigadier B G Courtis, moved to Grantham with the title Commander RCT TA, bringing with him staff responsibility on behalf of DGTM for the Special to Service standards of the whole of the RCT TA. The Depot and Training Centre TA was reorganized as HQ RCT TA and Depot RCT TA, the Headquarters continuing to command the Sponsored Group and the Depot providing centralized training and administrative facilities.

It was a period of continuing change, much of it driven by intractable financial and manpower constraints, briefly interrupted but never reversed by such major diversions as the Falklands campaign.

The 1983 Restructuring

The reorganization at Grantham in 1982 was followed almost immediately by major changes in the establishment and some role changes for all the Independent and Sponsored units. Independent and Sponsored transport regiments were placed on a standard establishment, mirroring for the first time the Regular Army. Headquarter squadrons were introduced and the Independent regiments increased by 49 officer posts and lost 379 soldier posts. At the same time the Sponsored units increased by 74 officers posts and lost 44 soldiers.

Many of the new establishments allowed very much greater flexibility in the employment of female officers and soldiers. Although they had served for many years with the TA they were generally limited to administrative, clerical and catering posts. The 1983 establishments saw a radical and welcome change of policy. Many – in some regiments all – posts were designated 'May be WRAC', allowing females the opportunity of filling all key appointments. The numbers of WRAC in a unit at any one time was controlled by a percentage figure. This varied according to role from none at all in the Port Squadron, through fairly limited numbers in road transport regiments, up to 50% in the UK Movement Control units. The number of WRAC increased sharply and the quality of recruit and of young officers, many of the latter joining from the University Officer Training Corps, was generally high and some were outstanding. Within a year or so the first WRAC officer was commanding a squadron and before long they were filling every type of appointment, including adjutants and squadron sergeant majors in all types of units. Major A N Notley, who in addition to her normal duties had filled the post of senior officer WRAC(V) for nearly ten years, was appointed MBE in the New Year's Honours List in 1990. In October the same year Major K M H George became the first WRAC officer serving with RCT TA to be promoted lieutenant colonel. On 1 April, 1992, all WRAC personnel serving with the RCT TA, other than clerks and chefs, rebadged on disbandment of the WRAC.

157 (Wales and Midland) Transport Regiment took over the role of supporting the Logistic Support Group from 160 Transport Regiment and barely a year later handed it on to 155 (Wessex) Transport Regiment. 160 Regiment became 4th Line transport under command of 2 Transport Group in the Rear Combat Zone with 262 Squadron deploying to 1st British Corps in the TTF role. The four independent Artillery troops formed as 270 Squadron, which, together with 283 MC Squadron from 162 MC Regiment, became 163 Transport and Movement Regiment under command of 2 Transport Group. RHQ 163 Regiment, formerly the UK MC regiment shed its six MC squadrons, which became independent, and re-roled moving to BAOR. The loss of the RHQ for the UK Sponsored MC squadrons was felt acutely and it had considerable implications for the span of command at Grantham, which was not to be rectified for another ten years. The reason was simple: a new RHQ was urgently needed but there was no question of any additional manpower being provided. On balance the BAOR task was considered operationally more important and UK was the loser.

Other major changes included the grouping of the four independent Traffic Regulating Centres as 280 TRC squadron under command of 162 MC Regiment, and the re-roling of the other two squadrons of the regiment as the 1st British Corps Movement Control Regiment.

Both the Movement Control Liaison Units, whose role had remained largely unchanged from Royal Engineer days, were enhanced. 496 MCLU, in support of the United Kingdom/United States L of C, was increased by fourteen officers and twelve WOs/SNCOs. 495 MCLU in BAOR was supplemented by a further thirty-four Liaison officers and watch-keepers and twelve SNCOs drawn from all Arms. It was retitled the British Support Command Liaison and Movement Staff TA, which cumbersome title was instantly abbreviated to 'The LAMS'. Lieutenant Colonel B D Emery TD, the Commanding Officer of 495 MCLU, was promoted Colonel as Commander of the enhanced unit. An eclectic bunch of experienced officers, most of whom had already had command of their squadron, battery or company, were recruited from all parts of the TA and, among other things, dinner nights became distinctly more colourful occasions with the infinite variety of the mess kits.

153 (Highland) Transport Regiment was redesignated 153 Artillery Support Regiment in recognition of the change of role and 216 (Tyne/Tees) Transport Squadron left 150 Transport Regiment and joined 2 Infantry Divisional Transport Regiment who had moved to Catterick from BAOR. This last was a grouping of some significance. Sponsored squadrons, such as 265 Port Squadron with 17 Port

Regiment and 287 MC Squadron with 29 Transport and Movement Regiment, had a very close relationship with the Regular unit they joined in war, but in peace they were firmly under command of HQ RCT TA for administration and military, as opposed to technical, training. 216 Squadron was part of the Divisional Regiment for all purposes and implicit in their second-line role was the assumption that they would be fully trained and instantly available on mobilization. A few years later a similar change of command affected 325 Air Despatch Troop, who left 155 (Wessex) Regiment and joined 55 AD Squadron at RAF Lyneham under command of 29 Regiment. During this period two changes of designation took place. The first, of great symbolic importance, happened in 1980. The widely disliked title, T and AVR, was discarded and the much cherished title of Territorial Army reintroduced. For many longer-serving members of the TA it had never been abandoned in daily usage. In the mid-1980s the title of Sponsored, adopted in 1967, was changed to Specialist. The change, which came out of the blue, was of less emotive significance except to the budget holders where the considerable stocks of recruiting and publicity material were rendered obsolete at a stroke!

Higher Level Training

Formation exercises at home and overseas played an increasingly important part in the training of the TA for war. Brigade and Divisional exercises were fairly frequent. The biannual NATO-wide WINTEX series involved the Movement Control Liaison units and representative Command cells from most other units. Similarly the SUMMER SALES series of Command Post Exercises in 1st British Corps invariably had their TA RHQs represented. Army level exercises were less frequent and involved years of planning. Exercise CRUSADER in 1980, the largest exercise since the 1967 reorganization, affected almost all units of the RCT TA. 20,000 TA troops were deployed to BAOR. Within the inevitable constraints of peacetime financial control and the 15-day camp period, the mobilization and deployment plans were fully tested and many lessons were learnt, the most important one being that the plans worked and BAOR could be reinforced by a Territorial Army fit and ready to fight. For the TA it was in many senses a coming of age in their role as part of the Regular order of battle.

For the RCT TA it was particularly important. Together with individual reservists, they formed fifty percent of the Corps and provided many units that did not exist in the Regular Army. Exercise LIONHEART, held in 1984, incorporated the lessons learnt from CRUSADER and was on an even larger scale; it is covered in Chapter 10. For the first time volunteer individual regular reservists joined TA units to bring them to War Establishment. In the United Kingdom the increasing emphasis on Home Defence during the 1980s included the nationwide tri-service Exercise BRAVE DEFENDER in 1985. As second-line support for the Home Defence TA infantry battalions the Home Defence transport squadrons, commanded by the Recruit, Reception and Training Teams of the Independent regiments and Depot RCT TA, were mobilized with volunteer reservists. Lack of recent military experience, some of the reservists not having worn uniform since they finished their National Service in the 1950s, was partly compensated for by immense enthusiasm. Despite this, the OC of the RRTT and his small team had a demanding task in controlling squadrons up to 500 strong widely deployed throughout their District.

Local Connections

Throughout the period the strong historical connections enjoyed by the Independent units with their local community was maintained despite the much wider area covered by each regiment after the 1967 reorganization. In many cases squadrons or troops had replaced former RASC columns but the support given to and received from local authorities and organizations continued. Several regiments and squadrons were honoured with the Freedom of their city or town.

Throughout the life of the RCT the TA regiments played their full part in the ceremonial life of the Army. In addition to the Freedom parades, all Independent regiments from time to time contributed contingents to local military and civic occasions. 151 (Greater London) Regiment played an expanding role in the organization and marshalling of the Lord Mayor of London's Show, whilst 154 (Lowland) Regiment had the privilege of mounting guard at Edinburgh Castle. The band and drums of 150 (Northumbrian) Regiment, the Pipes and Drums of 152 (Ulster) Regiment, 153 (Highland) Regiment, 154 (Lowland) Regiment, and the Corps of Drums of 157 (Wales and Midland) Regiment were in constant demand beating retreats and playing at parades, tattoos and military displays throughout the UK and the Continent. At Grantham the recruit completed his course with a ceremonial parade. Relatives and friends came from all over the country and the inspecting officers ranged from commanding officers of the TA regiments to members of the Army Board.

The Jubilee Parade

The twenty-five years of the RCT TA since the reorganization of 1967 was marked by a review held at Grantham on 28 June, 1992. Fifteen contingents representing every RCT TA unit paraded in front of their Colonel-in-Chief, and the drive past included virtually every type of vehicle used by the Corps. With one thousand soldiers and five bands on parade, and over 3,500 spectators, it was a unique gathering of the volunteer family. It was also the last time that HRH Princess Alice would visit her Corps. To mark the 50th year of her personal association with the RASC and RCT, the Colonel of Volunteers, Colonel I W B McRobbie, presented, on behalf of all units, a specially commissioned crystal rose bowl.

Cadet Forces

In common with many Corps and Regiments, the RCT, like its predecessors the RASC, sponsored Army Cadet Force units, and many contingents wore the Corps badge. The number varied from time to time, mainly due to Regular Army reorganizations, but were usually in the region of eighty. In addition a small number of Combined Cadet Force contingents were also cap-badged RCT.

Quite apart from the intrinsic value of the ACF as a worthwhile and demanding youth organization, the benefit to the Services, especially in times of lean recruiting, has long been recognized. The help given to the ACF by Regular and TA units has been more than repaid by the numbers joining both parts of the Corps when they became adults. There was also a reverse flow, particularly from the TA to the ACF. A number of senior TA officers have commanded their County contingents and many officers and senior NCOs, having completed their TA service, moved on to the ACF as detachment commanders and adult instructors. Some TA officers, able to give the large amount of time required, successfully combined their TA duties with ACF appointments to the mutual benefit of both organizations. Regardless of cap badge, the RCT has always been well placed to give material assistance to the ACF by providing much-needed transport, and this has been particularly useful during annual camps.

ORGANIZATIONAL CHANGES FROM 1965-1980

Air Despatch

In 1965 1 and 3 AASOs were re-named 14 and 15 (AD) Regiments RCT respectively. The following year an Air Despatch Group Headquarters was set up to manage the technical aspects of the specialization worldwide. Air Despatch training, previously conducted by a training wing administered by 47 (AD) Squadron, was now in the hands of an Air Despatch Training Squadron. 22 (AD) Company RASC had moved to RAF Tangmere in 1963 and the Training Squadron was set up there, getting establishment approval in February, 1967.

The changing priorities for Defence in the late sixties affected the RAF as well as the Army, and many famous stations were ear-marked for closure in the interests of rationalization. The closure of RAF Tangmere resulted in 22 (AD) Squadron moving to Fairford, and then, in 1968, to RAF Thorney Island. There it joined the Air Despatch Training Squadron, which became the Air Despatch Training wing of the Army School of Transport. 47 (AD) Squadron, at Colerne, since the closure of Watchfield, now moved to RAF Lyneham. A Territorial Army Air Despatch unit, 395 (AD) Troop RCT, was formed in Bristol in 1970 and in the same year 55 (AD) Squadron absorbed 22 (AD) Squadron at RAF Thorney Island, 22 Squadron becoming a transport unit. In 1976 both 14 (AD) Regiment and 55 (AD) Squadron were disbanded. The 55 was perpetuated as a Training Squadron in the Depot Regiment. 47 (AD) Squadron remained at RAF Lyneham and came under command of 29 Transport and Movements Regiment as the Army's Air Despatch capability. On the closure of RAF Thorney Island the much-reduced Air Despatch Training wing joined 47 (AD) Squadron at Lyneham.

The Training Regiments

The Charter of the Transport Officer in Chief (Army) (TO in C(A)) included full responsibility for all transport and movement matters, and this placed the Army Mechanical Transport School under direct control. The Corps also took over the RE Training Centre at Longmoor to form the School of Transport. 1965 and 1966 were busy years for the new organization. Apart from the formation of the new Corps and the restructuring of training, the RCT Training Centre had to redeploy to temporary barracks so that Buller Barracks, Aldershot, could be rebuilt. Vacating a barracks that had been occupied by the Corps' predecessors since 1859 was a prodigious task, but the move to the Queen Elizabeth Barracks at Church Crookham went smoothly. By late 1966 the Headquarters was fully operational. 15 Driver Training Battalion had been disbanded and the now-renamed 6 and 12 Training Regiments RCT, at Yeovil and Aldershot respectively, undertook basic recruit and driver trade training. 11 Training Regiment was responsible for the Corps' Depot function, administration of the Corps Band, reception and selection of recruits and Horse Transport training by H Squadron at Beaumont Barracks, Aldershot.

The Ministry of Transport extended the Heavy Goods Vehicle (HGV) licensing scheme in 1968. Limited Crown exemption permitted Service drivers under 21 to hold an HGV licence, but driver training had to be restructured to cope with the new regulations. Within the Armed Services, only Qualified Testing Officers (QTOs) were authorized to carry out HGV testing. Responsibility for training and classifying QTOs was given to the MT Wing of the School of Transport. 1900 QTOs were classified in the first year. After the 1968 Defence Review the number of adult recruits coming into the new Corps was severely reduced. 6 and 12 Training Regiments amalgamated at Aldershot, retaining the title of 12 Training Regiment RCT. On completion of the Buller Barracks rebuild November, 1969, the Training Centre and its regiments returned home, and driver training became a fact of life in Aldershot, bringing the Corps into sharper focus with the local people of our home town.

At this time the appointment of Master Driver RCT was introduced. These were very experienced drivers of Warrant Officer rank and were located with Divisional Regiments RCT and CsRCT at District Headquarters. Their function was to monitor HTV testing and to ensure that the proper standards were achieved by QTOs in units of all Arms, in addition to advising units on driver training and road safety. This greatly widened the influence of the Corps over MT training in the Army as a whole.

The Horse Transport Squadron was disbanded in 1970, marking the end of an era in Corps history. 11 Training Regiment took on basic recruit regimental training, leaving 12 Regiment to conduct driver training. Both Maritime and Air Despatch Group Headquarters had already been disbanded, and their training wings came under the direction of the Commandant, School of Transport at Longmoor.

Redeployments of the 1970s

Several factors led to the reorganization of Army driver training during the early 1970s. Firstly, the growth of Army driver training in crowded urban areas of Aldershot led to increasing pressure from the local authorities. Secondly, it was decided to rehouse the MT Wing of the School of Transport on a surplus RAF airfield rather than rebuild either Longmoor or Bordon. Finally, tracked vehicle training was rationalized and passed to Director Royal Armoured Corps. TO in C(A) was given responsibility for the centralized training of basic wheeled vehicle drivers for the whole Army (except RE and REME). The new Army School of Mechanical Transport (ASMT) for Army driver training was eventually established at Normandy Barracks, Leconfield, in Yorkshire. It took under its wing another RAF Station at Driffield for Junior Soldier Driver Training. The RCT Officers' School, with technical training for non-MT employments and the Publications Section, moved from Longmoor to Aldershot. In March, 1971, the RCT Training Development Team formed at Longmoor with the task of examining the content and standards of RCT trade training. This embraced the 'systems' approach to training. Each phase of training was defined as a series of 'training objectives'. This ensured that each individual could be monitored and the course content matched to each stage of training. Junior Leaders' training continued at a new RCT Junior Leaders' Regiment based at Norton Manor Camp near Taunton. In 1978 the Regiment moved to Azimghur Barracks at Colerne in Wiltshire.

Norton Manor was later re-opened as the Junior Soldiers Infantry Battalion Barracks with 59 and 34 Squadrons RCT as junior soldier squadrons, but sadly, the Battalion was disbanded shortly afterwards.

Formation of 2 Transport Group

The run-down of the British presence in the Far East at the end of the sixties reduced the requirement for a number of Corps units, for example 15 (AD) Regiment which was disbanded in 1968. Without their Far Eastern units the Maritime and Air Despatch Groups had lost much of their rationale and were disbanded. The Corps focused more than ever before on NATO and Western Europe. It was apparent that there was a need to establish a logistic command and co-ordinating organization for the very large numbers of both Regular and Territorial mixed types of transport units and movement units that made up the elements of Logistic Support Force (LSF). This had a major TA element, with units located throughout the UK. These, on mobilization, in addition to the regular units, would support 3rd Division, which was at the time at the hub of the UK Strategic Reserve and the provider of the ACE Mobile Force component. There was also the additional need for such an organization to command the RCT Specialist units located conveniently in Wiltshire and Hampshire. To meet this dual requirement 2 Transport Group RCT was established at Bulford, with a Commander in the rank of Brigadier, who also commanded the LSF and was responsible for the training of the TA in their role, but not their peacetime administration. The Headquarters of the Group worked very closely with Headquarters of 3rd Division, and both Regular and TA elements of the LSF exercised regularly with the Division in UK and in NATO areas of responsibility.

The outline organization of 2 Group is given below. Space does not permit the detailing of the long TA Orbat, but the size of its commitment and the importance of its role in the LSF was of paramount importance.

27 Regt RCT	20 Maritime Regt	17 Port Regt	14 AD Regt
Tank tptrs &	200 Hovercraft	Marchwood	RAF Lyneham
MF Logistics	Trials Sqn		
Bulford			

Territorial Army
Transport & Movement Elements
from units throughout the UK

EXAMPLES OF HOME-BASED TRANSPORT UNITS

In July, 1965, HQ RASC Aldershot District was redesignated HQ 27 Regiment RCT and tasked with providing the headquarters element of the recently enlarged 'Logistic Support Unit' of the Allied Commander Europe's Mobile Force (Land) – AMF(L). In March, 1967, 27 Regiment was also tasked with the provision of transport support to that Force. In November, 1968, 42 Squadron was incorporated to provide the transport support and at the same time headquarters of 27 Regiment RCT moved from Aldershot, and 42 Squadron from Catterick, to Ward Barracks in Bulford Camp. At this time the Regiment's AMF(L) responsibility was to provide the command and control of the HQ Logistic Support Unit AMF(L) and to provide a transport squadron in support. The second in command of 27 Regiment was designated the Commanding Officer of the unit when deployed, but this arrangement ceased in 1974 when a Commanding Officer was established. From then on the second in command of 27 Regiment was designated as regimental Commanding Officer on deployment, the established Commanding Officer in turn being designated commander of the Logistic Support Group.

20 Squadron RCT

One of the best known of all the MT units of the RASC, now titled 20 Squadron RCT, can trace its history back to 1885. Its responsibilities, initially as the War Office Car Company, and later as the Ministry of Defence Car Squadron, had basically been the same since the Second World War, and indeed were throughout the War. The unit had a number of civilian drivers who were employed alongside their military colleagues. 20 Company moved to Regent's Park Barracks in 1946, providing a unique record of continuity of service.

After 1965, now as 20 Squadron it continued to provide the staff cars and supporting vehicles only for the Army Department of the Ministry of Defence (previously the War Office) and the staff cars, coaches and load carriers for HQ London District. In July, 1967, however, it also took over responsibility for the MOD Car and Van Pools, and for all the transport requirements for the Central Staffs and the other two Service Departments. Within this overall responsibility there was the special task of providing the vehicles and drivers, known as Her Majesty The Queen's Baggage Train. This task was to support Her Majesty's household with transport and also to support official visits to the United Kingdom by foreign heads of state. In addition, the unit also provided the cars and drivers for members of the Royal Family, visiting Royalty and Heads of State attending functions sponsored by any of the three Services in the UK and BAOR.

20 Squadron RCT maintained its special link with the Royal Household through the CRCT London District at Horse Guards. On 13 July, 1971 (at a ceremony, repeated eight years later in 1979) Her Majesty The Queen, accompanied by His Royal Highness The Duke of Edinburgh, inspected informally the drivers and vehicles of The Queen's Baggage Train at Buckingham Palace. The CRCT presented the Officer Commanding 20 Squadron and other officers and soldiers to Her

20 Company RASC on Horse Guards Parade prior to rebadging.

Majesty. Her Majesty and Prince Philip also spoke to the families of officers and soldiers who were invited to attend the parade.

Training Regiments and the Depot

There were a number of early changes in the Training Organization and two of these affected the Corps' relationship with the local people of Aldershot, bringing the Corps' role into sharper focus. With the ending of National Service and the introduction of the all-Regular Army, the training commitment had diminished considerably. 15 Driver Training Battalion at Blandford had been disbanded, and although 6 Driver Training Battalion, renamed 6 Driver Training Regiment, at Yeovil, was to last into the time of the RCT, it too was disbanded on 31 March, 1969. Its tasks were taken over by 12 Training Regiment, previously 1 Battalion, and driver training became a part of Aldershot life. Until 1966 12 Regiment was responsible for driver training only, but in that year regimental training was added to the task taken over from 11 Regiment, which, in turn, assumed the old title of the Depot. Recruits into the Corps therefore received training in one regiment, based in Aldershot.

Army School of Mechanical Transport

There was a further important change in 1977 when all responsibility for RCT driver training passed to the Army School of Mechanical Transport (ASMT) at Leconfield and 12 Regiment was disbanded. A new era in driver training had started and ASMT continued to meet all the RCT driver training requirements for the remainder of the lifetime of the Corps.

Trainee drivers and their instructors begin a session at the ASMT - Leconfield.

FREEDOM OF THE BOROUGH OF ALDERSHOT

On 22 April, 1970, the Freedom of the Borough of Aldershot, the home of the Corps, was conferred on the Corps by the Mayor, Aldermen and Burgesses of the Borough.

A parade to mark the occasion was held in the presence of The Representative Colonel Commandant Major General E H G Lonsdale, CB, MBE, and The Transport Officer in Chief (Army) Major General P F Claxton CB, OBE, the salute being taken by the Mayor of Aldershot. The parade consisted of six squadrons of marching troops (three squadrons from 12 Training Regiment and one each from 2 Transport Group, 7 Squadron and 17 Squadron) commanded by Lieutenant Colonel R J Royle. In addition to the troops on parade, a cavalcade of vehicles, provided by 3 Division Regiment RCT and 2 Transport Group, and representing a cross section of the activities of the Corps, drove past through the centre of Aldershot.

FREEDOM OF THE BOROUGH OF RUSHMOOR

As a result of local government reorganization, the Borough of Aldershot became the Borough of Rushmoor, and on 29 May, 1981, the Freedom of the new Borough was granted to all Regiments and Corps who had previously held the Freedom of Aldershot. These were the Corps of Royal Engineers, the Royal Hampshire Regiment, the Parachute Regiment, the Royal Corps of Transport, the Royal Army Dental Corps and the Army Catering Corps and the Army Physical Training Corps. A representative parade of all the Regiments and Corps was held in Rushmoor arena, attended by many who had been at their respective earlier Freedom Parades when granted by the Borough of Aldershot. The representative Colonel Commandant of the Royal Corps of Transport, Major General P Blunt, CB, MBE, GM received the new scroll on behalf of the Corps.

DISBANDMENT PARADE OF THE RCT. To commemorate the disbandment of the RCT a final parade was held through the streets of Aldershot. The salute was taken by Major General J D MacDonald, CB, CBE, accompanied by His Worship the Mayor of Rushmoor.

THE NEW CORPS IN GERMANY AND BELGIUM

General

In BAOR, as in other areas of the world where British troops were deployed, the effects of the McLeod Report recommendations and the formation of the RCT caused considerable change. The principal representatives of the new Corps were based at HQ BAOR in Rheindahlen and HQ 1 (BR) Corps in Bielefeld. Each was a brigadier and, though each experienced several changes in title over the years, their relationship to each other changed little.

The brigadier in HQ BAOR was responsible to the Commander in Chief BAOR for the efficiency of the RCT in BAOR as a whole, whilst the brigadier in HQ 1 (BR) Corps was responsible to the Corps Commander for the operational efficiency of the RCT in 1 (BR) Corps and for commanding the RCT Corps Troops units. By 1982 a new headquarters, HQ 2 Transport Group RCT was established, based in Dusseldorf, and took on responsibility for RCT transport units to the rear (west) of 1 (BR) Corps.

1 (BR) Corps Support

The RCT organization in the BAOR Divisions was particularly affected by the various changes in tactical concepts in BAOR after 1965 and their previously standardized organizations were tailor-made to meet the differing roles of each Division. Functional changes also took place within many types of transport and movements units since their initial formation. In the static chain in BAOR the advantages of combining transport units and movements cells were quickly recognized with the formation of combined Transport and Movements Regiments.

Despite the many organizational changes dictated on governmental, financial or military grounds, the Corps' responsibilities changed in degree only. The dual responsibility of supporting the operational role of the field force units in 1 (BR) Corps and its Divisions on the one hand, and the equally vital role of providing support to the infrastructure necessary to sustain the forces and their families in Germany on the other, led to the parallel and mutually dependent field force and static units being formed.

The primary RCT units directly supporting the Divisions' fighting formations were the Divisional Transport Regiments. These were responsible for the maintenance and resupply of the front line units and covered the carriage and distribution of virtually all the formation's requirements, including fuel, ammunition, rations and the multitude of stores necessary to sustain a modern army in the field. Other specialist units established to provide third-line support included tank transporter, fuel and nuclear delivery units.

Method of resupply within BAOR

During the whole period of confrontation with the Warsaw Pact the planned method of operation of the Corps in the event of war changed little until the introduction of the DROPS system (described in Chapter 10). This system, as practised on exercises, covered the periods of both the RASC and RCT. The primary role was the provision of Combat Supplies to 1 (BR) Corps and the most important commodity by volume was Royal Artillery ammunition. The method of operation was to move these

Combat Supplies forward in a series of 'loops', starting at a railhead, depot, or Corps supply park with third-line Corps road transport, transferring to second-line divisional transport and, in the case of Royal Artillery ammunition, frequently delivering direct to the gun lines. For other natures unit B echelon 4-ton vehicles collected from an RASC/RCT Delivery Point (DP) / Immediate Replenishment Group (IRG), close behind the front line.

The key was to deliver as quickly as possible, whilst retaining flexibility. Flexibility was always a problem as no radios were carried in our Corps vehicles and so the planned programme could only be altered at the start or finish of a 'loop'. These loops frequently took several hours to drive, so flexibility was never easy to achieve. Even when a limited scale of radios was introduced in the early 1960s (Larkspur), the only improvement was the ease of passing fairly up-to-date commodity states at the location of the radio; the driver could still not be contacted on the loop and told to change his route. This lack of radio, coupled with the assessed pace of the battle, resulted in the Royal Artillery planning only to be able to use two-thirds of the ammunition actually supplied to them, as it would be ground-dumped and lost to the enemy's advance in the withdrawal battle that 1 (BR) Corps planned to fight.

Speed of delivery was severely reduced by the need to cross-load at every Exchange Point (XP) where the loops joined. Initially this was a manpower-intensive movement of loose boxes, but by the 1970s Mechanical Handling Equipment (MHE) in the form of fork-lift trucks (FLT) and CALM (Crane Attachment Lorry mounted) were in extensive use to handle pallets weighing well over 1 tonne. To unload the six pallets from an 8-tonne truck still took over twenty minutes with the most competent of MHE operators. Loading within a Corps Supply field location often took over a day from the time that the vehicle entered empty until it was on the MSR loop again moving forward, loaded. The Second World War American 'Red Ball' approach of running the vehicle and its load through the complete re-supply chain and changing the driver at every loop XP was often considered, but it ran contrary to the British concept of a driver having a personal vehicle and being responsible for the loads it carried and through running was never implemented

RASC/RCT drivers were required to be trained to a very high standard. In the early years movement down the MSR was by 'packets' with an NCO in charge of each group of vehicles. However, by the mid-1970s single-vehicle movement was required in order to speed up the delivery times. This meant that a driver, who could be tired and anxious, drove by himself, or, if in luck, with a co-driver in the cab. Together they had to map-read through any diversions off the MSR, probably including some off-road driving past damaged obstacles, maintaining an air defence lookout and being prepared for an NBC attack. Once at the end of a loop they frequently had to follow unit tactical signs to a new, strange location. Even when they had successfully reported in, they still had to prepare a defensive position, camouflage and service their vehicle and take turns on sentry duty. Sleep could be a very rare commodity!

The following diagram shows the general organization of the RCT in 1 (BR) Corps from the late 1970s to the early 1990s. During this period 2 Armoured Division Transport Regiment RCT then in BAOR was exchanged with 3 Armoured Division Regiment RCT which was in the UK. 2 Regiment then carried out training in BAOR as part of its role in the Strategic Reserve.

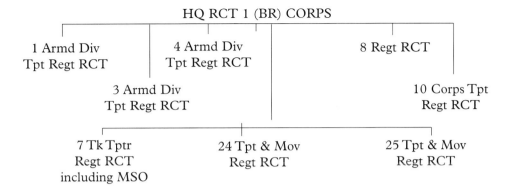

HQ RCT 1 (BR) CORPS

1 Armd Div
Tpt Regt RCT

4 Armd Div
Tpt Regt RCT

8 Regt RCT

3 Armd Div
Tpt Regt RCT

10 Corps Tpt
Regt RCT

7 Tk Tptr
Regt RCT
including MSO

24 Tpt & Mov
Regt RCT

25 Tpt & Mov
Regt RCT

The general organization of 2 Group RCT for the same period is shown in the diagram below:

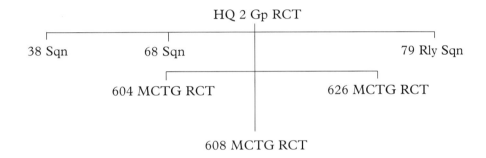

HQ 2 Gp RCT

38 Sqn

68 Sqn

79 Rly Sqn

604 MCTG RCT

626 MCTG RCT

608 MCTG RCT

Briefing Section Commanders.

Stalwart Platoon.

RCT Transport carrying bridging equipment on BAOR exercise.

8 Regiment RCT – Special Weapons Role

When 8 Transport Column RASC was formed in Nelson Barracks, Münster, in 1964, it assumed the role of the carriage of 1(BR) Corps special weapons, ie. nuclear, a task previously carried out by the Royal Artillery. Initially, two RASC companies, 5 and 13, carried the weapons and provided transport support to 570th US Army Artillery Group, the US custodians. Protection was provided by a dedicated mechanized battalion and the whole organization was given the title Weapons Support Group (WSG). In 1965 the WSG was joined by 604 Signal Troop which came under regimental command. On the formation of the Royal Corps of Transport on 15 July, 1965, the unit was retitled 8 Regiment RCT, moving to Portsmouth Barracks, Münster, in 1968 and consisting at that time of 5 Squadron, 13 Squadron, 604 Signals Troop and its REME workshop. In 1970 27 Squadron joined the Regiment from Bielefeld.

The Regiment was restructured on a number of occasions over the years and was expanded to incorporate ten platoons of Infantry, made up of RCT and Royal Pioneer Corps (RPC) soldiers, in 1981. Six of the platoons were found by the RPC, the remaining four by the RCT, who were given the task of close-escort troops to 13 and 27 Squadrons.

1986 saw a further reorganization of the Regiment when the four RCT close-escort troops were disbanded and this task was given to the remaining RPC troops which were reshaped into four defence platoons.

15 March, 1988, was the end of the Regimental role of special weapons movement. It was marked by a Regimental Parade which not only commemorated the re-role of the Regiment from its special weapons task, but also marked the disbandment of 604 Signal Troop and the removal from the Regimental establishment of the RPC platoons.

After the re-role 5 Squadron took over the nuclear baton and provided transport for 570th USAAG, but, in conjunction with 56 (SW) Battery RA, it also became responsible in war for forming field storage sites containing 1 (BR) Corps stocks of 155mm nuclear rounds. This task had two elements to it. The first was to provide a portion of the command of each of the two sites – in one OC 5 Squadron commanded the site, in the other the Battery Commander of 56 Battery RA, with the 21C of 5 Squadron as his alternate. The second element was the transport of the American custodians of the nuclear rounds, and this was carried out by 5 Squadron. Ironically, the RA drivers of 56 (SW) Battery drove the vehicles that carried the rounds. The involvement of OC 5 Squadron in the SW role meant that the Regimental Echelon was commanded in the field by the RQM.

Achieving fitness for the nuclear role involved a series of American-evaluated annual tests – Group Surety Evaluation (GSE), Brigade Surety Evaluation (BSE) and Nuclear Surety Inspection (NSI) – and the Annual Operational Test (AOT), a Field Training Exercise which was sponsored and assessed by HQ 1 Artillery Brigade. The Squadron completed its initial qualification for role in October, 1988.

In August, 1991, it was announced that all short-range nuclear weapons were to be removed from Europe, and in November the US Forces began outloading the Münster site, keeping 5 Squadron extremely busy until March, 1992. When the site was empty, 570th USAAG began rapidly to disband and, although there was a US Brigade Farewell Parade on 4 June, 1992 attended by a composite 5 Squadron Troop, there was no formal parade by the American Group at Münster. The Commanding Officer of 570th USAAG, Lt Col Guy Berry Jnr, was one of the very last Americans to leave, and on 30 June, 1992, presented farewell medallions to all members of the squadron on an informal parade in Portsmouth Barracks.

With the departure of the Americans, 5 Squadron re-roled to become HQ Squadron, and this marked the end of the Regiment's nuclear role.

The Static Organization

To provide the essential support from the Corps in maintaining British forces and their families in Germany in peacetime, non-field force static RCT units were located in garrisons throughout BAOR. Their task was to meet all general administrative transport requirements including the provision of school-children's buses, amenity transport to the local NAAFI and visits to the hospital or medical centre. Generally these tasks were carried out by locally recruited MCTG and MSO units. The background histories of these types of units are told in Chapter 6. In all cases, however, in addition to their day-to-day role of operating administrative transport, these units had a vital wartime role. Buses were readily convertible to an ambulance role and the carriage of routine administrative stores speedily transformed into the outloading of ammunition depots. The relatively distinct boundaries of responsibility between the 'field force' and 'static' transport units complemented one another in peacetime, the latter allowing the former to train for and refine its wartime role within 1 (BR) Corps.

The RCT also had an important role to play in such non-RCT units as Divisional Field Ambulances RAMC and the Headquarters and Signals Regiments of Division and Corps Headquarters. 14 Squadron formed part of HQ Regiment 1 (BR) Corps, in support of the Corps Headquarters, whilst 68 Squadron provided a similar role to 14 Squadron in support of HQ BAOR. Mention should also be made of a unique unit commanded and partially manned by RCT officers and soldiers – the Northern Army Group (NORTHAG)/2nd Tactical Air Force (2 ATAF) Transport Company. This unit, with British, German, Belgian and Dutch staff, was an excellent example of NATO co-operation providing transport for the multi-national headquarters in Rheindahlen.

The Lines of Communication

Since the end of the Second World War routine resupply from the UK home base to the British Forces in Germany was via the Channel Ports. 487 Movement Control Troop RCT was responsible for providing the movement control cover from 1965 until 1 April, 1970, when the unit was integrated into the new HQ RCT British Forces Antwerp. In 1973 HQ RCT moved to Emblem in Belgium, and was responsible for the planning and execution of British movements over the L of C in peace and war, its operational responsibilities stretching from the Channel Ports in the west to the Dutch/German border in the east. It also commanded the local Belgium civilian-manned 602 Transport Unit. Since very many units passed through Belgium and Holland into Germany to carry out their operational and training commitments, HQ RCT was continually engaged on the development of the L of C. There was an increasing number of command post exercises and field training exercises taking place each year and the support provided for these exercises between May and September was almost continuous. Many movement controllers seemed to live permanently at a port or airfield.

Introduction of Systems based on the ISO Container

The need to manage the BAOR Lines of Communication efficiently kept the Corps in the forefront of commercial developments in transport logistics. An important development in freight handling was the introduction of the International Standards Organization (ISO) container, and associated container ships, rail and road vehicles.

RCT Port Operators loading RCT Containers on to an LSL using Demag Crane and Rough Terrain Fork Lift Truck.

Vehicles of the RCT BAOR Freight Service.

By 1966 ISO commercial container traffic between the UK and Europe gradually superseded the loose freight on a specialized shipping system. BAOR was not slow in utilizing the new container system, and before the first one had reached Germany the BAOR Freight Service had been planned and introduced. This system provided a speedier delivery of ordnance stores within BAOR, using long-haul MCTG RCT road transport to interlink a number of Central Distribution Points (CDP). These were based on Ordnance depots, where RCT Local Transport Control Centres (LTCC) were established. This successful system reduced the average time for delivery of non-priority stores to BAOR from thirty to just four days.

THE GURKHA TRANSPORT REGIMENT

With the formation of the Royal Corps of Transport in July, 1965, it was intended that, as with other Corps units, the Gurkha Army Service Corps, then stationed in Singapore, Malaya and Hong Kong, should be retitled. It was discovered, however, that HQ Far East Land Forces had failed to seek the necessary approval of Her Majesty the Queen. All arrangements therefore had to be postponed and not until 1 November, 1965, did the Gurkha ASC became the Gurkha Transport Regiment (GTR).

At the end of 1966 the Regiment was at its peak with a strength of 1,268, including the Nepal Leave increment and men on Extra-Regimental Employment (ERE). Sadly the Redundancy Order following the Healey Defence Review in 1966 forecast many cuts for units in the Brigade of Gurkhas and the Regiment was directed to reduce its numbers to 806 by December, 1969. After the implementation of the Defence Review a period of consolidation for the Regiment took place. 31 Squadron from Singapore joined 28 Squadron in Hong Kong during 1971 and the last remnant of 34 Squadron, the Gurkha All Arms MT Training Wing, was absorbed by 31 Squadron and redesignated the Gurkha MT School.

CHAPTER 9

A Testing Time

Introduction. Equipment Developments in the Seventies; 612 Tank Transporter Unit MSO. Logistic Support Battalion, Allied Commander Europe's Mobile Force (Land) – (AMF(L). Northern Ireland; Transport Support; Movements. Hong Kong; The Gurkha Transport Regiment. Military Aid to the Civil Ministries (MACM). British Honduras – Belize. United Nations Force in Cyprus (UNFICYP). Operation CORPORATE – The Falkland Islands Campaign.

INTRODUCTION

The era that followed the introduction of the recommendations of the McLeod Report (outlined in Chapter 7) was not only one of continuing detailed reorganization and of re-equipping and absorption of new functions, but it was also to test the Corps thoroughly, under contrasting operational conditions. This chapter also describes some of the much-needed new equipment received in the seventies and some of the Corps' worldwide activities, ranging from examples of units' routine peacetime support tasks to the operations in Northern Ireland and the Falklands.

EQUIPMENT DEVELOPMENTS IN THE SEVENTIES

Crucial changes in armaments requiring increased ammunition support occurred in both artillery and tank weapons. The 105mm self-propelled (SP) Abbott artillery was replaced by the US 155mm S(PM109). Gun batteries were also raised from six to eight guns. The Chieftain tank (120mm gun) replaced the faithful Centurion (105mm gun). Battle groups became more mobile and rates of fire increased. The RCT needed to develop better systems and introduce more capable equipment to meet the challenges of faster handling and improved throughput. The 'one-man/one-box' handling of combat supplies was a legacy of the Second World War and was replaced by the concept of the 'unitized' load (a standard NATO pallet loaded with a predetermined mix of specified nature of combat supplies). The widespread introduction of Mechanical Handling Equipments and the fitting of a Crane Attachment Lorry Mounted to existing and new vehicles had helped to provide a dramatic improvement in handling capacity.

For example, at second line every fourth 4, 8 and 10-ton vehicle was now fitted with CALM. The great bulk of the existing fleet, however, was ill-fitted to cope with this new 'pallet/MHE' economy. Load beds and carrying capacities were so poorly incompatible with the pallet that the 4-ton Bedford RL and AEC 10-ton were effectively rendered obsolete, although many continued in *de facto* service for some years. The Stalwart 5-ton HMLC continued in Battle Group echelons.

A new logistic fleet was needed which was specifically designed for the pallet. Based on multiples of four tonnes, the concept proposed 4-tonne vehicles at first line, 8-tonne and 16-tonne at second and third line respectively. This provided a wide measure of compatibility throughout the echelons and lines of support system. At the same time the old 'jerrican economy' was replaced by a bulk fuel supply concept based on tankers and demountable bulk fuel tanks. These Unit Bulk Refuelling Equipments (UBRE), or 'fuel pods', were designed to fit on the 4 and 8-tonne vehicles modified with suitable cabs, exhausts and 'double pole' wiring to prevent sparks and enhance safety.

Inevitably the expense of new development and unit vehicle costs were constraints on the size, mobility levels and deployment of the new fleet. Compromises over the use of commercial designs, adapted for military use, were necessary, although the 8-tonne Medium Mobility Load Carrier was certainly a well-developed military special. A split of mobility levels was agreed, with a Medium Mobility Load Carrier fleet at second and third line, supported by a Low Mobility Load Carrier (LMLC) fleet at fourth line. Many of these vehicles were based on commercial designs and components. The development of better radial heavy-duty tyres dramatically improved lift capacity and cross-country performance without sacrificing convoy speeds. The prime limitations on lift shifted from bulk capacity to weight.

Other vehicle developments included a 'stretched' version of the 8-tonne MMLC offered by Bedford as a replacement for the old AEC Militants in 10 Regiment, while a 20-ton Scammell articulated tractor and trailer were used by 7 Regiment for the carriage of light armoured vehicles. The old Fordson 4-ton ambulance was replaced by a two-stretcher ambulance on the ³/₄-ton Land Rover chassis. Overall, technological and commercial improvements were a mixed blessing. More sophisticated systems could improve the driver's lot, but at the expense of less robust fittings and higher maintenance and repair levels.

Most of these modern features were later incorporated in the replacement for the Thorneycroft Antar tank transporter. The Antar, a product of the early 1950s oil industry, had been a faithful servant of the Corps but was expensive to maintain, indeed the maker, Thorneycroft, no longer existed. Moreover, in the 1970s the race between the West and the Soviet Union to develop a new generation of main battle tanks had hotted up. In Britain the prospect of massive sales to Iran of the new tank, then under development to follow Chieftain, complete with transporter trains, gave new impetus to what had been a Cinderella project. All was not smooth sailing and there was secrecy surrounding the tank project with its revolutionary Chobham armour. There was an initial underestimation of the tank's payload weight. The manufacturers were then faced with severe problems when the weight increase was announced after the release of the original trailer design specification! The development of a successful design was greatly helped by the fact that the Corps had many of its own officers of high technical ability serving throughout the various organizations involved, the Military Vehicle and Engineering Establishment, the Project Management teams, the Operational Requirements branch and the Corps' own technical branch, Transport 2 in Headquarters TO in C (Army), and the Training Logistics Development Team (TLDT). The Scammell Commander, as the new vehicle was called, was a great success. It had a much more powerful engine and improvements in all areas (even a radio/cassette for the crew), it could now maintain a comparable convoy speed with other vehicles and carry the heaviest service loads. Not only that, it could stop as well!

612 Tank Transporter Unit (MSO)

In BAOR on 1 January, 1973, 612 Tank Transporter Unit (MSO) RCT, in a major organizational change, was redesignated 16 Tank Transporter Squadron RCT and manned in part by RCT drivers. However, the new squadron retained an MSO component of two troops, which continued to maintain the proud traditions handed down to them from their founder members of the old Polish army, until being disbanded in 1987.

Logistic Support Battalion, Allied Commander Europe's Mobile Force (Land) – 1977

On 1 April, 1977, as part of the UKLF Restructuring Plan, 27 Regiment RCT became 27 Logistic Support Group Regiment RCT, and the Logistic Support Battalion AMF(L) was formed as an independent unit.

The Battalion was required to be rapidly deployable. It was a fully integrated, multi-cap-badged, multi-functional and multi-national AMF(L) unit. The role of the Battalion was to provide force-level logistic support to NATO's multinational rapid deployment brigade. There were seven contingency areas where the force could deploy, ranging from northern Norway to north-eastern Turkey. As an AMF(L) unit the Battalion deployed anywhere within Allied Command Europe (ACE) and was fully Arctic and warm-weather trained.

The Battalion had a permanent backbone structure of about 380 officers and men. On deployment this could swell to as many as 1,500, depending on the deployment area. The Unit consisted of a Battalion HQ, HQ Company, 42 Squadron RCT, AMF(L) Supply Company RAOC, AMF(L) Workshop REME, AMF(L) Medical Troop RAMC and 263 (Air Portable) Field Cash Office RAPC. In 1977 the Battalion also took under command for administrative purposes the UK tank transporter fleet, 414 Tank Transporter Unit RCT. On deployment the Battalion also assumed command of 50 MC Squadron RCT, a detachment from 21 PC Squadron RE and individual reinforcements from 28 Group RPC and Catering Branch HQ Southern District.

NORTHERN IRELAND

Introduction

The problems of Northern Ireland and the troubles stemming from them can be traced back to the 17th century and to the establishment of Scottish and English Presbyterian settlers in the north of Ireland, which was until then largely a Catholic community. The subsequent conflicts over religious differences in the north have, over three centuries, resulted in numerous hostile actions being perpetrated which have been enshrined in the folk history and culture of each community. In 1921 Ireland was partitioned into the six counties of Northern Ireland, commonly known as Ulster, and Eire in the south. Eire became the Republic of Ireland in 1948 and left the Commonwealth.

After partition the religious and cultural differences between the communities in Northern Ireland remained, polarizing further between Nationalists and Unionists, with all the underlying suspicions, antagonism and discrimination that defied every effort towards reconciliation. The Republican Catholics generally wished to have a united Ireland governed from Dublin, and the strongest demands for this, though not necessarily representing the views of all Catholics, came from Sinn Fein, the political branch of the Irish Republican Army (IRA). On the other hand the majority and dominant Protestant population were staunch in their loyalty to the Queen and the maintenance of the Union with Great Britain. A political resolution remained elusive, and the continuing antagonism and friction between the two factions manifested itself in sporadic acts of violence, both in Northern Ireland and on mainland Britain.

In 1969 the situation came to a head when a genuine civil rights protest movement was exploited to become a serious campaign of violence against the Royal Ulster Constabulary and the so-called 'B Special' auxiliaries. The Army was deployed to aid the civil powers but the violence escalated to envelop the military and the whole Protestant community in Northern Ireland. This ferocious campaign was led by a splinter group of the IRA – the Provisional Irish Republican Army (PIRA), known as the Provisionals. The aim of the Provisionals was to drive the British out of Ireland by any means. Violence soon spread to England.

Inevitably, retaliation against the PIRA and those thought to be supporting them started. Protestant Loyalist terrorist groups formed, on the excuse of protecting the Protestant community. This further exacerbated the situation, and tit for tat killings between the communities and outbreaks of serious rioting raised tensions and reduced what little chance there was of a peaceful solution. As always in such conditions, many innocent people of both communities, who only wanted to get on with their lives in peace, were caught up in these violent activities. Much intimidation, extortion and crime were directed against the general public by terrorist groups on both sides to raise money and gain support and compliance.

On 16 August, 1969, the 'Troubles', fanned by the annual march of the Protestant Apprentice Boys of Londonderry, and the counter-action by the Catholics of the Bogside area of the city in declaring a 'Free Derry' and establishing a 'no go' area, had become sufficiently serious for the Government to declare a State of Emergency. At this time the Army garrison in the Province consisted of HQ Northern Ireland District at Lisburn and three infantry battalions supporting logistic units scattered in various locations. The logistic organization was geared to supporting a peacetime garrison which had come to enjoy a gentle and pleasant lifestyle. This was to change rapidly. Large numbers of reinforcements of all arms and services, including 24 Air Portable Brigade, were hastily despatched to the Province. By the end of the year there were over 7000 troops in Northern Ireland compared with some 3000 before. Few would have imagined then that the Emergency would last beyond the life of the RCT itself. Over the years the Corps was involved in a continuous process of reinforcement, with changing tasks and organizations to support the needs of a force which was itself constantly responding to the changing political and security situation. Some examples of the Corps achievements are given in the following paragraphs; they illustrate the versatility, resourcefulness and courage of the many members of the RCT who helped it to make a major contribution to the work of the Army in Northern Ireland during these many years.

Transport Support

When the emergency began in 1969 RCT representation consisted of a small Transport and Movements Branch and 26 Squadron, both located at Lisburn. 26 Squadron had a long connection with Ireland, having been formed in the Curragh in 1888 and since the partition of Ireland in 1921 had been continuously based in the Province. The Squadron was tailor-made to meet the peacetime requirements of the

Province. Its capability was totally inadequate to meet the increased transport tasks which now faced the Corps and immediate reinforcement was essential.

The first RCT units sent to meet the requirement were 60 Squadron from Plymouth, 63 Parachute Squadron from Aldershot and a troop from 42 Squadron at Catterick. These units gave direct and immediate support to the infantry units to improve their mobility and flexibility. 26 Squadron was reinforced from a number of sources, including 65 Squadron, 14 Air Despatch Regiment and 18 Amphibious Squadron. When 18 Squadron was disbanded a short time later the manpower cover was used to increase the establishment of 26 Squadron. Until 1977, when a new 18 Squadron was formed, it was officially known as 18/26 Squadron RCT, claiming the only cavalry-type title in the Corps!

Some form of stability returned to the Province in 1970 and only 7 Squadron from Tidworth and 42 Squadron from Catterick remained to support the Garrison Squadron. This also had an additional troop, 416, added to provide non-operational transport support for troops in Londonderry.

In 1971 there was a marked deterioration in the situation and 65 Squadron arrived in the Province to be replaced by 60 Squadron in September. It was agreed at this time that RCT drivers should take over the driving of the ageing Humber one-ton

RCT-manned Humber 1 ton APC (Pig).

RCT-manned Saracen APC.

Armoured Personnel Carriers (APC), known as 'Pigs' from their appearance. In March, 1972, 3 Tank Transporter Squadron arrived from BAOR to fill this role, quickly gaining the confidence of the infantry units that they were supporting.

This increase in Corps responsibilities was soon followed by the formation of a support troop equipped with Saracen APCs in April, manned by soldiers from 1 Squadron, Colchester. Driving these vehicles was a distinct challenge to eighteen-year-old soldiers. There was limited visor vision on these vehicles and driving on narrow roads, flanked by thick hedges and with steep camber, proved difficult and added to the operational hazards.

The establishment by the IRA of 'no go' areas in Belfast and Londonderry in 1972 required a special operation to clear them. Operation MOTORMAN was mounted on 31 July. As a result 15 Squadron from Osnabruck joined 1 Squadron detachment in Londonderry, where a total of 110 Saracen APCs were deployed. The operation was successful, but in spite of this force levels continued to rise. By the beginning of 1973, there were 1,300 RCT all ranks at regimental and staff duty. There were over twenty infantry battalions deployed at this time.

The APCs were, on the whole, remarkably effective in their role. Not only in the rural areas were they being used for the sort of task for which they were originally designed, but even in the narrow and crowded streets of Belfast and Londonderry they performed adequately. Without doubt their use reduced casualties from small arms fire. When mined, they provided much better protection than Land Rovers and other soft-skinned vehicles. The major vulnerability was to anti-tank weapons, principally the Russian RPG 7. Fortunately few of these were in the hands of the IRA, and, when used, were often captured soon after.

Many lessons were learnt, or re-learnt, in operating APCs – the RASC had an APC squadron in BAOR in the late forties – but without doubt the greatest benefit was for section commanders. The very large number of small detachments manned by a section or less meant that, once deployed, squadron and troop commanders could exert very little immediate influence. The infantry company commander looked to the RCT section commander to produce the support he required and it was up to the junior NCO concerned to respond. Young (and some not so young) corporals, who, in the confines of barracks or on heavily controlled exercises in BAOR, had never really had the opportunity of being totally responsible for their command, found themselves completely on their own. In almost every case they reacted well, thrived on the responsibility and gained enormous confidence, capability and professionalism from their tours. The pressures of Ulster exposed their strengths and weaknesses very quickly. Squadron commanders also had the opportunity to get to know their men in a way that was not possible in barracks and many young soldiers were quickly identified as outstanding potential leaders.

Workshop support was provided by the APC Workshops, REME, at Moscow Camp, with detachments at Ballykinler and Londonderry in support of the other two squadrons. With over 400 Saracens and Humber one-ton vehicles, many fifteen or more years old, the workshop had a major task in keeping the fleet serviceable. It was a large workshop, 100 strong, which worked continuous twelve-hour shifts day and night throughout the year, in providing exceptional support. Vehicle availability was always high and invariably well exceeded the theoretical operational requirement of seventy percent on which both the manpower and spares scaling were based.

The whole APC organization, located at Moscow Camp, was supported by a small staff of a technical QM, an SQMS and a Master Driver (APCs). Overall control was the responsibility of the SO2 (Transport) on CRCT's staff who, with many other equally important tasks to be done, could only devote a very limited time to APCs. A case for the appointment of a deputy to command the APCs, with over 800 soldiers and the 450 APCs deployed in some seventy locations, was first rejected by the Ministry of Defence in 1973, only to be accepted in 1974.

It is doubtful whether any member of the Corps serving in Ulster will forget Moscow Camp, Belfast. This camp was set up in a small area of land taken over from Short Brothers in the heart of the docklands and used as a roulement (the tour rotation of units) battalion base. The Corps moved there in 1973 from HMS *Maidstone* and Palace Barracks, Hollywood. Legend has it that this site was used during the 1939-45 war as a Ministry of Supply Communications Office (MOSCO). A Property Services Agency official assumed it was Moscow that was being referred to and the name stuck! It is also the original test area for the 'Flying Bedstead' which developed into the Harrier Jump Jet.

Another troop with a special task was set up to provide support to the Royal Engineers. It was based at Antrim Bridging Camp with detachments at Castledillon and Ballykelly and equipped with a motley collection of vehicles, including dump trucks and pre-mix concrete trucks.

By 1979 the burden on the Corps of providing roulement support to Northern Ireland from the UK and BAOR was still continuing to have a detrimental effect on training, readiness and, to some extent, morale. In an attempt to rationalize the Emergency Tour Plot, it was decided to reduce the general transport commitment from a squadron to a large troop under the operational control of 26 Squadron RCT. 26 Squadron itself was tasked to man the detachment at Antrim. The roulement GT troop continued to run the Priority Freight Service and the operational reserve of troop carriers from its base in Moscow Camp.

The pace of RCT operations in Ulster varied enormously. Great efforts were made to reduce the force levels and introduce greater flexibility by earmarking units as 'on call' reinforcements, with the additional capability of changing roles as required. The first full roulement regiment, 4 Armoured Divisional Regiment, arrived in March, 1979, with its RHQ in Moscow Camp. At the same time CRCT Northern Ireland became Commanding Officer of the camp with the Camp Commandant and Staff Officer Grade 2 (APC), both RCT, answering directly to him.

Movements

The operations of Movements in Ulster posed many problems and the organization played a highly significant role in enabling the Army to meet its commitments. The main tasks were:

● Operational moves (either roulement or emergency) to and from the mainland or BAOR necessitating a permutation of civil ferry or RAF Air Support Command aircraft.

● Routine movement, including container traffic.

● Leave travel, including the processing of the concessional air fare scheme involving 2,400 applications per month.

● All Ulster-based TAVR and Cadet units training camps (which of necessity had to be taken outside the Province).

The scale of this effort is graphically illustrated by passenger statistics:

	Number of Unit Moves		
Period	**Major**	**Minor**	**Others**
January, 1969 – March, 1971	26	23	30
April, 1970 – March, 1971	64	40	40
April, 1971 – March, 1972	100	72	24

The total number of passengers for the 1971/72 period topped the 100,000 mark. The following year it was 169,000, broadly equivalent to the strength of the entire Army.

Over the years there was no let-up in the movements task in the Province, but methods and practice changed, either because of terrorist threats or because of new commercial practice. In 1978 it was decided to conduct routine ammunition re-stocking by using one of the new Landing Craft Logistic (LCL). The conventional Landing Ship Logistic (LSL) method required a massive operation to secure a berth in Belfast docks and escort the road convoy to the Command Ammunition Depot at Ballykinler. The LCL was able to discharge over the perfect sandy beach within the secure perimeter at Ballykinler. 26 Squadron with the GT roulement troop provided the shore-side support. Increasing use was made of civil air transport and the table below shows the increasing importance of containers. Figures for the period 1975 to

1979 were:

Year	Vehicles	Tons	Freight Containers
1975	7,325	10,839	Nil
1976	8,255	7,469	75
1977	8,944	2,087	428
1978	12,400	4,000	1,500
1979	13,220	600	8,084

	Passengers			
Year	RAF	Civil Air	LSL	Civil Sea
1975	41,000	49,797	18,199	26,017
1976	45,690	51,452	18,746	88,272
1977	48,210	48,196	18,428	93,781
1978	44,400	47,300	10,800	110,000
1979	36,839	110,167	11,137	54,587

Terrorist Activity in London

Sadly, the terrorism of Northern Ireland continued to be a hazard in the life of the Corps, even in London. On 10 October, 1981, Mr C W Liddiard, a civilian driver of 20 Squadron RCT, was badly hurt when driving a squadron bus carrying the Regimental band of the Irish Guards who were the target for an IRA bomb at Chelsea Barracks. In the attack two innocent civilians were killed and many of the bandsmen badly injured. The drivers of this unit, both military and civilian, were constantly in the public eye, with exacting individual responsibilities. Their record of personal efficiency is one of which they can be rightly proud.

HONG KONG

Gurkha Transport Regiment

In September and October of 1973 there were two special parades by the Regiment in Hong Kong. The first was for the Major General Brigade of Gurkhas and the second was for the farewell visit of the Colonel of the Regiment, Major General P G Turpin. It was at the second parade that the Regiment was presented with a personally signed photograph of Her Majesty by the Colonel of the Regiment. The Regiment presented the outgoing Colonel of the Regiment with a silver statuette of a Gurkha soldier in gratitude for the thirteen years during which he had held the appointment of Colonel of the Regiment, guiding the GASC and GTR through its formative years.

The Regiment was selected to take on a new commitment in 1975. Lieutenant J Longland and nineteen soldiers of the Regiment left Hong Kong for a tour of duty with the Korean Honour Guard. The Regiment was the first Corps unit to undertake this duty and thereafter continued to do so from time to time.

GTR APCs on IS duties with Infantry.

In 1976 the new establishment of the Regiment was confirmed and coupled with the move of the Headquarters to Gun Club Hill Barracks. On 1 September, 1976, the Regiment welcomed 29 Squadron and 415 Maritime Troop into the fold. Hong Kong Military Service Corps (HKMSC) soldiers were now a part of the Regiment and destined to play a significant role in Regimental duties in Hong Kong and abroad in the years to come. Only the family lines at Jubilee buildings remained at Sham Shui Po. In the latter part of the year the APC Troop was established. Initial training was done at the Gurkha Mechanical Transport School in Sek Kong. It was not long before training was under way with the APC Troop deploying with infantry battalions in the Internal Security Role (IS).

During the next few years the Regiment continued to immerse itself in Hong Kong Garrison duties, exercises, overseas commitments and in meeting a growing number of ERE appointments in UK. Detachments at RMAS Sandhurst, the Infantry Tactical Wing in Brecon and the Royal Engineers Training Depot at Chatham were examples of the places the soldiers could strive to work in. Every attempt was made to provide soldiers with a greater depth of military experience worldwide and this was to prove invaluable in the future. Overseas exercises for infantry battalions always had a detachment of GTR drivers to assist with transport and participate in general. Overseas exercises were also organized by the Regiment with GTR troops returning to Malaysia for Exercise ORCHARD ROAD. Later, other jungle training exercises took place in Brunei under the name of Exercise JUNGLE TROOPER.

A notable success during this period was the award of a Gurkha Commission (GCO) to Captain (QGO) Balkrishna Rana in appreciation of his skills and success within the Regiment. The GTR was naturally disappointed that, on receiving this promotion, he was posted to serve with 2/7 Gurkha Rifles. Later the Regiment was delighted to welcome back the most senior Gurkha of the Regiment, Major (GCO) Balkrishna Rana, into a succession of Regimental appointments. He was awarded the MBE for his services to the Regiment before retirement in 1992.

MILITARY AID TO THE CIVIL MINISTRIES (MACM) FIRE SERVICE STRIKES OF 1973

There were six separate fire service disputes involving the RCT during its lifetime. One of the first, in Glasgow in late 1973, was code-named Operation ATHENE. It started in the best of traditions with a signal from MOD late on a Friday afternoon to HQ Lowlands Area in Edinburgh Castle ordering the assembly of a tri-Service fire-fighting force to stand by to take over the Glasgow Fire Brigade. Only one officer was in the Headquarters, the Brigadier was away shooting, the COS on a course in the south of England and the G staff inspecting a TA exercise in Cyprus. It had been many years since the Services had been involved in a firemen's strike and there was no relevant experience on file. The hard-pressed G4 staff spent a frantic weekend writing a suitable operation order from scratch, sending impassioned pleas to MOD for anything they thought might be required and tracking down every UK Army Fire Officer. By the Monday morning a large group of units was starting to assemble, truckloads of firemen's helmets and clothing were being delivered from Civil Defence sources and eight Army Fire Officers arrived to assist with training. The Civil Defence fire engines, nicknamed 'Green Goddesses', were drawn from a depot at Lockerbie and were in sound condition even though they had not been used for many years.

It had been hoped that there would be several days to train, but events moved rapidly. By the Wednesday units were deploying to Glasgow and taking over the Glasgow Fire Stations. A hastily prepared but effective plan ensured accommodation by converting all the Glasgow TA drill halls into dormitories. Group catering 'meals on wheels' were arranged for both drill halls and fire stations. 154 (Lowland) Transport Regiment RCT (V) and its drill hall at Yorkhill Parade played a full part in all aspects of the operation. Fire-fighting skills improved with progression from stirrup pumps and buckets to the small water cannon on the Green Goddesses. Modifications to the Goddesses were soon devised and 'day glow' stripes were painted on the sides to improve visibility. Whether the arsonists took leave or the gods were kind is not known but the only fires were comparatively minor events. The success of the troops won the goodwill of the citizens of Glasgow and after nine days the firemen agreed to return to work while a settlement was negotiated and the troops were then withdrawn.

MACM in Ulster

In Northern Ireland, in addition to the Internal Security tasks covered earlier, the Corps was on several occasions deployed in Ulster on MACM duties. One such task occurred in May, 1977, when HQ 3 Divisional Regiment was sent to Ulster following

BP tanker in Northern Ireland with RCT Driver.

a threat by the Ulster Unionist Action Committee to call a general strike. The HQ established itself in Moscow Camp with a motley collection of HGV drivers wearing eleven different cap badges, including fifty men from the Royal Air Force. Their task was to be prepared to maintain the distribution of essential fuel supplies to roadside fuel stations, hospitals and vital industry. This was at the same time that transport for the 3,200 reinforcements had to be provided. Fortunately, the will to pursue industrial action was quickly lost, but MACM skills and procedures tested during this period were to be put to very effective use later.

In December, 1977, the Ulster firemen decided to go on strike. Twenty-three Civil Defence fire engines were collected from Glasgow by drivers from 26 Squadron and, manned by members of the Black Watch, went into action. They provided an effective fire service for a period of six weeks, including Christmas.

Perhaps the major operation in support of the civil power in Northern Ireland came in January, 1978, with the threatened strike by oil tanker drivers. Contingency plans became effective on Friday, 6 January, when a party of HGV1 RCT drivers, mainly from 16 Tank Transporter Squadron in BAOR, formally requisitioned a fleet of tankers from the oil company depots at 0300 hours. By 0730 tankers had been filled and were ready to operate. By the afternoon of Sunday, 8 January, 240,000 gallons of fuel had been delivered without accident, despite foul weather conditions with ice on the roads and freezing fog. The operation was so effective that the strikers went back to work on 9 January.

At the same time 26 Squadron had to provide a through-trucking service from UK RAOC depots to units in the Province because of a Transport and General Workers

306

Green Goddess *fire engines assembled after the strike was over.*

Union strike. Forty-ton tractors and trailers were hired on the mainland and a team from the Squadron operated round the clock using the Larne/Stranraer ferry across the Irish sea. This method proved very effective.

MACM – The Miners' Dispute

One of the bitterest MACM commitments involved the national miners' strike of 1984-1985. On 18 March, 1984, the Depot RCT TA were asked to host up to 1,500 civilian police personnel, on behalf of the Nottinghamshire Constabulary, in Prince William of Gloucester Barracks, Grantham. This entailed providing daily accommodation and feeding for the 1,500 policemen, in addition to an average of 200 TA soldiers undergoing military training, in a barracks equipped to accommodate a total of 850 all ranks. Feeding was a problem because of the hours that the police had to work. Extra catering staff were employed so that the kitchen could provide a twenty-four hours service. In addition, 1,500 boxed meals were required each day for the first ten weeks. The non-industrial civilian staff, comprising clerical officers, clerical assistants and typists, spent their lunch hours and evenings, outside their normal working hours, helping the catering staff prepare to pack these boxed meals. The dispute lasted for forty-six weeks during which a total of 130,000 policemen and 62,000 military passed through the system for accommodation and feeding at Grantham.

BRITISH HONDURAS – BELIZE

In 1973, in a move towards complete independence, British Honduras, which had become self-governing in 1964, adopted the name Belize. This further antagonized her western neighbour, Guatemala, who harboured a long-standing territorial grievance. Guatemalan military activity along the extensive common border triggered the precautionary reinforcement of the British Garrison which had remained there, and brought it up to two-infantry-battalion strength with supporting arms and services, including RCT Transport and Movements staff. Resupplying the outlying posts involved constant hard work, tasks made more difficult by the tropical conditions, including hurricanes, and the very high rainfall which caused frequent flooding and washed-away roads.

To provide greater logistic flexibility, the garrison was augmented in February, 1977, by a Ramped Powered Lighter (RPL) and soldiers for an operating detachment, provided by 17 Port Regiment on six-month tours. The craft was used to resupply the infantry company battle group based in the Toledo district. Later that year the Guatemalan border crisis flared up again and the garrison was doubled to 2000, including RAF Harriers and helicopters. Supply by road to the battle group in the south could take 24 hours plus, and was very damaging to the vehicles, whereas by sea it was only a 12-hour trip. Supplies could be delivered to the 'door' by RPL as the camp was beside the river, and the offshore islands gave some protection to the vessels during the tropical storms. This service was also greatly appreciated by the NAAFI for beer and soft drink resupply!

The RPL was obsolescent. It had first entered service in the late 1950s, designed for the Borneo Confrontation, but was specially retained there (withdrawn otherwise from British Army use) as it could negotiate the Belize rivers, shelter up them when hurricanes were forecast and, most importantly, be 'slipped' for local repair on a local civil-owned river slipway. The successor to the RPL, the RCL (Ramped Craft Logistic), was too heavy for the slipway and considered too wide and deep in draught for the rivers. Within one year the tropical conditions rendered an RPL a 'rust bucket', so one was returned to the UK (Marchwood) every year by civil ship as deck cargo for a 'base overhaul'. One repaired RPL was kept at Marchwood Military Port for immediate deployment to Belize in an emergency.

A second RPL was shipped out in December, 1977, followed by the formation of a proper transport and movements element at Airport Camp near Belize City. An MT troop, 404 Troop with 58 all ranks, was added to the existing Corps establishment of a Transport and Movements Office and the RPL detachment.

The uneasy border situation with Guatemala continued beyond the formal independence of Belize as a Republic in 1981. By June, 1983, with no prospect of the Guatemalan confrontation easing, the force in Belize had become more permanent. 404 Troop had been reinforced to over 70 strong and administrative transport support, including a VIP section with Safari Land Rovers, had been added to operational tasks.

To improve command and control, a Squadron HQ was added and RCT Belize became 24 Squadron RCT on 25 July, 1983, under the command of the senior RCT

RCT Ramped Powered Lighter off the coast of Belize.

officer. 404 Troop was split into A and B Troops which provided operational and administrative transport respectively. The Movement Control centre and RPL detachment completed the squadron.

Over the next ten years there were few changes to the routine or to the organization. At the end of 1984 the landing craft and harbour launch had been established as the third, or C, Troop. The harbour launch was eventually replaced by a more useful Landing Craft Vehicle and Personnel, with the continued task of resupplying the outlying bases. If for some reason the RPLs could not sail, the 200 miles to Punta Garda involved a 15-hour drive over a difficult road . Twice a year a resupply ship arrived to be discharged and reloaded with equipment and stores to be returned. Occasionally local water and road transport was provided to support visiting RN Ships.

Belize offered good opportunities for recreation and the summer temperatures above 110°F did not deter water sports enthusiasts from adventure training expeditions on the reefs along the coast, particularly on St George's Cay. Leave trips were also possible to Mexico, which one could drive to, the USA, Bermuda and the Bahamas, all of which did much to offset the difficult climatic and working conditions of the operational area.

United Nations Force in Cyprus (UNFICYP)

In 1974, after prolonged hostilities between Greek and Turkish military forces, UNFICYP established a buffer zone to be maintained and policed by UN forces to separate the opposing forces. Although Corps force commitments fluctuated periodically, they remained reasonably steady and operated effectively at one MT squadron, one port squadron working from Famagusta and an air movement cell/air despatch troop working from RAF Akrotiri. Tours for RCT units in Cyprus were usually relieved by units rotating through the island approximately every six months, and strengths were passed to the RLC with a view to reduction when the Corps responsibilities ended in 1993. Of particular note was the deployment during the Gulf War of a composite TA-manned squadron for the UNFICYP Tour. This released a Regular *RCT-driven refrigerator vehicle with UNIFICYP.*

The RCT Ammunition Ship Logistic St George. *The RCT GS Launch alongside is the* Hyperion, *both operating from the mole at Akrotiri.*

Squadron for the Gulf.

OPERATION CORPORATE – THE FALKLAND ISLANDS CAMPAIGN

Introduction

The Falkland Islands, situated in the South Atlantic Ocean about 400 miles north-east of Cape Horn, consist of two principal islands; and numerous other smaller islands which in total cover 4,700 square miles. The island of South Georgia, some 800 miles south-east of the Falkland Islands, and the South Sandwich Islands are administered from the Falkland Islands for convenience. The Falkland Islands were first settled in the eighteenth century by British, French and Spanish settlers, but by 1806 the Islands had been abandoned. They were largely uninhabited until 1833 when Captain Onslow of HMS *Clio* occupied Port Egmont and raised the Union Flag over the Islands. Since then they have been a British colony. In 1982 the population was estimated to be about 1,850, mostly involved in farming. They are mainly of British descent with some eighty percent born on the Islands. The only town is Stanley, with a population of just over 1,000. Argentina had been in dispute with Great Britain over the Falklands since the 19th Century, and in 1964 she had taken the dispute to the United Nations who referred the matter back to the two

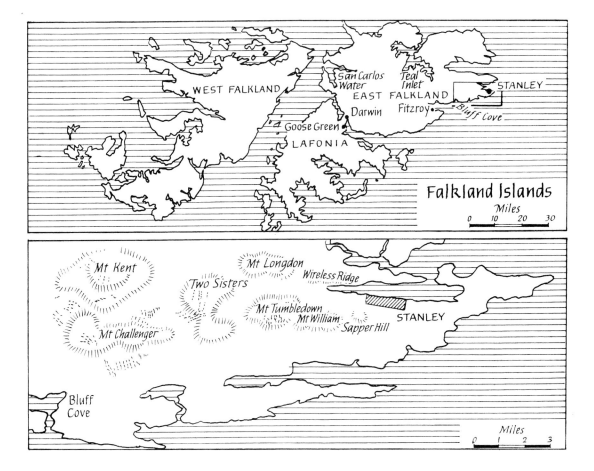

311

parties to settle. Inconclusive discussions had continued up to 1982.

At the end of March, 1982, the British Government reported to the UN that the situation in the area was potentially dangerous and that an Argentine task force was sailing towards the Islands. On 2 April it was confirmed that Argentine forces had invaded the Islands and had captured the Governor and the small force of Royal Marines. On 4 April South Georgia was also seized, although the small detachment of Royal Marines mounted a stiff resistance before being overwhelmed and captured. The British Government reaction was swift and decisive – a Task Force was sent to the South Atlantic to retake the Islands. The operation was given the code-name CORPORATE.

The mounting and support of the Task Force in the South Atlantic was a complex military operation, presenting enormous logistic problems. The lines of communication stretched 8,000 miles from the United Kingdom base, an average of twenty-one days' sailing time. There was no contingency plan involving the Falkland Islands; an operation of this magnitude outside Europe had never been foreseen. It was not until the night of 1-2 April that firm warning orders were issued and plans for an amphibious operation were developed.

The Corps played a major part in launching the operation from UK, particularly in the Movements role, the provision and organization of transport for outloading from depots, and in the considerable involvement of Marchwood Military Port. Subsequently, at sea and in the Falklands, these Port Operations tasks continued to be of paramount importance.

On 5 April, within three days of the fall of the Falkland Islands, a Naval task force with 3 Commando Brigade embarked, sailed from the UK. The Force included a number of Corps members, commando-trained, serving with the Commando Forces/3 Commando Brigade Royal Marines, including the Colonel A/Q, Colonel I S Baxter, the Commanding Officer of the Commando Logistic Regiment Royal Marines, Lieutenant Colonel I J Hellberg, and the entire Royal Marines Movement Staff, as well as a pilot with the Commando Air Squadron. These were in addition to the RCT supporting contingent from 17 Port Regiment RCT. Meanwhile Ascension Island, in the Indian Ocean, was being developed as a forward support base, using Wideawake Airfield to extend the limited facilities that already existed on the Island.

As the task force sailed south towards the so-called Total Exclusion Zone, the build-up of Argentine forces increased and it was decided to further reinforce the amphibious force with 5 Infantry Brigade. The deployment of a further 3,000 troops sorely pressed the available passenger shipping. The UK flag cruise liner fleet was not large and, with *Canberra* and *Uganda* already committed, the choice was narrowed to the *Queen Elizabeth II* and a collection of smaller and less suitable ships. After many high level discussions, the *Queen Elizabeth II* sailed for the South Atlantic on 12 May. Vehicles, stores and ammunition for 5 Brigade were aboard *Tor Caledonia*, the *Baltic Ferry*, *Nordic Ferry* and a helicopter 'carrier' *Atlantic Conveyor*. These left the UK between 9 and 12 May, 1982, with many stores support ships, mine countermeasure vessels and fuel tankers. Over fifty vessels were taken up from some thirty-three different companies. It represented one of the largest merchant fleets in the world, carrying over 100,000 tons of stores, 9,000 personnel and ninety-five assorted aircraft.

By the end of June some 5,800 passengers and 6,700 tons of cargo had been airlifted forward to Ascension Island. The RAF stations at Brize Norton and Lyneham were the principal mounting airfields. Freight and passengers were swiftly processed by RCT movements staffs and the Cargo Allocation Centre. Later in the operation an RCT movement control detachment was established to co-ordinate the movement and transit of Army units deploying and recovering through Ascension.

Marchwood Military Port, the home of 17 Port Regiment RCT, is the only UK port under military control, and provided a unique facility to mount operations. In a time of national emergency it could more easily be freed from legal restrictions governing the movement and storage of ammunition and explosives, and advantage was taken of this provision.

At 0900 hours on Friday 2 April, 1982, Transport and Movement Branch United Kingdom Land Forces was tasked to provide urgent transport assistance to move the assault packs of 3 Commando Brigade from depots at Kineton, Bicester and Donnington to shipping at Plymouth and Rosyth. Within twenty-five minutes the first vehicles were on the move from 27 LSG Regiment RCT at Aldershot on what was the beginning of three and a half months of frenzied outloading activity. By 1700 hours the same evening 140 vehicles were on the road and by the following morning this figure has reached 200.

Within the UK the operation was mainly one of road transport, moving stores to ports and airfields. About 100 civilian forty-foot flat-bed vehicles had to be hired, but later, when there was sufficient time to plan ahead, trains were used. Headquarters United Kingdom Land Forces also had to identify the thousands of different items of stores which made up the ships loads and arrange their collection from the length and breadth of the country, a formidable task by any standards. Volunteers from many RCT TA units assisted with the movement of stores to the ports and in other forms of support.

The main group of RCT soldiers actively involved in operations on the Falklands came from 17 Port Regiment RCT, providing specialist movement control and stevedore advice to cover the majority of the loading of ships. Marchwood Military Port was a large holding area for equipment and ammunition, for loading in Southampton docks. The smoothness with which requisitioned ships were prepared with an 'operational fit' for the South Atlantic was impressive to all. Each of the six Royal Fleet Auxiliary LSLs had detachments of soldiers from 17 Port Regiment RCT consisting of Port Operator detachments and crews for Mexeflote, a 125 ft powered raft with a capacity of 150 tonnes. In addition, the larger Roll On/Roll Off civilian ferries each took a detachment of port operators and associated mechanical handling equipment from the Port Regiment to assist in cargo offloading. In all the Regiment had two officers and 151 soldiers deployed with the Fleet. They received a thorough working-up period at sea off Ascension Island when the Fleet re-stowed its stores to reflect the latest plan, using Mexeflotes, the Royal Marine Landing Craft Utility (LCU) and every available helicopter. During the trip south from Ascension Island further redeployment of stores took place whilst the Fleet was at sea. This was no mean feat and was done by the onboard Port Operator detachments.

Helicopter Support Units

Elements of the Joint Helicopter Support Units (JHSU) were included in the Task Force. Three teams subsequently received the South Atlantic Medal with Rosette, including those on board *SS Atlantic Conveyor* when it was sunk by an Exocet missile. A team was also deployed to Ascension Island, and, during a nine-week period there, approximately 2,000 helicopter loads were 'hooked up', lifting an estimated

10,000,000 pounds of freight from the island out to south-bound ships.

The JHSUs were the youngest units in the RCT, being formed in 1982 to provide specialist ground-handling assistance to support the new RAF Chinook helicopters which had an enormous lift capacity. Two were raised, one in Germany in support of 1 (Br) Corps and the other in support of the UKMF(L), becoming fully operational in July, 1982. The units were jointly manned by Royal Corps of Transport and Royal Air Force personnel, with a small number from the Royal Electrical and Mechanical Engineers and the Army Catering Corps.

Outline of the Operations

On 25 April, the Royal Marines recaptured the island of South Georgia by amphibious assault. On 21 May 3 Commando Brigade landed at San Carlos Water on the north-west coast of East Falkland. Despite heavy air attacks, the brigade consolidated a beachhead, from which they were able to break out on 27 May. Subsequently, 2nd Battalion The Parachute Regiment decisively defeated a very much larger Argentine defending force in the notable action at Goose Green. This victory dealt a severe blow to the morale of the rest of the Argentine troops on the islands.

On 1 June 5 Infantry Brigade arrived at San Carlos. By 6 June 2nd Battalion The Parachute Regiment had disembarked and, together with the 2nd Battalion Scots Guards, who had landed at Fitzroy, were advancing inland. On 8 June the 1st Battalion the Welsh Guards suffered many casualties when the LSLs *Sir Galahad* and *Sir Tristram* were bombed at Fitzroy during disembarkation, *Sir Galahad* eventually sinking. Between 12-14 June, 3 Commando Brigade, from the mountains west of Stanley, captured Mount Longdon, Two Sisters and Wireless Ridge. 5 Infantry Brigade captured Mount Tumbledown and Mount William, and the enemy fled from Sapper Hill south-west of Stanley into the town. On 14 June, the Argentinians surrendered.

The Landing Tasks

Mexeflotes are normally carried attached to the sides of LSLs for ease of deployment and to utilize ship space. Prior to the initial landings at San Carlos on 20-21 May they were carried as deck cargo, for fear that the severe South Atlantic swell might tear off side-loaded equipment. On 21 May the rafts were unloaded in San Carlos Water with the initial landings as the first air attacks came in. Over the next two weeks the six Mexeflotes continued to work by day and night, frequently under fire. One estimate suggests that Mexeflotes moved over seventy-five percent of all stores. Frequently the rafts were overloaded and effectively running under water with only the palletized ammunition visible. Not once was a raft ever directly attacked, and if the Argentinians had appreciated the Mexeflote significance and sunk a few, then the course of the conflict could have been drastically affected. The LSLs left the war zone of San Carlos Water when they were not required for actual off-loading operations, leaving the raft crews to live off whichever ships they were operating from.

Throughout the short but intense twenty-four days of the land battle, resupply of combat supplies for, initially, 3 Commando Brigade and, additionally for the last two weeks, the reinforcing 5 Airportable Brigade, was undertaken by the Commando Logistic Regiment RM commanded by Lieutenant Colonel I J Hellberg RCT. This unique regiment is made up of the Commando Brigade logistic and medical sub-units group

An artists impression of an LSL being offloaded by helicopter and Mexeflote in San Carlos Water. (B V Wynn-Werninck)

to form a regiment of five squadrons manned by RN, RM and Army personnel. All are commando-trained and bonded strongly together by their loyalty to the green beret.

Limited shipping space resulted in the Regiment embarking at minimum manning levels, a fate also inflicted upon the logistic units of 5 Airportable Brigade whose task was initially envisaged by the MOD as little more than providing a garrison force as the enemy were expected to offer little opposition to 3 Commando Brigade. The Regiment, who also had to accept the task of holding a considerable number of POWs taken during the conflict and the medical care of enemy wounded, coped with their role magnificently despite frequent air attacks, the most difficult terrain and weather conditions, unexpected visits from the International Red Cross and an 8,000-mile L of C.

Apart from offloading in San Carlos Bay, LSLs were also used to ferry stores from the larger commercial ships further out to sea. During the San Carlos operations, the LSLs received their share of battle damage. Two had unexploded bombs lodged in them and one of these two vessels, RFA *Sir Lancelot*, had a second bomb skip off the water, enter the ship's structure, leave again and re-enter the water without exploding. After one attack Driver M Brough of 52 Port Squadron RCT was Mentioned in Despatches for his action in craning off an unexploded bomb from the *Sir Galahad* into an inflatable craft which had been filled with cornflake packets to cushion the bomb!

Later during the landings two forward distribution points were opened using nightly runs by RFA LSL and their associated side-carried Mexeflote raft. The one

Cargo offloaded at Port Stanley from the RCT-manned RCL and Mexeflote.

in the north at Teal Inlet was a considerable success, as was the southern location at Fitzroy (Bluff Cove) which was attacked on 7 June when both the *Sir Galahad* and the *Sir Tristram* were bombed, fifty-one people killed and forty-six injured. Thirty-three of those killed were from the 1st Battalion the Welsh Guards. Sergeant Boultby, of 51 Port Squadron RCT, the commander of the Mexeflote detachment, was unloading ammunition from the *Sir Tristram* at the time of the attack. He was awarded the Military Medal for his gallant efforts in rescuing survivors from the blazing *Sir Galahad* by Mexeflote. The vessel, burning from stem to stern as a result of the bombing, later sank.

After the ceasefire, probably the first of the task force ships into Port Stanley was the LSL RFA *Sir Percival*. She proudly flew the Army and RCT Fleet Ensigns alongside her own RFA Blue Ensign as a mark of respect for the co-operation received from the RCT soldiers serving in all the LSLs.

407 Troop RCT, an independent troop under command 27 LSG Regiment RCT, also took part in the operation. The troop was trained with the Volvo over-snow vehicles which were to prove equally versatile over the muddy ground conditions in the Falklands. On 1 June it landed in San Carlos Bay to assist in the setting up of a Brigade maintenance area in support of 5 Brigade. Volvo BV202 and requisitioned tractors were used to move the stores away from the beach and to set up dumps. Fuel became a serious problem and required careful control because the consumption of the Volvo BV202 was high and there were many other calls on fuel supplies.

407 Troop RCT manning Volvo BV202s and requisitioned tractors.

As the operation progressed, the troop moved into Port Stanley and took over captured Argentinian vehicles. Using these, the troop helped to clear up the mess left behind by the enemy.

29 Transport and Movements Regiment RCT had a major part to play in the UK mounting of the operation. They provided Movement Control Check Points (MCCP) and air transport liaison assistance at the airheads. In addition, individuals were tasked to augment movements staff in the MOD and HQ UKLF, stretching the Regiment's resources in manpower to its limits. Nineteen Movements staff also embarked on ships, tasked with liaison between ships crews and embarked servicemen, and with the consolidation and confirmation of stowage plans.

On 2 April 47 Air Despatch Squadron RCT became involved in Operation CORPORATE with crews on standby for operations with special forces. On 20 April the first airdrop of high-priority stores was made. For nineteen days the crews worked exceptionally long hours. Meanwhile, other crews learned how to lay mines from

RCT transport on the road between Port Stanley and Mount Pleasant airfield.

Hercules aircraft and fit Sidewinder missiles. During the second week of May the pattern of air despatch established itself with drops to both the task force and the assault group. Hercules aircraft needed two refuellings by Victor tankers which themselves had to be refuelled. There was a basic problem with in-flight refuellings (IFR): in level flight a Hercules going flat out on full throttle would not reach the slowest speed of the Victor tanker! IFR were achieved in a dive.

The Aftermath

After the conflict detachments of 17 Port Regiment, subsequently renamed 67 (FI) Port Squadron RCT, remained in the Falklands offloading the large amount of stores required to lengthen the runway at Port Stanley and to improve the accommodation. They assisted the Royal Engineers in their many tasks. Later Ramp Craft Logistic (RCL) manned by RCT soldiers were moved to the Falkland Islands as deck cargo on a heavy-lift ship, and used to assist the Mexeflotes in ferrying supplies ashore.

At the end of the operation several of the ships were designated for hospital and prisoner of war duties. Sergeant Hillyard on the MV *St Edmund*, a British Rail Sea Link ferry, had to give up his deluxe cabin with shower to Argentine General Menendez and Brigadier Joffre!

Taking up residence in an Argentine 20 ft ISO container, Warrant Officer Class 1 Roberts formed the Air Transport Liaison Detachment at Port Stanley airfield. This

FIPASS in Operation and Coastels in background. (Derek Balcombe)

was the start of our continuing commitment to what became the Joint Services Movement Staff of the Falkland Islands Logistic Battalion, now renamed the Supply and Movements Wing and serving at the Mount Pleasant airfield built in 1983 at a cost of £350 million. This enabled wide-bodied aircraft to fly direct from UK, greatly reducing flying time.

Three 'coastels' arrived in 1983; these huge second-hand ex-North Sea barges carried accommodation cabins for 900 men each and included ablutions, kitchens and recreation facilities. In 1984 a new port was built. This consisted of seven North Sea oil-rig support barges (specially modified in Belfast Docks) and called the Falklands Intermediate Port and Storage System (FIPASS) or 'Flexiport'. It provided accommodation and refrigerated storage enabling all-year-round port and storage facilities which Port Stanley could not offer. Chartered vessels, normally retained for storage and refrigeration, could be released, so saving £6 million annually.

As well as the RCT units involved in Operation CORPORATE, notable contributions were made by individual RCT officers and soldiers, including those who were working on the staffs of headquarters or detailed for special tasks. There are many stories of courage, fortitude and initiative displayed by those involved in Operation CORPORATE. The Corps has every reason to be proud of them.

The following Honours and Awards were given to members of the Corps for service during Operation CORPORATE:

DFC   Captain J G Greenhalgh, 656 Squadron AAC

MM   Sergeant D S Boultby, 51 Port Squadron, 17 Port Regiment RCT

Mention in Despatches

      Major A Todd, HQ Commando Forces RM

      Lieutenant D P Frankland, 51 Port Squadron, 17 Port Regiment RCT

      Lieutenant J G O Lowe, Instructor on Regular Career Course 29, Royal Military Academy Sandhurst

      Lance-Corporal K B Jones, 52 Port Squadron, 17 Port Regiment RCT

      Driver M Brough, 52 Port Squadron RCT

CBE   Brigadier D B H Colley, OBE, Ministry of Defence (DAP(A))

      Colonel I S Baxter, MBE, HQ Commando Forces RM

      Colonel J D Bidmead, OBE, HQ United Kingdom Land Forces

OBE   Lieutenant Colonel I J Hellberg, Commanding Officer, Commando Logistic Regiment RM

MBE   Major E L Barrett, HQ 3 Transport Group RCT
Major G J Yeoman, 20 Maritime Regiment RCT

      Major (Quartermaster) G N Groom, Transport 7, Logistic Executive (Army)

      Warrant Officer (Class 2) P D Williams, 47 Air Despatch Squadron RCT

      Warrant Officer (Class 2) D Moore, 47 Air Despatch Squadron RCT

BEM   Staff-Sergeant W F Blyth, HQ United Kingdom Land Forces

Commendations

Commander-in-Chief Task Force

      Sergeant A J Carter, 47 Air Despatch Squadron RCT

Corporal C H J Holdsworth, 47 Air Despatch

Squadron RCT

Commander-in-Chief Fleet

Captain G T Cook, 17 Port Regiment RCT

Captain D Hilditch, 3 Armoured Division Transport Regiment RCT

Warrant Officer (Class 2) J Mackenzie, 29 Transport and Movements Regiment RCT

Staff-Sergeant J W Storey, 68 Squadron RCT

Corporal A E Dimmick, 17 Port Regiment RCT

Commander-in-Chief United Kingdom Land Forces

Major J R Cawthorne, HQ United Kingdom Land Forces

Captain T J Murray, 17 Port Regiment RCT

Air Officer Commanding 38 Group RAF

Driver G J Hunt, 47 Air Despatch Squadron RCT

General Officer Commanding South East District

Corporal M Wilson, Joint Air Transport Establishment

CHAPTER 10

Towards a New Era

Introduction. Restructuring of Army training; BAOR: Tank Transporter Fleet Replacement; Training – Exercises LIONHEART 1984 and PLAIN SAILING 1989, The Logistic Shortfall Problem, Meeting the Transport Bill, Contract Hire. Northern Ireland. Military Aid to the Civil Ministries and Communities (MACM and MACC): The Ambulance Dispute – London, Winter Relief – 1990. The End of the Cold War – Germany: Berlin. Options for Change – Regular Army – Reserve Army. The Logistic Support Review.

INTRODUCTION

At the beginning of the eighties no one could have foreseen the astonishing and momentous political events within the Soviet Union that would take place in 1989, when Communism in Eastern Europe would collapse and the Berlin Wall be demolished. This would lead to the ending of the Cold War, the reunification of Germany and profound changes in the British Army and in NATO. As the decade opened though, the British Army was still committed to its long-standing NATO role in Europe and in BAOR this was the forefront of the Army's responsibilities and guided its thinking. Training in BAOR was maintained at a high level in response to the Cold War situation. Elsewhere in the world other commitments continued and the Corps was occupied with many of the ongoing tasks with which the Army was concerned in the seventies, as well as those that inevitably sprang up at short notice.

Some of the main activities and most important implications for the Corps in the eighties are outlined in this Chapter. It was a period of growing financial constraint but many improvements and refinements to doctrines, organizations and equipments were taking place, particularly in BAOR. By the end of the eighties the search for greater cost effectiveness in many shapes and forms within the Army was being relentlessly pursued by MOD, spurred on by political pressure within Government to reduce defence expenditure. This activity accelerated and expanded with the ending of the Cold War in November, 1989.

Earlier that year an initial study into the logistic support of the Army, with a view to reducing its cost, was put in hand by the Quartermaster General and the Master General of the Ordnance at the Ministry of Defence, and this developed into the Logistic Support Review (LSR) of 1990-91. As a result of the ending of the Cold War, however, the parameters for examination were greatly extended and the shape and size of the Armed Forces as a whole were to be studied under the Government policy of Options for Change. The effects that were to follow from these extensive studies, particularly for the Corps, are introduced later in this Chapter, and detailed subsequently in Chapter 12.

However, there was an unexpected and major diversion from the study processes started in 1989 with the advent of the Gulf War of 1990-91. This campaign not only substantially affected BAOR, from where the greater part of the Army element of the Force were found, but also involved considerable logistic support in every form from the UK and elsewhere. The War and the vital part played by the Corps, using the new equipment developed in the Eighties, is described in Chapter 11.

RESTRUCTURING OF ARMY TRAINING IN THE EIGHTIES

In the early 1980s the Women's Royal Army Corps was integrated into the Army's general trade structure. WRAC officers and junior ranks attended a variety of general and specialist RCT courses. In 1980 the RCT CVHQ moved from Bedford to Prince William of Gloucester Barracks at Grantham. Reorganized as the RCT TA Depot and Training Centre, it took on wider responsibilities for all aspects of TA Training. Following the Groom Report on the Individual Training Organization (ITO) in 1983, a Commander Training and Arms Director (CTAD), (later the Inspector General Doctrine and Training (IGDT)), assumed broad powers over all aspects of training including those of the Arms and Service Directors.

Organization of Training

Throughout the 1980s RCT training was split between the Training Group at Buller Barracks and the Army School of Mechanical Transport (ASMT), Leconfield. Adult recruits undertook a Common Military Syllabus Recruit (CMSR) at Buller, while Junior Leaders had forty-eight weeks at Colerne. Commandant ASMT was responsible to the DGTM for All Arms and RCT MT management, driver instructor and specialist vehicle training as well as driver training for ordinary and HGV licences, signals, advanced staff car, Master Driver and Qualified Testing Officers (QTO) training. The School of Transport undertook trade training for movement controllers, seamen and port operators at the Maritime Division of the School at Marchwood and Port Division at Gosport. HQ RCT TA supervised all TA training for the Corps' thirteen specialist units. The Independent TA Regiments used Grantham for Annual Camps, recruit training and numerous career and upgrading courses. The RCT TA Depot and Training Centre eventually came firmly under command of the newly-titled RCT Regular and Territorial Army Training Group at Aldershot.

Regular Army Training

The main responsibility for RCT recruit training throughout this period fell on the Depot and Training Regiment. It trained some 1300 recruits a year, as well as over 500 students on upgrading courses. 61 Depot Squadron held and administered recruits; 64 Squadron undertook induction and training; 65 Squadron ran military career courses, NCO Instructor Courses and the highly successful Potential Officer Cadet courses. The very last Passing Out Parade at Buller Barracks was on 19 March, 1993. For the Gulf War RCT TA units, Reservists and Battle Casualty Replacements were trained and prepared for desert operations. Training concentrated on NBC and Skill at Arms, but also covered desert navigation, aircraft recognition, the laws of Armed Conflict and the new small arms rifle. The introduction of the New Management Strategy in the late 80s led to increasing financial pressure on the Army's Training Organization. With an Executive Responsibility Budget of £18m, staff and unit commanders had to manage their own budget, run their training effectively and stay within budget! In 1991 young female recruits moved to Buller

Barracks at the end of basic training at the WRAC Training Centre at Guildford. They received induction training into the Corps before Phase II (trade training) at ASMT.

The School of Transport (later the School of Transportation) moved to Buller Barracks in 1977. The School ran six training divisions. In Aldershot were the Senior Division, responsible for the Advanced Transport Course, officer and senior rank civil management courses and the sub-unit commanders courses; the Junior Division, perhaps the busiest, covered junior officer training, including the newly-commissioned Young Officers Course and Captains Intermediate Transport Course; the TA Division, and the Movements and Railway Division. The Port and Maritime Divisions operated from Marchwood and Gosport respectively, with responsibility for training all port operator trades, navigation seamen and marine engineers. This included the Long Maritime Course for officers which included six months of intensive seamanship, navigation, sea survival, fire-fighting, damage control and radar training before 400 hours' supervised watch-keeping on a major vessel. Later, in 1985, the RCT Training and Logistic Development Team, which included the production and publishing of training pamphlets, was to be established. It was tasked to research, analyse and undertake trials of logistic transport doctrine and equipment development for the whole Army. The team soon built a well-deserved record of thorough and objective trialing and innovative conceptual development.

TA Training

It was widely accepted that the TA, particularly the Specialist units with no Regular permanent staff on establishment, lacked sufficient opportunity to keep their command and control procedures at peak efficiency. It was a potential weakness on mobilization. In 1983 the Commander RCT TA, Brigadier R E L Jenkins, introduced the Command and Control Trainer at Grantham. Modelled on the Battle Group Trainers at Bovington and Sennelager in BAOR, although less electronically sophisticated, it provided a simple and effective way of practising Command and Control procedures at any level from squadron up to complete formation. It was opened by the Inspector General TA and shortly afterwards visited by the Colonel-in-Chief. It consisted of a central map table with control consoles and, spread around the barracks, a series of command-post bunkers, all linked by simple but adequate communications. It was an instant success and has been continuously developing in scope and facilities since it was opened. In addition to every RCT TA regiment conducting their own weekend exercises, it has been used for wider logistic training by Regular courses from the Service Schools, Brigade and District headquarters for Home Defence Exercises, HQ BAOR and HQ Rear Combat Zone to exercise their TA units in the years when they were unable to go to BAOR, and by the Logistic Support Group. With decreasing opportunities for large field exercises either on the Continent or at home, the CCT is likely to play an increasingly important role in the future.

TA Recruiting and Retention

At this time the RCT TA mirrored the TA as a whole in the difficulties of recruiting and retention. In the Independent Regiments the pattern varied between regions. Some regiments were able to recruit to full establishment and over with soldiers, the undoubted attractions of driving playing a major part, and yet be chronically short of officers. Other regiments, able to pick their officers from plenty of aspiring candidates, found it harder to recruit sufficient soldiers. Specialist units, requiring a recruit to have the right type of driving licence before acceptance, rarely exceeded eighty percent of establishment. This was particularly so in the Movement Control units whose role and skills are difficult to explain to the potential recruit. Retention of the trained Volunteer proved an intractable problem. The pressures of job and family and the financial and other constraints on training with the proper equipment inevitably led to a waning of enthusiasm. In Independent regiments the average turnover was a third annually. In Specialist units, with less demand on time, the turnover rather less, at around seventeen percent. In both areas the result was a need for continuous recruiting.

Officers and Senior NCOs tending to serve for much longer periods experienced increasing pressures from their civilian employment in the eighties and early nineties. In Specialist units a particular difficulty was finding officers able to give the time for command at squadron level. With no Permanent Staff Administrative Officer, regular SNCOs or clerical staff, the amount of work they were required to do at home, in addition to fifty or sixty days a year training at Grantham, was inhibiting. The work at home was a known but unquantified factor. In 1989 the Commander RCT TA, Colonel A E W Stormer, commissioned a working party led by Lieutenant Colonel A S Feldman, who had just finished commanding 160 Regiment, to identify the size of the problem and make recommendations. The 'Feldman Report', based on a wide statistical survey of scores of current and former COs and OCs proved to be a most valuable document. It received wide circulation within the Ministry of Defence, many of the recommendations were adopted and it provided authentic evidence to support establishment cases for increases in permanent staff.

BAOR

New Tank Transporter Fleet Replacement

In 1984 the faithful but ageing Mighty Antar tank transporter in service with the Corps since the fifties was replaced by the high-technology Scammell Commander train in RCT Tank Transporter units, mainly located in BAOR. The Commander's 650 bhp Rolls Royce CV12 TCE diesel engine driving through a semi-automatic gear box produced a greatly enhanced performance compared to its predecessors. Transit times for operational movements were much speedier and the Commander was a quantum leap forward in the transportation of armoured vehicles. Not without its teething problems, it had by the early nineties reached sustainable reliability. It also provided considerably more comfort and hence less operating fatigue for the crew. These overall assets proved invaluable when subsequently the bulk of the vehicle fleet was deployed outside BAOR in their vital role in the Gulf War, lifting the Challenger 2 Main Battle Tanks (MBTs) of our Force under testing desert operating conditions.

Until the ending of the Cold War in 1989 the Corps tank transporter fleet in BAOR was vital to the General Deployment Plan (GDP) of 1st British Corps. Without it 1 (BR) Corps could not deploy to war and the daily tank transporter availability state was one of the Corps Commander's more important considerations, especially as there were no spare transporters or semi-trailers at depot stock. 7 Tank Transporter Regiment's total holdings were some 160 'trains'. The Chieftain Main Battle Tank (MBT) was too wide for movement by rail without extensive removal of

The new Tank Transporter – the Scammell Commander.

The first Mighty Antar delivered to the Army in September, 1951.

exterior equipment. The peacetime unit barracks were mostly well over 100 kilometres from the planned deployment area and road movement was required.

One of the first movements planned for 1 (BR) Corps when deploying for war was the use of 16 Tank Transporter Squadron at Fallingbostel to move the only RE Armoured Engineer Regiment of 1 (BR) Corps from its peace time base at Munsterlager. This location was outside the Corps area of operations and the lift required some forty-eight Centurion AVREs and 'Op rigged' (bridges mounted) Centurion and Chieftain AVLB into the GDP area. After deploying the Armoured Engineers, 16 Squadron would then concentrate upon Sennelager where all three Tank Transporter Squadrons were needed to deploy 1 (BR) Corps Covering Force armour from their peacetime barracks to the forward locations. Having deployed the Covering Force, all transporters would move westwards for a second time to pick up and deploy the armour of the Main Defensive Battle, which, if time was short, would already have started to move from its various barracks on its own tracks. Two regimental lifts were required to complete this deployment.

The tank transporters had one final but unquantifiable role and that was to recover battle-damaged tanks from the Covering Force battle at the east side of the Corps deployment area and transport these westwards, so that REME could then repair them. The tanks would then be available to deploy as part of the all-important final Corps Counter-Stroke battle. Tank recovery is a slow operation and if the Corps had gone to war there is little doubt that, in the fast-moving Covering Force battle, successful tank recovery on any large scale would have been a considerable problem.

Training – Exercise LIONHEART 1984

In September, 1984, Exercise LIONHEART, the second major reinforcement exercise since the end of the Second World War, saw the largest movement of military manpower and equipment across the English Channel since that time. This exercise was designed to practise the BAOR transition to war and war plans, and covered activity from the Continental Channel ports to the former inner German border involving the complete spectrum of RCT support.

The Exercise was dovetailed into:

● The reinforcement of 1(BR) Corps for its (normally) annual 'Field Training exercise' (FTX) Exercise SPEARPOINT; the majority of the reinforcements went forward to this exercise via the Corps Reinforcement Group (CRG) located at Sennelager.

● The activation of the UK Line of Communication (L of C) through airfields and the Channel ports in the UK and Belgium and along the designated 'tube' of routes through Belgium, the Netherlands and Germany; and

● The annual US Exercise REFORGER; in 1984 this exercise included the move of III (US) Corps from its base in Fort Hood, Texas, to its Assembly Area ('CRAFTY FOX') near Münster, in the middle of the British-designated military area of Germany – close behind the 1(BR) Corps Rear Boundary. III (US) Corps was the designated NATO Reserve Corps in the AFCENT (Allied Forces Central Europe, under SHAPE) area.

Following on from the successful Exercise CRUSADER of 1980, Exercise LIONHEART proved, for the Corps, that a number of lessons had been learned. In particular the need to create a more efficient port transit area for the reception of the many hundreds of vehicles arriving on the Continent by sea had been recognized, and with the cooperation of the Belgian Army a new convoy marshalling area was established near Zeebrugge. Prior planning and daily contact with both the Belgians and Dutch were key factors in ensuring that reinforcements passed smoothly through the Low Countries on their way to Germany. The manning of the L of C was also improved, with reinforcements from the Depot and Training Regiment RCT, the School of Transport, British Support Command Liaison and Movement staff (V) and a detachment of movement staff from RAF Lyneham. In this way full cover was provided from Zeebrugge through to the German border.

The UK L of C on the Continent was activated by the mobilization and deployment of Host Nation Movement and Traffic Control personnel with an increasing UK presence as the phases of Exercise LIONHEART developed through the declaration of the various NATO Alert Measures, ie.

● Military Vigilance and Simple Alert – the deployment of in-Theatre, Regular personnel – both Army and RAF.

● Reinforced Alert – Regular Army personnel mainly from the UK Army Training Organization (known as 'RED RUM' personnel) followed by Reserve Forces (Army and RAF) individuals and units.

Whilst road traffic provided most of the lift for normal day-to-day movement and exercises, transition to war and war would have involved the L of C movements staffs in considerable rail and air movement. Reinforcements, on light scales, would have been arriving from UK by air to collect their equipment and vehicles from the advanced base at Emblem before moving on into Germany.

Many thousands of non-combatants who were scheduled for evacuation to UK in the event of war, and arriving from BAOR and the Low Countries by train, would also have required processing. Later, in a similar way, battle casualties would have been arriving in one of ten scheduled ambulance trains for onward movement to the UK. All in all, any declaration of an official state of transition to war or move towards war itself would have created a massive movements task for the HQ RCT L of C movements staff.

Movement on the Continent was controlled by the Host Nations through a system of 'Movement Credits', which defined routes and timings. On crossing the Netherlands/German border, all UK (and some US Exercise REFORGER) reinforcements passed through the UK Staging Area at Leuth which was adjacent to one of the US Army pre-stocked vehicles and equipment depots. From Leuth, the designated UK reinforcements moved along the L of C to the 1(BR) Corps CRG at Sennelager and on to the Corps Exercise. Further 'realizm' was provided by the introduction of a river crossing of the River Rhine to the north of D;auusseldorf, simulating the destruction of the Rhine bridges. The ferries used were provided and operated by Germany army engineers.

The concurrent US Exercise REFORGER was significant in its overall effect on LIONHEART. The move from the Continental ports allocated to the US Forces (principally Rotterdam and Eemshaven in the Netherlands) of the US (III) Corps to its Assembly Area was parallel to the UK L of C 'tube', and did not conflict. However, the operational deployment of III (US) Corps by HQ AFCENT to the south of Germany later in the exercise crossed the UK L of C and had considerable effect on the last of the UK reinforcements moving to 1(BR) Corps and on the continuous movement of ammunition stores, vehicles and equipment to maintain the British Corps in the field. To de-conflict the various Movement priorities, HQ AFCENT created a multi-national Joint Movement Control Centre (North), the JMCC (N), which was located in the German Army Movement Headquarters in Münster. The UK was represented by in-theatre Regular Army staff with TAVR reinforcements. JMCC (N) was exercised for the first time during Exercise LIONHEART and proved invaluable in ensuring that national movement requirements were met according to the overall priorities allocated by HQ AFCENT on behalf of SHAPE.

Exercise FULL FLOW, the British Support Forces field training exercise in the Communication and Rear Combat Zones, incorporated the reinforcement of BAOR and RAF (Germany) by Regular, Territorial Army and Individual reinforcements. For Exercise SPEARPOINT, the field training exercise for 1 (BR) Corps, a total of 48,500 troops, 9,000 vehicles and 5,000 trailers and equipments were successfully moved, despite appalling weather conditions, from the United Kingdom using commercial shipping and aircraft as well as the RAF's Air Transport Force.

Overall, Exercise LIONHEART involved the use of military and civilian ships and aircraft, UK and Continental railways and military and civil police organizations of the five nations directly involved (UK, US, Belgium, Netherlands and Germany).

The War Plans for mobilisation and reinforcement of the British Army of the Rhine were realiztically practised and found to be generally sound and the co-operation and goodwill of the various host nations were tested to the limit and found to provide all the help needed and expected.

In terms of transition to war reinforcement plans, the UK level of participation represented approximately eighty percent of the Regular reinforcements and about fifty percent of the Territorial Army reserves. Over 8,400 RCT personnel were deployed on the exercise, of whom 3,834 were from the Territorial Army, and over six million miles were driven by RCT vehicles. The value of this exercise to the RCT, with their major contribution in both transport and movement tasks, was indisputable since it provided the most practical of opportunities for the Corps in Germany to practice its war role.

Other Training Exercises

In 1989 a further BAOR reinforcement exercise, PLAIN SAILING, took place, but this time it was only of limited scale and was designed primarily to practice movement along the L of C. Approximately 12,000 troops and 2,500 vehicles were involved, using fifty-nine aircraft sorties and sixty-two sailings on the normal commercial cross-channel ferries. This necessitated the participation of the complete Movement Control organization on the Continent augmented by the Territorial Army Movement Control units and individual reinforcements.

Frequent readiness and deployment exercises, such as QUICK TRAIN, ROCKING HORSE and ACTIVE EDGE, were very much a part of everyone's life in BAOR, and units were kept at constant readiness to deploy into the field. A general requirement was that units should be able to deploy from barracks, ready for war, in under six hours. Such had been the situation for very many years, and it was because of the high degree of readiness required that the bulk of the RCT's regular manpower was based in Germany. During the late 1980s, as government reductions in spending began to take effect and the General Deployment Plan adjusted, the formations based in Germany were reduced, and with them the number of RCT units in support. In addition, the detailed structure of each RCT unit was tailored to meet the specific requirements of the formation it supported, to make maximum use of the scarce Regular and Reserve manpower.

The Logistic Shortfall Problem

The Battle Attrition Study and Review of Ammunition Rates and Scales (BAS/RARS) in the eighties were extensive investigations into likely ammunition expenditure rates in high-intensity conflicts. These rates, on which logistic support provision was based, led to a reassessment of the BAOR war maintenance ammunition liability and the rates of replenishment artillery units would require. The quantity of ammunition was doubled and rates of fire of the guns increased by a factor of five. The balance of RCT second-line transport support significantly shifted in that almost 75% of available lift would be required to support the Royal Artillery and the remainder would be left in support of Brigades and Battle Groups.

These studies followed the first major BAOR Field Training Exercise to take place for some years, Exercise CRUSADER, held in 1980. Later experience gained during the Falklands campaign demonstrated clearly that the transport lift at all lines of transport support was inadequate up to a factor of three.

The logistic problem this presented to the RCT was compounded by other changes – the General Deployment Plans (GDPs) progressively moved the chosen ground for a main defensive battle forward from the River Weser area to the River Leine and then up to the inner German border. The problem that this longer L of C produced was further exacerbated by the removal of unit A2 Echelon vehicles from the teeth arms as a savings measure under the Army Restructuring Plan 1974. This effectively drew forward even more second-line RCT support to the Battle Groups to cover the gap created in the logistic resupply chain. Changes to the vehicle fleet and transportation systems were therefore essential, and, in order to increase the rates of replenishment over a longer L of C, vehicle load capacities had to be increased and mechanical handling equipment widely introduced into service. Although the palletization of loads had become standard, the movement of individual pallets by the current mechanical handling equipment was too slow to meet the increased demands of the Royal Artillery and more efficient means had to be found.

Meeting The Transport Bill

Bulk fuel carriers completely replaced the jerrican with the exception of a small holding of jerricans which had to be held at first line, predominantly by the Royal Armoured Corps.

A DROPS MMLC (Medium Mobility Load Carrier) in RCT use towing a DROPS trailer.
The Leyland vehicle is loaded with a flatrack containing MLRS (Multiple Launch Rocket System).

However, the major development was the introduction of DROPS technology at all lines of support mainly for the artillery ammunition resupply chain. DROPS, standing for Demountable Rack Offload and Pick-up System, was based on commercially developed and proven hydraulic lifting equipment used for waste disposal. This equipment, mounted on a commercial chassis with automatic gearbox and modified to give a medium mobility performance, together with a large trailer, virtually trebled lift capacity and reduced turnaround times by a factor of six.

After a successful development programme, the DROPS equipment was introduced into service during 1990 when the overall effects of the ending of the Cold War were emerging and just in time to see active service in the Gulf War. The details of its usage there are given in Chapter 11. Its lift capacity, speed and versatility made a significant contribution to the logistic effort and enabled planned restructuring of Corps Regular units and TA units in support of BAOR to go ahead. It was also introduced into the Royal Artillery for the first-line carriage of ammunition. At this stage, however, although the original problem of logistic transport shortfall in BAOR had been substantially overcome, the situation was soon to change completely as the Government re-assessed its defence policy with the ending of the Cold War. Options for Change, the Government's plan to meet the new world-wide defence situation was to affect the whole structure of the Army and its logistic support, and is introduced at the end of this Chapter. Concurrent with the development of DROPS, rail transfer equipment (RTE) was developed to enable the flat rack to be transferred from road to rail flats.

Rail transfer equipment.

Contract Hire

Not all developments related to RCT-owned equipment procured through the Service system. New ways of delivering capability were being explored. In 1987 twenty-eight Mercedes transporters and trailers were hired on contract from Ryder Trucks. These were straight commercial vehicles, hired for seven years, originally driven by the MSO drivers of 617 Tank Transporter unit and latterly by soldiers of 7 Tank Transporter Regiment RCT. This contract hire was one of the most significant developments of the decade and paved the way for the introduction of hire for all other types of administrative 'B' vehicles, often as a cost-saving measure (it being cheaper to hire the Mercedes than to buy, maintain, repair and replace a similar fleet), but also to provide vehicles that were no longer available through the procurement system.

While the Commander tank transporters were deployed on Operation GRANBY in the Gulf War, many of their lighter tasks back in BAOR were performed by the twenty-eight Mercedes transporters and trailers on contract hire.

To reinforce the value of this hire, thirteen of the Mercedes transporter trains were sent subsequently on Operation GRAPPLE in Yugoslavia, with the full backing of Ryders, since none of the thirty-five tonne tractors in service was considered suitable for the job.

A hired Mercedes Transporter and Trailer operated by 7 Tank Transporter Regiment.

NORTHERN IRELAND

In Northern Ireland there was little apparent political progress during the 1980s. For the Army the high manpower bill was becoming increasingly difficult to bear as it was having a debilitating effect on the whole field Army but particularly in BAOR. In the Province the Army did what it could by altering its operating procedures to reduce the overt surface travel which was manpower intensive, a simple administrative journey requiring a two-vehicle packet with five armed men as a minimum. Where possible plain or covert vehicles, needing only a driver, were adopted, while for operational unit moves the maximum use of helicopters was made. The introduction of the Boeing Chinook into RAF service greatly helped. In this way it was possible gradually to reduce the size of the RCT roulement force from a two-squadron regiment to a reinforced squadron. The squadron was to run the West Belfast Roulement Battalion APC fleet, provide a similar company lift for the Londonderry battalion, provide drivers for the EOD and ambulance APCs, operate the Freight Service and provide the Province Reserve GT lift. It also included a large REME element to man the Moscow Camp workshop. With a strength in excess of nearly 240 all ranks each roulement squadron tour made one complete BAOR squadron and elements of several others non-effective for nearly a year by the time that pre and post-tour training and leave were added to the tour itself. While fully supporting the Corps in the Province, successive Commanders RCT and Directors General of Transport and Movements made it plain to General Officers Commanding Northern Ireland and to Commanders Transport and Movements NI that they wished to reduce the roulement commitment to 150 as soon as practically possible.

The lower military profile of the Security Forces in the mid 1980s and a number of equipment developments made the 150-man roulement target look possible. The Humber Armoured 1-ton, the 'Pig', which incidently weighed ten times its nominal weight, was to be replaced. In Belfast and Londonderry its place was to be taken by the Land Rover Armoured Patrol Vehicle, or APV, which was based on Range Rover automotive parts and V8 petrol engine. This would be driven by the Infantry. The EOD 'Pigs' were to be replaced by an armoured Dodge van driven by RAOC personnel, and the Army's new wheeled APC, the GKN 'Saxon', was to be introduced, but in reduced numbers, to replace the 'Pig' reserve fleet. Savings in REME personnel were also anticipated.

On the strength of these changes the roulement squadron was to be reduced progressively and the first reduction was taken to coincide with the introduction of the APV in Belfast and Londonderry in 1985/86. All did not go well. The Royal Marines Commando and the Infantry Battalions which first operated the APV were unprepared for the intensive maintenance operation needed to keep the fleet of sophisticated vehicles operational. Nor were they able to come up with the total of nearly 150 trained drivers they would need to give each rifle section 'brick' a driver capable of coping safely with the high-powered, four-and-a-half ton, vehicle. Availability plummeted and the accident toll rose.

Commander Transport & Movements sent in a trouble-shooting team from the Roulement Squadron team and the resulting proposals were swiftly adopted. This amounted to the Corps managing servicing and maintenance and providing a core pool of experienced drivers. The accident rate fell and serviceability rapidly improved.

Elsewhere other problems were working against further reductions in Corps manpower. The new EOD armoured vans had increased in all-up weight and one of the two variants had exceeded the maximum limit for non-HGVs. This had serious implications for the standard and qualifications of the drivers, bearing in mind that these vehicles had to be driven safely at speed, as every deployment was an emergency. Chief Ammunition Technical Officer Northern Ireland and Commander Transport & Movements jointly recommended that RCT drivers should remain attached to the EOD teams and continue to drive the new vehicles in this responsible and prestigious duty. This prudent measure was accepted. The Corps in Northern Ireland therefore found itself meeting an unchanged commitment but with reduced manpower. Great credit is reflected on 26 Squadron and the successive roulement squadrons for the way in which the necessary adjustments were made with undiminished enthusiasm and commitment.

As the 1980s progressed the Corps found itself facing the indefinite prolongation of the major commitment of both permanent and roulement troops to the Northern Ireland garrison. The Army itself had settled into a routine which made increasing use of air and surface travel to move troops in and out of the Province rapidly, and more and more commercial logistic support was now provided from sources on the mainland. There was therefore an increasing emphasis on all aspects of Movements, whilst the leisure patterns of the garrison troops and their families also demanded a comparable travel bureau service. Local military operations were now frequently mounted as short set pieces of maximum effort, even comparatively simple engineer construction programmes. These meant that covert vehicles were exchanged for fully-manned 'green' vehicles and maximum security was laid on. Such operations typically lasted between two and four days – the massive manpower requirement could not be sustained longer – and required perfect co-ordination for success. Headquarters Northern Ireland normally delegated the detailed planning and operation control to one of the three Brigade headquarters. Commander Transport and Movements, Lieutenant Colonel M J I Cubitt, who had previously commanded 26 Squadron, found that his position as head of logistics Service staff in HQ Northern Ireland was not compatible with the need to do business frequently and easily at Brigade level where unit commanding officers were the people who mattered.

During the seventies the presence of an RCT Roulement Regiment in the theatre made an RCT CO and RHQ available to liaise with Brigade HQs and their commanding officers. In retrospect the real value of this arrangement was that it gave the Corps appropriate representation in matters of operational command and control which directly affected the way Corps units were able to do their main task – that of providing operational transport support. There was an increasing awareness of the *ad hoc* state of the Corps organization after nearly twenty years of improvisation. With no end to the military requirement in Northern Ireland in sight, it was necessary that the Corps in the Province should be organized on a more permanent and satisfactory footing, with a medium to long-term plan for unit administration, personnel management and internal affairs. To meet these requirements the solution was in forming a Transport and Movements Regiment from the Headquarters Staff, 26 Squadron, the Moscow Camp staff and the roulement units. Approval was given in 1988 to submit plans and proposals for the formation of this regiment. It was left to Lieutenant Colonel M G R Hodson to refine the planning, complete the detailed staff work and maintain the momentum which saw 21 Transport and Movements Regiment successfully formed. Long-term planning demanded much hard work with little immediate result, but this slowly produced undoubted benefits for the Corps.

First, new purpose-built accommodation for 26 Squadron, the Curragh Block, was opened in 1988. This latter became the new RHQ but the building was seriously damaged by a car bomb when terrorists penetrated the garrison security. Moscow Camp was eventually able to be given up.

MILITARY AID TO THE CIVIL MINISTRIES AND COMMUNITIES (MACM AND MACC)

The following paragraphs give examples of the types of MACM and MACC in which the Corps were involved.

MACM – The London Ambulance Dispute

Of the five ambulance disputes, Operation ORDERLY, which lasted from November, 1989, to March, 1990, is probably the best remembered, and London, because of its geographical location became the focal point for the dispute, which was based on pay and conditions of service. In late October, 1989, it was apparent that the Department of Health would not be able to cope with an all-out strike and contingency plans to employ service personnel, Metropolitan and City Police were prepared. Fortunately, G3 Operations, Medical and Transport Branches in Headquarters London District, Horse Guards had a week to plan the logistics and possible refresher training that might be required for a military response. As is normal, things always happen at short notice. Having allowed seven days to prepare, units found that on the Friday afternoon prior to the strike Ready for Deployment time was reduced to forty-eight hours.

HQ London District established a firm base at Chelsea Barracks and were able to muster a variety of sixty ambulances. It was quickly agreed that a policeman should ride in front of each ambulance as a local guide, troubleshooter and radio operator. The majority of drivers were found from 20, 56 and other RCT Squadrons, together with elements from the Household Cavalry, Foot Guards, Royal Artillery Band Woolwich and RAF. In the pre-deployment weekend Chelsea Barracks was a hive of activity with ambulances arriving from all over the United Kingdom. Medical stores were delivered, and some 500 individuals were processed and given refresher training. Everything had to be ready for deployment by 0900 hours Monday 6 November, 1989, and it was. Once deployed, the ambulance crews were based on local Police Stations throughout the London area and remained there until the dispute ended some four months later.

Reception at hospital accident and emergency departments was at first mixed and, in one case, hostile, but within a week all that had changed. With one or two exceptions, hospitals receiving patients were extremely helpful and, in some cases, crews even ate their Christmas dinners with the hospital staffs.

More than half the ambulance· tasks involved elderly people. Drivers and accompanying police officers were often confronted with the problem of getting patients out of high-rise blocks when lifts had failed. One twenty-seven stone patient who had been confined to his flat for many years was let down on a hoist via his bedroom window. The happiest events were drivers being called on to assist medics with live births which took place on twelve occasions whilst prospective mothers were being rushed to hospital.

The military ambulance was not designed for high-speed emergency journeys in heavy traffic and it is to the great credit of all drivers taking part in Operation ORDERLY that they handled the vehicles as well as they did. About a million and a half miles were driven by ambulances during the dispute, carrying some 62,100 various patients. The ambulance dispute clearly demonstrated the quality of the Corps' drivers when faced with a challenge. They proved to be attentive, resolute and caring when it mattered.

MACC – Winter Relief 1990

There were countless occasions when RCT units provided help to their local community, most during periods of harsh weather. One such example was Operation BARROW when high winds, heavy snow and severe icing on Wednesday 5 December, 1990, heralded the start of a ten-day period in which a large part of the Peak District and the East Midlands ground to a virtual standstill. Initial assistance of four self-drive Land Rovers was granted to the Lincolnshire Constabulary due to the paucity of their own cross-country vehicles. The heavy icing and high winds had a swift and progressively more serious effect on the National electricity grid. The Electricity Board were faced with the massive problem of providing emergency services and to this end the Services, already heavily committed to Operation GRANBY support, were required to assist. Four teams of four Land Rovers and four-ton vehicles were deployed to Nottingham, Derby, Mansfield and Newark-on - Trent. An Operations Room was manned on a twenty-four hour basis from Friday, 5 December until Friday, 14 December, 1990. Teams were progressively withdrawn and redeployed to other locations as the East Midland Electricity Board workload demanded.

The history of using the Armed Forces in the MACM and MACC roles indicates a great deal of success and highlights the Services' adaptability and resourcefulness under often difficult and conflicting conditions. The RCT always rose to their widely varying challenges with cheerfulness, good humour and, above all, professionalism. An often unsung record, but one that the Corps could be proud of.

THE END OF THE COLD WAR – GERMANY

Berlin

In 1989 the Soviet leader, Mikhail Gorbachev, withdrew his invasion forces from Afghanistan, these having been an obstacle in negotiating a reduction in East/West tension, and followed this action with the introduction of a more liberalized régime in the Soviet Union. Within some Eastern Bloc countries, including East Germany, those opposed to Communist rule took advantage of this relaxation to overthrow their own particular Communist régimes in an astonishing revolt, which was to lead to the ending of the Cold War and, in particular, the reunification of Germany.

The first manifestation of this ending was the breaching, by the citizens of East Berlin, of the hated Berlin Wall, which for twenty-eight years had symbolized the division between the Soviet Union and the Western Powers.

On 9 November, 1989, the people of Berlin awoke to find that this prominent dividing wall had been breached and free movement between East and West was once again possible. The swift removal of all but a few hundred yards of wall heralded, ironically, greater restrictions on military movement than before, and 62 Squadron in Berlin immediately became involved in this swiftly changing movements situation. A new 'control' never before experienced in Berlin, the *Verkehrskommandatur* (German Army Movement Control Group), arrived to insist on authorizing all military road moves within and outside the city. All tracked vehicles, when authorized, needed blue light German civil police escorts and could only leave Berlin via the railway system. Gone were the days of Chieftain main battle tanks patrolling the Kurfurstendamm, gone too were the days of slipping to the bank in the section armoured personnel carrier! Reunification and the withdrawal of Soviet troops, firstly to barracks, questioned the need for the continuance of the Berlin Military Train. However, it was not until 30 September, 1990, that the Soviet forces closed their office at Marienborn and the train could travel simply as a normal scheduled service without special documentation. This new-found freedom was also exercised by the *Reichsbahn* employees, who promptly went on strike for two days on 26 and 27 November, thereby halting the Berlin Military Train for the first time since the Berlin blockade.

The relative luxury provided by the Berlin budget receded as quickly as Germany's annual budget surplus was eaten up by the reunification bill. The first casualty of the new, financially aware UK Berlin Brigade was the Train. Its demise was followed rapidly by the equally expensive freight train, giving the already fully utilized transport assets additional tasks. Dates altered for a variety of political, economic and administrative reasons but the final Berlin Military Train ran to Berlin on 7 February, 1991, with many distinguished passengers present. Shortly afterwards, to mark the end of their service with the Berlin Military Train, the civilian catering crew were dined out by Army Catering Corps chefs. This last 'Berliner' journey was symbolic not only as a marker of contemporary changes within Germany, but rather in eastern Europe as a whole. Though its demise saddened those who had known and worked on the Train, it represented the new spirit of hope that emerged from the end of the Cold War.

Despite the increased restrictions, 62 Squadron's transport was required to go further and further afield in the name of the now high-profile UK Berlin Brigade. Humanitarian aid convoys to Smolensk and supporting the infantry on exercise in Soltau were but two of many new tasks for A Troop. The staff car drivers of B Troop were also brought down to earth when a request to replace their five-year-old Mercedes with the latest model was turned down. They had to settle for upgrading their smaller cars instead.

It was the Soviet Union, or at least its demise, which caused the greatest upheaval. Drawdown, the term used for the new imposed financial restrictions and ultimate withdrawal of the British Brigade in Berlin, was to be total. No one would escape to enjoy the cosseted social life previously enjoyed. However, immediate opportunities for those off duty were enhanced and, although reunification brought increased prices, Berlin now offered more variety for the discerning adventurer. Potsdam was only a few minutes drive away and the border with Poland only forty miles to the east. Travelling west, whereas the 'Corridor' used to cause lengthy delays and frustration, it was now the sheer weight of traffic which prevented a swift journey.

OPTIONS FOR CHANGE

Outline Effect – Regular Army

With the fall of the Berlin Wall and the collapse of the Soviet Union, the operational situation changed dramatically and the opportunity to achieve a 'peace dividend' was soon grasped by the Government, to be known as 'Options for Change'. As the straitjacket of superpower political stability was removed from Eastern Europe and the rest of the world, the nationalist and religious rivalries which had been suppressed came to the fore. It soon became obvious that, in addition to reducing force levels, they would also need to be restructured in order to cope with a new and more versatile role than had been the case under the General Defence Plan. The Army in Germany was thus reduced from three armoured divisions to one, with those units returning to the United Kingdom being used to form a mechanized division, designed to react rapidly to military crises either within or outside the NATO area. The primary role of the Germany-based division remained the defence of mainland Europe, although it could be deployed elsewhere if required.

This Options for Change re-assessment following the end of the Cold War, with its manpower ceilings and subsequent detailed staffing, resulted in an inability to man all the logistic units required to support both the new, armoured-biased and high-intensity conflict 1 (UK) Division, based in Germany, and the new mechanized-biased 3 (UK) Division based in the United Kingdom. In accordance with the post-Options for Change defence policy, which foresaw a greater probability of an out-of-area deployment of a division to intervene in low or medium intensity conflict, the decision was taken to under-implement 1 (UK) Division's logistic support at both second and third line in Germany in order to retain a balanced, comprehensive and manned logistic support for 3 (UK) Division in the United Kingdom. Consequently both one General Support and two Close Support Regiments, responsible for second-line support for 1 (UK) Division, each had two squadrons under-implemented and regular in-theatre third-line General Transport support was reduced to one DROPS squadron, itself in support of a Royal Artillery MLRS Regiment.

In the event BAOR-based British troops were deployed outside Germany well before the proposed force structure changes were announced. This deployment started in 1990/91 with the Gulf War, described in Chapter 11, and saw over ninety percent of the RCT in Germany deployed outside the theatre, in Northern Ireland, the Gulf and in UN roles, many soldiers and units finding themselves being used in a task for which few had trained. The UN roles are described in Chapter 12.

The Reserve Army

The RCT TA was affected to perhaps an even greater extent than the regular element of the Corps. Like the 1967 Defence Review, the plan was made within the Ministry of Defence in the greatest secrecy. Undoubtedly driven, although never officially admitted, by Treasury-imposed cash limits rather than defence commitments, there was virtually no consultation through the Chain of Command or with the TA itself. With some notable exceptions this was the same for most cap badges. Nor were the Territorial Auxiliary and Volunteer Reserve Associations consulted. When the Secretary of State for Defence eventually made his long-postponed announcement to the House on 10 December, 1991, the reductions came as a shock for all and a bitter blow to many well recruited and highly efficient units sentenced to be disbanded. The inexplicable anomalies and illogicalities of the reductions, particularly among the infantry battalions, resulted in a wave of protests, a widespread publicity campaign and subsequent changes.

The RCT TA was heavily hit, with initial reductions of 34% among the Independent units and 63% of the Specialist. All units were reduced in size. Among the Independents, 155 (Wessex) Regiment was to be disbanded, 153 (Highland) Regiment and 154 (Lowland) Regiment amalgamated as the Scottish Transport Regiment (Volunteers) and 213 (BAOR) squadron disbanded. In the Specialist units, 160 Transport Regiment and 163 Transport and Movements Regiments, a total of seven squadrons, were to be disbanded, together with a further four squadrons of 161 Ambulance Regiment and 162 MC Regiment. RHQ 162 MC Regiment remained, with a new role of commanding the UK Movement Control Squadrons, thus reversing the decision taken in the 1983 reorganization and filling a much-needed gap. The British Support Command Liaison and Movements Staff TA were amalgamated with 496 MCLU as the British Liaison and Movement Staff. In the process they were to be more than halved in size and lose their All Arms element.

The Secretary of State pledged that no eligible Volunteer who wished to stay in the TA would be discharged and the Ministry of Defence instructed units to tell their soldiers their personal future within 48 hours. It was an impossible order. Quite apart from the practical difficulty of contacting every soldier within the time, the information could not be given because it was not known.

The manpower ceiling for most, although not all, units had been published, but until such time as the new establishments had been written and agreed by the MOD the rank structure could only be guessed at. In the case of the RCT TA the coming Logistic Support Corps added a further complication. In the event Commanding Officers did their best and gave what assurances they could. It said much for the resilience of the Volunteers and the quality of the junior leadership that training continued throughout 1992 with nearly normal enthusiasm. This spirit was particularly evident in units due to be disbanded. Turnout for camp was good and to a man they determined to go out with style and on a high note.

Deciding the fate of each individual officer and soldier occupied much of 1992. At Grantham a series of preliminary grading boards for employability were held for all Specialist personnel throughout the summer. When the new establishments for the Royal Logistic Corps were approved in the autumn, posting boards were held to decide who was to stay, who had to leave the TA and who could be overborne for the next year or two. In the Independent regiments each Commanding Officer carried out a similar exercise for his own unit. Many long-serving officers and senior ranks had to leave and almost all did so with dignity and good grace. The coming formation of the RLC on 5 April, 1993, helped in this respect, because for many it provided a natural break point. Among those leaving, many of whom had a third clasp to their Territorial Decoration or Territorial Efficiency Medal, were those who had joined the TA after National Service some thirty years before. It was truly the end of an era. All disbanding units marked their demise with appropriate ceremony, including parades, church services and dinners.

THE LOGISTIC SUPPORT REVIEW (LSR)

Background

The Logistic Support Review (LSR) was simultaneous with Options for Change and was the first serious logistic study since 1975. Its seeds were sown in the Somerville Report of 1976 which resulted in the formation of the Logistic Executive (Army) at Andover. Somerville had brought together the professional and staff responsibilities of the RCT, RAOC and REME with some of QMG's own staff. Somerville recognized, however, that any major change to the logistic Corps should not be made until a 'generation after McLeod'. In the event, the impetus for a logistic review of some sort had been building up in the late 1980s. The LSR itself was in response to many pressures within the Army as a whole and the QMG's area in particular. Started in 1990, the review took nearly a year to complete its work and report to the Executive Committee of the Army Board (ECAB).

The aim of the LSR was 'to examine the Army's logistic support organization and systems to establish how the task of providing logistic support for the Army in peace, transition to war and war might be performed most efficiently and economically'. It looked across all areas of QMG's responsibility. Each of the three major logistic Corps (RCT, RAOC and REME) had a full Colonel representative on the Review; each headed up a team examining a function area not of their own Corps. The Teams visited and consulted widely, and made a large number of recommendations. Their final report was endorsed by the ECAB in June, 1991. The major recommendations were:

● There should be a two-corps structure for logistics, responsible respectively for Service Support and Equipment Support.

● There should be one Director General (DG) responsible for Service Support and one for Equipment Support.

● The QMG and the majority of his London staff should be relocated to Andover to form HQ QMG replacing the Logistic Executive (Army).

● An implementation plan should be produced.

A New Corps

The LSR recognized that 'supply and transport must be interdependent...together they constitute what the civilian world regards as the logistics function'. In essence, the Team recommended the formation of a new Logistic Support Corps encompassing the functions of the RCT, RAOC, RPC, ACC and the postal responsibilities of the RE. The new Corps was to be named The Royal Logistics Corps (The RLC), with its Director General (DG) designated Director General Logistic Support (Army) (DG LogSP(A)). The Report noted that the DG of the new Corps would own a Higher Level Budget of nearly £350m and the proposed Corps would:

● Constitute 14% of the Army's manpower strength and 20% of the TA.

● Total 27,000 officers and men, 75% in formed units with the balance serving elsewhere in the Army.

Retention of REME as a Separate Corps

REME as a Corps was to remain unchanged to carry out its same tasks on the ground with the Field Army, but with important additional equipment support functions. It was to form part of a broad-based Equipment Support Organization (ESO) with the DGEME becoming the Director General of Equipment Support (DGES). The ESO would embrace elements of other Arms and Services concerned with Equipment in Staff appointments, as part of its overall function, bringing together all Army Equipment Management Staffs.

Formation of the Implementation Team

Throughout this period there were momentous changes on the world scene. The Berlin Wall came down; the review of the Armed Forces, known as Options for Change, was put in hand to manage the expected reductions in all three Services (the so-called Peace Dividend); a study of officer careers was undertaken (the Grove Study) and the MOD's own internal structures were reviewed as part of the Prospect Study. On top of all this, Saddam Hussein invaded Kuwait and precipitated the Gulf War, and the drawdown from BAOR began. The work of all those involved in the formation of the new Corps and the disbandment of the old Corps had to be conducted against this backcloth. Many observers recalled the anxieties and concerns expressed during and after the earlier McLeod Study in 1964/65. Some wanted to redress some of the inconsistencies arising from McLeod's original separation of supplies and transport; others were keen to ensure that the new traditions and professional ethos built up by the RCT would not be lost through enforced and over-hasty amalgamation; the smaller Corps feared that their own unique traditions and professional skills would be irrevocably lost in the new Corps.

Once ECAB had agreed to the LSR's findings and recommendations, an LSR Implementation Team was formed to oversee the major elements of the implementation. A small Logistic Secretariat under the direction of Colonel G A Ewer was established at Andover in January, 1992, to take forward the detailed work of bringing together the doctrinal and operational policy aspects of the Forming Corps, and to develop those of the RLC. Major General D L Burden was nominated as the new Director General Logistic Support (Army) (DG LogSP (A)) and Brigadier R M Bullock as Deputy. The question of a Colonel-in-Chief for this huge new Corps was quickly resolved with the appointment of HRH The Princess Royal, with HRH The Duke of Gloucester and HRH The Duchess of Kent as Deputy Colonels-in-Chief. The formation of the new Corps was now in sight, and the details of the method of its creation, and the last activities of the RCT as a Corps in its own right are contained in Chapter 12.

Changes in the Training Organization

The LSR was closely followed by a fundamental Review of the Training Base (RTB) by Inspector General of Doctrine and Training (IGDT). It sought savings of money and manpower by a major rationalization of the training estate. Army Training Regiments (ATRs) formed up as part of Phase I of RTB. RCT recruits were directed to a new ATR at Pirbright in early 1993 to coincide with the formation of the RLC. RCT Junior Leader training was planned to move to Harrogate, but in the event, Army junior leader training ceased in favour of single-entry adult recruits. The last Passing Out Parade of RCT Junior Leaders was in February, 1992. During late 1992 and early 1993 the RCT Training Group refined plans to move instructors to ATR Pirbright in preparation for the first RLC recruit courses and to close Buller Barracks as a Training Centre.

It was agreed that the focus of RLC training would be at Deepcut near Camberley at the Princess Royal Barracks, re-named in honour of the new Corps' Colonel-in-Chief. The School of Transportation moved in the autumn of 1992 to complete RCT courses and to prepare for the new RLC courses. Working Groups from all the contributing Corps had already prepared comprehensive plans for the transfer and restructuring of training to meet the needs of the new Corps. HQ RCT TA remained the focus for RLC TA Training and was retitled HQ RLC TA. Port and Maritime training stayed at Marchwood in a new Combined Training Wing under command of the new Logistic Employment Training School organization at Deepcut. RCT Training at Buller Barracks effectively ceased on 5 April, 1993, and Brigadier A C Massey, the last Commander, handed over the barracks to 27 Transport Regiment RLC.

Throughout its short 27 years the RCT Training Organization unfailingly met the ever-changing operational needs of the Army. Undergoing many changes between formation in 1965 and amalgamation in 1993, the Group ensured that the officers and men of the RCT were well fitted to meet the challenges, new techniques and skills for the diverse tasks they had to undertake in peace and war. From operations in Aden, Northern Ireland, the Falklands and in the Gulf, professional and trained officers and soldiers of the RCT undertook a remarkable variety of operational roles around the world with undoubted success. This legacy of purposeful, well-motivated and highly respected training was passed proudly to the new Royal Logistic Corps.

CHAPTER 11

The Gulf War 1990 to 1991 – Operation Granby

Introduction. Deployment; Early Days – Opening the L of C; Initial RCT Order of Battle; The Outload Starts; TA Involvement. Deployment from NW Europe; By Sea and Air; Preparing for Operations; Support to the Desert Rats; Send more Tank Transporters! Command, Control and Concepts; Command and Control; Logistic Concept Development, Developing the Port of Entry and Building a Firm Base; 10 Transport Group; Baldrick Lines, GRANBY 1.5 and Massive Reinforcement; 27 Regiment joins the Fray; AMF(L) Logistic Battalion; Increasing Port Operations; Controlling both ends of the L of C; the Trawl for Manpower and Resources. The Build Up to War – Desert Deployment; The Desert Deployment starts; Reinforcement completed; Ambulance Support, Tank Transporter Operations; The Tasks; 16 Kilometres of Flashing Lights! Training and Regrouping for War; The Logistic regrouping Plan comes together; Reorganization – 1 ADTR's Story, Pushing forward the Lines of Communication; Support for the FFMA; The Battle Stocks move up; Deploying Ambulance Support; The Long Haul, War and Victory; Ready for War; One Hundred Hours; into Iraq; on to Kuwait; Tank Transporter Support; Casualties; The last L of C, Recovery and Return; Going Home; Getting it all back; The Gurkhas' Return; Some Lessons; Transport Operating Loops; Proven Professionalism.

INTRODUCTION

Operation GRANBY was the name given by the United Kingdom to the deployment of its Forces to the Middle East as part of an international alliance on an operation known initially as DESERT SHIELD and, later, as DESERT STORM. The deployment was in response to unanimous opposition by the international community at the United Nations to the invasion of Kuwait by Iraq on 2 August, 1990. Within two days the United States had deployed forces to Saudi Arabia with the initial aim of forestalling any further incursion into the Gulf area by Iraq, particularly against Saudi Arabia. On 8 August elements of the Royal Navy and the Royal Air Force were sent to the Gulf area. On 14 September the British Government announced that it would send 7 Armoured Brigade (The Desert Rats) from BAOR to operate with the American, Saudi Arabian and other Allied Forces. The Brigade was allocated supporting arms and logistic support grouped into a Force Maintenance Area (FMA). This initial element of the British Force became GRANBY 1. Because the name GRANBY 2 had been earmarked for a possible roulement of the Brigade Group at the end of six months the nickname GRANBY 1.5 was adopted for the commitment in December of massive reinforcement consisting of HQ 1 (British) Armoured Division, 4 Armoured Brigade, an Artillery Group, additional combat support and combat service support elements, making in all a strong armoured division with full logistic support.

This chapter highlights the extraordinary part played by the RCT in the Gulf War. The Corps was by far the largest single cap-badge in Theatre with wide-ranging roles that stretched it to the limits. In the event, the war was an operational and logistic triumph. A large number of complete RCT units were involved, with many individuals from the Corps playing key roles throughout the logistic processes of planning and implementation. There can be no doubt that the contribution made by the RCT for the logistic support of the Force was a decisive factor in the successful outcome of the operation.

An outline of the order of battle of the United Kingdom Forces and the Corps during the operation is given on p.367. These show the units which deployed with 7 Armoured Brigade under GRANBY 1, and the reinforced order of battle when the British Force was finally complete in the theatre after GRANBY 1.5. Formed RCT units are also shown in more detail, but, necessarily, there were many instances of units and sub-units being attached or detached to different regiments; these diagrams are at best a snapshot.

In addition to formed units, the Corps was strongly represented in many important posts. At the Ministry of Defence Colonel M F I Cubitt was the Director of Defence Logistic Movements (DDef Log Mov), a post tied to the RCT, and as such acted as Controller of the Defence Operational Movements Staff (DOMS). In crisis and war DOMS was formed on the nucleus of DDef Log Mov's small staff, considerably augmented by drawing on earmarked personnel, mostly from within the peacetime directorates of movements. DOMS was tasked with the procurement and allocation of all strategic transport resources, both civil and military, ships, aircraft, trains, inland water and road transport. Its functions included the allocation of terminal capacity such as ports and airheads, and the Controller was the resident adviser on strategic mobility to the Chiefs of Staff through the Director of Operations. Elsewhere Corps officers were strongly represented at the Joint Headquarters which had been formed at High Wycombe and at HQ BAOR and UKLF. Colonel J C Lucas, then Commander Transport & Movements HQ UKLF, was appointed Colonel Land Logistics, (handing over in November to Colonel W E J Allen) at the Joint Headquarters. At HQ BAOR Brigadier M W Betts as DQMG, and Brigadier N Muddiman as Commander Transport & Movements, were able to contribute directly to the planning and implementation during the mounting, deployment and sustainment of GRANBY from the Continent.

In the Gulf itself RCT officers and soldiers served on the staff of General Norman Schwarzkopf, the Allied Commander, and at Joint Forces Headquarters at Riyadh, in the FMA, at HQ 1 (BR) Division and both Brigade Headquarters. The key British logistic planners in the theatre were Corps members; Brigadier M S White commanded the Force Maintenance Area and Colonel G A Ewer was the Deputy Chief of Staff of 1 (BR) Armoured Division.

There were four main stages to the campaign;

● The initial deployment to the Gulf.

● The build-up of stocks and reinforcements and training and desert deployments leading up to the start of the air war.

● The 100-hour ground war.

● The aftermath and recovery of the Force.

In practice these stages overlapped and a full chronological account of each unit's part is not to be found in this story; rather it is a representative account of experiences and events as they affected many RCT units and individuals.

DEPLOYMENT

Early Days – Opening the Lines of Communication

Well before the Prime Minister's formal announcement of deployment on 14 September, many RCT officers and soldiers had been involved in highly secret planning teams at the MOD, Joint HQ High Wycombe and at UKLF and BAOR. In the MOD, DDef Log Mov, with the support of D Mov(A), Brigadier G E Bartlett, pressed the Director of Operations for authority to activate a DOMS cadre at the earliest opportunity. This was done on 5 August and contingency movements planning, involving the major commands, started straight away. Thus a framework of movement and logistic operations staff was activated in time to commence the massive task of devising detailed movement instructions, interpreting the ever-changing staff tables and priorities, and finding resources for the greatest deployment of British Forces, certainly since the Suez crisis and, arguably, since the Second World War. But during the first few weeks of August planning was seriously hampered by lack of declared long-term objectives. Initially GRANBY looked like being an RAF task with intervention authorized to last days rather than weeks. This reluctance to admit the possibility of any long-term commitment effectively prevented the accummulation of strategic transport or sustainable stocks. While the RAF build-up continued and looked like absorbing the entire Air Transport Force (ATF), the only ships DOMS was authorized to charter were for the use of USA shipping, as a gesture of 'solidarity'.

By the middle of August it was obvious that the allied intervention would be much longer than originally foreseen, and at last DOMS was able to persuade the Air Staff that shipping should be chartered to carry air weapons to the Gulf, releasing the ATF for other tasks. At the same time DOMS was asked to do movement staff checks on a number of Army and Royal Marine force options and it was clear that a major land involvement was becoming highly likely. DOMS was able to put in hand discreet preparation measures and, although no general chartering authority was in force, an unofficial short list of charter shipping was drawn up, such was the level of goodwill existing between D Mov(A) Staff and a number of reputable European shipping companies. In December, 1990, Brigadier M W Betts took over the appointment of DMov(A). When the order to deploy the first ground forces was given, the first ships were being loaded and were despatched within days.

At Marchwood Military Port (MMP) 17 Port and Maritime Regiment had been loading vessels for the RAF since early September and quickly responded to the new challenge, sending port operators to Cyprus and BAOR. 52 Port Composite Group was formed, with some soldiers sailing on the very first vessels to the Gulf, the LSLs *Sir Tristram* and *Sir Bedivere*. Included as part of this detachment was plant equipment and the three Rough Terrain Container Handlers (RTCH) which could only be despatched aboard the LSLs after removing mudguards and outer front wheels. Movement controllers from 29 Regiment flew out with port operators to open up the air and sea terminals at the Saudi Arabian Gulf port of Al Jubayl and to await the first British troops.

Initial RCT Order of Battle

It was obvious that the force would need a much larger than normal logistic organization to operate over such extended Lines of Communication (from the port of Al Jubayl to the eventual forward area of operations was a distance of some 350 kilometres). Unlike Western Europe, there was no railway infrastructure to support movement, so a strong element of third line road transport support was essential to sustain the extended resupply loop. It was decided, therefore, that the initial RCT support would consist of 1 Armoured Division Transport Regiment (1 ADTR), 10 Corps Transport Regiment (reinforced by 12 Squadron) and elements of 7 Tank Transporter Regiment and 54 Engineer and Ambulance Support Squadron. All were supported by their REME Regimental Workshops. To this were added port operating and movement control detachments from UK. The establishments of RCT regiments and squadrons had to be brought up to their war entitlements of personnel and equipment and elements of specialist units fused into the structure so that tailored support could be provided for 7 Armoured Brigade for desert operations.

The Outload Starts

In UK and BAOR especially there were intensive programmes to outload and redistribute stores to units and despatch them to departure airfields and seaports. New equipment and mobilization stocks were delivered to units. There were extra movement commitments in support of range and other work up training. Units deploying on GRANBY could not lift all their own scales of stores. A bold decision was taken to use ISO containers obtained from trade. In effect, this was the first major deployment of British Forces in which containers were used as the primary means of bulk movement. The recent arrival of DROPS vehicles into RCT field units and the use of the RTCH (inevitably known as 'wretches') from UK offered a workable concept for the deployment of containers forward on operations.

This ability to handle and deliver containers was not without a downside. Containers had to come into use to deliver stores rapidly from UK to BAOR on the 'just in time' principle. Because transit time was so short, under 24 hours, there was no need to track the containers or to know in detail what was in them. As a result no system existed for manifesting container contents in detail. However, transit time for a container from UK depot to FMA in the Gulf was almost a month, and, as more and more containers were filled and despatched, an ever-increasing proportion of precious and scarce material was at sea and lost to view. Although the Corps was quickly able to put together an effective system for tracking containers, a working system for providing visibility of the contents was never achieved, despite being a major preoccupation of QMG's staff. This was to have serious consequences. GRANBY units developed a lack of confidence in the supply chain which resulted in repeat or over-demanding, adding unnecessary tonnage to the hard-pressed Sea Train and Air Bridge.

The outload of stores and troops was a massive joint military and civil undertaking. Units of every sort were pressed into service including many RCT TA units on annual camps. From UK elements of 17 Port and Maritime Regiment and 29 Regiment, together with 1 and 7 Squadrons, were sent to assist BAOR. Transport support was also provided by 601 Transport Battalion of the Bundeswehr and the United States 501 Transport Battalion. 79 Railway Squadron came into its own and, by happy coincidence, 275 Railway Squadron (V) was training in BAOR at the time. Extensive use was also made of the excellent German railway infrastructure, especially for the outloading of ammunition from 3 Base Ammunition Depot (BAD) Bracht, 154 Forward Ammunition Depot (FAD) Wulfen and the Forward Storage Sites.

Territorial Army Involvement

All TA RCT units were involved in some way with operation GRANBY. Although individuals could not be mobilized, they could volunteer to join the Regular Army on a Short Service Volunteer Commission for officers or an 'S' type engagement for soldiers, and many did so. Almost two hundred volunteered to join 15 Squadron RCT, who were due to undertake a six-month tour with the United Nations in Cyprus in January, 1992. The troops of the squadron were needed for the Gulf and were replaced by two TA officers and one hundred soldiers who were commanded by the Regular SHQ. When volunteers were called for, the response from every Independent and Specialist unit was magnificent. Major D J Bowcock, a Retired Officer running Soldiers' Records at HQ RCT TA, was tasked with mobilizing the squadron. There was a considerable imbalance in age and rank, and after several weeks of preliminary work some 125 were called to Grantham for screening and attestation. A Temporary Mobilization Centre was set up staffed by a RAMC TA detachment from 202 General Hospital(V), the clerks of Soldiers' Records and the Army Recruiting Officer from Lincoln. In one very long and crowded weekend the final hundred were chosen, enlisted and handed over to Major S D Bragg OC 15 Squadron for brief training before flying to Cyprus. Their tour was thoroughly successful. Many lessons were learnt, not least that the Regular Army screening standards, designed to select a few 18-year-olds from many hundreds of applicants, needed some adjustment when applied to TA volunteers, many ten or more years older, who had experienced something of life. Duty officers at the Ministry of Defence and the RCT Manning and Record Office were gratifyingly co-operative in granting waivers to allow the ACTO to proceed. MOD observers had visited the TMC and Grantham was subsequently designated the mobilization centre for the whole of the Army, should the need arise again during the war.

Many hundreds of TA personnel in complete units and as individuals were involved in the outloading and mounting of Operation GRANBY in UK and BAOR, either during their annual camp or as volunteers for longer periods. 213 (BAOR) Transport Squadron, a TA unit based in Munchengladbach and recruited from UK nationals living in Germany, worked almost continuously over a protracted period providing transport support. 151 (Greater London) Regiment, on annual camp in BAOR, switched to outloading tasks and individuals stayed on in Germany after camp. Virtually all other Independent regiments provided drivers and vehicles in support of their Districts during the mounting phase. 275 Railway Squadron, on annual camp with 79 Railway Squadron, found themselves performing their mobilization role outloading depots for 7 Armoured Brigade deployment. 288 MC Squadron, reporting for annual camp in UK, were put on aircraft and flown complete to BAOR, and many individual Movement Control personnel volunteered for additional training and went to BAOR as *ad hoc* groups. 265 Port Squadron, camping at Marchwood, stowed ships with even greater urgency than usual. 496 Movement Control Liaison Unit, due to camp in late February, 1991, found themselves called in at very short notice a month early and deployed to assist the US forces outloading for DESERT STORM. Almost every member of the unit obtained leave of absence from their employer, or were, at considerable cost and inconvenience to themselves, able to rearrange their affairs in order to report for duty. That employers, during a severe economic recession, were so supportive was a most encouraging sign. It was some small but important recompense for the deep disappointment felt throughout the Territorial Army and by many Regulars that the Government had baulked at mobilizing the volunteers when it was increasingly obvious to all concerned that the Regular Army was stretched to the limit. The part played by 496 MCLU was subsequently recognized by the award of the United States Secretary of Defense commendation to Lieutenant Colonel S S Haywood TD, the Senior Officer of the unit.

DEPLOYMENT FROM NW EUROPE

By Sea and Air

The British Force and its equipment and stocks were deployed mainly by sea from the north German ports of Bremerhaven and Emden and from Marchwood Military Port (MMP). In BAOR a Port Task Group was established in order to co-ordinate the arrival by road and rail of vehicles, equipment, ammunition and stores for loading to ships. Between the period 28 September to 15 October thirty-three vessels were loaded with almost 4,000 vehicles and trailers, and 15,000 tons of cargo. DOMS was able to keep ahead of the demand for shipping, using the Baltic Exchange and the Government Freight Agents to charter, and there were no delays for want of shipping either in UK ports or in Germany. However, the proportion of British-flagged vessels offered at suitable rates was low and remained a concern. Of more immediate worry was the vast quantity of ammunition to be outloaded from British and German ports in peacetime, quantities which greatly exceeded peacetime safety limits, even after Government relaxation had been obtained. The only way round this was to use remote ports or quays and to resort to lightering and loading at anchor in roadsteads. This meant that fast and modern shipping such as the larger Ro-Ros and container ships could not be used for ammunition, the only available small ships with a self-loading capability being generally of the older 'tramp' type. The civilian stevedores who did the largest part of this dangerous and difficult stowing task throughout the autumn and winter months were magnificent.

Although a few soldiers were sent by sea to act as on-board escorts, the vast majority of the troops deployed by air from RAF Gutersloh and Hamburg civil airport using RAF Tristars, VC10s and Hercules, with some British Airways Tristars on charter. In UK the Air Mounting Centre (AMC) at South Cerney passed troops direct to RAF Lyneham. From the onset of Operation GRANBY 29 Regiment was tasked to give movements support to key UK units with small detachments in support of the SAS and other special forces. As September approached, the scale of the movements required became apparent and the AMC was fully activated. In the meantime, work at MMP continued unabated with the various phases of deployment merging into each other. 17 Regiment was operating at both ends of the sea train and scarcely drawing breath between each stage of the deployment. Job satisfaction and morale were nevertheless at an all-time high. The throughput of freight of all commodities, including vehicles, break bulk, ammunition and thousands of ISO containers, exceeded all previous records. Sheer statistics cannot reflect the often appalling conditions and long hours of work under which this work was achieved. In the Gulf weather conditions varied from near freezing temperatures at night, through bouts of torrential rain, to blistering heat. At one stage, port operators were operating in cargo holds at temperatures of 140 degrees Fahrenheit. For everyone hours of work were typically between eighty and ninety per week on twelve-hour shifts, seven days a week. To this was added the constant threat of air and chemical attack.

PREPARING FOR OPERATIONS

Support to the Desert Rats

For the RCT units warned for deployment to Saudi Arabia in support of 7 Armoured Brigade, preparations began immediately for Regiments to form up, prepare vehicles and equipment, and undergo rigorous individual training. In the case of 1 Armoured Division Transport Regiment, its role was the provision of second-line transport support to 7 Armoured Brigade. 2 Squadron was to give close support to the three battle groups, 33 Squadron supported 40 Field Regiment, Royal Artillery, and the RHQ had to command and administer the Brigade Maintenance Area (BMA). A troop of tippers and a troop of wheeled ambulances from 54 Squadron were tasked to provide direct support to the Brigade's Engineer Regiment and Field Ambulance. After a few hectic weeks in Bunde, the Regiment deployed to Saudi Arabia in early October, 1990. The vehicles travelled by ship, with the majority of the men moving by air. The first few days in the Gulf were spent 'marrying' the two together, getting acclimatized and continuing training. Work soon began in earnest, however, and the units deployed into the Brigade Maintenance Area (BMA) in the desert. By mid-November the Regiment began to replenish the Brigade on a daily basis and support its extensive operational training programme. Liaison between, and integration with, their respective battle groups, artillery and engineer regiments also kept squadrons busy. Much was learned in these initial few weeks and the procedures and skills that were eventually to be used in Iraq and Kuwait were developed.

Send More Tank Transporters!

Back in Germany all 7 Tank Transporter Regiment's vehicles were committed to the outload of armoured vehicles for GRANBY 1 to the ports of embarkation. A detachment of 120 men, twenty trains (tractor and trailer) and three solos (tractor only) deployed to Saudi Arabia in October. With the commitment of Headquarters 1 (UK) Armoured Division and 4 Armoured Brigade to the operation in November, the remainder of 7 Regiment was warned to deploy, leaving just fifteen trains to support BAOR.

COMMAND, CONTROL AND CONCEPTS

Command

In these early days, command and control arrangements were necessarily fluid as the Allied Forces built up. National contingents were all nominally under the command of the Saudi Commander-in-Chief. General Norman Schwarzkopf was nominated as the Military Commander for the Force and each nation had its own national commander. General Sir Peter de la Billiere assumed command of all United Kingdom Forces through British Forces Middle East (BFME), but answered to the Joint Headquarters in UK for national matters, just as General Schwarzkopf answered to his Joint Chiefs of Staff and President Bush. Despite all the potential for confusion and acrimony, both US and British Generals quickly established a fine relationship that stood the tests of many political and national sensitivities.

Liaison with US Forces

Liaison officers were established to resolve conflicting priorities over resources, especially road space. Initially the British were grouped with the US Marine Corps and developed a cheerful and workmanlike rapport over the use of dock facilities and port clearance with a great deal of mutual help. Meanwhile in London the increasing number of ships and aircraft being despatched to the Gulf raised concerns over the capacity of ports and airports in Saudi Arabia which would have to cope simultaneously with a much larger US operation. At this point the value of the personnel exchange scheme with the US Army was practically demonstrated. Under this long-standing arrangement two RCT majors and two warrant officers served with the US Transportation Corps at Fort Eustis, Virginia. Colonel Martyn Cubitt in DOMS had spent two years as S3 Operations with the US 7th Transportation Group at Fort Eustis. He found that his erstwhile American commanding officer was now Head of Movement Operations in US TRANSCOM and another US Army colleague, Colonel Tom Eanes, was in charge of the US terminal operations in Al Jubayl. Consequently such matters as the allocation of port capacity in principle were easily cleared up by telephone. The RCT exchange officer at the time was deployed to the Gulf with the US 7th Transportation Group which was commended for its major role in supporting the US Army's logistic operation.

Later, as part of the overall strategic plan for the ultimate liberation of Kuwait, 1 (UK) Division was transferred to the field command of US VII Corps. Such a transfer was inevitable once the Division was up to full strength and clearly needed for minefield breaching operations and the subsequent armoured thrust into Iraq. Deception played a major part in Allied planning and both transfers of command and actual geographic deployments were closely guarded secrets kept from both the Press (with a few exceptions) and the public at home. In particular, the potential threat of a major sea-borne assault was vigorously sustained throughout the Allied build-up and while the air war was prosecuted.

Logistic Concept Development

During these deployment and build-up phases the role of the FMA expanded dramatically, especially after the arrival of GRANBY 1.5. In effect the FMA's role moved from supporting a comparatively small armoured brigade to sustaining a hugely enlarged armoured division, complete with an artillery group and engineer group in direct support. New affiliations, operating procedures and operational concepts had to be developed very quickly as the line of communication stretched further and further into the desert. The establishment of logistic bases, pipelines and the Forward FMA (FFMA) were essential to this process; both US and UK Armies worked closely in formulating logistic plans and sharing the resources needed to achieve them. Of greatest importance was the interdependence of the transport operating loops of third-line RCT regiments from the FMA and the second-line divisional RCT regiments directly supporting the Division's front-line units. As these loops got longer, exceptional measures had to be devised to control and monitor the replenishment and stocking of combat and other supplies. With limited communications and the overriding need for security, the task was further complicated by the regrouping of combat and logistic units as operational plans were made and changed. Only the closest liaison and tight regimental control enabled the RCT to maintain its hold over the logistic chain from the port to front line.

DEVELOPING THE PORT OF ENTRY AND BUILDING A FIRM BASE

10 Transport Group

Meanwhile 10 Regiment became a Group with additional units placed under command. These included 12 Squadron from 8 Regiment, equipped with DROPS vehicles and a troop of 16 Squadron from 7 Regiment. 12 Squadron's role was primarily to carry water in the so-called 'Bean Cans' on flatracks, but DROPS also proved invaluable moving containers, Multiple Launch Rocket System (MLRS) and stores of all descriptions.

The Regiment took under command 52 Port Squadron and a movements squadron, initially 50 MC Squadron and later 59 MC Squadron. The final element of the Group was the Host Nation Transport Support Group. The Movement Control Centre (MCC) in Al Jubayl was established in the port with staff liaising closely with 52 Port Squadron and 10 Regiment to ensure that the process of offloading equipment and marrying it to units went as smoothly as possible. The Air Transport Liaison Officer (ATLO) staff dealt with the dramatic increase in the volume of work with a wide variety of aircraft in use. Freight arrived in Hercules from the RAF, from New Zealand, Spanish and Italian Air Forces, and, at one stage, a Soviet Antonov was in use. In addition, a number of civilian Jumbos, including one from Kuwait Airlines, were brought in to supplement the RAF Tristar and VC10 fleets. During the busy period between 28 September and 10 November 50 MC Squadron handled some 240 air sorties, as well as all the ships carrying the vehicles, containers and cargo. In those early days of the tour, late September, it was still very hot. Later there were relentless downpours, turning the ground to quagmire. It was a very busy and difficult time as the Force settled down with a stream of visitors and journalists. John Keegan of *The Daily Telegraph* reported back: '*The British logistic achievements fill a visitor with astonished pride. The pressure has been unrelenting but the prevailing atmosphere is one of utter calm and total competence.*'

Baldrick Lines

The primary task of 10 Regiment was the inload of ammunition, stores and equipment. In some ways even more demanding was the responsibility for the reception and administration of the Force as it arrived by air and sea. This very public task tested the ingenuity, tact and good humour of the Regiment to the limit. Most daunting was running the 2,000-bed camp, initially called 'Tented City', later christened universally 'Baldrick Lines' after the hapless manservant in the Blackadder TV series. This administrative commitment was undertaken in fine style with ingenuity and commonsense. It was one of the most remarkable RCT tasks of Operation GRANBY and the Corps earned high praise for its success.

GRANBY 1.5 AND MASSIVE REINFORCEMENT

27 Regiment Joins the Fray

After providing support to BAOR in GRANBY 1 from early September, 27 Regiment was warned as a later roulement for a planned GRANBY 2. Within days, however, the Regiment was brought forward for GRANBY 1.5 as third-line transport support to 1 (UK) Armoured Division. The Regiment was organized into HQ

Squadron, 7 and 42 Squadrons (from the AMF(L)) was equipped with a total of 104 x 14-tonne GS, 66 Squadron 32 x 22.5 Trucks Tanker Fuel (TTFs) and Regimental Workshops REME. There followed a strenuous period of reorganization, absorbing 8 Squadron's manpower, receiving individual reinforcements from over thirty different units including the Corps Band, retraining 66 Squadron from 8-tonne GS to TTF operations; and drawing and issuing equipment and stores. There was no time for collective training prior to deployment and, in the end, the Regiment had only one day in which to rehearse its operational role, and that was two days before the ground war began. The vehicles left by sea in late November, and the advance party, led by the Regimental Operations Officer, flew to Al Jubayl on 17 December. The main body followed by air between 28 December and 3 January, 1991. Within twelve hours of the first flight arriving, task vehicles had been located, retrieved and were on the road. The Regiment's role was to take over the transport details within the port area, releasing 10 Regiment to concentrate upon establishing a new logistic base – the Forward Force Maintenance Area (FFMA) alongside US Log Base Alpha. 42 Squadron cleared stores from the jetty to ordnance depots. 7 Squadron assisted in port clearance but became increasingly involved in supporting divisional training, the movement of priority freight, and the move to Alpha. 66 Squadron took over responsibility for running the FMA fuel point in the port area and collected fuel from the refineries at Dammam and delivered stocks to fuel installations from Al Jubayl to the FFMA.

AMF(L) Logistic Battalion in GRANBY

The flexibility of the AMF(L) Logistic Battalion was widely demonstrated during GRANBY. Not only was 42 Squadron RCT deployed under command of 27 Regiment RCT, but all the other permanent sub-units were involved to some extent during either GRANBY 1 or GRANBY 2. Corporal Mark Griffiths REME, of the AMF(L) Workshop REME, was awarded the Queen's Gallantry Medal during the conflict.

Increasing Port Operations

The demand for manpower and container-handling equipment in Saudi Arabia was reaching a peak at this time and more than 100 soldiers, nine container handlers and a variety of other equipment were now on the strength of 52 Port Squadron. A Mexeflote crew of six was despatched by 17 Regiment to Al Jubayl at the end of November, tasked to ensure the safe offload and storage of a workboat and two 126ft Mexeflote rafts sent to the Gulf as a contingency measure. A further two rafts were subsequently despatched. The workboat was employed in support of the harbour security plan and worked with the US Navy with the Mexeflote in reserve. The maritime tradesmen, when not tasked on the workboat, were employed alongside the port operators. Another Composite Port Troop, including crew for one of the two Ramp Craft Logistic (RCLs) in Cyprus, was deployed to Cyprus in January, 1991, to assist with the outload of RAF ammunition and equipment by sea from Akrotiri.

Controlling Both Ends of the L of C

From the end of August it had been necessary to augment DDef Log Mov's staff in DOMS to provide 24-hour cover, but, contrary to war plans, it was impossible for

D Mov(A) and D Mov (RAF) to shut down their normal business, although they did their best to help. DOMS sought, and received, RCT assistance from HQ DGTM and HQ UKLF. By October co-ordination among the various sea and airports of embarkation was improving and mobile phones and computer terminals were finding their way into the hands of the movements control operators on site. This enabled DOMS to better monitor the outward flow. Meanwhile air freight had become a major headache. The system for allocating priority to stores demands had all but vanished as most units were able to claim the highest priority. In addition the sea transit time exceeded the delivery criteria, automatically consigning many of these items to air freight. The RAF had up to twenty Hercules flying round the clock, augmented by VC10s and Tristars. To cope with outsized loads venerable Belfasts and gigantic Antonovs were chartered, in addition to the occasional availability of USAF C5 transports. Even this was not enough and an increasing number of chartered freighter aircraft were needed. Despite this the demand kept outpacing supply and a backlog of air freight steadily grew.

At South Cerney 55 MC Squadron was particularly busy. During the months of October and November, as the deployment for GRANBY 1 gained momentum, those working in the AMC faced a heavy workload, with shifts working day and night. During just one five-day period 385,000 pounds of equipment was processed, built

The main supply route from the Force Maintenance Area (FMA) to Forward Force Maintenance Area (FFMA).

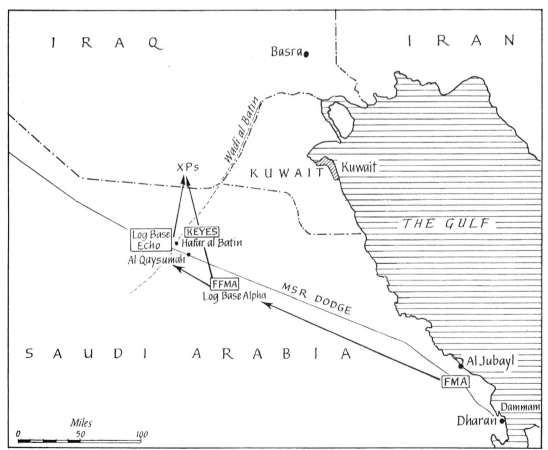

into twenty aircraft pallets and despatched to the Gulf. 59 MC Squadron returned from BAOR on 16 October and in November was tasked to take over the operations in the Gulf from 50 MC Squadron. By this time the majority of 7 Armoured Brigade was already in theatre. The Squadron still managed to arrive in time to offload some of the vessels it had helped to load in Germany! At MMP 17 Regiment was stretched in five ways: providing assistance in BAOR; receiving units in the Gulf; deploying units from UK; supporting the RAF in Cyprus; and meeting its routine commitments.

The Trawl for Manpower and Resources

By 8 November, eight weeks after the initial announcement, the deployment of 7 Armoured Brigade was complete. After seeing the logistic build-up, John Keegan of *The Daily Telegraph* reported back: '*If Saddam Hussein could see what I have seen, he would get out of Kuwait now!*' There was scarcely time to draw breath, however, before the announcement on 15 November that another brigade, plus full divisional headquarters and support, was to be deployed under GRANBY 1.5. 4 Armoured Division Transport Regiment (ADTR) was allocated as second-line transport support. It was reinforced by 38 Squadron from 2 Transport Group and 1 Squadron from UK, doubling the Regiment's normal peacetime establishment to over 1,000 all ranks. Further elements of 7 Tank Transporter Regiment and 54 Engineer and Ambulance Support Squadron were tasked. Preparations followed the pattern set by the earlier deployment, but this time the trawl for manpower and resources became global as more and more second and third-line assets were committed to GRANBY 1.5. This included all those initially earmarked for GRANBY 2 – the original roulement of GRANBY 1. Virtually every RCT unit in UK and BAOR, together with many overseas, were drawn into an ever-widening net as the demands for reinforcement grew. Extra staff were needed to match 24-hour shift manning in operational and movement planning teams at every level. To top it all, those arms units not involved in the deployment were still being sent on operational tours to Northern Ireland and Belize; overseas training and exercises continued unabated with all units expecting their normal level of RCT support. By now approximately half of the Joint Helicopter Support Unit (JHSU) was deployed in the desert on Operation GRANBY, whilst detachments in the Falkland Islands and in Northern Ireland continued to be maintained.

To release Regular RCT manpower RCT roulement tours were extended, some all-arms drivers were employed on peacetime routine tasks, contractors were brought in to operate freight services, over 100 RCT TA soldiers signed up for short Regular engagements to man a transport squadron for a UN tour in Cyprus and 496 Movement Control Unit (V) proudly manned ports and terminals for the US forces in UK to undertake the biggest outload of ammunition since the Second World War.

THE BUILD-UP TO WAR – DESERT DEPLOYMENT

The Desert Deployment Starts

The deployment of GRANBY 1.5 was effected between 16 December, 1990, and 10 January, 1991. As Christmas approached, it was clear that the initial aim of deterring

Saddam Hussein from attacking Saudi Arabia had been achieved, and that operations should now be directed towards his removal from Kuwait. The operational deployment of 1 (UK) Armoured Division began. Extra transport assets also began to arrive in theatre and the role of 1 ADTR changed. 2 Squadron continued to provide close support to the battle groups of 7 Armoured Brigade, but 33 Squadron lost its artillery support role and instead provided close support to the battle groups of 4 Armoured Brigade. The Base Maintenance Area (BMA) was disbanded as a Divisional Rear Area was established and the Commanding Officer reverted to his more usual role as Commander Transport of the Division.

Reinforcement Completed

As the year ended the lack of visibility of stores and containers in transit became more critical. In the air, despite DOMS taking reasonable measures to increase the number of chartered freighters, the demand for air freight continued to exceed expectations and outstripped supply. The backlog was to reach 500 tons before the situation was brought under control. At this critical time an ill-considered appeal to the public to send Christmas parcels to the troops resulted in the Forces Postal system being flooded by a massive response. Hundreds of tons of parcels added to the backlog of items to be forwarded by Movements. To make matters worse, many of these parcels were from anonymous donors and therefore had to be screened, in the interests of security, as 'suspicious' objects. Ultimately some fifty-two ISO containers were filled with these parcels to the embarrassment of the MOD, all virtually unnecessary as Servicemen were able to obtain all they needed from official sources, including NAAFI. The shipping process, however, was running smoothly and efficiently, from forecasting and chartering at DOMS to call forward, stow planning and actual loading.

The last reinforcement vessel departed on 9 January, 1991, and a cycle of resupply ships was already in train. By the end of this second deployment HQ BAOR Transport and Movements had coordinated the move from Germany of over 25,000 men on 277 air sorties and over 12,000 vehicles, 3,348 containers and approximately 62,000 tonnes of ammunition and general stores in 100 vessels. Together with the men and material from UK, the Gulf forces were soon to be on a sound operational and logistic footing. No emergency powers had been enacted either by UK or the Continental Host Nations.

Ambulance Support

Initially, only two ambulance troops of 54 Squadron had been tasked to support 7 Brigade in the Gulf, but the Ambulance Support Group of 16 Field Ambulance also provided fourth-line cover. As the commitment expanded to include support for 4 Armoured Brigade and 1 (UK) Armoured Division, it was obvious that additional ambulances and trained manpower was needed, together with an element for overall command and control. With RCT Regular manpower already heavily committed, the Gurkha Transport Regiment (GTR) offered men eager to help. Early in November, 1990, a composite ambulance squadron was formed from GTR assets in Hong Kong. As 28 (Ambulance) Squadron GTR, it deployed to UK during

November and December, 1990, and on 6 December 214 all ranks of 28 (Ambulance) Squadron GTR moved to Church Crookham to begin pre-deployment training and take on their specialist ambulances. A Group HQ was added with a Commanding Officer and other soldiers drawn from units throughout UK. The Gurkha Ambulance Group deployed in the comparative luxury of a Kuwait Airlines 747 in January.

TANK TRANSPORTER OPERATIONS

The Tasks

7 Regiment was joined by 414 Tank Transporter Unit from UK. Complete in theatre on 7 January, it was tasked with moving armour in support of the Division. Desert Detachment had rejoined the Regiment on Christmas Day and new arrivals swiftly took note of the Detachment's recent, relevant desert experience. Convoys of tank-transporters rolling up the desert supply routes became a familiar and impressive scene on the Nation's TV screens at home. Desert Detachment had already deployed 7 Brigade and various United States Marine Corps units to locations south of the Kuwait border so they could train for forthcoming operations. The Regiment then began the task of deploying the remainder of the Division, lifting everything from Bar Mine Layers to Challenger tanks. The Unipower Commander Tractor with a Crane Fruehauf 62-tonne Semi-Trailer proved more than equal to the task, carrying the heaviest up-armoured and bombed-up Challenger with ease. Although not designed for off-road use, the vehicles and crews were rarely defeated by desert conditions. The soldiers were superb, working continuously with little time for sleep, with so-called 'free time' spent preparing the vehicles for the next detail, a routine which continued for the next four months, with the Regiment never found wanting.

16 Kilometres of Flashing Lights!

Once the Division had completed training, 7 Regiment moved in to Concentration Area KEYES completing twenty-two loops on Routes DODGE and HORSE. Both exacted their toll on the vehicles and the REME Workshop's dedication ensured that the Regiment met the task. Movement slots on Route DODGE were at a premium. Often the Regiment would move in one packet of 160 vehicles or more, under the command of a squadron OC or 2IC. Booking in at RMP checkpoints at first raised a smile, then incredulity, followed quickly by respect! Sixteen kilometres of flashing amber lights in the rear-view mirror of the lead vehicle was a stirring sight. Driving standards on Route DODGE varied considerably. Fortunately 100 tonnes of fully laden Commanders would generally ensure that others kept well clear. On occasions reckless convoy-hopping by some Allied drivers led to appalling accidents and tragic loss of life. Royal Artillery and Royal Engineer units were also moved in preparation for artillery raids into Iraq and then delivered to their new locations close to the border. The Regiment then perfected the procedures that would be needed to carry the Armoured Delivery Group into Iraq and Kuwait. Ten trains deployed in support of the Divisional Recovery Plan for the operation.

7 Tank Transport Regiment moving fascine layers forward in support of Combat Engineers.

TRAINING AND REGROUPING FOR WAR

Training

In the Gulf an intensive period of preparation began as RCT regiments welcomed in the newly-arrived divisional units – advising and helping them adjust to the desert, running a reception area in the port of Al Jubayl and supporting what was now a highly demanding Divisional training programme. Christmas came and went. The British public responded with overwhelming generosity to the call for cards and gifts. It was a time to relax a little but also to feel a little homesick and apprehensive of what lay ahead. Rumours abounded and speculation grew. It was decided that the UK Force, originally teamed up with the US Marine Corps, would be placed under command of the US VII Corps. At the same time the Division began a series of complex and covert westward moves into its various staging areas and finalized its detailed preparations for war. The two Divisional Transport Regiments played a major role in all this activity – continuously outloading ammunition to various sites, providing fuel to the massive and 'thirsty' Division, operating with the different battle groups as they moved and trained, and running the divisional Delivery Point for a strength of 16,000. This was also a time to plan and prepare detailed orders for the war. The transport concept of operations was developed, setting out the roles of each regiment. A detailed transport plan in support of the overall Allied Operation DESERT STORM was refined. Everyone was briefed, rehearsed and geared up for his own task in the forthcoming operation.

The Logistic Regrouping Plan Comes Together

The main movement of stocks into the FFMA began on 3 January and over the next three weeks some 18,000 tonnes of ammunition, over 7 million litres of fuel and over 6,000 tonnes of other matériel were moved forward by 10 and 27 Regiments, supported by a large 'squadron' of local Saudi Arabian trucks under contract.

Divisional transport also helped in this task, joining the thousands of vehicles virtually nose-to-tail on the 'Tapline Road' (Route DODGE). On 21 January Brigadier White moved his HQ forward to the FFMA, 60 kms south-east of Hafar al Batin. Soon the FFMA held enough to ensure third-line support to the Division. The next task was to build up second-line stocks in the Divisional Maintenance Area (DMA) some 30 kms to the north-west. Even more stocks were being moved forward from Al Jubayl to ensure that the FFMA was always topped up. To maintain supplies of fuel and ease vehicle traffic, a Pipeline-over-the-Desert (PLOD) was built. To many RCT drivers the 'big picture' simply resolved itself into a seemingly endless succession of convoys, all-too-brief rests and then back on the road again. But gradually the logistic plan was achieved, with command well forward and the Division stocked, fuelled and armed. Some of the detailed stories that follow give a flavour of how it was done.

Reorganization – 1 ADTR's Story

Many RCT units were reorganized for the war. With its 1,500-tonne lift, 4 ADTR was tasked to support the artillery's two Direct Support regiments and three regiments of the General Support Group (with its heavy M109 guns and Multiple Launch Missile Systems (MLRS)). The concept was based on forward self-sufficiency. This was achieved by holding second-line transport and ammunition as far forward as possible. Squadrons therefore deployed under tactical control of their affiliated artillery requirements. With the anticipated ever-lengthening line of communication and the likely speed of the Division's advance into Iraq, the Regiment had to be prepared to establish and control artillery exchange points (AXPs) and refine its interface with third-line squadrons. It also had to run the Distribution Point (DP) for the newly-formed Artillery Group Administrative Area. The Royal Artillery had five regiments in support of the Division. It was decided to redistribute some RCT men and vehicles and allocate a squadron to support each artillery regiment or, in 38 Squadron's case, with its 14-tonners and DROPS, to the two heavy regiments. In early January the Regiment deployed seventy kilometres north-west of Al Jubayl into the Divisional Concentration Area. Unit vehicles were immediately tasked to outload ammunition and general stores from Al Jubayl up Route DODGE to the FFMA.

PUSHING FORWARD THE LINES OF COMMUNICATION

Trumpets are blown

Extract from a personal letter from General de la Billiére to the DGTM in February, 1991:

'Recently I visited a wet and cold FMA, to speak to Martin White about the quite

excellent work of the logistic Corps. They really are the heroes of the moment, yet their contribution tends to be overshadowed by the fighting echelon. Over the 21-day inload of the FMA for example, 10 Regiment RCT vehicles averaged 400 miles a day each, while during the present move of the Division, 7 Tank Transporter Regiment has moved 800 AFVs over the last ten days, with more to come. With only 55 men, the Port Squadron has unloaded 102 ships since arriving in theatre, turning round RORO ships in six hours, ammunition carriers in 24 hours and that leviathan Atlantic Conveyor *in even less…Logisticians are not very good at blowing their own trumpet, so I mention these statistics to do it for them.'*

At the other end of the Line of Communication the RCT were working wonders to ensure that sufficient ships and aircraft were chartered, the stores and equipment were marshalled, delivered, loaded and despatched so that nothing in theatre was delayed by anything for which the Corps had responsibility. As active hostilities approached, the main concern in DOMS was the preparation of adequate contingency measures. The Line of Communication over 4,500 miles was tenuous and the ability of our forces to sustain themselves in combat depended on it. A deterioration in the air situation could have resulted in charter crews refusing to fly into Saudi airspace. One aircraft diverted to Cairo and refused to go further. The situation was only resolved by a direct appeal by a Minister to the Chairman of the company. At sea, terrorist action or political allegiances could have resulted in the Suez Canal being closed, and Scud and air attacks in the Gulf in chartered shipping refusing to go within range. One timid captain approaching Al Jubayl turned his ship out to sea, protesting he was under attack by terrorists in a boat with a rocket launcher. On investigation the 'threat' turned out to be a bumboatman hoping to sell a carpet. Nevertheless, DOMS had to make sure that alternative systems were ready to swing into action. These would have involved cross-loading civil aircraft in safe airports and the use of Service aircraft for the forward leg. DOMS made sure that chartered shipping could round the Cape. To cope with the Gulf threat, trans-shipment was planned. Most of the RFA LSLs were retained in the Red Sea or Gulf waters, and a number of British flag vessels, which alone could be requisitioned to go forward, were spaced out prudently in the sea train. The shortage of British vessels of the right specification presenting themselves for charter remained a worry for this reason.

Support for the FFMA

The Allies launched a series of air attacks on 17 January to signify the start of the air war, and this brought a sharp change of emphasis. Saddam Hussein responded with retaliatory Scud missile attacks and key targets like the ports of Dhahran and Al Jubayl came under fire. Early fears of chemical attacks subsided, but troops continued to take full NBC precautions against the threat. The movements and port staff and transport units were still fully committed to handling inbound resupply flights and vessels. 27 Regiment deployed away from the port area to support the build up of the FFMA. 7 Squadron established an Administrative Harbour Area (AHA) on Route DODGE to provide a support for the Regiment's vehicles on the round trip between Al Jubayl and the FFMA. 42 Squadron remained in the port, becoming increasingly involved in tasks such as the building of the fuel pipeline from Al Jubayl forward to the Division. 66 Squadron exchanged its entire task vehicle fleet, handing over the 22.5 TTFs to 9 Squadron and receiving in their place a fleet of heavy articulated 30-cubic-metre tankers provided from local resources. These single-axle drive vehicles were in very poor condition and presented an enormous challenge to both drivers and the REME vehicle mechanics. By mid-February the quantity of stores arriving by sea had much reduced and, between 13 and 16 February, the Regiment conducted a phased move to the FFMA. By this time RHQ, 7 and 42 Squadrons and Workshops were in Log Base ALPHA; 66 Squadron was running the AHA and fuel points at Qaysumah and Al Jubayl (350 kilometres apart) and 77 Squadron remained at Al Jubayl, running Baldrick Lines and supporting the Regiment. Convoys continued to move stores from the Ordnance Depots at Al Jubayl to the FFMA, and on to DSA 4, a supply area to the west of the Wadi Al Batin.

The Battle Stocks Move Up

It was not until this late stage that 27 Regiment's role in the coming land battle was decided. 7 Squadron were to assist in establishing AXPs for 4 ADTR, 42 Squadron were to establish the XP for battle group natures for 1 ADTR, and 66 Squadron were to maintain an emergency resupply of fuel on wheels. On 19 February the troops were withdrawn from the MSRs and there was an opportunity to brief the drivers on their operational tasks and practise some simple procedures and drills. This was 27 Regiment's first day free of tasking since arriving in theatre. The Regiment completed a final stores lift from Al Jubayl before, on 22 and 23 February, vehicles were loaded with operational holdings ready for the move into Iraq. 42 and 7 Squadrons moved to Concentration Area ECHO on 24 and 24 February respectively, and joined the Divisional Administrative Area (DAA).

Deploying Ambulance Support

Deployment of the Gurkha Ambulance Group was straightforward. A complete ambulance troop moved to the most forward of the dressing stations and a half-troop deployed to the rearmost dressing stations. The remaining ambulances were tasked to collect from the helicopter landing sites and deliver to the reception wards of the field hospitals. Coach Troop was split equally between the field hospitals. Al Qaysumah, close to Wadi Al Batin, was selected as the forward airhead, so determining the location of the Forward Surgical Complex. The two field hospitals were sited in the desert next to the airhead. A new concept was trialled with an evacuation control point based on HQ 28 (Ambulance) Squadron GTR with Liaison Officers from each hospital. This created a single organization for command, control and administration for all assets for air and road casualty evacuation. This worked well on a series of casualty evacuation exercises, but the RAF concluded that the helicopters could be more effectively controlled from elsewhere. Sadly, the RAF Tasking Team was removed and the Squadron assumed command, control and administrative support for road casualty evacuation only.

The Long Haul

For the first three months of operation 10 Regiment had operated on a local basis from Al Jubayl. As the MSR extended, the task expanded to supporting the FFMA near Hafar al Batin, south of the point where the borders of Iraq, Kuwait and Saudi Arabia meet. Stores had to be moved yet again. During this phase the Regiment operated with RHQ in the rear, 17 Squadron halfway up the MSR manning a feeding and refuelling stop in the Administrative Harbour Area. Support Squadron was established in the FFMA in what was to become the Regiments' location on full deployment. The Regiment then moved up to the FFMA to support the Division, with 27 Regiment taking over the long haul, in effect becoming fourth line.

In five months of operation in the Gulf 10 Regiment alone completed more than four million kilometres. It moved and distributed millions of litres of fuel and water and 3,500 tonnes of ammunition and stores.

WAR AND VICTORY

Ready for War

The stage was now set. Pressing hard against the Iraq and Kuwait borders, units shook out into their start-points and made final preparations for war. Deception and secrecy should give the Allies the edge but the true strength and morale of the Iraqi army had not been tested. For most of the RCT officers and soldiers tensed for the battle this would be their first combat experience.

One Hundred Hours

It all began on 24 February, 1991. In the forefront of the Allied assault, 1 (UK) Armoured Division crossed the minefield breach into Iraq and set off on its now famous advance across the desert and into Kuwait. In 100 hours, the Division destroyed the equivalent of almost three Iraqi divisions, captured over 7,000 prisoners, (including two Iraqi divisional commanders) and covered almost 300 kilometres. RHQ 1 ADTR provided the reconnaissance party for the Divisional Rear Area and usually led all units in that grouping across the desert. It also planned the resupply by the second-line squadrons and coordinated the third-line assets from 10 Regiment and 27 Regiment operating in direct support of the Division. 9 Squadron (fuel), 8 Squadron (water), 7 Squadron (artillery ammunition) and 42 Squadron with battle group ammunition were under the tactical control of 1 ADTR and moved with the Divisional Rear Area grouping. The Immediate Replenishment Group (IRG) with each battle group kept the fighting echelons topped up with ammunition throughout, and, although usage was not high, the speed of movement kept IRGs busy and intimately involved. The replenishment of fuel became the most important and busiest task as the armoured formations moved forward at a speed unprecedented in modern warfare. Certainly it was much faster than the planners had foreseen. That no one ran out of fuel during the operations emphasizes the quality of planning, preparation and professionalism that went into this aspect of the RCT's support.

Into Iraq

The Allied offensive air operations had not interrupted RCT outloading tasks. Log Base *ECHO* had been inloaded from the FFMA and Al Jubayl. AXP 1 (ten kilometres south of the Iraq border) was stocked with 10,000 tons of artillery ammunition. During this time 4 ADTR moved three times, a fairly typical experience for most units. From 16 February the Royal Artillery continued to fire on Iraqi positions and 4 ADTR had its first opportunity to replenish guns firing in anger. 4 ADTR continued moving ammunition until 23 February when the squadrons loaded their trucks with one and a half day's supply of ammunition and rejoined their Royal Artillery units. On 24 February the Regiment's sub-units crossed the Iraq border and ground-dumped their vehicle ammunition stocks in preparation for the Breach Fire Plans. Trucks then returned to AXP 1 to reload and rejoin their units. Squadrons drove on through the minefield breach on the morning of 25 February before stopping in a staging area in a deserted Iraq position around midday, whilst 7 Armoured Brigade moved through them to cross its Line of Departure. During the next hours RHQ and the squadrons followed closely in the wake of the Royal Artillery in the rapid, left-hook advance through Iraq into Kuwait. Communications were awful, the weather appalling and navigation very difficult; yet the Regiment established two further AXPs (which were inloaded by the third-line transport of 10 and 27 Regiments) and, more importantly, kept the Royal Artillery resupplied with ammunition. By the end of 27 February most of the Regiment was located near the Kuwait border.

On to Kuwait

As the Allies pushed further into Iraq, Saddam Hussein's army fled ignominiously from Kuwait. In the face of this collapse, Saddam agreed to a ceasefire. 1 ADTR, with its sub-units still with their respective brigades, halted to the north-west of Kuwait City close to the Basra road. The ceasefire was effective from 0800 hours on 28 February. From 1600 hours the exhausted but triumphant squadrons joined the Divisional convoy crawling into Kuwait. Most rejoined their Regiments some forty kilometres north-west of Kuwait City. After a couple of days' rest, 4 ADTR gave up its artillery support role, adopting a more diverse transport role for the next month. This included running Divisional DPs in Kuwait and at Al Jubayl, recovering unexpended artillery ammunition from Iraq and Saudi Arabia, and moving combat supplies and captured Iraqi equipment to and from Kuwait.

Tank Transporter Support

Throughout the land war 7 Regiment ensured that the Division had fresh armour and crews nearby ready to reinforce the Brigades. This support was only needed on the tragic occasion when a platoon of British infantry in their Warrior armoured vehicles were mistakenly attacked by US A-10 aircraft. On the move through Iraq into Kuwait there was a great deal of stop-start-stop because of the Division's rapid progress. With the absolute air superiority won by the coalition, movement was carried out during the day. At night the Regiment moved into a laager and the Armoured Delivery Group unloaded to deploy a defensive screen to allow drivers to rest. After a long move through Iraq, 7 Regiment ended the war in the desert north of Kuwait City.

Casualties

Despite the worst fears of the planners, Allied casualties were mercifully light and helicopters were used for the majority of casualty evacuation. Some casualties were sent through the land evacuation chain and arrived safely at the General Hospital at Al Jubayl. All casualties, at some stage, were conveyed in Gurkha Ambulance Group transport. The Group performed extremely well, especially having taken on a new role, and proved their capacity for operating in any theatre of war. As a result of this successful operation, Captain (QGO) Krishnabahadur Gurung was awarded the MBE and Corporal Parsad Gurung received a Mention in Despatches for his sterling contribution in support of Dressing Station 5A in the desert. The ambulances remained roadworthy and kept up with their Dressing Stations during the rapid advance of the Division through Saudi Arabia, Iraq and finally Kuwait. Greater use was made of the CASEVAC system for Iraqi wounded, but at no time was it ever fully tested.

The Last L of C

On 27 February 7 and 42 Squadrons moved with the DAA into Iraq and followed the advance of the Division. A troop of local fuel tankers from 66 Squadron crossed 70 kilometres of sand tracks at night to establish a fuel XP at AXP1 by first light on 26 February. In the following days 7 Squadron completed two resupply trips for artillery ammunition from AXP1, and 42 Squadron returned to DSA 4 for a resupply of rations. By the time the ceasefire had been declared 42 Squadron had established an XP in the Divisional concentration area to the north-west of Kuwait City and 7 Squadron were already heavily employed in consolidating the artillery ammunition in the area of the breach operations. 27 Regiment was extended over a L of C stretching from Damman in the south, via Route DODGE and the line of the Division's advance, to the concentration area to the north-west of Kuwait City – a distance of 800 kilometres!

RECOVERY AND RETURN

Going Home

The war was over. Many RCT units rested wearily amid the blazing oilfields and wilful vandalism left by the Iraqi army. RCT second and third-line units drove south out of Kuwait during the last week of March, 1991, and filtered their vehicles into the Convoy Marshalling Area (CMA) beside Al Jubayl port. The soldiers began to fly out of theatre early in the first week of April, with the last ones departing on 7 April. 7 Regiment recovered Iraqi vehicles for intelligence and research purposes before moving the Division back to Al Jubayl. An Armoured Infantry Group was left in Kuwait for a while and was supported by Desert Detachment 2. The bulk of 7 Regiment returned to BAOR on 7 April, having moved over 7,000 vehicles, driven 2,700,000 kilometres and consumed millions of litres of fuel. A GT transport troop remained behind in Kuwait City as the Kuwait Transport Troop, part of the Kuwait Battle Group, eventually returning to UK and Germany on 5 June.

Getting It All Back

The sheer size of the recovery operation was too great for the in-theatre movement and port operations teams. As part of the overall Recovery Plan, the RHQ of 29 Transport and Movements Regiment RCT deployed from UK to Al Jubayl, assuming control of the movements assets in the theatre, 52 Port Squadron, 66 Squadron, and local civilian transport. Regrouped as the Logistic Support Regiment Middle East, immediate priority was given to the recovery of the troops. In early March, two desert airstrips were constructed in Kuwait to extract 4 and 7 Armoured Brigades back to Saudi Arabia, where they were held in transit camps prior to moving through the MCCP for their flights back to UK. In primitive conditions the MCCP processed an average of 1,000 people each day, although during the early stages, this figure often doubled. Despite the high public attention focused on return of troops by air, the long-term emphasis centred on the port. The vehicle parks were expanding by 300-400 vehicles every day and stocks of ammunition were literally piling up in the debombing areas. The shipping plot for the recovery left very little margin for error and the movers had to work extremely hard to meet the plan. Only after the pace of the recovery had abated in May were some of these RCT units able to thin out. By June the bulk of the recovery was complete and RHQ 29 Regiment started its own return to UK.

The Gurkhas' Return

By midday on 2 April, 1991, the life cycle of the Gurkha Ambulance Group was complete. All those who had deployed were safely recovered. A team spirit and single purpose had fused together drivers with medical staff, Gurkhas with British, and old hands with the inexperienced. These soldiers of the GTR were to return to Hong Kong with a Gulf medal to add to their UNFICYP medal of the previous year, much to the envy of their comrades in the Brigade of Gurkhas.

Some Lessons

Reflecting on the campaign, many of those involved felt that some operational lessons needed to be relearned. Training for general war in NW Europe had clearly proved highly effective for officers and men. The Corps expertise in all aspects of movement planning and control build-up to ensure speedy reinforcement of Europe from North America and of BAOR from UK was quite capable of coping with a very much longer strategic L of C in a different direction. However, 'just in time' logistics did not work well over 4,500 miles and the Army had forgotten how to operate from a forward base fed in bulk. The price for the lack of local control over demand and consumption was paid in RCT effort and by an increased burden on strategic transport assets, assets which would have been critical if the active war had been less favourable or less rapidly resolved.

Most vehicles and equipment stood up well to the rigours of the desert. Operating procedures had also stood the test well, although there was, at times, a temptation to reorganize to meet each new situation. Units soon found it better to stick to well-tried regimental and squadron structures whenever possible. The DROPS fleet performed outstandingly well and new roles were found for them almost every week. Best of all, they gave the British Army a battlefield delivery system for 20-foot ISO containers, much to the envy of the other Allied armies. Hardly surprising, low mobility vehicles, such as fuel tankers, performed very badly off anything but prepared roads. Attempts to exchange vehicles proved unworkable and unnecessary in practice – drivers were literally living in cabs and it would have been both impractical and highly unpopular to enforce vehicle exchanges. The satellite-based navigation Global Positioning System (GPS) was a remarkable success, with drivers and units easily meeting up at a ten-figure desert rendezvous at night. The main weakness in logistic units was, as always, inadequate communications, with units having to continue with the tried and tested systems of liaison officers and despatch riders.

Transport Operating Loops

The real difference between the logistic support of 1 (BR) Armoured Division in actual desert operations in the Gulf and the planned support for potential operations in BAOR was the third-line transport-operating loop of 750 kms. This is the equivalent distance from Bielefeld to Garmisch Partenkirchen and, in Europe, almost all of it on autobahns. In Saudi Arabia most of the route was barely the width of two large vehicles. There were many accidents, particularly involving US and other Coalition Force vehicles, and, sadly, many people died. For the British Forces the overall accident rate was remarkably low. Typically, the drivers were operating over thirty-six-hour loops for weeks on end. The problems of operating over such a long route are fairly obvious, primarily those of control, recovery and safety. Control could only be imposed by having the key elements of the regiment positioned at vital points along the route.

Proven Professionalism

The RCT had once again proved its high professionalism and unstinted commitment in support of the fighting man, earning genuine admiration and respect from the combat Arms and Allies it had supported so well throughout every stage of the campaign. Perhaps for the Corps, General Sir Peter de la Billiére summed it up succinctly in his letter to the DGTM praising the Corps with the words 'No RCT – no war!'

HONOURS AND AWARDS

The following Honours and Awards to members of the Corps were made for Service During Operation GRANBY.

QUEEN'S GALLANTRY MEDAL
    Corporal M J Driscoll
    Acting Captain P Shields

MENTION IN DESPATCHES
    Lieutenant Colonel P A D Evans OBE
    Major J M May
    Major J R Wallace MBE
    Corporal J V Baglee
    Corporal Pasad Gurung GTR

CBE   Brigadier M S White
    Colonel M F I Cubitt
    Colonel G A Ewer MBE

OBE	Lieutenant Colonel G J Haig
	Lieutenant Colonel R I Harrison
	Lieutenant Colonel K M Tutt

MBE	Major R G Beavis
	Major G Corani
	Major C J Harvey
	Major I M Hurley
	Major J G O Lowe
	Major R D Stocks
	Major D N Wright
	Captain H V Lewis
	Captain Krishnabahadur Guring GTR
	Warrant Officer Class 1 P R Bromley

BEM	Staff Sergeant G MacPherson
	Staff Sergeant T Mitchell
	Sergeant C Ward
	Corporal S D Bennett
	Corporal R Canavan
	Corporal P J Crabb
	Corporal G R Rennie
	Lance Corporal A Butterill
	Lance Corporal B G Mallaney

ANNEX A

FORMED RCT UNITS DEPLOYED ON OPERATION GRANBY

GRANBY 1

7 ARMOURED BRIGADE – RCT DEPLOYMENT

1 Armoured Divisional Transport
(Second line transport support)
74 Squadron (Sp Squadron)
2 Squadron (BG Sp)
33 Squadron (Arty Sp)
Two Troops of 54 Squadron
(Engr and Arty Sp)

10 Regiment Group
(Third line transport support)
Headquarters Squadron
9 Squadron (Fuel)
17 Squadron (GT)
12 Squadron (DROPS)
Troop of 16 Squadron (Tk Tptr)

50/59 Movement Control Squadron (from 29 Regiment)
52 Port Squadron (from 17 Port and Maritime Regiment)

GRANBY 1.5

1 (UK) ARMOURED DIVISION – RCT DEPLOYMENT

1 Armoured Divisional Transport Regiment
74 Squadron (Div Tps Sp)
2 Squadron (7 Armd Bde Sp)
33 Squadron (4 Armd Bde Sp)
One Troop 54 Squadron (Engr Sp) support)

4 Armoured Divisional Transport

76 Squadron (26 Fd Regt RA support)
19 Squadron (2 Fd Regt RA support)
1 Squadron (40 Rd Regt RA support)
38 Squadron (32/39 Heavy Regt RA

10 Regiment
Headquarters Squadron
9 Squadron (Fuel)
12 Squadron (DROPS)
17 Squadron
(General Transport)
Regimental Workshops
REME

27 Regiment
Headquarters Squadron
66 Squadron (Fuel)
42 Squadron (Battle
Group Exchange Point)

7 Squadron (Artillery
Exchange Point)

7 Tank Transporter Regiment
3 Squadron
16 Squadron
414 Tank Transporter Unit

50/59 Movement Control
Squadron
52 Port Squadron

Gurkha Ambulance Support Group
28 Ambulance Squadron Gurkha Transport Regiment
Troop 54 Squadron

COMMANDING OFFICERS AND SQUADRON COMMANDERS OF FORMED RCT UNITS COMMITTED TO OPERATION GRANBY

1 ARMOURED DIVISION TRANSPORT REGIMENT

Commanding Officer	Lieutenant Colonel G J Haig
OC 2 Squadron RCT	Major P McMahon
OC 33 Squadron RCT	Major J W O Lowe
OC 74 Squadron RCT	Major S M Loasby
OC Regiment Workshop	Captain D F Burgess REME

4 ARMOURED DIVISION TRANSPORT REGIMENT

Commanding Officer	Lieutenant Colonel D E Forrest (until 28.3.91)
Commanding Officer	Lieutenant Colonel G B L Fox
OC 1 Squadron RCT	Major A B Barton
OC 19 Squadron RCT	Major S Heaton
OC 38 Squadron RCT	Major I C Alexander
OC 76 Squadron RCT	Major M C Jones
OC Workshop REME	Captain T C Knee REME

7 TANK TRANSPORTER REGIMENT

Commanding Officer	Lieutenant Colonel K M Tutt
OC 3 Tank Transporter Squadron	Major J P Newis-Edward
OC 3 Tank Transporter Squadron	Major R A Dixon-Warren

OC 7 Tank Transporter Sqn Workshop	Major M J Clutson REME
OC 414 Tank Transporter Troop RCT	Captain A P Blomquist
OC Operation GRANBY 1 Detachment	Captain H V Lewis

10 CORPS TRANSPORT REGIMENT

Commanding Officer	Lieutenant Colonel P Chaganis
OC 9 Squadron	Major J A Goodall
OC 12 Squadron	Major J R Wallace
OC 17 Squadron	Major K B Anderson
OC Regiment Workshop	Captain D J Chadwick REME

17 PORT AND MARITIME REGIMENT

Commanding Officer	Lieutenant Colonel B Morris
Operations Officer (OC MMP)	Major G Corani
OC 52 Squadron RCT	Major I M Hurley
OC 51 Squadron RCT	Major N I F Appleton
OC 53 Squadron RCT	Major R A Tull

27 REGIMENT

Commanding Officer	Lieutenant Colonel P D Verge
OC 7 Squadron	Major L S Campbell
OC 42 Squadron	Major J G Askew
OC 66 Squadron	Major J J Little
OC 77 Squadron	Major R A Lukes
OC Workshops	Captain J D McDonald REME

29 REGIMENT

Commanding Officer	Lieutenant Colonel R I Harrison
OC 50 MC Squadron	Major P Allberry
OC 55 Squadron	Major D J Owen
OC 59 MC Squadron	Major J Hay

GURKHA AMBULANCE GROUP

Commanding Officer	Lieutenant Colonel I R Gunn
OC 28 (Ambulance) Squadron GTR	Major R J Gilroy

CHAPTER 12

The Final Years

Introduction. BAOR; Operations HANWOOD and GRAPPLE. RCT Organization in BAOR – HQ L of C; Air Trooping to Germany. UN Observer Missions. Northern Ireland. Final days of GTR. The New Regimental Structure. The Territorial Army. Formation. The Final Regimental Activities of the RCT.

INTRODUCTION

When the process of recovering the massive quantities of equipment used in the Gulf War in 1991 was barely completed, the eyes of the Corps were on its future as a founding member of The Royal Logistic Corps. This affected everyone in the Corps and the planning involved in the change was complex, with very many considerations and implications. Until the day of implementation in 1993, however, its tasks worldwide, covering many of its ongoing routine and operational activities, were still in place, whilst new commitments were also arising. All were against a background of imminent change, reorganization and personal uncertainties. Examples of some of these wide-ranging events, planning procedures and resulting decisions are given in the paragraphs that follow. These culminate in the final farewells to the Corps in which so many had been proud to serve during the period touched on by this volume, and contributed so much to its long history.

BAOR

In 1992/93, as the RCT in Germany was dramatically reducing in size, Operation GRAPPLE saw 17 Squadron RCT, heavily reinforced from other RCT units, deployed as part of the National Support Element (NSE), to support the 1st Battalion The Cheshire Regiment during the United Nations deployment to Yugoslavia. The war establishments of the units deployed on both Operation GRANBY and later on Operation GRAPPLE were heavily dependent upon reinforcement by reservists. Since the government was not prepared to call up RCT reservists, most units deploying had to be reinforced with regular manpower from other RCT units. The result was that many of the units that remained in Germany became non-effective.

For most RCT officers and soldiers the operational differences between being in a second, third or fourth-line unit become blurred. Many who had trained for a third or fourth-line role found themselves operating at second line in a completely different manner. They had to become familiar with new and unusual equipments very quickly. Without doubt the versatility and resilience of RCT officers and soldiers were greatly tested during the final years of the Corps involvement in Germany, but, without exception, units and soldiers benefited from the experience and rose to the challenges presented.

The UN and Former Republic of (FRY) Yugoslavia – Operations HANWOOD and GRAPPLE

The UN became involved in the conflict in Yugoslavia in September, 1991. The Security Council called for a complete weapon and military equipment embargo on Yugoslavia in an attempt to quell fighting between Serbia and Croatia. In November, 1991, the Security Council convened a meeting in Geneva between the fighting factions. From this meeting a ceasefire was called. The ceasefire broke down almost immediately causing the Security Council to send a small group of military and civil staff to the country. Their task was to ascertain the feasibility of deploying a peace-keeping force. This study was successful and in early 1992 the lead elements of the UN force deployed. The Corps' contribution to the United Nations Protection Force, Yugoslavia (UNPROFOR) provided support for two operations in the Yugoslavian theatre.

The commitment began with Operation HANWOOD, a Field Ambulance operating in support of UN Protection Forces deployed to Croatia following its secessionist war with Serbia. With one-third of Croatia's former territory in Serb hands, the UN Protected Areas covered a broad swathe from Vukovar and Osijek in the east to the strategic Maslenica Bridge on the Dalmatian coast road. The Corps provided soldiers, both as part of the Field Ambulance and as reinforcements, from 60 Squadron in Catterick. Operation HANWOOD ran from April, 1992, to October, 1993, before being withdrawn as the UK concentrated on a larger role in Bosnia-Herzegovina, Operation GRAPPLE.

A much greater commitment came in early November, 1992, when 17 Squadron deployed to Bosnia ahead of 1st Battalion The Cheshire Regiment. The mission was in support of the United Nations High Commission for Relief (UNHCR) delivering aid to an increasingly destitute civil population. The immediate logistic challenge was to support a battalion in Vitez, equipped with Warriors, accessible only over mountain tracks in an approaching winter. Having been warned for the operation as early as August, the Squadron was extensively prepared. With 80% of its personnel veterans of Northern Ireland and the Gulf, it was also well seasoned. The Squadron ORBAT had, however, been modified within the MOD, which presented the OC, Major Malcolm Hood, with an immediate problem. The absence of any suitable tankers meant that it was physically impossible to transport petrol to Vitez. The absence of a Corps officer from the initial reconnaisance had come home to roost! By the time,

10 Regiment RCT vehicles prepare to deploy on OP Grapple.

though, that the 9th/12th Royal Lancers and their Scimitars had deployed, so too had additional tankers, and the problem passed.

Initially based in Tomislavgrad on a six-month roulement tour, the Squadron was the sole second-line transport and movements focus in theatre and included within its ranks personnel from 7 Tank Transporter Regiment, 17 Port and Maritime Regiment, 29 Transport and Movements Regiment, 2 Group, and operators from 9 Squadron, also Bielefeld-based.

As winter closed in the pressing need was the inload of semi-permanent shelter and operational reserves. Whether moving the container city which became the home of the Cheshire Regiment, or inloading the bulk fuel installations, or hauling the armour, there was no option but to work as near round the clock as conditions allowed. The statistics tell the story, with well over 300,000 kilometres being notched up each month at an average speed of about fifteen kilometres per hour on narrow switchback routes in rain, wind, snow and ice. High vehicle availability and low accident rates told their own story. There were white out conditions in which the Squadron rescued civilian buses and their passengers from the snow drifts. Corporal Geordie Thornton and his men were forced to bivouac one night and take into their protection women and children fleeing the war zone without adequate clothing, food or shelter. On scarcely better days, convoys of upwards of thirty task vehicles with motorcycle and Land Rover escorts forced a passage through to Vitez and returned as far as conditions would permit. The abiding problem was one of time and space. Although distances were not unusually great, the difficulty of movement made for long and stressful days at the wheel.

Tomislavgrad was nominally a safe area, being fifteen kilometres from the front and largely significant as a staging post. On 8 January, 1992, the squadron base was accurately shelled for over two hours. Hard work has its own rewards and, with only about fifteen percent of the Squadron in location, it was the SHQ which took the battering and the OC's Land Rover acquired a few new spares in the process.

10 Regiment RCT Fuel Tankers prepare for OP GRAPPLE.

In February, with the opening up of the Mostar Road and a concentration of logistic assets on the coast, the Squadron moved back to a location some sixteen kilometres south-east of Split. This was the last home of the Squadron as an RCT unit, but it continued under UN colours before re-badging, and command passed to Major Richard Castell. The Squadron's greatest claim to fame was probably confounding the Staff calculations by doing more in less time than had been thought possible – but then the RCT was always rather good at that!

Berlin

As the rebuilding of East Berlin and a unified Germany began, the final chapter of the cold war story drew to a close when the Berlin Infantry Brigade drew down. However, 'no wall' did not mean 'no work' and 62 Squadron continued with its industrious support to the Brigade until it was disbanded as 62 Transport and Movements Squadron RCT on 1 April, 1993, and reformed as 62 Transport and Movements Squadron RLC.

RCT Organization in BAOR – HQ L of C

The HQ RCT L of C commitment based on Emblem, Belgium, lasted until 30 March, 1992, when the British Communication Zone was formally disbanded as part of the early closure measures associated with Options for Change. In a simple ceremony the Union Jack was lowered outside the headquarters and the camp was formally handed back to the Belgian Army. It soon became obvious, however, that, given the amount of equipment and vehicles to be returned to UK from BAOR as a result of drawdown, there would remain a continuing need for a movements presence to cover the Low Countries and northern France.

Headquarters RCT was therefore reorganized as a new unit – the United Kingdom Movement and Liaison Staff (Low Countries). This unit remained responsible for all movements in the Low Countries, including the four-day cycle of Landing Ship Logistics into Antwerp, and took on a number of liaison and staff planning tasks previously carried out by Headquarters British Communication Zone. 602 Transport Unit, however, was disbanded and their main task of moving containers and equipment to and from the exchange point in Moenchengladbach was put out to contract.

Air Trooping to Germany

The Air Trooping service to Germany remained largely unchanged for a little over 25 years, with Britannia Airways operating on contract out of Luton. On occasions where demand exceeded the number of available seats, *ad hoc* charter aircraft were arranged. Maximum use of the RAF Air Transport Fleet was also made in support of operational deployments, training overseas, and Arms Plot moves. The Britannia contract was to expire on 31 March, 1994, when a new carrier, British World Airlines, operating from Stansted, was awarded the contract. They were to provide an air-trooping service to RAF Bruggen, Munster, Osnabruck, Paderborn and Hanover. At the same time the weekly charter flights to Berlin were replaced by a discounted fare agreement, giving more flexibility for the drawdown of the Berlin Infantry Brigade until its closure at the end of 1994.

UN OBSERVER MISSIONS

Corps United Nations Military Observer (UNMO) commitments gave a wider scope for individuals to travel on a global scale and the RCT had personnel deployed in North Africa, the Middle East and the Far East.

Two Corps officers served in North Africa, coming under the jurisdiction of Operation MINURSO, the United Nations Mission for the Referendum in Western Sahara. Their task was to verify reduction and the positions of troops in the disputed zone, implement and supervise a repatriation programme and organize a free referendum, registering voters and proclaiming the final results. Operation MINURSO started in September, 1991, and observers served six-month tours.

In the Middle East the Corps had five Military Observers deployed in the border region of Iraq/Kuwait. These observers were primarily tasked with the maintenance of the demilitarized zone (DMZ) along the border region of the two countries. This tasking incurred secondary tasks such as the prevention of the entry of armed military personnel or military equipment into the DMZ. Covering an area some 200 kilometres long and ten kilometres deep, the 300-strong unarmed Military Observer force had to deal not only with the restraining of opposing armed troops, but also a considerable amount of mines and unexploded ordnance left from the conflict. The United Nations Iraq-Kuwait Observation Mission (UNIKOM) was established in April, 1991, and individuals posted to the UNIKOM served six-month tours.

In the Far East the Corps had six officers serving as Military Observers in Cambodia, where they were under the jurisdiction of the United Nations Transitional Authority in Cambodia (UNTAC). This body was established to maintain order throughout the period of organization and settlement over the composition of the new Cambodian government. A military observer posted to the UNTAC staff could be tasked with a multitude of different appointments, from the organization and the establishment of the UNTAC logistic network to the establishment and manning of border checkpoints, controlling the movement of weapons, ammunition and military stores across the Thai border as well as the supervision of the ceasefire and all related measures. The military observers deployed and remained unarmed throughout their six-month tour whilst operating from the UN base camp in Phnom Penh.

NORTHERN IRELAND

In 1992, as a lead into the formation of the new RLC, the RCT establishment was adjusted. By the end of that year there were 21 Transport and Movements Regiment, comprising RHQ, providing staff for HQ Northern Ireland, 26 Squadron, 49 Movement Control Squadron and 73 Squadron. Some units of other Corps scheduled to become RLC, were also placed under command, namely 22 Postal and Courier Squadron RE and RAOC Ordnance Depot (functional only until 5 April, 1993).

FINAL DAYS OF GTR

No sooner had all of the soldiers safely returned to Hong Kong from the Gulf when the Regiment was tasked to send a squadron to complete a United Nations tour in Cyprus. Despite the strain on manning and Hong Kong routine commitments, the

Regiment met the challenge. The contingent resurrected the name of 34 Transport Squadron GTR for this operational tour. The Squadron received much praise for the professional job done in Cyprus and Sergeant Subasing Gurung was awarded the BEM for his particular efforts.

In the latter days of the Corps the Regiment was blessed with positive news despite the bleak future for the Brigade of Gurkhas, with amalgamation and redundancy looming. On 30 August, 1992, the Colonel of the Regiment, Major General R M Llewellyn, was able to announce that Her Majesty was pleased to grant the Gurkha Transport Regiment a Royal Warrant. The name of the Regiment was to be the Queen's Own Gurkha Transport Regiment, bringing it in line with all other Brigade of Gurkhas' Regiments. The Regiment owes a great debt of gratitude to the Colonel of the Regiment who had strived to achieve this honour for the Regiment throughout his tenure of appointment. All badges and buttons were duly changed to reflect the new title and Commander British Forces Hong Kong Major General J P Foley, presided over an emotional and well executed Re-badging Parade on 27 February, 1993.

Other positive news in 1992 was the confirmation of the deployment of 28 Squadron to UK. This move was a part of the Options for Change package and secured a place for the Regiment in the future, if only at squadron level. 28 Squadron was to join 10 Regiment RLC operating in the DROPS role with a planned movement date of 15 November, 1993.

The planning by the Regiment for the necessary restructuring of the squadrons in the last few remaining years of service in Hong Kong was a difficult process, given the requirement for redundancy and the eventual demise of the HKMSC and the Regimental headquarters. The future of the Regiment, however, was to lie in the UK and 28 Squadron QOGTR would carry on the name of the Queen's Own Gurkha Transport Regiment with pride.

JHSU in Final Days

Although JHSU(UK) was housed and operated from the East Hangar at RAF Odiham, the hangar and buildings were condemned in 1988. It is hoped that a new

JHSU team on a training exercise.

hangar for JHSU on the southern side of the airfield will replace it. As a result of Options for Change JHSU(G) reduced from six teams to three teams in April, 1993, and moved to RAF Laarbruch. JHSU(UK) increased from four to seven teams, the UK and Germany parts of JHSU coming under command of a new Officer Commanding JHSU(UK). The whole organization in UK and Germany came under command of, and would be tasked by, Support Helicopter Force Headquarters (SHFHQ), based at RAF Benson.

An additional change is that military manpower, which until 1993 was drawn from the RCT driver trade, will be drawn from the Royal Logistic Corps Movements trade. Administrative support will be provided by 29 Transport Regiment RLC.

THE NEW REGIMENTAL STRUCTURE

Colonel C M Lake was established in May, 1992, as Regimental Colonel with formal responsibility for coordinating Regimental matters of the new Corps under the direction of a One-star Committee (almost immediately nicknamed 'the Famous Five'), which sought to draw together the many different strands of the forming Corps, on the basis that all Corps were equal, and to agree on its Regimental Structure. The Colonels Commandant were brought in, debatably at too late a stage, to assist and advise the Committee, and discussions covered almost every area of activity including training, uniforms, badges, accoutrements, messes, property, museums, bands, regimental marches, sports, organization and the future Institution. The status and continuance of official Associations, Affiliations and Freedoms had to be resolved in amicable and constructive ways between the Corps and with the agreement of those concerned. Each Corps formed its own Committees to manage the closure and post-formation affairs of the forming Corps [those of the RCT are described later in this Chapter]. Inevitably there were many hard bargains to be struck and, for each Corps, some disappointments over the loss of cherished traditions or much-loved items of dress. Where possible, historical precedent, goodwill and common sense all helped to bring the best of the Forming Corps to the development of the RLC.

Eventually decisions were finalized and the new Corps began to take shape building on its inheritance of the strengths and traditions from the Forming Corps. The new badge retained the eight-pointed star and crown of the RASC/RCT (giving the look and feel of the old badge to some 'old hands'), and incorporating distinctive elements of the other Corps. The motto 'We Sustain' was adopted from the ACC which fitted particularly well with QMG's declared aim 'to sustain the Army in peace and war'. The RLC was to be a mounted Corps, continuing the RCT tradition, and units would therefore be regiments, squadrons and troops. It was agreed that the ethos of the new Corps must be allowed to develop, but it must recognize the need for coherence through peace, transition to war and war. The RLC decided that, in view of 'operational imperatives, the supply and distribution strengths of the Corps lay at the heart of the new structure, and all Regular subalterns must therefore command in the field force'.

The Territorial Army

The Directors General and Directors of the five Forming Corps instructed their

TA/CVHQ Commanders to prepare an enabling plan for approval, and it was agreed by them that the focus for the TA would be at Grantham. The task of chairing the Joint Planning Committee RLC TA, as it was named, fell on the Commander RCT TA, Colonel C J Constable. He held the first informal round table meeting of the five Commanders at Grantham on 19 November, 1991. An outline plan of action was agreed and the JPC met formally on nine subsequent occasions, the Committee having been enhanced by the three Colonels TA of RE(PCS), RCT and RAOC. Much of the detailed planning was done by a working party at Chief of Staff level chaired by Lieutenant Colonel C H Jackman, Chief of Staff HQ RAOC TA. Shortly afterwards he became acting Commander RAOC TA and a full member of the JPC, when he moved the RAOC TA to Grantham from Deepcut in August, 1992. The Working Party was in turn supported by sub-committees covering all aspects of the formation. The TA were represented at all levels and played a full part in the decisions. A great deal of detailed work was involved and much of this was against a background of continuing uncertainty. Grantham had been nominated as the training focus for the RLC TA at an early stage, but, in the face of great pressure to reduce costs, this was once again thrown into the melting pot. Despite the fact that any alternative location was quite impractical to deal with the numbers involved, it was not until the personal intervention of the Quartermaster General that Grantham was finally confirmed.

Formation

The Royal Warrant was signed by HM The Queen on 18 March, 1993, and Colonel Lake was tasked to develop and organize the outstandingly successful Formation Parade at its new Headquarters at Deepcut on 5 April, 1993.

THE FINAL REGIMENTAL ACTIVITIES OF THE RCT

The Territorial Army Silver Jubilee

The Territorial Army marked the passing of the Corps by celebrating the Silver Jubilee of the Corps TA with a regimental day at the Prince William of Gloucester Barracks, Grantham, on 28 June, 1992. The focus of the day was the Jubilee Ceremonial Review, with over 1000 Volunteers on parade under the command of Colonel A S Feldman. Music was provided by the RCT Staff Band, 150 (Northumbrian) Transport Regiment RCT (V) Band, the pipers of 154 (Lowland) Transport Regiment RCT (V), 152 (Ulster) Ambulance Regiment RCT (V) and the Corps of Drums of 157 (Welsh) Transport Regiment RCT (V). Princess Alice, Duchess of Gloucester, took the salute with the Director General, Major General J D McDonald, the Representative Colonel Commandant, Major General I S Baxter, and Colonel C J Constable, Commandant HQ RCT TA in attendance. All RCT TA units were represented by their commanding officers and the family occasion was completed by regimental dinner nights in the various messes.

The Last Weekend and Regimental At Home

The final RCT Corps Weekend was celebrated at Buller Barracks in July, 1992. The 'At Home' followed the traditional pattern of a family reunion and fête, combined with static displays, sideshows, stalls and an arena events programme. Five Corps Bands were present – the Corps Staff Band, Corps of Drums, Pipers of the Gurkha Transport Regiment, Band of 150 Regiment, Pipes and Drums of 152 Ulster Ambulance Regiment and the Corps of Drums of 157 Regiment. Larger numbers than expected turned out and indifferent weather failed to dampen either enthusiasm or enjoyment.

The static displays demonstrated a wide range of Corps activities, particularly its success in the Gulf War. 27 Regiment proudly showed off captured Iraqi equipment and a video of their contribution to the victory. A unique collection of historic and modern equipment included prototypes and trials vehicles, and current RCT vehicles provided by HQ RCT TA. 21 Regiment brought a selection of vehicles used in Northern Ireland, including an armoured staff car. 20 Squadron displayed the Queen's Baggage vehicles. 17 Port and Maritime depicted their remarkable range of activities, vessels and equipment. Not to be outdone, 29 Transport and Movement Regiment and 63 Squadron arranged a fascinating display of RCT Airborne, Air Despatch and Movements units in realiztic surroundings. The wide variety of 'fun' sideshows and stalls were as popular as ever. The Corps Silver and Medal Collections were on show, as well as the Corps coaches and waggons. The Corps Museum opened, together with the popular RASC/RCT and Gurkha Transport Association stalls.

The arena programme included the Corps Staff Band, directed by Captain Ray Maycock, and a display by the Motor Cycle Display Team from 153 (Highland) Artillery Support Regiment, the Blue Arrows. Poor weather prevented the Silver

The RCT Moblile Recruiting Team Display at the Last Regimental Weekend.

Stars Freefall Parachute Display. A Parade of the Corps coaches and waggonettes was followed by the Tug-of-War Final between two very well matched teams from 47 Air Despatch Squadron and 17 Port and Maritime Regiment; after a hard-fought contest, the Despatchers won the day, making a 'deep impression' on 'God's Acre'!

The Director General, Major General J D MacDonald, presented the RASC/RCT Association Trophy for the best RCT-badged ACF Detachment in 1991-92 to 203 Brentwood Detachment. The RASC/RCT Association Annual Award for the Regular unit judged to have made the greatest contribution to the Corps during the year was presented to 29 Transport and Movements Regiment by the President of the RASC/RCT Association, Major General D B Braggins. As Representative Colonel Commandant, Major General I S Baxter awarded the Hemming Belt to Lance Corporal Bessey of 27 Regiment as the boxer who had contributed most to Corps Sport during the year. Princess Alice, Duchess of Gloucester made a moving presentation of the 'Young Soldier of the Year Award' to the families of members of the Corps who died during the Gulf War. The rain finally relented for the Beating Retreat and Finale, a memorable and emotional conclusion to the last Corps At Home.

The Final Corps Sunday

The following day the final Corps Sunday Service was held in the Corps Church of St Michael and St George. Monsignor J Mallon and the Reverend J Whitton conducted the traditional ecumenical service. The Lesson was read by Major General J D MacDonald and, as customary, the Books of Remembrance were displayed and pages turned during the Service. The Director General took the salute at the March Past on Steeles Road. The parade included squadrons from the Depot and Training Regiment, the Old Comrades, the Corps Staff Band, the Corps of Drums and the Corps of Drums of 157 Regiment. Later, at the Corps War Memorial in Buller Barracks, Major General I S Baxter led the Act of Remembrance and delivered an address before the Wreath-Laying Ceremony. A trumpeter from the Corps of Drums sounded the Last Post and Reveille.

FAREWELL VISITS AND TOURS

DGTM paid a final visit to the USA during the period 1-15 June, 1992. Visiting both CASCOM at Fort Lee and the US Army Transportation Centre at Fort Eustis, he gave a formal speech at the Army Birthday Ball hosted by the Sergeant Majors' Association. He later visited the US Transportation Command in St Louis and the Military Traffic Management Command in both Virginia and New Jersey.

At the end of November General and Mrs MacDonald undertook a three-week visit to Australia, New Zealand and Singapore. In Australia they were hosted by several senior Royal Australian Corps of Transport (RACT) officers, including Colonel Tim Winter, a former CO of 10 Regiment RCT before transferring to the Australian Army. DGTM was given a comprehensive tour of RACT units and facilities in South-East Australia before moving on to New Zealand for a whistle-stop tour of three days touring the military installations on both islands, attending the CGS's conference, meeting several senior Army officers and many officers and men of the Royal New Zealand Corps of Transport (RNZCT). The Far East tour finished with a two-day stopover in Singapore for courtesy calls on the senior logistic officers of the Singapore Army. In recognition of the contribution made to the RCT in Hong Kong by the Hong Kong Military Service Corps (HKMSC), DGTM was invited to become a Trustee of the HKMSC Trust Fund. He went to Hong Kong in early January, 1993, for the inaugural meeting. He also saw Commander British Forces and Commander Transport and Movements. The officers of the Queen's Own Gurkha Transport Regiment hosted a farewell lunch.

DGTM and Mrs MacDonald started their final visit to BAOR by attending the last RCT Ski Meeting in February, 1993. After taking part and presenting prizes, he became the first (and last) DGTM to travel to Berlin through the Czech Republic and the former German Democratic Republic to start a farewell tour of BAOR. Moving west, the General visited all BAOR-based units, ending up at HQ BAOR. After a courtesy call on the Commander-in-Chief, he returned for a series of regimental visits and farewell dinner nights to units in UK.

THE COMMEMORATIVE AND FAREWELL LUNCHES AND DINNERS

The final days of the Corps were marked by a series of lunches and dinners. On 19 November, 1991, a lunch was held at Regent's Park Barracks Officers Mess as a formal celebration of the 90th birthday of the Colonel-in-Chief. Hosted by Major General Bryan Colley as Representative Colonel Commandant, the lunch was attended by serving Colonels Commandant and past Colonels Commandant serving on Corps Committees. DGTM and other officers involved with Corps regimental affairs were also present. The occasion was marked by the presentation of a fine bench for the garden of her Royal Highness at Barnwell Manor.

The following year on 26 November, 1992, a farewell dinner was held at Buller. The principal guest was The Right Honourable Archie Hamilton MP, Minister of State for the Armed Forces. Senior guests included MGO, IGDT, GOC Southern District, GOC Scotland and CGRM, together with seventeen major-generals and many brigadiers holding key appointments throughout the Army. From February, 1993, social events increasingly became Corps family affairs. A dinner to mark the well-established association between the RCT and the Worshipful Company of Carmen was hosted by the Colonels Commandant at Buller Mess on 1 February, 1993. Guests included The Master, Sir Peter Levene, the serving Honorary Colonel Commandant RCT and other eminent Court Members of the Company. The Worshipful Company now has an association with the Royal Logistic Corps. In celebration of the Corps' many sporting traditions, a Sportsman's Dinner was held on 8 February at Buller hosted by DGTM. Attended by distinguished players past and present, the principal guests included Bobby Charlton, former England Soccer International, and Henry Cooper, former British, Commonwealth and European Heavyweight Boxing Champion. Ian Robertson, former International rugby player, now journalist and BBC commentator, gave an entertaining after-dinner speech. An auction of sporting memorabilia raised over £2000 for leukaemia research. On 18 February, 1993, the Inspector RCT, Brigadier D T Kinnear, held a well-attended lunch for past Inspectors of the RASC and RCT in Buller Mess Medal Room.

The Corps bade farewell to its Colonel-in-Chief, Princess Alice, Duchess of Gloucester, at a lunch held at Buller on 3 March. Past and Present Colonels Commandant and their wives attended, together with senior guests from the Training Group RCT, Regimental Headquarters and the RASC/RCT Association. Princess

Alice was presented with a silver candlestick by the Representative Colonel Commandant, Major General I S Baxter. Unable to celebrate its Bicentenary formally on 7 March, 1994, the Corps celebrated its 199th Anniversary with a dinner at Buller on 8 March. The principal guest was General Sir John Learmont, Quartermaster General, and the Colonels Commandant, TA Honorary Colonels and officers representing the chain of command throughout the Corps were present. A final Corps Dinner was held in Buller Mess on 2 April. There was a strong gathering of the Corps family as officers of the Corps and their ladies bade farewell to Major General and Mrs MacDonald. In addition to a leather-bound album containing the photographic story of his tour of duty, the Director General was presented with a coffee table made from an RCT Drum.

[handwritten annotation:] MAJ AND MAC A HARDING ATTENDED HE BEING THE ONLY TA OFFICER TO ATTEND — EXCEPT FOR THE COL OF VOLUNTEERS

CHAPTER 13

The Sporting Life of the Corps

INTRODUCTION

The Army Sport Control Board was formed on 20 November, 1918, by order of the Army Council, its principal aim being the control and conduct of sport in the Army. Before the formation of this Board the various sports in which the Army participated were controlled by separate committees. As an example, the Army Football Association is the oldest, celebrating its centenary in 1987. The strictest amateur principles were applied and the definition of a sportsman was detailed by the Board. Unit sport is the foundation of all sports played in the Army and it is from this source that the Corps and its predecessors have provided players to represent the Army, the Combined Services and their country, where their talents are ultimately on display to the nation and indeed to world audiences.

Because of lack of records and any form of organization compared with today, readers will appreciate the impossibility of producing information on Corps achievements prior to the twentieth century. As always, space is an inhibiting factor and therefore the mention of individuals has had to be restricted to those who represented their country, except in some cases where those who have represented the Army have been mentioned, without which their particular sport could not be included.

Association Football

There can be no doubt that Lieutenant K E Hegan is the Corps' most famous footballer. He was selected as a full English international against France, Belgium and Ireland in 1923 and 1924, as an amateur international at the Olympic Games in 1920 and on twenty other occasions from 1920 to 1932. Lieutenant T M R Briggs represented Scotland in 1928 as an amateur international and similarly Corporal J Vance for Ireland versus England in 1925 and Lance Corporal S G Waite for Wales versus England in 1937.

National Service after the 1939-1945 war saw the enlistment of many professional footballers into our Corps. Several played for their countries whilst they were serving. Private C Crowe was selected for the full England side during the 1960-1962 seasons; Lance Corporal K Cains, Lance Corporal D Emerson and Corporal R R Ardery were English Amateur Internationals in 1959-1961. Private J Little was a full Scottish International in 1954-56, as also were Private R Yeats (1960-1962), Lance Corporal A Gilzean (1959-1961), and Private A Young (1960-62). Our Army Challenge Cup winners are as follows:

Army Service Corps (Woolwich)	1913-14
RASC Training Establishment	1922-23
Training Centre RASC	1936-37
2 Training Battalion RASC	1961-62

| RCT Training Centre | 1972-73 |
| 10 Corps Transport Regiment RCT | 1988-89 |

Army Minor Units Cup winner:

| Depot and Training Regiment RCT | 1991-92 |

Athletics and Cross Country

Captain C R D Dugmore, represented Great Britain at the 1908 Olympic Games in both the triple jump and long jump. He was also the Irish AA 120 yards hurdles champion in 1912 and represented Ireland versus Scotland in 1912 in the same event. Lieutenant W H Summers, represented England versus Italy in the 100 metres in 1933.

As in other sports, National Service ensured that the Corps received its share of international athletes. Lance Corporal W G Nankeville, Lance Corporal Sandow and Second Lieutenant P H Valle all represented Great Britain in 1947 and 1948; Driver A James and Driver A Jones represented Wales in 1948 and 1960-61 respectively. 63 Parachute Squadron RCT were the Army Minor Units Athletics and Cross Country Champions in 1966 and 1967. 2 Armoured Division Transport Regiment were the initial winners of the Army Cross Country Relay Championships in 1979.

The golden years for Corps Tug-of-War were the thirties when RASC Feltham were Army Champions for five consecutive years from 1934-1938 inclusive, and also AAA champions. CSD Aldershot RASC, a very small supply depot, achieved a magnificent result in 1947 when they won the 110 stones Army Championship. 2 Training Battalion RASC were Army Champions (88 stones) in 1956 as were 5 Training Battalion RASC in 1959. Depot Battalion RASC were Army Champions (110 stones) in 1961, with 63 Parachute Squadron RCT not only winning the Army Championship (88 stones) in 1966 and 1968 but also achieving a magnificent double in 1968 when the Squadron also won the British national championship.

Boxing

Lieutenant J Courtis won the Inter-Services Light-Heavyweight Championship from 1924 to 1928 inclusive, also the Inter-Services Heavyweight Championship in 1928 and was a Bronze Medal winner for England in the 1924 Olympic Games. Second Lieutenant F Collinson represented Great Britain in 1971. At unit level, 15 Training Battalion RASC were Army Champions in 1957, 1958, 1959 and 1960, followed by 10 Regiment RCT being Army Champions in 1973, 1974, 1975 and 1977.

Canoeing

Lance Corporals B Jupp, S Warren and J Gregory all represented Great Britain in this arduous sport in 1966 and 1968, also Driver Stimpson in 1968. In 1965, 1966, 1968 and 1969, 63 Parachute Squadron RCT were the Army Long Distance Champions and were also the Army Sprint Champions in 1965 and 1966.

Cricket

The cricket ground in Buller Barracks, known as God's Acre, has seen many matches and performances since the first match played there in 1891. The ground and the excellent fixture list from the early days until the late 1930s was due to the interest and drive of Major General E H Fitzherbert.

A match between an Officers' side and an Other Ranks' side was played on 1 June, 1991 to mark the centenary of Corps cricket on God's Acre, and a year later the final Corps match was played on the Buller field on 30 August, 1992.

The doyen of Corps cricket over many years has been Brigadier W M E White who represented his county, Northamptonshire, the Army and Combined Services on many occasions since 1945, as well as being Captain and finally President of the Incogniti C C. Ferdie Marrison, a formidable personality, rose from Private through WO1(RSM) to Major and his career record of 646 wickets throughout the 1930s and 1940s stands as a monument to Corps cricket.

There is no record of a Corps player representing England whilst serving. F R Brown, a wartime officer, and J H Edrich, a National Serviceman, played for England both at home and on overseas tours captained England and were included in tours in Australia. M J K (Mike) Smith was a National Service Sergeant in 5 Training Battalion RASC in Aldershot in 1953 and played for the Corps. He had a distinguished career in first-class cricket, playing fifty matches for England, including twenty as Captain, and three overseas tours. He has since been a very able administrator and was awarded the OBE. He also played rugby for England.

The really halcyon days of Corps cricket were in the 1950s and 1960s. The fixture list, mostly of two-day matches against top Service and Civilian clubs, was excellent, and it was possible at times to field a side all with Army caps.

A worthy achievement by a unit was that of 27 Regiment RCT who were Army Cup winners in 1972.

Fencing

Major R D S Anderson RASC represented England versus USA in the Sabre event in 1930 and was also Epée and Sabre Army Champion in 1930 and 1931. Lieutenant R Craig fenced for Great Britain in 1968 (Olympics), 1969 and 1970.

Free Fall Parachuting

For most of its existence the Corps' Silver Stars Free Fall Parachute Display Team was based on 63 Parachute Company RASC and latterly at Colerne, the home of the Junior Leaders Regiment RCT/RAOC. The team competed all over the world, taking part in many displays and competitions, not only winning medals at all levels and disciplines but bringing high praise and publicity to the Corps. Captain R Card, WO2 G Raine, WO2 M Togher, Staff Sergeant J J Chandler and Sergeant R S Ackerman all represented the Army in the sixties and seventies, Staff Sergeant Chandler also representing Great Britain and Captain R Card being the Army Accuracy Champion in 1972.

Golf

The Corps has produced many Army Golf Champions, Lieutenant M R Gardner in 1936 and 1937, Lieutenant T F B Law in 1939, Major H B C Davies in 1951, Second Lieutenant M F Bonnallack in 1955 and Second Lieutenant M J Collinge in 1958. Many other officers have represented the Army. Second Lieutenant M F Bonnallack served as a National Service Officer in 1954-56. After his service, between 1961 and 1970, he won the Amateur and English Championships five times each and won or tied for the English strokeplay on four occasions. During this same period he was a member of the British Walker Cup team and in 1971 he captained the team to victory against the USA. Corps teams won the Army Golf Challenge Cup in 1937, 1938, 1952, 1955, 1969 and 1971.

Hockey

Those Corps players who have won International honours are Captain J D H Fisher for England in 1930, Second Lieutenant A J Dann for England in 1949-50 and Lieutenant G M Cutter for Great Britain and Wales in 1956-57. Many players have represented the Army and three players, Lieutenant G M Cutter, Sergeant S D Cook and Lieutenant D G Beckett the Combined Services in 1956-57.

Lawn Tennis

Although the Corps cannot claim any international honours in this sport, we have had Army champions on many occasions. Major J Puckle and Captain A Berger were the Army Regimental Doubles Champions in 1910 and a most praiseworthy achievement was that of SSM A V Baxter who was the Army Singles Champion (Other Ranks) in 1926 and 1927. Captain W Price was the Army Open Doubles Champion in 1927 with a partner from another regiment, as was Captain A Berger in 1929. WO1(RSM) F Marrison and SQMS P S Dundon were Army Doubles Champions (Other Ranks) in 1931. Second Lieutenant C A S Wyse and Private J Beresford won the Army Regimental Doubles Championship in 1961, as did Lieutenant B B Trinkwon and Second Lieutenant M F Hayes in 1968. Second Lieutenant M F Hayes was also the Army Singles Champion in 1967. After the Second World War Major General P G Turpin was undoubtedly the doyen of Corps tennis and has been the winner of the Corps Singles Championship both as a subaltern and major-general!

Modern Pentathlon

In the years 1949-1967 the Corps had strong teams in this exacting sport. Corporal I Lillywhite was a magnificent athlete and represented Great Britain in the 1968 Olympics, the Army in 1967, 1968 and 1969, the Combined Services in 1976 and in the World Pentathlon Championships in 1966 and 1967. Major R M Mortimer represented the Army in 1964, 1965 and 1966.

Motoring and Motor Cycling

The emphasis in this sport has had to be more on Motor Cycling than Motoring. Motor sport at national and international level is an immensely expensive business, beyond the facilities and assets of a regimental team. However, in the early 1980s Major D R Birrell produced a March 793 Super Vee racing car displaying Corps colours. With commercial sponsorship and with the support of a team of enthusiasts from 27 Regiment, he drove in a number of events successfully and in 1981 won the UK Super Vee Championship at Mallory Park.

An outstanding RASC motorcyclist before the Second World War was Sergeant, later Major,'Otto' Davies. He was representing the Army in the International Six Day

Trials in Salzburg in September, 1939, when war broke out. The team was in an unassailable winning position but had to be hustled out of the country before completing the last day. After the war at unit level 1 Training Battalion RASC were Army Motor Cycle Champions in 1961, 1 Divisional Regiment RCT in 1967 and 10 Regiment RCT in 1968 and 1970.

Throughout the time of the Royal Corps of Transport many expert motorcyclists represented the Corps at International level in trials and long distance cross country events. The most famous of all events, the International Six Day Trial/Enduro, was deemed to be the world championships of cross country competitions and the one event that all Corps and Army standard riders aspired to compete in. The Army team was selected from the best three riders in the Army and it is doubtful that there was ever a team sent to any of the International Six Day events throughout the Corps history that did not have an RCT cap-badged rider as a member. Sergeant George Webb and Sergeant Mick Soames are names that immediately spring to mind when talking about international riders who dominated Army motorcycling throughout the sixties and early part of the seventies, as are Bob Belton and Ken Applewhite. Other riders from Corps and Regiments throughout the Army were also highly rated and during 1977 a REME tradesman, Corporal Barraclough, was posted to 2 Infantry Divisional Transport Regiment RCT Workshop for a tour of duty attached to the RCT Regiment then based in Bunde. On the instigation of his Commanding Officer, Lieutenant Colonel I S Baxter, he subsequently transferred to the RCT.

Lieutenant Colonel Baxter was also instrumental in arranging for the re-enlistment of another young soldier, Private W Buckley, who had left the Army (10 Regiment RCT) some 12 months earlier to work as a civilian mechanic in a motorcycle shop in Bielefeld. WO2 Buckley later turned out to be one of the best trials riders ever to have served in the British Army, winning the Army motorcycle championships on no less than eight occasions.

Barraclough and Buckley rode at International level competition throughout 1979, competing in the Italian and French rounds of the European Enduro championships along with another Bunde-based motorcyclist, WO2 John Nightingale. Barraclough and Buckley also represented the Army in that year's International Six Day event held in Siegen, West Germany, Barraclough unfortunately retiring on day five with a collapsed rear wheel, while Buckley went on to finish, earning a bronze medal. Both riders went on to compete in a round of the European Enduro championships in Czechoslovakia in 1980, courtesy of approval from the Commanding Officer, with Land Rover and trailer, ample rations and duty coupons being provided.

Barraclough had by now been recognized as a competent motorcyclist and had attracted interest from the British importers of the Italian Cagiva motorcycle manufacturers. Cagiva sponsored Barraclough over a two-year period including two International Six Day motorcycle events at Brioude, France, in 1980 and the Italian island of Elba in 1981. France in 1980 was a wickedly difficult event with very few finishers from the week's arduous event. Barraclough was only one of a handful of British riders to complete the competition, thus justifying continued sponsorship from Cagiva throughout 1981. After promotion to Sergeant he continued to lead the Army Team in worldwide events until 1993. Buckley also represented the Army in the French event, but unfortunately crashed heavily on the third day, the damage to himself and machine resulting in retirement from the event. Motorcycling was then, as of course it still is today, very much a leisure pursuit, exercise and duties permitting. Motorcycling was interrupted only too frequently by long BAOR exercises and the occasional Northern Ireland tour.

Orienteering

The sport of Orienteering grew nationally in the 1970s and 1980s which resulted in it being encompassed as a recognized Army sport. Major M Roach represented Great Britain in Bulgaria in 1975 and represented the Army on several occasions in the 1970s. He was one of the original map-makers to produce fully resurveyed orienteering maps for competitions and surveyed over thirty maps of military training areas in the UK and Germany. Corps orienteering was dominated for many years by 8 Regiment RCT in BAOR and 27 Regiment RCT in the UK; towards the end of the 1980s 1 Armoured Division Transport Regiment RCT and 3 Tank Transporter Squadron RCT took over.

Riding and Coaching

The Corps' equestrian tradition stems directly from its early connections with horse transport and, apart from one or two individuals with privately owned horses, most of our success has been achieved by members of its mounted unit, the Animal Transport Training Company RASC, which later became H Squadron RCT. This unit was disbanded in Aldershot in March, 1970.

The Corps retained its tradition of driving horse-drawn transport when Major General Sir H Reginald Kerr KBE, CB, MC formed the RASC Coaching Club in 1923. The RASC, later RCT, coach appeared with success at major horse shows throughout the UK; it also supported meets of the Coaching Club of Great Britain and drove members of the Corps on sporting and social activities. The RCT Coaching Club was disbanded in 1973. Both the Corps and Kerr coaches are at present on loan to the Royal Logistic Corps.

Individually the Corps has had many expert horsemen. Brigadier J R Allen represented Great Britain in international Show Jumping events in 1951, as did Captain G G R Boon in 1959, 1960, 1961 and 1962 and Corporal A Oliver in 1955 and 1956. The RASC and RCT produced formidable teams in the 1960s comprising Major G G R Boon, Major T J Brown, Captain R A Hill, Sergeant R Graham and Corporal D Devereux. These riders produced continuous success, winning the Queen Elizabeth II Challenge Cup (Inter-Services Team Show Jumping) in 1960, 1961, 1962, 1965 and 1967.

Rugby Football

The Corps is able to boast of international players as well as many who have represented the Army and Combined Services. The first of the internationals was Lieutenant P E O'Brien-Butler ASC who won caps for Ireland against England, Scotland and Wales in 1897, 1898, 1899 and 1900, followed by Lieutenant J A Middleton RASC who represented England versus Scotland in 1922. Three outstanding National Servicemen were Private J D Currie who represented England, Barbarians, Oxford University and Gloucestershire in 1953; after his Army service he won 25 caps for England. Second Lieutenant S R Smith RASC represented England in 1954.

Captain J D Macdonald played eight times for Scotland in the 1960s, and as well as captaining his national side he represented the Army and the Barbarians. Captain Macdonald reached the rank of major-general and was the last Director General of the RCT before absorption into the Royal Logistic Corps in 1993. Another outstanding player in the 1960s was Captain G Lilley, a fast and fearless back row forward, who won twelve Army caps in addition to playing for the Combined Services and the Barbarians. Captain J M Bowles played regularly for the Army from 1969 to 1980 and the Combined Services from 1972 to 1980, and had the honour of captaining both the Army and Combined Services, including their match against the Australian touring side.

We have never won the Army Cup, although two Corps teams, 1(BR) Corps Transport Column RASC and 63 Parachute Squadron RCT, reached the final. 63 Squadron was a minor unit reaching the final of a major competition, losing only 9-5 against 1st Battalion the Duke of Wellington's Regiment, a truly outstanding achievement.

Corps units competed every season for the Goodfellow Cup and the Eassie Sevens. The winners of the Corps Championship in BAOR and the Goodfellow Cup, confined to UK units, played each other for the Major General Sir Cecil M Smith trophy to decide the season's Corps Champions. All three trophies had been presented by distinguished Corps officers.

Sailing

From 1957 the Corps regularly provided Army team members mainly in dinghy and offshore events. Since 1976 the RCT team was placed first or second each year in the Army Championships for offshore events, and Corps boats were selected to represent the Army in the Joint Services Offshore Race in 1980 and 1981. In a short period the Corps has made an outstanding contribution to Army sailing and many members have taken part in national and Army events.

The Corps owned three offshore yachts based in BAOR, all named *St Christopher*. The last yacht, *St Christopher V,* was purchased in 1992 and was transferred to The Royal Logistic Corps. Sailing was established as a major adventure training activity in BAOR. Each year over three hundred RCT soldiers in BAOR participated in this activity and sailed in the Corps yacht to a large number of foreign ports.

Skiing and Luge

Birdwood Barracks, Bunde, in BAOR, the home of 2 and, later, 1 Armoured Division Transport Regiment RCT was the focus of RCT skiing throughout the life of the Corps, the regimental team regularly representing the RCT at Army championships. The team were the Army Ski Champions, winners of the Princess Marina Cup, four times in 1973, 1975, 1982 and 1986, and several individuals represented the Army, Combined Services and national teams over the years.

Four individuals have been outstanding. Lance Corporal (later Staff Sergeant) K A Oliver represented Great Britain in 1969, 1970, 1971, 1972 (Olympics), 1976 (Olympics) and 1980 (Olympics). He was the British and Army 15km Cross Country Champion in 1969, 1971, 1973, 1974 and 1978, the British and Army 20km Biathlon Champion in 1971, 1973, 1977 and 1978, the British and Army 10km Biathlon Champion in 1974 and 1977 and the British and Army 30km Cross Country Champion in 1977, and the winner of many other international events. Lance Corporal (later Staff Sergeant) I M White was the Army Downhill Champion in 1972, 1974 and 1976, Army Slalom Champion in 1972, 1975, 1976, 1978, 1979 and 1980, Army Alpine Champion in 1972, 1975 and 1976 and the Combined Services Downhill Champion in 1972, 1974 and 1979; he was selected as the Army Team Captain in 1981, the first time an NCO has ever been awarded this distinction. Corporal C McIvor represented Great Britain at the 1980 and 1984 Olympics, also Corporal M Watkins at the 1984 and 1988 Olympics.

A major achievement by junior NCOs was that of Lance Corporal A Simpson who represented Great Britain in the Junior Biathlon World Championships in 1989 and was the British Junior Biathlon Champion in 1990; also Lance Corporal J Lock who skied for Great Britain in 1988.

Members of the Corps have also had some outstanding results in the comparatively new discipline of Luge, a sport which involves sliding feet first on a sled along a convoluted corridor of ice. Captain Stephanie McGowan represented Great Britain from 1990 to 1992 in world-wide events and another female athlete, Driver C Dawson, has been selected for Luge training with the ultimate goal of the 1998 Olympics.

Skill at Arms

It is unfortunate that no records exist of Corps achievements prior to 1948. The Army Rifle Association was founded in 1893 and there can be no doubt that ASC and RASC individuals and units reached the highest level of competition at Bisley.

In 1948 Private K Finlay won the title of Champion Young Soldier of the Year, followed by Captain E W H Brooks winning the King's Prize, Bisley, in 1949. The 1950s produced great success for Corps marksmen. Sergeant J E White won the Queen's Medal and was TA Champion in 1953 but the achievements of Captain C G F Platfoot were almost unlimited. He was not only a fine rifle and pistol shot but he trained many unit teams. He was a member of the Army Rifle VIII in 1956, 1957, 1958 and the Army Revolver VIII in 1956, 1958, 1960 and was the Inter-Services Rifle Champion and winner of the Queen Mary Medal in 1958. Major H J Aldred was a member of the Army SMG VIII for ten consecutive years from 1958 to 1967 inclusive, was the SMG Individual Champion at Bisley in 1962 and 1964, and was the Inter-Services XX Champion in 1954. Lieutenant Colonel M G M Crosby RASC was Captain of the Army VIII for five consecutive years from 1957 to 1961 inclusive, Major J M Riches RCT was the Army Long and Short Range Target Rifle Match Champion in 1966 and 1974, Lieutenant J E C Lewis RCT won the National Rifle Association Silver Medal and Bisley Cup in 1968 and was the Army Long and Short Range Target Rifle Match Champion in 1969 and Second Lieutenant M Rees RCT won the Young Officers' Cup and ARA Spoon in 1978.

There were several notable team achievements with splendid performances by the Gurkha Transport Regiment. 34 Squadron GTR won the Squadron Shield (All Arms) at Bisley in 1968, the Regimental team won the King Edward VII Cup, the 1st Army Cup and the Duke of Connaught Cup in 1968 and followed this triple success by winning the ARA Unit Rifle Match, Bisley, in 1972. 31 Squadron GTR won the Young Soldiers' Small-bore Match in 1977 and 28 Squadron GTR won the Malta Command Cup in 1978. All these Corps successes were achieved at Bisley, scene every year of the fiercest all arms and inter-service competition.

Twenty-nine members of the Corps have reached the Army Rifle 100 to shoot off for the Queen's Medal to become the individual Army Rifle Champion. Only one has achieved this ultimate distinction, Driver Deobahadar Rana in 1986.

Major D J Owen RCT was selected as Adjutant of the British Army Rifle Team for its tour of Canada in 1990 and Captain of the team for its 1993 tour. The honour of Captain had also been granted to Brigadier M J Squire OBE in 1989.

Squash

Not many Corps players of distinction appeared until the 1970s, although Lieutenant P W Le Gros RASC represented England in 1945, also Lieutenant P F Fuente RASC in 1946, 1947 and 1948, and Lieutenant Colonel (later Major General) P G Turpin RASC played for the Army in 1952. Captain (later Major) D J Le Cheminant RCT, Lieutenant (later Major) I R Mosedale RCT, Captain R P Broad RCT and Lance Corporal P Costigan all represented the Army regularly from the mid-1970s to the early 1990s.

Swimming

Although the Corps has had no internationals, fifteen swimmers represented the Army during the period 1926-1939 and a further fourteen swam for the Army during 1948-1968.

CHAPTER 14

The Regimental Life and Organization of the Corps

Regimental Affairs

Up to 1960 Regimental Affairs were conducted privately by the Corps, largely through the Chain of Command where appropriate, and through volunteers operating from within the Committee system. The HQ Officers' Mess, the Association and the Benevolent Fund had some paid for staff and all administrative expenses were met from Regimental Funds. These informal arrangements developed into a structure which lasted with comparatively minor changes to the 1990s. In 1960 the Army Board formally accepted the need for Regimental Headquarters throughout the Army and, more importantly, funded manpower to support them.

The original Buller Officers' Mess.

The Regimental Headquarters

The Corps Regimental Headquarters was founded in Buller Barracks with two main sections. The Regimental Secretary headed a Secretariat to run the affairs of the Institution. The Controller, originally in London, moved to Aldershot in 1975 and ran the affairs of the Association and the Benevolent Fund.

The Secretariat provided the focal point of RCT regimental activities and coordinated Corps domestic affairs. This included Corps funds, Corps property, the Corps Journal (*The Waggoner* from 1953), *The Review* and the *RCT Officers' Handbook*, museum, library and medal collection, Corps history, records, archives and memorials, policy aspects of the Headquarters Mess, and the Band. RHQ also provided the specialist staff for the maintenance and safeguarding the regimental traditions. The Secretariat ensured that Colonels Commandant and the Head of the Corps could exercise control over domestic regimental matters with the benefit of the continuity and experienced staff of Retired Officers. Control was effected largely through a number of committees reporting to the Committee of Management of the Institution and coordinated by the Council for Regimental Affairs when required. The senior appointment in the staff of RHQ RCT was that of Secretary, a Retired Officer Grade II, the first incumbent being Colonel J R Burgess TD from 1960 to his untimely death in harness in 1972. Brigadier D W E Hancox served from 1972 to 1982, handing over to Brigadier B G E Courtis in 1982. Colonel J A Newcombe filled the role of Regimental Secretary for six months after the early retirement of Brigadier Courtis. Lieutenant Colonel J G Hambleton took on the task from 1990 to the formation of the Royal Logistic Corps on 4 April, 1993. In October, 1992, an Assistant Secretary, Lieutenant Colonel C J Doland, was appointed to help with the transition. He then became the Secretary of the RASC/RCT Institution. As such, he conducted all the detailed staff work that resulted in the successful formation of the new Corps Institution that continues to cater for those officers who wish to remember with pride their service within the RASC and RCT.

The Regimental Association

The RASC/RCT Association formed an integral part of RHQ RCT and was responsible for the administration of Association branches throughout the United Kingdom and the operation of the RASC/RCT Benevolent Fund. From 1927 to 1944 the Association was run by a Secretary, but from 1945 onwards the post became that of Controller when it was held by Colonel H M Wright, OBE, 1945 to 1952; Brigadier Farquharson-Roberts CBE, 1952 to 1960; Colonel E (Jock) Marshall OBE, 1960 to 1975; Colonel R F Discombe OBE, 1975 to 1981; Brigadier D Cardle, 1981 to 1991. The incumbent from 1991 has been Lieutenant Colonel R E Wills.

Major General Sir Cecil Smith (Retired) leads the Association March Past at the Annual Corps Week, Church Parade, Aldershot.

The Committees

By 1982 the Committee structure of the Institution, the Association and the Benevolent Fund were well established and proved well able to carry out the business of the Corps, making effective use of a wide cross-section of officers and soldiers from within the Corps as Committee members. There were two significant changes over the period. Firstly, the Committees of the Institution reorganized to form the Museum Trust, the Medal Trust and the Central Property and Disbanded Units Trust. These changes, together with the creation of the Council for Regimental Affairs, created a valuable and responsive forum which was to help make the final, and difficult decisions over the future when the Corps was due to be amalgamated with other Corps to form the RLC.

The second change was perhaps of greater significance to the Institution. The Trustees of the Benevolent Fund decided to allow an amount of money from the One-Day's Pay Scheme to be transferred to the Clayton Trust for use in support of Corps activities. This money was not required for Benevolence and this highly effective formula took effect for three years until 1992. In all, a sum of some £350,000 was transferred. But for this, many of the activities and acquisitions on the winding-up of the Corps could not have been achieved. This initiative by the Trustees of the Benevolent Fund contributed, in a large part, towards an effort from 1983/84 aimed at establishing the Clayton Trust as the Capital Fund of the Corps outside that required for Benevolence. Major General W M Allen and Major General D B H Braggins were the driving forces behind this initiative to establish a firm financial base for a wide variety of Corps activities. In the event it proved a most timely initiative. Treasurers over this period were Lieutenant Colonel S Hoyle 1966 to 1979, and Major M D Isherwood 1979 to 1991.

The Regimental Museum and the Corps Journal

The post of Editor of the Journal and Curator of the Museum within the RHQ had been combined since its establishment in 1960. The pressure on the incumbent was always great. These were compounded by changes within the printing industry, the donation of more and more items of personal memorabilia from officers, soldiers and their families to the Museum or the archives. Major C W P Coan, 1977 to 1987, and Lieutenant Colonel M H G Young, 1987 to 1993, together with regular and invaluable help from a number of loyal Friends of the Museum, brought both Journal and the Museum up to date with modern display and conservation techniques. The Centenary issue of *The Waggoner* was published in 1991. Its resounding success gave rise to a book, *Waggoners Way*, compiled with extracts from articles and photographs from Journals of the previous 100 years and previously unpublished archive photographs. Over 1,300 copies were sold, a record for any Corps book.

The Medal Collection

The RCT Medal Collection was reorganized during the return to the new HQ Officers' Mess in the newly rebuilt Buller Barracks in 1969. Lieutenant Colonel G T Pearce MBE was appointed Corps Numismatist and was able to oversee its display in a specially prepared Medal Room within the new mess. The collection was substantially enhanced over the years with the addition of the display of neck decorations, a mobile case for the Victoria Cross and George Cross displays, and four mobile cases holding additional acquisitions not yet incorporated chronologically into the Central Display. Over many years Professor R M Graveson, a Corps officer during the Second World War, had been a keen collector of Corps medals and, as a result, he became a Trustee of the RCT Medal Trust. His generous loans and gifts of medals to the Corps were much appreciated; as a final act he bequeathed a large number of important and prestigious medals to the Corps on his death in 1991. The RCT Medal Trust was established in 1986. The aims of the Trust, together with the details of entitled recipients, have been written into the new Trust Deed which incorporates all the requirements of the Institution of the RASC/RCT on the end of the Corps on 4 April, 1993.

The DALTON VC

Perhaps the most important addition to the Collection was the purchase of the Victoria Cross won by Assistant Commissary J L Dalton at Rorke's Drift in 1879. A sum of £84,000 was raised by the family of the Corps after a spirited Corps-wide campaign for contributions organized by the Regimental Headquarters. The medal was auctioned by Spinks in 1986 and purchased by the Corps for £64,000. The Spinks family, who owned the medal, were most conscious of its importance to the Corps and contributed to the cost. The balance of the Funds was donated to assist in the maintenance of the Medal Collection.

Regimental Publications

A Corps Journal was first published in 1891 with the aim of promoting *esprit de corps* and presented an account of regimental and unit life in the Corps. It included regimental and unit news, accounts of professional activities, sports, domestic occurrences and reports of the Regimental Association and its regional branch activities. The style was conservative but managed to keep abreast of the times, finally adopting a new title, *The Waggoner* in March, 1953. The archive collection of journals now provides an invaluable record of the Corps history and source of information for the casual and serious student alike.

There was such a demand for space in the Journal for reports and articles of current regimental and domestic interest that professional matters tended to be crowded out. To remedy this *The Quarterly* was first published in October, 1905, entirely devoted to professional articles. It was dedicated to the encouragement of officers to take a greater interest in the professional aspect of their careers and to study and discuss all manner of problems likely to be faced by the Corps in war. There was a break in publication between 1914 and 1920, but it then continued, with the exception of 1928, until 1939. In this period it had become a valuable addition to the official Royal Army Service Corps training manuals.

After the Second World War a successor to *The Quarterly* was revived under the title of *The Review* which was first published in 1948. This covered a wide variety of subjects and provides an admirable insight to the current professional activities and concerns of the RASC and RCT.

In addition to publications of a periodical nature, the Corps has from time to time published works in the interest of recording the history of the Corps and its members, and those produced before 1983 are included in the bibliography. However, during the 1980s and 1990s a number of new books and pamphlets were published, which added to the efforts of many Corps members to leave a full record of Corps activities. Among these were:

A Short History of the Royal Corps of Transport and its Predecessors 1794-1981	Maj C W P Coan
History of the Royal Corps of Transport and Museum Guide	Maj C W P Coan
The Turn of the Wheel	Maj Gen P G Turpin (1988)
Eyewitness in Zululand	Lt Col I H W Bennett (1989)
Wait for the Waggon (pamphlet)	Lt Col I G Thomas/Maj C W P Coan (1986)
The Unknown Fleet	Lt Col R K Cooley (1993 (nationally)
History of the Corps Band (pamphlet)	Lt Col I G Thomas (1993(locally)
Waggoner's Way	Lt Col M H G Young (1993)

The Histories of Air Despatch and of the Army Service Corps in the First World War, by Col M F I Cubitt and Lt Col M H G Young respectively, are being written as this history goes to the publishers.

Clubs

The Corps has been fortunate that, in addition to its formal social life, it has been able to enjoy a wide variety of clubs, such as the Officers' Lunch Club, the Waggon Club, the RASC/RCT Officers' Luncheon Club, the Movement Control Officers' Club, the QM's Association of the RASC/RCT and Air Despatch Reunion Dinners. The Corps Masonic Lodge 'Nil Sine Labore', founded in 1898, continued its activities and in 1993 opened its membership to members of the RLC. Although all these clubs and associations are privately organized and funded, they reflect the comradeship engendered over the years within a number of organizations and

The RASC Coaching Club – Major George Boon driving Her Majesty the Queen, 1959.

activities. These clubs have continued to flourish and the future looks good with a refreshingly open approach to accommodating the changing circumstances and the needs of the clubs and their members over the coming years.

The Royal Hospital Chelsea

The Royal Hospital Chelsea was founded in 1682 by King Charles II as a retreat for veterans of the regular army who had become unfit for duty, either after 20 years' service or as a result of wounds. The provision of a hostel, rather than some system of pensions, was undoubtedly inspired by the Hotel des Invalids in Paris, founded by Louis XIV.

The building was designed by Sir Christopher Wren and was intended to house all Army pensioners; however, it soon became evident that there were considerably more old soldiers who were entitled to 'pension' than had been estimated when building began. Thus James II established a money pension for the overflow who were known as Out-Pensioners, to distinguish them from the In-Pensioners who lived in the Royal Hospital. The In-Pensioners number some 385 and are drawn from Army pensioners of good character who will have served a minimum of 12 years and/or may be in receipt of a service disability pension. Normally not less than 65 years of age, they will also be of single status.

On entry into the Royal Hospital they surrender their service pensions *in toto* and in return receive free board and lodging, clothing and medical care. Leave of absence is freely granted. Uniform is worn within the grounds and civilian clothes may be worn outside. The ceremonial dress for In-Pensioners of scarlet coat and tricorne hat is a modern version of the service dress of Marlborough's time. Meals are served restaurant-style in the Great Hall for all but the most infirm who are served in their Long Wards.

The term 'Hospital', as we understand it today, is a misnomer. Originally intended as a retreat for veteran soldiers, most of whom had suffered injury or wounds, we would now see it as a Hospice or Rest Home for our retired soldiers. In this context, medical support is one of the most important aspects of the Royal Hospital and a fully staffed 100-bed Infirmary, under the control of the Physician and Surgeon and his two assistant Medical Officers, provides every possible care and support to all residents.

From the outset, In-Pensioners have been allocated a berth, or cubicle, in a Long Ward some 200 feet in length. Originally berths measured six foot square, but in recent years have been enlarged to nine foot square with ceilings and air-conditioning, thus providing greater peace and privacy. Berths are furnished with a bed, table, wardrobe, chest of drawers, chair, television point and radio headphones.

Charles II intended that the Royal Hospital should be organized on military lines, but without the rigours of military discipline, and this has continued through the centuries. Management, from its earliest days, has been undertaken by a Board of Commissioners appointed directly by the crown and the Paymaster General has always been the Chairman. The Governor and Lieutenant Governor are assisted by an Adjutant, three Medical Officers, a Chaplain, Quartermaster and five retired officers, styled Captains of Invalids, who command the five Companies of In-Pensioners. The In-Pensioners themselves fill the Company rank structure, and, with others who volunteer for duties such as clerks, guides, library and museum assistants, to name a few of the duties, approximately 120 In-Pensioners, and the Royal Hospital itself, benefit from their continuing activity and interest in life generally.

Considerable emphasis is placed on their welfare and recreation. In addition to their own Club, they are able to follow their spare-time interests and hobbies; there are allotments for those who wish to garden, an Arts and Crafts centre, a library, bowls, putting and croquet. Much emphasis is placed on regimental links and many outings are arranged by them. Other benefactors arrange outings to the Races, Chelsea Association Football Club, Lords, and many other visits of an historical or general interest are arranged, including a Battlefield tour each year. The first Corps pensioners to join the Royal Hospital were:

Royal Waggon Train – Andrew Parker. Became In-Pensioner 1858. Died 1872. Age 83.
Army Service Corps – John Stean. Became In-Pensioner 1873. Died 1875. Age 46.
Military Train – James Bonwell. Became In-Pensioner 1878. Died 1881. Age 61.
RASC – C Bushell. Became In-Pensioner 1926. Died 1935.

MANAGING CHANGE – DECISIONS FOR THE FUTURE

The conduct of Regimental Affairs developed steadily from the first meeting of the ASC Officers Club in 1910. Since then the Corps' predecessors established many effective and resilient structures for the management of Regimental life and the maintenance of its traditions and history. These culminated in the establishment of a small Regimental Headquarters designed to look after Corps responsibilities and dedicated to maintaining comradeship through Association Branches and effecting distribution of benevolence to those in need. This organization stood the test of time and was in a good position to cope with its most severe test as it faced major reorganization under Options of Change.

Once it became clear that the RCT would not survive in its current structure, the Council for Regimental Affairs was to be convened in 1991 under the Chairmanship of the Representative Colonel Commandant, Major General I S Baxter. Through this Council, the affairs of the Corps were managed in detail by four main Trusts (the Benevolent Fund, the Association, the Clayton Trust and the Institution). Regular and detailed briefings of the Council were made by the Director General and the Staff of Transport 1 on the Army Board's decisions arising from Options for Change. The Trustees considered a number of key subjects and their decisions were subsequently endorsed by the Council. In particular, the following were reviewed:

Bicentenary Arrangements
Disposal of Property.
Regimental Museum.
RCT Medal Collection.
Finance.
Sport.
The Surviving RASC/RCT Regimental Structure.

Bicentenary

In 1989, plans had been put in hand to prepare for the Bicentenary of the Formation of the Royal Waggoners on 7 March, 1794. The first meeting of the Bicentenary

Committee was held in February, 1990, under the chairmanship of the Director General, Major General C E G Carrington. As it became clear that the Corps, as a separate entity, would not survive into 1994, plans were adjusted. The Bicentenary Committee agreed to leave social events to the successor Corps, and to concentrate wholly on leaving a permanent record of the service given by the RCT and its predecessors since 1794. Decisions relating to the Bicentenary are summarized below:

Memorials

Bicentenary memorials, stones and tablets were commissioned for the National Army Museum, within the Corps Church of St Michael and St George and on the War Memorial within Buller Barracks. All were completed and formally unveiled before April, 1993.

The Corps Collect

The Collect is a short prayer used in the liturgy of public worship. In a standard form but with varying content it is appointed for a particular day, function or event and at those Divine Services celebrated by the Corps family throughout the years, Collects fitted to a corporate desire, have been said.

The Corps Collect said by all members of the Royal Corps of Transport is:

Almighty God, our Heavenly Father, who knows no barriers of land, sea, or air in reaching out in mercy to all thy children;

Grant unto us of the Royal Corps of Transport, that we may triumph over all difficulties in the service of our comrades, so that with them we may play our part in the cause of peace and the safety of all peoples.

Grant too, that remembering at all times the trust put in us, we may be strengthened to face alike the monotony of routine, and the excitement of danger with high courage and constant skill.

And thus in all our journeyings and in all perils by land, sea and air, may we ever know thy help and comfort.

Through Jesus Christ our Lord, Amen.

Painting

An oil painting was commissioned from Mr Johnny Jonas to commemorate 200 years of support to the British Army from the Royal Waggoners through to the Royal Corps of Transport. The painting was set in Spain during the Peninsula Campaign in the year 1812, just before the battle of Salamanca. Private Twigg of the Royal Waggon Train, whose General Service Medal and 13 bars are held within the Medal Display, would have been serving during this period. The original picture is now in The Royal Logistic Corps Headquarters Officers Mess, Deepcut.

Silver

The Committee sought to commission a silver centrepiece which would stand out from the Corps' existing and impressive silver. Six options were considered, including a modern piece designed by the Corps Silversmiths, A Edward Jones Ltd. In the event, a design based on the Drums and accoutrements of the Corps Band and the Corps of Drums was finally selected and the contract awarded to A Holt and Son. Mr Holt, senior, had served as a driver within the RASC in 1945.

History

Finally the Committee ensured that the Bicentenary Budget would be sufficient to enable a history of the Corps to be produced covering the years from 1794 to 1993. This would then complete the set of histories covering the years from 1982 to 1993.

Property

A series of Boards of Officers were convened to review the Corps Property. These Boards recommended what should be kept in Trust, gifted to the new Corps or disposed of to Corps Members.

Silver Furniture and Paintings

Items valued at £1,000 or above were to be held in trust by the Corps and placed in the care of the new Corps but protected by a loan agreement. A number of items of smaller value, but of particular historical significance, were added to this category. Items of less than £1,000 were gifted to the RLC. A small balance of items of comparatively low value, but of nostalgic significance, were offered for sale to Corps members.

Library

The Regimental Headquarters arranged for a valuation of the Library. The Board recommended the dispersal of the library to the RLC, to the Archives or for disposal.

Museum of Army Transport

The Council ruled that ten prestigious vehicles should be brought to account and protected by Trust. The balance of vehicles were gifted to the National Army Museum to ensure the protection of the RCT vehicle display at the Museum of Army Transport at Beverley. A few items were retained., in particular Field Marshal Lord Montgomery's Rolls Royce and all the Corps coaches, carts and carriage.

The RCT Medal Collection

The Medal Collection was protected by Trust. It is now displayed in the RLC HQ Officers' Mess at Deepcut under the technical control of the Medal Sub-Committee of the Institution of the RASC/RCT with Lieutenant Colonel G T Pearce as Numismatist.

Finance

The monies accrued by the RASC/RCT Association and the RASC/RCT Benevolent Fund were retained by these Trusts with whom the responsibility for comradeship and the alleviation of need continues to rest. The Trusts no longer benefit from income from a One Day's Pay Scheme. The balance of Corps money is concentrated on a new Institution of the RASC/RCT Trust which incorporates the monies and responsibilities of the Clayton Trust, the RCT Aldershot Institution Rebate Fund (formally based on profits from the old ASC Lemonade factory in Aldershot!) and the Disbanded Units Fund. From the accumulated wealth of the new Institution Trust, a gift of £100,000 was made to the RLC on behalf of the RCT element within the new Corps.

Sport

Arrangements for the merger of all RCT sports with those of the new Corps were delegated to Sports Chairmen and their Committees. This included the right to allocate trophies and residual monies to the new Corps so that continuity could be maintained within each sport. All major sporting trophies, therefore, remain in use within their appropriate sport. Before the Corps disbanded, a number of sports tours and matches of significance were arranged. Cricketers were able to celebrate their 100th anniversary with a centenary match on the Buller pitch in 1992; this was in addition to their last tour of the Channel Islands. The Corps Tennis Club hosted a match against the RAOC with a Dinner to commemorate the 80th Anniversary of the first Corps Championships in 1912. Finally, the Corps Rugby team managed a last tour of America before passing this tradition over to the care of the new Corps.

The Residual Regimental Structure and Organization

Once the plans for Options for Change were firm, the Regimental Council coordinated the plans of the Trustees in order to produce a new Corps Committee and Trust Structure which could manage Corps affairs within the new circumstances. Trust documents and charters were adjusted to ensure that responsibilities could be carried forward to both retired members of the Corps as well as those serving members who transferred into the RLC. There was also a need to meet legal and moral responsibilities which remained with the Corps for both its people and its property and much work was done to identify the best interests of all concerned. Under the respective chairmanship of Major General I S Baxter (Institute of the RASC/RCT), Major General D H Braggins (The RASC/RCT Association), and Major General W Bate (The RASC/RCT Benevolent Fund), the work necessary to adjust the Corps structure and close down Trusts and Committees was put in hand. The move of the Museum and the Medal Collection from Buller Barracks to Deepcut was an emotional event for many. Some found it difficult to come to terms with such deep-rooted changes, however inevitable in the changing world. At the very least, it must be said that these changes were managed with skill and care by highly experienced officers at the heart of the Corps who sought to ensure the survival of its great legacy of tradition and history.

Relationships with the Royal Logistic Corps

It was apparent at an early stage that the RCT would not wish to transfer all its

400

residual responsibilities to the new Corps. At the same time, however, the Ministry of Defence was not prepared to fund manpower for RASC/RCT matters beyond the post of Controller and two clerks. This was sufficient to cope with Association and Benevolent matters but not those responsibilities previously encompassed in the Charter of the Institution and its various Trusts. The new office of the Institution of the RASC/RCT was, therefore, privately funded with two part-time staff to administer the run-down to the new structure. Within a year or so, the RLC was able to take on the bulk of the work in accounting for all Corps property, artefacts and archives. This left a small voluntary staff, under the part-time Secretary, to maintain social events, the *Waggoner Newsletter* and provide a central point of contact for retired members of the Corps and for serving members of the RLC with previous service in the Corps.

A FLAG IS LOWERED AND A FLAG IS RAISED

The Corps saw many changes to its location, title and organization since the raising of the Royal Waggoners on 7 March, 1794, for service in Flanders, but finally established its first roots in Aldershot in 1856 and, since then, remained proudly in the Army's order of battle despite many changes to its structure.

The RCT celebrated the Freedom of the Borough of Rushmoor for the final time on 17 February 1993, proudly exercising its right to march through the streets of Aldershot. The Corps Staff Band and Corps of Drums led contingents from:

The Depot and Training Regiment RCT
17 Port and Maritime Regiment RCT
29 Transport and Movements Regiment RCT
41 Squadron RCT
63 Airborne Squadron RCT
The Aldershot Branch of the RASC/RCT Association

They were followed by an excellent cavalcade of representative historic and modern Corps vehicles. The salute was taken outside the Princes Hall by the Worshipful Mayor of Rushmoor, Councillor Roger Kimber and the Director General Transport and Movements, Major General J D MacDonald CB CBE. At a reception at Buller Officers' Mess, the Mayor presented the Corps with a bound biography of Stefan Kurylak, a former Councillor and Polish-born RCT soldier who made it his life's work to help his old country. The DGTM presented a silver figurine of a Royal Waggon Train Officer to the Borough. In thanking the Corps on behalf of the Council, the Mayor affirmed, 'You will always remain Freemen of this Borough!'

At one minute before midnight on Saturday 4 April, 1993, the Royal Corps of Transport Headquarters Sergeants' Mess proudly lowered the Royal Corps of Transport flag in Buller Barracks for the last time. The next day, in the presence of its new Colonel-in-Chief, HRH The Princess Royal, the Royal Logistic Corps no less proudly raised its own flag at Deepcut.

ANNEXES AND APPENDICES

BATTLE HONOURS

A Battle Honour is a distinction given to selected units of the British Army present during a distinguished action, battle or campaign.

This distinction and the continuing enactments of the many forms of ceremonial observed to mark and celebrate these honours enhances that unique quality which sets a regiment apart from others – regimental pride.

The naming of battle honours on the colours or standards of a regiment are a constant reminder of the deeds and glories of a soldier's antecedents. Regimental pride as a tangible asset in the beginning is built on with discipline, training and comradeship and becomes a reality by the courage and resolution of the individual when death is preferable to cowardice. Upon such foundations are battle honours won.

On the appropriate pages of this book there are the records of five battle honours of the predecessors of the Royal Corps of Transport.

These honours were awarded to the Royal Waggon Train and the Military Train, but neither organization carried colours or standards and no relative embellishments were evident on their dress.

The absence of any logistical appreciation for the needs of their Army by successive governments and the constant reductions of the defence budget continued throughout the 19th Century. With each new designation of a hurriedly formed transport organization, antecedents were not remembered and ceremonial connected with previously gained honours was of no consideration.

It is not easy to detect when regimental pride in the predecessors of the Royal Corps of Transport developed. Given the settled and calculated existence which the Army Service Corps enjoyed from 1888 and the performance of the well-trained units it provided in South Africa in the Boer War 1899-1902, this is a reasonable moment in time. It did not have the advantage of the enthusiastic cavalry charges of the Military Train, but it built on personal performance, devotion to duty, discipline and the competence of commanders at all levels to achieve a position of status in the Army. These attributes are not a combination for glory but they would certainly lead the way to regimental pride.

If there were any approved system or code of rules for the award of battle honours before 1882 it has not been discovered. In that year Major General Sir Archibald Alison, a notable military historian, presided over a committee to consider the claim of regiments going back over a hundred years. In the findings there was no mention of those battle honours already awarded.

The battle honours of the Royal Waggon Train and the Military Train were awarded before 1882. They were properly given and authentically quoted in the Army Lists of the times. Once given, they cannot be taken away without any formal action and the succession of the Royal Corps of Transport to its predecessors is not in question.

Precedent exists in the case of claiming the battle honours of predecessors and is indeed apparent on each occasion a line regiment or cavalry regiment changes its title on amalgamation.

The battle honours of the Corps are:

ROYAL WAGGON TRAIN

PENINSULA
'in commemoration of their services during the late war in Portugal, Spain and France under Field Marshal, the Duke of Wellington'

HORSE GUARDS 6 April, 1815

WATERLOO
'in commemoration of their distinguished services on the 18 June, 1815'

HORSE GUARDS 14 December, 1815

MILITARY TRAIN

LUCKNOW
'in commemoration of their recent services in restoring order in Your Majesty's Indian Dominions' (Listed in Relief of Lucknow and Capture of Lucknow)

HORSE GUARDS 8 August, 1863

TAKU FORTS AND PEKIN
'in commemoration of their services in China in 1860'

HORSE GUARDS 4 November, 1861

NOTE: At the time of the awards of these distinctions the Regular Army was administered from an office at the Horse Guards, Whitehall, by the Secretary at War, the Adjutant-General and the Quartermaster-General, with civilian staff.

HONOURS AND AWARDS

Awards of The Victoria Cross

The Victoria Cross, the most highly coveted decoration which it is possible for any sailor, soldier or airman, of any rank, to obtain, was instituted by Queen Victoria in 1856 at, it is said, the suggestion of the Prince Consort.

The Cross was traditionally and for many years manufactured from the bronze guns captured in the Crimea, but this supply was exhausted in 1942. Originally the ribbon, 38mm wide, was blue for Royal Navy and red (actually a crimson or claret) for the Army, but with the formation of the Royal Air Force in 1918 a crimson ribbon was adopted for all recipients.

There are five members of the predecessors of the Royal Corps of Transport who have been awarded the Victoria Cross

Farrier M Murphy
2 Battalion Military Train   15 April, 1858   Azimghur

Private S Morley
2 Battalion Military Train   15 April, 1858   Azimghur

Assistant Commissary J L Dalton
Commissariat and Transport Department   22 January, 1879   Rorke's Drift

Second Lieutenant A C Herring
Army Service Corps, attd 6 Battalion
Northampton Regiment   23 March, 1918   Montagne Bridge, Jussy

Private R G Masters
Army Service Corps,
attd 141 Field Ambulance   9 April, 1918   Bethune

AWARDS OF THE ALBERT MEDAL AND THE GEORGE CROSS

The Albert Medal was established by Queen Victoria in 1866 for the distinguished and many heroic acts performed in saving life at sea. In 1877 the awards were extended to cover similar acts on land.

King George VI instituted the George Cross in September, 1940, to acknowledge the outstanding gallantry of the civilian population in the war of that time. The civilian award would have the same status as the Victoria Cross and would take precedence next in line after that medal.

Following an announcement in the House of Commons on the 21 October, 1971, those who held the Albert Medal were able to exchange it for the George Cross. Thus three recipients of the Albert Medal were given the opportunity to exchange, the others being deceased – Geoffrey Rackham and Walter Cleall exchanged, Thomas Walton declined.

Albert Medal
Lieutenant Sidney Albert Rowlandson ASC	21 May, 1916	France
Mech Staff Sergeant Thomas Michael Walton ASC	21 May, 1916	France
Private Alexander Anderson ASC	21 May, 1916	France
Private Joseph Thomas Lawrence ASC	21 May, 1916	France
Major Lewis Collingwood Bearne DSO ASC	30 June, 1918	France
Private Albert Edward Usher ASC	30 June, 1918	France
Private Arthur Johnson ASC	30 June, 1918	France
Driver Alfred Horne ASC	30 June, 1918	France
Lieutenant Geoffrey Rackham ASC	27 October, 1918	France
Walter Cleall	11 August, 1919	Cardiff

George Cross
Driver Joseph Hughes RASC	21 March, 1946	Lyemun Barracks Hong Kong

GENERAL ORDERS, DECORATIONS AND MEDALS AWARDED FOR GALLANTRY TO MEMBERS OF THE ROYAL CORPS OF TRANSPORT AND ITS PREDECESSORS

The first awards for gallantry in action were those gained at Azimghur during the Indian Mutiny in 1858 by Farrier M Murphy and Private S Morley of the 2nd Battalion Military Train. The details of these awards and other Victoria Crosses, Albert Medals and George Cross are recorded herein. Below is a numerical listing of gallantry awards from the institution of the Distinguished Conduct Medal in 1845 until the disbandment of the Royal Corps of Transport in 1993.

The first award was made to:
Ashanti 1873-74
Staff Sergeant Thomas Brookhouse DCM
Army Service Corps.

The last award was made to:
Falkland Islands 1982
Captain J G Greenhalgh DFC
Royal Corps of Transport.

Medal	Instituted	Numbers Awarded
VICTORIA CROSS – 'most auspicious bravery or pre-eminent act of valour or self-sacrifice or extreme devotion to duty in the face of the enemy	**1856** For all ranks	5
ALBERT MEDAL – 'heroic acts on land and sea by those who endanger their own lives in saving or endeavouring to save the lives of others'	**1866** For all (at sea) **1877** For all (extended to include on land)	10
GEORGE CROSS – 'for acts of heroism or of the most conspicuous courage in circumstances of extreme danger'	**1940** For all. The award to members of the Fighting Services is confined to actions for which purely military honours are not normally granted	1

DISTINGUISHED SERVICE ORDER –

'distinguished service under fire or under conditions equivalent to service in actual contact with the enemy'	**1866** For Officers	313

MILITARY CROSS –

1914 – 'distinguished and meritorious service in time of war' 1920 – changed to 'gallant and distinguished service in action'	**1914** For Captains and below and Warrant Officers – Extended to include substantive Majors	585

DISTINGUISHED FLYING CROSS –

'an act or acts of valour, courage or devotion to duty performed whilst flying in active operations against the enemy'	**1918** For Officers and Warrant Officers of the Air Forces	4

AIR FORCE CROSS –

'an act or acts of valour, courage or devotion to duty whilst flying though not in active operations against the enemy'	**1918** For Officers and Warrant Officers of the Royal Air Force – extended to include other individuals who render distinguished service to aviation in actual flying	9

DISTINGUISHED CONDUCT MEDAL –

'for distinguished conduct in the field'	**1845** For Sergeants **1854** For NCOs and men	377

GEORGE MEDAL –

'awarded in similar circumstances to the George Cross but not so outstanding to merit that award'	**1940** For all	19

MILITARY MEDAL –

'for individual acts of bravery in the field brought to notice by the recommendation of the Commander-in-Chief	**1916** For NCOs and men – extended to include Warrant Officers	1999

DISTINGUISHED FLYING MEDAL –

'awarded in the same conditions as is the Distinguished Flying Cross'	**1918** For NCOs and men of the Air Forces	9

AIR FORCE MEDAL –

'awarded in the same conditions as is the Air Force Cross'	**1918** For NCOs and men and to others in the same conditions as the Air Force Cross	1

THE QUEEN'S GALLANTRY MEDAL

'for exemplary acts of bravery'	**1974** 'intended primarily for civilians, but members of HM Forces are also eligible for actions for which purely military honours are not normally granted'	2

Civil Honours

The highest honour that a civic authority can bestow is the grant of the Freedom of the Borough to individuals or regiments. This is used to recognize distinguished achievements in service to the nation or to the community. The bond between the civic authorities and the units they have honoured is marked by the unique distinction of marching through the streets of the Borough on ceremonial occasions with band playing, drums beating, bayonets fixed and, where appropriate, colours flying.

The Freedom of the Borough of Aldershot

In recognition of the distinguished record of the Royal Corps of Transport and its long and continuous association with the Borough, Aldershot Borough Council conferred the Freedom of the Borough of Aldershot upon the Corps on 22 April, 1970. The ceremony took place in the Aldershot Recreation Ground in front of a large audience of local citizens and cheering school children. The Representative Colonel Commandant, Major General EHG Lonsdale CB MBE, accepted the Freedom on behalf of the Corps and the Mayor of Aldershot, Councillor JJ Town-Clear presented the Corps with an illuminated scroll and a silver casket. The Corps presented the Borough with a pair of silver candelabra. Exercising their new right as Freemen, the Corps marched through the streets of Aldershot with 'bands playing, drums beating and bayonets fixed'.

The Freedom of the Borough of Rushmoor

On 29 May, 1981, the Freedom of the new Borough of Rushmoor was conferred upon the RCT, and other Regiments and Corps who had received the Freedom of the Borough from the former Aldershot Borough Council. An impressive and unique ceremony was held in Rushmoor Arena and, to mark the occasion, each of the participating Regiments and Corps was presented with an individual illuminated scroll bearing the resolution passed by the Council at the Special Meeting held on 19 May, 1981. As Representative Colonel Commandant, Major General P Blunt, CB, MBE. GM accepted the scroll and signed the Roll of Honorary Freemen on behalf of the Corps. The scroll had been designed to fit into the original presentation silver casket to which had been added the Rushmoor Coat-of-Arms and an inscription recording the fact that the Freedom of the Borough of Rushmoor had been conferred upon the Corps. Later that day all the Regiments and Corps involved in the ceremony paraded through the Borough and past the Princes Hall where the salute was taken by the Worshipful Mayor of Rushmoor, Councillor M H Garrood.

Many units of the Corps were so honoured with the grant of Freedoms in the United Kingdom. In addition to Aldershot and Rushmoor, Haverfordwest, Southport, Eccles, Birkenhead, Port Talbot, Gosport, Tynemouth and Sefton were among Boroughs which granted Freedoms. In Germany the towns of Duisburg, Hamm and Spandau marked their post-war associations with Corps units by granting similar Freedoms.

THE REGIMENTAL BAND

The first band to be formed was that of the Royal Waggon Train in 1799 whose barracks were in Mitcham Road in Croydon. *The Chronicle of Croydon* by J Corbett Anderson, records the fact that 'the band was a very fine one and, by its splendid performances, used to contribute much to the happiness of Croydonians'.

The uniforms of this band and others of the Corps predecessors followed closely to that prescribed in the clothing regulations of the times. Exceptionally, the Blackamoors of the Royal Waggon Train Band wore picturesque dress corresponding between Turk and Zouave with short red jackets embroidered in gold, very loose trousers and high Turkis (Turbans).

A marching band and string band were formed in 1888, being wholly maintained by the Corps officers; it was known as the Army Service Corps Voluntary Band, Aldershot. The Band continued to be maintained by the officers of the Corps as a private venture until it was given official recognition in 1938.

In March, 1984, the Band were honoured by being selected to accompany Her Majesty the Queen and His Royal Highness Prince Philip during a State visit to the Kingdom of Jordan. The Band played at a series of events including the Royal Garden Party, the Royal Reception and a television concert at the Palace of Culture – part of the King Hussein Sports City. There were also more informal concert engagements to 'support' British Week. The overall visit was a great success. The King and his senior officers were very impressed with the Band and the Director of Music, Major Kenny, made a further special visit to Amman to discuss the engagement of a British Band Master, or Director Instructor, to assist and advise the Jordanian Armed Forces Band Services. Captain P G Butler of The King's Own Scottish Borderers, when appointed to the post, paid special tribute to the Director of Music and the Corps Band and suggested that it was the tremendous impression that they had made upon the King and his courtiers that had brought about his appointment.

From 1939 onwards it increased considerably in size until 1956 when it received the status of a major staff band and, on the formation of the Royal Corps of Transport, continued to be stationed in Aldershot at the home of the Corps in Buller Barracks.

The Band carried out many public engagements and, until interrupted by active service as drivers in the Gulf War, it had played at the famous Horse of the Year Show on thirty-nine consecutive occasions. Eight days after the cease-fire in the Gulf the band played at the liberation party of the British Ambassador in Kuwait.

For many years there had been a wish throughout the Corps to improve the dress of the band by replacing the Number 1 Dress hat. Finally, a blue Shako with the white and red pompom was decided upon and officially approved in 1974 thus confirming a link with the Military Train who wore that design with distinction from 1856 to 1869.

There were four other bands in the Corps supported by the Territorial Army. 150 Regiment RCT (V) was established with an official TA Band. No less than three bands of Pipes and Drums existed in 152 Regiment RCT(V), 153 Regiment RCT(V)

The band and drums of the RCT at Buller Barracks wearing the new Shako headdress.

and 154 Regiment RCT(V). The Junior Leaders Regiment of the Corps maintained a Corps of Drums as a musical hobby, supported entirely by the regiment. The quality and performance of this Corps of Drums was an inspiration to the young soldiers and led directly to the establishment and maintenance of a strong Corps of Drums at Buller Barracks which performed regularly with the Staff Band.

The Regimental March was first played in 1875 when for the first time the Army Service Corps were invited to march past at a review of troops in Aldershot in honour of the Sultan of Zanzibar. Having no special tune for this purpose, the Commander-in-Chief, the Duke of Cambridge, ordered 'Wait for the Waggon' to be played. It remained the Corps March Past, with a few unauthorized embellishments, for seventy years, when, to relieve the repetitive nature of the melody, a second element, the 'South Africa Trek Song' was added. Having been approved by the Royal Military College of Music and authorized by Army Orders, the new regimental march was first played on VJ DAY, 15 August, 1945, and the title 'Wait for the Waggon' was retained.

Directors of Music

Since 1945 Directors of Music were:

Maj J F Dean	1947-1962
Maj D K Walker	1962-1969
Maj W Allen MBE	1969-1978
Maj T A J Kenny	1978-1987
Maj D Marshall	1987-1990
Maj R Maycock	1990-1993

BADGES OF THE CORPS

Origins

A badge of the Royal Waggon Train which formed in 1802 was shown in illustrations of the time on the tilts of waggons. The device was the cypher 'GR' surmounted by a crown within a red circular patch bearing the title 'Royal Waggon Train'. In 1812 personnel of the Royal Waggon Train were issued with the new pattern shako for light dragoons. This was adorned with a red and white plume in front with below it a black cockade and a central white rosette. The subsequent shako of 1831 had a metal plate described as 'gilt Maltese Cross having the letters RWT'.

The Military Train shako bore a black horsehair plume and a plate with 'the double gilt oak branch enclosing a garter with the words Military Train and the number of the battalion inside the garter' Later the battalion number was replaced by a lion and a crown. The last design of shako, in 1869, was worn by the first Army Service Corps and the new badge consisted of 'a gilt laurel wreath surmounted by a crown enclosing the Garter inscribed with its motto, 'Honi soit qui mal y pense', within which the letters ASC were entwined'.

The Land Transport Corps wore no badge of distinction but each Wing of the

410

Corps, each dedicated to the support of one of the six Divisions of the Army, was distinguished by a different divisional colour, these colours 'pervading as much as possible on their clothing, equipment and carriages'.

In 1878 the last shako was replaced by a cloth-covered helmet. These were ornamented by a plate formed of the eight-pointed star of India surmounted by a crown, many Corps and Regiments using the same plate. The size and material of these plates varied, officer's plates being gilded, and in all cases the centrepiece of the star varied as the title of Corps changed. The crown also altered from Royal (Victorian) to the Imperial (Tudor) crown. The Imperial crown survived the reigns of four monarchs and became known as the King's crown. A badge, made of stamped brass, clearly modelled on the helmet plate, was introduced for wear on the field service cap in 1894 and this, with minimum variations, evolved into the cap badge of the Royal Corps of Transport.

There were two major changes when the ASC became a Royal Corps in 1918. The ASC cypher in the centre of the badge was replaced by the royal cypher, and the Corps title was added within a scroll, beneath the Garter and imposed on the laurel leaves. Also in 1918 colour was introduced for the officers' badge when the central field on which the royal cypher was mounted was made red and the Garter became blue. In 1949 the star of the officer's badge was changed to white metal.

During WW2 attempts were made to substitute shiny metal cap badges with dull 'bronzed' badges in the interests of concealment and camouflage. For similar reasons the practice grew up in Northern Ireland during the post-war troubles of blackening cap badges and in the end inconspicuous embroidered cloth badges were issued for operational wear. All the original hat badges of the Corps throughout its life are shown at the beginning of the book.

The Corps Motto

The Army Service Corps was using the motto 'For Queen and Country' in 1892. It appeared underneath the Corps badge on the frontispiece of the Army Service Corps journal which was founded the previous year. This motto was short-lived. A committee was formed representing all ranks on the instigation of the commander ASC in Aldershot, Lieutenant Colonel Ernest Grattan, who had previously founded the journal. The latin 'Nil Sine Labore' was proposed and accepted as the new motto in August, 1892, a free translation being 'Nothing worthwhile is achieved without hard work'.

FLAGS

A blue and white flag of the Army Service Corps flew at Ladysmith in 1900 during the Boer War outside the headquarters of the 8th Brigade Supply and Transport Company commanded by Captain Philip Scott ASC. The colours blue and white have been associated with the Royal Corps of Transport and its predecessors since the days of the Military Train in 1856 and since then these colours have always been present on the Corps flag. In 1894 another colour, gold, was added to the blue and white to represent the gold lace of the tunic.

The early arrangement of the tricoloured flag was to show 'blue to the mast and white to the blast' with the gold in the middle. During Allenby's campaign in Palestine in 1916-1918, where the flag was frequently used, the white in the fly quickly became drab and indistinguishable from the gold and the practice grew up of reversing the flag with white to the mast. After the war this was adopted first in Bulford and then in Aldershot in 1921.

In 1945 it was noted that with three vertical stripes it was conventional to have the lightest colour in the centre and the darkest to the mast. With the order of the colours thus changed the Corps badge was added, being emblazoned on the white in the centre panel. By 1946, however, it was noted that the arrangement contravened heraldic law by defacing a metal, the white 'silver' panel, with another metal, the gold of the badge. The RASC flag thus came to its final style with gold to the mast and white once again to the blast.

In 1965 a new flag was introduced for the Royal Corps of Transport. This had three colours arranged in seven horizontal stripes. Blue predominated as the background with narrower white and red stripes. The red stripe symbolized the new duties inherited from the Corps of Royal Engineers. The Corps badge was emblazoned in the centre on the blue field, satisfying heraldic convention.

Fleet Ensigns

WD (RASC/RCT) FLEET ENSIGN

In 1890 the Admiralty authorized the flying of 'a Blue Ensign of Her Majesty's Fleet with the Badge of such other Military Services, on the Fly thereof, namely two crossed swords', when the WD Fleet changed from civilian to military control and came largely under the command of the Transport Department of the MOD. The ASC operated vessels flying this flag in the First World War and in 1941 the RASC took on overall control of the WD Fleet, which then changed its name to the RASC Fleet. In 1965 it was retitled the RCT Fleet on the formation of that Corps. Soldiers of the RASC & RCT serving in one of the maritime units wore the Fleet Ensign at either shoulder (shoulder flash) in all forms of working dress uniform. This was introduced in 1944.

The Army Ensign

The Defence Council approved the Army Ensign in Army Order 53 of 1966. The design is as per the WD (RASC/RCT) Fleet Ensign, but with the addition of the Army Cypher, first approved for use by King George VI in 1939, superimposed upon the Crossed Swords and to be flown in place of the RCT Fleet Ensign when the vessel is under the command of a commissioned officer. Major B V Wynn-Werninck of the Corps produced the original drawings for the Ensign which were given to the Royal Naval Dockyard at Portsmouth. Three were made in the flag-loft and it was first flown on LCT Mk VIII's HMAV (Her Majesty's Army Vessels – a new title that was introduced with this Ensign) *Abbeville, Akyab* and *Audemer* during Exercise Waggon Trail on 5 June, 1967.

APPOINTMENTS

The nomination of a Director of Supplies and Transport in 1915 established an appointment to which officers of the Army Service Corps, Royal Army Service Corps and Royal Corps of Transport were duly promoted General Officer and head of their respective Service.

Previously the appointment to the head of their Service varied in title as well as rank as the Army sought to recognize and install an established Supply and Transport system.

Director of Supplies and Transport

1915	Major General S S Long, CB.
1916	Major General Sir Alban Crofton-Atkins, CB, CMG.
1919	Major General W K Tarver, CB, CMG.
1919	Major General Sir Evan Carter, KCB, MVO.
1921	Major General P O Hazelton CB, CMG.
1925	Major General G F Davies, CB, CMG, CBE.
1929	Major General Sir Evan Gibb, KCB, CB, CMG, DSO.
1933	Major General C W McLeod, CB, CBE, DSO.
1937	Major General M S Brander, CB, OBE.
1940	Major General R T Snowden-Smith, CB, CBE.
1943	Major General Sir Reginald Kerr, KBE, CB, MC.
1946	Major General F S Clover, CBE.
1948	Major General Sir Cecil Smith, KBE, CB, MC.
1951	Major General H C Goodfellow, CB, CBE.
1954	Major General W H D. Ritchie, CB, CBE.
1957	Major General Sir William Roe, KBE, CB.
1960	Major General P G Turpin, CB, CBE.
1963	Major General Sir John Potter, KBE, CB.

Transport Officers in Chief (Army)

1965	Major General Sir John Potter, KBE, CB.
1966	Major General E H G Lonsdale, CB, MBE.
1969	Major General P F Claxton, CB, OBE.
1971	Major General V H J Carpenter, CB, MBE.
1973	Major General P Blunt, CB, MBE, GM.
1976	Major General P H Benson, CBE.

Director-General of Transportation

1977	Major General P H Benson, CBE.

Director-General of Transport and Movements

1978	Major General P H Benson, CBE.

1978	Major General F J Plaskett, CB, MBE.
1981	Major General W M Allen, CB.
1982	Major General D H Braggins, CB.
1985	Major General D B H Colley, CB, CBE.
1989	Major General C E G Carrington, CB, CBE.
1990	Major General J D MacDonald, CB, CBE.

Director of Movements (Army) post 1965

1966	Major General Sir John Potter, KBE, CB.
1968	Major General J R Reynolds, CB, OBE.
1971	Major General W Bate, CB, OBE, DL.
1973	Major General V H J Carpenter, CB, CBE.
1975	Major General F J Plaskett, CB, MBE.

CORPS OFFICERS HOLDING OTHER GENERAL OFFICER APPOINTMENTS

In 1888 General Sir Redvers Buller, the Quartermaster-General decided that a new Army Service Corps should be formed. At that time the senior ranking officer in the new Corps was Colonel H S E Reeves, CB.

The First World War – 1914-1918 saw the Corps with one Lieutenant General and nine Major Generals serving in the Army.

In 1982 Lieutenant General Sir Paul Travers, KCB, became Quartermaster-General, the first to be appointed from the Corps.

Marked with an asterisk are those officers who also served as Directors of the Corps, as listed above, otherwise all listed below served in senior command, Staff or Corps appointments worldwide. Those marked † held the appointment of Inspector of the Corps in the rank of Major General, the appointment being downgraded to Brigadier in 1960.

Major General Sir Bertram Rowcroft and Major General W S Tope became the first and second Directors of the Royal Electrical and Mechanical Engineers in 1942 and 1947 respectively.

Date of Appointment

Major General Sir Herbert N Bunbury, KCB.
| The first Major General in the Corps. | |
| Major General i/c Administration, Irish Command. | 1907 |

Major General Sir Charles E Heath, KCB, CVO.
Director of Transport and Remounts, The War Office.	1907
Director of Quartering, The War Office	1914
Deputy Quartermaster General, The War Office	1916

Major General C A Hadfield.
| Major General i/c Administration, South Africa Command. | 1909 |
| Major General i/c Administration, Irish Command. | 1911 |

Lieutenant General Sir Frederick T Clayton, KCMG, KCB.
    Major General appointments:
    Director of Supplies, The War Office.   1906
    Major General i/c Administration, South Africa Command.   1911
    Director of Supplies, BEF and Inspector of QMG Services in France.   1914
    Lieutenant General appointment:
    Inspector General of Communications, Western Front   1915

Major General Sir Frederick W B Landon, KCMG, CB.
    Director of Transport and Movements, The War Office.   1913
    Chief Inspector QMG Services, The War Office.   1918

Brigadier General Sir Charles H Bridge, KCMG, CB.
    Retired 1903.
    Re-employed Inspector of Remounts.   1906
    Head of Mule Purchasing Commission in USA.   1914
    Granted honorary rank of Major General.   1918

Major General P E F Hobbs, CB, CMG.
    DA and QMG The First Army.   1915

Major General F F Johnson, CB, OBE, DL.
    Major General i/c Administration, Southern Command.   1915

Major General F W B Koe, CB, CMG.
    Inspector General of Communications, Middle East.   1916

Major General Sir William B Boyce, KCMG, CB, DSO.
    Director of Transport, British Armies in France.   1914

Major General H N Sargent, CB, CBE, DSO.
    DA and QMG, First Army Corps 1914.   1914
    Granted honorary rank of Major General, Reserve and Fifth Army.   1919

Major General Sir Reginald Ford, KCMG, CB, DSO.
    DQMG, British Forces in France and Flanders.   1918

⋆Major General Sir Evan Carter, KCMG, CB, MVO.
    Director of Supplies, British Armies in France.   1915

Major General F M Wilson, CB, CMG.
    Director of Supplies and Transport, Rhine Army.   1918
    Director of Supplies and Transport, India.   1921

Major General N G Anderson, CB, CMG, DSO.
    Assistant Director of Supplies and Transport, Eastern Command.   1921

Major General H N Foster, CMG, CBE.
    Assistant Director of Supplies and Transport, Southern Command.   1927

Lieutenant General Sir Humphrey Gale, KBE, CB, CVO, MC.
 Major General i/c Administration, Home Forces.   1940
 Chief Administrative Officer, Supreme HQ, Allied Expeditionary Force. 1944
 Granted honorary rank of Lieutenant General.   1947

★Major General M S Brander, CB, OBE
 Major General i/c Administration, Eastern Command.   1940

†Major General C Le B Goldney, CB, CBE, MC.
 Director of Supplies and Transport, Middle East.   1941

Major General W D'A Collings, CB, CBE.
 Director of Supplies and Transport, British Army of the Rhine.   1945

Major General Sir Bertram Rowcroft, KBE, CB.
 Director of Mechanical Engineering, War Office.   1942

Major General W S Tope, CB, CBE.
 Director of Mechanical Engineering, Middle East.   1943
 Director of Mechanical Engineering, The War Office.   1946

†Major General H M Whitty, CB, OBE.
 Director of Supplies and Transport, Central
 Mediterranean Forces (Italy).   1944
 Middle East.   1946

†Major General E H Fitzherbert, CB, DSO, MC.   1940

†Major General T W Richardson, CB, CBE. 1943

★Major General Sir Cecil Smith, KBE, CB, MC
 DQMG(AE) GHQ Middle East.   1943
 Major General i/c Administration, Western Command.   1944
 Major General Q SHAEF.   1944
 Major General i/c Administration, Northern Command.   1945
 General officer Commanding in Chief, HQ Northern Command.   1947
 Chief of Staff, HQ Northern Command.   1947

★Major General Sir Reginald Kerr, KBE, CB, MC
 Major General Administration, Far East Land Forces   1946
 Major General i/c Administration, Eastern Command   1942

†Major General W J F Eassie, CB, CBE, DSO.   1951

†Major General G A Bond, CB, CBE.   1954

†Major General A F J Elmslie, CB, CBE.   1957

Major General J E Witt, CB, CBE, MC.
 Director of Supplies and Transport, Middle East.   1950

416

★Major General W H D Ritchie, CB, CBE.
    Director of Quartering, The War Office.   1952

★Major General P G Turpin, CB, CBE.
    Director of Movements (Army).   1963

Major General D H V Buckle, CB, CBE.
    Director of Supplies and Transport, Middle East.   1953
    Major General i/c Administration, Middle East.   1956

★Major General Sir William Roe, KBE, CB.
    Major General i/c Administration, HQ Rhine Army.   1954

Major General C H Stainforth, CB, OBE.
    Chief of Staff, Southern Command   1965
    General Officer Commanding Aldershot District.   1966
    South East District.   1968

★Major General P Blunt, CB, MBE, GM
    Assistant Chief of Defence Staff (Personnel and Logistics).   1977

Lieutenant General Sir Paul Travers, KCB.
    Vice Quarter Master General (Major General).   1979
    General Officer Commanding South East District.   1981
    Quarter Master General.   1982

Major General I S Baxter, CBE.
    Assistant Chief of Defence Staff (Logistics).   1987

Major General A L Meier, OBE.
    Director General of Military Services (Intelligence).   1991

COLONELS COMMANDANT

In April, 1921, His Majesty King George V approved the appointment of Colonels Commandant to the Administrative Corps – Royal Army Service Corps, three: Royal Army Medical Corps, one: Royal Army Ordnance Corps, one: Royal Army Veterinary Corps, one. Similar appointments already existed in the Royal Regiment of Artillery and the Corps of Royal Engineers. The first three Majors Generals of the Royal Army Service Corps to fill the appointments were approved by His Majesty on 23 September, 1921. This number has been raised in 1950 to four, in 1969 to five and in 1981 to six.

The main responsibilities of the Colonels Commandant are to safeguard the traditions and customs of the Corps, to protect its interests and integrity, to foster *esprit de corps* and to further its influence and image.

Related to the more recent appointments are those of the predecessors of the Royal Army Service Corps.

Captain James Poole was named as Captain Commandant for the Royal Waggoners 1794-1795.

Lieutenant Colonel Digby Hamilton was Lieutenant Colonel Commandant of the Corps of Waggoners in August, 1799. When the title of Royal Waggon Train was adopted and Digby Hamilton was promoted, he became Colonel Commandant, an appointment which was to last until the disbandment of 1833.

In April, 1855, when the Land Transport Corps was raised Colonel William M S McMurdo was Colonel and Director of that Corps until 1857 when it was disbanded and the Military Train formed with Colonel McMurdo continuing as its first Colonel Commandant. In 1860 he was succeeded by Colonel John Clarke Kennedy and later by Colonel George Erskine.

Between 1869, when the Military Train was disbanded, until 1921 there was no appointment relating to Colonel Commandant.

Years of Appointment	Name	Representative Colonel Commandant
1921-26	Maj Gen (Hon Lt Gen) Sir Frederick T Clayton KCB, KCMG	
1921-30	Maj Gen Sir Frederick W B Landon KCMG, CB	
1921-33	Maj Gen Sir Evan E Carter KCMG, CB, MVO	
1927-35	Maj Gen P E F Hobbs CB, CMG	1933-34
1930-38	Maj Gen Sir Reginald Ford KCMG, CB, DSO – who became the first Representative Colonel Commandant in 1932	1932, 1937
1933-47	Maj Gen Sir Evan Gibb KBE, CB, CMG, DSO	1935, 1938
1935-42	Maj Gen W K Tarver CB, CMG	1936
1938-44	Maj Gen C W MacLeod CB, CMG, DSO	1939
1942-49	Maj Gen M S Brander CB, OBE	1947
1944-54	Lt Gen Sir Humphrey Gale KBE, CB, CVO, MC	1946, 1949, 1953
1947-50	Maj Gen E H Fitzherbert CBE, DSO, MC	1948
1949-59	Maj Gen Sir Reginald Kerr KBE, CB, MC	1950, 1954, 1956
1950-59	Maj Gen Sir Cecil Smith KBE, CB, MC	1952, 1957, 1959
1950-55	Maj Gen F S Clover CB, CBE	1951
1954-63	Maj Gen H C Goodfellow CB, OBE	1955, 1958
1955-59	Maj Gen H M Whitty CB, OBE	
1959-64	Maj Gen W H D Ritchie CB, CBE	1960, 1964
1959-64	Maj Gen D H V Buckle CB, CBE	1961
1960-65	Maj Gen G A Bond CB, CBE	1962
1963-67	Maj Gen Sir William Roe, KBE, CB	1963
1964-69	Maj Gen A F J Elmslie CB, CBE	1965
1964-70	Maj Gen A T de Rhe-Philipe CB, OBE (Late Corps of Royal Engineers)	1966
1965-75	Maj Gen P G Turpin CB, OBE	1967, 1969
1967-73	Maj Gen Sir John Potter KBE, CB	1968
1969-74	Maj Gen E H G Lonsdale CB, MBE	1970
1969-72	Maj Gen C H Stainforth CB, OBE	1971

1971-75	Brig R A J Eggar CBE	1972
1971-78	Maj Gen J R Reynolds CB, OBE, ERD	1973
1973-80	Maj Gen P F Claxton CB, OBE	1974
1974-86	Maj Gen W Bate CB, OBE, DL	1975, 1977, 1982, 1986
1975-88	Maj Gen V H J Carpenter CB, MBE	1976, 1978, 1985
1976-90	Maj Gen P Blunt CB, MBE, GM	1979, 1981, 1987
1979-90	Maj Gen P H Benson CBE	1980, 1983, 1988
1981-91	Maj Gen F J Plaskett CB, MBE	1984, 1989
1981-83	Lt Gen Sir Paul Travers KCB	
1986-93	Maj Gen D H Braggins CB	1990
1988-93	Maj Gen D B H Colley CB, CBE	1991
1989-93	Maj Gen I S Baxter CBE	1992
1991-93	Maj Gen C E G Carrington CB, CBE	

Honorary Colonels Commandant

1974-78	Maj (Hon Col) R N Levitt OBE, TD
1988-91	Col Sir Christopher Leaver GBE, JP
1991-93	Sir Peter Levene KBE

COLONELS IN CHIEF

As recognition for its work in South Africa, the Army Service Corps was honoured by the appointment of HRH the Duke of Connaught and Strathearn as Colonel on 2 September, 1902. This appointment continued until 1932 during which time King George V had conferred the prefix 'Royal' on the Army Service Corps. In 1932 HRH the Duke of Connaught and Strathearn assumed the title Colonel in Chief of the Royal Army Service Corps. At the time of his death in 1942 he had maintained a close association with the Corps lasting forty years.

On 20 February, 1942, King George VI appointed HRH Prince Henry, Duke of Gloucester, as Colonel-in-Chief of the Royal Army Service Corps and later, on its formation, he became the first Colonel in Chief of the Royal Corps of Transport on 15 July, 1965. The death of Prince Henry on 10 June, 1974, was a great blow to the Corps. He had been a staunch supporter of the Corps and a most valued adviser during the war years and after, particularly in the years leading up to the formation of the new Corps. During the declining years of his life, when his strength failed him, HRH the Princess Alice, Duchess of Gloucester had taken on the role of deputy to her husband and had won the respect and admiration of the Corps for the wholehearted way in which she had taken on this onerous task. It was with the greatest satisfaction that the Corps received the news on 8 February, 1975, that Her Majesty had appointed Princess Alice Colonel-in-Chief of the Royal Corps of Transport. Her gracious presence at many Corps and Regimental occasions will long be remembered with affection.

ALLIANCES AND AFFILIATIONS

In December, 1920, HM King George V approved the alliance of the Army Service Corps of the Dominion of Canada, of the Commonwealth of Australia, of New Zealand and of the Union of South Africa with the Royal Army Service Corps in recognition of their close collaboration during the Great War. Later, in 1930, His Majesty approved an alliance with the Ceylon Supply and Transport Corps, which a year later was renamed the Ceylon Army Service Corps.

Commonwealth Armies

The Second World War strengthened the ties and affiliations between the sister Corps which survived the dismantling of the Empire. As they evolved and developed their supply and transport systems to meet their needs, Commonwealth armies were able to use their friendships and liaison to learn from each other. The Corps continued to maintain its alliances with its sister Corps in Australia, Canada, New Zealand, India, Pakistan, Sri Lanka and Malaysia. Over many years Directors General renewed personal and professional links and it was a rare year when contact was not made between the Corps and at least one of the allied Corps. Regular contacts were made and maintained with the Indian Army by Major PC Malins MBE MC.

Gurkhas

The Gurkha Transport Regiment has continued to be an approved affiliated Regiment. As the Queen's Own Gurkha Transport Regiment, a new title granted in 1993, the Regiment has become affiliated to The Royal Logistic Corps.

The Worshipful Company of Carmen

A formal association established initially with the Worshipful Company of Carmen in 1975 has continued to flourish within the Corps. Regular dinners, including a Tenth Anniversary Dinner in the presence of Her Royal Highness the Princess Royal, together with the annual awards to the winner of the Carmen Sword, have established a fine relationship. The Corps was pleased to recommend that this should continue into the future with the new Corps.

MEMORIALS TO THE ROYAL CORPS OF TRANSPORT AND ITS PREDECESSORS

Memorials of various form and dedication mark the presence of the Corps and its predecessors at those campaigns and battles endured by the British Army from 1794 to 1993. On the memorials in the village squares of the country, in the cathedrals and churches of the nation and War Graves throughout the world our soldiers will for ever be remembered, and their names are in many cases recorded among all others who gave their lives. For example:

> Those of the Royal Waggon Train who died at Waterloo are remembered by a plaque fixed to a barn wall at Hougoumont Farm.

All Saints Church in Ladysmith has a memorial to those who lost their lives during the siege in 1899-1900.

All Saints Church in Baghdad with a memorial for those who died in Mesopotamia in 1915-1924.

In the record of the events and places where such memorials are to be found it would be fitting to start in Aldershot where predecessors of the Corps were stationed from 1856 adjacent to and in Buller Barracks. As this was then the home of the Corps for well over a hundred years, it was appropriate to distinguish the Church of St George (now St Michael and St George) in the military garrison as the spiritual home of the Corps in which place many generations of our soldiers worshipped. Among the many Corps memorials in that church are those which start with the Egyptian campaign of 1882, through the small wars which followed, then the Boer War, the Great War, Second World War, Malayan Emergency and other associated records. Those shown below are on the official Register of Corps Memorials throughout the world.

UNITED KINGDOM

ALDERSHOT (Hants)   Church of St Michael & St George displays many Corps memorials

Buller Barracks. The Corps War Memorial and various commemorative plaques.

BELFAST (N Ireland)   St Ninian's Church, Whitehouse. Plaque dedicated to 257 Company RASC.

BORDON (Hants)   Church of the Sacred Heart. Statue of St Patrick ex Longmoor and the garrison RC Church Bordon.

BRISTOL (Avon)   Bristol Cathedral. Plaque of 2nd Battalion Military Train.

CAMBERLEY (Surrey)   Royal Military Academy, Sandhurst. ASC Memorial in the Memorial Chapel and 30 Corps RASC Memorial at the main entrance.

DARLINGTON (Co Durham)   North Cemetery. The grave of Farrier M Murphy VC. 2nd Battalion Military Train.

DEEPCUT (Hants)   Royal Logistic Corps Museum. Movement Control Memorial by the entrance.

DOWN AMPNEY (Wilts)   All Saints Church. Air Despatch Memorial for D Day and Arnhem.

LECONFIELD (Humberside)	The Garrison Church. Memorial windows, ex St Martins Garrison Church at Longmoor.
LONDON	St George's Chapel, Westminster Cathedral. Second World War Memorial plaque.
	National Army Museum, Chelsea. Memorial plaque to the RCT and its predecessors.
	Horse Guards Memorial, Westminster, The Guards Division including RASC units.
	St Matthew's Church, Fulham. Plaque in memory of ASC of the Great War.
	St Paul's Cathedral. Transvaal Defence Memorial 1880-1881 includes ASC names.
SLEDMERE (N Yorkshire)	Wagoners Reserve Memorial. The 'Wagoners' of the Army Service Corps who died in the Great War.
SOUTHPORT (Merseyside)	St Cuthbert's Church cemetery. The grave of Private R G Masters VC, Army Service Corps. A citation of his action hangs in the Botanic Gardens Museum at Churchtown.
TIDWORTH (Hants)	St Patrick's Church. RCT Memorial on pulpit.

OVERSEAS

BELGIUM

Antwerp	St Boniface Church RASC Memorial window, originally in St Christopher's in Grobbendonk.
Ypres	St George's Chapel. RASC Memorial.
Waterloo	Hougoumont Farm. A plaque to members of The Royal Waggon Train.

BERMUDA

St George	RASC wharf. RASC Memorial plaque on the wall of the Department of Marine and Ports.

CYPRUS

Dhekelia	Garrison Church. RASC Memorial window.

FRANCE **Somme**	Martinpuich village. 47th (London) Division Memorial. The Divisional Train ASC names thereon.
Normandy	Arromanches. D-Day
	Granges near Dives sur Mer. 6th Airborne Division Memorial. RASC badge and names.
	Barent (near Ranville). Memorial brass plaque of 224 Parachute Field Ambulance including its RASC Transport Platoon.
GERMANY **Bielefeld**	St Michael's Church, Catterick Barracks. RCT Memorial lectern and plaque.
	617 Tank Transporter Squadron RCT. Polish standard, unit memorial in 7 Transport Regiment RLC Officers' Mess.
Gutersloh	St Mark's Church, Princess Royal Barracks. RCT stained glass window ex St Dennis Barracks, Munsterlager. Also smaller stained glass 'cap badge' window, from St George's Church, Bielefeld.
Paderborn (Sennelager)	The Church of St John and St Christopher, Dempsey Barracks. Stained glass window of St Stanislav, Polish Imperial Eagle and RCT badge – a memorial to those of the Mixed Service Organization serving with the RASC and RCT.
GIBRALTAR	Alameida Gardens. Duke of Wellington Memorial including the Royal Waggon Train 1820.
HONG KONG **Gun Club Barracks**	The grave of Driver Joseph Hughes GC in Happy Valley ex Lyemun Barracks.
IRAQ **Baghdad**	Memorial panel in a church to those serving in Mesopotamia 1915-1924.
ADEN	Graves of soldiers of 60 Squadron RCT.
ITALY **Venice**	Memorial to RASC Water Transport personnel. Church of St George, Campo Santi Apostoli, Dorsoduro.

The grave of Driver Joseph Hughes GC in Happy Valley ex Lyemun Barracks.

JAMAICA
Newcastle Hill Station RASC plaque on wall.

MALAYSIA
Penang/Ipoh   RASC plaque which the Planters Association used in a
                         ceremony to remember those who died during the
                         emergency.

NETHERLANDS
Oosterbeek   Air Despatch Memorial for the RASC members who died
                         at Arnhem.

PAKISTAN
Chaklala   Memorial to those of the ASC and RASC who died 1906
                         to 1927.

Colonel N Beard laying a wreath at the Silent Valley Cemetery, Aden, on the graves of soldiers of 60 Squadron, Royal Corps of Transport, killed in 1967. (N Beard)

SINGAPORE

Tanglin   St George's Church. RASC Memorial plaque replacing that which was lost during the departure from Singapore in 1971.

SOUTH AFRICA

Chievely   Memorial includes names of those in the ASC, 1899-1902.

Ladysmith   ASC plaque in the Church of All Saints.

Port Elizabeth Grave of James Dalton VC.

TURKEY

Gallipoli   War Memorial which includes members of the ASC.

UKRAINE

Crimea   Cathcart Hill Memorial. A tablet, part of the whole, listing members of the Land Transport Corps.

In early 1994 the RASC/RCT Memorials Sub-Committee were given the task of extending their existing record of Corps memorials to include all memorials of the

RASC and the RCT or their predecessors which contain either a Corps crest or the name of the Corps or a unit of the Corps. This record will not normally include personal memorials except where the individual received a significant award for gallantry. The record is maintained in a Memorials Register and that which appears is a record at the time of the publication of this book.

Comments from those who observe this record would be welcomed, particularly to help identify other Corps memorials, and should be passed to the Secretary, RASC/RCT Institution.

Bibliography

1. *The Royal Army Service Corps, a History of Transport and Supply in the British Army.* Volume 1 by Sir John Fortescue (1660-1902), published by Cambridge University Press, 1930.
2. *Wellington's Army in the Peninsula (1808-1814)* by Michael Glover.
3. *The Predecessors of the Royal Army Service Corps, 1757-1888* by Lieutenant Colonel C H Massé MC, published by Gale and Polden, 1948.
4. *Britain and Her Army* by Correlli Barnett.
5. *The Royal Army Service Corps* (Famous Regiments Series) by Graeme Crew, published by Leo Cooper Ltd, 1970.
6. *Citizen Soldiers of the Royal Engineers Transportation and Movements and The Royal Army Service Corps 1859-1965* by Colonel G Williams OBE, published by The Camelot Press Ltd (1966).
7. *The Early History of Transport and Supply* by Fortescue.
8. *The Life of General Sir Redvers Buller* (2 Volumes) by Colonel C H Melville, published by Edward Arnold & Co, 1923.
9. *A Victorian Soldier: His Life and Times* by A E Clarke Kennedy.
10. *From Horse to Helicopter* by Brigadier John Sutton and Colonel John Walker, published by Leo Cooper, 1990.
11. *The River War* (The Nile) by Sir Winston Churchill.
12. *System of Land Transport during Operations in Sudan.* Report by the Senior Commissariat PRO Officer, WO33/45/
13. *Notes of Transport and Camel Corps 1887* by Burn.
14. *With the ASC in South Africa* by Sir Wodehouse Richardson, published 1903.
15. *Military Transport* by Lieutenant Colonel G A Furze, 1879.
16. *Eyewitness in Zululand* by Ian Bennett, published 1989.
17. *The Royal Army Service Corps: A History of Transport and Supply in the British Army.* Volume 2 by Colonel R H Beadon (1903-1920), published by Cambridge University.
18. *The Report of the Royal Commission on the War in South Africa.* (6 Volumes).
19. *History of Transport Services in the Egyptian Expeditionary Force 1916-1918* by Lieutenant Colonel G E Badcock, published 1925.
20. *The Turn of the Wheel: The History of the Royal Army Service Corps 1919-1939* by Major General P G Turpin CB, OBE, MA, FCIT, published by Barracuda Books, 1988.
21. *The Story of the Royal Army Service Corps 1939-1945*, published by G Bell and Sons Ltd, 1955.
22. *The Story of the Royal Army Service Corps and the Royal Corps of Transport 1945-1982*, published by Leo Cooper in association with Secker and Warburg, 1983.
23. *Transport Saga* – Pickfords Ltd.

COLOUR PICTURES

Frontispiece   The Colonel-in-Chief, Her Royal Highness Princess Alice.

1. The Royal Waggoners raised by Royal Warrant, 7 March, 1794. Institution of the Royal Corps of Transport (IRCT)

2. An Officer of the Royal Waggon Train, 1803. (IRCT).

3. A Field Officer, a Subaltern and a Veterinary Officer of the Royal Waggon Train, 1822-1827. (IRCT)

4. The Royal Waggon Train moving a barge loaded with a Company of the 95th of Foot on the Royal Military Canal, Hythe, 1809. (H J Compton)

5. Private Brewster driving an ammunition waggon through the gates of Hougoumont Farm to supply the 3rd Guards during the Battle of Waterloo. (IRCT)

6. The action at Azimghur during the Indian Mutiny (an artist's impression). (IRCT)

7. Captain, Commissariat Staff Corps, 1859-1869. (IRCT)

8. Assistant Commissary, Control Department, 1869-1875. (IRCT)

9. A painting of the *Braemar Castle,* sunk whilst trooping in the Aegean in 1916. (IRCT)

10. A painting by Michael Turner, Guild of Aviation Artists, depicting York freighters at RAF Gatow, Berlin, in 1948 during the Berlin Air Lift. (Royal Air Force Club, London)

11. Her Majesty the Queen receiving the Keys of the City of Portsmouth from Lieutenant Colonel T C Street, the Commanding Officer of 20 Maritime Regiment, RCT, at the start of her official visit to that city in 1977. (IRCT)

12. Her Majesty the Queen inspecting the Queen's Baggage Train which is provided by 20 Squadron RCT.

13. Crane Attachment Lorry Mounted (CALM) fitted to an 8-tonne Bedford TM; also a JCB 410 Rough Terrain Fork Lift Tractor (RT FLT) unloading ammunition. (IRCT)

14. RCT Port Operations - Marchwood Military Port. (R Grevatte-Ball)

15. RCT Railway Operations in Germany. (IRCT)

16. The Berlin Military Train with the RCT Movement Control Train Staff. (IRCT)

17. HRH Prince Philip, Duke of Edinburgh, inspecting the Royal Staff cars at Buckingham Palace, accompanied by Major General V H J Carpenter CB, MBE, the Representative Colonel Commandant RCT. (IRCT)

18. Schoolchildren in BAOR boarding RCT school buses with MCTG drivers. (IRCT)

19. RCT-manned Bedford TM 8-tonne Medium Mobility Load Carrier (MMLC). (IRCT)

20. RCT-manned Bedford TM 14-tonne MMLC. (IRCT)

21. RCT JCB loading ammunition on standard NATO pallets onto a Demountable Rack Offload and Pickup System (DROPS). (IRCT)

22. A view of the enlarged Military Port at Marchwood showing three Landing Ships

Logistic (LSL). (R Grevatte-Ball)

23. RAF Chinook with underslung 20-tonne container load in the Falklands Campaign. (IRCT)

24. Ammunition being unloaded from a merchant ship to an RCT-manned Mexeflote raft in the Falklands Campaign. (IRCT)

25. Offloading Mechanical Handling Equipment (MHE) at Al Jubayl prior to receiving main stocks. (IRCT)

26. A convoy of 35-tonne Leyland Crusaders each carrying two FV430 Armoured Personnel Carriers led by a Leyland DROPS vehicle. (Martin White)

27. Convoy Marshalling Area, Al Jubayl.

28. B Troop of 38 Squadron RCT loaded and ready to move forward. (Martin White)

29. DROPS vehicle loading with ammunition. (Martin White)

30. RHQ and Workshop of 27 Regiment RCT moving into location. (Martin White)

31. A Scammell Commander of 7 Tank Transporter Regiment moving trucks forward. (Martin White)

32. Commander 4 Brigade, Brigadier Christopher Hammerbeck, and officers and NCOs of 38 Ambulance Squadron GTR meet Corporal Parsad Gurung. (Martin White)

33. Officers and NCOs of 28 Ambulance Squadron GTR.

34. Artillery Units on the move, carried by 7 Tank Transporter Regiment RCT. (Martin White)

35. 17 Squadron RCT running the Administrative Harbour Area on the Main Supply Route (MSR) Dodge. (Martin White)

36. Supplies moving on the MSR. (Martin White)

37. All-important fuel tankers coping with desert conditions. (Martin White)

38. A unit of 10 Regiment RCT refuelling en route. (Martin White)

39. A DROPS vehicle taking and filling a water tank. (Martin White)

40. A DROPS vehicle delivering water to a flexible (pillow) tank. (Martin White)

41. The RCT Medal Collection - general view. (IRCT)

42. The RCT Medal Collection showing the Victoria Cross case. (IRCT)

43. Ex-RASC/RCT In-Pensioners, The Royal Hospital, Chelsea. (The Royal Hospital)

44. Major General J D MacDonald CB, CBE, the last Director of the RCT, in 1992, with Regimental Sergeant Major R W Cass and In-Pensioner Sergeant C Varley MVO, MBE, formerly RSM at the RCT Training Centre. (IRCT)

General Index

Bold indicates the top level of the index. *Italics* refer to a map or picure

435

445

Index of Names

The ranks shown are the highest known
Italics indicate reference to pictures

447